AMERICAN CRIMINAL LAW

JOHN M. SCHEB, J.D., LL.M.
Judge, Florida Court of Appeal, Second District (Ret.)
Distinguished Professorial Lecturer, Stetson University, College of Law

JOHN M. SCHEB II, Ph.D.
Professor of Political Science
University of Tennessee, Knoxville

West Publishing Company
Minneapolis/St. Paul New York Los Angeles San Francisco

Copyediting: Christianne Thillen
Text Design: Lois Stanfield,
LightSource Images
Composition: Carlisle Communications, Ltd.

Cover image: Tom Pressly, REFLECTIONS OF JUSTICE
acrylic on canvas, 48″ × 36″, Art and the Law 1983
Photo courtesy of West Publishing Corp.
Eagan, Minnesota
Photo credits appear after Index

WEST'S COMMITMENT TO THE ENVIRONMENT
In 1906, West Publishing Company began recycling materials left over from the production of books. This began a tradition of efficient and responsible use of resources. Today, up to 95 percent of our legal books are printed on recycled, acid-free stock. West also recycles nearly 22 million pounds of scrap paper annually—the equivalent of 181,717 trees. Since the 1960s, West has devised ways to capture and recycle waste inks, solvents, oils, and vapors created in the printing process. We also recycle plastics of all kinds, wood, glass, corrugated cardboard, and batteries, and have eliminated the use of Styrofoam book packaging. We at West are proud of the longevity and the scope of our commitment to the environment.

Production, Prepress, Printing and Binding by West Publishing Company.

Explanatory Note
The authors have attempted to present the general principles of criminal law in this textbook. However, because of the variance in state statutes and court decisions from state to state, it is recommended that students and officers consult with their legal advisors before assuming that principles of law applicable in other states exist in their state.

British Library Cataloguing-in-Publication Data. A catalogue record for this book is available from the British Library

Printed in the United States of America

03 02 01 00 99 98 97 96 8 7 6 5 4 3 2 1 0

Library of Congress Cataloging-in-Publication Data
Scheb, John M. (John Malcolm), 1926–
American criminal law / John M. Scheb, John M. Scheb II.
p. cm.
Includes index.
ISBN 0-314-08669-4 (soft)
1. Criminal law—United States. I. Scheb, John M. 1956–
I. Title.
KF9219.S338 1996
345.73—dc20
[347.305] 95-37702
CIP

DEDICATED TO
JOHN M. SCHEB III
(Born April 2, 1992)

About The Authors

John M. Scheb was born in Orlando, Florida in 1926. He entered the practice of law in 1950. He served as municipal judge in Sarasota, Florida from 1957 to 1959. From 1959 to 1970, he served as City Attorney for the city of Sarasota. In 1974, he was appointed to the Florida District Court of Appeal, 2nd district, a position he held until his retirement in 1992. Judge Scheb is now Distinguished Professorial Lecturer at Stetson University College of Law in St. Petersburg. He holds the B.A. from Florida Southern College, the J.D. from the University of Florida, and the LL.M. from the University of Virginia.

John M. Scheb II was born in Sarasota, Florida in 1955. He attended the University of Florida from 1974 to 1982, receiving the B.A., M.A., and Ph.D. in political science. He is now Professor of Political Science and Director of the Social Science Research Institute at the University of Tennessee, Knoxville. Professor Scheb is co-author, with Otis H. Stephens, Jr., of *American Constitutional Law* (West Publishing Co., 1993). He is also co-author, with William Lyons and Lilliard E. Richardson, Jr., of *American Government: Politics and Political Culture* (West Publishing Co., 1995).

CONTENTS

PREFACE

This book represents the first half of Scheb and Scheb, *Criminal Law and Procedure,* 2nd edition (West Publishing Co., 1994). Since that book was published, we received numerous suggestions that it be reissued in two volumes: one dealing with substantive criminal law, the other dealing with criminal procedure. This volume, which deals with the substantive aspect, thus contains the first thirteen chapters of *Criminal Law and Procedure.*

To capture some of the more important recent developments that have taken place since *Criminal Law and Procedure,* 2nd edition, was published in January 1994, we have added a fourteenth chapter entitled "Recent Developments in the Criminal Law." Chapter 14 focuses on the creation of new crimes and the interpretation of existing laws to cope with societal changes. We begin with an examination of current criminal law issues involving the exercise of constitutional rights and close with a brief summary of the landmark Federal Crime Bill of 1994.

In addition to the persons we acknowledged in *Criminal Law and Procedure,* 2nd edition, we wish to thank Loretta Maxwell, a Ph.D. student in the Department of Political Science at the University of Tennessee, Knoxville, and Jean E. Moore, an Instructor at the University of Tennessee College of Law, for their research assistance on this project.

Much of the credit for this book belongs to the staff at West Publishing Company who provided excellent assistance and support throughout the project. We especially thank our editor, Joan Gill, developmental editor, Becky Stovall, and our production editor, Tamborah Moore. Working with these professionals made the task of producing a textbook infinitely easier and more pleasant.

Finally, we would like to thank our wives, Mary B. Scheb and Sherilyn Claytor Scheb, for their patience and support, without which the project could not have been undertaken, much less completed.

We hope this book is useful to students and teachers of criminal law. Naturally, we assume full responsibility for any errors contained herein.

John M. Scheb
John M. Scheb II
August 2, 1995

Reviewers and Affiliations

Jerry C. Armor, Calhoun Community College, Decatur, AL

Sherry Biddinger-Gregg, Indiana State University, Terre Haute, IN

Elaine Cohen, Broward Community College, Fort Lauderdale, FL

Paul Falzone, California State University-Sacramento, Sacramento, CA

Barbara May, Montgomery County Community College, Telford, PA

Robert W. Peetz, Midland College, Midland, TX

Bob Plesha, Lakewood Community College, St. Paul, MN

Chet Zerlin, Miami-Dade Community College, Coral Gables, FL

AMERICAN CRIMINAL LAW

PART I

INTRODUCTION TO THE CRIMINAL JUSTICE SYSTEM

CHAPTER 1

FUNDAMENTALS OF CRIME, LAW, AND PUNISHMENT

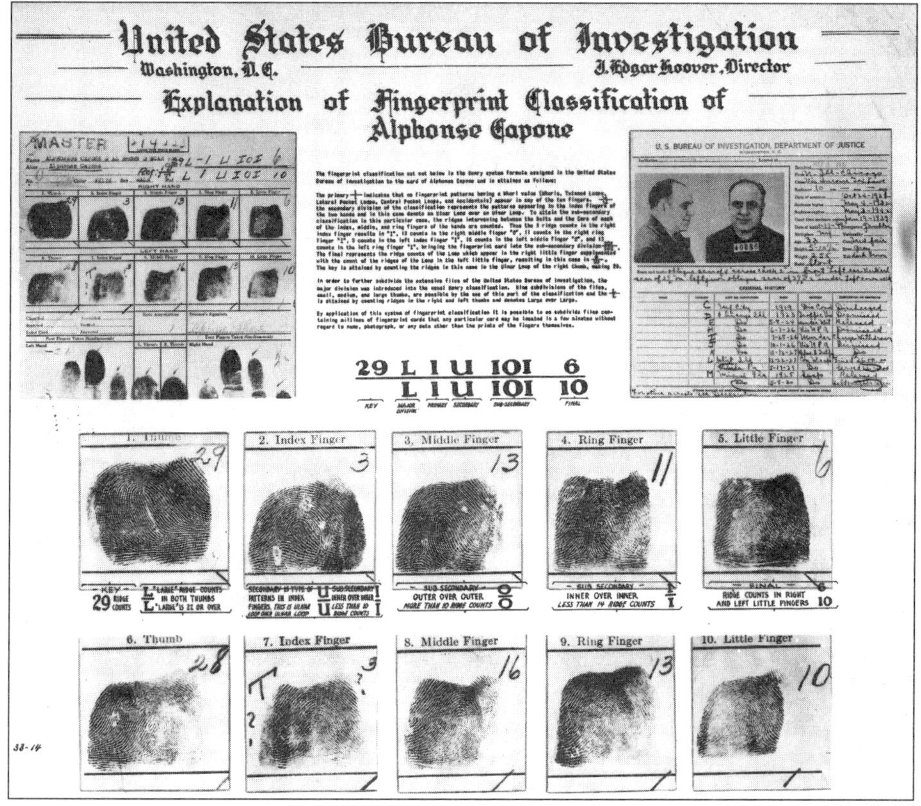

CHAPTER OUTLINE

Introduction
What Is a Crime?
Civil and Criminal Law
Constitutional Limitations
Substantive and Procedural Criminal Law
The Origins and Sources of the Criminal Law
Criminal Punishment
Why Do People Commit Crimes?
The Seriousness of the Current Crime Problem
Conclusion

INTRODUCTION

The fundamental problem facing any society is how to control the actions of individuals that threaten the life, liberty, and property of other individuals as well as society's collective interests in order, peace, safety, and decency. Societies have developed a number of informal means of achieving this control, including family structures, social norms, and religious precepts. On the other hand, law is a formal means of achieving social control. In general, law can be defined as a body of rules prescribed and enforced by government for the regulation and protection of society. Criminal law is that branch of the law that prohibits certain forms of conduct and imposes penalties on those who engage in prohibited behavior.

WHAT IS A CRIME?

Every crime involves a wrongful act (*actus reus*) specifically prohibited by the criminal law. For example, in the crime of battery, the *actus reus* consists in the striking or offensive touching of another person. Even the failure to take action can be considered a wrongful act, if the law imposes a duty to take action in a certain situation. For example, in many jurisdictions, one who fails to report an instance of child abuse to the proper authorities may be guilty of an offense.

In most cases the law requires that the wrongful act be accompanied by criminal intent (*mens rea*). Criminal intent does not refer to one's motive or reason for acting, but merely to one's having formed a mental purpose to act. To convict a person of a crime, it is not necessary to know *why* a person committed a crime. It is only necessary to show that the individual intentionally committed a prohibited act. An unintentional act is usually not a crime, although, as we will discover, there are exceptions to this principle. Moreover, in certain instances, one may be held criminally responsible irrespective of intent. Crimes of this latter nature are classified as strict liability offenses. A good example of a strict liability offense is selling liquor to a minor. (Strict liability offenses and elements of crimes generally are discussed in Chapter 4.)

Nullen Crimen, Nulla Poena, Sine Lege

A person cannot be convicted of a crime unless he or she committed a specific offense against a law that provides for a penalty. This principle is expressed in the maxim *nullen crimen, nulla poena, sine lege,* a Latin phrase that means "there is no crime, there is no punishment, without law." A related principle of American law is the proscription of *ex post facto* laws. Under the United States Constitution (Article I, Sections 9 and 10), an act cannot be made a crime retroactively. To be criminal, an act must be illegal at the time it was committed.

Felonies and Misdemeanors

Criminal law distinguishes between serious crimes, known as felonies, and less serious offenses, called misdemeanors. Generally speaking, felonies are offenses

FORM 1. COMPLAINT—SUMMONS FOR MISDEMEANOR OR PETTY MISDEMEANOR

STATE OF MINNESOTA DISTRICT COURT
COUNTY OF ____ ____ JUDICIAL DISTRICT

____________,) COMPLAINT—SUMMONS
Plaintiff,) FOR
vs.) MISDEMEANOR OR
) PETTY MISDEMEANOR
____________,)
Defendant.) District Court File No. _____

COMPLAINT

The Complainant being duly sworn, makes complaint to the above-named Court and states that Complainant believes there is probable cause to believe that the above-named Defendant committed the offense described below. The Complainant states that the following facts established PROBABLE CAUSE:

The above facts constitute Complainant's basis for believing that the above-named Defendant, on the ___ day of _____, 19___ at __________,
(location)
in the above-named County, committed the following described

OFFENSE

Charge: _____ in violation of Section: ______

(description)

THEREFORE, Complainant requests that the Defendant, subject to bail or conditions of release where applicable,

(1) be arrested or that other lawful steps be taken to obtain the Defendant's appearance in court; or

(2) be detained, if already in custody, pending further proceedings; and that the Defendant otherwise be dealt with according to law.

____
(Name of Complainant)
Complainant

Being duly authorized to prosecute the offense charged, ________________ hereby approves this
(Prosecuting Attorney)
Complaint.

____
(Prosecuting Attorney)
Name:
Attorney License No.:
Title:
Address:
Telephone No.:

FINDING OF PROBABLE CAUSE

From the above sworn facts, and any supporting affidavits or supplemental sworn testimony, I, the Issuing Officer, have determined that probable cause exists to support, subject to bail or conditions of release where applicable, Defendant's arrest or other lawful steps to be taken to obtain Defendant's appearance in Court, or Defendant's detention, if already in custody, pending further proceedings. The Defendant is therefore charged with the above-stated offense.

SUMMONS

THEREFORE YOU, THE ABOVE-NAMED DEFENDANT, ARE HEREBY SUMMONED to appear on the ___ day of _______, 19___, at ___ o'clock ___ m., before the above-named Court at
____
(Room Number) (Place) (Address)
to answer this complaint.

IF YOU FAIL TO APPEAR in response to this Summons, a warrant for your arrest may be issued.

This Complaint—Summons was sworn to, subscribed before, and issued by the undersigned authorized Issuing Officer this ___ day of _____, 19 .

____
Issuing Officer*

Sworn testimony has been given before the Issuing Officer by the following witnesses:

*The name and title of the Issuing Officer should be printed or stamped following the Issuing Officer's signature.
[Effective for criminal actions commenced or arrests made after 12 o'clock midnight January 1, 1990.]

FIGURE 1.1 A Form for Filing a Criminal Complaint. Source: *Minnesota Rules of Court, State and Federal, 1991.* (West Publishing Co., 1991), p. 216.

THE ELEMENTS OF A CRIME

Normally, the following elements must be present to constitute a crime:

1. Actus reus, *or wrongful act.* There must be some specific act of commission or omission by the accused. Unlike the religious concept of sin, a crime must involve more than evil thoughts.
2. Mens rea, *or guilty mind.* Generally speaking, an act cannot be regarded as criminal unless accompanied by an intention to commit the prohibited act. Thus a person who was insane at the time of committing an offense cannot be held criminally liable for his or her actions.
3. *Concurrence of action and intent.* Society does not punish a person for merely entertaining an evil intention, nor for committing an unavoidable act. Rather, for a crime to occur, there must be a concurrence between the *actus reus* and *mens rea.*
4. *Harm.* To constitute a crime, an act must cause harm to a legally recognized interest such as an individual's person, property or reputation, or societal interests in order, safety, peace, morality, and health.
5. *Causation.* There must be a causal relationship between the act and the harm suffered. Thus, for example, if Bunny Burns stabs Jimmy Johnson and the latter soon dies from a preexisting disease, Bunny Burns would not ordinarily be found guilty of murder. Of course, she could be found guilty of a lesser felony such as mayhem or aggravated assault.

for which the offender can be imprisoned for more than one year; misdemeanors carry jail terms of less than one year. Common examples of felonies include murder, rape, kidnapping, arson, assault with a deadly weapon, robbery, and grand larceny. Typical misdemeanors include petit theft, simple assault and battery, public drunkenness, disorderly conduct, prostitution, gambling, and various motor vehicle infractions.

Crime: An Injury Against Society

Our legal system regards crimes not merely as wrongs against particular victims but as offenses against the entire community. Indeed, there does not have to be an individual victim for there to be a crime. For example, it is a crime to possess cocaine, even though it is unlikely that a particular individual will claim to have been victimized by another person's use of the drug. It is a crime because society, through its governing institutions, has made a collective judgment that cocaine use is inimical to the public welfare.

Because crime is an injury against society, it is government, as society's legal representative, that brings charges against persons accused of committing crimes. In the United States, we have a federal system, that is, a division of power and responsibility between the national and state governments. Both the national government and the states enact their own criminal laws. Thus both the national and state governments may prosecute persons accused of crimes. The national government initiates a prosecution when a federal (national) law has been violated; a state brings charges against someone who is believed to have violated one of its laws.

The Role of the Crime Victim

Because the government prosecutes criminals on behalf of society, the victim of a crime is not a party to the criminal prosecution. By filing a complaint with a law enforcement agency, a victim initiates the process that leads to prosecution, but once the prosecution begins, the victim's participation is primarily that of being a witness. Quite often victims feel lost in the shuffle of the criminal process. They sometimes feel that the system is insensitive or even hostile to their interests in seeing justice done. As we shall see, some states are now taking steps to address victims' concerns. But fundamentally, the victim is a secondary player in the criminal justice system. The principal parties in a criminal case are the prosecution (i.e., the government) and the defendant (i.e., the accused person). There are situations, however, in which the victim may have another remedy—a civil suit to recover damages for losses or injuries suffered.

Civil and Criminal Law

The criminal law is not the only body of law that regulates the conduct of individuals. The civil law provides remedies for essentially private wrongs, offenses in which the state has a less direct interest. Most civil wrongs are classified as breaches of contract or torts. A breach of contract occurs when a party to a contract violates the terms of the agreement. A tort, on the other hand, is a wrongful act that does not violate any enforceable agreement but that nevertheless violates a legal right of the injured party. Common examples of torts include wrongful death, intentional or negligent infliction of personal injury, wrongful destruction of property, trespass, and defamation of character. As noted earlier, a crime normally entails intentional conduct. A driver who accidentally hits and kills another person with his or her car would not necessarily be guilty of a crime, depending on the circumstances (see discussions of manslaughter and vehicular homicide, Chapter 6). If the accident resulted from the driver's negligence, he or she would have committed the tort of wrongful death, and would be subject to a civil suit for damages.

The criminal and the civil law often overlap. Thus, conduct that constitutes a crime may also involve a tort. For example, suppose Randy Wrecker intentionally damages a house belonging to Harvey Homeowner. Wrecker's act may well result in both criminal and civil actions being brought against him. Wrecker may be prosecuted by the state for the crime of willful destruction of property and also may be sued by Homeowner for the tort of wrongful destruction of property. The state would be seeking to punish Wrecker for his antisocial conduct, whereas Homeowner would be seeking compensation for the damage to his property. The criminal case would be designated *State v. Wrecker* (or *People v. Wrecker,* or even *Commonwealth v. Wrecker,* depending on the state); the civil suit would be styled *Homeowner v. Wrecker.*

Constitutional Limitations

Under our system of government, the prohibitions of the criminal and civil law are subject to limitations contained in the federal and state constitutions. Thus the First Amendment to the U.S. Constitution prohibits government from using the civil or criminal law to abridge freedom of speech. For example, the United States Supreme Court has interpreted the First Amendment to limit the ability of public officials to sue their critics for the torts of libel and slander. *New York Times v. Sullivan,* 376 U.S. 254, 84 S.Ct. 710, 11 L.Ed.2d 686 (1964). In the criminal law context, the Supreme Court has said that one cannot be punished merely for advocating violence unless there is "imminent lawless action." *Brandenburg v. Ohio,* 395 U.S. 444, 89 S.Ct. 1827, 23 L.Ed.2d 430 (1969). The First Amendment also has important implications for the crimes of obscenity and indecency.

Other important constitutional principles limit the authority of government to define certain conduct as criminal. Among them is the right of privacy, which relates to abortion and a wide range of sexual conduct that traditionally was defined as criminal. We discuss these limitations in some detail in Chapter 3.

Substantive and Procedural Criminal Law

As we have noted, there can be no prosecution, and no punishment, except as provided by law. Our criminal law prescribes both substantive and procedural rules governing the everyday operation of the criminal justice system. Substantive criminal law prohibits certain forms of conduct by defining crimes and establishing the parameters of penalties. Procedural criminal law regulates the enforcement of the substantive law, the determination of guilt, and the punishment of those found guilty of crimes. For example, while substantive law makes the possession of heroin a crime, the procedural law regulates the police search and seizure that produce the incriminating evidence. The substantive law makes premeditated murder a crime; the procedural law determines the procedures to be observed at trial and, if a conviction results, at sentencing.

The Origins and Sources of the Criminal Law

Many antisocial acts classified as crimes have their origin in the norms of primitive societies. Certain types of behavior have been universally condemned by mankind since ancient times. Acts such as murder, rape, robbery, and arson are considered *mala in se,* or inherent wrongs. Other acts that the modern criminal law regards as offenses are merely *mala prohibita;* they are offenses only because they are so defined by the law. Many so-called victimless crimes, such as possession of marijuana or gambling, are generally not regarded as offensive to universal principles of morality. Rather, they are wrong simply because the law declares them wrong. In the case of *mala prohibita* offenses, the legislature has reached a judgment that certain conduct, while not contrary to universal moral principles, is nevertheless incompatible with the public good.

Development of Law in the Western World

There is a general consensus that law developed in Western civilization as leaders began formalizing and enforcing customs that had evolved among their peoples. Eventually, informal norms and customs came to be formalized as codes of law. The Code of Hammurabi regulated conduct in ancient Babylonia some two thousand years before Christ. In the seventh century B.C., Draco developed a very strict code of laws for the Athenian city-states. Even today, one hears strict rules or penalties characterized as being "Draconian." These developments influenced the Romans in their development of the Twelve Tables in the fifth century B.C. And, of course, long before the time of Jesus, the Hebrews had developed very elaborate substantive and procedural laws.

In the first century A.D., the Code of Justinian was promulgated throughout the Roman Empire. The Code of Justinian became very influential in determining the evolution of law on the European continent. The Napoleonic Code, promulgated under Napoleon Bonaparte in 1804 as a codification of all the civil and criminal laws of France, was based in large part on the Code of Justinian. The Napoleonic Code became a model for a uniform system of law for the nations of Western Europe. It is for this reason that the legal systems of Western Europe are often said to be "Roman law" systems. Roman law systems are based on the primacy of statutes enacted by the legislature. These statutes are integrated into a comprehensive code designed to be applied by the courts with a minimum of judicial interpretation.

Development of the English Common Law

American criminal law is derived largely from the English common law, which dates from the eleventh century. Prior to the Normal Conquest of 1066, English law was a patchwork of local laws and customs, often applied by feudal courts. William the Conqueror, the first Norman king of England, dispatched royal judges who traveled the country settling disputes based on the common customs of the people (hence the term *common law*). By 1300 the decisions of the royal judges were being recorded to serve as precedents to guide judges in future similar cases. The common-law doctrine of following precedent, known as *stare decisis,* remains an important component of both the English and American legal systems. As the centuries passed, coherent principles of law and definitions of crimes emerged from the decisions of the judges. Thus, in contrast to Roman law systems, which are based on legal codes, the common law developed primarily through judicial decisions.

By 1600, the common-law judges had defined the crimes of murder, manslaughter, mayhem, robbery, burglary, arson, larceny, rape, suicide, and sodomy as felonies. They had also begun to develop a number of lesser offenses known as misdemeanors. In contrast to the criminal law that was developing on the continent, England developed trial by jury and trained barristers to argue cases on an adversarial basis. A "barrister" is a lawyer permitted to cross the "bar" in the courtroom that separates the bench from the spectators. Thus, in England, a barrister is a trial lawyer. Although we do not use the term *barrister* in the United States, we do refer to licensed attorneys as having been "admitted to the bar."

As representative government developed in England, the dominance of the common-law courts diminished. Parliament came to play a significant role in the formation of the criminal law by adopting statutes that revised and supplemented the common law. However, the adversarial system of justice continued and the basic English felonies remain today defined essentially as they were by the common-law judges centuries ago.

Development of the American Criminal Law

Our criminal laws came basically from the common law as it existed at the time that America proclaimed its independence from England in 1776. After independence, the new American states adopted the English common law to the extent that it did not conflict with the new state and federal constitutions. However, the federal government did not adopt the common law of crimes. From the outset, federal crimes were defined by statutes passed by Congress. Of the fifty states in the Union, Louisiana is the only one whose legal system is not based ultimately on the common law. Rather, it is based primarily on the Napoleonic Code.

The new American judges and lawyers were greatly aided by *Blackstone's Commentaries,* published in 1769, in which Sir William Blackstone, a professor at Oxford, codified the principles of the common law. Blackstone's seminal effort was a noble undertaking, but it had the effect of demystifying English law. Consequently, Blackstone's encyclopedic treatment of the law was less than popular among English barristers, who by this time had developed a close fraternity and took great pride in offering their services to "discover the law." In America, however, *Blackstone's Commentaries* became something of a "legal bible."

As the American nation developed, most common-law definitions of crimes were superseded by legislatively defined offenses in the form of statutes. These criminal statutes, or codes, for the most part retain the offenses defined by the common law. However, criminal statutes and codes often go far beyond the common law in prohibiting offenses that are *mala prohibita.* Criminal offenses can also be defined by regulatory agencies where such authority has been specifically delegated by Congress or a state legislature. When authorized by state constitutions or acts of state legislatures, cities and counties may adopt ordinances that define certain criminal violations.

Although the majority of states have abolished all, or nearly all, common-law crimes, and replaced them by statutorily defined offenses, the common law remains a valuable source of interpretation. This is because legislatures frequently use terms known to the common law without defining such terms. For example, in proscribing burglary, the legislature may use the term *curtilage* without defining it. In such an instance, a court would look to the common law, which defined the term to mean "an enclosed space surrounding a dwelling."

The Model Penal Code (MPC)

The American Law Institute (ALI) is an organization of distinguished judges, lawyers, and academics who have a strong professional interest in drafting model codes of laws. In 1962, after a decade of work that produced several tentative drafts, the ALI published its Proposed Official Draft of the Model Penal Code (MPC). The MPC consists of general provisions concerning criminal liability, sentences, defenses, and definitions of specific crimes. The MPC is not law; rather, it is designed to serve as a model code of criminal law for all states. It has had a significant impact on legislative drafting of criminal statutes, particularly during the 1970s when the majority of the states accomplished substantial reforms in their criminal codes. Additionally, the MPC has been influential in judicial interpretation of criminal statutes and doctrines, thereby making a contribution to the continuing development of the decisional law. In this text, we illustrate many principles of law by representative statutes from federal and state jurisdictions; however, in some instances where the MPC is particularly influential, the reader will find references to specific provisions of the MPC.

Sources of Procedural Law

The procedural criminal law is promulgated both by legislative bodies, through enactment of statutes, and by the courts, through judicial decisions and the development of rules of court procedure. The U.S. Supreme Court prescribes rules of procedure for the federal courts. Generally, the highest court of each state, usually called the state supreme court, is empowered to promulgate rules of procedure for all the courts of that state.

In addition to the common law, statutes, regulations, and ordinances, the federal and state constitutions contribute to the body of substantive and procedural law. The U.S. Constitution, for example, defines the crime of treason. U.S. Const. Art. III, Sec. 3. The Constitution has much to say about criminal procedure, most notably as it relates to search and seizure, U.S. Const. Amend. IV, the protection against compulsory self-incrimination, U.S. Const. Amend. V, the right to counsel, U.S. Const. Amend. VI, and the right to trial by an impartial jury, U.S. Const. Amend. VI. Of course, the responsibility for "fleshing out" the general principles of criminal procedure contained in the federal and state constitutions rests primarily with the courts by deciding specific cases presented to them. Also, through the adoption of statutes, the Congress and the state legislatures provide additional details in this area.

Due Process of Law

By far the broadest, and probably the most important, constitutional principle relating to criminal procedure is found in the due process clauses of the Fifth and Fourteenth Amendments to the Constitution. The same principle can be found in some provision of every state constitution. Reflecting a legacy that can be traced to the Magna Charta (1215), such provisions forbid the government from taking a person's life, liberty, or property, whether as punishment for a crime or any other reason, without due process of law. Due process refers to those procedural safeguards necessary to assure the fundamental fairness of a legal proceeding. Many essential elements of due process are found in the Bill of Rights of the Constitution (e.g., the right to a trial by an impartial jury, the right to counsel, and the freedom from unreasonable searches and seizures).

Other important due process protections are not specifically mentioned in the Constitution. For example, it is fundamental that in a criminal case the defendant is presumed innocent, and the prosecution must establish the defendant's guilt beyond a reasonable doubt. *In re Winship*, 397 U.S. 358, 90 S.Ct. 1068, 25 L.Ed.2d 368 (1970). While no one seriously challenges the reasonable doubt standard as an essential element of due process, other traditional characteristics of criminal trials, such as the twelve-member jury and the requirement of a unanimous verdict finding the defendant guilty of a crime are not always viewed as necessary elements of constitutional due process. *Williams v. Florida*, 399 U.S. 78, 90 S.Ct. 1893, 26 L.Ed.2d 446 (1970); *Apodaca v. Oregon*, 406 U.S. 404, 92 S.Ct. 1628, 32 L.Ed.2d 184 (1972). Consequently these traditional elements of criminal procedure have been modified in a number of states.

CRIMINAL PUNISHMENT

During the colonial period of American history, and indeed well into the nineteenth century, the death penalty was often inflicted for a variety of felonies including rape, arson, and horse theft. Likewise, such corporal punishments as flogging or being placed in a pillory were common. Now that officially sanctioned corporal punishment is no longer administered to those convicted of crimes in this country, criminal sanctions entail one or more of the following:

1. **The death penalty.** Although the Supreme Court's decision in *Furman v. Georgia,* 408 U.S. 238, 92 S.Ct. 2726, 33 L.Ed.2d 346 (1972), temporarily halted the imposition of the death penalty, capital punishment returned in 1977 when the state of Utah placed convicted murderer Gary Gilmore in front of a firing squad. Since then, the administration of the death penalty has become more common. Currently, thirty-six states as well as the federal government have statutes providing for capital punishment, either by electrocution, the gas chamber, the firing squad, or by lethal injection. The Supreme Court has held that the death penalty is a legitimate punishment, but only for the crime of murder. *Coker v. Georgia,* 433 U.S. 584, 97 S.Ct. 2861, 53 L.Ed.2d 982 (1977). Although the public largely supports the death penalty for the crime of premeditated murder, the penalty remains controversial among criminologists. The evidence to support the hypothesis that capital punishment is a general deterrent to murder seems tenuous at best.
2. **Incarceration.** This is the conventional mode of punishment prescribed for those convicted of felonies. Under federal and state law, felonies are classified by their seriousness, and convicted felons may be imprisoned for periods ranging from one year to life. Incarceration is usually available as a punishment for those convicted of the more serious misdemeanors, but for only up to one year in most jurisdictions. While it was originally thought to be an effective means of rehabilitation, most criminologists now view incarceration simply as a means of isolating those persons who pose a serious threat to society. The U.S. Department of Justice reported that the number of inmates in federal and state prisons reached an all-time high in 1992, with 883,593 persons incarcerated. Indeed, prison populations grew approximately 150 percent between 1980 and 1992. This tremendous increase reflects the fact that during the 1980s federal and state sentencing laws were amended to increase the length of prison terms given to convicted felons. Unfortunately, many prisons are now seriously overcrowded to the point that courts must limit the number of inmates that can be confined.
3. **Monetary fines.** Fines are by far the most common punishment for those convicted of misdemeanors. Felons are likewise often subject to fines in addition to, or instead of, incarceration. Usually, the law allows the sentencing judge to impose a fine, a jail term, or some combination of the two. A number of felonies, especially serious economic crimes, now carry very heavy fines. For example, violations of federal banking and securities laws are punishable by fines running into the millions of dollars.
4. **Community service.** This sanction is becoming more attractive as a punishment for less serious crimes, especially for juveniles and first-time offenders. Community service is generally regarded as a more meaningful sanction than the imposition of a fine. It is also viewed as less likely than incarceration to promote future criminal behavior. The theory underlying community service is that an offender will become aware of his or her

obligations to the community and how his or her criminal conduct violated those obligations.

5. **Probation.** This alternative to incarceration is common for first-time offenders, except in cases involving the most serious crimes. Probation is usually conditioned on restrictions on the probationer's everyday conduct. Arguably, it has the advantage of placing the individual in the supervision of the government while keeping him or her away from the possibly crime-inducing environment of the prison. Unfortunately, the success of probation has often been hindered by inadequate staffing, resulting in inadequate supervision of probationers.
6. **Loss of civil rights.** Federal and state statutes deprive convicted felons of certain rights, most notably the right to vote and to hold public office. In recent years, however, the courts have held that incarcerated criminals do retain certain fundamental constitutional rights, such as the right to freely exercise their religious beliefs. *Cruz v. Beto,* 405 U.S. 319, 92 S.Ct. 1079, 31 L.Ed.2d 263 (1972). Even where courts have recognized the constitutional rights of prisoners, they have generally restricted the scope of these rights in light of the overriding necessity for security and discipline in the prison environment. *Bell v. Wolfish,* 441 U.S. 520, 99 S.Ct. 1861, 60 L.Ed.2d 447 (1979).

Sentencing Persons Convicted of Crimes

Sentencing takes place after the accused has been convicted of a crime. Sentences for particular crimes are spelled out in the statutes, although typically these statutes allow for considerable discretion on the part of the judge or jury imposing the sentence. In an effort to reduce disparities in sentencing, the federal government and some states have developed sentencing guidelines, a subject discussed in Chapter 2.

WHY DO PEOPLE COMMIT CRIMES?

For centuries it was widely believed that people who committed crimes were "touched by the devil." In modern times, we tend not to ascribe criminal behavior to metaphysical causes but to factors that can be observed, examined, and explained. The science of criminology is devoted to identifying the causes and effects of criminal behavior. Criminology is far from a merely academic concern—our understanding of the causes of criminal behavior affect the policies we follow in attempting to prevent and control crime.

In the nineteenth century, criminologists like Cesare Lombroso (1835–1909) began to examine crime as a biologically based phenomenon, arguing that some people are "born criminal types." Most contemporary criminologists reject such biological models of crime in favor of theories that stress environmental factors. Today most criminologists would concede that there are multiple causes of crime.

Fundamentally, it must be recognized that the existence of crime is a function of the criminal law itself, for, by definition, there can be no crime without criminal law. As more forms of conduct have become prohibited by law, the incidence of crime has increased. Currently, the federal government defines more than 2,800 distinct criminal offenses; the number of offenses designated by state and local governments is even greater. Much behavior not traditionally regarded as criminal has been incorporated into modern criminal codes. For example, numerous federal and state laws now criminalize actions that threaten the natural environment and the public health (see Chapter 10). Consequently, the traditional concept of what constitutes a crime has been greatly expanded.

Undoubtedly, the overwhelming majority of Americans regard themselves as law-abiding citizens. Yet many of these people routinely commit crimes they do not regard as morally wrong, such as underreporting their income for tax purposes, smoking marijuana, betting on football games, or speeding on interstate highways. Many so-called upperworld crimes are regarded by their perpetrators simply as shrewd business practices (e.g., consumer fraud, insider trading in stocks, price fixing, or violations of health and safety regulations).

Criminologists have focused most of their attention on why people commit crimes that are *mala in se,* such as offenses against persons like murder, rape, robbery, and aggravated assault. Of lesser magnitude are the crimes against property such as grand larceny, burglary, forgery, and fraud. Criminologists have also examined why some people are much more likely than others to commit these economic crimes.

As noted, *mala in se* offenses like murder, rape, mayhem, burglary, robbery, and arson have existed from the very outset of human experience. Some would say that such behavior flows from human nature itself. But the prevalence of crime in modern society requires more explanation than unfavorable characterizations of human nature. Social scientists have, not surprisingly, placed great emphasis on sociological, economic, and political factors. Many have stressed the decline of religion and the nuclear family as agents of socialization, the alienation of the individual from an impersonal mass society, and the emergence of huge cities that provide subcultures conducive to crime and frequent opportunities to commit crimes. Others have pointed to the lessening of criminal penalties and the increased restrictions placed on law enforcement by courts. Still others have cited the existence of massive unemployment and poverty in a society that has so much wealth and that places so much importance on individual affluence. In dealing with a phenomenon as complex as crime, most social scientists agree that all these hypotheses are quite plausible.

Criminals as Rational Actors

During the Age of Enlightenment, the Italian criminologist Cesare Beccaria (1738–1794) argued that crimes are rational acts committed by rational individuals who believe that the benefits of committing a crime outweigh the disadvantages of doing so. The widespread belief in the deterrent effect of punishment is based on this rationalistic view of criminal behavior. If criminals are rational actors who calculate the costs and benefits of their actions, then making punishment swift, certain, and severe ought to deter people from committing crimes. Of course, the constitutional requirement of due process and the constitutional prohibition against "cruel and unusual punishments" militate against swift, certain, and severe punishment. Moreover, it is doubtful that all or even most criminals rationally assess the costs and benefits of their acts. Certainly crimes of passion, which are impulsive acts of violence committed by people whose emotions have run away with them, are by definition not rational acts. But it is also difficult to understand how the numerous rapes, assaults, kidnappings, child molestations, and homicides that occur today are the result of rational thought by rational people, even if these crimes are carefully planned. Nevertheless, most people believe that, to the extent that criminal conduct is rational, crime would be lessened by strengthening law enforcement agencies, removing impediments to police investigations, expediting trials, limiting appeals, and enhancing criminal penalties. Clearly, the American public is apprehensive about crime and tends to support all of these strategies. Of course, the courts of law owe their primary allegiance to the Constitution, not to public opinion.

THE SERIOUSNESS OF THE CURRENT CRIME PROBLEM

While crime is generally perceived as having worsened over the last three decades, it is very difficult to know exactly the scope of the problem. Since the 1930s the Federal Bureau of Investigation (FBI) has published the Uniform Crime Reports (UCR). These are based on standardized definitions of certain key "index crimes" reported to state and federal law enforcement agencies. With the exception of theft, these index crimes do not include misdemeanor offenses. Moreover, the actual occurrence of crime exceeds reported crime by an unknown margin that probably varies markedly across jurisdictions. It is well known that people in large cities are much less likely to report crimes than are residents of suburbia or small towns. Similarly, reportage probably varies according to the nature and severity of crimes. For example, the victims of rape, embarrassed by what has happened to them and reluctant to experience the difficulties of a criminal trial, often let their attacks go unreported. Victims of motor vehicle theft, on the other hand, are very likely to report their misfortunes since there is little stigma attached to being a victim of theft and it is often necessary to report losses to secure reimbursement from insurance companies. Consequently, the UCR gives us a very fuzzy picture of the incidence of crime in America.

More accurate and useful than the Uniform Crime Reports are victimization surveys in which representative samples of people are asked whether they have been the targets of criminal activity. The victimization studies done by the Bureau of the Census under sponsorship of the Law Enforcement Assistance Administration (LEAA) in the 1970s revealed that the actual incidence of crime far surpassed that reported to the FBI. These victimization studies also revealed much about the demographics of crime victimization in America. Except for rape and purse snatching, men tend to be victims of both violent and economic crime more frequently than do women. Young people also tend to be disproportionately victimized, as do African Americans and other ethnic and racial minorities. However, it must be recognized that, given the pervasiveness and degree of randomness of crime, no one is exempt from potential victimization. In 1987, the U.S. Department of Justice released a report predicting that five out of six twelve-year-olds would be the victims or intended victims of crimes during their lifetimes.

TABLE 1.1 Crime Rates, 1983, 1991, and 1992 (number of offenses per 100,000 persons)

Crime	1983	1991	1992	% Change in Rate 1983–1992	% Change in Rate 1991–1992
Murder	8.3	9.8	9.3	+12%	−5%
Forcible rape	33.7	42.3	42.8	+27%	+1%
Robbery	217	273	264	+22%	−3%
Aggravated assault	279	433	442	+58%	+2%
Burglary	1338	1252	1168	−13%	-7%
Larceny	2869	3229	3103	8%	−4%
Motor vehicle theft	431	659	631	+47%	−4%

Source: Federal Bureau of Investigation, *Crime in the United States, 1992.*

According to the National Crime Victimization survey, Americans twelve and over experienced nearly 19 million criminal victimizations involving violence or personal theft during 1992. Additionally, some 15 million household crimes (primarily burglaries) were committed. Nearly one quarter of the nation's households experienced some form of criminal victimization during 1992. Table 1.1 compares crime rates over time. It shows that the murder rate rose 12 percent between 1983 and 1992, but actually declined by 5 percent between 1991 and 1992. The highest rate of increase over the ten-year period is in aggravated assault, which increased 58 percent between 1983 and 1992. The only crime that showed a decrease over the period was burglary, which declined 13 percent. In looking at short-term changes between 1991 and 1992, violent crimes (with the exception of murder) showed slight increases. Property crimes evidenced a significant decline.

In the early 1990s, the American public became extremely concerned about the crime problem. Some think that constant accounts of real crime in the media as well as dramatic portrayals of fictional crime on TV and in the movies give people an exaggerated sense of the dangers of crime. But to people living in the nation's inner cities who are afraid to leave their homes after dark, crime represents a very real danger. Clearly, crime remains a serious social, legal, and political problem for this country.

Conclusion

One of the more tragic aspects of the crime problem is that many Americans are losing faith in the ability of their government to protect them from criminals. Indeed, in some areas of the country victims are unlikely even to report crimes to the police. Some victims are unwilling to endure the difficulties of being a witness. Others simply believe that the perpetrator will not be apprehended, or if so, will not be punished.

Our state and federal governments are severely constrained both by legalities and practicalities in their efforts to fight crime. Not only is the specter of "a cop on every corner" distasteful to most Americans, it is well nigh impossible to achieve even with unlimited public resources, let alone in this age of fiscal retrenchment.

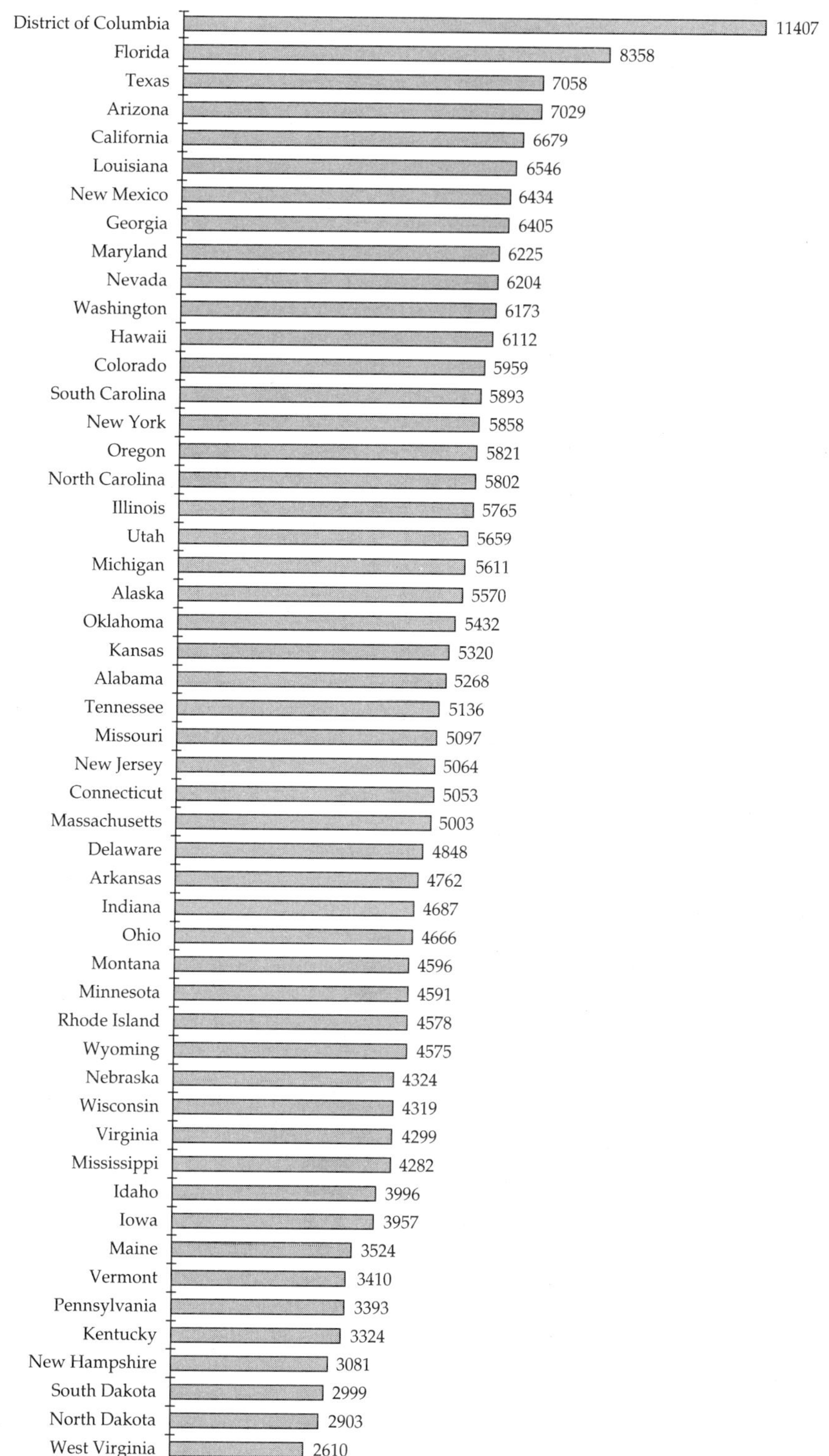

FIGURE 1.2 Serious Crimes Known to Police per 100,000 population, 1989. Source: U.S. Department of Commerce, Bureau of the Census, 1990.

Obviously, one of the most serious problems currently facing law enforcement is the massive importation of illegal drugs into this country. How many personnel, aircraft, and ships would it take to stem the flow of cocaine, heroin, and marijuana across our borders? Are we willing, indeed are we able, to commit such massive resources to the fight against drug smuggling?

Currently, the nation's prison system is filled beyond its capacity, yet the public is demanding that more convicted criminals be incarcerated and for longer periods of time. Yet the public appears unwilling to provide the revenues needed to build the additional prisons necessary to house these inmates.

Finally, society must confront the problem of the constitutional limitations on crime definition and law enforcement. Judges do have considerable discretion in interpreting the commands of the state and federal constitutions. Yet, if these documents are to be viable protections of our cherished liberties, we must accept the fact that they place significant constraints on our efforts to control crime. For instance, to what degree is the public willing to allow the constitutional protection against unreasonable searches and seizures to be eroded? To what degree are we willing to sacrifice our constitutionally protected privacy and liberty in order to speed up the ferreting out of crime? Perhaps this is the fundamental question of criminal law and procedure in a society that prides itself in preserving the rights of the individual.

QUESTIONS FOR THOUGHT AND DISCUSSION

1. What are the chief distinctions between the civil and criminal law, and why do they often overlap?
2. To what extent is the English common law significant in contemporary American criminal law?
3. What is the essential difference between the substantive and procedural criminal law? Can you give examples of each?
4. How does the U.S. Constitution affect the ability of a legislature to define certain conduct as criminal?
5. What social, economic, and psychological factors cause individuals to commit serious crimes?
6. In what ways does the prevalence of illegal drug use contribute to the crime problem? Would crimes such as burglary, larceny, robbery, and murder diminish in frequency if drugs like heroin and cocaine were legalized?
7. Why is it difficult to obtain a clear statistical picture of crime in the United States? What suggestions would you offer to expedite a more accurate assessment of crime in America?
8. What means of punishment for criminal offenses exist in your state? Is capital punishment available for persons convicted of first-degree murder? Which punishments, if any, do you think are most effective in controlling crime in your state?

CHAPTER 2

THE ORGANIZATION OF THE CRIMINAL JUSTICE SYSTEM

CHAPTER OUTLINE

INTRODUCTION

In every modern country, criminal justice is a complicated process involving a plethora of agencies and officials. In the United States, criminal justice is particularly complex, due largely to the existence of federalism, the constitutional division of authority between the national and state governments. Under this scheme of federalism, the national government operates one criminal justice system for the purpose of enforcing the criminal statutes adopted by Congress; each of the fifty states has its own justice system for enforcing its own criminal laws. As a result of this structural complexity, it is difficult to provide a coherent overview of criminal justice in America. Each system is to some extent unique, in terms of both substantive and procedural law. Yet there are a number of similarities: All fifty-one criminal justice systems in the United States involve law enforcement agencies, prosecutors, defense attorneys, courts of law, and corrections agencies. All follow certain general procedures beginning with arrest and, in some cases, ending in punishment. Finally, all systems are subject to the limitations of the United States Constitution, as interpreted by the United States Supreme Court.

LAW ENFORCEMENT AGENCIES

Law enforcement agencies are charged with the task of enforcing the criminal law. They have the power to investigate suspected criminal activity, to arrest suspected criminals, and to detain arrestees until their cases come before the appropriate courts of law. We expect law enforcement agencies not only to arrest those suspected of crimes but also to take steps to prevent crimes from occurring. In the United States there are nearly forty thousand federal, state, and local agencies involved in law enforcement and crime prevention.

At the national level, the Federal Bureau of Investigation is the primary agency empowered to investigate violations of federal criminal laws. Located in the Department of Justice, the FBI is by far the most powerful of the federal law enforcement agencies, with broad powers to enforce all of the many criminal laws adopted by the Congress. The FBI currently employs more than 25,000 people, including nearly eleven thousand agents spread out over fifty-six field offices in the United States and twenty-one foreign offices. Its annual budget exceeds 2.3 billion dollars. The FBI uses the most sophisticated methods in crime prevention and investigation.

In addition to the FBI, a number of federal agencies have law enforcement authority in specific areas. Among them are the Bureau of Alcohol, Tobacco, and Firearms; the Drug Enforcement Administration; the Customs Service; the Immigration and Naturalization Service; the Bureau of Postal Inspection; and the Secret Service.

Many states have their own counterparts to the FBI. Similarly, every state has a number of state agencies responsible for enforcing specific areas of the law, ranging from laws governing traffic safety to laws governing agricultural importation, from casino gambling to the dispensing of alcoholic beverages.

At the local level, we find both county and municipal law enforcement agencies. Nearly every county in America has a sheriff. In most states, sheriffs are elected to office and exercise broad powers as the chief law enforcement officers of their respective counties. In some areas, particularly the urban Northeast, many of the powers traditionally exercised by sheriffs have been assumed by state or metropolitan police forces. However, in the rest of the country, especially in the rural areas, sheriffs (and their deputies) are the principal law enforcement agents at the county level. More than twenty thousand cities and towns have police departments. Local police are charged with enforcing the criminal laws of their states, as well as of their municipalities. Although the county sheriff usually has jurisdiction within the municipalities of the county, generally he or she concentrates enforcement efforts on those areas outside municipal boundaries.

In addition to providing law enforcement in the strictest sense of the term, local law enforcement agencies are heavily involved in order maintenance or "keeping the peace," hence the term *peace officers*. Often, keeping the peace involves more discretion than merely applying the criminal law.

PROSECUTORIAL AGENCIES

While law enforcement agencies are the "gatekeepers" of the criminal justice system, prosecutors are central to the administration of criminal justice. They determine whether to bring charges against suspected criminals. They have enormous discretion, not only in determining whether to prosecute but also in determining what charges to file. Moreover, prosecutors frequently set the tone for plea bargaining and have a powerful voice in determining the severity of sanctions imposed on persons convicted of crimes. Accordingly, prosecutors play a crucial role in the criminal justice system.

The chief prosecutor at the federal level is the Attorney General, who is the head of the Department of Justice. Below the Attorney General are a number of United States Attorneys, each responsible for a specific geographical area of the country. The United States Attorneys in turn have a number of assistants who handle most of the day-to-day criminal cases brought by the federal government. The Attorney General and the United States Attorneys are appointed by the president, subject to the consent of the Senate. The assistant U.S. Attorneys are federal civil service employees.

In addition to the regular federal prosecutors, Congress has provided for the appointment of special prosecutors (or "independent counsel") in cases involving alleged misconduct by high government officials. By far the most infamous such case was "Watergate," which resulted in the convictions of several high-ranking officials and the resignation of a president. But there have been several cases where, under congressional direction, a special prosecutor has been appointed. One of the more dramatic instances was the Iranian arms scandal of 1986. There, a special prosecutor was assigned to investigate shipments of arms to Iran and subsequent diversion of profits from the arms sales to rebel forces in Nicaragua.

Each state likewise has its own attorney general and a number of assistant attorneys, plus a number of district or state's attorneys at the local level.

Generally speaking, local prosecutors are elected for set terms of office. In most states local prosecutors act autonomously and possess broad discretionary powers.

Cities and counties also have their own attorneys. These attorneys sometimes prosecute violations of city and county ordinances, but increasingly their function is limited to representing their cities or counties in civil suits and giving legal advice to local councils and officials. These city and county attorneys are generally appointed by the governing bodies they represent.

DEFENSE ATTORNEYS

It is axiomatic in American criminal law that individuals accused of any crime, no matter how minor the offense, have the right to employ counsel for their defense. U.S. Const. Amend. VI. Beginning in the 1960s, the United States Supreme Court greatly expanded the right to counsel by requiring states to provide attorneys to indigent defendants. *Gideon v. Wainwright,* 372 U.S. 335, 83 S.Ct. 792, 9 L.Ed.2d 799 (1963); *Argersinger v. Hamlin,* 407 U.S. 25, 92 S.Ct. 2006, 32 L.Ed.2d 530 (1972). In some states an indigent person who requests counsel at public expense has an attorney from the private bar appointed to represent him or her. Many states, however, have chosen to handle the problem of indigent defense by establishing public defender's offices. Like public prosecutors, public defenders are generally elected to set terms of office.

THE COURTS

Courts of law are the centerpieces of the federal and state criminal justice systems. It is their responsibility to determine both the factual basis and legal sufficiency of criminal charges and to insure that criminal defendants are provided due process of law.

Basically, there are two kinds of courts: trial and appellate courts. Trial courts conduct criminal trials and various pretrial and posttrial proceedings. Appellate courts hear appeals from the decisions of the trial courts. While trial courts are primarily concerned with ascertaining facts, determining guilt or innocence and imposing punishments, appellate courts are primarily concerned with matters of law. Appellate courts serve both to correct legal errors made by trial courts and to develop law when new legal questions arise.

Jurisdiction

The first question facing a court in any criminal prosecution is that of jurisdiction, the legal authority to hear and decide the case. A court must have jurisdiction, over both the subject matter of a case and the parties to a case, before it may proceed to adjudicate that controversy. The jurisdiction of the federal courts is determined both by the language of Article III of the Constitution and by statutes enacted by Congress. The jurisdiction of the state courts is determined by the respective state constitutions and statutes. Essentially, the federal courts adjudicate criminal cases where defendants are charged with violating federal criminal laws; state courts adjudicate alleged violations of state laws.

The Federal Court System

Article III of the U.S. Constitution provides that "The judicial Power of the United States shall be vested in one supreme Court, and in such inferior Courts as the Congress may from time to time ordain and establish." Under this authority Congress has created the federal court system comprising a number of trial and appellate tribunals. These courts handle prosecutions for violations of federal statutes. In addition, federal courts sometimes review convictions from state courts where defendants raise issues arising under the U.S. Constitution.

Federal District Courts The principal trial court in the federal system is the United States District Court. There are district courts in ninety-four federal judicial districts around the country. A criminal trial in the district court is presided over by a judge appointed for life by the president with the consent of the Senate. Pretrial proceedings in the district courts and trials of misdemeanors are often handled by federal magistrates, who are appointed by federal district judges.

The district courts were created by an act of Congress in 1789. Since then, Congress has created specialized courts to handle specific kinds of cases (e.g., the United States Court of International Trade and the United States Claims Court).

The United States Courts of Appeals The intermediate appellate courts in the federal system are the United States Courts of Appeals (also known as circuit courts). Twelve geographical circuits (and one "federal circuit") cover the United States and its possessions. Figure 2.1 indicates the geographical distribution of the circuit courts. The circuit courts hear both criminal and civil appeals from the district courts and from "quasi-judicial" tribunals in the independent regulatory agencies. Generally, decisions of the courts of appeals are rendered by panels of three judges who vote either to affirm or to reverse the lower court decisions under review. There is a procedure by which the circuit courts provide *en banc* hearings, where all judges assigned to the court participate in a decision. Like their counterparts in the district courts, federal appeals court judges are appointed to life terms by the president with the consent of the Senate.

Military Tribunals Crimes committed by persons in military service are prosecuted in proceedings before courts-martial, with appeals decided by the Court of Military Appeals in Washington, D.C. Only under conditions of martial law do military tribunals have the authority to try civilians. *Ex parte Milligan*, 71 U.S. (4 Wall.) 2, 18 L.Ed.281 (1866). Article 1, Section 8 of the U.S. Constitution grants Congress the authority to regulate the armed forces. Under this authority, Congress has enacted the Uniform Code of Military Justice (UCMJ), 10 U.S.C.A. §§ 801–940. The UCMJ gives courts-martial jurisdiction to try all offenses under the code committed by military personnel. Notwithstanding this grant of authority, the United States Supreme Court held in 1969 that military jurisdiction

The Thirteen Federal Judicial Circuits

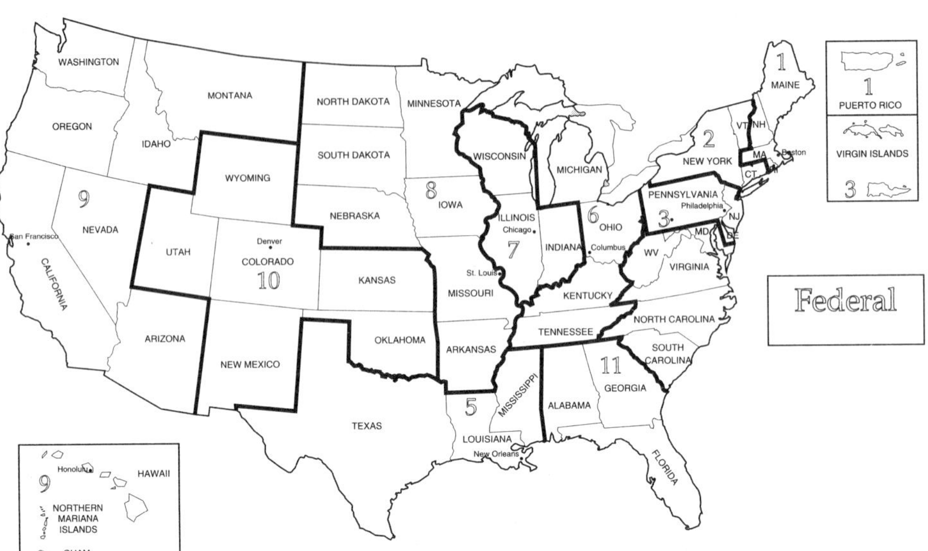

FIGURE 2.1 The Federal Judicial Circuits. Source: *Federal Reporter*, 2d Series (West Publishing Co.).

was limited to offenses that were service connected. *O'Callahan v. Parker*, 395 U.S. 258, 89 S.Ct. 1683, 23 L.Ed.2d 291 (1969). The *O'Callahan* decision had the effect of greatly narrowing military jurisdiction over offenses committed by servicepersons. In 1987 the Court, in a 5–4 decision, overruled *O'Callahan* and said that military jurisdiction depends solely on whether an accused is a military member. *Solorio v. United States*, 483 U.S. 435, 107 S.Ct. 2924, 97 L.Ed.2d 364 (1987). Thus courts-martial may now try all offenses committed by service persons in violation of the UCMJ.

Decisions of courts-martial are reviewed by military courts of review in each branch of the armed forces. In specified instances appeals are heard by the United States Court of Military Appeals. The Court of Military Appeals is staffed by civilian judges who are appointed to fifteen-year terms by the president with the consent of the Senate.

The United States Supreme Court. The highest appellate court in the federal judicial system is the U.S. Supreme Court. The Supreme Court has jurisdiction to review, either on appeal or by writ of *certiorari*, all the decisions of the lower federal courts and many of the decisions of the highest state courts. Naturally, the Supreme Court is able to review only a very small percentage of the numerous criminal cases decided by lower courts.

The Supreme Court is staffed by nine justices who, like district and circuit judges, are appointed for life. These nine individuals have the final word in

JURISDICTION OVER CRIMES COMMITTED ON INDIAN RESERVATIONS

Article I, Section 8 of the U.S. Constitution mentions Indian tribes as being subject to Congressional legislation. Congress has provided that federal courts have jurisdiction over specified offenses committed by Native Americans on Indian reservations. 18 U.S.C.A. § 1153. At the same time, Congress has permitted certain states to exercise jurisdiction over such offenses. 18 U.S.C.A. § 1162. Furthermore, offenses committed by one native American against another on a reservation are generally subject to the jurisdiction of tribal courts, unless the crime charged has been expressly made subject to federal jurisdiction. *Keeble v. United States*, 412 U.S. 205, 93 S.Ct. 1993, 36 L.Ed.2d 844 (1973).

Courts of the state where an Indian reservation is located, not federal courts, have jurisdiction over crimes on the reservation where the offense is perpetrated by a non-Indian against a non-Indian, but non-Indian defendants charged with committing a crime on a reservation are subject to federal jurisdiction if the victim was a member of the tribe. *United States v. Antelope*, 430 U.S. 641, 97 S.Ct. 1395, 51 L.Ed.2d 701 (1977).

determining what the U.S. Constitution requires, permits, and prohibits in the areas of law enforcement, prosecution, adjudication, and punishment. The Supreme Court also promulgates procedural rules for the lower federal courts to follow in both criminal and civil cases.

State Court Systems

Each state has its own independent judicial system. These courts handle more than 90 percent of criminal prosecutions in the United States. State judicial systems are characterized by enormous variation in structure, but every state has one or more levels of trial courts and at least one appellate court. Some states, like North Carolina, have adopted tidy, streamlined court systems (see fig. 2.2). Other states' court systems are extremely complex, as is the case in Texas (see fig. 2.3). In complexity, most states fall somewhere between the two extremes.

STAGES IN THE CRIMINAL PROCESS

Certain basic procedural steps are common to all criminal prosecutions, although specific procedures vary greatly among jurisdictions. As cases move through the system from arrest through adjudication and, in many instances, toward the imposition of punishment, there is considerable attrition. Of any one hundred felony arrests, perhaps as few as twenty-five will result in convictions. This "sieve effect" occurs for a number of reasons, including insufficient evidence, police misconduct, procedural errors, and the transfer of young offenders to juvenile courts.

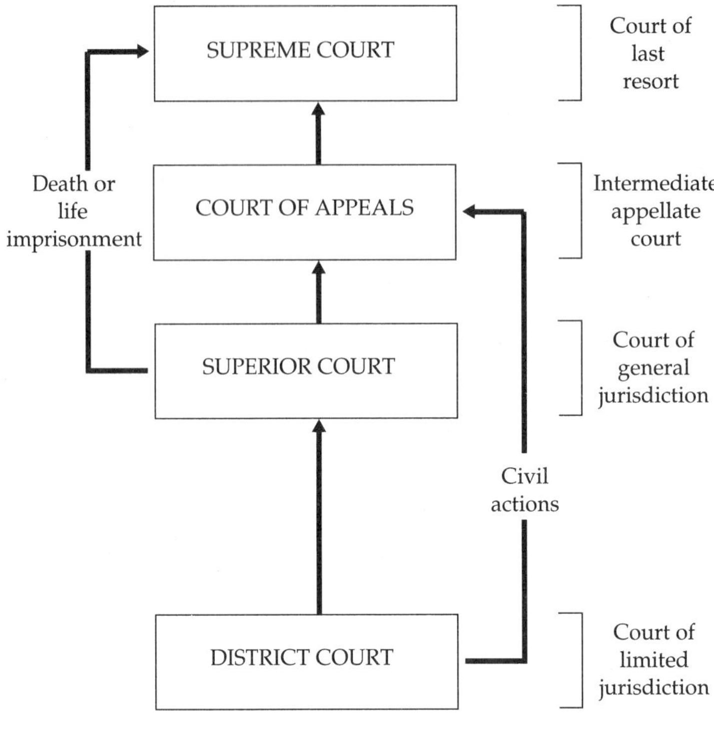

FIGURE 2.2 North Carolina Court System. Source: U.S. Department of Justice/National Center for State Courts.

Search and Seizure

Search and seizure normally occur prior to arrest. Searches are directed at locating evidence of crime; seizures occur when searches are fruitful. Like all activities of law enforcement, search and seizure is subject to constitutional limitations. The Fourth Amendment to the U.S. Constitution, enforceable against the states through the due process clause of the Fourteenth Amendment, explicitly protects citizens from unreasonable searches and seizures. *Mapp v. Ohio,* 367 U.S. 643, 81 S.Ct. 1684, 6 L.Ed.2d 1081 (1961). The Supreme Court has interpreted this protection as requiring law enforcement officers to have specific grounds for conducting searches, either "probable cause" or the less stringent standard of "reasonable suspicion." *Terry v. Ohio,* 392 U.S. 1, 88 S.Ct. 1868, 20 L.Ed.2d 889 (1968). Furthermore, the Court has held that officers must obtain warrants authorizing searches unless "exigent circumstances" make it impossible to obtain a warrant and also preserve evidence of crime. *Carroll v. United States,* 267 U.S. 132, 45 S.Ct. 280, 69 L.Ed. 543 (1925). There are several well-defined types of searches, each subject to a distinct set of constitutional rules. The limited investigatory stop, the "stop-and-frisk," the border search, the search incident to a lawful arrest, and electronic eavesdropping are examples of types of searches that have been addressed by the courts.

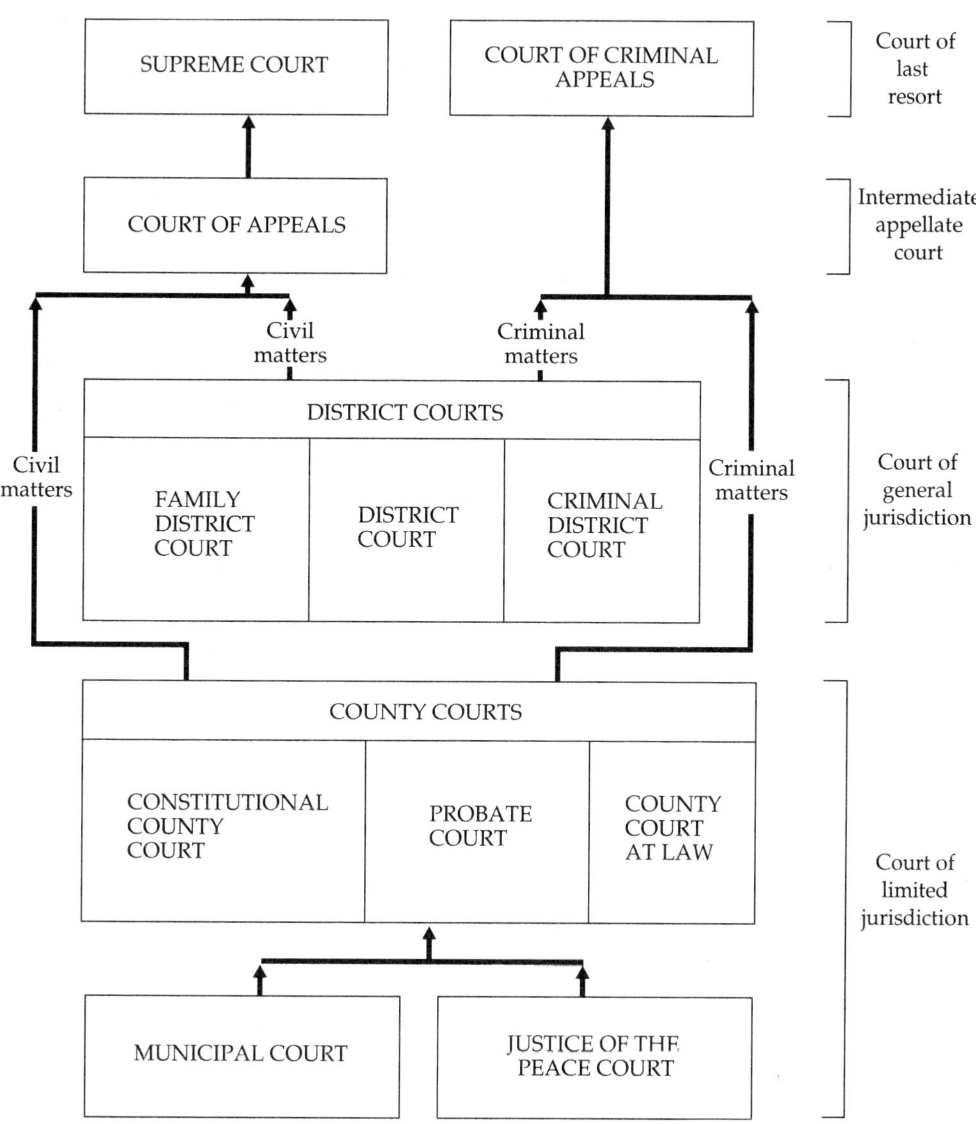

FIGURE 2.3 The Texas Court System. Source: U.S. Department of Justice/National Center for State Courts.

To enforce the protections of the Fourth Amendment, the Supreme Court has fashioned a broad "exclusionary rule" that bars the fruits of illegal searches and seizures from being used as evidence in criminal trials. *Weeks v. United States,* 232 U.S. 383, 34 S.Ct. 341, 58 L.Ed. 652 (1914); *Mapp v. Ohio,* 367 U.S. 643, 81 S.Ct. 1684, 6 L.Ed.2d 1081 (1961). Recent decisions by the Court have narrowed somewhat the scope of this exclusionary rule. See, for example, *United States v. Leon,* 468 U.S. 897, 104 S.Ct. 3405, 82 L.Ed.2d 677 (1984). Nevertheless, because it excludes from many cases evidence that is both reliable and probative, the exclusionary rule remains controversial.

Arrest and Interrogation

Arrest consists of taking into custody a person suspected of having committed a crime. Arrests can be made on the basis of warrants issued by magistrates or indictments handed down by grand juries. More commonly, arrests are made by police who observe commission of a crime or have probable cause to believe a crime has been committed, but face exigent circumstances that prevent them from obtaining an arrest warrant. When an officer restricts a person from leaving the officer's presence or formally places that person under arrest, a number of constitutional protections come into play. These include the well-known *Miranda* warnings given to suspects in custody advising them of their constitutional rights. *Miranda v. Arizona,* 384 U.S. 436, 86 S.Ct. 1602, 16 L.Ed.2d 694 (1966).

The investigative tool of police interrogation takes many forms—from direct questioning to the use of subtle psychological techniques. Subject to narrow exceptions, custodial interrogation is not permitted until the suspect has been issued the *Miranda* warnings and has either waived those rights or has obtained counsel. A Fifth Amendment analogue of the Fourth Amendment exclusionary rule requires that confessions obtained by police through custodial interrogation must be excluded from evidence unless they meet these constitutional criteria. *Miranda v. Arizona,* 384 U.S. 436, 86 S.Ct. 1602, 16 L.Ed.2d 694 (1966).

An individual arrested for a minor misdemeanor is generally released from police custody and ordered to appear in court at a later date to answer the charge. If the arrest is for a major misdemeanor or felony, the individual is usually held in custody pending an initial appearance before a judge or magistrate.

Initial Appearance

Under the Constitution, a person accused of a crime has the right to a "speedy and public trial." U.S. Const., Amend. 6. This includes the right to be brought before a judge to be formally apprised of the charges. In addition to reading the charges, the judge at the first appearance attempts to ascertain whether the defendant is represented by an attorney. If not, and the defendant is indigent, the judge generally appoints counsel. Finally, the judge determines whether the accused is to be released from custody pending further proceedings. A defendant who merits pretrial release can be released either on bail or on his or her own recognizance. In deciding whether to grant pretrial release, and whether to require that the defendant post a bond to assure the court the defendant will appear to answer the charges, a judge must weigh the seriousness of the alleged crime as well as the defendant's prior record and ties to the community.

Summary Trials for Minor Offenses

In the case of minor misdemeanors, including many traffic violations, trials are often held in a summary fashion without the use of a jury, usually at the defendant's first appearance in court. The U.S. Supreme Court has held that a jury trial is not constitutionally required unless the defendant is subject to incarceration for more than six months. *Duncan v. Louisiana,* 391 U.S. 145, 88 S.Ct. 1444, 20 L.Ed.2d 491 (1968). In such cases, we might question whether the traditional presumption of innocence applies. In a summary trial the charges are read, the defendant is asked to plead to the charges, and a verdict is reached, often within a few minutes. In most such cases, defendants do in fact plead guilty, but even when they protest innocence, they are seldom accquitted. This is largely because judges are much more inclined to take the word of the arresting officer over that of the accused, and rarely are there any additional witnesses. Although a person charged with any criminal offense has the right to retain counsel to represent him or her at a summary proceeding, most defendants charged with minor misdemeanors are not represented by counsel. A principal reason is the expense of retaining a lawyer. The Supreme Court has said that indigent persons do not have a right to counsel at public expense unless they are actually sentenced to more than six months in jail. *Scott v. Illinois,* 440 U.S. 367, 99 S.Ct. 1158, 59 L.Ed.2d 383 (1979).

The Grand Jury

According to the Constitution, "no person shall be held to answer for a capital, or other infamous crime, unless on a presentment of indictment of a Grand Jury . . ." U.S. Const. Amend. 5. The grand jury, not to be confused with the trial jury, is a body that considers evidence obtained by the prosecutor in order to determine whether there is probable cause to hold a trial. As a mechanism designed to prevent unwarranted prosecutions, the grand jury dates back to twelfth-century England.

Each federal judicial district maintains a grand jury. These grand juries comprise twenty-three jurors. Grand juries are also maintained in many state jurisdictions, although the Supreme Court has held that states are not required to use grand juries in charging criminal defendants. *Hurtado v. California,* 110 U.S. 516, 4 S.Ct. 111, 28 L.Ed. 232 (1884).

Grand jury proceedings are typically closed to the public. The prosecutor appears before the grand jury with a series of cases he has built against various defendants. Witnesses are called and physical evidence is presented. If the grand jury believes that a given case is substantial, it hands down an indictment, or "true bill." In the overwhelming majority of cases, grand juries hand down indictments against persons as requested by prosecutors, leading some to question the utility of the grand jury procedure as a means of guarding against arbitrary or unwarranted prosecution.

The Preliminary Hearing

About half of the states, especially those that entered the Union more recently, have dispensed with the ancient institution of the grand jury. They have opted instead for charging defendants in a fashion that is less cumbersome and arguably more protective of the innocent. Under the more modern approach, the prosecutor files an accusatorial document called an "information" containing the charge against the accused. A preliminary hearing is then held in which a judge or magistrate must determine whether there is probable cause to hold the defendant for trial. At the preliminary hearing, the prosecutor presents physical evidence and testimony designed to persuade the judge that probable cause exists. The defense attorney, whose client is also usually present, generally exercises the right to cross-examine the prosecution's witnesses. In addition, the defense may, but seldom does, present evidence on behalf of the defendant at that time.

A number of states, for example, Tennessee and Georgia, use the grand jury mechanism, supplemented by an optional preliminary hearing. This hybrid model provides a double check against the possibility of unwarranted prosecution.

Arraignment

The arraignment is the first appearance of the defendant before the court that has the authority to conduct a trial. At this stage the defendant must plead to the charges that have been brought. The defendant has four options: (1) to plead guilty, in which case guilt will be pronounced and a date set for sentencing; (2) to plead not guilty, in which case a trial date will be set; (3) to plead *nolo contendere,* or no contest, which is tantamount to a plea of guilty; (4) to remain silent, in which case the court enters a plea of not guilty on behalf of the accused.

Plea Bargaining

Only a small proportion (perhaps 5 percent) of felony cases ever reach the trial stage. Many cases are dropped by the prosecutor for lack of evidence. Some cases may be dropped due to obvious police misconduct. Others are dismissed by judges at preliminary hearings, usually for similar reasons. Of the cases that reach the arraignment stage, only about 10 percent result in trials. In the other 90 percent, defendants enter pleas of guilty, often in exchange for concessions from the prosecution. To avoid trial, which is characterized by both delay and uncertainty, the prosecutor often attempts to persuade the defendant to plead guilty, either by reducing the number or severity of charges, or by promising not to seek the maximum penalty allowed by law. This controversial practice is known as plea bargaining.

Under a plea bargain, a charge of possession of cocaine with intent to distribute may be reduced to simple possession. First-degree murder, which may carry a death sentence, might be reduced to second-degree murder, which carries a term of imprisonment. A series of misdemeanor charges stemming from an altercation in a bar might be reduced to single charge of disorderly conduct.

The U.S. Supreme Court has upheld the practice of plea bargaining against claims that it violates the due process clauses of the Fifth and Fourteenth Amendments. *Brady v. United States,* 397 U.S. 742, 90 S.Ct. 1463, 25 L.Ed.2d 747 (1970); *North Carolina v. Alford,* 400 U.S. 25, 91 S.Ct. 160, 27 L.Ed.2d 162 (1970). However, because there is always a danger of coerced guilty pleas, especially when defendants are ignorant of the law, it is the judge's responsibility to ascertain whether the defendant's guilty plea is voluntarily and knowingly entered. *Boykin v. Alabama,* 395 U.S. 238, 89 S.Ct. 1709, 23 L.Ed.2d 274 (1969).

Pretrial Motions

Typically, a number of pretrial motions are available to both the defense and prosecution in a criminal case. Of particular importance are these motions:

- To dismiss the charges against the accused
- To inspect evidence in the hands of the prosecution
- To suppress evidence because of alleged illegalities in gathering it
- To change the venue of a trial in order to protect the accused from prejudicial pretrial publicity
- To obtain a continuance (postponement) of the trial
- To inspect the minutes of grand jury proceedings
- To ask for psychiatric evaluation of the accused
- For closure of pretrial proceedings (again, to protect the right of the accused to a fair trial)

Jury Selection

The Supreme Court has held that defendants in both state and federal prosecutions have the right to a jury trial if they are subject to more than six months incarceration. *Duncan v. Louisiana,* 391 U.S. 145, 88 S.Ct. 1444, 20 L.Ed.2d 491 (1968). Potential trial jurors (venirepersons) are selected typically, but not universally, from the rolls of registered voters. The actual process of jury selection, known as *voir dire,* consists of questioning potential jurors to determine their suitability for jury duty. In the federal courts, *voir dire* is conducted primarily by the judge; in the states, it is typically conducted by the attorneys for both sides. In all jurisdictions, attorneys may challenge jurors they find to be unsuitable. Attorneys may exercise a limited number of peremptory challenges, which are generally granted as a matter of course. However, peremptory challenges may not be based solely on the race of a prospective juror. *Batson v. Kentucky,* 476 U.S. 79, 106 S.Ct. 1712, 90 L.Ed.2d 69 (1986). Unlike peremptory challenges, challenges for cause must be supported by reasons acceptable to the court. There is, however, considerable discretion in the court's allowance of such challenges. While peremptory challenges are limited in number, there is no set limit to the number of challenges for cause.

Trial Procedures and Adjudication

The criminal trial is a formal and complex adversarial encounter between the government and the accused. The trial is governed by rules of evidence and procedure that are designed to develop the case in an orderly fashion and assist the fact finder (judge or jury) in reaching the correct result. After opening statements by counsel, the prosecution, through the introduction of testimony and physical evidence, attempts to prove the guilt of the accused beyond a reasonable doubt. The purpose of the defense is to create reasonable doubt about the government's case. In some cases the defense relies solely on cross-examination of the prosecution's witnesses to establish doubt. In most cases, the defense introduces evidence to contradict the evidence against the defendant or to discredit the government's witnesses. Witnesses called by each side are subject to cross-examination, and physical evidence is subject to inspection and challenge. During closing arguments counsel attempt to persuade juries of the merits of their positions. Following this, the trial judge instructs the jury on the relevant points of law and the jurors' responsibilities in reaching a verdict. Where a jury returns a verdict of guilty, defense counsel frequently moves the court for a new trial or other relief.

Sentencing

After the guilt of the accused has been determined, sentence is imposed by the court. Very often, a separate court appearance is scheduled to allow for a presentence investigation before imposing sentence. In imposing sentences, judges generally must follow statutory requirements governing the type and severity of sentence for particular crimes. Types of sentences include probation, incarceration, work release, monetary fines, community service, and, of course, death. Different statutory approaches govern the length of prison sentences that courts may impose. Indeterminate sentencing occurs when individuals are incarcerated for periods of time to be determined by correctional agencies. Determinate sentencing occurs when statutes specify prison terms for particular crimes. In most jurisdictions, judges are able to impose particular sentences within broad parameters defined by statutes. In recent years, we have witnessed two trends away from broad judicial discretion in the area of sentencing. First is the tendency for legislatures to require imposition of flat or mandatory sentences. Second, some juridictions have developed sentencing guidelines to address the problem of sentencing disparity.

Congress enacted the Sentencing Reform Act of 1984 to "provide certainty and fairness in meeting the purposes of sentencing, avoiding unwarranted sentencing disparities among defendants with similar records who have been found guilty of similar criminal conduct while maintaining sufficient flexibility to permit individualized sentences also warranted by mitigating or aggravating factors. . . ." 28 U.S.C.A. § 992(b)(1)(B). Where unusual circumstances exist, federal appellate courts have permitted district courts to exercise wide discretion in determining upward or downward departures from the recommended sentences.

Even before the federal government adopted sentencing guidelines, Minnesota, in 1980—followed by a few other states—adopted its own guidelines through legislation. The experience of these states, along with that of the federal courts, has over the past few years given impetus to a number of state efforts in enacting similar guidelines.

Appeal and Discretionary Review

Federal law and the laws of every state provide those convicted of crimes a limited right to appeal their convictions to higher tribunals. Appellate courts generally confine their review of convictions to legal, as distinct from factual, issues. While appellate courts review the legal sufficiency of evidence, they do not attempt to second-guess the factual determinations of trial judges and juries. Rather, appellate courts review such procedural issues as denial of fair trial, denial of counsel, admission of illegal evidence, and improper jury instructions.

Appellate courts focus on errors of consequence, often overlooking so-called harmless errors.

When convictions are upheld on appeal, defendants may petition higher appellate courts for further review. Such review is available at the discretion of the higher court. The Supreme Court receives thousands of petitions each year from defendants whose convictions have been affirmed by the United States Courts of Appeals or the highest appellate tribunals of the states. Naturally, the Supreme Court is able to review only the small percentage of these cases that present important issues of law.

Postconviction Relief

A person who has been convicted of a crime, has exhausted all normal appellate remedies, and is confined to prison may still challenge his or her conviction, sentence, or conditions of confinement by filing a petition for a writ of *habeas corpus*. *Habeas corpus* is an ancient common-law device that permits judges to review the legality of someone's confinement. In modern American criminal procedure, *habeas corpus* has become a way for prisoners who have exhausted all other avenues of appeal to obtain judicial review. A federal prisoner petitions the appropriate federal district court for *habeas corpus* relief. Under most state statutes, state prisoners may file *habeas corpus* petitions or other similar petitions for postconviction relief with the appropriate state courts.

Under federal law, a state prisoner may petition a federal district court for *habeas corpus relief* if he or she wishes to raise federal constitutional issues, for example, the alleged denial of the Sixth Amendment right to be represented by counsel. The power of federal courts to issue *habeas corpus* in state cases can be traced to an act of Congress adopted just after the Civil War. See *Ex parte McCardle*, 74 U.S. (7 Wall.) 506, 19 L.Ed. 264 (1869).

There is no statutory limit to the number of federal *habeas corpus* petitions a prisoner may file; in several cases, prisoners have brought numerous petitions requiring many years to resolve. The denial or grant of *habeas corpus* relief by a federal district court is subject to appeal in the U.S. Court of Appeals. The circuit court's ruling is subject to review by the Supreme Court on a discretionary basis. Thus it can take several years to finally resolve one federal *habeas corpus* petition, especially if the petition raises difficult constitutional claims where the law is not yet fully settled. If a state prisoner were permitted to raise each of many issues in separate federal *habeas corpus* petitions, it could take decades to resolve all of the claims. It is for this reason that the Supreme Court has moved recently to require prisoners to raise all claims in their first *habeas corpus* petition. The Court has said that, unless there are exceptional circumstances, failure to do so constitutes an abuse of the writ of *habeas corpus*. *McCleskey v. Zant*, 499 U.S. 467, 111 S.Ct. 1454, 113 L.Ed.2d 517 (1991).

THE CORRECTIONS SYSTEM

As with courts, there is a federal corrections system and fifty separate state corrections systems. Each of these systems is responsible for supervising those persons sentenced to prison by courts of law. Originally, prisons were conceived as a place for criminals to reflect on their misdeeds and repent, hence the term *penitentiary*. In the twentieth century, the emphasis has been on rehabilitation through psychological and sociopsychological methods. Unfortunately, these efforts have been less than successful. Ironically, prisons appear to "criminalize" individuals more than rehabilitate them. Inmates are exposed to an insular society with norms of conduct antithetical to those of civil society. As "total institutions," prisons do not encourage individuals to behave responsibly; furthermore, prisons provide an excellent opportunity for spreading of criminal techniques. It is probably unrealistic to expect rehabilitation programs to succeed in such an environment. Today, prisons are generally regarded as little more than a way to punish and isolate those persons deemed unfit to live in civil society.

The federal and state prison systems are currently undergoing a crisis. There is simply not enough space to house inmates. The public continues to demand stiffer sentences for convicted felons, but legislators (and taxpayers) are often unwilling to pay the price of constructing more prisons. In many state prisons, cells originally designed for one or two inmates now house three or four prisoners.

In many instances federal courts have ordered prison officials to reduce overcrowding so as to comply with the federal constitutional prohibition against "cruel and unusual punishments." U.S. Const. Amend. 8. Aside from the threat of federal judicial intervention, overcrowded prisons are more likely to produce inmate violence and even riots.

In addition to prisons, corrections systems include agencies that supervise probation, parole, community service, and other forms of alternative sentences (see Chapter 18). With burgeoning prison populations, these alternatives to incarceration are assuming more importance and consuming more resources, especially at the state level.

Conclusion

The American system of criminal justice is an extremely complicated one. The primary reason for this complexity is the principle of federalism, which refers to the division of political and legal authority in this country among one national government and fifty state governments. The national government and each of the fifty states has its own criminal laws, as well as its own law enforcement agencies, prosecutors, courts, and prison systems. No two systems are exactly alike. Indeed, there is tremendous variation from one jurisdiction to the next, both in terms of the substantive criminal law and the practices and procedures used by the various components of the criminal process. Yet, despite their substantive and procedural differences, all jurisdictions share two basic goals: to protect society from crime and, at the same time, to protect the rights of the individual suspected of having committed an offense. Much of the conflict and inefficiency inherent in our criminal justice system stems from the need to balance these two competing objectives.

QUESTIONS FOR THOUGHT AND DISCUSSION

1. How does the concept of federalism complicate the criminal justice process in the United States?

2. What provisions of the United States Constitution protect a defendant at the following stages of the criminal process?
   a. A pre-arrest police search of the suspect's home designed to seize incriminating evidence
   b. A police interrogation of the suspect at the station house
   c. A magistrate's determination whether to grant pretrial release to a person arrested on a felony charge
   d. A judge's determination whether to appoint an attorney for a defendant who claims to be too poor to afford a lawyer
   e. A prosecutor's decision whether to file a formal accusation or information charging the defendant with one or more felonies
   f. A trial judge's determination to accept the defendant's plea of guilty at arraignment
   g. A judge's determination of the nature and extent of punishment to be imposed on a convicted felon

3. Compare and contrast the functions of trial and appellate courts in deciding criminal cases. How are they similar? How are they different?

4. How would you account for the recent trend toward curtailing judicial discretion in criminal sentencing?

PART II

THE SUBSTANTIVE CRIMINAL LAW

CHAPTER 3

Constitutional Limitations on the Prohibition of Criminal Conduct

CHAPTER OUTLINE

INTRODUCTION

Under a parliamentary system, such as those in Great Britain, Italy, Japan, and most of the world's democracies, the statutes enacted by the legislature are by definition the supreme law of the land. There is no overarching authority, except for the will of the people expressed through the ballot box, to limit exercises of legislative power. In the wake of the American Revolution, the founders were as wary of a parliamentary system as they were of a monarchy. The framers of the Constitution understood that unbridled power to make and enforce criminal prohibitions constitutes a serious threat to liberty. Thus, they framed a Constitution that delimits the power of Congress and state legislatures to enact criminal statutes. For example, Article III, Section 3 provides that the crime of treason against the United States "shall consist only in levying War against them, or in adhering to their Enemies, giving them Aid and Comfort." By circumscribing the crime of treason, the framers sought to prohibit the federal government from using the offense to punish political dissenters. Incidentally, treason is the only crime actually defined in the Constitution; all other crimes are defined by the common law, state and federal statutes, or both.

The Importance of Judicial Review

Constitutional limits on the enactment and enforcement of criminal statutes do not depend for their vitality only upon the voluntary compliance of legislators, prosecutors, and police officers. Under the doctrine of judicial review, courts are empowered to declare null and void laws that violate constitutional principles. In a landmark decision in 1803, the Supreme Court first asserted the power to invalidate legislation that is in conflict with the Constitution. *Marbury v. Madison,* 5 U.S. (1 Cranch) 137, 2 L.Ed. 60 (1803). Speaking for the Court in *Marbury,* Chief Justice John Marshall said, "It is emphatically the province and duty of the judicial department to say what the law is." 5 U.S. (1 Cranch) at 177, 2 L.Ed. at 175. Although the power of judicial review is generally associated with the Supreme Court, all courts of record, whether state or federal, may exercise the power to strike down unconstitutional legislation. It is doubtful whether constitutional limitations on governmental power would be meaningful in the absence of judicial review.

Unconstitutional *"Per Se"* and Unconstitutional "As Applied"

Throughout this textbook, we will be discussing constitutional limitations on the criminal justice system. Many of these principles are procedural in nature, imposing restrictions and obligations on law enforcement, prosecution, adjudication, and sentencing. In this chapter we are concerned only with those constitutional provisions that place limits on the substantive criminal law, both in the types of laws that legislatures are barred from enacting and the situations in which police and prosecutors are barred from enforcing existing statutes.

A statute may be declared unconstitutional on its face, in that it inherently trenches on some constitutionally protected liberty or exceeds the constitutional powers of government. Alternatively, a law that is facially valid, such as an ordinance prohibiting disorderly conduct, may be declared unconstitutional as applied if it is enforced in a way that impermissibly restricts or punishes the exercise of constitutional rights.

BILLS OF ATTAINDER AND *EX POST FACTO* LAWS

Two historic abuses of the English Parliament that the Framers of the Constitution sought to correct were bills of attainder and *ex post facto* laws. A bill of attainder is a legislative act inflicting punishment on an individual, or a group of easily identifiable individuals. *United States v. Brown,* 381 U.S. 437, 85 S.Ct. 1707, 14 L.Ed.2d 484 (1965). Laws of this character are antithetical to the basic principle that a person accused of wrongdoing is entitled to a fair trial in a court of law.

An *ex post facto* law is one that retroactively (1) makes an innocent act illegal; (2) increases the punishment for a criminal act; or (3) decreases the standard of proof required to convict a defendant of a crime. *Calder v. Bull,* 3 U.S. (3 Dall.) 386, 1 L.Ed. 648 (1798). Because the essence of the *ex post facto* law is retroactivity, it is flatly inconsistent with the principle of legality, which holds that individuals are entitled to know in advance if particular contemplated conduct is illegal.

Article I, Section 9 of the Constitution prohibits the Congress from adopting bills of attainder and *ex post facto* laws. Article I, Section 10 extends these same prohibitions to the state legislatures. These categorical injunctions probably account for the fact that there have been relatively few judicial decisions striking down laws on these grounds.

THE BILL OF RIGHTS

While the original Constitution contained few express limitations on legislative power, the Bill of Rights added several important constraints on the Congress. For criminal law, the most significant of these are the First Amendment freedoms of expression, religion, and assembly; the Second Amendment protection of "the right to keep and bear arms"; the Fifth Amendment Due Process Clause; the Eighth Amendment Cruel and Unusual Punishments Clause; and the Ninth Amendment guarantee of "rights retained by the people."

Although legislation is normally presumed by courts to be constitutional, the Supreme Court has recognized that "there may be narrower scope for the operation of the presumption of constitutionality when legislation appears on its face to be within a specific prohibition of the Constitution, such as those of the first ten amendments." *United States v. Carolene Products Co.,* 304 U.S. 144, 151 n. 4, 58 S.Ct. 778, 783 n. 4, 82 L.Ed. 1234, 1241, n. 4 (1938). Effectively, this means that government must carry the burden of proving that its enactment does not offend the Constitution.

Application of the Bill of Rights to State and Local Laws

The Bill of Rights begins with the injunction that "*Congress* shall make no law . . ." [emphasis added]. Unlike certain provisions in the original, unamended

Constitution, the Bill of Rights makes no mention of limitations on the state and local governments. Throughout much of the nineteenth century, the Bill of Rights was viewed as imposing limitations only on the Congress, having no effect on state legislatures or local governing bodies. The Supreme Court officially adopted this view in a landmark decision in 1833. *Barron v. Baltimore,* 32 U.S. (7 Pet.) 243, 8 L.Ed. 672 (1833). Under this interpretation of the Bill of Rights, citizens had to look to their state constitutions and state courts for protection against state and local actions that infringed on their rights and liberties.

The ratification of the Fourteenth Amendment in 1868 provided a justification for extending the scope of the Bill of Rights to apply against the states. Section 1 of the Fourteenth Amendment enjoins the states from depriving "any person of life, liberty, or property, without due process of law." It also prohibits states from adopting laws that "abridge the privileges and immunities of citizens of the United States."

In a series of decisions, the Supreme Court has held that the Due Process Clause of the Fourteenth Amendment makes enforceable against the states those provisions of the Bill of Rights that are "implicit in the concept of ordered liberty." *Palko v. Connecticut,* 302 U.S. 319, 58 S.Ct. 149, 82 L.Ed. 288 (1937). This doctrine of "selective incorporation" has been employed by the Court to enforce the procedural guarantees of the Bill of Rights in state criminal prosecutions. For example, in *Wolf v. Colorado,* 338 U.S. 25, 69 S.Ct. 1359, 93 L.Ed. 1782 (1949), the Court said that the Fourth Amendment protection against unreasonable searches and seizures is applicable to state and local, as well as federal, law enforcement authorities. Similarly, in *Duncan v. Louisiana,* 391 U.S. 145, 88 S.Ct. 1444, 20 L.Ed.2d 491 (1968), the Court held that the Fourteenth Amendment requires states to observe the jury trial requirement of the Sixth Amendment.

In addition to incorporating the procedural protections of the Bill of Rights into the Fourteenth Amendment, the Court has extended the substantive limitations of the Bill of Rights to the states. In 1925 the Supreme Court recognized that the First Amendment protections of free speech and free press applied to state as well as federal laws. *Gitlow v. New York,* 268 U.S. 652, 45 S.Ct. 625, 69 L.Ed. 1138 (1925). Likewise, in 1934 the Court said that the First Amendment guarantee of free exercise of religion is enforceable against state and local governments. *Hamilton v. Regents of the University of California,* 293 U.S. 245, 55 S.Ct. 197, 79 L.Ed. 343 (1934).

Since the process of selective incorporation began in 1897, (see *Chicago, Burlington and Quincy R.R. v. Chicago,* 166 U.S. 226, 17 S.Ct. 581, 41 L.Ed. 979 (1897)), the Court has incorporated virtually all the provisions of the Bill of Rights into the Fourteenth Amendment, making them applicable to the state and local governments. The Federal Constitution, and in particular the Bill of Rights, now stands as a barrier to the enactment or enforcement of unreasonable or oppressive criminal laws, whether they are enacted by Congress, a state legislature, or a local governing body.

THE FIRST AMENDMENT FREEDOM OF EXPRESSION

Perhaps the most treasured of our liberties, and the rights most essential to maintaining a democratic polity, are the First Amendment freedoms of speech and press. Often, freedom of speech and freedom of the press are referred to jointly as freedom of expression. Although the concept of free expression is fundamental to our democratic society, the Supreme Court has said that the First Amendment has "never been thought to give absolute protection to every individual to speak whenever or wherever he pleases, or to use any form of address in any circumstances that he chooses." *Cohen v. California,* 403 U.S. 15, 19, 91 S.Ct. 1780, 1785, 29 L.Ed.2d 284, 290 (1971). The task of the courts, of course, is to strike a reasonable balance between the right of expression and the legitimate interests of society in maintaining security, order, peace, safety, and decency. In what has become a classic phrase, Justice Oliver Wendell Holmes, Jr., observed that the "most stringent protection of free speech would not protect a man in falsely shouting fire in a theater, and causing a panic." *Schenck v. United States,* 249 U.S. 47, 51, 39 S.Ct 247, 249, 63 L.Ed. 470, 473 (1919). Moreover, the Supreme Court has said that certain types of speech are so inherently lacking in value as not to merit any First Amendment protection.

> There are certain well defined and narrowly limited classes of speech, the prevention and punishment of which have never been thought to raise any constitutional problem. These include the lewd and obscene, the profane, the libelous, and the insulting or "fighting" words—those which by their very utterance inflict injury or tend to incite an immediate breach of the peace. It has been well observed that such utterances are no essential part of any exposition of ideas, and are of such slight social value as a step to truth that any benefit that may be derived from them is clearly outweighed by the social interest in order and morality. *Chaplinsky v. New Hampshire,* 315 U.S. 568, 571, 62 S.Ct 766, 769, 86 L.Ed. 1031, 1035 (1942).

Advocacy of Unlawful Conduct

One of the most basic and perplexing problems posed by the First Amendment is whether speech advocating unlawful conduct may itself be made unlawful. The Supreme Court first encountered this problem in *Schenck v. United States, supra,* where an official of the Socialist Party appealed from a conviction under the Espionage Act of 1917, 40 Stat. at L. 217, 219. Charles T. Schenck had been convicted of participating in a conspiracy to cause insubordination in the military services and to obstruct military recruitment at a time when the United States was at war. The "conspiracy" consisted of activities surrounding the mailing of a leaflet to draftees urging them to resist induction into the military. The Supreme Court upheld Schenck's conviction, saying that

> the question in every case is whether the words used are used in such circumstances and are of such a nature as to create clear and present danger that they will bring about the substantive evils that Congress has a right to prevent. It is a question of proximity and degree. When a nation is at war many things that might be said in time of peace are such a hindrance to its effort that their utterance will not be endured so long as men fight, and that no court could regard them as protected by any constitutional right. 249 U.S. at 52, 39 S.Ct. at 249, 63 L.Ed. at 473.

The Supreme Court first invoked the "clear and present danger" doctrine to reverse a criminal conviction in a case involving a Georgia man who had been prosecuted under a state law prohibiting "any attempt, by persuasion or otherwise" to incite insurrection. *Herndon v. Lowry,* 301 U.S. 242, 57 S.Ct. 732, 81

L.Ed. 1066 (1937). Since then, the doctrine has been used by state and federal courts to reverse numerous convictions where persons have been prosecuted for merely advocating illegal acts.

The modern Supreme Court has refined the clear and present danger doctrine so that public advocacy may be prohibited only in situations when there is "imminent lawless action." *Brandenburg v. Ohio*, 395 U.S. 444, 89 S.Ct 1827, 23 L.Ed.2d 430 (1969). Today, it is questionable whether the courts would uphold a conviction in circumstances similar to those in the *Schenck* case. The courts would most likely find that mailing a leaflet or standing on a street corner urging resistance to the draft—activities that were fairly common during the Vietnam War—are not fraught with "imminent lawless action" and therefore do not constitute a clear and present danger.

Symbolic Speech and Expressive Conduct

Freedom of expression is a broad concept embracing speech, publication, performances, and demonstrations. Even the wearing of symbols is considered to be constitutionally protected "symbolic speech." *Tinker v. Des Moines Independent Community School District*, 393 U.S. 503, 89 S.Ct. 733, 21 L.Ed.2d 731 (1969). The Supreme Court has recognized a wide variety of conduct as possessing "sufficient communicative elements to bring the First Amendment to play." *Texas v. Johnson*, 491 U.S. 397, 404, 109 S.Ct. 2533, 2539, 105 L.Ed.2d 342, 353 (1989). The Court has accorded First Amendment protection to, among other things, "sit-ins" by blacks to protest racial segregation, *Brown v. Louisiana*, 383 U.S. 131, 86 S.Ct. 719, 15 L.Ed.2d 637 (1966); the wearing of American military uniforms by civilians to protest the Vietnam War, *Schacht v. United States*, 398 U.S. 58, 90 S.Ct. 1555, 26 L.Ed.2d 44 (1970); and "picketing" over a variety of issues, *Amalgamated Food Employees Union v. Logan Valley Plaza, Inc.*, 391 U.S. 308, 88 S.Ct. 1601, 20 L.Ed.2d 603 (1968).

Without question, the most controversial applications of the concept of expressive conduct have been the Supreme Court's decisions holding that the public burning of the American flag is protected by the First Amendment. In *Texas v. Johnson, supra*, the Court invalidated a Texas statute banning flag desecration. Gregory Johnson had been arrested after he publicly burned an American Flag outside the Republican National Convention in Dallas in 1984. The Supreme Court's decision to reverse Johnson's conviction and strike down the Texas law resulted in a firestorm of public criticism of the Court as well as the enactment of a new federal statute. The Flag Protection Act of 1989, amending 18 U.S.C.A. § 700, imposed criminal penalties on anyone who knowingly "mutilates, defaces, physically defiles, burns, maintains upon the floor or ground, or tramples upon" the American flag. In *United States v. Eichman*, 496 U.S. 310, 110 S.Ct. 2404, 110 L.Ed.2d 287 (1990), the Supreme Court invalidated this federal statute as well, saying that "punishing desecration of the flag dilutes the very freedom that makes this emblem so revered, and worth revering." 496 U.S. at 319, 110 S.Ct. at 2410, 110 L.Ed.2d at 296.

"Fighting Words" and Threats to Public Order

One type of expression that sometimes transgresses the criminal law is public speech that threatens the public peace and order. The Supreme Court has said that

> no one would have the hardihood to suggest that the principle of freedom of speech sanctions incitement to riot . . . When clear and present danger of riot, disorder, interference with traffic upon the public streets, or other immediate threat to public safety, peace, or order appears, the power of the State to prevent and punish is obvious. *Cantwell v. Connecticut,* 310 U.S. 296, 308, 60 S.Ct. 900, 905, 84 L.Ed. 1213, 1220 (1940).

At the same time, government "may not unduly suppress free communication of views . . . under the guise of conserving desirable conditions." *Cantwell v. Connecticut, supra.* Again, the problem for courts is to strike a reasonable balance between legitimate competing interests in the context of the particular facts in the case at hand.

In *Feiner v. New York,* 340 U.S. 315, 71 S.Ct. 303, 95 L.Ed. 295 (1951), the Supreme Court upheld a disorderly conduct conviction stemming from an incident in which a street-corner speaker excited a hostile crowd by insulting President Truman and the mayor of New York. Writing for the Court, Chief Justice Vinson noted that "It is one thing to say that the police cannot be used as an instrument for the suppression of unpopular views and another thing to say that, when as here the speaker passes the bounds of argument or persuasion and undertakes incitement to riot, they are powerless to prevent a breach of the peace." 340 U.S. at 321, 71 S.Ct. at 306, 95 L.Ed. at 300.

As noted previously, the Supreme Court has held that so-called fighting words are unprotected by the Constitution. *Chaplinsky v. New Hampshire, supra.* Fighting words are "those personally abusive epithets which, when addressed to the ordinary citizen, are, as a matter of common knowledge, inherently likely to provoke violent reaction." *Cohen v. California,* 403 U.S. at 20, 91 S.Ct. at 1785, 29 L.Ed.2d at 291.

"Hate Speech"

Would a public cross-burning by the Ku Klux Klan in a black neighborhood qualify as fighting words, or would it be considered expressive conduct protected by the First Amendment? What about the display of swastikas by Nazis parading through the streets of a predominantly Jewish city? Would police be justified in these instances to make arrests for incitement to riot? These questions became more than hypothetical during the 1980s, when the country witnessed a resurgence of racist organizations, and cities and states countered with laws proscribing "hate speech." One such law, a St. Paul, Minnesota, ordinance, provided:

> Whoever places on public or private property a symbol, object, appellation, characterization or graffiti, including, but not limited to, a burning cross or Nazi swastika, which one knows or has reasonable grounds to know arouses anger, alarm or resentment in others on the basis of race, color, creed, religion or gender commits disorderly conduct and shall be guilty of a misdemeanor.

In *R.A.V. v. St. Paul,* 505 U.S. ____, 112 S.Ct. 2538, 120 L.Ed.2d 305 (1992), the Supreme Court declared this ordinance unconstitutional in the context of a criminal prosecution of a white teenager who burned a cross on the front lawn of a black family's home. Lest the public be tempted to conclude that the Supreme Court condoned racially motivated cross-burnings, the Court stated:

> Let there be no mistake about our belief that burning a cross in someone's front yard is reprehensible. But St. Paul has sufficient means at its disposal to prevent such

behavior without adding the First Amendment to the fire. 505 U.S. at ____, 112 S.Ct. at 2550, 120 L.Ed.2d at 326.

Obscenity

Traditionally, state and local governments have proscribed speech, pictures, films, and performances regarded as obscene, generally classifying these as misdemeanor offenses. Despite challenges to the constitutionality of such obscenity laws, the Supreme Court has held that obscenity is beyond the pale of the First Amendment, and thus subject to criminal prosecution. *Roth v. United States,* 354 U.S. 476, 77 S.Ct. 1304, 1 L.Ed.2d 1498 (1957).

The problem for the legislatures, police, prosecutors and courts is to determine what is obscene and therefore unprotected by the First Amendment. The Supreme Court has held that for expression to be obscene, it must (1) appeal to a prurient interest in sex; (2) depict sexual conduct in a patently offensive way; and (3) lack serious literary, artistic, political or scientific value. *Miller v. California,* 413 U.S. 15, 93 S.Ct 2607, 37 L.Ed.2d 419 (1973). Despite this test, arguably, the concept of obscenity remains somewhat vague. Yet the Supreme Court has made it clear that obscenity refers only to "hard-core" pornography. *Jenkins v. Georgia,* 418 U.S. 153, 94 S.Ct. 2750, 41 L.Ed.2d 642 (1974). (The "intractable obscenity problem," as it has been called, is dealt with more fully in Chapter 8.)

Nude Dancing

Every state has a prohibition against indecent exposure. Generally, these statutes are applied in situations where individuals expose themselves in public or private to unwilling viewers. But what if the exposure takes place by mutual consent, such as in a night club that features nude dancing? The Supreme Court has recognized that this form of entertainment is entitled to First Amendment

CASE IN POINT

OBSCENITY

Billy Jenkins managed a movie theater in Albany, Georgia, in which the film "Carnal Knowledge" was being shown. The film, which starred Jack Nicholson, Candice Bergen, Art Garfunkel, and Ann-Margret, appeared on many critics' "Ten Best" lists for 1971. On January 13, 1972, local law enforcement officers entered the theater, pursuant to a warrant, and seized the film. Jenkins was later convicted of distributing obscene material and was fined $750 and sentenced to 12 months probation. By a divided vote, the Georgia Supreme Court affirmed the conviction. On appeal, the United States Supreme Court reversed Jenkins' conviction, holding that "Carnal Knowledge" simply was not hard-core pornography and was thus protected under the First Amendment standards delineated in *Miller v. California.*

Jenkins v. Georgia, 418 U.S. 153, 94 S.Ct. 2750, 41 L.Ed.2d 642 (1974).

protection under certain circumstances, but has also expressed a willingness to uphold reasonable regulations, especially involving establishments that serve alcoholic beverages. *Doran v. Salem Inn,* 422 U.S. 922, 95 S.Ct. 2561, 45 L.Ed.2d 648 (1975). In *Barnes v. Glen Theatre, Inc.,* 501 U.S. 560, 111 S.Ct. 2456, 115 L.Ed.2d 504 (1991), the Court upheld an Indiana statute requiring that night club dancers wear "pasties" and "G-strings" when they dance. In an opinion expressing the view of three justices, Chief Justice Rehnquist observed that

> the governmental interest served . . . is societal disapproval of nudity in public places among strangers. The statutory prohibition is not a means to some greater end, but an end in itself. It is without cavil that the public indecency statute is "narrowly tailored"; Indiana's requirement that the dancers wear at least pasties and a G-string is modest, and the bare minimum necessary to achieve the state's purpose. 501 U.S. at ____, 111 S.Ct. at 2463, 115 L.Ed.2d at 515.

Profanity

Although in *Chaplinsky v. New Hampshire, supra,* the Supreme Court specifically enumerated profanity as being among those categories of speech so lacking in value as not to merit First Amendment protection, this view no longer prevails. In *Cohen v. California, supra,* the Supreme Court invalidated the "offensive conduct" conviction of a man who entered a courthouse wearing a jacket emblazoned with the slogan "Fuck the Draft." Writing for the Court, Justice Harlan opined that

> the state has no right to cleanse public debate to the point where it is grammatically palatable to the most squeamish among us. Yet no readily ascertainable general principle exists for stopping short of that result if we were to affirm the judgment below. For, while the particular four-letter-word being litigated here is perhaps more distasteful than others of its genre, it is nevertheless often true that one man's vulgarity is another's lyric. Indeed, we think it is largely because government officials cannot make principled distinctions in this area that the Constitution leaves matters of taste and style so largely to the individual. 403 U.S. at 25, 91 S.Ct. at 1788, 29 L.Ed.2d at 294.

Notwithstanding the Supreme Court's decision in *Cohen v. California,* most states and many cities retain laws proscribing profanity. These laws are seldom enforced and even more rarely challenged in court.

FREEDOM OF ASSEMBLY

The First Amendment specifically protects the "right of the people peaceably to assemble." Yet, as we have seen, one of the most important purposes of the criminal law is to maintain public peace and order. Sometimes these values come into conflict, as in the civil rights struggle of the 1960s, when public demonstrations became an important part of a powerful political movement. See, for example, *Cox v. Louisiana,* 379 U.S. 559, 85 S.Ct. 476, 13 L.Ed.2d 487 (1965); *Adderley v. Florida,* 385 U.S. 39, 87 S.Ct. 242, 17 L.Ed.2d 149 (1966); *Walker v. City of Birmingham,* 388 U.S. 307, 87 S.Ct. 1824, 18 L.Ed.2d 1210 (1967).

In one classic case, *Edwards v. South Carolina,* 372 U.S. 229, 83 S.Ct. 680, 9 L.Ed.2d 697 (1963), the Supreme Court reversed the breach-of-the-peace convictions of 187 black citizens who were arrested after they refused to disperse a peaceful civil rights demonstration on the grounds of the state capitol. The Court, per Justice Stewart, found that the "circumstances in this case reflect an exercise of . . . constitutional rights in their most pristine and classic form." 372 U.S. at 235, 83 S.Ct. at 683, 9 L.Ed.2d at 702.

As the *Edwards* decision indicates, governments may not ban assemblies in the public forum as long as they are peaceful and do not impede the operations of government or the activities of other citizens. Yet, in order to promote the interests of safety, order and peace, governments may impose reasonable time, place, and manner regulations on public assemblies. The character of a given place and the pattern of its normal activities determine the type of time, place, and manner regulations that the courts consider reasonable. *Grayned v. City of Rockford,* 408 U.S. 104, 92 S.Ct. 2294, 33 L.Ed.2d 222 (1972). For example, a restriction against the use of sound amplifiers in close proximity to a courthouse or library might well be judged reasonable, while a ban on "picketing" on the steps of the same buildings would not. In imposing time, place, and manner regulations, governments must be careful not to deprive demonstrations or protests of their essential content by imposing excessive or unnecessarily burdensome regulations. *United States v. Grace,* 461 U.S. 171, 103 S.Ct. 1702, 75 L.Ed.2d 736 (1983).

Free Exercise of Religion

The value of freedom of religion is so deeply rooted in American culture that rarely have legislatures sought to impinge directly on that right. Yet from time to time lawmakers have sought to prevent certain unpopular religious groups from proselytizing. The Supreme Court has been quick to invalidate such efforts. In one leading case, the Court struck down a state statute that made it a misdemeanor for any person to solicit door-to-door for religious or philanthropic reasons without prior approval from local officials, who were authorized to make determinations as to whether solicitors represented bona fide religions. The law was successfully challenged by a member of the Jehovah's Witnesses sect who was prosecuted for engaging in door-to-door proselytizing without a permit. *Cantwell v. Connecticut, supra.*

Much more problematic are government attempts to enforce criminal statutes designed to protect the public health, safety, and welfare against religious practices deemed inimical to these interests. Does the right to freely exercise one's religion permit one to violate an otherwise valid criminal statute? In 1878, the Supreme Court answered this question in the negative by upholding the prosecution of a polygamist. *Reynolds v. United States,* 98 U.S. (8 Otto) 145, 25 L.Ed. 244 (1878). More recently, however, the Supreme Court granted to members of the Old Order Amish sect an exemption to the Wisconsin compulsory education law. The Court found that the law significantly interfered with the Amish way of life and thus violated their right to freely exercise their religion. *Wisconsin v. Yoder,* 406 U.S. 205, 92 S.Ct. 1526, 32 L.Ed.2d 15 (1972).

CASE IN POINT

FREE EXERCISE OF RELIGION

Douglas Clifford was convicted of driving without a license, as required by Washington law, 46.20.021. On appeal, he claimed that the state requirement that he obtain a license violated his right to free exercise of religion in that "to accept the licensing requirements of the State is to put the State on a footing equal or superior to God, absolutely contrary to my convictions." The Washington Court of Appeals, Division 3, affirmed the conviction. Although accepting the sincerity of Clifford's religious objections to the law, the court sustained the constitutionality of the statute as applied. The court observed that "the licensing statute serves a compelling state interest in law enforcement as well as a compelling state interest in highway safety." The court further observed that "any exemption to the licensing requirement carved out for religious reasons . . . would eventually be requested by a potentially unlimited number of members of their religious community."

State v. Clifford, 787 P.2d 575 (Wash. App. 1990).

Unusual Religious Practices

Several state courts have decided cases arising from unusual forms of worship. The Tennessee Supreme Court upheld the validity of a statute making it a crime to handle poisonous snakes in religious ceremonies against the claim that the law violated the right to free exercise of religion guaranteed by the state constitution. *Harden v. State,* 216 S.W.2d 708 (Tenn. 1949).

In a decision that cuts the other way, the California Supreme Court reversed the convictions of several members of the Native American Church for possession of peyote. *People v. Woody,* 394 P.2d 813 (Cal. 1964). In the court's view, the sacramental use of peyote was central to the worship of the Native American Church, and thus protected by the First Amendment. Similarly, an Oklahoma appellate court recognized the right of members of the Native American Church to use peyote in religious rituals. *State v. Whitehorn,* 561 P.2d 539 (Okl. Crim. App. 1977). Yet the appellate court cautioned against the nonsacramental use of the drug, which would still be subject to criminal prosecution.

In 1990, the U.S. Supreme Court held that the sacramental use of peyote by members of the Native American Church was *not* protected by the Free Exercise Clause of the First Amendment. *Employment Division v. Smith,* 494 U.S. 872, 110 S.Ct. 1595, 108 L.Ed.2d 876 (1990). This decision by the Nation's highest court means that state courts that have granted such protection may wish to reconsider their positions. However, in our federal system, state courts are free to provide greater levels of protection to individual rights under the terms of their state constitutions than those provided by the federal constitution.

Refusal of Medical Treatment

One of the more troubling and tragic situations in which the Free Exercise Clause potentially comes into conflict with the criminal law involves the refusal of medical treatment. Certain religious groups, such the Christian Scientists, believe that physical healing is to be achieved through spiritual power. Thus, when faced with an illness or injury, they are likely to refuse medical treatment. Other groups, such as the Jehovah's Witnesses, believe that blood transfusions are specifically enjoined by Scripture.

The courts have recognized the right of a competent adult to refuse medical treatment on religious grounds, even if the refusal results in death. See, for example, *In re Estate of Brooks,* 205 N.E.2d 435 (Ill. 1965); *In re Milton,* 505 N.E.2d 255 (Ohio 1987). It is another matter entirely when parents refuse to allow medical treatment for their children. The Supreme Court has recognized that

> parents may be free to become martyrs themselves. But it does not follow that they are free in identical circumstances, to make martyrs of their children before they have reached the age of full legal discretion when they can make that choice for themselves. *Prince v. Massachusetts,* 321 U.S. 158, 170, 64 S.Ct. 438, 444, 88 L.Ed. 645, 654 (1944).

Accordingly, courts seldom allow freedom of religion as a defense to a criminal charge stemming from a situation in which parents refused to seek or allow medical treatment for their children. In one recent case, a member of the Christian Scientist faith was prosecuted for involuntary manslaughter after failing to seek medical treatment of her daughter's meningitis, which turned out to be fatal. The California Supreme Court rejected the defendant's free exercise of religion defense, saying that "parents have *no* right to free exercise of religion at the price of a child's life." *Walker v. Superior Court,* 763 P.2d 852 (Cal. 1988).

THE RIGHT TO KEEP AND BEAR ARMS

There are numerous criminal prohibitions—at the federal, state, and local levels—against the sale, possession, and use of certain types of firearms. "Gun

---

CASE IN POINT

FREE EXERCISE OF RELIGION

After receiving a number of complaints about the practice of animal sacrifice associated with the Santeria religion, the city of Hialeah, Florida adopted an ordinance making it an offense to "unnecessarily kill, torment, torture, or mutilate an animal in a public or private ritual or ceremony not for the primary purpose of food consumption." Practitioners of Santeria sued to challenge the constitutionality of the ordinance. On June 11, 1993, the United States Supreme Court unanimously declared the ordinance unconstitutional. Writing for the Court, Justice Anthony Kennedy observed that "the laws in question were enacted by officials who did not understand, failed to perceive, or chose to ignore the fact that their official actions violated the Nation's essential commitment to religious freedom."

Church of the Lukumi Babula Aye, Inc. v. City of Hialeah, 508 U.S. ___ , 113 S.Ct. 2217, 124 L.Ed.2d 472 (1993).

---

control" laws are seen by many as antithetical to the "right to keep and bear arms." The Second Amendment to the U.S. Constitution provides:

> A well regulated Militia, being necessary to the security of a free state, the right of the people to keep and bear arms shall not be infringed.

In *United States v. Miller,* 307 U.S. 174, 59 S.Ct. 816, 83 L.Ed 1206 (1939), the Supreme Court upheld a federal law criminalizing the interstate shipment of sawed-off shotguns, saying that "the right to keep and bear arms" had to be interpreted in relation to the "well regulated militia." The Court concluded that possession of sawed-off shotguns had no reasonable relationship to serving in the militia. In recently reaffirming *Miller,* the Court said that "the Second Amendment guarantees no right to keep and bear a firearm that does not have some reasonable relationship to the preservation or efficiency of a well regulated militia." *Lewis v. United States,* 445 U.S. 55, 65 n.8, 100 S.Ct. 915, 921 n.8, 63 L.Ed.2d 198, 209 n.8 (1980). Like the federal constitution, many state constitutions contain language dealing with the right to keep and bear arms. Yet state courts tend to give wide latitude to state and local gun control laws.

THE DOCTRINES OF VAGUENESS AND OVERBREADTH

The Fifth Amendment to the U.S. Constitution provides that "no person . . . shall be deprived of life, liberty or property without due process of law." The two fundamental aspects of due process are "fair notice" and "fair hearing." The principle of fair notice implies that a person has a right to know whether particular contemplated conduct is illegal. The Supreme Court has emphatically stated, "No one may be required at peril of life, liberty or property to speculate as to the meaning of penal statutes." *Lanzetta v. New Jersey,* 306 U.S. 451, 453, 59 S.Ct. 618, 619, 83 L.Ed. 888, 890 (1939). A criminal law that is excessively vague in its proscriptions offends this principle, and is thus invalid under the Due Process Clause of the Fifth or Fourteenth Amendments (depending on whether it is a *federal* or *state* statute). However, we must realize that the vagueness doctrine is "designed more to limit the discretion of police and prosecutors than to ensure that statutes are intelligible to persons pondering criminal activity." *United States v. White,* 882 F.2d 250, 252 (7th Cir. 1989). Accordingly, the Supreme Court has held that the requisite specificity of criminal statutes may be achieved through judicial interpretation. *Rose v. Locke,* 423 U.S. 48, 96 S.Ct. 243, 46 L.Ed.2d 185 (1975). As interpreted by the Seventh Circuit Court of Appeals in *United States v. White,* "provided that conduct is of a sort widely known among the lay public to be criminal. . . , a person is not entitled to clear notice that the conduct violates a *particular* criminal statute." [emphasis in original] *United States v. White, supra* at 252.

In a landmark decision, the Supreme Court struck down a Jacksonville, Florida, ordinance that prohibited various forms of vagrancy including loitering and "prowling by auto." *Papachristou v. Jacksonville,* 405 U.S. 156, 92 S.Ct. 839, 31 L.Ed.2d 110 (1972). Writing for the Court in *Papachristou,* Justice Douglas objected to the "unfettered discretion" the ordinance placed in the hands of the police, allowing for "arbitrary and discriminatory enforcement of the law." (For further discussion of the vagueness doctrine as it relates to the crimes of vagrancy and loitering, see Chapter 11.)

CASE IN POINT

THE RIGHT TO KEEP AND BEAR ARMS

Part I, Article 2-a of the New Hampshire Constitution provides: "All persons have the right to keep and bear arms in defense of themselves, their families, their property and the state." At the same time, a New Hampshire statute proscribes possession of firearms by convicted felons. RSA 159:3. Scott Smith, who was convicted in the Rockingham Superior Court of being a felon in possession of a firearm, challenged the constitutionality of the statute. The New Hampshire Supreme Court affirmed the conviction and sustained the validity of the statute, saying, "the State constitutional right to keep and bear arms is not absolute and may be subject to restriction and regulation. . . . The governmental interest served by the statute, protection of human life and property, is patently significant."

State v. Smith, 571 A.2d 279, 281 (N.H. 1990).

Closely related to the concept of vagueness, the doctrine of overbreadth was developed exclusively in the context of the First Amendment. It is concerned with the precision of a criminal law that potentially infringes on First Amendment freedoms. Thus a law that forbids people from congregating on the street and engaging in speech that is "annoying" to passersby is overbroad. *Coates v. City of Cincinnati,* 402 U.S. 611, 91 S.Ct. 1686, 29 L.Ed.2d 214 (1971). The overbreadth of the law may permit police to make arrests for constitutionally protected conduct, such as political speech, as well as unprotected activity, such as fighting words.

The doctrine of overbreadth enables a person to contest the legality of a law imposing restrictions on First Amendment freedoms even when he or she has not been charged with violating the law. It also permits the person being prosecuted to challenge the facial constitutionality of the law, even though his or her actions might not be constitutionally protected, on the ground that the law might be applied in the future against activities protected by the First Amendment. This controversial doctrine was designed to bring to the courts' attention laws that have a "chilling effect" on the exercise of First Amendment rights.

In the 1980s, the Supreme Court appeared to be retreating somewhat from the overbreadth doctrine. In *New York v. Ferber,* 458 U.S. 747, 102 S.Ct. 3348, 73 L.Ed.2d 1113 (1982), for example, the Court rejected an overbreadth challenge to a child pornography statute that criminalized child pornography well beyond the legal test of obscenity delineated in *Miller v. California, supra.* Although expressing concern that the statute might possibly be applied to punish constitutionally protected artistic expression, the Court concluded that the law was not "substantially overbroad" and that impermissible applications of the statute should be addressed on a case-by-case basis. According to the *Ferber* Court, a statute should not be invalidated for overbreadth if its legitimate reach "dwarfs its arguably impermissible applications." 458 U.S. at 773, 102 S.Ct. at 3363, 73 L.Ed.2d at 1133.

THE PROHIBITION AGAINST CRUEL AND UNUSUAL PUNISHMENTS

The Eighth Amendment prohibits the imposition of "cruel and unusual punishments." This principle applies both to the procedures by which criminal sentences are imposed, *Furman v. Georgia*, 408 U.S. 238, 92 S.Ct. 2726, 33 L.Ed.2d 346 (1972), and to the substantive laws that define punishments. For example, in *Coker v. Georgia*, 433 U.S. 584, 97 S.Ct. 2861, 53 L.Ed.2d 982 (1977), the Supreme Court invalidated a provision of a state death penalty law that allowed capital punishment in cases of rape. Writing for the plurality, Justice White concluded that "the death penalty, which is 'unique in its severity and its irrevocability,'is an excessive penalty for the rapist who, as such, does not take human life." 433 U.S. at 598, 97 S.Ct. at 2869, 53 L.Ed.2d at 993. Generally, however, in Eighth Amendment cases, the Supreme Court does not rule on the validity of a statute, but rather confines its inquiry to the constitutionality of a particular sentence. For example, in *Solem v. Helm*, 463 U.S. 277, 103 S.Ct. 3001, 77 L.Ed.2d. 637 (1983), the Supreme Court vacated a life sentence without possibility of parole imposed under a state habitual offender law. The Court found that life imprisonment without parole was significantly disproportionate to the defendant's crimes, all of which were nonviolent in nature.

On occasion, the Eighth Amendment has even been employed to limit the definition of crimes. In *Robinson v. California*, 370 U.S. 660, 82 S.Ct. 1417, 8 L.Ed.2d 758 (1962), the Supreme Court, relying on the Cruel and Unusual Punishments Clause, struck down a state law that made it a crime for a person to be "addicted to the use of narcotics." The Court found it unacceptable that an individual could be punished merely for a "status" without regard to any specific criminal conduct. In effect, the Court "constitutionalized" the traditional requirement that a crime involve a specific *actus reus*.

CASE IN POINT

THE VAGUENESS DOCTRINE

Dan D. Robinson was convicted of failing to "securely confine or restrain a vicious dog," an offense under Ohio R.C. § 955.22(D)(1).Under 955.11(A)(4)(a)(iii), a "vicious dog" included any dog that belonged to "a breed that is commonly known as a pit bull dog." On appeal, Robinson challenged the law as excessively vague in that it failed to define the meaning of *pit bull*. An Ohio appellate court rejected the challenge, saying that although the statute lacked a specific definition, "mathematical certainty is not always essential to constitutionality." The court concluded that the statute "refers to those animals which display the physical characteristics generally conforming to the various standards normally associated with pit bulls."

State v. Robinson, 541 N.E. 2d 1092, 1097 (Ohio App. 1989).

The Constitutional Right of Privacy

Although there is no mention of "privacy" in the text of the Constitution, the Supreme Court has held that a sphere of intimate personal conduct is immune from legislative interference. In its first explicit recognition of this "meta-textual" constitutional right, *Griswold v. Connecticut,* 381 U.S. 479, 85 S.Ct. 1678, 14 L.Ed.2d 510 (1965), the Court relied in part on the Ninth Amendment, which provides that:

> The enumeration in the Constitution, of certain rights, shall not be construed to deny or disparage others retained by the people.

In the *Griswold* case, the Supreme Court invalidated as applied to married couples a state law proscribing the use of birth control devices. In *Eisenstadt v. Baird,* 405 U.S. 438, 92 S.Ct. 1029, 31 L.Ed.2d 349 (1972), the Court extended the principle to protect single individuals from a similar anti-contraception statute. Writing for the Court in *Eisenstadt,* Justice Brennan stated that the right of privacy is "the right of the individual, married or single, to be free from unwarranted governmental intrusion into matters so fundamentally affecting a person as the decision whether or not to beget a child." 405 U.S. at 453, 92 S.Ct. at 1038, 31 L.Ed.2d at 362.

Abortion

The Supreme Court's *Griswold* and *Eisenstadt* decisions paved the way for its landmark abortion decision in *Roe v. Wade,* 410 U.S. 113, 93 S.Ct. 705, 35 L.Ed.2d 147 (1973). In *Roe,* per Justice Blackmun, the Court held that the right of privacy was broad enough to include a woman's decision to terminate her pregnancy. This 7–2 decision invalidated the Texas antiabortion statute, and rendered unenforceable similar laws in most states. The essential holding in *Roe v. Wade* was reaffirmed by the Supreme Court in 1992, albeit by a 5–4 vote. *Planned Parenthood v. Casey,* 505 U.S. ____ , 112 S. Ct. 2791, 120 L.Ed.2d 674. The shrinking Supreme Court majority favoring the constitutional right to abortion and the continuing "pro-life" and "pro-choice" demonstrations around the country attest to the extremely controversial nature of the right to abortion. (The abortion issue is discussed more thoroughly in Chapter 6.)

Sexual Conduct

In 1986, the Supreme Court declined to extend the right of privacy to protect homosexual conduct between consenting adults. In *Bowers v. Hardwick,* 478 U.S. 186, 106 S.Ct. 2841, 92 L.Ed.2d 140 (1986), the Court upheld a Georgia statute making sodomy a crime. However, the Court did not address the question of whether the state could enforce its sodomy law against private heterosexual activity between consenting adults. Under a strict interpretation of the right of privacy, sexual relations between consenting adults would not be subject to governmental prohibition. Such a principle could, of course, invalidate long-standing (and still fairly prevalent, if seldom enforced) proscriptions against sodomy, adultery, fornication, and seduction. It might also raise serious questions as to the validity of statutes proscribing incest, bigamy, and prostitution, which are nearly universal among the American states (see Chapter 8).

The Right to Die

As we noted previously in the context of free exercise of religion, courts have held that competent adults have the right to refuse medical treatment in some circumstances. It is now well-established that a competent adult with a terminal illness has the right to refuse medical treatment that would unnaturally prolong his or her life. See, for example, *Satz v. Perlmutter,* 379 So.2d 359 (Fla. 1980). Under certain circumstances courts have allowed the family of a comatose individual to direct removal of extraordinary means of life support. See, for example, *In re Quinlan,* 355 A.2d 647 (N.J. 1976), cert. denied, 429 U.S. 922, 97 S.Ct. 319, 50 L.Ed.2d 289 (1976).

The so-called right to die, if extended beyond the right of a terminally ill person to refuse artificial means of life support, runs headlong into criminal prohibitions against suicide and, potentially, homicide. As yet, courts have been unwilling to extend the right of privacy this far. For example, in *Gilbert v. State,* 487 So.2d 1185 (Fla.App. 1986), a Florida appeals court rejected Roswell Gilbert's "euthanasia" defense to the charge that he committed premeditated murder against his wife, who suffered from osteoporosis and Alzheimer's disease (see Chapter 6).

Equal Protection of the Laws

The Fourteenth Amendment of the U.S. Constitution forbids states from denying persons "equal protection of the laws." The Due Process Clause of the Fifth Amendment has been interpreted to impose a similar prohibition on the federal government. *Bolling v. Sharpe,* 347 U.S. 497, 74 S.Ct. 693, 98 L.Ed. 884 (1954). Most state constitutions contain similar requirements. On occasion, the concept of equal protection has been used to challenge the validity of criminal statutes. For example, in *Loving v. Virginia,* 388 U.S. 1, 87 S.Ct. 1817, 18 L.Ed.2d 1010 (1967), the Supreme Court relied on the Equal Protection Clause of the Fourteenth Amendment in striking down a state statute that criminalized interracial marriage. The effect of *Loving* was that any law that criminalized conduct solely on the basis of the race of the parties was rendered null and void. In *Eisenstadt v. Baird, supra,* the Court invoked the Equal Protection Clause in striking a Massachusetts law that criminalized the use of birth control devices by single persons, but not by married couples. And in *Craig v. Boren,* 429 U.S. 190, 97 S.Ct. 451, 50 L.Ed.2d 397 (1976), the Court invalidated an Oklahoma law that forbade the sale of beer containing 3.2 percent alcohol to females under the age of eighteen and males under the age of twenty-one. The Court concluded that the state lacked a sufficient justification for discriminating between the sexes in the availability of the contested beverage.

STANDARDS OF JUDICIAL REVIEW

At a minimum, a criminal law that touches on constitutionally protected interests must be "rationally related to furthering a legitimate government interest." *Massachusetts Board of Retirement v. Murgia*, 427 U.S. 307, 96 S.Ct. 2562, 49 L.Ed.2d 520 (1976). For example, a state law that makes it a crime for a person to perform surgery without a license is obviously a rational means of advancing the state's legitimate interests in public health and safety. Thus, even though the law deprives lay persons of their right to make contracts freely, and discriminates against those unable to obtain a license, there is little doubt it would withstand judicial review under the "rational basis test."

Criminal laws that infringe "fundamental rights" such as First Amendment freedoms are judged by a more stringent standard of review. Such laws are subject to "strict judicial scrutiny," which means, in effect, that they are presumed to be unconstitutional. To survive judicial review, government must show that the challenged law furthers a compelling government interest. *Shapiro v. Thompson*, 394 U.S. 618, 89 S.Ct. 1322, 22 L.Ed.2d 600 (1969). This is a heavy burden for the government to carry. Consequently, many laws subjected to strict judicial scrutiny are declared unconstitutional. However, the application of strict scrutiny is not necessarily equivalent to a declaration of unconstitutionality. For example, in *New York v. Ferber, supra,* the Supreme Court upheld a child pornography law that impinged on the First Amendment freedom of expression because, in the view of the Court, the law served a compelling interest in protecting children from the abuse typically associated with the pornography industry.

THE IMPORTANCE OF STATE CONSTITUTIONS

Under our federal system of government, the highest court of each state possesses the authority to interpret with finality its state constitution and statutes. A decision by a state court is not subject to review by the United States Supreme Court, except insofar as the state law on which it is based is being challenged as a violation of the federal constitution and/or statutes. Since every state constitution contains language protecting individual rights and liberties, many state court decisions implicate both state and federal constitutional provisions. Under the relevant language of their constitutions and statutes, state courts are free to recognize greater (but not lesser) protections of individual rights than are provided by the U.S. Constitution as interpreted by the federal courts. As a result of the increased conservatism of the federal judiciary, and in particular the Supreme Court, over the last decade, there has been a resurgence of interest in state constitutional law as it relates to civil rights and liberties.

In *Michigan v. Long*, 463 U.S. 1032, 1040, 103 S.Ct. 3469, 3476, 77 L.Ed.2d 1201, 1214 (1983), the U.S. Supreme Court said that "when a state court decision fairly appears to rest primarily on federal law, or to be interwoven with the federal law, and when the adequacy and independence of any possible state law ground is not clear from the face of the opinion, we will accept as the most reasonable explanation that the state court decided the case the way it did because it believed that federal law required it to do so." However, the Court also indicated that "if the state court decision indicates clearly and expressly that it is alternatively based on bona fide separate, adequate, and independent grounds, we, of course, will not undertake to review the decision." 463 U.S. at 1041, 103 S.Ct. at 3476, 77 L.Ed.2d at 1214 (1983).

Michigan v. Long effectively invited the state courts to consider the parallel provisions of their state constitutions independently. Some state courts have accepted the invitation. For example, in *In re T.W.*, 551 So.2d 1186 (Fla. 1989), the Florida Supreme Court struck down as a violation of the right of privacy a statute that required parental consent in cases where minors sought abortions. The constitutionality of a similar law had been upheld on federal grounds by the U.S. Supreme Court in *Planned Parenthood v. Ashcroft*, 462 U.S. 476, 103 S.Ct. 2517, 76 L.Ed.2d 733 (1983). In *T.W.*, the Florida Supreme Court made it clear that it was basing its decision on an amendment to the Florida Constitution that (unlike the federal constitution) explicitly protects the right of privacy. Similarly, in *State v. Kam*, 748 P.2d 372 (Hawaii 1988), the Hawaii Supreme Court adopted an interpretation of its state constitution that affords considerably broader protection to pornography than that provided by the U.S. Constitution. Finally, in *Williams v. City of Fort Worth*, 782 S.W.2d 290 (Tex. 1989), a Texas appellate court struck down as a violation of the state equal rights amendment a city ordinance prohibiting females, but not males, from publicly exposing their breasts! These decisions, and many others like them, mean that a person interested in constitutional limitations on the prohibition of criminal conduct must not ignore the provisions of state constitutions that parallel the U. S. Constitution.

CONCLUSION

The constitutional limitations discussed in this chapter have a direct bearing on the legislative definition of crimes, especially with respect to offenses against public morality (discussed in Chapter 8) and offenses against public order (discussed in Chapter 11). The well-established power of judicial review sustains both the constitutional rights of the individual and the rule of law. These rights and principles impose serious constraints on the definition of criminal conduct and the enforcement of the criminal law.

QUESTIONS FOR THOUGHT AND DISCUSSION

1. Can you think of a hypothetical example of a bill of attainder? What about an *ex post facto* law?
2. Is it possible for the criminal law to define the crime of obscenity, precisely enough to avoid the "vice of vagueness" or the problem of overbreadth?
3. Can a municipality enforce an ordinance totally banning religious organizations from canvassing neighborhoods in search of new members? What about an ordinance that prohibits such canvassing between the hours of 8 P.M. and 8 A.M.?
4. Should the constitutional right of privacy invalidate criminal statutes that proscribe homosexual conduct between consenting adults?

5. Would the constitutional right of privacy provide a defense to a charge of possession of obscene materials where videotapes were viewed only by the defendant in the privacy of his or her home?
6. John Masters, a licensed psychotherapist, has been charged with violating a new state statute making it a crime for "any licensed psychologist, psychiatrist, or psychotherapist to have sexual intercourse with a patient during the existence of the professional relationship." Masters is challenging the constitutionality of the statute on two principal grounds: (a) that it intrudes on his right of privacy; and (b) that it violates the Equal Protection Clause of the Fourteenth Amendment in that it fails to apply the same prohibition to other health-care professionals. Do you think Masters is likely to prevail in his challenge to the statute? If you were a judge faced with these constitutional questions, how would you be inclined to rule? What additional information would you need to render your decision?
7. Could a father who, without judicial approval, unplugs the respirator sustaining the breathing of his comatose, terminally ill child be prosecuted for murder?
8. Would a law making it an offense for a person to carry prescription medicine in other than the original labeled container meet the rational basis test?
9. How does the doctrine of judicial review affect the power of a state legislature to define criminal conduct? Would the constitutional limitations on legislative power be as stringent without the power of courts to declare laws unconstitutional?

A NOTE ON READING AND BRIEFING CASES

Beginning with this chapter, each chapter in this book includes a number of excerpted decisions by appellate courts. We have chosen these decisions to illustrate some of the important concepts and principles described in the chapters. Some instructors may wish to have their students "brief" some or all of these cases. Whether or not the instructor assigns it, students may find briefing cases useful in learning material and preparing for examinations.

A case brief is simply a summary of a court decision, usually in outline format. Typically, a case brief contains the following elements:

1. The name of the case, the court deciding the case, and the date of the decision
2. The essential facts of the case
3. The key issue(s) of law involved (or those applicable to a point of law being considered)
4. The holding of the court
5. A brief summary of the court's opinion, especially as it relates to the key issue(s) in the case
6. Summaries of concurring and dissenting opinions, if any

Students may also wish to make a note of any questions or comments they have at the end of the brief.

CASES

BRANDENBURG V. OHIO

Supreme Court of the United States, 1969.
395 U.S. 444, 89 S. Ct. 1827, 23 L.Ed.2d 430.

[In this landmark case, the U.S. Supreme Court considers whether, and under what circumstances, the advocacy of unlawful conduct is protected by the First Amendment.]

PER CURIAM.

The appellant, a leader of a Ku Klux Klan group, was convicted under the Ohio Criminal Syndicalism statute for "advocat[ing] . . . the duty, necessity, or propriety of crime, sabotage, violence, or unlawful methods of terrorism as a means of accomplishing industrial or political reform" and for "voluntarily assembl[ing] with any society, group, or assemblage of persons formed to teach or advocate the doctrines of criminal syndicalism." . . . He was fined $1,000 and sentenced to one to 10 years' imprisonment. The appellant challenged the constitutionality of the criminal syndicalism statute under the First and Fourteenth Amendments to the United States Constitution, but the intermediate appellate court of Ohio affirmed his conviction without opinion. The Supreme Court of Ohio dismissed his appeal, sua sponte, "for the reason that no substantial constitutional question exists herein." It did not file an opinion or explain its conclusions. Appeal was taken to this Court, and we noted probable jurisdiction. . . .

The record shows that a man, identified at trial as the appellant, telephoned an announcer-reporter on the staff of a Cincinnati television station and invited him to come to a Ku Klux Klan "rally" to be held at a farm in Hamilton County. With the cooperation of the organizers, the reporter and a cameraman attended the meeting and filmed the events. Portions of the films were later broadcast on the local station and on a national network.

The prosecution's case rested on the films and on testimony identifying the appellant as the person who communicated with the reporter and who spoke at the rally. The State also introduced into evidence several articles appearing in the film, including a pistol, a rifle, a shotgun, ammunition, a Bible, and a red hood worn by the speaker in the films.

One film showed 12 hooded figures, some of whom carried firearms. They were gathered around a large wooden cross, which they burned. No one was present other than the participants and the newsmen who made the film. Most of the words uttered during the scene were incomprehensible when the film was projected, but scattered phrases could be understood that were derogatory of Negroes and, in one instance, of Jews. Another scene on the same film showed the appellant, in Klan regalia, making a speech. The speech, in full, was as follows:

"This is an organizers' meeting. We have had quite a few members here today which are—we have hundreds, hundreds of members throughout the State of Ohio. I can quote from a newspaper clipping from the Columbus, Ohio, Dispatch, five weeks ago Sunday morning. The Klan has more members in the State of Ohio than does any other organization. We're not a revengent organization, but if our President, our Congress, our Supreme Court, continues to suppress the white, Caucasian race, it's possible that there might have to be some revengeance taken.

"We are marching on Congress July the Fourth, four hundred thousand strong. From there we are dividing into two groups, one group to march on St. Augustine, Florida, the other group to march into Mississippi. Thank you."

The second film showed six hooded figures, one of whom, later identified as the appellant, repeated a speech very similar to that recorded on the first film. The reference to the possibility of "revengeance" was omitted, and one sentence was added: "Personally, I believe the nigger should be returned to Africa, the Jew returned to Israel." Though some of the figures in the films carried weapons, the speaker did not.

The Ohio Criminal Syndicalism Statute was enacted in 1919. From 1917 to 1920, identical or quite similar laws were adopted by 20 States and two territories. In 1927, this Court sustained the constitutionality of California's Criminal Syndicalism Act, the test of which is quite similar to that of the laws of Ohio. . . . The Court upheld the statute on the ground that, without more, "advocating" violent means to effect political and economic change involves such danger to the security of the State that the State may outlaw it. But [this view] has been thoroughly discredited by later decisions. . . . These later decisions have fashioned the principle that the constitutional guarantees of free speech and free press do not permit a State to forbid advocacy . . . [unless it] is directed to inciting or producing imminent lawless action and is likely to incite or produce such action. As we said in Noto v. United States, "the mere abstract teaching . . . of the moral propriety or even moral necessity for a resort to force and violence, is not the same as preparing a group for violent action and steeling it to such action." A statute which fails to draw this distinction impermissibly intrudes upon the freedoms guaranteed by the First and Fourteenth Amendments. It sweeps within its condemnation speech which our Constitution has immunized from governmental control. . . .

Measured by this test, Ohio's Criminal Syndicalism Act cannot be sustained. The Act punishes persons who "advocate or teach the duty, necessity, or propriety" of violence "as a means of accomplishing industrial or political reform"; or who publish or circulate or display any book or paper containing such advocacy; or who "justify" the commission of violent acts "with intent to exemplify, spread or advocate the propriety of the doctrines of criminal syndicalism"; or who "voluntarily assemble" with a group formed "to teach or advocate the doctrines of criminal syndicalism." Neither the indictment nor the trial judge's instructions to the jury in any way refined the statute's bald definition of the crime in terms of mere advocacy not distinguished from incitement to imminent lawless action.

Accordingly, we are here confronted with a statute which, by its own words and as applied, purports to punish mere advocacy and to forbid, on pain of criminal punishment, assembly with others merely to advocate the described type of action. Such a statute falls within the condemnation of the First and Fourteenth Amendments. The contrary teaching of Whitney v. California [1927] . . . cannot be supported and that decision is therefore overruled.

Reversed.

Mr. Justice BLACK, concurring . . .

Mr. Justice DOUGLAS, concurring . . .

Miller v. California

Supreme Court of the United States, 1973.
413 U.S. 15, 93 S. Ct. 2607, 37 L.Ed.2d 419.

[In this case the U.S. Supreme Court articulates a three-part test for determining what is obscene.]

Mr. Chief Justice BURGER delivered the opinion of the Court.

This is one of a group of "obscenity-pornography" cases being reviewed by the Court in a reexamination of standards enunciated in earlier cases involving what Mr. Justice Harlan called "the intractable obscenity problem." . . . Appellant conducted a mass mailing campaign to advertise the said illustrated books, euphemistically called "adult" material. After a jury trial, he was convicted of violating California Penal Code 311.2(a), a misdemeanor, by knowingly distributing obscene matter, and the Appellate Department, Superior Court California, County of Orange, summarily affirmed the judgment without opinion Appellant's conviction was specifically based on his conduct in causing unsolicited advertising brochures to be sent through the mail in an envelope addressed to a restaurant in Newport Beach, California. The envelope was opened by the manager of the restaurant and his mother. They had not requested brochures; they complained to the police.

The brochures advertise four books entitled "Intercourse," "Man-Woman," "Sex Orgies Illustrated," and "An Illustrated History of Pornography," and a film entitled "Marital Intercourse." While the brochures contain some descriptive printed material, primarily they consist of pictures and drawings very explicitly depicting men and women in groups of two or more engaging in a variety of sexual activities, with genitals often prominently displayed.

I

This case involves the application of a State's criminal obscenity statute to a situation in which sexually explicit materials have been thrust by aggressive sales action upon unwilling recipients who had in no way indicated any desire to receive such materials. This Court has recognized that the States have a legitimate interest in prohibiting dissemination or exhibition of obscene material when the mode of dissemination carries with it a significant danger of offending the sensibilities of unwilling recipients or of exposure to juveniles. . . . It is in this context that we are called on to define the standards which must be used to identify obscene material that a State may regulate without infringing the First Amendment as applicable to the States through the Fourteenth Amendment. . .

II

This much has been categorically settled by the Court, that obscene material is unprotected by the First Amendment. . . . "The First and Fourteenth Amendments have never been treated as absolutes." . . . We acknowledge, however, the inherent dangers of undertaking to regulate any form of expression. State statutes designed to regulate obscene materials must be carefully limited. . . . As a result, we now confine the permissible scope of such regulation to works which depict or describe sexual conduct. That conduct must be specifically defined by the applicable state law, as written or authoritatively construed. A state office must also be limited to works which, taken as a whole, appeal to the prurient interest in sex, which portray sexual conduct in a patently offensive way, and which, taken as a whole, do not have serious literary, artistic, political, or scientific value.

The basic guidelines for the trier of fact must be: (a) whether "the average person, applying contemporary community standards" would find that the work, taken as a whole, appeals to the prurient interest, . . . (b) whether the work depicts or describes, in a patently offensive way, sexual conduct specifically defined by the applicable state law, and (c) whether the work, taken as a whole, lacks serious literary, artistic, political, or scientific value. We do not adopt as a constitutional standard the "utterly without redeeming social value" test of Memoirs v. Massachusetts; . . . that concept has never commanded the adherence of more than three Justices at one time. . . . If a state law that regulates obscene material is thus limited, as written or construed, the First Amendment values applicable to the States through the Fourteenth Amendment are adequately protected by the ultimate power of appellate courts to conduct an independent review of constitutional claims when necessary. . . .

We emphasize that it is not our function to propose regulatory schemes for the States. That must await their concrete legislative efforts. it is possible, however, to give a few plain examples of what a state statute could define for regulation under the second part (b) of the standard announced in this opinion supra:

(a) Patently offensive representations or descriptions of ultimate sexual acts, normal or perverted, actual or simulated.

(b) Patently offensive representations or descriptions of masturbation, excretory functions, and lewd exhibition of the genitals.

Sex and nudity may not be exploited without limit by films or pictures exhibited or sold in places of public accommodation any more than live sex and nudity can be exhibited or sold without limit in such public places. At a minimum, prurient, patently offensive depiction or description of sexual conduct must have serious literary, artistic, political, or scientific value to merit First Amendment protection. . . .

Under the holdings announced today, no one will be subject to prosecution for the sale or exposure of obscene materials unless these materials depict or describe patently offensive "hard core" sexual conduct specifically defined by the regulating state law, as written or construed. We are satisfied that these specific prerequisites will provide fair notice to a dealer in such materials that his public and commercial activities may bring prosecution. . . .

It is certainly true that the absence, since Roth, of a single majority view of this Court as to proper standards for testing obscenity has placed a strain on both state and federal courts. But today, for the first time since Roth was decided in 1957, a majority of this Court has agreed on concrete guidelines to isolate "hard core" pornography from expression protected by the First Amendment. . . .

This may not be an easy road, free from difficulty. But no amount of "fatigue" should lead us to adopt a convenient "institutional" rationale—an absolutist, "anything goes" view of the First Amendment—because it will lighten our burdens. "Such an abnegation of judicial supervision in this field would be inconsistent with our duty to uphold the constitutional guarantees." . . . Nor should we remedy "tension between state and federal courts" by arbitrarily depriving the States of a power reserved to them under the Constitution, a power which they have enjoyed and exercised continuously from before the adoption of the First Amendment to this day. . . .

III

Under a national Constitution, fundamental First Amendment limitations on the powers of the States do not vary from community to community, but this does not mean that there are, or should or can be, fixed, uniform national standards of precisely what appeals to the "prurient interest" or is "patently offensive." These are essentially questions of fact, and our nation is simply too big and too diverse for this Court to reasonably expect that such standards could be articulated for all 50 States in a single formulation, even assuming the prerequisite consensus exists. When triers of fact are asked to decide whether "the average person, applying contemporary community standards" would consider certain materials "prurient," it would be unrealistic to require that the answer be based on some abstract formulation. The adversary system, with lay jurors as the usual ultimate factfinders in criminal prosecution, has historically permitted triers-of-fact to draw on the standards of their community, guided always by limiting instructions on the law. To require a State to structure obscenity proceedings around evidence of a national community standard" would be an exercise in futility. . . .

It is neither realistic nor constitutionally sound to read the First Amendment as requiring that the people of Maine or Mississippi accept public depiction of conduct found tolerable in Las Vegas, or New York City. People in different States vary in their tastes and attitudes, and this diversity is not to be strangled by the absolutism of imposed uniformity.

IV

The dissenting Justices sound the alarm of repression. But, in our view, to equate the free and robust exchange of ideas and political debate with commercial exploitation of obscene material demeans the grand conception of the First Amendment and its high purposes in the historic struggle for freedom. It is a "misuse of the great guarantees of free speech and free press." . . . The First Amendment protects works which, taken as a whole, have serious literary, artistic, political or scientific value, regardless of whether the government or a majority of the people approve the ideas these works represent. "The protection given speech and press was fashioned to assure unfettered interchange of ideas for the bringing about of political and social changes desired by the people." . . . But the public portrayal of hard core sexual conduct for its own sake, and for the ensuing commercial gain, is a different matter.

One can concede that the "sexual revolution" of recent years may have had useful byproducts in striking layers of prudery from a subject long irrationally kept from needed ventilation. But it does not follow that no regulation of patently offensive "hard core" materials is needed or permissible; civilized people do not allow unregulated access to heroin because it is a derivative of medicinal morphine.

Vacated and remanded.

Mr. Justice DOUGLAS, dissenting.

. . . Today the Court retreats from the earlier formulations of the constitutional test and undertakes to make new definitions. This effort, like the earlier ones, is earnest and well-intentioned. The difficulty is that we do not deal with constitutional terms, since "obscenity" is not mentioned in the Constitution or Bill of Rights. And the First Amendment makes no such exception from "the press" which it undertakes to protect nor, as I have said on other occasions, is an exception necessarily implied, for there was no recognized exception to the free press at the time the Bill of Rights was adopted which treated "obscene" publications differently from other types of papers, magazines, and books. So there are no constitutional guidelines for deciding what is and what is not "obscene." The Court is at large because we deal with tastes and standards of literature. What shocks me may be sustenance for my neighbor. What causes one person to boil up in rage over one pamphlet or movie may reflect only his neurosis, not shared by others. We deal here with problems of censorship which, if adopted, should be done by constitutional amendment after full debate by the people. . . .

. . . The idea that the First Amendment permits government to ban publications that are "offensive" to some people puts an ominous gloss on freedom of the press. That test would make it possible to ban any paper or any journal or magazine in some benighted place. The First Amendment was designed "to invite dispute," to induce "a condition of unrest," to "create dissatisfactions with conditions as they are," and even to stir "people to anger." The idea that the First Amendment permits punishment for ideas that are "offensive" to the particular judge or jury sitting in judgment is astounding. No greater leveler of speech or literature has ever been designed. To give the power to the censor, as we do today, is to make a sharp and radical break with the traditions of a free society. The First Amendment was not fashioned as a vehicle for dispensing tranquilizers to the people. Its prime function was to keep debate open to "offensive" as well as to "staid" people. The tendency throughout history has been to subdue the individual and to exalt the power of government. The use of the standard "offensive" gives authority to government that cuts the very vitals out of the First Amendment. As is intimated by the Court's opinion, the materials before us may be garbage. But so is much of what is said in political campaigns, in the daily press, on TV or over the radio. By reason of the First Amendment—and solely because of it—speakers and publishers have not been threatened or subdued because their thoughts and ideas may be "offensive" to some. . . .

Mr. Justice BRENNAN, with whom Mr. Justice STEWART and Mr. Justice MARSHALL join, dissenting. . . .

Coates v. Cincinnati

Supreme Court of the United States, 1971
402 U.S. 611, 91 S. Ct. 1686, 29 L.Ed.2d 214.

[Here the U.S. Supreme Court applies the vagueness and overbreadth doctrines to a local ordinance.]

Mr. Justice STEWART delivered the opinion of the Court.

A Cincinnati, Ohio, ordinance makes it a criminal offense for "three or more persons to assemble . . . on any of the sidewalks . . . and there conduct themselves in a manner annoying to persons passing by . . . ." The issue before us is whether this ordinance is unconstitutional on its face.

The appellants were convicted of violating the ordinance, and the convictions were ultimately affirmed by a closely divided vote in the Supreme Court of Ohio, upholding the constitutional validity of the ordinance. . . . An appeal from that judgment was brought here and we noted probable jurisdiction. . . . The record brought before the reviewing courts tells us no more than that the appellant Coates was a student involved in a demonstration and the other appellants were pickets involved in a labor dispute. For throughout this litigation it has been the appellants' position that the ordinance on its face violates the First and Fourteenth Amendments of the Constitution. . . .

In rejecting this claim and affirming the convictions the Ohio Supreme Court did not give the ordinance any construction at variance with the apparent plain import of its language. The court simply stated:

> The ordinance prohibits, inter alia, "conduct . . . annoying to persons passing by." The word "annoying" is a widely used and well understood word; it is not necessary to guess its meaning. "Annoying" is the present participle of the transitive verb "annoy" which means to trouble, to vex, to impede, to incommode, to provoke, to harass or to irritate.

We conclude . . . that the ordinance "clearly and precisely delineates its reach in words of common understanding. It is a "precise and narrowly drawn regulatory statute [ordinance] evincing a legislative judgment that certain specific conduct be . . . proscribed.' " . . .

Beyond this, the only construction put upon the ordinance by the state court was its unexplained conclusion that "the standard of conduct which it specifies is not dependent upon each complainant's sensitivity." . . . But the court did not indicate upon whose sensitivity a violation does depend—the sensitivity of the judge or jury, the sensitivity of the arresting officer, or the sensitivity of a hypothetical reasonable man.

We are thus relegated, at best, to the words of the ordinance itself. If three or more people meet together on a sidewalk or street corner, they must conduct themselves so as not to annoy any police officer or other person who should happen to pass by. In our opinion this ordinance is unconstitutionally vague because it subjects the exercise of the right of assembly to an unascertainable standard, and unconstitutionally broad because it authorizes the punishment of constitutionally protected conduct.

Conduct that annoys some people does not annoy others. Thus, the ordinance is vague, not in the sense that it requires a person to conform his conduct to an imprecise but comprehensible normative standard, but rather in the sense that no standard of conduct is specified at all. As a result, "men of common intelligence must necessarily guess at its meaning.". . .

It is said that the ordinance is broad enough to encompass many types of conduct clearly within the city's constitutional power to prohibit. And so, indeed, it is. The city is free to prevent people from blocking sidewalks, obstructing traffic, littering streets, committing assaults, or engaging in countless other forms of antisocial conduct. It can do so through the enactment and enforcement of ordinances directed with reasonable specificity toward the conduct to be prohibited. . . . It cannot constitutionally do so through the enactment and enforcement of an ordinance whose violation may entirely depend upon whether or not a policeman is annoyed.

But the vice of the ordinance lies not alone in its violation of the due process standard of vagueness. The ordinance also violates the constitutional right of free assembly and association. Our decisions establish that mere public intolerance or animosity cannot be the basis for abridgement of these constitutional freedoms. . . . The First and Fourteenth Amendments do not permit a State to make criminal the exercise of the right of assembly simply because its exercise may be "annoying" to some people. If this were not the rule, the right of the people to gather in public places for social or political purposes would be continually subject to summary suspension through the good-faith enforcement of a prohibition against annoying conduct. And such a prohibition, in addition, contains an obvious invitation to discriminatory enforcement against those whose association together is "annoying" because their ideas, their lifestyle, or their physical appearance is resented by the majority of their fellow citizens.

The ordinance before us makes a crime out of what under the Constitution cannot be a crime. It is aimed directly at activity protected by the Constitution. We need not lament that we do not have before us the details of the conduct found to be annoying. It is the ordinance on its face that sets the standard of conduct and warns against transgression. The details of the offense could no more serve to validate this ordinance than could the details of an offense charged under an ordinance suspending unconditionally the right of assembly and free speech. The judgment is reversed.

Mr. Justice BLACK. . . .

Mr. Justice WHITE, with whom the Chief Justice and Mr. Justice BLACKMUN join, dissenting.

The claim in this case, in part, is that the Cincinnati ordinance is so vague that it may not constitutionally be applied to any conduct. But the ordinance prohibits persons from assembling with others and "conduct[ing] themselves in a manner annoying to persons passing by . . . ." . . . Any man of average comprehension should know that some kinds of conduct, such as assault or blocking passage on the street, will annoy others and are clearly covered by the "annoying conduct" standard of the ordinance. It would be frivolous to say that these and many other kinds of conduct are not within the foreseeable reach of the law.

It is possible that a whole range of other acts, defined with unconstitutional imprecision, is forbidden by the ordinance. But as a general rule, when a criminal charge is based on conduct constitutionally subject to proscription and clearly forbidden by a statute, it is no defense that the law would be unconstitutionally vague if applied to other behavior. Such a statute is not vague on its face. It may be vague as applied in some circumstances, but ruling on such a challenge obviously requires knowledge of the conduct with which a defendant is charged. . . .

Our cases, however, recognize a different approach where the statute at issue purports to regulate or proscribe rights of speech or press protected by the First Amendment. . . . Although a statute maybe neither vague, overbroad, nor otherwise invalid as applied to the conduct charged against a particu-lar defendant, he is permitted to raise its vagueness or unconstitutional overbreadth as applied to others. And if the law is found deficient in one of these respects, it may not be applied to him either, until and unless a satisfactory limiting construction is placed on the statute. . . . The statute, in effect, is stricken down on its face. This result is deemed justified since the otherwise continued existence of the statute in unnarrowed form would tend to suppress constitutionally protected rights. . . .

Even accepting the overbreadth doctrine with respect to statutes clearly reaching speech, the Cincinnati ordinance does not purport to bar or regulate speech as such. It prohibits persons from assembling "conduct[ing]" themselves in a manner annoying to other persons. Even if the assembled defendants in this case were demonstrating and picketing, we have long recognized that picketing is not solely a communicative endeavor and has aspects which the State is entitled to regulate even though there is incidental impact on speech. . . .

In the case before us, I would deal with the Cincinnati ordinance as we would with the ordinary criminal statute. The ordinance clearly reaches certain conduct but may be illegally vague with respect to other conduct. The statute is not infirm on its face and since we have no information from this record as to what conduct was charged against these defendants, we are in no position to judge the statute as applied. That the ordinance may confer wide discretion in a wide range of circumstances is irrelevant when we may be dealing with conduct at its core.

I would therefore affirm the judgment of the Ohio Supreme Court.

Griswold v. Connecticut

Supreme Court of the United States, 1965.
381 U.S. 479, 85 S. Ct. 1678, 14 L.Ed.2d 510.

[In this case, the U.S. Supreme Court reviews a state law making it a crime, even for married couples, to use birth control devices.]

Mr. Justice DOUGLAS delivered the opinion of the Court.

Appellant Griswold is Executive Director of the Planned Parenthood League of Connecticut. Appellant Buxton is a licensed physician and a professor at the Yale Medical School who served as Medical Director for the League at its Center in New Haven—a center open and operating from November 1 to November 10, 1961, when appellants were arrested.

They gave information, instruction and medical advice to married persons as to the means of preventing conception. They examined the wife and prescribed the best contraceptive device or material for her use. Fees were usually charged, although some couples were serviced free. . . .

The appellants were found guilty as accessories and fined $100 each, against the claim that the accessory statute as so applied violated the Fourteenth Amendment. The Appellate Division of the Circuit Court affirmed. The Supreme Court of Errors affirmed that judgment. . . .

. . . We do not sit as a super-legislature to determine the wisdom, need and propriety of laws that touch economic problems, business affairs, or social conditions. This law, however, operates directly on an intimate relation of husband and wife and their physician's role in one aspect of that relation.

The association of people is not mentioned in the Constitution nor in the Bill of Rights. The right to educate a child in a school of the parents' choice—whether public or private or parochial—is also not mentioned. Nor is the right to study any particular subject or any foreign language. Yet the First Amendment has been construed to include certain of those rights.

[Previous] . . . cases suggest that specific guarantees in the Bill of Rights have penumbras, formed by emanations from those guarantees that help give them life and substance. Various guarantees create zones of privacy. The right of association continued in the penumbra of the First Amendment is one, as we have seen. The Third Amendment in its prohibition against the quartering of soldiers "in any house" in time of peace without the consent of the owner is another facet of that privacy. The Fourth Amendment explicitly affirms the "right of the people to be secure in their persons, houses, papers, and effects, against unreasonable searches and seizures." The Fifth Amendment in its Self-Incrimination Clause enables the citizen to create a zone of privacy which government may not force him to surrender to his detriment. The Ninth Amendment provides: "The enumeration in the Constitution, of certain rights, shall not be construed to deny or disparage others retained by the people."

The Fourth and Fifth Amendments were described in Boyd v. United States . . . as protection against all governmental invasions "of the sanctity of a man's home and the privacies of life." We recently referred in Mapp v. Ohio . . . to the Fourth Amendment as creating a "right to privacy, no less important than any other right carefully and particularly reserved to the people." . . .

We have had many controversies over these penumbral rights of "privacy and repose." . . . These cases bear witness that the right of privacy which presses for recognition here is a legitimate one.

The present case, then, concerns a relationship lying within the zone of privacy created by several fundamental constitutional guarantees. And it concerns a law which, in forbidding the use of contraceptives rather than regulating their manufacture or sale, seeks to achieve its goals by means having a maximum destructive impact upon that relationship. Such a law cannot stand in light of the familiar principle, so often applied by this Court, that a "governmental purpose to control or prevent activities constitutionally subject to state regulation may not be achieved by means which sweep unnecessarily broadly and thereby invade the area of protected freedoms." . . . Would we allow the police to search the sacred precincts of marital bedrooms for telltale signs of the use of contraceptives? The very idea is repulsive to the notions of privacy surrounding the marriage relationship. . . .

Mr. Justice GOLDBERG, whom the Chief Justice and Mr. Justice BRENNAN join, concurring.

. . . Although the Constitution does not speak in so many words of the right of privacy in marriage, I cannot believe that it offers these fundamental rights no protection. The fact that no particular provision of the Constitution explicitly forbids the State from disrupting the traditional relation of the family—a relation as old and as fundamental as our entire civilization—surely does not show that the Government was meant to have the power to do so. Rather, as the Ninth Amendment expressly recognizes, there are fundamental personal rights such as this one, which are protected from abridgment by the Government though not specifically mentioned in the Constitution. . . .

Although the Connecticut birth control law obviously encroaches upon a fundamental personal liberty, the State does not show that the law serves any "subordinating [state] interest which is compelling" or that it is "necessary . . . to the accomplishment of a permissible state policy." The State, at most, argues that there is some rational relation between this statute and what is admittedly a legitimate subject of state concern—the discouraging of extra-marital relations. It says that preventing the use of birth-control devices by married persons helps prevent the indulgence by some in such extra-marital relations. The rationality of this justification is dubious, particularly in light of the admitted widespread availability to all persons in the State of Connecticut, unmarried as well as married, of birth-control devices for the prevention of disease, as distinguished from the prevention of conception. . . . But, in any event, it is clear that the state interest in safeguarding marital fidelity can be served by a more discriminately tailored statute, which does not, like the present one, sweep unnecessarily broadly, reaching far beyond the evil sought to be dealt with and intruding upon the privacy of all married couples. . . .

"Adultery, homosexuality and the like are sexual intimacies which the State forbids . . . but the intimacy of husband and wife is necessarily an essential and accepted feature of the institution of marriage, an institution which the State not only must allow, but which always and in every age it has fostered and protected. It is one thing when the State exerts its power either to forbid extra-marital sexuality . . . or to say who may marry, but it is quite another when, having acknowledged a marriage and the intimacies inherent in it, it undertakes to regulate by means of the criminal law the details of that intimacy." . . .

In sum, I believe that the right of privacy in the marital relation is fundamental and basic—a personal right "retained by the people" within the meaning of the Ninth Amendment. Connecticut cannot constitutionally abridge this fundamental right, which is protected by the Fourteenth Amendment . . . [The] convictions must therefore be reversed.

Mr. Justice HARLAN, concurring in the judgment. . . .

Mr. Justice WHITE, concurring in the judgment. . . .

Mr. Justice BLACK, with whom Mr. Justice STEWART joins, dissenting.

. . . I get nowhere in this case by talk about a constitutional "right of privacy" as an emanation from one or more constitutional provisions. I like my privacy as well as the next one, but I am nevertheless compelled to admit that government has a right to invade it unless prohibited by some specific constitutional provision. For these reasons I cannot agree with the Court's judgment and the reasons it gives for holding this Connecticut law unconstitutional. . . .

I realize that many good and able men have eloquently spoken and written, sometimes in rhapsodical strains, about the duty of this Court to keep the Constitution in tune with the times. The idea is that the Constitution must be changed from time to time and that this Court is charged with a duty to make those changes. For myself, I must with all deference reject that philosophy. The Constitution makers knew the need for change and provided for it. Amendments suggested by the people's elected representatives can be submitted to the people or their selected agents for ratification. That method of change was good for our Fathers, and being somewhat old-fashioned I must add it is good enough for me. . . .

Mr. Justice STEWART, whom Mr. Justice BLACK joins, dissenting.

Since 1879 Connecticut has had on its books a law which forbids the use of contraceptives by anyone. I think this is an uncommonly silly law. As a practical matter, the law is obviously unenforceable, except in the oblique context of the present case. As a philosophical matter, I believe the use of contraceptives in the relationship of marriage should be left to personal and private choice, based upon each individual's moral, ethical, and religious beliefs. As a matter of social policy, I think professional counsel about methods of birth control should be available to all, so that each individual's choice can be meaningfully made. But we are not asked in this case to say whether we think this law is unwise, or even asinine. We are asked to hold that it violates the United States Constitution. And that I cannot do. . . .

CHAPTER 4

Elements of Crimes; Parties to Crimes

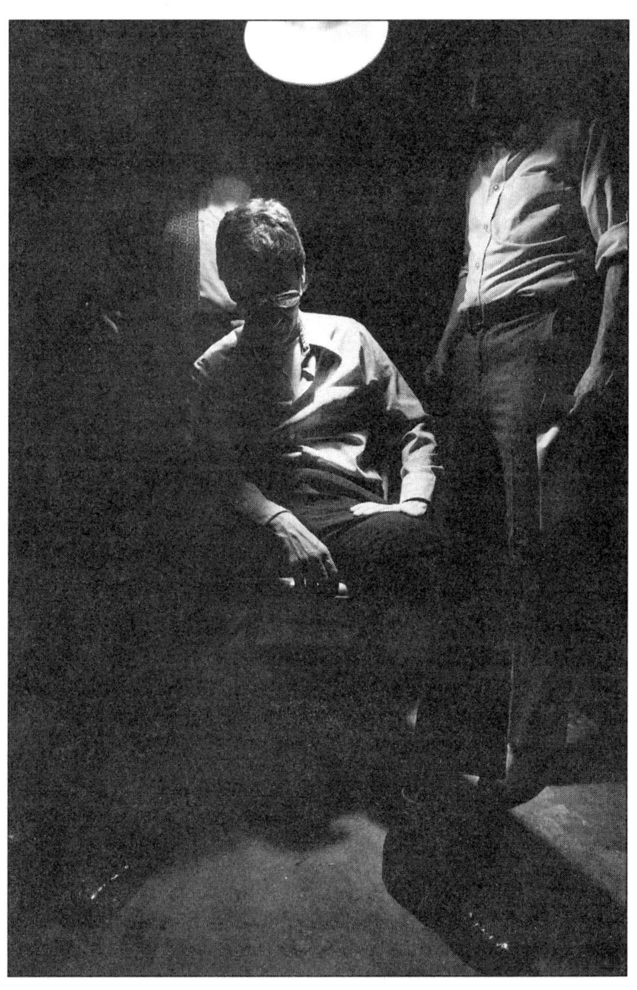

CHAPTER OUTLINE

Introduction
What Constitutes a Criminal Act or Omission?
The Nature of Criminal Intent
Parties to a Crime
Conclusion

Cases
Morissette v. United States
State v. Ferguson
State v. Starks

INTRODUCTION

As we explained in Chapter 1, the essential elements of a crime are a physical act, often referred to as the *actus reus* (wrongful act) and the intent or state of mind, frequently called the *mens rea* (guilty mind). To establish that a defendant is guilty of a crime, the prosecution must prove the defendant committed some legally proscribed act or failed to act when the law required certain action. It is also essential to prove that such act or failure to act occurred with a simultaneous criminal intent. It would be contrary to our common-law heritage to punish someone who accidentally or unwittingly committed an act without any intent to commit a crime. Likewise, a person cannot be punished for a mere intention, however wrongful that intention may be. Certain regulatory and public welfare offenses are classified as strict liability crimes and are exceptions to the common-law concept of requiring proof of a defendant's criminal intent. They came into prominence during the Industrial Revolution and today they form a significant part of the substantive criminal law.

In addition to the basic requirement of establishing a physical act and intent, in some instances the prosecution must establish that certain circumstances existed at the time the act was committed. For example, in the trial of a homicide offense, the prosecution must prove a causal relationship between the defendant's act and the victim's death. Also, in some sexual battery offenses the prosecution must establish that the defendant's acts occurred without the victim's consent.

The terms commonly used in modern criminal law (such as felony, misdemeanor, principal, and accessory) are derived from the common law. An understanding of their history leads to a better understanding of their function in contemporary American criminal law and procedure in federal and state court systems.

WHAT CONSTITUTES A CRIMINAL ACT OR OMISSION?

To fulfill the requirements of the criminal law, the actor must willfully commit a proscribed physical act or intentionally fail to act where the law requires a person to act. Courts have generally held that some outward manifestation of voluntary conduct must occur to constitute the required physical act. Consider two hypothetical examples:

- A enters B's house or strikes B. A has quite obviously committed an "act."
- A hands B a glass of liquid to be given to C. Unknown to B, A added poison to the glass of liquid before handing it to B. B gives the liquid to C, who drinks it and dies. Here A has acted through B, an innocent agent; thus A has committed the "act."

Even a person's failure to act can satisfy the requirements of a physical act in the criminal law. Remember that to be guilty of a crime for failure to act, there must have been a legal duty to act in the first place. Such a duty can arise in one of three ways: (1) by relationship of the actor to the victim, for example, a parent-child or husband-wife; (2) by a statutory duty; or (3) by contract between the actor and the victim. Consider these examples:

- A, an expert swimmer, is lying on the beach when he sees a young girl, unrelated to him, struggling to stay afloat and crying for help. A disregards her cries and she drowns. Is A criminally liable? The answer is no, for although we may agree that A had a strong moral obligation to attempt to save the child, there was no legal obligation that he do so. If, on the other hand, A was the child's parent or guardian, or a lifeguard on duty, then A's omission to act would most likely qualify as a criminal act.
- B receives an annual income of $50,000 from operation of her business. She fails to file a federal income tax return as required by the laws of the United States. Is B's omission a criminal act? Clearly it is, for she has violated a statutory obligation, the breach of which is punishable by law.
- C, a surgeon, undertakes to perform an operation on a patient for a fee. Before completing the operation, C decides to cease his efforts. As a result of such inattention, the patient dies. Would C's failure to complete what he undertook professionally qualify as an act within the meaning of the criminal law? Yes, because C had a contractual relationship with his patient.

Finally, we must realize that the requisite criminal act or omission must be voluntarily accomplished by the actor. The rationale for the requirement of a voluntary act is simple: Only those persons whose acts result from free choice should be criminally punished. Most acts are voluntary. For example, when you raise your hand it is considered a voluntary act, but when your hand moves as a result of a muscle spasm, it is not a voluntary act. Likewise, movements

CASE IN POINT

THE *ACTUS REUS* REQUIREMENT

Law officers found two whiskey stills and all the paraphernalia for making liquor on the defendant's land. Seeing no activity, they drove away. As they did, they met a car driven by the defendant heading toward the property. The car contained a quantity of sugar and other indicators of the illegal activity the officers suspected. The defendant committed no act of making liquor in the presence of the officers, but on the basis of what they observed, they arrested the defendant and he was convicted of making liquor unlawfully.

On appeal, the South Carolina Supreme Court reversed the conviction, observing, "the evidence overwhelmingly tends to show an intention to manufacture liquor. . . But intent alone, not coupled with some overt act . . . is not cognizable by the court. [T]he act must always amount to more than mere preparation, and move directly toward the commission of the crime." Citing respectable textbook authority, the court explained that the law does not concern itself with mere guilty intention, unconnected with any overt act.

State v. Quick, 19 S.E.2d 101 (S.C. 1942)

committed by a person who is unconscious, or acts by someone having an epileptic fit or sleepwalking are not regarded as voluntary acts. On the other hand, a driver who takes sleeping pills before beginning to operate an automobile and then falls asleep at the wheel would generally be held criminally responsible for a traffic accident, because the driver voluntarily committed the act of taking the pills.

Possession as a Criminal Act

In certain crimes possession alone is the wrongful act. For example, in the offense of carrying a concealed weapon, possession of the weapon concealed from ordinary observation is the wrongful act. Likewise, possession of contraband such as illegal drugs or untaxed liquors constitutes the wrongful act element of certain offenses.

There are two classes of possession: actual and constructive. Actual possession exists when a person has something under his or her direct physical control. Examples of actual possession are when an item is on your person or within your reach or located in a place where you alone have access. Constructive possession, on the other hand, is a more difficult concept because it is based on a legal fiction. A person who has the power and intention to control something either directly or through another person is said to be in constructive possession. The exact meaning of these terms is usually determined by the context of the situation. The difficulty is exacerbated when two or more persons are in joint possession of the premises or vehicle where an object is found. Consider the following examples:

- A and B rent and jointly share an apartment. A police search yields contraband drugs found on the coffee table in the living room used by both A and B. Can both be charged with possession of the contraband? They probably can: Possession by both A and B can be inferred, since the drugs are in plain view and located in a place to which both have access.
- Under the same circumstances of a shared apartment, drugs are found in a privately owned, closed container in a dresser drawer where only A keeps clothing and valuables. Since B has no access to this area, the law does not infer that B has constructive possession of the contents in the drawer. Of course, there may be circumstances under which the prosecution could prove that B actually had rights to the drugs, knowledge of their whereabouts, and access to them. Then the prosecution could establish that B was in constructive possession of the contraband.

Status as a Criminal Act

"Status" refers to a person's state of being, and ordinarily the state cannot criminalize a person's status. This principle was highlighted by the U.S. Supreme Court in *Robinson v. California,* 370 U.S. 660, 666–667, 82 S.Ct. 1417, 1420, 8 L.Ed.2d 758, 762–763, (1962), where the Court, in declaring unconstitutional a California statute that made it an offense for a person "to be addicted to the use of narcotics," states that

> we deal with a statute which makes the "status" of narcotic addiction a criminal offense, for which the offender may be prosecuted "at any time before he reforms."... We hold that a state law which imprisons a person thus afflicted as a criminal, even though he has never touched any narcotic drug within the State or been guilty of any irregular behavior there, inflicts a cruel and unusual punishment in violation of the Fourteenth Amendment.

The issue of when a criminal statute proscribes status, as opposed to conduct, can be very close. This is illustrated by the Supreme Court's decision in *Powell v. Texas*, 392 U.S. 514, 88 S.Ct. 2145, 20 L.Ed.2d 1254 (1968). Powell was a chronic alcoholic who was convicted of being drunk in public. Four justices held that defendant Powell was punished for being in a public place on a particular occasion while intoxicated, and not for his status as a chronic alcoholic. A fifth justice concurred in affirming Powell's conviction. As you study Chapter 11 concerning offenses against public order and safety, consider whether a statute that makes it a crime to be a vagrant offends the principle that a person's status cannot be criminalized.

THE NATURE OF CRIMINAL INTENT

The common law developed the doctrine that there should be no crime without a *mens rea* or "guilty mind." This element is customarily referred to as the criminal intent and, as noted, to constitute a crime there must be a concurrence of the *actus reus* or "act requirement" with a person's criminal intent. See, for example, *People v. Leckner*, 500 N.E.2d 721 (Ill. App. 1986). "Strict liability" offenses discussed in a later topic are an exception to this principle.

Criminal intent must be distinguished from motive. To obtain a conviction, a prosecutor must establish the defendant's criminal intent, but not necessarily the defendant's motive for committing a crime. A person's motive often equates with an impulse, an incentive, or a reason for certain behavior, and proof of one's motive may assist in establishing criminal intent. To illustrate, if the prosecution relies on circumstantial evidence to establish the defendant's guilt in a homicide case, the fact that the defendant had vowed "to get even" with the victim may be a relevant factor in the proof. Yet the failure to establish a defendant's motive is not material to proof of guilt, because the law prohibits criminal acts, not bad motives. Moreover, good motives do not exonerate you from a crime. Thus, a person who steals food simply to give it to a poor hungry family is probably well-motivated in doing so. Nevertheless, such a person would be guilty of a crime because of his or her act and intent.

The basic reason the law requires proof of a criminal intent as well as an act or omission is to distinguish those acts or omissions that occur accidentally from those committed by a person with a "guilty mind." As the court observed in *In re Hayes*, 442 P.2d 366, 369 (Cal. 1968), "an essential element of every orthodox crime is a wrongful or blameworthy mental state of some kind."

General and Specific Intent

Traditionally, courts distinguish the intent requirement of various crimes by describing them as requiring either "general" or "specific" intent. General intent is the intent presumed from the act the defendant commits. It refers to an actor's physical conduct in the sense that the actor intends the consequences of his or her voluntary actions.

For example, a person who fires a pistol at another is presumed to have intended either to kill or at least to injure the victim. Where a crime requires only proof of a general intent, the fact finder (i.e., the judge or jury) may infer the defendant's intent from the mere act itself. Thus, the prosecution does not have to prove that the defendant had any specific intent when the act was committed. An Indiana appellate court recently explained the concept of general intent quite well: "General intent exists when from the circumstances the prohibited result may reasonably be expected to follow from the offender's voluntary act, irrespective of a subjective desire to have accomplished such result." *Myers v. State,* 422 N.E.2d 745, 750 (Ind. App. 1981).

Criminal statutes that prohibit particular voluntary acts are generally classified as "general intent" statutes. See *State v. Poss,* 298 N.W.2d 80 (S.D. 1980). Statutory words such as *willfully* or *intentionally* generally indicate that the offender must only have intended to do the act and not to accomplish any particular result. To illustrate: A statute that makes it arson for a person to willfully and unlawfully damage by fire any dwelling defines a general intent crime. See *Linehan v. State,* 476 So.2d 1262 (Fla. 1985).

A specific-intent crime, on the other hand, is one in which the actor intends a particular result. Thus, a crime that requires a specific intent prohibits an act done with an intent beyond that which ordinarily accompanies an act. Again, in the context of the crime of arson, if the statute read that it was an offense for any person "willfully and with the intent to injure or defraud the insurance company to set fire to any building," then the prosecution would be required to prove that the defendant had the specific intent to injure or defraud the insurance company when the proscribed act was perpetrated.

Assume State X charged a defendant with burglary of a dwelling under a statute defining the offense as "the unauthorized entry of a dwelling by a person with the intent to commit theft therein." Three basic elements must be established to convict the defendant. First, the state must prove the defendant made an unauthorized entry. Second, it must prove that the entry was into a dwelling house. Finally, it must establish that the defendant made such unauthorized entry with the intent to commit a theft therein. Because the statute defines a specific-intent crime, the state must prove that the defendant intended certain definite consequences to follow an entry into the dwelling, that is, to commit a theft. Intent, of course, is a state of mind. Nevertheless, it can be (and almost always is) inferred from the defendant's actions and surrounding circumstances. Therefore, if some of the dwelling owner's property had been moved and other items left in disarray, the inference would be that the defendant who made an unauthorized entry intended to commit theft from the dwelling. And this would be true whether the defendant did in fact commit a theft within the dwelling.

The Model Penal Code Approach to Intent

The Model Penal Code (MPC) was drafted in 1962 by the American Law Institute, an organization composed of prominent lawyers, judges, and academics. The MPC is not law, but it represents a modern criminal code greatly influencing the reform of criminal statutes in the majority of states. The MPC rejects the common-law terms for intent and instead proposes four states of mind: purposeful; knowing; reckless; and negligent. It defines a purposeful act as one taken with an intent to cause a particular result, while a knowing act is one taken when the result is practically certain to occur, although causing that result is not the purpose for doing the act. The MPC defines a reckless act as one taken in disregard of a substantial risk and a negligent act as one taken by a person who fails to perceive the substantial risk of harm that may result from it. M.P.C. § 2.02.

The MPC classification of culpability is analytical, and each category is clearly defined, whereas over the years the common-law classifications of specific and general intent have become subject to considerable variations in court decisions in various jurisdictions. Nevertheless, in reading cases, you will find that most courts cling to the common-law classifications of specific and general intent. Two reasons come to mind: First, the law is traditional and based on precedent; and second, most appellate court judges probably completed their legal education before the MPC classification became well known. In any event, you should be familiar with both the common-law and MPC classifications.

The Doctrine of Transferred Intent

When a person intends to commit one criminal act but accomplishes another, the law implies that the necessary criminal intent for the second wrongful act is present. For example, if A aims a gun at B intending to kill B but misses and kills C instead, A's intent to kill B is transferred to C, the victim. This is the doctrine of transferred intent, in which the defendant's original intent is transferred from one against whom it was directed to the one who suffered the consequences. The doctrine does not require one fact to be presumed based upon finding of another fact. Rather, under this concept it becomes immaterial whether the accused intended to injure a person who is actually harmed. If the accused acted with the required intent toward someone, that intent suffices as the required element of intent for the crime charged. *State v. Locklear,* 415 S.E.2d 726 (N.C. 1992).

The concept of the doctrine of transferred intent is designed to hold a person who is committing a dangerous illegal act responsible for the consequences to the innocent victim. The doctrine is most frequently applied in homicide cases, even though some courts have had difficulty justifying its application where no actual intent to kill a third party is evidenced. Yet, application of the doctrine seems to achieve just results and, perhaps more importantly from the viewpoint of the prosecution, it obviates the need to establish that it was predictable A's actions directed against B would result in injury to C, an innocent victim. Of course, the actor must have had a criminal intent in the first place. Thus, if a parent lawfully administering punishment to a child accidentally strikes an innocent bystander, there is no criminal intent to transfer.

The Importance of Determining the Intent Required

It is essential to determine whether a particular offense is a general-intent or a specific-intent crime. First, the intent requirement determines the proof required of the prosecution. Second, in certain crimes the intent required determines whether particular defenses are available to the defendant.

The "Strict Liability" Offenses

While common-law crimes consist of a criminal act or omission known as the *actus reus* and the mental element known as the *mens rea*, legislative bodies have the power to dispense with the necessity for the mental element and authorize punishment of particular acts without regard to the intent of the actor. At this point, acquaintance with two terms becomes important. *Mala in se* offenses are "wrongs in themselves," while *mala prohibita* refers to "offenses deemed wrong by statute." In the common-law felonies of murder, rape, robbery, larceny, etc., the proscribed conduct is considered *mala in se*, and the intent is deemed inherent in the offense. This is true even if the statute now proscribing such criminal conduct fails to specify intent as an element of the offense. On the other hand, many criminal statutes proscribe conduct not deemed criminal at common law, and these offenses are generally classified as *mala prohibita*. Statutes of this type generally proscribe commission or omission of acts through neglect and do not require proof of criminal intent.

These *mala prohibita* offenses are commonly referred to as strict liability offenses. For the most part, they include "regulatory" or "public welfare" types of offenses often tailored to address unique problems created by the Industrial Revolution and present-day technology. Some of the earliest examples of strict liability are seen in cases involving sale of liquor and adulterated milk. See, for example, *Barnes v. State*, 19 Conn. 398 (1849); *Commonwealth v. Boynton*, 84 Mass. (2 Allen) 160 (1861). Examples of strict liability offenses today include traffic regulations, food and drug laws, and laws prohibiting the sale of liquor and cigarettes to minors. Today, strict liability offenses constitute a substantial part of the criminal law.

In *Morissette v. United States*, 342 U.S. 246, 255–256, 72 S.Ct. 240, 246, 96 L.Ed. 288, 296–297 (1952), the Supreme Court commented on strict liability offenses and observed:

> These [public welfare offenses] do not fit neatly into any of such accepted classifications of common-law offenses. . . . While such offenses do not threaten the security of the state . . . they may be regarded as offenses against its authority, for their occurrence impairs the efficiency of controls deemed essential to the social order as presently constituted. In this respect, whatever the intent of the violator, the injury is the same, and the consequences are injurious or not according to fortuity. Hence, legislation applicable to such offenses, as a matter of policy, does not specify intent as a necessary element. The accused, if he does not will the violation, usually is in a position to prevent it with no more care than society might reasonably expect and no more exertion than it might reasonably exact from one who assumed his responsibilities. Also, penalties commonly are relatively small, and conviction does no grave damage to an offender's reputation. Under such considerations, courts have turned to construing statutes and regulations which make no mention of intent as dispensing with it and holding that the guilty act alone makes out the crime.

The definition of *mala prohibita* as referring to acts not essentially involving moral wrong can be deceptive. For example, having consensual sexual relations with a minor is generally considered a strict liability offense, and the offender can be held criminally responsible even if the minor claims to be and has the appearance of an adult. Of course, in this instance the offender's conduct would clearly be termed a moral wrong as well as a criminal offense.

In the chapters that follow, note that as penalties for statutory offenses become heavier, courts are reluctant to dispense with proof of intent. This is true in environmental crimes (Chapter 10) and in some serious motor vehicle violations. For example, many state courts have addressed the issue of whether proof of a criminal intent is necessary to convict of the statutory crime of driving with a revoked or suspended license. In *Jeffcoat v. State,* 639 P.2d 308 (Alaska App. 1982), the Alaska Court of Appeals held that even though the statute is silent, the element of *mens rea* must be read into it by implication. Several other state courts agree. On the other hand, in *State v. Antonsen,* 525 A.2d 1048 (Me.1987), the Supreme Court of Maine held that such a statute does not require proof of a culpable mental state, thereby aligning that state with the courts in several other states.

PARTIES TO A CRIME

Historically, the common law classified parties to crimes as either principals or accessories. Principals were persons whose conduct involved direct participation in a crime; accessories were accomplices or those who gave aid and comfort to principals.

Common law had three categories of crimes: treason, felonies, and misdemeanors. The highest-ranked crime under the English common law was treason. Treason consisted of killing the monarch or the monarch's high ministers or giving aid and comfort to the enemies of the Crown. Under the common law, all parties involved in a crime of treason were considered principals.

Given the history of the English monarchy, the American colonists were understandably conscious of the potential for abuse in enforcing the common law for treason. Thus, the framers of the Constitution provided that "Treason against the United States, shall consist only in levying war against them, or in adhering to their Enemies, giving them Aid and Comfort." U.S. Const. Art. 3, Sec. 3. Moreover, to emphasize the need to protect citizens from the abusive power of government, the framers also provided that "No Person shall be convicted of Treason unless on the Testimony of two Witnesses to the same overt Act, or on Confession in open Court." U.S. Const. Art. 3, Sec. 3.

The common law classified crimes other than treason as felonies and misdemeanors. Felonies were very serious crimes: At times, a person found guilty of a felony could be deprived of all worldly possessions and suffer either death or lengthy imprisonment. Because of the serious nature of felonious conduct, and because all persons involved might not be equally guilty, the common law developed a number of technical distinctions among the various participants. To comprehend present criminal law regarding participants in a crime, a basic knowledge of the common-law scheme is essential.

At common law, a person directly involved in committing a felony was classified as a principal; a person whose conduct did not involve direct participation was classified as an accessory. Principals were further classified by the degree of their participation. A person who directly or through the acts of an innocent agent actually committed the crime was a principal in the first degree. A principal in the second degree was a person not directly involved but actually

CASE IN POINT

THE *MENS REA* REQUIREMENT

The defendant was convicted under a statute that made it an offense to fondle or caress the body of a child under sixteen years "with the intent to gratify the sexual desires or appetites of the offending person or . . . to frighten or excite such child." On appeal, the Indiana Supreme Court noted that the strongest evidence in favor of the prosecution was that both the defendant's daughters admitted that during playfulness the father touched and came in contact with one of his daughter's breasts. There was, however, no evidence that this was done with the intent to gratify the sexual desires of the defendant or to frighten the child.

In reversing the defendant's conviction the court observed: "A crime has two components—an evil intent coupled with an overt act. The act alone does not constitute the crime unless it is done with a specific intent declared unlawful by the statute in this state. . . There must also be proved beyond a reasonable doubt, the specific intent at the time of touching to gratify sexual desires or to frighten the child as stated in the statute."

Markiton v. State, 139 N.E.2d 440 (Ind. 1957).

or constructively present at the commission of the crime who aided and abetted the perpetrator. The concept of actual presence is self-explanatory; however, the concept of constructive presence requires further explanation. To be constructively present, you must be sufficiently close to render assistance to the perpetrator. For example, if a man led a woman's escort away from her so that another man could sexually attack the woman, the man who led the escort away would probably be constructively present at the crime and would be classified as a principal in the second degree because he was aiding and abetting a crime. To aid and abet another in the commission of a crime means to assent to an act or to lend countenance or approval, either by active participation in it or by encouraging it in some other manner. *State v. Myers,* 158 N.W.2d 717 (Iowa 1968).

An accessory at common law was classified as either an accessory before or after the fact. An accessory before the fact procured or counseled another to commit a felony, but was not actually or constructively present at the commission of the offense. An accessory after the fact knowingly assisted or gave aid or comfort to a person who had committed a felony.

Because misdemeanors were far less serious than felonies, the common law found no necessity to distinguish between participants. As in the case of treason, all participants in misdemeanor offenses were regarded as principals.

Accessories to felonies were not regarded as being as culpable as the principals, so they were punished less severely at common law. Moreover, the common law gave accessories some significant technical advantages. A party had to be charged as a principal or as an accessory, and a principal had to be tried first. If the principal was found not guilty, the accessory could not be tried for the offense.

The Modern American Approach

Federal law stipulates that "Whoever commits an offense against the United States or aids, abets, counsels, commands, induces, or procures its commission, is punishable as a principal." 18 U.S.C.A. § 2(a). The federal statute reflects the law of most of the states insofar as it abolishes the distinction between principals and accessories before the fact.

The trend in American criminal law has been to abolish both the substantive and procedural distinctions between principals and accessories before the fact. As early as 1872, California enacted a statute defining principals as "all persons concerned in the commission of a crime, whether it be felony or misdemeanor, and whether they directly commit the act constituting the offense, or aid and abet in its commission, or, not being present, have advised and encouraged its commission." West's Ann. Cal. Penal Code § 31. As explained by the Supreme Court of Appeals of West Virginia in *State v. Fortner,* 387 S.E.2d 812, 822 (W.Va. 1989):

> Being an accessory before the fact or a principal in the second degree is not, of itself, a separate crime, but is a basis for finding liability for the underlying crime. . . . In essence, evidence of such complicity simply establishes an alternative theory of criminal liability, i.e., another way of committing the underlying substantive offense.

Even though the common-law distinction between principals and accessories before the fact has been largely abolished, the concept of accessory after the fact as a separate offense has been retained by many jurisdictions. Modern statutes view an accessory after the fact as less culpable than someone who plans, assists, or commits a crime. Thus, statutes generally define accessory after the fact as a separate offense and provide for a less severe punishment.

CASE IN POINT

AIDING AND ABETTING

Both Walter Godinez and Julio Montes were indicted for murder, attempted armed robbery, and armed violence. Montes' case was tried separately before a judge. The evidence revealed that Eduardo Soto was shot to death on April 28, 1986, in Chicago, Illinois. Montes confessed that Walter Godinez attempted to rob Soto and shot him while the defendant Montes acted as a lookout. Montes was convicted.

On appeal, Montes argued several points, including his contention that the evidence failed to establish his guilt on the basis of accountability. The court rejected his contention, stating that "the defendant said that he knew that Godinez intended to rob Soto two days before the shooting and again on the night of the shooting. On both occasions he agreed to act as lookout; and he knew that Godinez was armed with a revolver. Acting as a lookout is an act aiding and abetting the commission of the offense."

People v. Montes, 549 N.E.2d 700, 707 (Ill. App. 1989).

Under the law of most states, a lawful conviction as an accessory after the fact requires proof that the defendant knew that a felony had been committed by the person aided or assisted. The gist of being an accessory after the fact lies essentially in obstructing justice, and a person is guilty when he or she knows that an offense has been committed and receives, relieves, comforts, or assists the offender in order to hinder his or her apprehension, trial, or punishment. *United States v. Barlow*, 470 F.2d 1245 (D.C. Cir. 1972). Federal law, however, does not distinguish whether the person assisted has committed a felony or a misdemeanor. 18 U.S.C.A. § 3.

Because of a wife's duty at common law to obey her husband, a woman who gave aid and comfort to her husband was exempt from the law governing accessories after the fact. While this exemption no longer prevails, some state statutes exempt spouses and other classes of relatives from penalty for being accessories after the fact. For example, Florida law prevents the prosecution as an accessory after the fact of any person standing in the relation of husband or wife, parent or grandparent, child or grandchild, brother or sister, either by blood or marriage. West's Fla. Stat. Ann. § 777.03.

CONCLUSION

The concepts discussed in this chapter are basic to an understanding of the criminal law in the United States. At this stage, such fundamental concepts as the *actus reus* and the *mens rea* seem abstract; however, they will become more concrete as we relate them to the various offenses discussed in later chapters.

Common-law crimes were considered *mala in se* or wrongs in themselves and required proof of a general or specific intent. In contrast, many modern statutory offenses are classified as *mala prohibita*, simply because a legislative body has classified them as such wrongs.

The elements of crimes will be of continuing relevance throughout the text. In contrast, the background concerning the designation of parties to crimes is largely of historical importance. The trend in modern criminal law is to treat as principals all parties to crimes, whether perpetrators or accomplices. This approach may be debatable but society has found it necessary, and this principle is firmly ingrained in modern criminal law.

QUESTIONS FOR THOUGHT AND DISCUSSION

1. Distinguish between the concepts of motive and intent in the criminal law. Can you cite an instance where a person would be guilty of a crime despite his or her good motives?
2. Does the proliferation of strict liability crimes offend the basic principles of criminal liability outlined in Chapter 1?
3. Should the criminal law punish a person whose mere carelessness, as opposed to willfulness, causes harm to another?

4. Is there a justification for the criminal law not punishing a person for failing to act when there is a clear moral duty to act?
5. Has the moral integrity of the criminal law been jeopardized by the increasing number of offenses for which a person can be convicted without proof of any criminal intent?
6. What justifies the criminal law making mere possession of contraband articles illegal? Would this rationale extend to criminalizing the mere possession of such innocent items as a screwdriver, pliers, or ice pick that could be used to commit burglary?
7. Why is the common-law doctrine distinguishing between principals and accessories before the fact of diminished importance in contemporary criminal law?
8. Is it fair to assess the same degree of fault and impose the same punishment on an accomplice as on a perpetrator?
9. Is there a valid reason to exempt close family relatives from punishment as accessories after the fact to felonious conduct?
10. I. N. Mate, a prisoner in a state institution, was visited by his long-time friend, Sol Toolmaker. Mate had previously told Toolmaker how much he wanted to escape from the prison. So on this occasion, Toolmaker brought Mate two small saws. Mate hid the saws in a place where he thought they would not be found by the prison guards, but the guards promptly discovered and confiscated the saws. The warden turned this evidence over to prison's legal counsel with a request that charges be prepared against Mate for attempting to escape from prison. Assuming Mate intended to escape from prison, did his conduct constitute a criminal act?
11. A.H., a juvenile, was adjudged delinquent on the basis that he became a principal by having aided and abetted O.M., another juvenile, in committing a robbery. The victim, Ms. Turista, was seated on a bench waiting for the bus when the two young males (A.H. and O.M.) approached. O.M. began to struggle with Ms. Turista and grabbed her purse. A.H. stood by, doing nothing during the incident. The two juveniles then ran away together. At the adjudicatory hearing, the detaining officer testified that A.H. agreed to discuss the matter with officers because "he said he didn't do anything wrong." On appeal, A.H. contends that his adjudication of delinquency based on his being an aider and abettor was in error because there was no evidence that he intended to participate or that he assisted in any way in committing the robbery. Do you think A.H.'s conduct made him a principal in the robbery? If you were an appellate judge, on the basis of this scenario, would you vote to overturn A.H.'s adjudication of delinquency?

CASES

MORISSETTE v. UNITED STATES

Supreme Court of the United States, 1952.
342 U.S. 246, 72 S.Ct. 240, 96 L.Ed. 288.

[In this case the U.S. Supreme Court rules that where the intent of the accused is an ingredient of the offense charged, its existence may not be presumed but must be proved by the evidence.]

Mr. Justice JACKSON delivered the opinion of the Court.

. . . On a large tract of uninhabited and untilled land in a wooded and sparsely populated area of Michigan, the government established a practice bombing range over which the Air Force dropped simulated bombs at ground targets. These bombs consisted of a metal cylinder about 40 inches long and eight inches across, filled with sand and enough black powder to cause a smoke puff by which the strike could be located. At various places the range signs read "Danger—Keep Out—Bombing Range." Nevertheless, the range was known as good deer country and was extensively hunted.

Spent bomb casings were cleared from the targets and thrown into piles "so that they will be out of the way." They were not stacked or piled in any order but were dumped in heaps, some of which had been accumulating for four years or upwards, were exposed to the weather and rusting away.

Morissette, in December of 1948, went hunting in this area but did not get a deer. He thought to meet expenses of the trip by salvaging some of these casings. He loaded three tons of them on his truck and took them to a nearby farm, where they were flattened by driving a tractor over them. After expending this labor and trucking them to market in Flint, he realized $84.

Morissette, by occupation, is a fruit stand operator in summer and a trucker and scrap iron collector in winter. An honorably discharged veteran of World War II, he enjoys a good name among his neighbors and has no blemish on his record more disreputable than a conviction for reckless driving.

The loading, crushing and transporting of these casings were all in broad daylight, in full view of passers-by, without the slightest effort at concealment. When an investigation was started, Morissette voluntarily, promptly and candidly told the whole story to the authorities, saying that he had no intention of stealing but thought the property was abandoned, unwanted and considered of no value to the government. He was indicted, however, on the charge that he "did unlawfully, wilfully and knowingly steal and convert" property of the United States of the value of $84, in violation of 18 U.S.C. § 641. . . . Morissette was convicted and sentenced to imprisonment for two months or to pay a fine of $200. The Court of Appeals affirmed, one judge dissenting.

On his trial, Morissette, as he had at all times told investigating officers, testified that from appearances he believed the casings were cast-off and abandoned, that he did not intend to steal the property, and took it with no wrongful or criminal intent. The trial court, however, was unimpressed, and . . . refused to submit or to allow counsel to argue to the jury whether Morissette acted with innocent intention. It charged:

> "And I instruct you that if you believe the testimony of the government in this case, he intended to take it. . . . He had no right to take this property. [A]nd it is no defense to claim that it was abandoned, because it was on private property. . . . And I instruct you to this effect: That if this young man took this property (and he says he did), without any permission (he says he did), that was on the property of the United States Government (he says it was), that it was of the value of one cent or more (and evidently it was), that he is guilty of the offense charged here. If you believe the government, he is guilty. . . . The question on intent is whether or not he intended to take the property. He says he did. Therefore, if you believe either side, he is guilty."

Petitioner's counsel contended, "But the taking must have been with a felonious intent." The court ruled, however, "That is presumed by his own act."

The Court of Appeals suggested that "greater restraint in expression should have been exercised," but affirmed the conviction because "[a]s we have interpreted the statute, appellant was guilty of its violation beyond a shadow of doubt, as evidenced even by his own admissions." Its construction of the statute is that it creates several separate and distinct offenses, one being knowing conversion of government property. The court ruled that this particular offense requires no element of criminal intent. This conclusion was thought to be required by the failure of Congress to express such a requisite.

... Stealing, larceny, and its variants and equivalents, were among the earliest offenses known to the law that existed before legislation; they are invasions of rights of property which stir a sense of insecurity in the whole community and arouse public demand for retribution, the penalty is high and, when a sufficient amount is involved, the infamy is that of a felony, which, says Maitland, is " ... as bad a word as you can give to man or thing." State courts of last resort, on whom fall the heaviest burden of interpreting criminal law in this country, have consistently retained the requirement of intent in larceny-type offenses. If any state has deviated, the exception has neither been called to our attention nor disclosed by our research.

Congress, therefore, omitted any express prescription of criminal intent from the enactment before us in the light of an unbroken course of judicial decision in all constituent states of the Union holding intent inherent in this class of offense, even when not expressed in a statute. Congressional silence as to mental elements in an act merely adopting into federal statutory law a concept of crime already so well defined in common law and statutory interpretation by the states [does not mean that intent is not required as an element of the crime]. Nor do exhaustive studies of state-court cases disclose any well-considered decisions applying the doctrine of crime without any intent to such enacted common-law offenses.

The government asks us by a feat of construction radically to change the weights and balances in the scales of justice. The purpose and obvious effect of doing away with the requirement of a guilty intent is to ease the prosecution's path to conviction, to strip the defendant of such benefit as he derived at common law from innocence of evil purpose, and to circumscribe the freedom heretofore allowed juries. Such a manifest impairment of the immunities of the individual should not be extended to common-law crimes on judicial initiative....

We hold that mere omission from § 641 of any mention of intent will not be construed as eliminating that element from the crimes denounced....

Congress has been alert to what often is a decisive function of some mental element in crime. It has seen fit to prescribe that an evil state of mind, described variously in one or more such terms as "intentional," "willful," "knowing," "fraudulent" or "malicious," will make criminal an otherwise indifferent act, or increase the degree of the offense of its punishment. Also, it has at times required a specific intent of purpose which will require some specialized knowledge or design for some evil beyond the common-law intent to do injury.... In view of the care that has been bestowed upon the subject, it is significant that we have not found, nor has our attention been directed to, any instance in which Congress has expressly eliminated the mental element from a crime taken over from the common law.

The section with which we are here concerned was enacted in 1948, as a consolidation of four former sections of Title 18.... We find no other purpose in the 1948 re-enactment than to collect from scattered sources crimes so kindred as to belong in one category. Not one of these had been interpreted to be a crime without intention and no purpose to differentiate between them in the matter of intent is disclosed. No inference that some were and some were not crimes of intention can be drawn from any difference in classification or punishment.... [E]ach is, at its least, a misdemeanor, and if the amount involved is $100 or more each is a felony. If one crime without intent has been smuggled into a section whose dominant offenses do require intent, it was put in ill-fitting and compromising company. The government apparently did not believe that conversion stood so alone when it drew this one-count indictment to charge that Morissette "did unlawfully, willfully and knowingly steal and convert to his own use."

Congress, by the language of this section, has been at pains to incriminate only "knowing" conversions. But, at common law, there are unwitting acts which constitute conversions. In the civil tort, except for recovery of exemplary damages, the defendant's knowledge, intent, motive, mistake, and good faith are generally irrelevant. If one takes property which turns out to belong to another, his innocent intent will not shield him from making restitution or indemnity, for his well-meaning may not be allowed to deprive another of his own.

Had the statute applied to conversions without qualification, it would have made crimes of all unwitting, inadvertent and unintended conversions. Knowledge, of course, is not identical with intent and may not have been the most apt words of limitation. But knowing conversion requires more than knowledge that defendant was taking the property into his possession. He must have had knowledge of the facts, though not necessarily the law, that made the taking a conversion. In the case before us, whether the mental element that Congress required be spoken of as knowledge or as intent, would not seem to alter its bearing on guilt. For it is not apparent how Morissette could have knowingly or intentionally converted property that he did not know could be converted, as would be the case if it was in fact abandoned or if he truly believed it to be abandoned and unwanted property.

It is said, and at first blush the claim has plausibility, that, if we construe the statute to require a mental element as part of criminal conversion, it becomes a meaningless duplication of the offense of stealing, and that conversion can be given meaning only by interpreting it to disregard intention. But here again a broader view of the evolution of these crimes throws a different light on the legislation. . . .

The purpose which we here attribute to Congress parallels that of codifiers of common law in England and in the states and demonstrates that the serious problem in drafting such a statute is to avoid gaps and loopholes between offenses. It is significant that the English and state codifiers have tried to cover the same type of conduct that we are suggesting as the purpose of Congress here, without, however, department from the common-law tradition that these are crimes of intendment.

We find no grounds for inferring any affirmative instruction from Congress to eliminate intent from any offense with which this defendant was charged.

As we read the record, this case was tried on the theory that even if criminal intent were essential its presence (i) should be decided by the court (ii) as a presumption of law, apparently conclusive, (iii) predicated upon the isolated act of taking rather than upon all of the circumstances. In each of these respects we believe the trial court was in error. . . .

Reversed.

STATE v. FERGUSON

Supreme Court of South Carolina, 1990.
302 S.C. 269, 395 S.E.2d 182.

[In this case the South Carolina Supreme Court considers whether the distribution of cocaine is a strict liability offense and, if not, whether the trial court's jury instruction to the contrary constitutes a reversible error.]

TOAL, Justice:

On November 3, 1988, deputy sheriff Douglas Pernell of Dillon County phoned an individual known as the "Fatman" (an unidentified co-conspirator with the appellant) concerning the receipt of bribes in exchange for illegal police protection. The "Fatman" told Pernell that Ferguson (a.k.a. "Dino") would deliver the bribe monies. Pernell then spoke with Ferguson, who informed Pernell that he needed more time to come up with the requisite amount of money and that Pernell should come back later. Implicitly, Ferguson then changed his mind and offered to bring Pernell $250.00 in cash and a quantity of cocaine instead of the usual $500.00 cash amount.

Ferguson met with Pernell approximately ten minutes later at a post office, bringing him a shoe polish box containing $250.00 and a bag of cocaine. Two . . . officers witnessed the transaction. Upon giving Pernell the box, Ferguson said, "It's all there." . . .

Ferguson argues that the trial court committed two charging errors warranting reversal. He complains that, as to both the bribery offense and the distribution of cocaine offense, the trial court failed to properly charge the jury on the required criminal intent, or mental state of the defendant. Ferguson bases his arguments on the basic premise in criminal law that ordinarily, in order to establish criminal liability, a criminal intent of some form is required. This premise is rooted in the maxim *actus non facit reum nisi mens sit rea.* For example, the mental state required to be proven by the State for a particular crime might be purpose (intent), knowledge, recklessness, or criminal negligence. Of course, the legislature, if it so chooses, may make an act or omission a crime regardless of fault. . . . These crimes are referred to commonly as "strict liability" offenses. Whether an offense is a strict liability offense, and if not, what kind of criminal intent is required to satisfactorily show a commission of that offense, are questions of legislative intent. . . .

As for the bribery charge, we simply disagree with Ferguson's contention. The trial court charged the jury, in pertinent part:

> Thirdly, the defendant is charged with violating a statute which reads 'whoever corruptly gives to any officer, including police officers, any gift, or gratuity with the intent to influence such officer's act or judgment on any matter which is pending before him shall be guilty of an offense.' Corruptly, when used in that statute, simply means dishonestly. It means an effort to procure dishonest activities of the person to whom the gratuity or gift is offered to get him to fail to perform his duties in whatever office he is holding and whatever duty he is required to exercise. . . .

We hold that the jury was adequately instructed as to the mental state required for the bribery offense.

We agree that the trial court committed error, however, in ruling, in effect, that there is no mental state required for the offense of distribution of cocaine. We held in *State v. American Agricultural Chem. Co.,* 118 S.C. 333, 337, 110 S.E. 800 (1922) that:

> In offenses at common law, and under statutes which do not disclose a contrary legislative purpose, to constitute a crime, the act must be accompanied by a criminal intent, or by such negligence or indifference to duty or to consequences as is regarded by the law as equivalent to a criminal intent.

A reading of the entire statutory scheme convinces us that the legislature intended to place a mental state requirement in the offense contained in S.C. Code Ann. § 44–53–370(a) (1985).

Having held that the legislature did not intend this serious offense to be a strict liability crime, we now turn to what kind of mental state is required to be proven in order to show a violation of § 44–53–370(a). We are guided in this decision by our ruling in *State v. Freeland,* 106 S.C. 220, 91 S.E. 3 (1916). In *Freeland,* the alleged offense was illicit possession of cocaine. No mental state requirement was mentioned in the statute. The trial court instructed the jury that, if the defendant did not know that she had cocaine in her possession, she should be acquitted. This Court held, regarding an attack on this charge:

> [t]he instruction was really too favorable to defendant, in that it did not eliminate the possibility of willful or negligent want of knowledge. If she was culpably ignorant of the fact, her ignorance would not excuse her. . . .

The instant case is therefore controlled, in our view, by *Freeland.* Hence, the State must show that a given defendant was at least criminally negligent when he/she manufactured, distributed, or dispensed a controlled substance in order to prove a violation of § 44–53–370(a).

Nevertheless, although we find error, we hold that such was harmless in this case, in light of the overwhelming evidence that Ferguson was well aware that he was distributing cocaine. *State v. Mitchell,* 286 S.C. 572, 336 S.E.2d 150 (1985). For instance, Ferguson specifically told Pernell, "I've got $250.00 and the white stuff" when setting up their rendezvous at the post office. . . . Ten minutes later, Ferguson then delivered a shoe polish box to Pernell at the post office containing $250 cash and a quantity of cocaine with $250 written on it. Under these circumstances, it strains credulity past the breaking point to adhere to Ferguson's theory that he was just an honest delivery man with no knowledge or reason to know he was distributing cocaine.

Accordingly, the judgment of the lower court is AFFIRMED.

GREGORY, C.J. and HARWELL, CHANDLER, and FINNEY, J.J., concur.

STATE v. STARKS

Supreme Court of Kansas, 1991.
249 Kan. 516, 820 P.2d 1243.

[In this case the Kansas Supreme Court considers whether there is sufficient evidence to support charges of possession of marijuana with intent to sell within 1,000 feet of an elementary or secondary school and conspiracy to sell marijuana.]

SIX, Judge.

This criminal case arises from a "reverse sting" drug operation. The case concerns the determination of probable cause during a preliminary hearing.

The State Appeals the preliminary hearing order of dismissal. . . .

The trial court, at the conclusion of the preliminary hearing, dismissed the charges against defendant Terry L. Starks and Ricky L. Casey for possession of marijuana with intent to sell within 1,000 feet of an elementary or secondary school (K.S.A. 1990 Supp. 65–4127b[e]) and against Starks for conspiracy to sell marijuana (K.S.A. 21–3302 and K.S.A. 1990 Supp. 65–4127b).

We disagree with the disposition of the intent to sell charge. We agree that the dismissal of the conspiracy charge against Starks was proper.

Facts

Starks, Casey, and Jon A. Heter were charged with possession of marijuana with intent to sell within 1,000 feet of an elementary or secondary school (count I) and conspiracy to sell marijuana (count II). Their arrests were the result of a "reverse sting" operation conducted by the Reno County Drug Enforcement Unit and the Kansas Bureau of Investigation (KBI). A reverse sting occurs when law enforcement officials sell drugs to individuals who seek to purchase a large quantity for resale. Once the drugs are purchased from the undercover agent, the purchasers are arrested for drug possession, often with intent to sell.

The reverse sting, in the present case, began when a confidential informant told a sheriff's detective that Heter wanted to purchase a large quantity of marijuana. The KBI agreed to supply the marijuana. Special Agent Atteberry was sent to Hutchinson to act as an undercover agent.

Atteberry and a confidential informant arranged a meeting with Heter at a Hutchinson motel. According to Atteberry, Heter and a drug connection originally planned to purchase five kilos of marijuana for the price of a quarter pound of cocaine and $1,500. Heter told Atteberry that he did not know if the connection could obtain the cocaine. Heter agreed with Atteberry to buy five kilos of marijuana for $7,500 ($1,500 per kilo). Heter then left to show the connection a sample of the marijuana, stating he would return in 15 minutes with the money to complete the transaction. He did not return. Atteberry later learned that Heter believed that there were undercover police around the motel.

Atteberry met with Heter at Heter's residence the following day. They agreed to complete the transaction that evening at the residence, which was located 96 feet from Liberty Middle School.

Atteberry's Testimony

The State relied heavily on Atteberry's testimony. Atteberry testified that Heter stated the connection did not have a driver's license; consequently, another individual would drive the connection to Heter's residence. According to Heter, a vehicle would pull all the way to the back of a neighbor's driveway on the east, and the connection would bring $9,000 to exchange for the marijuana. The connection did not want to meet Atteberry.

The complex arrangements among Heter, the connection, and the driver were related by Atteberry. Heter planned on paying Atteberry $7,500 for five kilos of marijuana; however, the connection was told the price was $9,000. Heter wanted Atteberry to return $1,500 to him after the connection left. Heter and his connection intended to deceive the driver regarding the quantity of marijuana purchased. Atteberry testified:

> "Earlier, one of our conversations that Mr. Heter asked how much five kilos of marijuana weighed, and I replied eleven pounds. He believed it to be ten pounds. His deal with his connection was for ten pounds of marijuana for $9,000, so his inten-

tions, what he stated was that he was going to cut one of the bricks in half and keep the one pound and him and his connection was going to meet later and split that one pound, but the connection did not want the driver of the vehicle to know that they were splitting the one pound up."

Atteberry also related Heter's statements regarding the driver's involvement:

"He stated that, that as I stated earlier, that Heter replied that he was charging his buddy a little bit more and that they're in it together on this, the driver and the connection. He says, I'm trying to make a little off it, 'cause he stated he was selling, Heter was selling the marijuana to his connection for $9,000, and at that time the connection was selling some of this marijuana to the driver of the car."

Atteberry testified that: (1) Heter stated his connection was leaving for Texas the following day to sell the marijuana; (2) Heter intended to sell some of the marijuana to make money to fix up his car; and (3) marijuana was currently selling for $60 per quarter ounce or $200 per ounce in the Hutchinson area.

The Reverse Sting

While Atteberry, Heter, and the informant waited for the connection to arrive, Atteberry brought in five kilos of marijuana. Heter picked out one of the kilos, cut it in half, and placed one half kilo under his chair. The remaining four and one-half kilos were placed next to the chair.

A brown Maverick, announced by its noisy muffler, pulled into the neighbor's driveway on the east side of Heter's residence. Heter went to the rear of the residence and returned to the living room carrying a large wad of money clutched with both fists. Heter and Atteberry began counting the money. The $9,000 cash pile had a strong odor of marijuana.

Law enforcement officers, listening to the conversation over the informant's body transmitter, moved in when they heard the money being counted. Heter was in the living room. A KBI agent testified that he observed a subject, identified as Casey, attempt to exit the back door of the residence. The agent illuminated Casey with a flashlight and ordered him into the house. Casey ran to the basement. Later, Casey informed the police officers that he was told to go to the basement and that he did not know what was going on. Casey had no driver's license.

Starks was slumped down low behind the wheel in the Maverick when apprehended.

After being Mirandized, Heter agreed to talk to the police. According to police, Heter stated that he had spoken with Casey about the $9,000 and about buying the five kilos of marijuana. Casey came to Heter's residence, brought $9,000, and the transaction took place. Heter claimed he was just the "middle man."

Starks, after being Mirandized, also agreed to talk to the police. According to police, Starks stated he (1) had no knowledge of any drug transaction; (2) was Casey's friend; (3) had been called by Casey and asked for a ride; (4) picked up Casey and took him to Heter's residence at Casey's direction; (5) did not know Heter; and (6) did not notice Casey carry anything into the residence.

Heter, Casey, and Starks did not testify at the preliminary hearing. Neither Casey's nor Starks' names were mentioned by Heter before the arrest.

The State admitted that neither Casey nor Starks actually possessed the marijuana. The State argued that Casey and Starks aided and abetted Heter's possession of marijuana with intent to sell and was criminally responsible under K.S.A. 1990 Supp. 21–3205.

The trial court bound Heter over for trial on both count I (possession with intent to sell) and count II (conspiracy to sell). Casey was bound over for trial on count II. The trial court dismissed count I against Casey and Counts I and II against Starks. The State then dismissed count II against Casey.

Probable Cause

If, from the evidence presented at the preliminary hearing, it appears that a crime has been committed and there is probable cause to believe the defendant committed the crime, the magistrate shall bind the defendant over for trial. . . .

Count I—Possession of Marijuana With Intent to Sell

The State argues that the trial court erred when it found insufficient evidence to establish probable cause that Starks and Casey aided and abetted Heter in possessing the marijuana with intent to sell.

Starks argues that he did not know Heter and did not have any idea of the transaction among Heter, Casey, and Atteberry. . . .

The evidence presented at the preliminary hearing was sufficient to establish probable cause that Starks and Casey aided and abetted Heter in possessing the marijuana with intent to sell within 1,000 feet of an elementary or secondary school.

The distance of 96 feet from Heter's residence to Liberty Middle School is not contested.

K.S.A. 1990 Supp. 21–3205(1) provides that a person is criminally responsible for a crime committed by another if the person charged intentionally aids, abets, advises, hires, counsels, or procures the other to commit the crime. Mere association with the person who commits the crime or mere presence in the vicinity is insufficient to establish guilt as an aider and abettor. However, when a person knowingly associates with an unlawful venture and participates in a way which indicates the person is willfully furthering the success of the venture, there is sufficient evidence of guilt to go to the jury. . . .

Starks stated to the police officer that he: (1) simply gave Casey a ride to Heter's residence; (2) did not know Casey and Heter were conducting a drug transaction; and (3) did not see Casey carry anything into the residence.

Casey stated to police that he was told to go down in the basement and that he did not know what was going on.

In contrast, Atteberry testified that Heter told him the driver and the connection were "in it together." According to Heter, Casey planned to sell some of the marijuana to Starks. Casey and Heter did not want Starks to know that they were purchasing 11 pounds rather than 10 pounds. Atteberry also testified that Casey brought the money into Heter's house in a large wad that smelled of marijuana. In addition, Atteberry testified Heter (1) told Atteberry he was selling the marijuana to Casey for $1,500 more than Heter paid; and (2) planned to sell his portion of the split one pound in order to have money to fix his car.

The KBI agent testified that Starks was slumped down in the car seat and that Casey attempted to flee the residence.

There is a conflict between the statements of Starks and Casey, and the testimony of Atteberry. Looking at all the evidence, viewed in the light most favorable to the prosecution, the evidence is sufficient to cause a person of ordinary prudence and caution to entertain a reasonable belief that Starks and Casey willfully furthered the success of Heter's possession of the marijuana with intent to sell. The jury could find that Casey knowingly provided the money necessary for Heter to possess the marijuana with intent to sell and that Starks knowingly provided the transportation.

Count II—Conspiracy to Sell Marijuana

K.S.A. 21–3302(1) provides: "A conspiracy is an agreement with another person to commit a crime or to assist to commit a crime. No person may be convicted of conspiracy unless an overt act in furtherance of such conspiracy is alleged and proved to have been committed by him or by a co-conspirator."

The State contends that the trial court improperly weighed the evidence, finding it "too thin" to bind Starks over on count II. The State argues that Atteberry's testimony provides sufficient evidence that Starks was involved in the agreement between Casey and Heter to sell marijuana. Starks counters that the evidence was insufficient to support a finding of probable cause that Starks was involved in the agreement.

A review of the evidence indicates that Starks did not enter into an agreement to sell marijuana.

Atteberry testified that Heter told him Starks and Casey were in it together. Starks planned on purchasing some of the marijuana from Casey. There was no testimony concerning either the quantity Starks intended to purchase or what Starks intended to do with the marijuana after the purchase. There was no testimony that Starks knew what Casey intended to do with the marijuana. The only evidence of an agreement involving Starks relates to his intention to purchase an unknown quantity from Casey. The evidence is not sufficient to establish probable cause of an agreement to sell marijuana.

We affirm the trial court's dismissal of the count II charge against Starks for conspiracy to sell marijuana (K.S.A. 21–3302 and K.S.A. 1990 Supp. 65–4127b).

We reverse the trial court's dismissal of the count I charges against Starks and Casey for possession of marijuana with intent to sell within 1,000 feet of an elementary or secondary school (K.S.A. 1990 Supp. 65–4127b[e]).

Affirmed in part and reversed in part. . . .

CHAPTER 5

INCHOATE OFFENSES

CHAPTER OUTLINE

Introduction
Attempt
Solicitation
Conspiracy
Conclusion

Cases

Bucklew v. State
State v. Keen
Gomez v. People

INTRODUCTION

The word *inchoate* means underdeveloped or unripened. Thus, an inchoate offense is one involving activities or steps preparatory to the completion of a crime. There are three such offenses: attempt, solicitation, and conspiracy. Although preparatory to commission of other offenses, they are separate and distinct crimes. During the 1800s each was recognized as a misdemeanor at common law; however, this was too late to become a part of the common law under the reception statutes adopted by most new American states. Most American jurisdictions now define these offenses by statute, frequently classifying them as felonies.

Why Criminalize Preparatory Conduct?

Inchoate offenses were originally created by the courts in response to the need to prevent commission of serious crimes. The development of the law in this area has been primarily through the courts. Frequently the courts have found difficulty in determining when mere noncriminal activity has reached the stage of criminal conduct. Yet, by recognizing an actor's design toward commission of an offense, the law permits police to apprehend dangerous persons who have not yet accomplished their criminal objectives. Consequently, by making certain preparatory conduct illegal, the law gives law enforcement officers an opportunity to terminate such conduct at an early stage.

ATTEMPT

Of these inchoate crimes, attempt is probably the most frequently charged. "Attempt," of course, means an effort to accomplish a particular purpose. A criminal attempt consists of an intent to commit a specific offense and an act that constitutes a substantial step toward the commission of that offense. *People v. Tuczynski*, 378 N.E.2d 1200 (Ill. App. 1978). Thus, as explained in an early New York opinion, whether an attempt to commit a crime has been made depends on both the actor's mind and conduct. *People v. Moran*, 25 N.E. 412 (N.Y. 1890).

No particular federal statute proscribes the offense of attempt. In general, federal courts have recognized the requisite elements of attempt as (1) an intent to engage in criminal conduct, and (2) the performance of an act that constitutes a substantial step toward the completion of the substantive offense. See *United States v. Manley*, 632 F.2d 978 (2d Cir. 1980), *cert. denied*, 449 U.S. 1112, 101 S. Ct. 922, 66 L.Ed.2d 841 (1981).

State penal codes often specifically provide for attempts to commit the most serious crimes such as murder. The remaining offenses are then covered by a general attempt statute. A typical statute that covers all attempts provides "Whoever attempts to commit an offense prohibited by law and in such attempt does any act toward the commission of such an offense, but fails in the perpetration or is intercepted or prevented in the execution of the same, commits the offense of criminal attempt." West's Fla. Stat. Ann. § 777.04(1). The requirement of an act contemplates an act that constitutes a substantial step toward commission of an offense. While the quoted statute makes no distinction between felony or misdemeanor offenses, statutes in some states limit the crime of attempt to attempts to commit felonies or certain specified crimes.

The Requisite Criminal Intent

To find a defendant guilty of the crime of attempt, most courts require the prosecution to prove that the defendant had a specific intent to commit the intended offense, frequently referred to as the "target crime." Most courts reason that one cannot attempt to do something without first forming the specific intent to accomplish that particular act. See, for example, *Thacker v. Commonwealth,* 114 S.E. 504 (Va. 1922). The rationale for this majority view seems to be that an attempt involves the concept of intended consequences by the actor. One state supreme court disagrees on whether specific intent is always required. In 1983, the Florida Supreme Court found it illogical to require proof of a specific intent for the successful prosecution of an attempt to commit a crime when the target crime only required proof of a general intent. *Gentry v. State,* 437 So.2d 1097 (Fla. 1983). Under this view the prosecution must prove a specific intent to convict a defendant of an attempted premeditated murder, a specific-intent crime. On the other hand, it would only have to prove the defendant had a general intent to commit an attempted battery, a general-intent crime. As pointed out in Chapter 4, a general intent is usually inferable from the actor's conduct and the surrounding circumstances. In any event, it seems that courts should require proof of at least the type of intent that must be established in prosecuting the target crime.

What Constitutes a Substantial Step toward Commission of a Substantive Offense?

As noted earlier, the "act" element in the crime of attempt requires an act that constitutes a substantial step toward the commission of an offense. The Model Penal Code distinguishes preparatory conduct from an attempt by allowing conviction for the crime of attempt, where the actor engages in "an act or omission constituting a substantial step in a course of conduct planned to culminate in the commission of the crime." M.P.C. § 5.01. Federal courts follow this test. *United States v. Mandujano,* 499 F.2d 370, 376 (5th Cir. 1974), cert. denied, 419 U.S. 1114, 95 S.Ct. 792, 42 L.Ed.2d 812 (1975).

Many state statutes also include the term *substantial* in defining the act requirement. Where they do not, courts usually imply that the act must constitute a substantial step toward commission of a substantive offense. In either instance, it becomes necessary to distinguish between mere preparatory acts of planning or arranging means to commit a crime and those acts that constitute a direct movement toward commission of an offense. The question is: How close must that act be to accomplishment of the intended crime? Appellate courts have taken various approaches to determining what constitutes such a substantial step. This issue frequently turns on the specific factual situation involved. An early, and demanding, test held that an actor must have engaged in the "last proximate act necessary to accomplish the intended crime," but most courts have now rejected that test. See, for example, *People v. Parrish,* 197 P.2d 804, 806 (Cal. App. 1948). Some courts apply a more realistic test that holds that the actor's conduct must be "within dangerous proximity to success." New York courts have summed it up in a practical manner, opining simply that an accused's conduct must be "very near" to the completion of the intended crime. *People v. Mahboubian,* 544 N.Y.S. 2d 769 (N.Y. 1989).

Attempts in Relation to Substantive Crimes

Generally, when a criminal act completes a substantive crime, the attempt usually merges into the target offense. The actor is then guilty of the substantive crime, rather than merely an attempt to commit it. Thus, a person who is successful in an attempt to commit murder is guilty of murder.

The Model Penal Code proposes that an accused who "purposely engages in conduct which would constitute the crime if the attendant circumstances were as he believed them to be" is guilty of an attempt. M.P.C. § 5.01(1)(a). While many state statutes track this Model Penal Code language, it may be debatable whether the law should pursue a conviction for an attempt to commit a crime that is legally impossible to commit.

Moreover, there can be no attempt to commit certain crimes because some substantive offenses by definition embrace an attempt. To illustrate, take the statutory crime of uttering a forged instrument. This offense is usually defined as

CASE IN POINT

A Judicial Construction of "Substantial Step"

Defendant, Mark Molasky, was charged with attempted murder of Ellis and Ellen Denos. At Molasky's trial the evidence revealed that while he was imprisoned for various sexual offenses, the Denoses sought to adopt Molasky's son. Molasky opposed their action, and while the Denoses were in the process of adoption, he had a conversation with Ricky Holt, a fellow inmate, concerning payment, time, and manner in which Holt was to kill Ellis and Ellen Denos. Molasky was convicted of second-degree murder and appealed, arguing the evidence was insufficient to establish that he was guilty. The Missouri Supreme Court pointed out that the Missouri statute on general attempts was patterned after Section 5.01 of the Model Penal Code, and before a defendant could be guilty of an attempt it must be established that the defendant's actions constituted a "substantial step" toward the target crime. The court found that the evidence disclosed a solicitation by Molasky, but it was not accompanied by other corroborating action to indicate a seriousness of purpose. There was no payment of money or furnishing Holt with a picture or other identification of the potential victims. The court observed that "given factually different circumstances, a solicitation could support an attempt charge. Here, however, this burden has not been met."

State v. Molasky, 765 S.W.2d 597, 602 (Mo. 1989).

CASE IN POINT

THE LAW OF ATTEMPT

Defendant was found guilty of attempting to escape from prison. He appealed, contending that the state failed to prove beyond a reasonable doubt that he had committed an overt act as required by law. He characterized his actions as preparatory steps indicative only of an intention to attempt an escape. The Supreme Judicial Court of Maine rejected his contention and affirmed his conviction. "[T]here was undisputed evidence that a dummy was found in defendant's cell; that defendant was in an unauthorized area attempting to conceal his presence; and that a rope ladder was found in a paper bag close to where he was concealed. [Defendant] had gone far beyond the preparation stage."

State v. Charbonneau, 374 A.2d 321, 322 (Me. 1977).

including an attempt to pass a forged instrument to someone to obtain something of value. Therefore, one who makes such an attempt would be guilty of uttering a forged instrument, not merely an attempt to do so. In effect, the attempt is subsumed by the very definition of the substantive crime. Needless to say, it would be redundant to charge someone with attempting to attempt to commit a given crime.

Defenses to the Crime of Attempt

Generally, a defendant cannot be found guilty of attempt if it is legally impossible to commit the offense attempted. For example, a man who assaults a mannequin dressed as a woman would not be guilty of attempted rape. Yet, this example must be distinguished from similar situations. A person who fires a pistol at another's shadow, believing it to be an intended victim, could be prosecuted for attempted homicide. Likewise, a woman who picks another's pocket intending to steal money may be found guilty of attempted theft, even if the victim's pocket is empty. In these instances courts have said that although it was factually impossible to commit the crime, it was legally possible to do so. Admittedly, the distinction is a close one.

New York law currently provides that it is no defense to a prosecution for attempt that the crime charged to have been attempted was factually or legally impossible to commit, if it could have been committed had the circumstances been what the defendant believed them to be. N.Y. McKinney's Penal Law § 110.10. The trend is toward finding an attempt to commit a crime in instances where the actor's intent has been frustrated merely because of some factor unknown at the time. Thus, if the accused believed a victim was alive when shooting at the victim, an attempt to kill a dead person constitutes an attempt under New York law. *People v. Dlugash*, 363 N.E.2d 1155 (N.Y. 1977).

Some jurisdictions have laws providing that it is a defense to the crime of attempt if the defendant abandons an attempt to commit an offense or otherwise prevents its consummation. See, for example, Vernon's Tex. Ann. Penal Code §

15.04(a). If recognized as a defense, abandonment must be wholly voluntary. It cannot be the result of any outside cause like the appearance of the police on the scene. See, for example, *People v. Walker,* 191 P.2d 10 (Cal. 1948) (en banc), *aff'd on rehearing,* 201 P.2d 6 (1948), *cert. denied,* 336 U.S. 940, 69 S. Ct. 744, 93 L.Ed. 1098 (1949).

SOLICITATION

By the 1800s, the common law specified that a person who counseled, incited, or solicited another to commit either a felony or a misdemeanor involving breach of the peace committed the offense of solicitation. A person was guilty of solicitation even if the crime counseled, incited, or solicited was not committed. *State v. Blechman,* 50 A.2d 152 (N.J. 1946).

The offense of solicitation is now defined by statute in most American jurisdictions. The statutory definition in Illinois is typical: "A person commits solicitation when, with intent that an offense be committed, other than first-degree murder, he commands, encourages, or requests another to commit the offense." Illinois S.H.A. 720 ILCS 5/8–1. The gist of the offense remains the solicitation, so the offender may be found guilty irrespective of whether the solicited crime is ever committed.

Some statutes stipulate that the crime solicited must either be a felony or fall within a certain class of offenses. See, for example, Vernon's Tex. Penal Code Ann. § 15.03(a). In contrast, the Model Penal Code takes the position that solicitation of any offense is a crime. M.P.C. § 5.02.

Commission of the crime of solicitation does not require direct solicitation of another; it may be perpetrated through an intermediary. In *State v. Cotton,* 790 P.2d 1050 (N.M. App. 1990), the court reversed a defendant's conviction of criminal solicitation because there was no evidence that the defendant ever communicated the solicitation to the person he intended to solicit to commit a crime. The court, however, recognized that solicitation could be perpetrated through an intermediary and offered the following example:

> If A solicits B in turn to solicit C to commit a felony, A would be liable even where he did not directly contact C because A's solicitation of B itself involves the commission of the offense. Where the intended solicitation is not in fact communicated to an intended intermediary or to the person sought to be solicited, the offense of solicitation is incomplete; although such evidence may support, in proper cases, a charge of attempted criminal solicitation. 790 P.2d at 1055.

In contrast, the Model Penal Code states that "It is immaterial . . . that the actor fails to communicate with the person he solicits to commit a crime if his conduct was designed to effect such communication." M.P.C. § 5.02(2).

The Requisite Criminal Intent

The language of statutes making solicitation a crime may not seem to require the prosecution to establish the defendant's specific intent. Most courts, however, hold that to commit solicitation the solicitor must have specifically intended to induce or entice the person solicited to commit the target offense. See, for example, *Kimbrough v. State*, 544 So.2d 177 (Ala. Crim. App. 1989). The prosecution should at least establish that the actor who solicits someone to commit a crime had the requisite intent for the crime solicited.

The Rationale for Making Solicitation a Crime

In explaining why its penal code makes solicitation an offense, a California appellate court offered two reasons: first, to protect individuals from being exposed to inducement to commit or join in the commission of crime; and second, to prevent solicitation from resulting in the commission of the crime solicited. *People v. Cook*, 199 Cal.Rptr. 269 (Cal. App. 1984).

Most students of the criminal law would concede that solicitation should be a criminal offense. But, you might ask, is it more serious than the inchoate crime of attempt? The Tennessee Supreme Court has suggested that it is not, stating: "There is not the same degree of heinousness in solicitation as in attempts, nor is solicitation as likely to result in a completed crime, there not being the same dangerous proximity to success as found in attempts." *Gervin v. State*, 371 S.W.2d 449, 451 (Tenn. 1963). In taking the contrary point of view, the Connecticut Supreme Court said:

> The solicitation to another to [commit] a crime is as a rule far more dangerous to society than the attempt to commit the same crime. For the solicitation has behind it an evil purpose, coupled with the pressure of a stronger intellect upon the weak and criminally inclined. *State v. Schleifer*, 121 A. 805, 809 (Conn. 1923).

Solicitation Distinguished from Other Inchoate Crimes

The offenses of solicitation and attempt are different crimes, analytically distinct in their elements. Although each is an inchoate offense, solicitation is complete when the request or enticement to complete the intended offense is made; and it is immaterial if the solicitee agrees, if the offense is carried out, or if no steps were taken toward consummation of the offense. Mere solicitation is generally not sufficient to constitute an attempt, because attempt requires proof of an overt act to commit the intended criminal act. This principle was succinctly explained by the Idaho Supreme Court when it said: "The solicitation of another, assuming neither the solicitor or solicitee proximately acts toward the crime's commission cannot be held for an attempt." *State v. Otto*, 629 P.2d 646, 650 (Idaho 1981).

Solicitation is distinguished from conspiracy because while solicitation requires an enticement, conspiracy requires an agreement. Sometimes a solicitation may result in a conspiracy, and some courts have looked upon the offense as "an offer to enter into a conspiracy." See, for example, *Commonwealth v. Carey*, 439 A.2d 151, 155 (Pa. Super. 1981).

Defenses to the Crime of Solicitation

Generally, the fact that the solicitor countermands the solicitation or the fact that it was impossible for the person solicited to commit the crime are not defenses to

CASE IN POINT

THE LAW OF SOLICITATION

Defendant Roger Gardner, an alleged contract killer, subcontracted the killing of Alvin Blum to a man named Tim McDonald for a fee of $10,000. Gardner met with McDonald and gave him some expense money, a gun, and ammunition. In talking with McDonald, Gardner said that he (Gardner) would first kill a man named Hollander, and if this did not create the desired result then McDonald would be directed to kill Blum. Gardner's attempts were foiled when he was arrested and charged with solicitation to murder. It turned out that McDonald was a police informant whose assistance led to Gardner's arrest. On appeal, Gardner argued that he did not commit the crime of solicitation because he did not actually direct McDonald to proceed with the murder of Blum or pay him all of the money he had promised. In affirming Gardner's conviction the Maryland Court of Appeals said:

> What Gardner fails to take into account is that the crime of solicitation was committed when he asked McDonald to commit the murder. Neither a final direction to proceed nor fulfillment of conditions precedent (paying of the money) was required. The gist of the offense is incitement. [W]e agree that the crime of solicitation was committed.

Gardner v. State, 408 A.2d 1317, 1322 (Md. 1979).

a charge of solicitation. However, in some states, it is a defense if the defendant can affirmatively establish that after soliciting another person to commit an offense, the defendant prevented commission of the crime under circumstances manifesting a complete and voluntary renunciation of his or her criminal purpose. The Model Penal Code provides that it is a defense to a charge of solicitation if there has been a timely, complete, and voluntary renunciation of the accused's criminal purpose. M.P.C. § 5.02 (3). Some states have adopted this position. See, for example, Ky. Rev. Stat. § 506.020.

CONSPIRACY

At common law, conspiracy consisted of an agreement by two or more persons to accomplish a criminal act or to use unlawful means to accomplish a noncriminal objective. The gist of the offense was the unlawful agreement between the parties, and no overt act was required. *State v. Carbone,* 91 A. 2d 571 (N.J. 1952).

Today the offense of conspiracy is generally defined by statute in all jurisdictions. Most state laws define the elements of the offense along the lines of the common law. Typically, the Florida law states: "Whoever agrees, conspires, combines, or confederates with another person or persons to commit any offense commits the offense of criminal conspiracy." West's Fla. Stat. Ann. § 777.04(3). On the other hand, federal law (with some exceptions) requires an overt act in a conspiracy to commit an offense or defraud the United States. 18 U.S.C.A. § 371.

A number of states also require proof of an overt act in order to convict someone for conspiracy. Texas law, for example, provides: "A person commits criminal conspiracy if, with intent that a felony be committed, (1) he agrees with one or more persons they or one or more of them engage in conduct that would constitute the offense, and (2) he or one or more of them performs an overt act in pursuance of the agreement." Vernon's Tex. Penal Code Ann. § 15.02(a). Note that the Texas statute also requires an intent that a felony be committed, whereas in most states it is only necessary to prove an intent to commit a criminal offense.

Because of the variations encountered in statutory language, in reviewing any statute defining conspiracy it is necessary to determine at the outset (1) the type of the offense or unlawful activity the statute proscribes, and (2) whether it requires proof of an overt act in furtherance of the parties' agreement.

Why the Offense of Conspiracy? The Perceived Danger of Group Action

Why is conspiracy considered an offense distinct from the substantive offense the conspirators agree to commit? Perhaps one of the most cogent responses to this question was articulated by the late U.S. Supreme Court Justice Felix Frankfurter. In *Callanan v. United States,* 364 U.S. 587, 593–594, 81 S.Ct. 321, 325, 5 L.Ed.2d 312, 317 (1961), the late justice observed:

> Concerted action both increases the likelihood that the criminal object will be successfully attained and decreases the probability that the individuals involved will depart from their path of criminality. Group association for criminal purposes often, if not normally, makes possible the attainment of ends more complex than those which one criminal could accomplish . . . . Combination in crime makes more likely the commission of crimes unrelated to the original purpose for which the group was formed. In sum, the danger which a conspiracy generates is not confined to the substantive offense which is the immediate aim of the enterprise.

The Required Act and Intent in Conspiracy

In general, the *actus reus* of the crime of conspiracy is the unlawful agreement. Where an overt act is required, such act need not be a substantial movement toward the target offense. For example, in California, where the law requires an overt act, the courts have said that an overt act tending to effect a conspiracy may merely be a part of preliminary arrangements for commission of the ultimate crime. *People v. Buono,* 12 Cal. Rptr. 604 (Cal. App. 1961). In fact, a single act such as a telephone conversation arranging a meeting has been held to be sufficient proof of an overt act. *United States v. Civella,* 648 F.2d 1167 (8th Cir. 1981), *cert. denied,* 454 U.S. 867, 102 S. Ct. 330, 70 L.Ed.2d 168 (1981).

Statutes frequently fail to encompass the intent requirement in the offense of conspiracy. This difficulty is compounded by failure of the courts to clearly define the intent required for a conviction. In general, the prosecution must prove that a defendant intended to further the unlawful object of the conspiracy, and such intent must exist in the minds of at least two of the parties to the alleged conspiracy. *People v. Cohn,* 193 N.E. 150 (Ill. 1934). Many courts refer to the crime as requiring a specific intent. See, for example, *People v. Marsh,* 376 P.2d 300 (Cal. 1962). As previously noted with respect to attempts, such intent may be inferable from the conduct of the parties and the surrounding circumstances. While many federal court decisions have not required proof of a specific intent, the U.S. Supreme Court has said that in federal prosecutions there must be proof of at least the criminal intent necessary for the requirements of the substantive offense. *United States v. Feola,* 420 U.S. 671, 95 S. Ct. 1255, 43 L.Ed.2d 541 (1975).

Some Common Misconceptions about the Crime of Conspiracy

Contrary to some popular views, the participants in a conspiracy need not even know or see one another as long as they otherwise participate in common deeds.

CASE IN POINT

CONSPIRACY TO DELIVER CONTROLLED SUBSTANCES

In a non-jury trial, Brian Smith was found guilty of conspiracy to deliver lysergic acid diethylamide (LSD). On appeal, he argued that the evidence was insufficient to support his conviction because there was no proof beyond a reasonable doubt (1) that he agreed to engage in delivery of LSD, and (2) that he intended that it be delivered. The appellate court rejected both contentions and affirmed Smith's conviction.

On February 16, 1988, Corporal Cook, working undercover, agreed to purchase fifty doses of LSD from Bruce Erickson at a park in the City of Snohomish, Washington. Erickson asked Smith for a ride to go there, ostensibly to meet David Hensler (who owed Smith $600, a sum Smith very much wanted to collect). When Smith and Erickson arrived in Smith's vehicle, the officer approached the car and asked Erickson if he had LSD. When Erickson produced a bag of LSD, the officer asked Smith if he had tried it. Smith replied "he was going to college . . . and couldn't afford to get messed up, but that his wife had taken some of it, and . . . 'it really [messed] her up.'" At that point Corporal Cook agreed to purchase the LSD, handed the money to Erickson, and arrested both Smith and Erickson.

In affirming Smith's conviction, the appellate court first pointed out that "a formal agreement is not necessary to the formation of a conspiracy." Then the court observed that although Smith's primary purpose in giving Erickson a ride to the park was to meet Hensler, his secondary purpose was to assist in delivering LSD. In finding the evidence sufficient to show that Smith intended to assist Erickson, the court opined, "there was evidence not only of knowledge of Erickson's unlawful purpose, but an agreement to assist with the plan by providing the necessary transportation . . . Here there were two overt acts: first, that Smith drove Erickson to Snohomish knowing, according to Corporal Cook, Erickson's purpose for the trip; and second, that Smith provided encouragement for the sale by assuring the officer of the potency of the drug . . . We hold that there is sufficient evidence to convince a rational trier of fact beyond a reasonable doubt that Smith agreed to transport Erickson to Snohomish for the common purpose of delivering LSD."

State v. Smith, 828 P.2d 654, 656, 657 (Wash. App. 1992).

The essence of the offense is the mutual agreement of the parties to the conspiracy, not the acts done to accomplish its object. Moreover, the agreement need not be explicit. In fact, it seldom is. In most instances, the agreement is implied from the acts of the parties and the circumstances surrounding their activities. Furthermore, all the conspirators do not have to join in the conspiracy at the same time.

Conspiracy Distinguished from Aiding and Abetting and Attempt

As noted in Chapter 4, aiding and abetting someone in the commission of a crime makes a person either a principal or an accessory before the fact. Conspiracy is a separate offense and must be distinguished from aiding and abetting. Conspiracy involves proof of an agreement between two or more persons, an element often present, but not essential, in proving that a defendant aided and abetted a crime. On the other hand, aiding and abetting requires some actual participation. *Shedd v. State*, 87 So.2d 898 (Miss. 1956), *cert. denied*, 352 U.S. 944, 77 S. Ct. 262, 1 L.Ed. 2d 237 (1956). Conspiracy differs from the crime of attempt in that it focuses on intent, whereas attempt places more emphasis on the defendant's actions.

Spousal Conspiracies

Because the common law regarded a husband and wife as one person for most purposes, a husband and wife could not be guilty of conspiring with one another. Since the trend of the law in recent years has been to recognize the separate identities of the spouses, there appears to be no valid reason to continue the common-law approach. See, for example, *People v. Pierce*, 395 P.2d 893 (Cal. 1964).

Conspiracy Does Not Merge into the Target Offense

Conspiracy is regarded as a separate and distinct crime; therefore, it usually does not merge into the target offense. As the New Jersey Supreme Court has pointed out, a conspiracy may be an evil in itself, independent of any other evil it seeks to accomplish. *State v. Lennon*, 70 A.2d 154 (N.J. 1949). A pragmatic consideration is that by not merging conspiracy into the target offense, the law can more effectively deter efforts of organized crime.

The Range of Conspiracies in Our Society

The range of conspiracies cuts across socioeconomic classes in society. Traditionally, state prosecutions for conspiracy have been directed at criminal offenses such as homicide, arson, perjury, kidnapping, and various offenses against property. In recent years an increasing number of both state and federal conspiracy prosecutions have been related to illicit drug trafficking. In addition to the large number of narcotics violations, federal prosecutions include a variety of conspiracies not found under state laws. Among these are customs violations, counterfeiting of currency, copyright violations, mail fraud, lotteries, and violations of antitrust laws and laws governing interstate commerce and other areas of federal regulation. Recently, a number of federal prosecutions have involved conspiracies to deprive persons of their civil rights or equal protection of the law.

Defenses to the Charge of Conspiracy

Where a statute requires proof of an overt act as an element of the crime, an alleged conspirator may defend by showing withdrawal from the conspiracy before commencement of such an act. Where an overt act is not required, a more difficult issue is presented. In some states, statutes specifically provide for the defense of withdrawal and renunciation. As an illustration, Missouri law specifies: "No one shall be convicted of conspiracy if, after conspiring to commit the offense, he prevented the accomplishment of the objectives of the conspiracy under circumstances manifesting a renunciation of his criminal purpose." Vernon's Mo. Ann. Stat. § 564.016(5)(1).

In the absence of statutory authority, courts have been reluctant to approve a person's withdrawal as a defense. One of the difficulties in approving withdrawal as a defense is that even though a conspirator withdraws, the criminal objective of the conspiracy may proceed. Therefore, it seems reasonable to require that a person who would rely on such defense not only renounce any criminal purpose but also take the necessary steps to thwart the objective of the conspiracy. To accomplish this result, the conspirator would probably have to notify law enforcement authorities of the pertinent details of the conspiracy. In any event, if an accused is allowed to offer such a defense, the defendant has the burden of establishing his or her withdrawal from the conspiracy.

Entrapment, a defense to be examined in Chapter 13, may under some circumstances be a defense to conspiracy. *Stripling v. State,* 349 So. 2d 187 (Fla. App. 1977), *cert. denied,* 359 So. 2d 1220 (Fla. 1978).

The *Pinkerton* Rule; Wharton's Rule

In *Pinkerton v. United States,* 328 U.S. 640, 66 S.Ct. 1180, 90 L.Ed 1489 (1946), Pinkerton was charged with conspiring with his brother for tax evasion, including some offenses allegedly committed by his brother during times that Pinkerton was incarcerated. The trial court instructed the jury that it could find Pinkerton guilty if it found he was a party to a conspiracy and that the offenses were in furtherance of the conspiracy. Pinkerton was convicted and upon review the U.S. Supreme Court upheld his conviction, stating that a member of a conspiracy is liable for all offenses committed in furtherance of the conspiracy. The Court did indicate that a different result may occur if the offenses were not reasonably foreseeable as a natural consequence of the unlawful agreement of the conspirators. This has come to be known as the "*Pinkerton* Rule." It is based on the theory that conspirators are agents of each other, and just as a principal is bound by the acts of his agents within the scope of the agency relationship, so is a conspirator bound by the acts of his co-conspirators. *United States v. Troop,* 890 F.2d 1393 (7th Cir. 1989). Obviously, the doctrine has broad implications, and not all courts have accepted it.

Another legal doctrine, Wharton's Rule, is named after Francis Wharton, a well-known commentator on criminal law. The Rule is an exception to the principle that a conspiracy and the target crime do not merge. Wharton's Rule holds that two people cannot conspire to commit a crime such as adultery, incest, or bigamy since these offenses require only two participants. The rationale is that, unlike the usual conspiracy, which is often like a wheel with many spokes, the offenses named do not endanger the public generally. Wharton's Rule has been applied in many state and federal courts, but it has its limitations. In holding the rule inapplicable to various federal gambling offenses under the Organized Crime Control Act of 1970, the Supreme Court pointed out that the rule itself is simply an aid to determination of legislative intent and must defer to a discernible legislative judgment. *Iannelli v. United States,* 420 U.S. 770, 786, 95 S.Ct. 1284, 1294, 43 L.Ed.2d 616, 628 (1975).

Some Unique Aspects of the Offense of Conspiracy

The courts regard conspiracy as a partnership in crime, and view each conspirator as an agent of the others. It follows that each will be held responsible for the acts of the others within the context of their common design. *Commonwealth v. Thomas,* 189 A.2d 255 (Pa. 1963), *cert. denied,* 375 U.S. 856, 84 S.Ct. 118, 11 L.Ed.2d 83 (1963). This principle permits an exception to the rule of evidence that ordinarily excludes hearsay statements from being used in a trial over the defendant's objection. Indeed, statements by a co-conspirator in furtherance of the conspiracy made during the pendency of the conspiracy may be admitted into evidence. Statements that have been found to be "in furtherance of" the conspiracy include statements to inform other conspirators of the activities or status of the conspiracy and those identifying other conspirators. Federal courts have upheld the use of statements as to the sources or purchaser of controlled substances. See, for example, *United States v. Patton,* 594 F.2d 444 (5th Cir. 1979). Before receiving this type of evidence, a court must receive independent evidence that a conspiracy has been committed. In some instances courts receive the hearsay evidence subject to it being tied into the offense by independent evidence of the conspiracy. Court procedures in this area are very technical evidentiary matters. A principal problem is for the court to determine the scope of the conspiracy and the inception of the conspirator's participation.

The Supreme Court of Hawaii properly characterized the judicial approach to conspiracy when it stated:

> In the eyes of the law conspirators are one man, they breathe one breath, they speak one voice, they wield one arm, and the law says that the acts, words, and declarations of each, while in the pursuit of the common design, are the words and declarations of all. *Territory v. Goto,* 27 Hawaii 65 (1923).

Courts have held that once formed, a conspiracy continues to exist until consummated, abandoned, or otherwise terminated by some affirmative act. *Cline v. State,* 319 S.W.2d 227 (Tenn. 1958).

These unique aspects are significant. They assist the prosecution in proof of cases that otherwise might be unprovable. Perhaps the law has established these exceptions in recognition of the difficulties of prosecuting persons involved in conspiracies, which are generally formed in secret.

CASE IN POINT

FIRST AMENDMENT CONCERNS IN A CONSPIRACY PROSECUTION

American involvement in the Vietnam conflict and the attendant military draft engendered considerable controversy in the 1960s. Dr. Benjamin Spock, the well-known "baby doctor," and several others were convicted of conspiracy to counsel registrants to resist the military draft. In reversing his conviction, the United States Court of Appeals for the First Circuit observed that while Spock was one of the drafters of a call to resist duties imposed by the Military Selective Service Act of 1967, "his speech was limited to a condemnation of the war and the draft, and lacked any words or content of counseling." Thus, the court concluded that Spock's actions lacked the clear character necessary to imply specific intent under the strict standards of the First Amendment.

United States v. Spock, 416 F.2d 165 (1st Cir. 1969).

Criticism of the Conspiracy Laws

There has been an increased tendency in recent years to prosecute defendants for conspiracies as well as target crimes. The offense of conspiracy is a potent weapon in the hands of the prosecutors, particularly in coping with the problem of organized crime. But since the intent requirement and the form of agreement required are somewhat imprecise, some commentators have criticized the offense and the activities of certain prosecutors, particularly where an overt act is not required. The most basic criticism is that prosecutors, judges, and juries are given too wide a latitude in finding a defendant guilty because a conspiracy is easier to prove than specific criminal acts. Additionally, some critics argue that conspiracy prosecutions chill or effectively abolish First Amendment rights of free expression.

CONCLUSION

Inchoate offenses often pose substantial problems for law enforcement agencies, courts, and legislative bodies. Police and courts often have great difficulty determining the stage at which an act tends toward commission of a crime so as to qualify as criminal attempt. There remains controversy whether it should be a criminal offense to solicit another person to commit a crime, irrespective of whether the solicited offense is a felony or a misdemeanor. Conspiracy too is problematic. Some statutes extend criminal liability beyond legislatively defined crimes to include injuries to the public health and morals, making the offense of conspiracy vulnerable to the criticism that the law is converting civil wrongs into criminal conduct.

Despite the problems associated with inchoate offenses, there remains strong support for criminalizing conduct directed toward future injuries to society. Criminalizing preparatory conduct permits the timely intervention of law enforcement agencies to restrain dangerous persons and prevent intended crimes.

QUESTIONS FOR THOUGHT AND DISCUSSION

1. What is the justification for criminalizing attempt, solicitation, and conspiracy?
2. How does the criminal law distinguish between mere preparatory conduct and the overt act required for a criminal attempt? Can you think of a situation in which preparatory conduct would not constitute a criminal attempt?
3. Should it be a defense to a charge of attempt that the accused voluntarily abandoned the attempt?
4. Would impotency be a legitimate defense to a charge of attempted rape?
5. What is the rationale for making solicitation a crime even where a solicitor's requests are completely unheeded?
6. Which do you think poses a more serious threat to society: an attempt or a solicitation to commit murder? Why?
7. Should statutes defining conspiracy require proof of an overt act in furtherance of the conspirators' agreement? Why or why not?
8. Given the First Amendment protections of freedom of expression and association, can members of a revolutionary political organization be prosecuted for conspiring to overthrow the government of the United States?
9. Would a person who offers a bribe to someone believed to be a juror, but who is not a juror, be guilty under a statute making it an offense to offer bribes to jurors?
10. What is the evil the offense of conspiracy is designed to combat?
11. Leo Lothario was having an affair with Lucy Slarom, a woman separated from her husband, Joe. One night while Lothario and Lucy were playing tennis in her backyard, Joe appeared on the scene. Lothario demanded he leave, but Joe declined and sat in one of the yard chairs. Lothario went to the garage, picked up a rifle, pointed it at Joe, and from a distance of approximately seventy-five feet, fired a shot in the direction of Joe. The bullet missed Joe by about eighteen inches. Lothario explained to the police that he was simply trying to scare Lucy's estranged husband so he would not bother her. On the strength of these facts, do you think there is a basis to charge Lothario with attempted murder?
12. John and Jane were running a student loan "scam." They were convicted of soliciting several students to make false applications in exchange for a "cut" of the loan proceeds and also for aiding and abetting those same students in making false applications for loans. On appeal, they argue that the solicitation charges merged into their convictions for aiding and abetting the making of the false applications. The state responds that John and Jane were guilty of both crimes because the solicitation offenses were completed before John and Jane assisted the students in making the false applications. How should the appellate court rule on this appeal? Why?

CASES

BUCKLEW V. STATE

Supreme Court of Mississippi, 1968.
206 So.2d 200.

[This case deals with an attempt to commit a crime.]

ROGERS, Justice:

This is an appeal from a judgement of conviction of attempted embezzlement from the Circuit Court of Jones County, Mississippi, wherein the mayor of the City of Laurel was fined in the amount of $816.05. The testimony in this case shows that sometime in the summer of 1965 Henry Bucklew, the mayor of Laurel, Mississippi, called a representative of Kelly-Lowe Dodge, Inc., an automobile repair shop, advised them that he had a jeep which belonged to the Pest Control Department of the City of Laurel, and asked whether or not they could repair it. Kelly-Lowe Dodge, Inc., repaired the jeep and purchased tires and chains for it. The repair bill, including labor and parts, amounted to $816.05.

Kelly-Lowe submitted its bill by mail to the City of Laurel on November 25, 1965. When the clerk saw the bill he recognized that it was not an obligation of the city and took it to the mayor. The mayor advised the clerk that he would "take care of it." Some time later, John Jacobs, who was in charge of what is known as the Pest Control Department of the City of Laurel, was requested by the mayor to sign the bill which had been submitted by Kelly-Lowe. In the meantime, the city clerk had requested a copy of this bill from the repair shop "for the files" of the City of Laurel. Later, the mayor was indicted by the grand jury of Jones County for the crime of an attempt to commit embezzlement. The bill for repairs to the jeep was never finally submitted to the city for payment by the mayor or anyone else. The testimony shows that the city clerk had an understanding with the mayor and city commissioners that before bills could be paid by the city it was necessary for the heads of the various departments to approve the payment before they were submitted to the clerk for payment. Thereafter, the mayor or commissioner to whom the bill had been referred would indicate his approval of the bill by signing his name to the approval sheet attached to the bill. The city clerk would then prepare a check in the payment of the amount indicated and return it to the mayor for his signature. Before the check could be cashed it required the signature of the clerk. In the absence of the mayor it was necessary for one of the commissioners to sign checks with the clerk before they could be paid.

The testimony showing the approval of Mr. Jacobs by affixing his signature on the bill is the only testimony showing the intention of the mayor after the bill had been turned over to him by the clerk, except that an auditor testified that the mayor told him that he approved the bill by mistake. The original bill was not offered in evidence.

The defendant, Henry Bucklew, was indicted under section 2122, Mississippi Code 1942 Annotated (1956).

When the State had concluded its testimony, the defendant made a motion to exclude the evidence offered on behalf of the State and requested the court to direct the jury to find the defendant not guilty, for the reason that the State had not shown that the defendant had committed an overt act toward the commission of the crime of embezzlement as charged in the indictment. The court overruled this motion and defendant rested his case, without introducing testimony in his behalf and without having testified in his own defense. The issue is, therefore, clearly defined: Did the State show that the defendant committed an overt act in an attempt to commit the crime of embezzlement?

Under the general law it has been pointed out that an attempt to commit a crime consists of three elements: (1) an intent to commit a particular crime; (2) a direct ineffectual act done toward its commission; and (3) the failure to consummate its commission. . . . Our statutory law requires proof of an overt act in order to sustain a conviction of an attempt to commit a crime.

The pertinent part of section 2017, Mississippi Code 1942 Annotated (1956), is as follows:

> Every person who shall design and endeavor to commit an offense, and shall do any overt act toward the commission thereof, but shall fail therein, or shall be prevented from committing the same, on conviction thereof, . . .

This Court is in accord with the general law as to the essential elements of the crime of "attempt to commit a crime." We have held that the law requires that the State establish criminal *intent* as an element to the crime of attempt "to commit a crime."...

We have also held that there must be an *overt act* done toward the commission of the crime in order to establish the crime of "attempt to commit a crime."...

We have no trouble with the third element, since the Legislature has provided for this element by enactment of section 2018, Mississippi Code 1942 Annotated (1956). This law prevents prosecution for the "attempt to commit an offense, when it shall appear that the crime intended or the offense attempted was perpetrated. . . ."

We have held that the mere intention to commit a crime is not punishable. . . . The intention must therefore be coupled with an overt act. But, what is meant by the requirement that the State prove "an overt act"? . . .

In *Williams v. State,* 209 Miss. 902, 48 So.2d 598 (1950), the defendant was convicted of attempting to commit larceny by the "pigeon dropping" game. The Court there said:

> The necessary elements of an attempt are the intent to commit, and the overt act toward its commission. . . . The rule is well recognized that "whenever the design of a person to commit crime is clearly shown, slight acts done in furtherance of this design will constitute an attempt.". . .

In that case, however, the testimony showed that the various acts of preparation had been concluded and that the defendant then went to the place to receive the money. This Court held that this was a sufficient overt act to establish an attempt.

In the case of *Stokes v. State,* 92 Miss. 415, 46 So. 627 (1908), this Court pointed out that where one attempted to procure another to kill a third party, and in furtherance of his design took a gun, loaded it and went with the party to a point where the killing was to occur, but was arrested, his act was sufficient to establish an attempt to commit a crime.

The records in the foregoing cases indicate that the defendants had reached a point in the proceedings to commit a crime beyond mere preparation, so that they had actually begun to commit the alleged crime. In *Williams* the defendant had done everything necessary to commit a crime except receive the money, and in *Stokes* the defendant had performed his part in the crime of murder and there was nothing left for him to do in furtherance of the crime.

In *State v. Lindsey,* 202 Miss. 896, 32 So.2d 876 (1947), this Court held that stalking, chasing and running after the prosecuting witness, in a lonesome and secluded place in the country was not a sufficient overt act on which to base a charge of attempt to "forcibly ravish her." In that case we said:

> The gravamen of the offense of an attempt to commit a crime is fixed by the statutory requirement that the defendant must do an overt act toward the commission thereof and be prevented from its consumation. . . .

It is contended by the State in the instant case that the appellant, defendant in the court below, accomplished the required overt act by having the department head of the Pest Control Department sign the bill submitted by Kelly-Lowe Dodge, Inc. An examination of the testimony in this case, however, shows that if all the State attempted to prove was true, the acts done by the defendant were mere acts in preparation to the submission of the bill to the clerk for payment. The testimony shows that it was necessary for the mayor to sign the bill before submitting it to the clerk for payment, and the proof shows that the mayor did not submit the bill to the clerk for payment. Moreover, there is nothing in the record to show that there was any extraneous cause that prevented the mayor from attempting to collect the amount due to the automobile company. Moreover, the record shows that the mayor told the auditor that the bill had been signed through a mistake. Therefore, if the mayor had intended to defraud the City, the record shows that he had abandoned his purpose before attempting to collect the funds from the city treasury. . . .

From the foregoing facts, and our study of the law in this case, we have come to the conclusion that the proof here shown does not sustain the charge of "an attempt to embezzle" funds from the City of Laurel by the appellant.

We pause to point out that the law, like religion, holds out a promise to those who would commit crime and sin that if they voluntarily resist temptation so as to recant and desist before attempting to carry into effect their evil purpose, they will not be held accountable for mere evil intent. On the other hand, facts such as we have in this case prove the rule that those in high places should not only avoid wrongdoing, but should avoid the appearance of evil, because, although the law will not punish for mere evil intent, public opinion will convict and will certainly condemn.

Inasmuch as the law does not punish for the mere appearance of evil, we conclude that the testimony in this case does not establish an attempt to commit a crime, for the reason that it does not show an *overt act* on the part of the appellant to commit the crime charged, before it is shown that he abandoned his alleged purpose. We are, therefore, constrained to hold that the judgement of the trial court must be reversed, and the appellant, Henry Bucklew, discharged.

Judgment reversed and appellant discharged.

ETHRIDGE, C.J., and JONES, Inzer and SMITH, JJ., concur.

STATE V. KEEN

North Carolina Court of Appeals, 1975.
214 S.E.2d 242.

[This case deals with solicitation.]

Defendant was charged in a bill of indictment with soliciting Blaine Bacon and Ben Wade to kill and murder Susan Page Keen, wife of defendant.

Evidence for the State is summarized as follows. Blaine Bacon first saw Patrick Alan Keen, the defendant, on the afternoon of 12 September 1973. Defendant brought his Volkswagen bus into Bacon's garage to be repaired. Bacon examined the vehicle, told defendant that he did not have the necessary parts, and suggested that defendant return the next day. Defendant returned the next day and Bacon proceeded to repair the vehicle. Defendant asked Bacon if he knew "someone with few scruples and in need of some money." Defendant replied that he wanted his wife killed so that he could collect the proceeds from an insurance policy in her name. He agreed to pay Bacon $5,000.00 from the proceeds of policy.

Defendant told Bacon the death of his wife must occur before 1 October since that was the expiration date of her life insurance policy. At the close of the conversation Bacon asked the defendant to give him a few days to consider the proposition and to contact him the following Monday.

Defendant had purchased a $100,000.00 policy on his wife's life dated 1 July 1973, and was the named beneficiary. Defendant paid the quarterly premium for the months of July, August, and September but did not pay the premium due 1 October 1973, and the policy lapsed on 31 October.

Bacon immediately attempted to contact several law enforcement officers with whom he had become acquainted when he had worked as an informer or undercover agent. He finally reached a U.S. Treasury agent and informed him of what defendant had said. The agent advised him to keep in contact. Bacon's actions thereafter were generally directed by law enforcement officers. On Friday, the defendant again visited Bacon, told him of the urgency of the time factor, and sought a definite answer as to whether Bacon would kill Mrs. Keen. Defendant informed Bacon that she was in Fayetteville and said he could go there and "blow her brains out." Bacon again told the defendant to wait until Monday for an answer.

The following Monday afternoon, defendant met Bacon at his garage. Ben Wade, an agent of the State Bureau of Investigation, was concealed in Bacon's rear office so that he could overhear their conversation. At this meeting defendant again stressed the importance of time and asked Bacon when he was going to kill Mrs. Keen. Bacon replied that accidents were not his style but that he had discussed the matter with a friend who was a professional killer. Bacon told the defendant that his friend was an expert at making deaths appear accidental and that he would be in Asheville the following Friday. On Wednesday defendant visited Bacon again. The two established Friday morning as their meeting time, and defendant was asked to bring a picture of his wife.

On that Friday the two men drove in defendant's van to a motel in Asheville. They went to a room where Wade, posing as a professional killer, was waiting. A wireless transmitter was taped to Wade's back for the purpose of recording the conversation. Tapes of the conversation were introduced at trial for the purpose of corroboration.

At the motel defendant told Wade that his wife was in Fayetteville and gave him her address. He also gave him a photograph and physical description of her. He told Wade that his wife's death must appear accidental and must occur prior to the cancellation of her life insurance policy on the first of October. Defendant volunteered to raise the fee for the killing to $6,000.00 and the method of payment was discussed. With respect to "front money," defendant said that he had no cash but did have a motorcycle, a Volkswagen bus, and a five-acre tract of land to which titles could be signed over to Bacon who, in turn, could transfer them to Wade. Wade replied that he wanted the titles transferred that day and instructed defendant to put the vehicles in Bacon's name and the property in Wade's name. He told defendant he would wait at the motel until 2:30 that afternoon.

At the conclusion of the conversation, defendant left the room. Police immediately placed him under arrest. Upon being arrested defendant replied, "Oh my God how did you find out about it so fast?"

Defendant testified, in substance, as follows. He did not originally intend to have his wife killed but Bacon implanted the idea in his mind. After he and Bacon discussed the life insurance policy in Mrs. Keen's name, Bacon suggested that defendant "knock her off" and collect on the policy. Bacon volunteered to kill Mrs. Keen for $5,000.00. When Bacon telephoned and told him that his friend had arrived, defendant indicated to Bacon that he wanted to call off the thing and did not care to visit Bacon's friend. Bacon responded that his friend had come all the way to Asheville, would be very upset if defendant did not at least talk with him and might seek vengeance on defendant. Defendant, although he had no intention of following through with the plan, proceeded to the motel in order to talk the other men out of it. He was frightened and answered Wade's questions because of his fear.

The jury found defendant guilty and judgment was entered imposing a sentence of confinement of not less than five nor more than ten years. . . .

VAUGHN, Judge.

In support of his contention that the court should have granted his motion for judgment of nonsuit, defendant argues that the State's own evidence shows that: " . . . the defendant was (1) entrapped and (2) that there was the interposition of a resisting will thereby making the commission of a crime impossible."

We hold that defendant's contentions on entrapment were properly submitted to the jury with instructions from the court which were correct in law and manifestly fair to defendant.

Defendant argues that there could have been no completion of the crime since all parties with whom he spoke were connected with law enforcement. The answer is that the interposition of a resisting will, by a law enforcement officer or anyone else, between the solicitation and the proposed felony is of no consequence. This is so "because the solicitation was complete before the resisting will of another had refused its assent and cooperation.". . . Defendant was not charged with the crime of conspiracy, a crime which was not completed because of the failure of Bacon, in fact, to concur in defendant's scheme to murder defendant's wife. The crime of solicitation to commit a felony is complete with the solicitation even though there could never have been an acquiescence in the scheme by the one solicited.

Defendant also contends that his conviction of solicitation to commit murder cannot be punished by imprisonment for more than two years. We concede that the applicable statute . . . and the reported cases leave some lack of certainty as to what crimes may be designated and punished as "infamous."... It appears, nevertheless, to be settled that conspiracy to murder is an infamous offense and punishable as a felony....

The crime of which defendant was convicted is but one step away from conspiracy to murder—and that step is not one defendant could have taken. If Bacon had concurred in defendant's scheme to murder the latter's wife, the conspiracy would have been complete. Bacon's rejection of defendant's atrocious scheme does not render defendant's conduct any less "infamous" than it would have been if his offer had been accepted. We hold that the punishment imposed does not exceed that authorized by law.

We have considered the other contentions made in defendant's brief and find them to be without merit.

No error.

MARTIN and ARNOLD, JJ., concur

GOMEZ V. PEOPLE

Colorado Supreme Court, 1963.
381 P.2d 816.

[This case involves conspiracy to commit larceny.]

MCWILLIAMS, Justice.

Joyce Gomez and Roberta Taylor were jointly tried and convicted by a jury of conspiring on November 1, 1960, to commit the crime of larceny from the person of one Edward Cook. By the present writ of error Gomez alone seeks reversal of the judgment and sentence entered pursuant to the verdict of the jury.

The only assignment of error pertains to the sufficiency of the evidence, Gomez contending that the trial court erred in refusing to direct a verdict in her favor and, a fortiori, that the evidence does not support the subsequent determination by the jury that she is guilty of the crime of conspiracy. From a careful review of the record we conclude that her contention is without merit. However, inasmuch as the legal sufficiency of the evidence has been challenged, it becomes necessary to review the record before us in some detail in order to give meaning to our conclusion that here is evidence to support the verdict.

The evidence adduced by the People established the following:

1. That Cook, a locomotive engineer, got off work at about midnight on November 1, 1960, and he was going via automobile from the roundhouse at 40th Avenue and Williams Street in Denver to his home in southwest Denver when he encountered Gomez and Taylor at 26th Avenue and Welton Street;
2. That Cook at this time had approximately $340 in his wallet, $75 of which was secreted in an inside compartment of the wallet, the balance of the currency being in the wallet proper;
3. That Cook had this comparatively large amount of money on his person because this was his pay day, and he had cashed his pay check, getting "paid in ten dollar bills";
4. That while Cook was stopped for a traffic light at 26th Avenue and Welton Street, Gomez and Taylor with no invitation opened the right-hand door of his car and proceeded to deposit themselves on the front seat;
5. That Gomez, who was seated immediately next to Cook, asked or "ordered" him to drive on, stating: "Help us out; this girl's [Taylor's] husband is going to kill her," and that one of the two women stated that Taylor's husband was armed with a gun;
6. That Cook promptly proceeded to drive for several blocks, but when he got over his "surprise" stopped the car and ordered the two women to leave his car;
7. That the two refused to leave, whereupon Cook got out of his car, went around it and opened the right-hand door, and with only little difficulty succeeded in getting Taylor out of the automobile;
8. That with his back turned to Taylor he then proceeded to forcibly evict Gomez from his car, that she initially resisted, but after considerable

struggle he was able to pull her out of his car by the coat collar;

9. That about this time he realized for the first time that his wallet which he carried in his left rear trousers pocket was missing;
10. That Gomez and Taylor then broke and ran, whereupon he gave hot pursuit, and after a four-to-five-block chase espied the two crouching down on the floor of the front seat of an abandoned automobile;
11. That he opened the left-hand front door of this auto and saw Taylor and Gomez "down on the floor board attempting to hide";
12. That as he was in the act of pulling Taylor out of the car as the police arrived, whereupon Gomez got out of the front door on the right-hand side of the vehicle, crying "rape";
13. That a subsequent search of this auto by the police revealed 26 ten-dollar bills under the front seat in such a position that they could not have been accidently "dropped there," because they were a foot or so back under the seat;
14. That search of Cook's automobile by the police thereafter disclosed that his wallet was "pushed down in the crack on the [front] seat quite a ways"; and
15. That though Cook's wallet still contained the $75 hidden in the inside compartment, the remainder of his currency was missing.

The foregoing resume demonstrates quite clearly to us that the trial court did not commit error in submitting the case to the jury, and that actually there is ample evidence to support the jury's verdict.

True, there was evidence to the contrary. Although Taylor elected not to testify, Gomez did testify in her own behalf, and her testimony was radically different from that of Cook in virtually all particulars, as under the circumstances might well be expected. However, no good purpose would be served by detailing Gomez's testimony, as it did no more than create a conflict in the evidence and thereby pose a disputed issue of fact properly to be resolved by the jury.... There being competent evidence, both of a direct and circumstantial nature, to support the jury's determination, we are not at liberty to set it aside.

In support of the general proposition that a conspiracy "need not be proved directly, but may be inferred by the jury from the facts proved."...

The judgement is affirmed.

FRANTZ, C.J. and DAY, J., concur.

C H A P T E R 6

OFFENSES AGAINST PERSONS

CHAPTER OUTLINE

Introduction
The Common-Law Background
The American Development
Assault and Battery
Mayhem
Homicide
Suicide
Sexual Battery
Sodomy
Abortion
Child Abuse
Spouse Abuse; Abuse of the Elderly
False Imprisonment and Kidnapping
Conclusion

Cases

State v. Towers
Furr v. State
Manuel v. State
Commonwealth v. Graves
State v. Studham
State v. Rothenberg
State v. Snider

INTRODUCTION

Every civilized society attempts to protect its people from injury or death at the hands of wrongdoers. Imposing criminal sanctions is society's way of protecting human life from those whose conduct it cannot tolerate. As the English common law developed, the judges created offenses to protect individuals from conduct that society concluded was wrongful and injurious. These basic offenses as defined by English common law were inherited by the American colonists. Since then, many social changes have occurred in America, and federal and state statutes have redefined many of these offenses and have created new ones. In this chapter, we examine the common-law crimes against persons and discuss their statutory development in the United States. We also explore some representative statutes defining present-day offenses against persons.

THE COMMON-LAW BACKGROUND

By the time of the English colonization in America, the common law had identified four groups of offenses against persons. These consisted of: (1) the assaultive crimes, that is, assault, battery, and mayhem; (2) the homicidal crimes of murder, manslaughter, and suicide; (3) sexual offenses of rape, sodomy, and abortion; and (4) the offenses known as false imprisonment and kidnapping. Murder, manslaughter, rape, sodomy, and suicide were common-law felonies; the remaining offenses named were classified as misdemeanors.

THE AMERICAN DEVELOPMENT

Early substantive criminal law in America was essentially a continuation of the English common law of crimes. By the 1800s, however, America's quest for representative government and its penchant for definiteness and certainty, combined with the standards of written constitutions, resulted in legislative definition of crimes. Defining offenses against persons became primarily a state rather than a federal legislative function, and the new states basically followed the common-law themes with variations deemed necessary in the new social and political environment.

As the United States became urbanized, more densely populated, and increasingly mobile, the areas of conduct statutorily defined as criminal offenses against persons required revision and, in many instances, an enlargement. Under modern statutes, assault and battery have been classified according to their seriousness, the character of the victim, and the environment in which these crimes are committed. Homicidal offenses, too, have been divided into classifications of murder and manslaughter based on the degree of the offender's culpability, and a new offense of vehicular homicide has been created to cope with the dangers inherent in motor vehicle traffic. At early common law, suicide was punished by causing the forfeiture of the decedent's goods and chattels to the king. See *State v. Willis,* 121 S.E.2d 854 (N.C. 1961). Suicide statutes are now designed primarily to punish those who would attempt or assist in self-destruction.

In recent years, contemporary moral standards have caused the offense of rape to be expanded into a more comprehensive offense of sexual battery, with new emphasis on the victim's age and vulnerability. At the same time, enforcement of laws proscribing sodomy has declined, and abortion, a common-law crime, has become a woman's constitutional right. Finally, while the offense of false imprisonment is essentially the same as at common law, the crime of kidnapping serves a much different role in American society than it did under the English common law.

ASSAULT AND BATTERY

Assault and battery, while commonly referred to together, were separate offenses at common law. An assault was basically an attempted battery consisting of an offer to do bodily harm to another by using force and violence; a battery was a completed or consummated assault. *State v. Maier,* 99 A.2d 21 (N.J. 1953). Although an actual touching was not required, words alone did not constitute an assault. *Herrington v. State,* 172 So. 129 (Miss. 1937). The common law made no distinction between classes or degrees of assault and battery but dealt with aggravated cases more severely.

Modern Statutory Development

Today all jurisdictions make assault an offense, and most make battery a crime as well. Assault is usually defined by statute, as is battery. Sometimes the term *assault and battery* is used to indicate one offense. Simple assaults and batteries generally remain misdemeanors, while those perpetrated against public officers (e.g., fire and police personnel) are frequently classified as felonies. Legislatures commonly classify as felonies more egregious assaultive conduct as aggravated assault, aggravated battery, and assault with intent to commit other serious crimes.

The California Penal Code defines an assault as "an unlawful attempt, coupled with a present ability, to commit a violent injury on the person of another." West's Ann. Cal. Penal Code § 240. It imposes increased penalties for an assault committed upon a person engaged in performing the duties of a peace officer, fire fighter, lifeguard, process server, paramedic, physician, or nurse, West's Ann. Cal. Penal Code § 241(b); and, like most states, makes it a felony to commit an assault with a deadly weapon or with force likely to produce great bodily injury. West's Ann. Cal. Penal Code § 245. Many states classify this latter offense as aggravated assault. For example, under Florida law, a person who commits an assault with a deadly weapon without intent to kill or an assault with an intent to commit a felony is guilty of aggravated assault, a felony offense. West's Fla. Stat. Ann. § 784.021.

Again, the California Penal Code defines as battery "any willful and unlawful use of force or violence upon the person or another." West's Ann. Cal.

Penal Code § 242. The code also specifies increased punishment for batteries committed against specific classes of officers, West's Ann. Cal. Penal Code § 243; against transportation personnel, West's Ann. Cal. Penal Code § 243.3; or when committed on school property, West's Ann. Cal. Penal Code § 243.2. Consistent with its handling of aggravated assaults, Florida law classifies a battery resulting in great bodily harm, permanent disability, or permanent disfigurement, or one committed with a deadly weapon as an aggravated battery, an even more serious felony than aggravated assault. West's Fla. Stat. Ann. § 784.045.

While most assault and battery prosecutions occur under state laws, the federal government also has a role in this area. Federal statutes proscribe assault within the maritime and territorial jurisdiction of the United States. 18 U.S.C.A. § 113. Federal courts have held that the statute covers the entire range of assaults, *United States v. Eades*, 615 F.2d 617 (4th Cir. 1980), *cert. denied*, 450 U.S. 1001, 101 S. Ct. 1709, 68 L.Ed.2d 203 (1981), and that the word *assault* includes acts that would constitute batteries under most state laws. *United States v. Chaussee*, 536 F.2d 637 (7th Cir. 1976). Additional federal statutes proscribe assaults on federal officers engaged in the performance of official duties, 18 U.S.C.A. § 111, and assaults of foreign diplomatic and other official personnel. 18 U.S.C.A. § 112.

Common Illustrations of Assault and Battery

Statutory definitions vary, but under most statutes a simple assault would include a threat to strike someone with the fist, or a missed punch. Firing a shot in the direction of a person, throwing a rock at someone but not hitting them, or threatening someone with a weapon would probably all qualify as aggravated assault.

A battery, on the other hand, involves some physical contact with the victim. Some common illustrations of a simple battery would include hitting or pushing someone, a male hugging and kissing a female—or even an offensive touching, if against her will—using excessive force in breaking up a fight, intentionally tripping another individual, or using excessive force (by a parent or teacher) in disciplining a child. The acts referred to as constituting aggravated assault, if completed, would most likely be prosecuted as aggravated batteries.

A frequently litigated issue in prosecutions for aggravated assault and aggravated battery is whether the instrument used by the defendant is a dangerous weapon capable of producing death or great bodily harm. Throwing someone out of a window, or using an air pistol, a hammer, a club, or an ice pick—and under some circumstances, even the fist—have been found to qualify. Courts generally reason that the test is not whether great bodily harm resulted, but whether the instrument used was capable of producing such harm.

The Burden of the Prosecution

The proof required to establish assaultive offenses is dependent on the statutory language of the offense. However, to convict a defendant of simple assault or battery, the prosecution generally need only prove the act and the defendant's general, but not specific, intent. In aggravated assault and aggravated battery prosecutions, courts have arrived at different interpretations of the intent requirement, but usually proof of the defendant's general intent is sufficient. In contrast, if a defendant is prosecuted for committing an assault or battery "with the intent to do great bodily harm" or "with the intent to commit a specific felony, e.g., murder," courts usually require the prosecution to prove the defendant's specific intent to accomplish those results.

Defenses to Charges of Assault and Battery

Many forms of conduct involving intentional use of physical force do not constitute batteries. In many instances there is an express or implied consent of the person against whom the physical force is exerted. Reasonableness is the test applied in sports contests and friendly physical encounters. Everyday examples include such contact sports as football, in which the participants obviously consent to forceful bodily contact. The physician who performs surgery with consent of the patient provides another example of physical contact that, if properly applied, does not constitute a battery. Reasonableness is also the test applied to interpersonal relationships. Thus, while a person may imply consent to a friendly kiss or caress, seldom could a person imply consent to an act of violence, even when done under the guise of affection. A teacher may discipline a pupil, and a police officer or prison guard may use reasonable force to effect an arrest or preserve order. Often the degree of force used by teachers, police officers, and correction officials is regulated by statutory law, and an excessive use of force may constitute a battery. See *State v. Mendoza*, 258 N.W.2d 260 (Wis. 1977). Likewise, parents and guardians and those standing *in loco parentis* have a right to impose reasonable punishment when disciplining a child, but must take into consideration the child's age, health, size, and all other relevant circumstances. Parents who inflict injury on a child or who impose excessive punishment may be guilty of committing a simple or even an aggravated battery. *State v. Thorpe*, 429 A.2d 785 (R.I. 1981). They may also be subject to prosecution under modern statutes proscribing child abuse.

A person charged with battery may defend by showing that the touching or hitting was unintentional, that the physical force used was reasonable, or that the action was taken in self-defense. Self-defense is subject to qualifications, as explained in Chapter 13. Defenses applicable to the offense of battery generally apply as well to a charge of assault. The theory is that a person who fails to make physical contact with another can defend on the same basis of reasonableness or self-defense as a person who successfully commits a battery.

A Variation in Criminal Offenses: The New Crime of Stalking

By the end of the 1980s, police and legislators were receiving complaints from victims and their families and friends that persons were being continually harassed by conduct consisting of continued surveillance and threats, often with the intent to cause a person targeted to reasonably fear for his or her safety. Law enforcement officers refer to this type of behavior as "stalking." Many prosecutors felt that the traditional protections of the criminal law were not always sufficient to protect victims from the needless torment caused by this conduct, and they urged legislators to adopt appropriate statutes to combat the problem.

California enacted a stalking law in 1991, and by 1993 a majority of the states had enacted laws making stalking a crime. These laws often stipulate that to be

CASE IN POINT

Assault With a Deadly Weapon

Rasor, a police officer, stopped a vehicle and attempted to arrest the driver, Jackson, for driving while intoxicated. As he did, a fight broke out between the officer and Jackson. At that point the defendant, Lloyd Gary, a passenger in Jackson's car, approached the two combatants, removed the officer's pistol, and pointed it at Rasor and Jackson.

Gary was convicted of assault with a deadly weapon. On appeal, he argued that the trial judge erred in not directing the jury to return a verdict of not guilty because the evidence showed no attempt to commit a physical injury. The Arizona Supreme Court rejected Gary's argument, saying "The pointing of a gun may constitute 'an assault' . . . and it is not necessary to show in addition that there was an intent to do physical harm to the victim."

State v. Gary, 543 P.2d 782, 783 (Ariz. 1975).

guilty of the offense a person must willfully, maliciously, and repeatedly follow or harass another and make a credible threat against that person. The Illinois statute is one of the toughest new laws against stalking. Chapter 38 of the Criminal Code was amended, making it a felony to stalk and a more serious felony to be guilty of aggravated stalking, and now provides:

> § 12–7.3
>
> (a) A person commits stalking when he or she transmits to another person a threat with the intent to place that person in reasonable apprehension of death, bodily harm, sexual assault, confinement or restraint, and in furtherance of the threat knowingly does any one or more of the following acts on at least 2 separate occasions:
>
> (1) follows the person, other than within the residence of the defendant;
>
> (2) places the person under surveillance by remaining present outside his or her school, place of employment, vehicle, other place occupied by the person, or residence other than the residence of the defendant.
>
> § 12–7.4
>
> (a) A person commits aggravated stalking when he or she, in conjunction with committing the offense of stalking, also does any of the following:
>
> (1) causes bodily harm to the victim;
>
> (2) confines or restrains the victim; or
>
> (3) violates a temporary restraining order, an order of protection, or an injunction prohibiting the behavior described in . . . [the Domestic Violence Act of 1986].

Stalking laws have been criticized as being excessively vague. It remains to be seen how stalking statutes will be construed by the courts and whether challenges to their constitutionality will prevail. As the number of prosecutions under these new laws increases, judicial activity in this area is likely.

MAYHEM

At common law, mayhem consisted of willfully and maliciously injuring another so as to render the victim less able in fighting, either in self-defense or in ability to annoy an adversary. To obtain a conviction for mayhem, it was only necessary to establish that the act was committed with a general intent. *Terrell v. State*, 8 S.W. 212 (Tenn. 1888). The crime of mayhem has been extended to include injuries that disfigure a person. Most states only require proof of a general intent that may be presumed from the offender's act of maiming the victim. Some, however, require proof of the actor's specific intent to maim or disfigure the victim.

Two appellate decisions illustrate the applicability of mayhem statutes. In Texas, a man who found his wife committing an act of adultery cut off her paramour's sex organ with a razor. The defendant was found guilty of mayhem under a Texas statute, and his conviction was affirmed on appeal. *Sensobaugh v. State*, 244 S.W. 379 (Tex. Crim. App. 1922). In another instance, a defendant deliberately struck another man, and as a result of the battery the victim lost his eye. The defendant's conviction under a New Mexico penal statute was affirmed on appeal. *State v. Hatley*, 384 P.2d 252 (N.M. 1963).

California statutes classify mayhem in two categories: basic and aggravated. The statute defining mayhem states:

> Every person who unlawfully and maliciously deprives a human being of a member of his body, or disables, disfigures, or renders it useless, or cuts or disables the tongue, or puts out an eye, or slits the nose, ear, or lip, is guilty of mayhem. West's Ann. Cal. Penal Code § 203.

While mayhem appears to be a general-intent offense, aggravated mayhem is a specific-intent crime because Section 205 refers to the intent to do some further act such as "to permanently disable the victim," or to achieve some additional consequences beyond the act of mayhem. West's Ann. Cal. Penal Code § 205; *People v. Daniels*, 537 P.2d 1232 (Cal. 1975).

In *People v. Ferrell*, 267 Cal. Rptr. 283 (Cal. App. 1990), the defendant was a stranger to the victim. Yet, she came looking for her by name at the address furnished her by a friend from jail. When the defendant approached the victim, she knocked the phone from the victim's hand and shot her in the neck. Defendant's conviction for aggravated mayhem was upheld by the appellate court, which concluded the jury could reasonably have inferred that the defendant intended both to kill the victim, and if she did not die, to disable her permanently.

Mayhem statutes are less common today because many of the acts formerly prosecuted under laws proscribing mayhem are now prosecuted as other statutory crimes (e.g., aggravated battery and attempted murder).

HOMICIDE

The word *homicide* means the taking of the life of one human being by another. The English common law recognized both criminal and noncriminal homicides. Criminal homicide embraced the crimes of murder and manslaughter; noncriminal homicide included those killings of humans deemed either justifiable or excusable. The killing of a human being was common factor in all classes of homicide; however, the state of mind of the perpetrator was significant in determining whether an offense had been committed, and if so, the category of that offense.

At common law, murder was the unlawful killing of one person by another with "malice aforethought." The required malice could be either express or implied. *State v. Robinson*, 78 So. 933 (La. 1918). There were no degrees of murder.

Manslaughter at common law was the unlawful killing of one human being by another when no malice was involved. *State v. Boston*, 11 N.W.2d 407 (Iowa 1943). There were two categories: voluntary and involuntary. *People v. Richardson*, 293 N.W.2d 332 (Mich. 1980). Voluntary manslaughter consisted of an intentional, unlawful killing that occurred in the heat of passion due to some adequate provocation. *Cottrell v. Commonwealth*, 111 S.W.2d 445 (Ky. 1937). Involuntary manslaughter was the unintentional killing of another by gross, or wanton negligence of the accused. *People v. Campbell*, 212 N.W. 97 (Mich. 1927). Simply stated, the difference between the two was that the former was intentional while the latter was unintentional. *Wiley v. State*, 170 P. 869 (Ariz. 1918).

At common law, homicide was justifiable if performed by the command or permission of the law; it could be excusable if it occurred through accident or when committed for necessary self-protection. *State v. Brown*, 126 A.2d 161 (N.J. 1956).

The American Approach to Homicide

With some variations, the basic scheme of common-law homicide has been carried over into the statutory law of American jurisdictions. Most states, however, classify murder as either first or second degree. Murder in the first degree is usually defined as requiring either *malice aforethought* or *premeditation*. Second-degree murder commonly requires proof that the accused was guilty of *imminently dangerous* or *outrageous* conduct, albeit not malicious in the common-law sense of malice aforethought.

All states make manslaughter a crime, although some statutes abolish the distinction between voluntary and involuntary manslaughter. Moreover, modern statutes extend the offense of manslaughter to embrace a person's responsibility for death resulting from an omission to act where the law imposes such a requirement.

Modern criminal codes generally provide that it is justifiable homicide for one to take another's life by authority of the law (e.g., an executioner performing a duty). It is usually considered excusable homicide if death results from the inadvertent taking of another's life when the actor is not guilty of criminal negligence (e.g., death occurring from an unavoidable traffic accident).

The overwhelming majority of homicide prosecutions are brought under state laws. However, federal statutes provide jurisdiction over the killing of certain officers and employees of the United States engaged in performance of their official duties, 18 U.S.C.A. § 1114, as well as certain foreign officials, 18 U.S.C.A. § 1116. Federal statutes classify criminal homicide as murder in the first degree, felony murder, and manslaughter. 18 U.S.C.A. § 1111–1112.

First-Degree Murder. The California Penal Code illustrates a modern statutory approach to homicide. It defines murder as the "unlawful killing of a human being, or a fetus, with malice aforethought" but stipulates that death of the fetus is not murder when an abortion is performed with the mother's consent. West's Ann. Cal. Penal Code § 187. The malice required by the code may be either express or implied. When a deliberate intention is manifested to take a person's life unlawfully the malice is considered express; it may be implied when no considerable provocation appears or under other circumstances indicating malice. West's Ann. Cal. Penal Code § 188.

In defining degrees of murder, the California code states:

> All murder which is perpetrated by means of a destructive device or explosive, knowing use of ammunition designed primarily to penetrate metal or armor, poison, lying in wait, torture, or by any other kind of wilful, deliberate, and premeditated killing, or which is committed in the perpetration of, or attempt to perpetrate, arson, rape, robbery, burglary, mayhem . . . is murder of the first degree; and all other kinds of murder are of the second degree. West's Ann. Cal. Penal Code § 189.

The penalties in California and other jurisdictions for first-degree murder are the most severe, with decreasing penalties provided for second-degree murder and manslaughter.

First-degree murder is the highest classification of homicide. It contemplates a true "intent to kill" and usually requires proof of either malice aforethought or premeditation. Thus, to obtain a conviction, the prosecution must establish the defendant's specific intent to take another's life.

The California Supreme Court has said that "when a defendant with a wanton disregard for human life, does an act that involves a high degree of probability that it will result in death, he acts with malice aforethought." Moreover, the court opined that "willful, deliberate, and premeditated" as used in the statute indicates its intent to require as an essential element of first-degree murder substantially more reflection "than the mere amount of thought necessary to form the intention to kill." *People v. Cruz*, 605 P.2d 830, 834 (Cal. 1980). The Pennsylvania Supreme Court has defined malice aforethought more elaborately, saying it is "not only a particular ill will, but a hardness of heart, cruelty, recklessness of consequences, and a mind regardless of social duty." *Commonwealth v. Buzard*, 76 A.2d 394, 396 (Pa. 1950) (citing *Commonwealth v. Drum*, 58 Pa. 9 (1868)). Such malice may be expressed or may be implied from the circumstances under which a homicidal act is performed.

Many jurisdictions define first-degree murder in terms of the "premeditated intent" of the offender. Florida, for example, classifies a homicide as a first-degree murder if the unlawful killing of a human being is "perpetrated from a premeditated design to effect the death of the person killed or any human being." West's Fla. Stat. Ann. § 782.04.

Initially, you may think of a premeditated act as requiring a lengthy period of deliberation. Indeed, dictionaries commonly define *premeditation* as a conscious and deliberate preplanning over a period of time. Judicial decisions defining premeditation, however, emphasize that although it requires thought beforehand, no particular length of time is required. The length of time necessary to deliberate, or to form a specific intent to kill, need only be time enough to form the required intent before the killing. It matters not how short that time may be, *State v. Davis*, 260 A.2d 587 (Conn. 1969), *vac'd. in part*, 408 U.S. 935, 92 S. Ct. 2856, 33 L.Ed. 2d 750 (1972), as long as the process of premeditation occurs at any point before the killing. See, for example, *State v. Corn*, 278 S.E. 2d 221(N.C. 1981).

The prosecution may establish either malice aforethought or premeditation by a variety of evidentiary facts and circumstances. These include threats, quarrels, and expressions of ill will, as well as the nature of the weapon used, the presence or absence of adequate provocation, previous difficulties between the parties, the manner in which the homicide was committed, the nature of the wound inflicted, and the manner in which it was inflicted.

Felony Murder. The common law developed a doctrine that where an accused was engaged in the commission of a felony and a homicide occurred, the felonious act was regarded as a substitute for the proof of malice aforethought required to find the defendant guilty of murder. Thus, it became felony murder where an accused unintentionally killed a human being while committing, or attempting to commit, such common-law felonies as burglary, arson, rape, or robbery. The theory was that if a killing resulted, even though unintentional or accidental, the required malice was carried over from the original felony. Consequently, the felon would be found guilty of murder.

Although of dubious ancestry, the felony murder doctrine has been incorporated into most criminal codes in the United States. See *People v. Aaron*, 229 N.W.2d 304 (Mich. 1980). With the proliferation of crimes classified as felonies, legislatures have generally limited its applicability to felonies involving violence or posing great threat to life or limb (e.g., rape, robbery, kidnaping, arson, and burglary). See, for example, West's Ann. Cal. Penal Code § 189. Recently some have sought to equate certain

CASE IN POINT

First-Degree Murder: Evidence of Premeditation

Defendant Phillip Lee Young suggested to his two companions that they rob and kill John Cooke in order to obtain money to buy liquor. After the three men used a ruse to gain entry to Cooke's house, Young stabbed Cooke twice in the chest, and one of the companions stabbed the victim several times in the back. Cooke died as a result of the injuries.

A jury found Young guilty of first-degree murder and he appealed. After explaining that first-degree murder is the unlawful killing of a person with malice and with premeditation and deliberation, the North Carolina Supreme Court rejected Young's contention that the evidence was insufficient to support a conviction.

State v. Young, 325 S.E.2d 181 (N.C. 1985).

felonious drug offenses with violent felonies. Some statutes even provide for degrees of felony murder depending on the seriousness of the felony attempted or perpetrated by the accused, and whether the accused is present at the scene when the killing occurs. See, for example, West's Fla. Stat. Ann. § 782.04.

Felony murder statutes have produced much litigation in the criminal courts. Some of the questions raised include

- Can a felon who perpetrates an offense be guilty of felony murder where the victim of the intended offense kills a co-felon?
- Should the felon committing a crime such as robbery be guilty of felony murder if a police officer mistakenly kills the felon's intended victim?
- Can a felon be guilty of felony murder when a co-felon accidentally kills a bystander or a police officer?

Most courts have held that the doctrine of felony murder does not extend to a killing stemming from the commission of the felony if it is directly attributable to the act of someone other than the defendant or those actively participating with the defendant in the unlawful enterprise. Nevertheless, courts have arrived at different solutions to these and other problems of felony murder laws.

Perhaps questions such as these led the Michigan Supreme Court in 1980 to abrogate the felony murder doctrine. After commenting on how its prior decisions had already significantly restricted the doctrine, the court concluded that the rule that substitutes the intent to commit the underlying felony for the malice element of murder had to be abolished. Its abrogation of the doctrine does not make irrelevant the fact that a death occurred in the course of a felony. Rather, the court noted that a jury can properly infer malice from evidence that a defendant intentionally set in motion a force likely to cause death or great bodily harm. Michigan juries, however, are no longer required to find malice if they are satisfied from all the evidence that it does not exist. *People v. Aaron,* 299 N.W.2d 304 (Mich. 1980).

A cogent argument can be made that the felony murder rule violates the basic requirement of moral culpability in the criminal law. Moreover, critics of the doctrine point out that under the early common law, conviction of a felony was punishable by death. Consequently, they note, when a death occurred in the commission of a felony and the accused was guilty of felony murder, no additional consequences resulted. Not so today, because no felony except for murder committed under aggravating circumstances is punishable by death. Nevertheless, the felony murder doctrine is well established in most jurisdictions. With legislatures perceiving the need to take a "hard line" on crime, it is doubtful that many will be motivated to repeal felony murder statutes. Courts, therefore, will most likely become increasingly conscious of the need to strictly interpret such statutes. Observing that it is the commission of a specified felony that supplants the requirement of premeditation for first-degree murder, the Florida Supreme Court declared that for the felon to be guilty of felony murder there must be some causal connection between the homicide and the underlying felony. *Bryant v. State,* 412 So.2d 347 (Fla. 1982).

Second-Degree Murder. In many jurisdictions second-degree murder is a residual classification applied to unlawful homicides not evidenced by malice aforethought or premeditation, not occurring in conjunction with other felonies, and not falling within the statutory definition of manslaughter. See, for example, West's Ann. Cal. Penal Code § 189. More commonly, second-degree murder is defined in terms of the defendant having a "depraved mind or heart." Florida statutes define second-degree murder as a killing "perpetrated by any act imminently dangerous to another and evincing a depraved mind regardless of human life, although without any premeditated design to effect the death of any particular individual." West's Fla. Stat. Ann. § 782.04. Florida courts have said that an act is imminently dangerous to another and evinces a depraved mind if a person of ordinary judgment would know it is reasonably certain to kill or cause serious bodily injury to another and is done from ill will, hatred, spite, or an evil intent, so as to indicate an indifference to human life. See, for example, *Marasa v. State,* 394 So.2d 544 (Fla. App. 1981). Second-degree murder is a general-intent crime. *Gentry v. State,* 437 So.2d 1097 (Fla. 1983).

In practice, convictions for second-degree murder often reflect a "jury pardon." A classic example is when the state prosecutes a defendant for first-degree murder and the jury determines that the circumstances surrounding the killing do not show malice aforethought, premeditation, or are simply not sufficient to justify the penalty, often death. In such an instance a jury sometimes returns a verdict for the lesser offense of second-degree murder, always a noncapital felony. We might generalize that second-degree murder convictions often occur when a jury is convinced the defendant acted recklessly or even outrageously, but with no intent to take the victim's life.

Manslaughter. As noted, there were two classes of manslaughter at common law: voluntary and involuntary. California, like many states, preserves that distinction and defines manslaughter as the "unlawful killing of a human being without malice." It enumerates three categories: voluntary, involuntary, and vehicular. Voluntary manslaughter refers to instances where death of the victim occurs upon a sudden quarrel or in the heat of passion. Involuntary manslaughter is where a death occurs from the commission of a lawful act that might produce death, in an unlawful manner, or without due caution and circumspection. The third category, vehicular homicide, involves death resulting from the perpetrator driving a vehicle while in the commission of an unlawful act not amounting to a felony, and with gross negligence, or driving a vehicle in the commission of a lawful act that might produce death in an unlawful manner, and with gross negligence. West's Ann. Cal. Penal Code § 192.

Many other states define manslaughter without categorizing it as voluntary or involuntary. Still other state legislatures have defined manslaughter by degrees. New York law, for example, provides that a person who recklessly causes the death of another person, or commits an unlawful abortional act on a female that causes her death, or a person who intentionally causes or aids another to commit suicide commits manslaughter in the second degree. McKinney's N.Y. Penal Law § 125.15. However, a person who inflicts certain intentional serious injuries that cause death of another under circumstances that do not constitute murder may be guilty of the more serious offense of manslaughter in the first degree if he or she (1) acts under influence of extreme emotional

CASE IN POINT

SECOND-DEGREE MURDER: EVIDENCE OF DEPRAVED INDIFFERENCE

The state charged a fifteen-and-a-half-year-old boy with murder in the second degree under Section 125.25(2) of the New York—McKinney's Penal Law, which provides: "A person is guilty of murder in the second degree when: . . . (2) Under circumstances evincing a depraved indifference to human life, he recklessly engages in conduct which creates a grave risk of death to another person, and thereby causes the death of another person." The evidence at trial revealed the defendant loaded a mix of "live" and "dummy" shells at random into the magazine of a 12-gauge shotgun and then pumped a shell into the firing chamber, not knowing whether it was a "dummy" or "live" round. He next raised the gun to his shoulder and pointing it directly at the victim exclaimed, "Let's play Polish roulette," and asked, "Who is first?" Then the defendant pulled the trigger, discharging a live round into a thirteen-year-old victim's chest, resulting in the eventual death of the victim.

On appeal, the court first distinguished the crime of second-degree murder by depraved indifference from manslaughter, by saying that it must be shown that the actor's reckless conduct is imminently dangerous and presents a grave risk of death, whereas in manslaughter the conduct need only present the lesser "substantial risk" of death. Then pointing out that the defendant had an intense interest in and a detailed knowledge of weapons and analogizing the incident to a macabre game of chance, the New York Court of Appeals held the evidence was legally sufficient to support the defendant's conviction of second-degree murder.

People v. Roe, 542 N.E.2d 610 (N.Y. 1989).

disturbance, or (2) commits an unlawful abortional act that causes the death of a female pregnant for more than twenty-four weeks unless it is an abortional act deemed justifiable by statutory exceptions. McKinney's N.Y. Penal Law § 125.20.

Irrespective of whether a statute classifies manslaughter as voluntary, involuntary, or by degree, certain situations generally fall within the definition of the offense. Common examples include a death resulting from mutual combat, or killing someone by use of excessive force while defending yourself or a family member or acting in defense of your property.

The intent that must be established to obtain a conviction of manslaughter may depend on the nature of the charge. To establish voluntary manslaughter, the prosecution may have to establish the defendant's specific intent. On the other hand, in a prosecution for involuntary manslaughter, the defendant's intent need only be general and may be inferred from the defendant's act and surrounding circumstances.

Often a charge of involuntary manslaughter is based on allegations of criminal negligence. A highly publicized example of this arose from a tragic accident occurring in the film industry. In 1982, some Hollywood moviemakers shooting a scene for the movie "The Twilight Zone" used a helicopter that

CASE IN POINT

Spousal Adultery Not Available to Reduce Murder of Former Cohabitant to Manslaughter

David McCarthy was convicted of the murder of Adrianne Neal, with whom he had enjoyed a long-standing romantic relationship. McCarthy and Neal never married, but cohabited for several years and even had two children out of wedlock. Eventually Neal terminated the relationship, and she and the children moved to their own apartment. Several months later, McCarthy entered the apartment and discovered Neal in bed with another man. McCarthy shot both of them, but only Neal died. At trial, McCarthy's defense counsel sought to obtain a conviction for the lesser offense of manslaughter on the ground that McCarthy was acting under serious provocation as a result of "spousal adultery." Counsel requested that the jury be instructed on voluntary manslaughter in addition to murder. The trial judge denied the request, reasoning that the absence of a marital relationship precluded the use of such an instruction.

On appeal, the Illinois Supreme Court upheld the defendant's conviction. The court refused to enlarge the concept of spousal adultery as a basis for considering a lesser degree of homicide to include a relationship between former co-habitants which had effectively ended.

People v. McCarthy, 547 N.E.2d 459 (Ill. 1989).

crashed on the set, decapitating an actor and a child and crushing another child. The state prosecuted the director and four of his associates for involuntary manslaughter, claiming they were guilty of criminal negligence. The defendants argued that the tragic deaths resulted from an unforeseeable accident. The media reported in May 1987, after a dramatic five-month trial, that a jury found them all not guilty.

Provocation frequently comes into play in the trial of manslaughter cases. Provocation that would cause a reasonable person to lose control may be sufficient to convert an otherwise intentional killing of another to manslaughter. Mere words, however gross or insulting, are not sufficient to constitute provocation. Rather, to reduce a homicide from murder to manslaughter, it must generally be shown that there was sufficient provocation to excite in the defendant's mind such anger, rage, or terror as would obscure an ordinary person's reasoning and render the person incapable of cool reflection. *Hardin v. State,* 404 N.E.2d 1354 (Ind. 1980). A classic example: discovering one's spouse in an act of adultery with significant sexual contact taking place. See, for example, *Tripp v. State,* 374 A.2d 384 (Md. App. 1977).

Modern statutes often define manslaughter as consisting of the negligent performance of a legal duty or the doing of a lawful act in an unlawful manner. In addition to the more common instances, courts have upheld manslaughter convictions under such statutes for death occurring because of criminal negligence of medical practitioners or because of parental failure to provide medical

CASE IN POINT

MANSLAUGHTER BY CULPABLE NEGLIGENCE

William Burge and Juanita Calloway became involved in an argument over the fact that Calloway was apparently sleeping with one of her sons. When Calloway displayed a knife, Burge pulled a gun that he carried to kill snakes that lurked in the walls of his house. Burge pointed the gun at Calloway and cocked it. Burge then pushed Calloway in an attempt to get her into his car. When he did, Calloway's hand hit the gun and it went off, severely wounding Calloway. While driving her to the hospital, Burge ran out of gas and called an ambulance. Calloway died en route to the hospital.

Despite his plea of self-defense, a jury found Burge guilty of manslaughter by culpable negligence. In affirming the conviction, the Mississippi Supreme Court rejected the defendant's contentions of self-defense and excusable and justifiable homicide. The court observed that the jury could reasonably have determined that although the victim was holding a knife the defendant was not in danger of great personal injury.

Burge v. State, 472 So.2d 392 (Miss. 1985).

attention or adequate nourishment for their children. See, for example, *People v. Ogg,* 182 N.W.2d 570 (Mich. App. 1970). The California Supreme Court held that a parent of a seriously ill child who makes only provision for prayer may be guilty of such criminal negligence as to justify finding the parent guilty of involuntary manslaughter or child endangerment. *Walker v. Superior Court,* 763 P.2d 852 (Cal. 1988), *cert. denied,* 491 U.S. 905, 109 S.Ct. 3186, 105 L.Ed.2d 695 (1989).

Vehicular Homicide. The carnage on American highways has caused many states to enact statutes making vehicular homicide a specific felony, rather than opting to rely on prosecutors charging a defendant with manslaughter for causing a traffic death. The Florida statute is typical and reads:

> "Vehicular homicide" is the killing of a human being by the operation of a motor vehicle by another in a reckless manner likely to cause the death of, or great bodily harm to, another. West's Fla. Stat. Ann. § 782.071.

The Florida Supreme Court has said that in enacting the statute the legislature created a separate offense with a lesser standard of proof than is required for conviction under the state's manslaughter statute. Thus, the statute enables the prosecution to secure a conviction where the state is unable to meet the level of proof otherwise required in establishing manslaughter. Therefore, the court said the state could charge a defendant with manslaughter for operating a motor vehicle in a culpably negligent manner that causes the death of a human being or could proceed under vehicular homicide, a lesser included offense. *State v. Young,* 371 So.2d 1029 (Fla. 1979).

Justifiable and Excusable Homicide. As in most jurisdictions, California classifies nonculpable homicide as excusable or justifiable. It is excusable when committed by accident or misfortune or in doing any other lawful act by lawful means, with usual and ordinary caution, and without any unlawful intent. It may also be excusable when committed in the heat of passion, or on sudden and sufficient provocation, or on sudden combat where no dangerous weapon is used and the killing is not done in a cruel or unusual manner. West's Ann. Cal. Penal Code § 195.

Examples of excusable homicide include killing someone when resisting attempts to murder or inflict great bodily injury upon a person; or when in defense of a person's home under certain circumstances; or in some instances of self-defense where there is a reasonable ground to apprehend imminent danger of great bodily harm to a person's self or spouse, parent, or child. See West's Ann Cal. Penal Code § § 196–197; *People v. Collins,* 11 Cal.Rptr. 504 (Cal. App. 1961).

When death is inflicted by public officers in obedience to a court judgment or in discharge of certain other legal duties, or when necessarily committed in apprehending felons, homicide is considered justifiable. West's Ann. Cal. Penal Code § 196; *People v. Young,* 29 Cal.Rptr. 595 (Cal. App. 1963).

A New Concern in the Law of Homicide. Another area of contemporary concern has resulted from technological advances in medicine that have enabled physicians to use sophisticated life-support systems to prolong life for indefinite periods. In a landmark case involving Karen Quinlan, the New Jersey Supreme Court in 1976 reviewed the request of Karen's parents to remove the life-support systems sustaining the life of their daughter, who lay in a comatose state with no reasonable medical probability of regaining a sapient existence. The court said

CASE IN POINT

VEHICULAR HOMICIDE: CRIMINAL LIABILITY FOR SECOND ACCIDENT

On the evening of February 14, 1987, Gary Dawson was a passenger in a car driven by Richard Peaslee, Jr., on a snow-packed, icy road in Maine. As a result of Peaslee's intentional "fishtailing," the car went out of control and overturned, throwing Dawson onto the road. Dawson, unable to move, lay on the road where he was run over by another vehicle several minutes later. Dawson died before help arrived on the scene. A jury found Peaslee guilty of vehicular manslaughter, and he appealed.

In affirming Peaslee's conviction, the Maine Supreme Court rejected his contention that he was not criminally responsible for the second accident. "The separate accidents were not independent of each other," said the court, "because Dawson would not have been lying immobile on the road in the path of the other car were it not for Peaslee's conduct." Moreover, the court concluded that "[w]hether Dawson was killed by the first or second impact makes no difference."

State v. Peaslee, 571 A.2d 825 (Me. 1990).

that withdrawal of such life-support systems, under the circumstances, would not constitute a criminal homicide. *In re Quinlan,* 355 A.2d 647 (N.J. 1976).

A significant body of decisional law is now developing on the issue of when life-sustaining measures should be initiated and when they may be removed. Generally, a competent adult who is terminally ill may decide to forgo such extraordinary measures or may order such measures discontinued. There are, however, varying judicial opinions as to when, under what circumstances, and by whom discontinuance may be ordered for minors and incompetents. Statutes in several states now address many of the problems in this area; yet, there is no statutory or judicial consensus on the procedures to effectuate discontinuance. Moreover, the issue of whether removal of life supports extends to discontinuance of hydration and nourishment as well as respirators and similar life-prolonging devices has only recently surfaced. These problems involve moral, ethical, and religious concerns that must be considered in the development of any viable policy in this area by legislators and judges. Courts have been cautious not to allow criminal prosecutions where life-sustaining medical procedures have been discontinued in good faith based on competent medical advice and consent of a competent patient and the patient's family. See, for example, *Barber v. Superior Court,* 195 Cal.Rptr. 484 (Cal. App. 1983).

Prosecutorial Burdens in Homicide Cases

To obtain a conviction in a homicide case, the prosecution must carry a number of burdens.

Requirement That Victim Was "Alive" before Homicidal Act. By definition, a criminal homicide consists of someone taking another person's life. It follows that before the accused can be found guilty of a homicidal crime, the prosecution must establish that the victim was alive before the accused's criminal act. In most instances this is not too difficult, but it can present a real problem. Consider, for example, the killing of a fetus. Under common law a child was not considered born until the umbilical cord had been severed, and the child's circulation became independent of its mother.

In the highly publicized case of *Keeler v. Superior Court,* 470 P.2d 617 (Cal. 1970), the California Supreme Court held that in enacting its homicide statute, the legislature intended it to have the settled common-law meaning that to be the subject of homicide a fetus must be "born alive." Consequently, the court overturned a murder conviction where the defendant stomped on a pregnant woman's abdomen, thereby causing the death of her fetus. As a result, California amended section 187 of its penal code that defines murder to include the present language, "the unlawful killing of a human being, *or a fetus,* with malice aforethought [emphasis added]."

Absent legislative reform, most courts today would probably follow the view taken by the California court prior to the legislative amendment to section 187.

The* Corpus Delicti *Requirement. In addition to establishing that a human being was alive before a killing took place, the prosecution must always establish the *corpus delicti,* or body of the crime. The *corpus delicti* consists of the fact that a human being is dead and that the death was caused by the criminal act or agency of another person. *State v. Feuillerat,* 292 N.W.2d 326 (S.D. 1980). Some argue that the *corpus delicti* requirement is simply a technicality that impedes the search for truth. Others contend that by requiring some independent evidence to link a defendant to the crime charged ensures that no one is convicted based on a mistake or fabricated confession. As of now, the rule is firmly implanted in American law. To prove the *corpus delicti,* the prosecution must show by either direct or circumstantial evidence, independent of the accused's statements, that the victim died as a result of a criminal act. Usually, the victim's body is available for medical examination and a physician can testify as to the cause of death. If the deceased's body is not recovered *and* the victim's death cannot be determined to have resulted from a criminal act, a conviction cannot be lawfully obtained. Consider the case of *Ex parte Flodstrom,* 277 P.2d 101 (Cal. 1954). There, it could not be determined if a baby died from the mother's alleged homicidal act or whether death occurred as a result of natural causes. Consequently, since there was no evidence available to establish the *corpus delicti,* the appellate court discharged the accused mother from custody on the ground that she was being held to answer charges of murder without probable cause.

The "Proximate Cause" of the Victim's Death. To hold a defendant responsible for the death of a victim, the prosecution must establish that the victim's death was "proximately caused" by the defendant. This means that the victim's death must have been the natural and probable consequence of the defendant's unlawful conduct. See *Hamrick v. People,* 624 P.2d 1320 (Colo. 1981).

Where A shoots or physically beats B, or A pushes B out of a window or overboard from a boat, or A administers poison to B, medical evidence can usually establish the cause of the victim's death. Killings, however, can be accomplished in hundreds of ways. For example, death may be precipitated by fright or shock or by other means not involving physical contact with the victim. The accused's acts or omissions need not be the immediate cause of the victim's death as long as the death results naturally from the accused's conduct. *State v. Leopold,* 147 A. 118 (Conn. 1929).

Some situations present perplexing issues for medical experts and courts. For example, a defendant fired a shot into the water about six feet from a boat occupied by two boys. When a second shot struck nearer to the boat than the first, one of the boys leaped out of the boat into the water. The boat capsized with the remaining boy in it. Both boys drowned. The defendant argued that he could not be guilty of causing the death of the boy who drowned when the boat overturned. The Tennessee Supreme Court rejected his contention and upheld the defendant's conviction for involuntary manslaughter, concluding that it was his shots, not the act of the boy who caused the boat to capsize, that caused the decedent's death. *Letner v. State,* 299 S.W. 1049 (Tenn. 1927).

In another instance, a wife who had been severely beaten by her husband in the past was impelled by fear of another beating at his hands to jump from a moving automobile. She died from injuries sustained. Her husband was charged with her murder and was found guilty of the lesser offense of manslaughter. On appeal, the Florida Supreme Court upheld the conviction. *Whaley v. State,* 26 So.2d 656 (Fla. 1946).

When Death Occurs. Just as it is necessary to determine that a homicide victim was alive before the injury that caused death, it is also necessary to establish that death has, in fact, occurred. In most instances, the classic definition will suffice: Death occurs when the heart stops beating and respiration ends. However, technological advances have rendered this definition obsolete as the sole means of determining when death occurs. Many state legislatures have now adopted a definition of "brain death" that specifies that irreversible cessation of total brain functions constitutes death. In other instances, courts have adopted the new definition. See, for example, *In re Bowman,* 617 P.2d 731 (Wash. 1980). In November 1992, the Florida Supreme Court held that an encephalic newborn whose heart was beating and who was breathing was not considered "brain dead" for purposes of an organ donation. *In re: T.A.C.P.,* 609 So.2d 588 (Fla. 1992).

The "One Year and a Day" Rule. Another obstacle to the prosecution of homicide cases can be the common-law "one year and a day" rule. Under this ancient common-law doctrine, if more than a year and a day intervened between the injury inflicted by the accused and the victim's death, the person who caused the injury could not be held criminally responsible for the victim's death. *State v. Moore,* 199 So. 661 (La. 1940). This inflexible rule has been continued because of uncertainties of medical science in establishing the cause of a victim's death after a lengthy period had elapsed.

In this age of advancing medical technology, the "one year and a day" rule has little relevance and has been rejected or revised either by statute or judicial decision in many jurisdictions. The California Penal Code now states: "To make the killing either murder or manslaughter, it is requisite that the party die within three years and a day after the stroke received or the cause of death administered." West's Ann. Cal. Penal Code § 194. Other jurisdictions have abrogated the rule by judicial fiat. In that vein, the North Carolina Supreme Court recently observed that for a court to remain oblivious to advances in medical science when considering whether to apply an ancient common-law rule would be "folly." *State v. Hefler,* 310 S.E.2d 310 (N.C. 1984). Nevertheless, where such temporal requirements have not been abrogated, the prosecution must establish that the victim's death occurred within the prescribed common-law or statutory period.

This is another instance where the rationale for the strict common-law rule no longer exists. The sophistication of modern medicine leaves little reason for continued adherence to the common-law rule. In light of widespread criticism of the "year and a day" rule, legislatures should either adopt a statute along the lines of the California enactment or just abolish the rule. Increasingly, legislatures have recognized the obsolescence of the "year and a day" rule. Florida did so in 1988; Georgia in 1991.

Defenses to Homicidal Crimes

Defendants charged with murder or manslaughter frequently plead either self-defense or insanity. These defenses are discussed in detail in Chapter 13. Where an accused defends against a charge of manslaughter, the "heat of passion" defense discussed earlier may be available in some instances, as would be the defense of reasonable care or accidental killing in others.

SUICIDE

The early English common law defined the offense of suicide as the intentional taking of a person's life by self-destruction. Suicide was not only regarded as being contrary to nature, it was looked upon as an offense against the biblical commandment, "Thou shalt not kill." Suicide was a species of felony punishable by forfeiture of the decedent's goods and chattels because it deprived the king of one of his subjects. *May v. Pennell,* 64 A. 885 (Me. 1906).

In the United States, the thrust of statutory criminal law has been to make it an offense to cause or aid another person to commit suicide. As of 1993, a majority of the states had laws making assisted suicide a crime. New York law provides that a person is guilty of manslaughter in the second degree if he or she "intentionally causes or aids another person to commit suicide." McKinney's N.Y. Penal Law § 125.15. In Texas, a person who, with intent to promote or assist in the commission of suicide, aids or attempts to aid another to commit suicide is guilty of a misdemeanor. If the actor's conduct causes a suicide or an attempted suicide that results in serious bodily injury, the offense becomes a felony. Vernon's Tex. Penal Code Ann. § 22.08.

The Michigan Experience

Michigan, and several other states, had no laws against assisted suicide. This was dramatized on June 4, 1990, when a fifty-four-year-old woman suffering from Alzheimer's disease took her life by pressing a button that injected a lethal substance into her system through use of a suicide machine developed by Dr. Jack Kevorkian, a retired Michigan pathologist. Murder charges filed against the doctor were dismissed on the ground that Michigan had no law against assisted suicide and the prosecutors failed to show that the doctor tripped the device used to effect the death.

After several additional instances of assisted suicide of terminally ill patients, the Michigan legislature enacted and the governor on December 16, 1992, signed a bill banning assisted suicide. The new law took effect on April 1, 1993, and set a fifteen-month period to allow the legislature to address the problem in more depth. The new law provides a four-year prison sentence and $2,000 fine for violators. On August 17, 1993, Dr. Kevorkian was arraigned on charges of violating the new law for assisting in the suicide of a man suffering from Lou Gehrig's disease. Kevorkian attacked the Michigan law as being unconstitutional.

Competing Values in Suicide Laws

Laws against assisted suicide bring into play significant policy issues and require legislatures to carefully balance competing claims of individual liberty, ethics, and the interest of society. Some proponents of allowing assisted suicide argue that it simply enables a person who has a rational capacity to make a choice. Those who reject this view urge that the state has an interest in the preservation of life, and that some individuals may die needlessly as a result of misdiagnosis. Moreover, they argue that allowing assisted suicide leads to an indifference to the value of life.

SEXUAL BATTERY

There are early biblical accounts of the offense of rape; however, the law of rape, as it exists today, has its roots in the early English common law. It was a felony for a male to have unlawful carnal knowledge (i.e., sexual intercourse) of a female by force and against her will. This is usually referred to as "common-law rape" or "forcible rape." In later stages of the English law, it became a statutory offense for a man to have carnal knowledge of a female child under ten years of age with or without the child's consent. This latter offense came to be known as "statutory rape." See *State v. Keturokis,* 276 N.W. 600 (Iowa 1937).

The common-law offenses required penetration, however slight, of the female's sexual organ by the male sexual organ; no emission of seed was required. At common law, there was a conclusive presumption that a male under age fourteen could not commit the crime of rape. *Foster v. Commonwealth,* 31 S.E. 503 (Va. 1898).

Common-law rape contemplated unlawful intercourse; therefore, a husband could not be guilty of raping his wife. Although this so-called marital exception is of somewhat dubious judicial origin, it is generally credited to the writings of Sir Matthew Hale, who served as Lord Chief Justice in England from 1671 to 1676. Of course, in egregious cases the husband could be charged with assault or battery of his wife. Furthermore, a husband or even another woman could be charged as an aider or abettor if he or she assisted or procured another man to rape his wife.

In March 1991, England's Court of Appeal dismissed an appeal by a man who was convicted of an attempted rape of his estranged wife. In delivering the opinion of the five-judge court, the Lord Chief Justice observed that a rapist remains a rapist irrespective of his relationship with his victim, and that the centuries-old legal doctrine that a husband could not be guilty of raping his wife no longer represented the law considering the position of a wife in contemporary society.

The American Approach

The new American states followed the common-law scheme in statutorily defining rape; however, two principal changes occurred. First, many states explicitly rejected the common-law presumption that males under age fourteen could not commit the offense. Second, legislatures in most states made consensual intercourse with a young female an offense if the female was younger than sixteen or eighteen, rather than ten. Some, however, added the qualification that the female must have been "of previous chaste character." See, for example, West's Fla. Stat. Ann. § 794.05. A female of previous chaste character is generally defined as one who has not previously voluntarily indulged in sexual intercourse outside of marriage.

American courts divided on the intent required for a defendant to be guilty of rape. Some held that no intent other than that evidenced by the doing of the act of intercourse was needed. See, for example, *Walden v. State,* 156 S.W.2d 385 (Tenn. 1941). Others required proof of the defendant's specific intent. See, for example, *Thomas v. State,* 95 P.2d 658 (Okl. Crim. App. 1939).

Courts in American jurisdictions struggled with the requirements of "force" and "consent" in the law of forcible rape. When focusing on these elements some judges instructed juries that "in order for the defendant to be found guilty of rape, you must find that the woman resisted to her utmost." Later cases recognized that it was not necessary for a female victim to resist to the utmost; rather, the degree of resistance came to be regarded as a relative matter dependent on all the circumstances surrounding the incident. Yet, courts continued to recognize that resistance generally had to be more than a mere negative verbal response by a female.

All courts recognized that to constitute common-law rape, sexual intercourse had to be without the female's consent. It was presumed, however, that there could be no consent by a woman who was asleep, unconscious, or mentally incapable. Moreover, consent obtained by fraud or impersonation or through pretext was invalid. Thus, if a man impersonated a woman's husband and caused her to submit to sexual intercourse, he would be guilty of rape. Likewise, a physician who had intercourse with female patients who were not conscious of the nature of the doctor's acts because of the treatments being administered, was properly found guilty of rape. *People v. Minkowski*, 23 Cal.Rptr. 92 (Cal. App. 1962).

In contrast to common-law rape, the elements of force and consent were irrelevant in statutory rape because the purpose of these statutes was to protect young women from all acts of sexual intercourse. See, for example, *State v. Horton*, 39 S.E.2d 222 (S.C. 1946). Some jurisdictions allowed a man to defend against a charge of statutory rape on the basis that he was mistaken about the female's age; others held a defendant strictly liable even if he made a good faith and reasonable inquiry to determine the victim's age. This latter concept of a "strict liability" offense was discussed in Chapter 4. A California law making statutory rape a crime was challenged on the basis of gender discrimination, since only males could be prosecuted for the offense. The United States Supreme Court rejected the challenge. *Michael M. v. Superior Court*, 450 U.S. 464, 101 S. Ct. 1200, 67 L.Ed.2d 437 (1981).

While most jurisdictions held that the prosecution could obtain a conviction in a rape case based on the uncorroborated testimony of the victim, many courts instructed juries to the effect that "a charge of rape is easily made by a woman and difficult to refute by a man," a statement also attributed to England's Lord Hale. Consequently, when the complainant was the only witness who testified to the act, juries were frequently admonished to "rigidly scrutinize" the victim's testimony. Furthermore, in rape prosecutions it became common for courts to admit evidence of the female complainant's general reputation for sexual immorality and to allow inquiry concerning her prior specific sexual acts. This latter practice probably accounts for the fact that in all too many instances rape became an unreported crime. Indeed, many women came to believe that they were being denied the protection of the law and at the same time were made to feel guilty for having been raped.

Reform in the American Law of Rape

During the late 1970s and the 1980s, protests led to a number of statutory and judicial reforms in the law of rape. Initially, many such protests were by women's groups who complained of traumatic encounters between female victims and police, prosecutors, defense attorneys, and courts. In all too many instances, they contended, a female rape victim was degraded and made to feel ashamed for the assault she suffered. As societal awareness increased, significant changes in the law were accomplished. Before examining a modern criminal code proscribing sexual offenses, you should become aware of the more significant legislative and judicial reforms in this area.

A Gender-Neutral Offense. The offense of sexual battery has evolved from the crime of rape and is now frequently defined by statute in gender-neutral terms. These new statutes embrace all types of sexual impositions and do not limit the offense to the common-law concept of vaginal rape of a female. Instead, they proscribe anal, oral, or vaginal penetrations by a sex organ or by another object, excepting acts performed for *bona fide* medical purposes. The offender and victim may be of either sex. As we will explain under gender-neutral statutes in a later section, in appropriate circumstances a husband may be charged with rape of his wife.

Classification of Offenders. The trend of the newer statutes has been to divide the offense of sexual battery into various classifications. Thus, sexual contacts other than intercourse are proscribed. Punishment varies according to the type of sexual conduct or contact, the character and extent of force used, and the age and vulnerability of the victim. Those who commit sexual batteries against the helpless, and those who take advantage of their position of familial or supervisory authority, can be singled out for special punishment. These reforms have achieved more just results in punishing offenders. Furthermore, proper classification of offenses has led to convictions where merited by the evidence.

Rape Shield Laws. One of the most significant legal reforms concerning rape has been the enactment of "rape shield laws" by a majority of the states. In a prosecution for rape (or sexual battery), these laws preclude presentation of evidence of a victim's prior sexual activity with anyone other than the defendant. Even where the defendant seeks to introduce evidence of prior relations with a victim, some statutes require such evidence to be first presented to the court *in camera* for a determination as to whether the evidence of the defendant's prior relationship with the victim is relevant to the victim's consent.

By 1993 most states had enacted rape shield laws based on the theory that a victim's prior sexual activity does not prove whether the victim has been violated in the instance for which the defendant stands accused. Thus, in *State v. Madsen*, 772 S.W.2d 656 (Mo. 1989), the Missouri Supreme Court held that neither evidence of a victim having a "live-in" boyfriend or having two illegitimate children was relevant in a prosecution for rape. But can a female victim offer testimony of a prior rape to explain her conduct in failing to resist an attacker? In *Raines v. State*, 382 S.E.2d 738 (Ga. App. 1989), the appellate court found this to be appropriate.

In interpreting the applicability of rape shield laws to some unusual factual situations, courts have faced some difficult judgments. In a Massachusetts decision, the court ruled that a defendant charged with rape should have been allowed to question the complainant as to whether she had sexual intercourse with anyone else on the night of the attack. The court concluded that such evidence would not constitute an attack on the complainant's credibility. Rather, the court held that such evidence tended to support the defendant's theory that someone else had attacked the complainant and that she had wrongly accused him. *Commonwealth v. Fitzgerald,* 590 N.E.2d 1151 (Mass. 1992).

A Virginia appellate court ruled that evidence that a victim did not report the alleged rape until a month after the incident, when she learned that she had contracted gonorrhea, was admissible to show ill will of the complainant. The court found that such evidence did not relate to sexual conduct of the victim and was therefore not barred by the Virginia rape shield statute. *Evans v. Commonwealth,* 415 S.E.2d 851 (Va. App. 1992).

The Resistance Requirement. Significant judicial reforms have also occurred. For example, courts no longer insist that a woman must "resist to the utmost" in order to establish that her sexual privacy has been violated. This is consistent with the advice of law enforcement officers who frequently caution women that violent resistance to a rapist's attack may result in the victim's serious injury or death. In considering whether a victim's resistance has been overcome, courts find it appropriate to consider several factors. The extent of the offender's force and violence remains important. So, too, is the psychological and emotional stress of a female victim whose sensibilities are outraged by fear of violation of her bodily integrity. See, for example, *State v. Studham,* 572 P.2d 700 (Utah 1977).

Testimony of Victims. Courts have also come to realize that there is no unique reason to single out the testimony of a sexual battery victim and instruct juries that it deserves more scrutiny than the testimony of other crime victims. See, for example, *Marr v. State,* 494 So.2d 1139 (Fla. 1986). The low conviction rate for persons accused of rape belies the need for special scrutiny for the uncorroborated testimony of a rape victim. In fact, data compiled by the Federal Bureau of Investigation revealed that of the FBI's four violent crimes (murder, forcible rape, robbery, and aggravated assault), rape has the highest rate of acquittal or dismissal. See *People v. Rincon-Pineda,* 538 P.2d 247 (Cal. 1975).

A Modern Statutory Treatment of Sexual Offenses

Michigan has modern, comprehensive laws that classify criminal sexual conduct by various degrees, depending on whether it involves sexual penetration or sexual contact with another person as well as other factors. It defines "sexual penetration" as sexual intercourse, cunnilingus, fellatio, anal intercourse, or any other intrusion, however slight, of any part of a person's body or of any object into the genital or anal openings of another person's body; but emission of seed is not required. "Sexual contact" is defined as including the intentional touching of the victim's intimate parts or the intentional touching of the clothing covering the immediate area of the victim's intimate parts, if that intentional touching can reasonably be construed as being for the purpose of sexual arousal or gratification. Mich. Comp. Laws Ann. § 750.520a(k)(l).

Section 520(b) deals with first-degree criminal sexual conduct and provides:

1. A person is guilty of criminal sexual conduct in the first degree if he or she engages in *sexual penetration* with another person and if any of the following circumstances exists:

(a) That other person is under 13 years of age.
(b) That other person is at least 13 but less than 16 years of age and any of the following:
  (i) The actor is a member of the same household as the victim.
  (ii) The actor is related to the victim by blood or affinity to the fourth degree.
  (iii) The actor is in a position of authority over the victim and used this authority to coerce the victim to submit.
(c) Sexual penetration occurs under circumstances involving the commission of any other felony.
(d) The actor is aided or abetted by 1 or more other persons and either of the following circumstances exists:
  (i) The actor knows or has reason to know that the victim is mentally incapable, mentally incapacitated, or physically helpless.
  (ii) The actor uses force or coercion to accomplish the sexual penetration. Force or coercion includes but is not limited to any of the circumstances listed in subdivision (f)(i) to (v).
(e) The actor is armed with a weapon or any article used or fashioned in a manner to lead the victim to reasonably believe it to be a weapon.
(f) The actor causes personal injury to the victim and force or coercion is used to accomplish sexual penetration. Force or coercion includes but is not limited to any of the following circumstances:
  (i) When the actor overcomes the victim through the actual application of physical force or physical violence.
  (ii) When the actor coerces the victim to submit by threatening to use force or violence on the victim, and the victim believes that the actor has the present ability to execute these threats.
  (iii) When the actor coerces the victim to submit by threatening to retaliate in the future against the victim, or any other person, and the victim believes that the actor has the ability to execute this threat. As used in this subdivision, "to retaliate" includes threats of physical punishment, kidnapping, or extortion.
  (iv) When the actor engages in the medical treatment or examination of the victim in a manner or for purposes which are medically recognized as unethical or unacceptable.
  (v) When the actor, through concealment or by the element of surprise, is able to overcome the victim.
(g) The actor causes personal injury to the victim, and the actor knows or has reason to know that the victim is mentally incapable, mentally incapacitated, or physically helpless.
(h) The other person is mentally incapable, mentally disabled, mentally incapacitated, or physically helpless, and any of the following:
  (i) The actor is related to the victim by blood or affinity to the fourth degree.
  (ii) The actor is in a position of authority over the victim and uses this authority to coerce the victim to submit.

2. Criminal sexual conduct in the first degree is a felony of the first-degree. . . . Mich. Comp. Laws Ann. § 520(b).

Second-degree criminal sexual conduct follows substantially along the lines of the preceding section, but instead of penetration it makes *sexual contact* with a victim's intimate parts unlawful. Violation is a second-degree felony. Mich. Comp. Laws Ann. § 750.520(c).

Third-degree criminal sexual conduct includes two of the same elements as a first-degree offense (i.e., penetration and use of force or coercion), but does not include the element that the defendant was aided and/or abetted in the act by one or more persons. Mich. Comp. Laws Ann. § 750.520(d).

Fourth-degree criminal sexual conduct involves sexual *contact* with another person involving force or coercion, or where the actor knows or has reason to know that the victim is mentally incapable, mentally incapacitated, or physically helpless, or the victim is under jurisdiction of the department of corrections and the actor is associated with that department. It is a serious misdemeanor. Mich. Comp. Laws Ann. § 750(e).

Note that the Michigan law makes no distinction as to the sex of the actor or victim. It broadly defines sexual penetration and sexual contact and divides the offense of criminal sexual conduct into degrees considering the conduct of the actor and the vulnerability of the victim. Thus, it embodies many of the changes that are reforming the law of rape in the United States.

The Trend to Eliminate the Marital Exception

As noted, Lord Hale, the famous English jurist of the seventeenth century, wrote that a husband could not be guilty of the rape of his wife. A wife, he explained, had given herself in marriage to her husband. It was as simple as that. To support this rationale the common-law courts offered such reasons as (1) the wife is a chattel belonging to her husband; (2) a husband and wife are "one" and obviously a husband cannot rape himself; and (3) by marriage the wife irrevocably consents to intercourse with her husband on a continuing basis.

Whatever value this principle had in seventeenth-century England, its justification is no longer viable in contemporary American society. Despite the fact that the rationale for it is outmoded, until recently "Hale's Rule" was universally accepted by American courts.

By the 1980s the so-called marital exception rule began to erode. In 1981, the New Jersey Supreme Court held that the state's rape statute that used language "any person who has carnal knowledge of a woman forcibly against her will" did not except from its operation a husband who was living apart from his wife. *State v. Smith*, 426 A.2d 38 (N.J. 1981). One justice who concurred in the result would have gone even further:

> Whatever may have been common law rule in seventeenth century England in the time of Sir Matthew Hale, it never was the law of this State that there was a marital exemption from the law of rape and that a husband could not be guilty of the rape of his wife. 426 A.2d at 47 (Sullivan, J. concurring).

By the beginning of the 1990s about half of the states had either abrogated or modified the marital exception. Some states created a new offense of "spousal rape" carrying lesser penalties than the traditional rape statutes. See, for example, Ariz. Rev. Stat. § 13–1406.01. Some criticize this approach as tending to minimize spousal rape. In 1990, Louisiana made rape a gender-neutral offense by redefining it as "the act of anal or vaginal sexual intercourse with a male or female person committed without the person's lawful consent." Oklahoma continued to define rape as "an act of sexual intercourse involving vaginal or anal penetration accomplished with a male or female *who is not the spouse of the perpetrator.* Okl. Stat. Ann. Tit. 21, § 1111(b)(4). A few states will allow prosecution of a husband for rape of his wife only if the wife has filed for divorce or other termination of their legal relationship and the couple are living apart.

Pending adoption of gender-neutral sexual battery statutes, some courts are addressing challenges to traditional rape statutes on constitutional grounds. In *People v. Liberta,* 474 N.E.2d 567 (N.Y. 1984), New York's highest court rejected such traditional rationales for the marital exception as implied consent and "wife as property." The court termed the notion of implied consent as "irrational and absurd" and emphasized that a married woman should have the same right to bodily autonomy as a single woman. It dismissed any idea of the wife being property of the husband because the state recognizes that wives and husbands are separate legal entities. In rejecting any distinction between marital and nonmarital rape, appellate courts in other states have relied on constitutional arguments similar to those expounded by the New York court. See, for example, *Shunn v. State,* 742 P.2d 775 (Wyo. 1987).

Reform in this area is not without problems. There is considerable apprehension that any criminalization of sexual acts within a marriage may lead to threats and unfounded charges by unhappy wives. Some argue that prosecution of a husband for rape may make reconciliation of marital differences impossible. Furthermore, they contend proof of guilt will be difficult to obtain because of the usual lack of corroborating evidence of the incident. Be that as it may, marriage in contemporary society is looked upon as a partnership, and neither spouse should be legally permitted to commit a sexual battery or any other offense against the other spouse. In light of prevailing values, a marriage contract should not be deemed a license to enforce sex on demand by a forcible encounter with one's spouse. The solution lies primarily with legislative bodies. At a minimum, statutes should be amended to provide there is no marital exception between husbands and wives who live separate and apart by agreement or judicial decree.

Prosecutorial Burdens

As in all criminal cases, the prosecution must prove the *corpus delicti,* that is, the fact that the crime has been committed. Proof that an act of sexual intercourse has taken place with the victim is usually sufficient in a rape case. Additionally, in a statutory rape case, proof must be offered of the age of the female, and in some instances, age of the male. In sexual battery prosecutions, proof of the defendant's general intent is usually sufficient, absent a statute requiring proof of specific intent.

One of the common problems in sexual battery prosecutions is the lack of independent eyewitness testimony. Consequently, it frequently becomes the victim's word against the defendant's word. Thus, police and prosecutors place paramount importance on a "fresh complaint" by a victim. Preservation of semen, photographs of bruises, torn clothing, and even pubic hairs become valuable evidence to corroborate a victim's testimony. Seldom is the credibility of a complaining witness as vital as in sexual battery prosecutions. To appear in court and testify concerning a sexual assault is a traumatic experience for a victim of sexual assault. This is particularly true for young children. To assist youngsters,

CASE IN POINT

Does Asking One's Attacker to Wear a Condom Constitute Consent?

In May 1993, in Travis County, Texas, Joel Valdez, a 28-year-old defendant who was charged with rape, claimed that the female with whom he admittedly had sexual intercourse had asked him to wear a condom. Valdez testified that he complied with the woman's request, and that accordingly they were simply "making love." But the 26-year-old complainant explained that she pleaded with her attacker to wear a condom only to protect herself from AIDS. The jury in Austin, Texas found Valdez guilty of rape, implicitly finding that asking the attacker to wear a condom does not constitute consent to sexual intercourse.

many courts permit them to illustrate their testimony through the use of anatomically detailed dolls. See *State v. Lee,* 459 N.E.2d 910 (Ohio App. 1983).

Rape Trauma Syndrome

In 1974, the term *rape trauma syndrome* was coined by psychiatrists to describe a recurring pattern of physical and emotional symptoms experienced by rape victims. Since then prosecutors have sought to introduce expert testimony at rape trials to establish that a victim's symptoms are consistent with that of the syndrome. This type of evidence has particular relevance to prosecutions where the defendant claims consent of the victim as a defense. On review of convictions, appellate courts have disagreed on whether such evidence is admissible. The Kansas Supreme Court allowed the introduction of psychiatric testimony that a rape victim suffered from rape trauma syndrome, noting that such expert evidence is relevant where the defendant claims consent. *State v. Marks,* 647 P.2d 1292 (Kan. 1982). The supreme courts in Montana and Arizona have reached a similar conclusion. *State v. Liddell,* 685 P.2d 918 (Mont. 1984); *State v. Huey,* 699 P.2d 1290 (Ariz. 1985). An Ohio appellate court held that such expert psychiatric testimony is admissible where its value outweighs its prejudicial impact. The court noted that expert opinion of this type assists laypersons in interpreting reactions of a victim, especially in child rape cases. *State v. Whitman,* 475 N.E.2d 486 (Ohio App. 1984).

There is respectable judicial authority to the contrary. In 1982, the Minnesota Supreme Court ruled that the rape trauma syndrome is not a fact-finding tool but rather a therapeutic tool and that admission of expert testimony on the subject at a rape trial is erroneous. *State v. Saldana,* 324 N.W.2d 227 (Minn. 1982). Several other appellate courts have held that expert testimony concerning the syndrome is not admissible to prove that a rape in fact occurred. For example, in *People v. Pullins,* 378 N.W.2d 502 (Mich. App. 1985), the court held evidence of rape trauma syndrome inadmissible to establish that a rape in fact occurred. This came the year after the Missouri Supreme Court in *State v. Taylor,* 663 S.W.2d 235

(Mo. 1984), concluded that such testimony was beyond that proper basis of expert opinion. The subject remains controversial and there is much to be written yet.

New York's highest court recently concluded that the scientific community has now generally accepted that rape is a highly traumatic event that triggers the onset of certain identifiable symptoms. The court agreed that expert testimony of the rape trauma syndrome may be admitted to aid the jury's understanding of the victim's behavior after the assault. Nevertheless, the court observed that identifiable symptoms in rape victims do not indicate whether an incident did or did not occur; thus trial judges cannot allow such testimony to be introduced for such purpose. *People v. Taylor,* 552 N.E.2d 131 (N.Y. 1990).

Can a defendant charged with rape introduce expert testimony concerning the rape trauma syndrome to establish that a rape did not occur? In *Henson v. State,* 535 N.E.2d 1189 (Ind. 1989), the defense presented a witness who testified to seeing the victim dancing and drinking at a bar on the evening after the alleged rape. The defense then sought to introduce expert testimony on the subject, but the trial judge would not allow it. The state supreme court ruled that the testimony must be permitted because it would be unfair to allow the prosecution to present expert testimony on rape trauma syndrome but deny a defendant the same opportunity.

Defenses to Charges of Sexual Battery

Beyond a general denial of the charges, the most common defense asserted in a rape case is that the victim consented. For consent to be a defense, it must be voluntarily given before the sexual act. As pointed out previously, the defense of consent is not available where the victim is unconscious, asleep, or mentally deficient.

The defense of consent would not be valid in a case of voluntary sexual battery (i.e., statutory rape), since persons under a certain age are legally incapable of consent. Moreover, it is usually not a defense to a charge of voluntary sexual battery that the defendant believed that the victim was above the prohibited age. Most courts hold this to be true even if the victim's age or appearance was misrepresented by the victim. If the statute under which the defendant is being prosecuted for voluntary sexual battery requires proof of the victim's prior chastity, then proof of the victim's unchastity is a defense.

Impotency (i.e., the inability to engage in sexual intercourse) can be asserted as a defense to a charge of rape. The majority of cases where the defense of impotency is asserted involve charges against young males and men who have reached an advanced age. This defense, however, is seldom successful.

Finally, if the statute under which the defendant is prosecuted requires proof of a specific intent, the defendant may show an inability to form such intent due to voluntary intoxication (see Chapter 13).

SODOMY

Consensual sodomy is not a crime against a person, but in the jurisdictions that retain this offense, it is considered an offense against morality (for further discussion, see Chapter 8). Nonconsensual sodomy, on the other hand, is very definitely a crime against a person, falling under the category of rape or sexual battery.

Abortion

Abortion has been legally defined as the willful bringing about of the miscarriage of a pregnant woman. It was a common-law misdemeanor for a woman who was "quick" with child to have an abortion. The stage of being quick referred to the point during a woman's pregnancy when the fetus stirred in the womb.

Most American jurisdictions adopted statutes along the lines of the common law in proscribing abortion. There was a tendency, however, to spell out that an abortion was justified if physicians found it essential to save the mother's life. More liberal statutes allowed abortions to be performed when one or two physicians advised it was necessary to prevent serious injury to the mother. By 1970 a few states had even repealed criminal penalties for abortions where they were performed under medical supervision in the very early stages of a woman's pregnancy.

The 1960s and 1970s, a period of liberalized views on sexual practices, witnessed a clamor for liberalization of abortion laws. But before significant reforms occurred in the States, the U.S. Supreme Court entertained a challenge to the constitutionality of a Texas law that permitted abortion only on medical advice that it was necessary to save the mother's life. In a landmark 7–2 decision in 1973, the Court in *Roe v. Wade*, 410 U.S. 113, 93 S. Ct. 705, 35 L.Ed.2d 147 (1973), held that a fetus was not a "person" within the meaning of the Fourteenth Amendment to the United States Constitution. Therefore, the fetus was not entitled to the constitutional protection of the law granted persons. The Court then extended its views on privacy by holding that a woman's personal right of privacy was involved in the decision whether to abort a fetus. The Court's decision had the effect of invalidating most state laws proscribing or regulating abortions. A decision whether to abort during the first trimester of a pregnancy, the Court said, was a matter between the woman and her physician without state regulation. After the first trimester, procedures for abortion could be regulated when "necessarily related to maternal health." In the final trimester, when the fetus has become "viable," the state may prohibit abortion except "when it is necessary, in appropriate medical judgment, to preserve the life or health of the mother."

The controversial issue of abortion has philosophical, religious, ethical, medical, and political dimensions. As part of the national debate, Congress in the early 1980s considered but rejected a constitutional amendment to restrict abortions. A more conservative Supreme Court has modified *Roe* to allow states greater leeway in regulating abortions in such areas as waiting periods and required counseling. In the wake of one of these decisions, *Planned Parenthood v. Casey*, 505 U.S. ____, 112 S.Ct. 2791, 120 L.Ed.2d 674 (1992), supporters of abortion rights clamored for Congress to adopt a statute that would codify the holding in *Roe v. Wade*. Upon assuming office, President Clinton issued an executive order eliminating a number of restrictions on abortion counseling in federally funded clinics that had been imposed by the prior administration.

CHILD ABUSE

During the 1980s complaints of child abuse increased dramatically. Many cases involve commission of assault, battery (or aggravated categories thereof), or some category of sexual assault or sexual battery. Nevertheless, with the rise of neglect, abuse, and violence against children, many states have enacted specific child abuse laws to cover a broader range of abusive behavior.

McKinney's New York Penal Law § 260.10(1) provides:

> A person is guilty of endangering the welfare of a child when: He knowingly acts in a manner likely to be injurious to the physical, mental or moral welfare of a child less than seventeen years old or directs or authorizes such child to engage in an occupation involving a substantial risk of danger to his life or health.

Statutes now commonly require medical professionals and social workers to report instances of suspected child abuse to the enforcement authorities. When such cases of child abuse reach the courts, they often involve legal issues as to whether parents, social workers, and others who discuss these matters with an abused child are to be permitted to testify in court concerning communications with the child. Moreover, expert testimony of physicians, psychologists, and social workers is often relied upon to explain a child's sometimes curious behavior that may grow out of certain types of abuse.

The widespread drug problem has led to prosecutions of women for child abuse where during pregnancy the mothers-to-be ingested cocaine and demonstrable medical effects were present in their children at birth. Courts have generally declined to hold that such action constitutes child abuse. See e.g., *State v. Gethers*, 585 So.2d 1140 (Fla. App. 1991); *State v. Gray*, 584 N.E. 2d 710 (Ohio 1992).

SPOUSE ABUSE; ABUSE OF THE ELDERLY

Legislatures and courts have also been giving increased attention to the problem of spouse abuse and abuse of the elderly. Many of these abuses constitute criminal violations of traditional statutes previously discussed; however, laws have been enacted in many states to provide for issuance of court injunctions to protect spouses from domestic violence and provide for arrest of those who violate these orders. In other instances legislatures have provided for enhanced penalties for those who commit crimes of violence against elderly persons.

FALSE IMPRISONMENT AND KIDNAPPING

In recognition of the need to protect an individual's freedom of movement, the common law developed two misdemeanor offenses: false imprisonment and kidnapping. False imprisonment consisted of confining someone against the person's will, while kidnapping involved forcibly abducting and taking a person to another country. See *Smith v. State*, 23 N.W. 879 (Wis. 1885).

The Statutory Offense of False Imprisonment

Not all states have adopted statutes making false imprisonment an offense. Those that have generally classify it as a misdemeanor and define it much as did the common law. Typically, the Texas statute states: "A person commits an offense if he intentionally and knowingly restrains another person." Vernon's Tex. Penal Code Ann. § 20.02(a). Texas law declares the offense to be a misdemeanor but provides that if the offender recklessly exposes the victim to a substantial risk of serious bodily injury it becomes a felony. Vernon's Tex. Penal Code Ann. § 20.02(c). Usually, a prosecution for false imprisonment only requires proof of a defendant's general intent, although this depends on the particular statute.

Some Common Scenarios of False Imprisonment. Four hypothetical situations illustrate the crime of false imprisonment:

- A police officer takes a person into custody under an unlawful arrest.
- A prison warden fails to release a prisoner who has served his or her term.
- A storekeeper detains a customer when the storekeeper has a hunch the customer has shoplifted but has no reasonable basis for such suspicion.
- An overzealous male suitor refuses to allow his female companion to leave his apartment without yielding to his sexual demands.

False Imprisonment Not a Commonly Charged Offense. In recent years false imprisonment has not been a commonly charged offense. Three reasons chiefly account for this:

- Serious charges involving restraint of a person frequently reveal elements constituting the statutory offense of kidnapping.
- Persons claiming to have been falsely imprisoned often seek to recover damages in a civil suit, rather than press criminal charges.
- Upon close investigation many restraints undoubtedly are determined to have been imposed based on authority, or at least a reasonable belief that there was authority to have restrained the complaining party.

Modern Statutory Treatment of Kidnapping

Unlike false imprisonment, the crime of kidnapping is a serious felony universally proscribed by state and federal jurisdictions. It plays a far greater role in our society than it did at common law.

Under modern legislation it is not necessary, as it was at common law, that the victim of kidnapping be taken to another country. The elements of the crime are necessarily dependent on the precise wording of the statute in a particular jurisdiction, but in general, to constitute kidnapping there must be an unlawful taking and forcible carrying away (sometimes called "asportation") of a victim without that person's consent. Intimidation and coercion can substitute for the required force, and even where consent has been given, it must have been voluntarily given by a person who has the capacity to consent. Therefore, young children and incompetent persons cannot legally consent to an act of asportation.

Some states classify kidnapping as either simple kidnapping or kidnapping for ransom. Others classify the offense by degrees. In New York, kidnapping in the second degree is a felony that merely involves the abduction of another person. McKinney's N.Y. Penal Code § 135.20. Kidnapping in the first degree is a more serious felony, and the statute proscribing it states:

> A person is guilty of kidnapping in the first degree when he abducts another person and when:
>
> 1. His intent is to compel a third person to pay or deliver money or property as ransom, or to engage in other particular conduct, or to refrain from engaging in particular conduct; or
> 2. He restrains the person abducted for a period of more than twelve hours with intent to:
>
>   (a) Inflict physical injury upon him or violate or abuse him sexually; or
>   (b) Accomplish or advance the commission of a felony; or
>   (c) Terrorize him or a third person; or
>   (d) Interfere with the performance of a governmental or political function; or
> 3. The person abducted dies during the abduction or before he is able to return or to be returned to safety. McKinney's N.Y. Penal Code § 135.25.

The Requirement of "Asportation" in Kidnapping. The asportation or movement of the victim distinguishes the crime of kidnapping from the offense of false imprisonment. One of the more commonly litigated issues in kidnapping prosecutions concerns the extent of movement of the victim required to meet this element of the crime. In recent years courts have tended to limit the scope of kidnapping statutes by deciding that the required movement of a victim must be something more than that inherent in or incidental to the commission of another felony. The proliferation of court decisions on this subject may be the result of the tendency of prosecutors to levy multiple charges against a criminal defendant for conduct arising out of a single criminal episode.

When is the offender's movement of a victim in conjunction with an independent offense such as assault, rape, or robbery sufficient to constitute an independent offense of kidnapping? If the movement is merely incidental to a crime and does not involve an additional significant risk to the victim, courts generally will not sustain a conviction for kidnapping in addition to the other offense. Recent appellate court decisions are instructive. In 1978, the New Hampshire Supreme Court held that a defendant was properly convicted as an accomplice of a defendant who forced a woman into a car and drove her to an apartment where the principal defendant assaulted her. *State v. Goodwin*, 395 A.2d 1234 (N.H. 1978). In the same vein, two years later, the North Carolina Supreme Court sustained a kidnapping conviction where a handyman forced a woman off the street and into her home for purposes of sexually assaulting her. *State v. Adams*, 264 S.E.2d 46 (N.C. 1980).

Two 1983 appellate court decisions addressed the problem, expounding a somewhat different approach. The Florida Supreme Court held that the statutory requirement of "confining, abducting, or imprisoning another person . . . with intent to commit or facilitate commission of any felony" does not include movement

CASE IN POINT

RAPE AND KIDNAPPING: REQUIRED RESISTANCE IN FACE OF THREATS

Late one night after leaving work, a woman responded to a request by two men to assist them in getting their car off the road. When she began to leave both men grabbed her, ordered her into the back seat of the car, and threatened to kill her unless she cooperated. The men told her that they had escaped from prison and were holding her as a hostage. They then drove their victim to a tent, disrobed her, and forced her to submit to sexual acts with each of them. When they drove her back to her car the next morning, they told her that they would kill her if she reported the incident to the police.

The defendants were convicted of rape, kidnapping, and several other offenses. On appeal, they argued that the victim had cooperated in their endeavors, hence they were not guilty of either rape or kidnapping. The Indiana Supreme Court rejected their contentions and explained that the resistance necessary to protect against sexual attack is dependent on all circumstances. Further, the court noted that a victim need not physically resist after being confronted with threats and being in fear of injury.

Ballard v. State, 385 N.E.2d 1126 (Ind. 1979).

or confinement that is inconsequential or inherent in the nature of the felony. *Faison v. State,* 426 So.2d 963 (Fla. 1983). In applying this rationale a California appellate court held that moving a robber's victim across a room or from one room to another was an insufficient movement to meet the requirement for kidnapping. *People v. John,* 197 Cal. Rptr.340 (Cal. App. 1983).

Federal Kidnapping Laws. Perhaps the most notorious kidnapping to have occurred in the United States was the abduction of the infant son of Charles A. Lindbergh, the "Lone Eagle" who, in 1927, made the first nonstop solo flight across the Atlantic Ocean. The Lindbergh baby was abducted from the family home in New Jersey in 1932. Bruno Richard Hauptman was convicted of the crime after a spectacular trial and was executed in 1936. The Lindbergh kidnapping led to a demand for federal laws to enable the Federal Bureau of Investigation to become involved in the apprehension of kidnappers. This, in turn, led to sweeping changes in state and federal laws on kidnapping. The Federal Kidnapping Act, commonly called the Lindbergh Law, provides:

> Whoever unlawfully seizes, confines, inveigles, decoys, kidnaps, abducts, or carries away and holds for ransom or reward or otherwise any person, except in the case of a minor by a parent thereof . . . shall be punished by imprisonment. . . . 18 U.S.C.A. § 1201(a).

Subsection (b) of the statute raises a presumption that if the kidnapped victim is not returned within twenty-four hours after the taking, then the defendant did, in fact, take the victim across state lines. This presumption effectively allows the federal government to bring federal agents into the investigation of an alleged kidnapping promptly.

A recent federal statute makes hostage taking an offense, 18 U.S.C.A. § 1203, while other federal statutes make it a crime to knowingly receive, possess, or dispose of any money or property that has been delivered as ransom for a victim of a kidnapping, 18 U.S.C.A. § 1202, or for a bank robber to avoid apprehension by forcing someone to accompany him. 18 U.S.C.A. § 2113(e).

Defenses to Charges of False Imprisonment and Kidnapping

It is not false imprisonment for a person to detain another under authority of the law. Thus, an officer, or even a private citizen, who makes a lawful arrest or a jailer who detains a prisoner lawfully committed to custody are not guilty of an offense. Likewise, a parent who reasonably disciplines a child or a teacher who reasonably restrains a pupil would not be guilty of false imprisonment.

Consent, also, can be a defense to false imprisonment or kidnapping. Of course, the consent must not have been induced by threat, coercion, or misrepresentation and must have been given by a person competent to give consent. A person who relies on consent as a defense has the burden of establishing the validity of such consent.

The Problem of Child-Snatching

In recent years marital disputes have given rise to many serious problems concerning the custody of children of divorced or separated parents. The term *child-snatching* is now commonly applied to situations in which one parent deliberately retains or conceals a child from the other parent. The problem has resulted partly from the ability of one parent to seize a child from the custodial parent, travel to another state, and petition the court in the latter state for custody of the child. This activity is now being curbed by several approaches:

- In many states trial judges include a provision in a divorce judgment requiring court approval to remove a child from the state where the divorce is granted. Violation may subject the offending party to being held in contempt of court, or in some states, to be prosecuted for a felony.
- The Uniform Child Custody Jurisdiction Act (UCCJA), proposed in 1968 and now in force in all fifty states, generally continues jurisdiction for custody in the home or resident state of the child. Cooperation between the courts in the different states is becoming increasingly effective in preventing "judge shopping."
- The majority of states have made child-snatching a felony, thereby subjecting violators to extradition for prosecution in the state where the offense occurs.
- The Parental Kidnapping Prevention Act (PKPA), 28 U.S.C.A. § 1738A, enacted by Congress in 1980 addresses the problem of interstate child abduction.
- Federal and state governments, as well as religious and civic organizations and the media, have initiated programs for identifying children and for collecting and disseminating information on missing children.

CONCLUSION

Crimes against persons usually result in either death or injury to the victim. Victims of violent personal crimes who survive often suffer emotional and psychological damage, as well as physical injury. Additionally, offenses resulting in death or injury frequently have long-lasting social and economic effects on the victim. Consider the economic plight of a family in which a working parent is disabled by a penniless assailant; or the strains imposed on a marital union in which the young bride was sexually assaulted or kidnapped and ravished as a teenager.

Over the centuries the assaultive, homicidal, sexual, and detention crimes have been a stable base for prosecuting those whose antisocial conduct offended the basic norms of civilized people. Yet, society changes and laws must change to cope with the needs of a dynamic society.

Many searching questions must be examined in respect to offenses against persons. For example: Is it justifiable to find a thief guilty of murder simply because a co-felon kills a victim during commission of the theft? Should the marital exception in the law of rape be eliminated to make it possible to charge a husband with raping his wife? If so, must the courts employ different standards of determining the elements of consent and force? Are there other biases against female victims of sexual assault that must be addressed? By whom: legislatures or the courts? Is there any solution to end the divisive struggle over legalized abortion? Is the defendant who moves a victim during commission of a felony likely to be pressured into pleading guilty to a charge to avoid a threatened prosecution for kidnapping the victim?

Indeed, offenses against persons are the crimes from which people probably suffer the most direct consequences. Understandably, the prosecution of serious offenders attracts more public interest than other actions in the criminal justice system.

As you study succeeding chapters discussing the procedural aspects of the criminal law, consider not only the rights of the defendant, but also the rights of society and the rights of the victims of crimes.

QUESTIONS FOR THOUGHT AND DISCUSSION

1. What are the essential differences between the offenses of assault and battery under modern statutes?
2. Shortly before midnight, a man is driving through a residential area in an attempt to get his wife, who is in labor, to the hospital. The posted speed limit is 30 MPH, but the anxious husband is driving 50 MPH. In a dark area, the car strikes and kills a ten-year-old boy who is playing in the middle of the street. Can the driver be convicted of (a) manslaughter or (b) vehicular homicide?
3. Is it legitimate for a jury to find a defendant guilty of manslaughter in a case where there is evidence of premeditation, simply because members of the jury feel that the defendant was somewhat justified in taking the life of the victim?
4. How can the prosecution establish the *corpus delicti* in a murder case when the body of the victim cannot be found?

5. Given the scope of the constitutional right of privacy discussed in Chapter 3, how can a state make it a crime for a person to attempt suicide or to aid another in such an attempt?

6. Why has the common-law doctrine of felony murder become controversial among courts and legal scholars in recent years?

7. Can a state make it a crime to kill a viable fetus, notwithstanding the Supreme Court's decision in *Roe v. Wade?*

8. A male who has been diagnosed with acquired immune deficiency syndrome (AIDS) engages in sexual intercourse with a female. He does not inform the female that he has AIDS. As a result, the female contracts AIDS and dies from the disease some two years later. Under the laws of your state, could the male be convicted of a homicidal act?

9. What interests does the law seek to protect in proscribing (a) forcible rape; (b) statutory rape?

10. Which statutory and judicial reforms of the 1970s and 1980s in the law of rape were the most significant from the standpoint of a female victim? Why?

11. Is there any justification for courts to continue following "Hale's Rule" that creates a "marital exception" in the law of rape?

12. A store manager observes Lucy Grabit stuffing a pair of nylon hose into her purse before going through the check-out counter in a supermarket. The manager detains her and promptly directs his employee to call the police. Is the store manager guilty of false imprisonment? Why?

13. Several college freshmen enter the dean's private office and remain there for several hours. They refuse to let the dean leave until he yields to their demands to allow unrestricted visitation in all dormitories. Under contemporary criminal statutes what offense, if any, have the students committed? Explain.

14. Defendant was convicted of battery under a statute that provides: "A person commits a battery when he either intentionally or knowingly, and without legal justification, makes physical contact of an insulting or provoking nature with an individual." The evidence disclosed that one morning the male defendant picked up a female friend whom he had invited to have breakfast with him. En route to the restaurant he unbuttoned her blouse, placed his hand on her breast, and after she removed his hand and asked him to stop, he again placed his hand on her breast. On appeal, the defendant argues that his conviction should be reversed because his acts were not insulting, there was no struggle, and the female did not testify that she was traumatized or disturbed by his acts. Moreover, he points out that the evidence disclosed that after the incident the female complainant remained with him and accompanied him to a restaurant where they had breakfast together. Should the appellate court reverse this conviction on the ground that the evidence is insufficient? Why or Why not?

15. Defendant and her husband have two sons, ages 5 and 3. Without notifying her husband, she left the family home with both children at a time when no court proceedings were pending concerning either their marriage or custody of their children. Two weeks later, and without the wife's knowledge, the husband

obtained a court order granting him custody of the two children. An arrest warrant was eventually issued for the wife and she was arrested in another state and brought back to her home state, where she now faces prosecution under a statute that provides: "Whoever, being a relative of a child . . . without lawful authority, holds or intends to hold such a child permanently or for a protracted period, or takes or entices a child from his lawful custodian . . . shall be guilty of a felony." The wife's attorney stipulates that the facts are correct as stated, but contends the wife cannot be convicted of parental kidnapping under the quoted statute. What result do you think should occur? Why?

16. A nineteen-year-old woman returns home from an evening at the beach. She tells her mother that she has been raped and sodomized by an attacker she doesn't know. Some hours later, the woman identifies her attacker to her mother, and they notify the police. At trial the prosecution seeks to admit testimony of the rape trauma syndrome to explain the victim's reticence in promptly identifying her attacker. The defense objects. Should the court allow expert testimony on this subject to explain the reactions of the female victim in the hours following her attack and to explain why she may initially have been unwilling to report the defendant who attacked her? Why or why not?

CASES

STATE v. TOWERS

Supreme Court of Maine, 1973.
304 A.2d 75.

[This case involves the offense of aggravated assault and battery.]

WERNICK, Justice.

Defendant has appealed from a judgment of the Superior Court (Penobscot County) embodying his conviction, on October 15, 1971, of the offense of assault and battery, high and aggravated in degree. . . .

Evidence produced at the trial, jury-waived, warranted the following factual conclusions.

Defendant had visited a friend's house to return a car bed. The complaining witness, a thirteen year old girl, was in the house "babysitting" for a child two years of age and an infant of six months. She had known defendant as a neighbor for approximately half a year, and in all of her prior contacts with him he had always acted toward her as a gentleman. Defendant and the complaining witness engaged in conversation for about fifteen minutes. Then, while complainant was holding the six months old infant, who was crying, under her right arm, defendant took hold of her and kissed her on the cheek and lips. She immediately asked him "to leave me alone," but defendant continued to hold her and proceeded to touch her breasts and place one of his hands between her legs in contact with her "private part" from outside her clothing. The complainant told defendant to "stop," whereupon defendant did stop and with the remark to complainant: "Don't tell anybody," he left the house. The complainant did not mention the incident until the following morning, almost twenty-four hours later, when she told her mother. The complainant waited because when she had returned home, she found that "everybody was around."

Defendant's single contention on appeal is that, within the legal meaning of "high and aggravated," the finding of an aggravated degree of assault and battery may not here stand as a matter of law. Defendant points to the fleeting nature of the incident insofar as he ceased his actions upon the second request by complainant. He further mentions that there were no physical injuries inflicted and maintains that the psychological impact upon the girl must have been minimal since she waited almost twenty-four hours before she reported what had transpired.

In *State v. Bey*, 161 Me. 23, 206 A. 2d 413 (1965) this Court observed that assault and battery may become "high and aggravated in nature" by the presence of "circumstances of aggravation, such as . . . great disparity between the ages and physical conditions of the parties, a difference in the sexes, indecent liberties or familiarities with a female, the purposeful infliction of shame and disgrace, . . ." . . .

State v. Rand, 156 Me. 81, 161 A. 2d 852 (1960) involved a factual situation so remarkably similar to the instant case that, for purposes of the appropriate application of controlling legal principles, the cases must be held indistinguishable. Sustaining a conviction of assault and battery, high and aggravated in nature, we said in *Rand:* "What intention could the respondent have had other than an evil intention to indulge his own lustful desires? By his indecent acts he violated the person and dignity of the child in a manner abhorrent to society." . . .

Under the combined import of *State v. Bey* and *State v. Rand* the present adjudication that defendant had committed an assault and battery, high and aggravated in degree was legally warranted.

The entry is:

Appeal denied.

FURR v. STATE

Supreme Court of Arkansas, 1992.
308 Ark. 41, 822 S.W.2d 380.

[In this case the Arkansas Supreme Court considers the sufficiency of evidence to sustain a conviction for first-degree murder.]

NEWBERN, Justice.

The appellant, Jesse Robert Furr, was convicted of murder in the first degree and sentenced to life imprisonment in connection with the shooting death of his stepmother, Ruth Furr. He argues the Trial Court erred by refusing to direct a verdict in his favor because there was insufficient evidence that he possessed the necessary purposeful mental state. We affirm the conviction.

Furr lived with his father and stepmother near Huntsville. On the day the killing occurred, Furr got off work at 12:30 P.M., went home, and began drinking beer. His father and stepmother, and others present, were also drinking. Eventually, everyone except Furr and his stepmother left the house.

According to Furr's testimony, the two began discussing the family's financial problems, and he told his stepmother, "Well, if you ain't got no money, why don't you get rid of some of these guns?" He picked up a .22 caliber pistol, cocked it, and began pointing it around the room. Furr testified his finger accidentally hit the trigger, the gun went off, and the bullet struck his stepmother who was standing some five feet away from him at the kitchen sink.

Furr testified that after the shooting he saw that his stepmother was not breathing and he panicked. He took some money, two pistols, and his stepmother's truck and left for Midland, Texas, where his mother lived. He testified he was afraid to call the police because he was on parole for a burglary committed in Texas and knew he could not possess any weapons.

Furr was apprehended in Texas and brought back to Arkansas. After being advised of his rights, Furr admitted his responsibility for the shooting but stated it was an accident. The sheriff testified Furr told him he had been drinking the day of the shooting and had a "buzz." He further told the officer "[I] was acting crazy with a .22 caliber revolver, pointing it around," and "I pointed it at her and touched the trigger and it went off." Furr first told the sheriff he was standing across the room from his stepmother when the gun went off, but later said, "I could have been closer than I previously said."

Chief medical examiner, Dr. Fanny Malak, testified the victim was shot once behind the left ear, and the bullet traveled down towards the right ear and entered the brain. A large amount of gunpowder residue was found inside and outside the wound. An autopsy revealed multiple fractures of the skull. According to Dr. Malak, gases had entered and expanded inside the brain leading to increased pressure there. The pressure caused a crack in the roof of the victim's left eye, and the eye was visibly swollen and discolored as a result. Based on the gunpowder residue inside the wound and the multiple fractures of the skull, Dr. Malak inferred that the gun had touched the victim's scalp when fired.

The jury was instructed on premeditated and deliberated capital murder and the lesser included offenses of murder in the first degree, murder in the second degree, and manslaughter.

Murder in the first degree is purposely causing the death of another person. Ark. Code Ann. § 5–10–102(a)(2) (Supp. 1001). "A person acts purposely with respect to his conduct or a result thereof when it is his conscious object to engage in conduct of that nature or to cause such a result." Ark. Code. Ann. § 5–2–202(1) (1987).

On appeal from denial of a directed verdict, this Court reviews the evidence in the light most favorable to the appellee, in this case the State, and affirms if there is any substantial evidence to support the conviction. . . . Evidence is substantial if it is of sufficient force and character to compel reasonable minds to reach a conclusion, passing beyond suspicion and conjecture. . . .

Intent is seldom capable of proof by direct evidence and must usually be inferred from the circumstances surrounding the killing. . . . The intent necessary for first degree murder may be inferred from the type of weapon used, the manner of its use, and the nature, extent, and location of the wounds. . . .

The evidence with respect to Furr's purposeful mental state at the time of the crime, viewed in the light most favorable to the State, was substantial. From Dr. Malak's expert testimony that the gun used in the shooting was fired at close, or point blank, range the inference could easily be drawn that it was the purpose of the person firing to kill the victim. One is presumed to intend the natural and probable consequences of one's act. . . . The jury was free to determine the weight to be given the expert testimony, and they could reject or accept all or any part of it they believed to be true. . . .

The State also presented evidence that Furr stole some money, a truck, and two guns from his stepmother after the shooting and then fled the scene. Furr testified he had no intent to return the money or the guns. A jury could reasonably conclude from this evidence that Furr purposely killed his stepmother for financial reasons.

Furr claimed his finger accidentally hit the trigger, and the gun went off, but the trier of fact is not required to believe the testimony of any witness. This is especially true when the witness is the accused. . . .

We find the evidence supporting the conviction to have been substantial. The record of trial has been examined for error in accordance with our Rule 11(f), and we have found no errors prejudicial to Furr.

Affirmed.

Manuel v. State

District Court of Appeal of Florida, Second District, 1977.
344 So.2d 1317.

[This case deals with second-degree murder.]

OTT, Judge.

Appellant was convicted of second-degree murder. We reverse and remand for the imposition of a sentence of manslaughter for reasons hereinafter stated.

On the night of March 26, 1976, Robert Jackson, 10, was playing with Wendell Elliott, 13, in the vicinity of Janie Mae Hayes' house. The house fronted on Ohio Street in Lake Wales. The boys were playing "chase"—a game which rewards silence and stealth. They were playing so quietly and the night was so dark that a woman sitting on a nearby porch was unaware of their presence.

Earlier that night, Louise Manuel, wife of the appellant, had come to Ms. Hayes' house and accused a lodger, Ella Mae Kindrick, of having an affair with her husband. An argument ensued, after which Mrs. Manuel left the area.

The appellant was in a bar when he heard that his wife had been involved in a tiff. He obtained his .32 caliber pistol and began walking down Ohio Street toward the Hayes house. Upon reaching the area in front of the Dunlap house—two doors from the Hayes house—Manuel stopped walking when he saw Ella Mae Kindrick on the Dunlap front porch. He said to her, "Who's doing this to my wife?" . . . "Who's that messing with my wife?" He then fired a single shot into the ground.

After firing the first shot, Manuel proceeded to a lightpost (the light was broken) in front of the house between the Dunlap and Hayes houses. At this point, Wendell Elliott, having heard the shot, ran from the rear of the Hayes house to a point about three feet from Manuel. Once there, Wendell called for Robert, but received no answer. The record contains no indication that Wendell attempted to warn Manuel that Robert was in the area.

About three minutes after firing the first shot, Manuel fired another shot. According to Ms. Kindrick, from her vantage point on the Dunlap porch she could not tell exactly in which direction Manuel had pointed the pistol when he fired the second shot. On direct examination, Wendell Elliott testified that he could not tell at what, if anything, Manuel was aiming. On cross-examination, however, Wendell testified that the gun was pointed in the general direction of an area on the far side of Ms. Hayes' front yard where a trash barrel and other garbage containers were located. Nothing in his testimony indicated he could actually see the trash barrel and other garbage containers. Nothing in his testimony indicated he knew where Robert Jackson was at the time the second shot was fired.

The deputy sheriff who took Manuel into custody testified that Manuel asked about Jackson's condition and stated that he had not intended to hit the boy and was sorry about it. According to this deputy, Manuel did not indicate whether or not he knew the boy was in the area, but did say that "he knew he hit the boy when he shot" and that "the boy got in the way."

The testimony was uncontradicted that Ohio Street was very badly lit, especially in the area where the boys were playing. A police photographer who arrived soon after the shooting testified that one could not see where to walk without a flashlight.

The record is somewhat sparse with regard to Manuel's mental state. The deputy who took Manuel into custody testified that Manuel stated that "he had got his pistol to try to protect his wife, stop the fight, keep anybody from hurting her."

The statute governing murder in the second degree, Section 782.04(2), Florida Statutes, provides in relevant part:

> The unlawful killing of a human being, when perpetrated by any act imminently dangerous to another and evincing a depraved mind regardless of human life, although without any premeditated design to effect the death of any particular individual, shall be murder in the second degree.

The Florida Standard Jury Instruction for murder in the second degree provides as follows:

> An act is one imminently dangerous to another and evincing a depraved mind regardless of human life if it is an act (or a series of acts) which
>
> 1. a person of ordinary judgment would know is reasonably certain to kill or do serious bodily injury to another;
> 2. is done from ill will, hatred, spite or an evil intent, and
> 3. is of such a nature that the act itself indicates an indifference to human life.

Number 2 above amounts to what is frequently termed malice. The depravity of mind required in second degree murder has been equated with malice in the commonly understood sense of ill will, hatred, spite or evil intent. . . .

Within the category of second degree murder there exist varying gradations of cases. The reason for this is that some acts are simply more depraved than others. For example, in *Weaver v. State,* 220 So.2d 53 (Fla. 2d DCA 1969), the court found the evidence to overwhelmingly support a finding of malice. In *Weaver,* the victim was a police officer. He was responding to the scene of a domestic dispute at the Weaver household. When Weaver resisted the officer's illegal attempt to enter his home, the officer maced Weaver. Weaver then disarmed the police officer, pursued him, ignored the officer's pleas for mercy, expended all the bullets in his gun in shooting the officer in the back and made an immediate res gestae exclamation acknowledging the killing. The court found these facts furnished more than a sufficient basis for a finding of the requisite depravity of mind. . . .

Another "strong" case is that of *Grissom v. State,* 237 So.2d 57 (Fla. 3d DCA 1970). In *Grissom,* the defendant, a junior high school student, was disciplined by a teacher for a rule violation. Upon being disciplined, the defendant threatened to return and kill the teacher. A short time later he did return armed with a handgun and fired two shots at the teacher, wounding but not killing him. While fleeing the building after shooting the teacher, he fired one shot up a stairway in the school building. That shot struck and killed a student standing on the stairs.

Second degree murder convictions were also upheld in cases involving the pointing of a weapon at a vital area of the body before the weapon discharged. In *Edwards v. State,* 302 So.2d 479 (Fla. 3d DCA 1974), the court found that the act of the defendant in pointing his gun at the victim's head, waiting until the victim had taken three steps backward, and then firing the gun, to be both depraved and imminently dangerous. See *State v. Bryan,* 287 So.2d 73 (Fla. 1973).

In *Hines v. State,* 227 So.2d 334 (Fla. 1st DCA 1969), the defendant had pointed a shotgun at the head of the deceased. The defendant stated that he "had a gun" and that she (the deceased) "should go out . . . and act like a squirrel and if he killed her . . . it wouldn't be no accident." The gun discharged striking the deceased in the face and killing her. The court found that even if it accepted the defendant's contention that the gun had fired upon closing the breach that such an act committed while a gun is purposely pointed at the head of another from a very short distance certainly implied malice.

The instant case contrasts with the "pointed gun" cases in that Manuel pointed his gun in a direction (toward the garbage area) where one would think a shot could not result in harm to any person. In addition, the lack of any substantial evidence of malevolence directed toward any person strongly suggests to this court that Manuel's conduct, while certainly culpable and inexcusable, falls far short of malice.

The statute governing manslaughter, Section 782.07, Florida Statutes, provides in relevant part:

> The killing of a human being by the . . . culpable negligence of another, without lawful justification . . . shall be deemed manslaughter.

The Florida Standard Jury Instruction for manslaughter defines culpable negligence as follows:

> Culpable negligence is negligence of a gross and flagrant nature and consists of more than a mere failure to use ordinary care. Culpable negligence is consciously doing an act or following a course of conduct which any reasonable person would know would likely result in death or great bodily injury to some other person, even though done without the intent to injure any person but with utter disregard for the safety of another.

In *Savage v. State,* 152 Fla. 367, 11 So.2d 778, 779 (1943), the court defined culpable negligence as that conduct which showed a

> . . . gross and flagrant character, evincing reckless disregard of human life or of the safety of persons exposed to its dangerous effects; or that entire want of care which would raise the presumption of indifference to consequences; or such wantonness or recklessness or grossly careless disregard of the safety and welfare of the public, or that reckless indifference to the rights of others, which is equivalent to an intentional violation of them.

In the manslaughter area, one distinct line of cases involves accidental shootings in which manslaughter convictions were not upheld. As with the second degree murder cases, these "accident" cases are not all alike; some illustrate more serious and reprehensible conduct than do others. . . . [A] . . . "totally accidental" case was that of *Walsingham v. State,* 272 So. 2d 215 (Fla. 2d DCA 1973). There, the defendant was holding a rifle on his lap in his bedroom while examining it. The rifle accidentally discharged. The bullet passed through a door and a wall and eventually struck one of defendant's children, killing him. . . .

Two other "accident" cases, a bit stronger on the facts, were *Parker v. State,* 318 So.2d 502 (Fla. 1st DCA 1975), and *Sharp v. State,* 120 So.2d 206 (Fla. 2d DCA 1960). In *Parker,* the defendant was "fooling around" by waving his pistol around in the cab of a moving truck. At one point, he waved the pistol past the decedent's head when it went off. The fact that the defendant had the hammer positioned in the safety notch and believed the gun would not fire was considered an important factor.

In *Sharp,* the defendant intentionally pointed a loaded shotgun in the direction of a crowd for the purpose of restoring order. He then stumbled and the gun fired accidently, killing a man. An important factor in the defendant's not being convicted was his bad leg which apparently precipitated the stumbling and resultant firing of the gun.

One step beyond the "accident" cases are those in which the actual shooting was certainly accidental, but the act fits within the culpable negligence standard. In *Williams v. State,* 336 So. 2d 1261 (Fla. 1st DCA 1976), a conviction for manslaughter was upheld. In that case there had been a bar fracas in which the appellant had been involved. During a lull in the fighting a vehicle in which the victim was riding arrived at the bar. When the driver of the vehicle pulled a shotgun out of his trunk the appellant—observing this—took his shotgun out of his truck and held it pointed toward the ground. As he shifted his grasp the shotgun discharged.

In *McBride v. State,* 191 So.2d 70 (Fla. 1st DCA 1966), a conviction for manslaughter was also upheld. The court found that the defendant "needlessly [had] on his person a deadly weapon which he brandished ... in a careless and reckless manner." The court stated that the defendant "set the stage for the tragedy which ultimately followed (an accidental shooting) even though he may have had [no] intention of killing the decedent." ...

It is submitted that the facts in the instant case, although clearly indicating more culpable conduct than the facts of the non-manslaughter "accident" cases, supra, are not sufficient to warrant a conviction for second degree murder. Rather, if the *McBride* or *Williams* facts do not fall within second degree murder, i.e., they do not make out a prima facie case of a depraved mind, then it is inescapable that the facts in the instant case fall far short of second degree murder. In the instant case there was no evidence that the appellant either observed the victim or had any notice (actual or constructive) of his possible presence.

Thus, the noiseless playing of the victim, the inky blackness of the night and the lack of demonstrated ill will on the part of the appellant point more toward culpable negligence than the evincing of a depraved mind regardless of human life.

REVERSED and REMANDED.

HOBSON, Acting C. J., and SCHEB, J., concur.

COMMONWEALTH V. GRAVES

Superior Court of Pennsylvania, 1983.
310 Pa. Super, 184, 456 A.2d 561.

[This case involves the crime of third-degree murder.]

VAN der VOORT, Judge:

A jury found appellant guilty of third degree murder for the death of Lynette Weston, age 10, and of first degree murder for the death of Lloyd Weston, age 10, and recommended a death sentence on the first degree murder conviction....

... [A]ppellant argues ... that all of the evidence of guilt presented in this case is circumstantial and insufficient to prove beyond a reasonable doubt that he is the individual who committed these two homicides.

Initially, we note that circumstantial evidence may be sufficient to establish, beyond a reasonable doubt a crime, and that the accused was responsible for the crime.... Here, the Commonwealth's evidence established the following.

The appellant had been caring for the victims on the night when they were strangled to death. At 4:45 A.M., Daniel Anderson left the Weston home, leaving appellant alone with the children. At 7:10 A.M., the victims were discovered dead by their mother; appellant was not on the premises. No one else had been seen entering the house between 4:45 A.M. and 7:10 A.M. After several calls, appellant was advised of the children's deaths. He claimed that he was forced to leave the house. A sample of appellant's pubic hair was found to be consistent with a hair found on the female victim. A bathrobe which appellant had been wearing earlier contained blood stains, consistent with the type of the female victim and inconsistent with appellant's type. Dried blood was found under the finger nails of the female victim (its type was not determinable); fresh scratches were found on appellant's upper body. Such scratches did not match appellant's girl friend's nails and she denied having made them. Scratch marks found on the male victim were consistent with the characteristics of appellant's finger nails.

We find that the evidence was sufficient beyond a reasonable doubt to show that appellant was responsible for the death of the two young victims. We must also inquire whether the Commonwealth proved the requisite intent for the killing of Lynette Weston ... and for the premeditated killing of Lloyd Weston....

The evidence, as it differs between the two deaths does not appear to support the different verdicts: murder in the third degree (Lynette) and murder in the first degree (Lloyd). A jury's verdict in a criminal case will not be set aside merely because it appears to be inconsistent with another verdict of the jurors. So long as the challenged verdict is supported by the evidence we will not on review delve into the thought process of the jury. . . .

Murder of the third degree has been defined as "an unlawful killing with malice expressed or implied, but absent any specific intent to take a life." . . . As to the death of Lynette Weston we find no need to expound on the facts already given; they clearly show the existence of malice.

The conviction for murder of the first degree for the death of Lloyd Weston requires a little more discussion. The trial court . . . found the fact that the victim had been manually strangled to death raised a presumption that the murder was both intentional and malicious. Appellant argues that the verdict was based on conjecture that the killing occurred to "silence a witness" who viewed the first crime.

Where there is no direct or concrete evidence of a specific intent to kill the fact-finder must look to the act itself and all the surrounding circumstances. . . . It is the law of this Commonwealth that premeditation and deliberation may be found where there is a conscious effort to cause death; this design can be formed in a very short time. . . . Where a deadly force is knowingly applied by a defendant to his victim, the intent to kill may be as evident as if the defendant had verbally announced his intent. . . . *[Commonwealth v.] Meredith* offers special guidance to this case; there the defendant was convicted of the beating death of a two and one half (2 ½) year old child. On appeal, it was held that the number and severity of blows, the size and age of the victim permitted a finding that a deadly force had been applied to a vital part of the body and allowed the jury to infer an intent to kill. Likewise here, we believe the jury was entitled to find, where a ten year old child is strangled to death, the specific intent to kill required for a conviction for first degree murder.

Judgment of sentence affirmed.

State v. Studham

Supreme Court of Utah, 1977.
572 P.2d 700.

[This case deals with the crime of rape.]

CROCKETT, Justice:

Defendant, Clyde Lloyd Studham, appeals from a jury conviction of rape. . . .

The prosecutrix, Janis ________, had lived with defendant in a meretricious relationship beginning in November, 1972. A son, Chad ________, was born on September 14, 1973. The relationship between Janis and the defendant had terminated in December of 1974 and the defendant was under a court order not to annoy or visit her.

At approximately 4:00 A.M. on the morning of March 5, 1976, Janis was awakened at her apartment by a knocking and ringing of her doorbell. Defendant, who had been drinking, was at the door and he said he wanted to talk to her, but she refused to let him in. He kicked the door open and entered; and he remained in the apartment for about two hours, during which there was some kissing and amorous advances.

The prosecutrix testified that in his efforts to force sexual intercourse upon her defendant threatened her, pinned her to the floor during a struggle, put his hand over her mouth so that she had difficulty breathing, and forced intercourse upon her against her will. She did not scream or attempt to run from her apartment, which she said was due to its futility and the fact that her young son was asleep in the adjoining room.

After the defendant left, she called her mother, who reported the incident to the police. Deputy Lester Newren of the Salt Lake County Sheriff's office came to investigate. Janis's only visible injuries were a bruised face and cut lip; and there were blood stains on her bathrobe. Pursuant to his questioning and investigation, he took the prosecutrix to St. Mark's Hospital where she was examined by Dr. John Corkrey. Later in the day the defendant was arrested and charged with this offense.

Defendant's argument that the evidence is not sufficient to prove his guilt beyond a reasonable doubt is: that it rests almost solely upon her own self-interested testimony; that it is inherently improbable and inconsistent because, though she claims force, and denies consent, she did not scream, or try to escape from the apartment even though during the time he was there she had opportunity to do so.

Most crimes are committed in such secrecy as can be effected; and that is particularly so of this type of offense. Therefore, the question of guilt or innocence often depends upon the weighing of the credibility of the victim against that of the accused. Accordingly, the rule is that if there is nothing so inherently incredible about the victim's story that reasonable minds would reject it, a conviction may rest upon her testimony alone.

In regard to the failure of the victim to make an outcry, this is to be said: Whether an outcry was made, or should have been made, depends upon how practical and effective it might have been. It is evidence which may be received and it is one of the circumstances to be considered as bearing upon the critical issue of consent. But mere failure to make such an outcry does not render a conviction unsupportable.

The essential element in rape is the forcing of intercourse upon a woman "without her consent" and "against her will." It is sometimes said that those terms mean essentially the same thing, but this is not true because such an act might occur in circumstances which would be "without her consent" but which would not necessarily involve overcoming her will and her resistance, both of which must be proved. In that regard there has often been much preoccupation with and stress placed upon the matter of the physical confrontation between the accused and the victim; and it has sometimes been said that she "must resist to the utmost" or other expressions of that import. But that view no longer obtains. Even though it is necessary that the rape be against the victim's will, manifest by a determined effort on her part to resist, it is not necessary that it be shown that she engaged in any heroics which subjected her to great brutality or that she suffered or risked serious wounds or injuries.

What we think is a sounder view recognizes that the bruising and terrorizing of the senses and sensibilities can be just as real and just as wrong as the beating and bruising of the flesh; and that the law should afford a woman protection, not only from physical violence, but from having her feelings and sensibilities outraged by force or fear in violation of what she is entitled to regard and protect as the integrity of her person. Accordingly, in determining whether the victim's will and resistance were overcome, it is appropriate to consider that this may be accomplished by either physical force and violence, or by psychological or emotional stress imposed upon her, or by a combination of them. As to the degree of resistance required: The victim need do not more than her age and her strength of body and mind make it reasonable for her to do under the circumstances to resist. In this case there is a reasonable basis in the evidence upon which the jury could believe beyond a reasonable doubt that that test was met.

In urging that the court committed error in refusing to instruct the jury that rape is easy to charge and difficult to defend against, defendant asserts that it was particularly applicable here because, in addition to the lack of corroboration, and their prior difficulties, there existed the possibility of malice behind the charge. We are aware that such an instruction in abstract terms and not focused upon the particular evidence in the case has been given without it being prejudicial error. Nevertheless, such an instruction is not looked upon with favor since it is in the nature of a directive to the jury as to how they should evaluate evidence, rather than a statement of law. Under our procedure the judging of the evidence should be left exclusively to the jury and the trial judge should neither comment thereon nor give any indication as to what he may or may not think as to the quality of the evidence. In any event, we see no reason to believe that the failure to give such an instruction in this case was error. . . .

Affirmed. No cost awarded.

STATE v. ROTHENBERG

Supreme Court of Connecticut, 1985.
195 Conn. 253, 487 A.2d 545.

[This case examines the sufficiency of the evidence to support Rothenberg's conviction for sexual assault and unlawful restraint.]

PETERS, Chief Justice.

... After a trial to the court, the defendant was found guilty ... and judgment was rendered accordingly. The defendant appeals from the judgment against him.

The trial court reasonably found the following facts. The defendant and the complainant met at a bar in Southbury during the early morning hours of August 23, 1981. The complainant recognized the defendant as someone she had met there previously. They danced. The defendant asked the complainant to accompany him to a party at a friend's condominium in Woodbury. Somewhat reluctantly, the complainant agreed and drove to the condominium in her own car.

When the couple arrived at the condominium, it appeared to be empty. In fact, however, the two bedrooms, although their doors were closed, were occupied throughout the events that then transpired. The owner of the condominium was in one bedroom and two guests were in the other.

After a brief tour of the condominium, the complainant and the defendant sat on a couch in the living room. They kissed and the defendant gave the fully clothed complainant a back rub. The complainant, at the defendant's request, gave him a back rub while he was clad only in his undershorts.

The complainant then told the defendant that she wanted to leave, but he told her that she could not go. On the pretext of wanting to use the bathroom, the complainant ran to and partially opened the front door of the condominium. The defendant closed the door and forcibly prevented her from leaving by holding her arms. The complainant could not persuade the defendant to let her leave the condominium but was allowed to use the bathroom, where she remained for approximately thirty minutes until she looked for a way to escape or a weapon. During this time, the defendant alternately promised that he would let the complainant leave and threatened to wake up his friend to join the harassment of the complainant if she did not leave the bathroom.

As the complainant emerged from the bathroom, the defendant took her by the arms and pulled her, struggling, to the living room couch. Fearing injury if she were to resist further, the complainant then submitted. The defendant sexually assaulted the complainant several times before finally releasing her.

The unseen occupants of the bedrooms in the condominium remained there throughout the night. One did not hear either the defendant or the complainant at all. The others heard sounds of conversation when the defendant and complainant first entered the condominium, but soon thereafter fell asleep and heard nothing further.

The defendant does not deny the occurrence of the sexual activity but contends that the state failed to prove that it was anything other than consensual. ...

The defendant claims that the evidence adduced at trial to support his conviction was insufficient in two respects. First, the defendant argues that the complainant's testimony that the defendant restrained and sexually assaulted her was unbelievable as a matter of law in light of the totality of the evidence at the trial. Second, the defendant claims that the evidence showed that he lacked the criminal intent necessary to a finding of guilt. We find neither assertion persuasive.

... [T]he defendant claims that the complainant's account of the events at the condominium is fatally undermined by the evidence given by the occupants of the bedrooms. The complainant testified that the defendant had "slammed" the front door during her escape attempt and had "yelled" at her while she was in the bathroom. The other people in the condominium testified that they had heard nothing beyond normal conversation and had slept throughout the incident. According to the defendant, the juxtaposition of this evidence necessarily validates his contention that the complainant's continued presence in the condominium and participation in the sexual activity was consensual.

The defendant's argument fails to recognize that, in determining the credibility of witnesses, the trier of the facts may properly believe all or part of the testimony of a witness.... The contours of the determination of credibility are uniquely shaped by the trial court and are not reviewable on appeal. "The trier of the facts determines with finality the credibility of witnesses and the weight to be accorded their testimony." ... The trial court could have believed the complainant's testimony that the defendant prevented her from leaving, and forcibly imposed himself upon her, without giving significant weight to her account of how loudly the defendant spoke or how noisily he closed the door. Alternatively, the court could have disbelieved the testimony of the occupants of the bedrooms. Viewing the evidence, as we must, in the light most favorable to sustaining the judgment of the trial court, ... we conclude that the trial court could reasonably have found that the evidence established the defendant's guilt beyond a reasonable doubt....

The defendant's second claim of insufficiency of the evidence relies upon the trial court's own finding that the complainant's conduct was ill-advised and subject to misconstruction. The trial court did find that the complainant "committed a serious error in judgment when she accompanied the defendant, a young man whom she knew only slightly, to an unknown location, where she really had no idea what might confront her. And once there, she compounded her error in judgment by her voluntary conduct in engaging in intimate physical contact with the defendant, who was almost completely unclothed. In the Court's view, this was a foolhardy act of very poor judgment that was subject to misinterpretation by a young man, such as the defendant, as indicative of a willingness to engage in more explicit sexual conduct. I am satisfied in my own mind that this is essentially what happened. The defendant did misconstrue the complainant's conduct and concluded that she would, in fact, be a willing participant in further sexual activity." According to the defendant, this finding proves that he was mistaken about the complainant's consent and therefore lacked the mental state necessary to commit the charged offenses.

This argument would be compelling had the trial court's opinion ended where the defendant's quotation stops. The trial court went on, however, to find that "[w]hen the complainant sought to withdraw from the situation, a situation that was developing beyond her expectations, the defendant was unwilling to permit her to do so. And he thereafter forced his attentions on the complainant and compelled her to engage in sexual intercourse against her will. The defendant failed to recognize that consensual sexual relations are one thing, forced sexual intercourse is something altogether different. The term 'consensual sexual relations' means full consent, and that clearly implies that a party should always be free to decline to go beyond a certain point. This the complainant tried to do. The defendant refused to honor this decision of the complainant and permit her to leave. For this he must be and is found guilty of both offenses as charged in the information." The trial court's finding in its totality makes it clear that the complainant's unambiguous request to leave the condominium disabused the defendant of any misinterpretation of her wishes. The defendant's conduct thereafter was knowingly coercive. A temporary misunderstanding about consent does not give irreversible license to compel sexual intercourse. There was ample evidence to support the trial court's finding and the defendant's conviction.

The defendant's second claim of error is that the trial court should have excluded testimony about his prior sexual history, just as the court upheld objections to similar questions asked of the complainant on her cross-examination. Under General Statutes Section 54-861, evidence of the sexual history of a sexual assault victim is now admissible only in clearly and narrowly defined circumstances established in a separate hearing. The defendant urges us to hold that the policy represented by that statute is as applicable to defendants as it is to complaining witnesses. In either case, he maintains, the prejudicial effect of evidence of prior sexual conduct, in the absence of special circumstances, far outweighs its probative value.

The defendant questions the admissibility of evidence concerning his prior activities at the Southbury bar and his prior visits to the condominium with other women whom he had met at that bar. Although the defendant objected at trial to the admission of this testimony, he did not then advance the reasoning upon which he now relies. In the main, his objections were devoid of any specific grounds. On the one occasion when a special objection was taken, the defendant's proferred grounds were that the challenged question was beyond the scope of cross-examination and argumentative. In response to that claim, the trial court noted that the evidence was admissible because it was relevant to the defendant's credibility, motive and intent. . . .

On this record, it would be improper to find error. We recognize that the defendant's argument has much to commend it; especially in light of the recent enactment of General Statutes Section 54–86f. . . . We therefore agree that defendants, like sex crime victims, should be shielded from unnecessarily prejudicial evidence of their prior sexual conduct. Appellate review of evidentiary rulings of the trial court is, however, limited to the specific legal issue raised by the objection of trial counsel. . . . The purpose of requiring trial counsel to object properly is not merely formal but serves the important function of alerting the trial court to error while there is time to correct it without ordering a retrial. . . . In the absence of an objection in the trial court on the grounds of prejudice, we find no error in the admission of the challenged evidence. . . .

STATE V. SNIDER

Court of Appeal of Iowa, 1991.
479 N.W.2d 622.

[In this case the Iowa Court of Appeals considers whether there is sufficient evidence to support the defendant's conviction for false imprisonment.]

SACKETT, Judge.

. . . Iowa Code section 710.7 (1989), False Imprisonment, states:

> A person commits false imprisonment when, having no reasonable belief that the person has any right or authority to do so, the person intentionally confines another against the other's will. A person is confined when the person's freedom to move about is substantially restricted by force, threat or deception.

The facts, taking the evidence in light most favorable to the verdict, are the defendant had been drinking for a considerable period in a bar where the victim worked as a bartender. The defendant and the victim were the last people in the bar when the victim told the defendant her boyfriend was coming. She asked the defendant to finish his drink so she could close the bar. The defendant went behind the bar, grabbed the victim by the arms, took her from behind the bar and pushed her about ten feet to a pool table. Once at the pool table, he pushed her backward against the table and held her against her will for no more than fifteen minutes. He then left the bar. Her boyfriend arrived two minutes later and called the police. The defendant was arrested.

The essential elements of false imprisonment are (1) detention or restraint against one's will, and (2) the unlawfulness of such detention or restraint. . . .

The term *confines or removes* in defining kidnapping under section 710.1 requires no minimum period of confinement or distance of removal, but does require more than the confinement or removal that is an inherent incident of commission of the crime. . . .

Section 710.7 specifies a person is confined when the person's freedom to move about is substantially restricted. The words *substantially restricted* do not appear in the kidnapping statute. . . .

We first look to whether the period of confinement or distance of removal exceeded that which would normally be incidental to an assault. . . . To do so, we assess whether the confinement or removal was significantly independent from the assault because it either (1) substantially increased the risk of harm to the victim, (2) lessened the risk of detection, or (3) significantly facilitated the defendant's escape following the assault.

Holding the victim against the pool table did not lessen defendant's risk of detection or facilitate his escape. The defendant had been at the bar for some time. He was known by the victim. The bar area where the victim was held was open to the public. The victim had told the defendant her boyfriend was coming to help her close up. Consequently, the longer the defendant stayed in the bar and held the victim down, the more likely he would be detected.

A pivotal question is whether holding the victim against the pool table substantially increased her risk of harm. The victim was harmed by the assault. The defendant was convicted of assault. He has not appealed that conviction. The State has the burden to show the confinement or movement was not merely incidental to the assault. . . . In *[State v.] Rich,* 305 N.W.2d at 745, the court determined a defendant's movement of a victim a short distance from a mall into a restroom was not in and of itself sufficient confinement or removal within the meaning of Iowa Code section 710.1. The factors that raised the defendant's actions to a removal and confinement in Rich, are not present here. The facts of this case do not show the victim's freedom was substantially restricted. We reverse the conviction for false imprisonment.

REVERSED AND DISMISSED.

All judges concur except HABHAB and DONIELSON, JJ., who dissent.

HABHAB, Judge (dissenting).

I respectfully dissent from the majority's reversal and dismissal of Snider's conviction for false imprisonment. I believe the evidence was sufficient to generate a jury question on the issue. . . .

Forcible confinement for almost fifteen minutes is not merely incidental to the initial assault. Additionally, the facts show the confinement was separate from the assault. . . . The confinement itself was substantial. . . . Unlike the majority, I do not find the confinement against the victim's will merged into the assault charge. I believe both offenses were separate.

The evidence supports submission of both assault and false imprisonment charges to the jury. I would find the trial court did not err in denying the motion for directed verdict on the false imprisonment charge.

I would affirm.

DONIELSON, J., joins this dissent.

CHAPTER 7

CRIMES AGAINST PROPERTY AND HABITATION

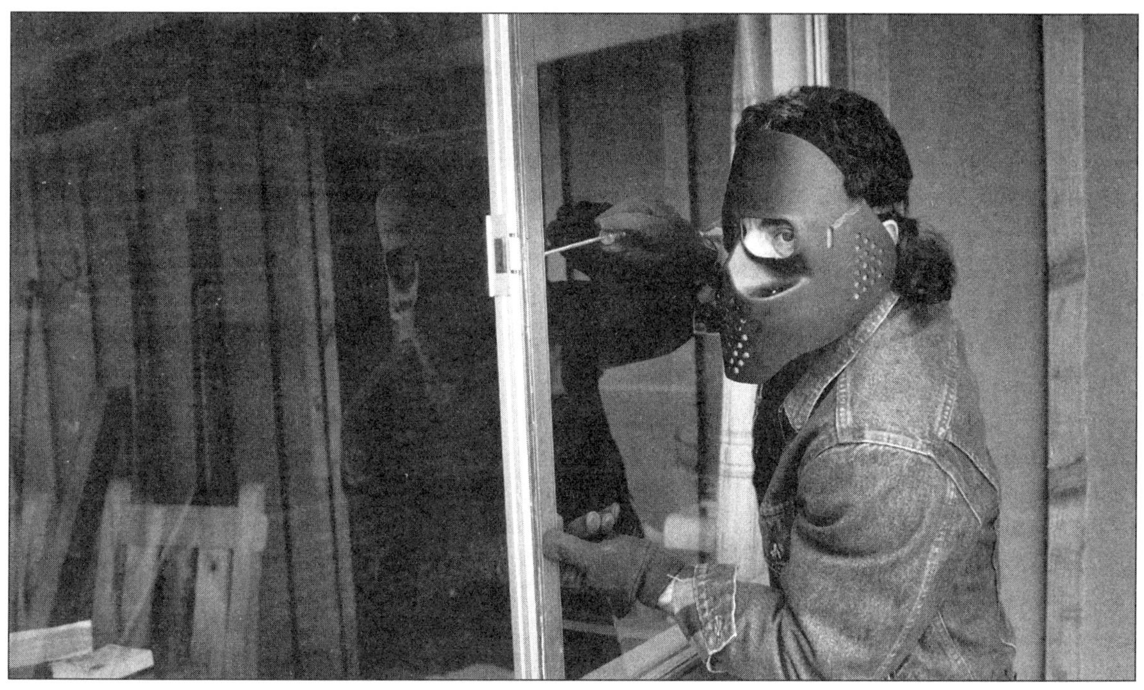

CHAPTER OUTLINE

Introduction
The Common-Law Background
The Basic Common-Law Property Offenses Dealing with Theft
The Modern Approach to Theft Offenses
The Offense of Robbery
Forgery and Uttering a Forged Instrument
Worthless Checks; Credit Card Fraud
Habitation Offenses
Malicious Mischief
Extortion
Defenses to Crimes Involving Property
Conclusion

Cases

State v. Richard
Jones v. Commonwealth
State v. Gomez
State v. Feldt
Fox v. State
State v. Tonnisen

INTRODUCTION

Private property is a basic tenet of American law. In the early history of the new America, property interests beyond raw land were often meager, consisting primarily of those possessions necessary for survival. Dwellings for most people were modest. At that time, enforcement of the law was largely dependent on "self-help." As the new nation developed, property interests became a vital part of the American economy, and professional law enforcement became the rule and not the exception. The public law recognized the need to deter people from infringing on the property interests of others and to punish transgressors. In today's affluent society and with the rapid technological advances of the past few decades, crimes against property have assumed even greater significance. In this chapter we examine the background of basic common-law property and habitation offenses and provide a sampling of the present-day statutory crimes in this area.

THE COMMON-LAW BACKGROUND

When the common law emerged, England was an agrarian country with relatively little commercial activity. Possession of private property was an important concept; but beyond the right to occupy a dwelling, property interests of most people consisted largely of what the law refers to as "tangible" property (i.e., such things as animals, cooking implements, and tools). The "intangible" property interests that are often referred to legally as "choses in action" (e.g., stocks, bonds, notes, and other evidences of wealth of such great economic importance in contemporary society), were either nonexistent or of little significance.

The common-law offenses involving property reflect the environment in which they matured. It was a very serious offense for someone to permanently deprive another of the possession of personal property, whether through stealth or through force, violence, or intimidation. Thus larceny and robbery were felonies, yet it was of far less consequence to cheat someone by the use of false tokens or false weights and measures. When it came to such breaches of ethics as misrepresentations and violations of trust, the common law generally left victims to their civil remedies. This view gave rise to such early maxims as *caveat emptor,* meaning "let the buyer beware." Since commercial transactions were not a major concern, forgery remained a misdemeanor. Likewise, extortion and malicious mischief were also misdemeanors, because the conduct involved in these offenses did not qualify for the severe punishment meted out for felonies. Finally, offenses concerning the rights of landholders were dealt with largely through the civil law.

THE BASIC COMMON-LAW PROPERTY OFFENSES DEALING WITH THEFT

The early common law recognized two offenses dealing with theft: larceny and receiving stolen property. The theft offenses of "false pretenses" and embezzlement were created by statutes passed by the English Parliament.

Larceny

The basic common-law offense against infringement of another's personal property was larceny, the crime from which all other property offenses developed. Larceny was a felony that consisted of (1) the wrongful taking and carrying away of (2) the personal property of another (3) with the intent to permanently deprive the other person of the property. *State v. Griffin,* 79 S.E.2d 230 (N.C. 1953). Many terms used in reference to larceny are not commonly used today. The taking was called the "caption," the carrying away, the "asportation," and the personal property had to have a "corporeal" (i.e., a physical) existence. The wrongful act of taking was described as a "trespass," while the intent to permanently deprive the victim of the property was known as the *"animus furundi."*

To constitute common-law larceny, the taking had to be a deprivation of the owner's or possessor's interest in personal property. Real estate and the property attached to it were not subject to larceny; neither were trees nor crops wrongfully severed from the land. But, if the owner of property had already severed crops and a thief carried them away, it was larceny because the thief was carrying away personal property rather than merely infringing on the owner's real property. *State v. Collins,* 199 S.E. 303 (S.C. 1938).

These distinctions are difficult to appreciate today, but they were significant in the development of the common law, where wrongs concerning a person's land gave rise to chiefly civil, as opposed to criminal, remedies. Also, at common law, anyone wrongfully deprived of possession of personal property was entitled to recover damages based on the tort (civil wrong) of conversion. Thus, there was overlap between the crime of larceny and the tort of conversion.

As the common law developed, personal property consisted largely of tools, household items, and domestic animals. Items such as promissory notes were not subject to larceny because they represented intangible legal rights; coins and bills were, because they had a physical existence.

A taking by a person who had a lawful right to possession was not larceny. As we will discuss later, this led Parliament to enact the crime of embezzlement. Since the property had to be taken from another, a co-owner or partner did not commit larceny by taking jointly owned property. *State v. Kusnick,* 15 N.E. 481 (Ohio 1888). Nor did a spouse commit larceny by taking the other spouse's property, because at common law spouses were considered one. *State v. Phillips,* 97 N.E. 976 (Ohio 1912).

To find an accused guilty of larceny, it was necessary to prove that the taker carried the property away. This was required to show termination of the owner's right of possession and possession by the wrongdoer. *Driggers v. State,* 118 So. 20 (Fla. 1928). This element was usually satisfied by even a slight removal of the property. *State v. Williams,* 97 S.W. 562 (Mo. 1906). It was also essential to prove the taker's intent to permanently deprive the owner of the property. See *Hubbard v. State,* 41 So.2d 1 (Miss. 1949). A person could not be convicted for just borrowing or using property under a reasonable belief of a right of possession. Consequently, a man who temporarily took another's horse would not be guilty of larceny because there was no intent to permanently deprive the owner of the horse. See *In re Mutchler,* 40 P. 283 (Kan. 1895). Furthermore, had a man taken a horse that reasonably appeared to be the taker's own, the taker would likely have been acting under a *bona fide* mistake of fact, hence not guilty of larceny. Yet, a person who secured possession of goods through trickery could be found guilty of larceny if there was proof that the trickster intended to deprive the owner of the goods. *Murchison v. State,* 26 So.2d 622 (Ala. App. 1946).

Receiving Stolen Property

The common-law offense of receiving stolen property was a misdemeanor consisting of knowingly receiving possession and control of personal property belonging to another with the intent to permanently deprive the owner of possession of such property. See *Engster v. State,* 10 N.W. 453 (Neb. 1881). In contrast, the crime of larceny was a common-law felony, except where property of a very minor value was involved. *People v. Burke,* 145 N.E. 164 (Ill. 1924).

False Pretenses and Embezzlement

Many technical and often subtle distinctions developed in the common-law crime of larceny. Perhaps one reason for this was the reluctance of courts to find a thief guilty of larceny since the penalty at early common law was death. As commerce became more significant in England, the crime of larceny was not adequate either to deal with those who obtained financial advantage through false pretenses, or to deter or punish servants who fraudulently appropriated property that rightfully came into their possession. Consequently, by the late 1700s, the English Parliament created two supplemental misdemeanor offenses:

CASE IN POINT

RECEIVING STOLEN PROPERTY: SUFFICIENT EVIDENCE TO CONVICT

Defendant Lynn Belt was convicted of receiving stolen property in violation of Utah Code Ann. 76–6–408(1) (Supp. 1989), which makes it a crime for a person to receive property of another "knowing that it has been stolen or believing that it probably has been stolen. . . . with a purpose to deprive the owner thereof." Belt appealed, contending the evidence was legally insufficient to support his conviction.

The evidence revealed the defendant purchased videocassette recorders from Sgt. Illsley of the Metro Major Felony Unit during an undercover operation involving purchase and sale of stolen property. Defendant met Illsley at an empty parking lot, where Illsley offered the new recorders to the defendant at a very low price, explaining that the store name and serial numbers had been cut off. Defendant replied, "I don't want to hear about the serial number or store names—just do our business." Illsley testified that at one point the defendant said, "I wish you wouldn't cut the serial numbers off. That makes it look hot." The Court of Appeals of Utah held that the evidence was sufficient for the jury to have found that the defendant believed the goods he purchased were stolen and affirmed Belt's conviction.

State v. Belt, 780 P.2d 1271 (Utah App. 1989).

false pretenses and embezzlement. The offense of false pretenses came into being in 1757, 30 Geo. 2, ch. 24, before the American Revolution. The offense thereby became a part of the common law of those states that adopted it with the statutory modifications made by Parliament prior to the American Revolution. See *State v. McMahon,* 140 A. 359 (R.I. 1928). Embezzlement, on the other hand, did not become a statutory crime until 1799, 39 Geo. 3, ch. 85, too late to become part of the common law adopted by the new American states. By subsequent enactments, Parliament broadened the scope of embezzlement.

False pretenses (actually "obtaining property by false pretenses") was usually directed at a seller who obtained someone else's property by (1) the accused obtaining wares or merchandise of another (2) by false pretenses and (3) with the intent to cheat or defraud the other person. *State v. Tower,* 251 P. 401 (Kan. 1926). Parliament's enactment of the offense of false pretenses during the industrial revolution represented an important development in the English law of crimes. Since false pretenses became an offense just prior to the American Revolution, few English decisions became a part of the common law adopted by the new American states. Yet the English law in this area influenced American legislation and judicial decisions.

In contrast to larceny, embezzlement occurred where an accused who had lawful possession of another's property (e.g., a servant or employee) wrongfully appropriated the property. *Murchison v. State,* 26 So.2d 622 (Ala. App. 1946). A series of enactments by the English Parliament brought not only servants and employees, but also brokers, bankers, lawyers, and trustees within the scope of embezzlement. Thus, an embezzlement occurred when someone occupying a position of trust converted another's property to his or her own use, *State v. Griffin,* 79 S.E.2d 230 (N.C. 1953), whereas larceny required proof of a wrongful taking and carrying away of the personal property of another. Nevertheless, to convict a defendant of embezzlement, it was necessary to prove that the accused intended to defraud the victim. *People v. Hurst,* 28 N.W. 838 (Mich. 1886).

THE MODERN APPROACH TO THEFT OFFENSES

A review of the various technical distinctions that developed in the common-law offenses of larceny, receiving stolen property, false pretenses, and the early statutory offense of embezzlement makes it obvious that significant reforms were needed. A redefinition of these basic property offenses was required to cope with the various aspects of theft in American society. Modern theft ranges from the theft of vehicles, shoplifting, and looting to such sophisticated forms of theft as credit card frauds, various scams, theft of trade secrets, and computer-related crimes. Indeed, theft is a nationwide problem that must be dealt with by both state and federal authorities.

Federal Approaches

Congress has enacted a series of statutes comprehensively proscribing theft and embezzlement. The first, 18 U.S.C.A. § 641, provides:

CASE IN POINT

LARCENY COMMITTED THROUGH A PHONY NIGHT-DEPOSIT BOX

A Massachusetts jury convicted Brian Donovan and Robert Grant of larceny. Evidence introduced at trial showed that they had constructed a phony night-deposit box and attached it to the wall of a bank building. The box was constructed of heavy-gauge steel just like a real depository. Seven depositors lost an estimated $37,000 by making deposits to the phony box. Although the phony box was never recovered, a witness testified that he overheard defendants in a bar talking about the phony deposit box as "a helluva'n idea." Another witness stated that Grant had admitted to her that he had robbed a bank using a phony deposit box. On appeal, the Massachusetts Supreme Court rejected defendants' contentions that certain testimony had been improperly admitted into evidence and that the evidence produced at trial was legally insufficient to prove the crime of larceny.

Commonwealth v. Donovan, 478 N.E.2d 727 (Mass. 1985).

> Whoever embezzles, steals, purloins, or knowingly converts to his use or the use of another, or without authority, sells, conveys or disposes of any record, voucher, money, or thing of value of the United States or any department or agency thereof, or any property made or being made under contract for the United States or any department or agency thereof; or
>
> Whoever receives, conceals, or retains the same with intent to convert it to his use or gain, knowing it to have been embezzled, stolen, purloined or converted;
>
> Shall be fined. . . .

The purpose of 18 U.S.C.A. § 641 is to place in one part of the criminal code crimes so kindred as to belong in one category. The Supreme Court has said that despite the failure of Congress to have expressly included the common-law intent requirement for larceny, Section 641 should not be construed to eliminate that intent requirement from the statute. The statute has been held to apply not only to larceny and embezzlement but also to all instances in which a person may obtain wrongful advantage from another's property. *Morissette v. United States*, 342 U.S. 246, 72 S. Ct. 240, 96 L.Ed. 288 (1952). Another federal statute provides penalties for embezzling or unlawfully taking the contents of any vehicle moving in interstate commerce. 18 U.S.C.A. § 659. Federal appellate courts have characterized the intent requirements under this statute as the intent to appropriate or convert the property of the owner. Furthermore, the federal appellate courts have said that a simultaneous intent to return the property or make restitution does not make the offense any less embezzlement. See, for example, *United States v. Waronek*, 582 F.2d 1158 (7th Cir. 1978).

A variety of other federal statutes concern embezzlement and theft by public officers or employees of the United States and custodians of federal funds, bank examiners, and bank officers and employees. See 18 U.S.C.A. §§ 641–665.

State Approaches

All states have enacted statutes expanding the common-law concept of larceny to include all types of tangible and intangible property. Historically, the states maintained numerous statutes basically adopting the concepts of common-law larceny, receiving stolen property, false pretenses, and embezzlement. As new problems developed, legislative bodies attempted to fill in the gaps by creating new offenses. As a result, numerous statutory offenses proscribing various forms of stealing and dishonest dealings were enacted. Often these statutes have been confusing; in some instances, they have been contradictory.

In recent years many states have replaced their various statutes with a consolidated theft statute that proscribes stealing in very broad terms. These new statutes make it unlawful for a person to commit any of the common-law offenses mentioned as well as other crimes, and they scale penalties based on the amount and character of the property stolen.

Florida, for example, passed the Florida Anti-Fencing Act in 1977. Despite its narrow title, the new act defines theft as including all of the common-law offenses, a number of former statutory offenses, possession of property with altered or removed identifying features, and dealing in stolen property (i.e., fencing). West's Fla. Stat. Ann. § 812.012–037. The law says that:

> A person commits theft if he knowingly obtains or uses, or endeavors to obtain or to use, the property of another with intent to, either temporarily or permanently:
> (a) Deprive the other person of a right to the property or a benefit therefrom.
> (b) Appropriate the property to his own use or to the use of any person not entitled thereto. West's Fla. Stat. Ann. § 812.014(1).

Under the simplified, yet comprehensive, theft statute, the phrase "obtains or uses" replaces the old common-law requirements of "taking and carrying away" with any manner of (a) taking or exercising control over property; (b) making any unauthorized use, disposition, or transfer of property; (c) obtaining property by fraud, willful misrepresentation of a future act, or false promise; (d) by conduct previously known as stealing, larceny, purloining, abstracting, embezzlement, misapplication, misappropriation, conversion, obtaining money or property by false pretense, fraud, or deception; or (e) other conduct similar in nature. West's Fla. Stat. Ann. § 812.012 (2). "Property of another" is generally construed to mean that the victim either owned or had a right to custody of the property taken. See *R. C. v. State,* 481 So.2d 14 (Fla. App. 1985).

As in other modern statutes, the Florida statute defining theft includes tangible as well as intangible property. The seriousness of the offense is categorized by the value or type of property stolen. Grand theft in the first degree, the most serious felony, involves stealing property valued at $100,000 or more, while grand theft in the second degree, a somewhat less serious felony, involves theft of property valued at $20,000 or more, but less than $100,000. It is grand theft of the third degree and a lesser felony if the property stolen is either valued at $300 or more, but less than $20,000 or if the property falls into any of the following classes: a will, codicil, or other testamentary instrument; a firearm; a motor vehicle; livestock; a fire extinguisher; 2,000 pieces or more of citrus fruit; or property taken from an identified construction site. West's Fla. Stat. Ann. §

812.014 (2)(a)(b)(c). Note the emphasis placed not only on the value of items stolen and their character but also on the importance of local economic interests. Except for the specified articles, theft of property having a value under $300 is petit theft, a misdemeanor, but a person who commits petit theft and who has previously been convicted two or more times commits a felony of the third degree. West's Fla. Stat. Ann. § 812.014(2)(d). West's Fla. Stat. Ann. § 812.014(2)(d).

Theft remains a specific-intent crime, but like many of the newer theft statutes, the Florida statute simply refers to "the intent to deprive." According to the Florida Supreme Court, this simply means the "intent to steal" and *not* the intent to *permanently* deprive the owner of the property. *State v. Dunmann*, 427 So. 2d 166 (Fla. 1983). In *Dunmann*, the court also held that the enactment of the omnibus theft statute (§ 812.012 *et seq.*) by implication repealed Florida's so-called joyriding statute. Additionally, the court has ruled that because the definition of theft contained in this statute includes an *endeavor* to commit theft, the crime is fully proved when an attempt, along with the requisite intent, is established. *State v. Sykes*, 434 So.2d 325 (Fla. 1983) (see Chapter 5).

Computer Crime: New Offenses to Cope with High-Tech Crime

Once the use of computers became common in today's society, they soon became tools employed by criminals to commit a variety of offenses. Indeed, the pervasiveness of computers poses some unique challenges to law enforcement agencies and prosecutors. Most computer crimes violate laws defining theft, fraud, embezzlement, etc. at the state level and often, mail fraud at the federal level. Nevertheless, starting with Florida in 1978, nearly every state has adopted some form of laws specifically defining computer crimes. These laws define such terms as *access, computer program, computer software, data base, computer hacking, financial instrument,* and other terms used in modern computer parlance, and address such activities as computer manipulation, theft of intellectual property, telecommunications crimes, and software piracy. They also create such offenses as computer fraud, computer trespass, and theft of computer services.

Section 18.2–152.3 of the Virginia Computer Crimes Act provides:

> Any person who uses a computer or computer network without authority and with the intent to:
> 1. Obtain property or services by false pretenses;
> 2. Embezzle or commit larceny; or
> 3. Convert the property of another shall be guilty of the crime of computer fraud.

Depending on the value of property or services actually obtained, the offense is either a felony or a serious misdemeanor. Additional Virginia statutes make computer trespass, invasion of privacy by computer, and theft of computer services offenses.

A Unique Prosecutorial Burden in Theft Offenses

Except where statutorily specified articles are stolen, theft offenses are usually classified as grand or petit theft based on the value of goods stolen. Usually

CASE IN POINT

UNAUTHORIZED ACCESSING A VOICE MAIL BOX VIOLATES A STATE STATUTE PROHIBITING UNLAWFUL USE OF A COMPUTER

Defendant, Andrea M. Gerulis, was convicted in a bench trial of two counts of unlawful use of a computer and two counts of violating a statute that criminalized intentionally obtaining various electronic services "available only for compensation" by deception, unauthorized connection, etc. Defendant was ordered to make restitution. The evidence before the trial court revealed that the defendant deposited and retrieved information from voice mailboxes (VMBs) of a hospital and a telephone message company without authority from either to do so. By altering passwords she thereby prevented authorized users from using their VMBs. The defendant appealed, contending the evidence was insufficient to sustain her convictions.

The appellate court found that VMBs are high speed data processing devices that perform memory functions and therefore are "computers" within the meaning of the statute, and the defendant's disruption of normal use of the VMBs violated the statute. The court then addressed the defendant's convictions for theft of services. The court observed that the prosecution had charged the defendant under a statute that makes it an offense if a person "intentionally obtains services for himself or for another which he knows are available only for compensation." Because the evidence revealed that the VMBs the defendant accessed were provided by the hopsital and message company without charge for their employees, the court found that the defendant's mere intent to obtain free services did not violate that statute. Accordingly, the court affirmed the defendant's convictions for unlawful use of a computer, reversed her convictions for theft of services, and remanded the case to the trial court to modify the restitution order imposed as defendant's sentence.

Commonwaelth v. Gerulis, 616 A.2d 686 (Pa. Super. 1992).

grand theft is a felony. Therefore, the prosecution must establish the value of goods or services stolen. The determining factor is generally the market value at the time and in the locality of the theft. *State v. Kimbel,* 620 P.2d 515 (Utah 1980). This may be shown by proof of the original market cost, the manner in which the property stolen has been used, and its general condition and quality. *Negron v. State,* 306 So.2d 104 (Fla. 1974). Judges customarily instruct juries that if the value of the property cannot be ascertained, they must find the value to be less than that required for grand theft. But consider the theft of a credit card. Holders of these cards usually have set credit limits available to them on proper signature. Therefore, a credit card has no market value in lawful channels for a third person. In *Miller v. People,* 566 P.2d 1059 (Colo. 1977), the Colorado Supreme Court held that the amount that could be purchased on the stolen card in the "illegitimate" market could be considered in determining whether a defendant was guilty of felony theft.

In any event, proof of value is very important in a theft case because it can often mean the difference between the defendant being convicted of a misdemeanor or a felony, or even of a felony of various degrees.

The Offense of Robbery

At common law, robbery was a felony that consisted of (1) a taking of another's personal property of value (2) from the other person's possession or presence (3) by force or placing the person in fear and (4) with the intent to permanently deprive the other person of that property. *Houston v. Commonwealth,* 12 S.E. 385 (Va. 1890). In reality, robbery was an aggravated form of larceny where the taking was accomplished by force or threats of force with the same specific-intent requirement as in common-law larceny. To constitute robbery, the violence or intimidation had to overcome the victim's resistance and precede or accompany the actual taking of property. *State v. Parker,* 170 S.W. 1121 (Mo. 1914). Property in the victim's dwelling or vicinity was regarded as being in the victim's possession. See *Hill v. State,* 60 N.W. 916 (Neb. 1894). To illustrate a significant difference between larceny and robbery: A person who spirited a man's wallet from his pocket would be guilty of larceny, but if the victim resisted and the thief took the wallet by force or violence, the offense constituted robbery.

Statutory Approaches to Robbery

In some respects robbery is an offense against the person, because it usually involves an assault or battery. See, for example, *State v. Shoemake,* 618 P.2d 1201 (Kan. 1980). Yet it involves a taking of property also and is generally classified as an offense against property.

A federal statute makes it an offense to take, or attempt to take, by force and violence or intimidation from the person or presence of another, any property or money belonging to or in the care of a bank, credit union, or savings and loan association. 18 U.S.C.A. § 2113(a).

Federal jurisdiction is established where the bank is a federally chartered institution or where its deposits are federally insured. *United States v. Harris,* 530 F.2d 576 (4th Cir. 1976). The statutory offense varies from the common-law crime of robbery in that the government need only establish the defendant's general intent. *United States v. Klare,* 545 F.2d 93 (9th Cir. 1976), *cert. denied,* 431 U.S. 905, 97 S. Ct. 1699, 52 L.Ed.2d 390 (1977).

Robbery is an offense in every state. Many states have enacted statutes simply defining it as did the common law, a practice sometimes referred to as codifying the common law. Other states classify robbery according to degree, with the seriousness of the offense usually based on whether the assailant is armed, the degree of force used, and, in some instances, on the vulnerability of the victim. The value of the property taken does not usually affect the degree of the crime of robbery, as it does that of theft.

The Colorado Criminal Code provides a good illustration of classification of robbery offenses: "A person who knowingly takes anything of value from the person or presence of another by the use of force, threats, or intimidation commits robbery." West's Colo. Rev. Stat. Ann. § 18–4–301(1). This is "simple robbery" in contrast to the statutory offense of "aggravated robbery." The Colorado statute further provides:

> (1) A person who commits robbery is guilty of aggravated robbery if during the act of robbery or immediate flight therefrom:
> (a) He is armed with a deadly weapon with intent, if resisted, to kill, maim, or wound the person robbed or any other person; or
> (b) He knowingly wounds or strikes the person robbed or any other person with a deadly weapon or by the use of force, threats, or intimidation with a deadly weapon knowingly puts the person robbed or any other person in reasonable fear of death or bodily injury; or
> (c) He has present a confederate, aiding or abetting the perpetration of the robbery, armed with a deadly weapon, with the intent, either on the part of the defendant or confederate, if resistance is offered, to kill, maim, or wound the person robbed or any other person, or by the use of force, threats, or intimidation puts the person robbed or any other person in reasonable fear of death or bodily injury. West's Colo. Rev. Stat. Ann. § 18–4–302.

Under Colorado law, robbery of the elderly or handicapped is punishable the same as the offense of aggravated robbery. West's Colo. Rev. Stat. Ann. § 18–4–304.

The Colorado Supreme Court has said that the gist of the crime of robbery under the Colorado statutes is "the putting in fear and taking of property of another by force or intimidation." *People v. Small,* 493 P.2d 15 (Colo. 1972). Aggravated robbery is distinguished from simple robbery by the fact that an accomplice or confederate is armed with a dangerous weapon with intent, if resisted, to maim, wound, or kill. The court said that simple and aggravated robbery are but two degrees of the same offense. *Atwood v. People,* 489 P.2d 1305 (Colo. 1971). The intent the prosecution is required to prove is simply the perpetrator's intent to force the victim to give up something of value. *People v. Bridges,* 612 P.2d 1110 (Colo. 1980). Property is taken from the "presence of another" under Colorado law when it is so within the victim's reach, inspection, or observation that he or she would be able to retain control over the property but for the force, threats, or intimidation directed by the perpetrator. *People v. Bartowsheski,* 661 P.2d 235 (Colo. 1983).

The Temporal Relationship of Force to the Taking

Is it essential that the element of violence or intimidation occur before or at the same time as the taking of the victim's property? State appellate courts are divided on this issue, often based on the specific statutory language. Note that the Colorado statute in addressing aggravated robbery includes the language "if during the act of robbery or immediate flight therefrom." The Colorado Supreme Court has said that force used in robbery need not occur simultaneously with the taking. *People v. Bartowsheski,* 661 P.2d 235 (Colo. 1983). Other courts have agreed. In *Hermann v. State,* 123 So.2d 846 (Miss. 1960), a defendant, after stealthily obtaining gasoline, made a getaway from a filling station by pointing a deadly weapon at the attendant. The attendant stuck his hand through the window of the vehicle but was pushed away by the offender. The Mississippi Supreme Court held that this act of pushing the victim away constituted the force element of robbery. Again, in *People v. Kennedy*, 294 N.E.2d 788 (Ill. App. 1973), the court held that while the taking may be without force, the offense is robbery if the departure with the property is accomplished by the use of force.

In 1986, the Florida Supreme Court held that defendants who used force while fleeing a retail store after committing theft in the store could not be convicted of robbery. The court followed the traditional common-law view that the use of force must occur before or at the same time as the taking of property. *Royal v. State*, 490 So.2d 44 (Fla. 1986). The state legislature promptly amended the statutory definition of robbery to add that "an act shall be deemed in the course of committing the robbery *if it occurs in an attempt to commit robbery or in flight after the attempt or commission.*" [emphasis added] West's Fla.Stat. Ann. § 812.13(3)(b).

A New Statutory Offense: Carjacking

Recognizing the serious threat that forcible auto theft poses to persons and their motor vehicles, and after a nationwide spree of "carjacking," Congress enacted

CASE IN POINT

ARMED ROBBERY: IS AN UNLOADED GUN A "DANGEROUS WEAPON"?

On the morning of July 26, 1984, Lamont Julius McLaughlin and a companion, both wearing masks, entered a bank in Baltimore. McLaughlin brandished a handgun and told those in the bank to put up their hands and not to move. While McLaughlin held the gun, his companion leaped over the counter and stuffed several thousand dollars into a brown paper bag. Police officers were waiting outside and promptly arrested the pair. It was then determined that McLaughlin's gun was not loaded.

McLaughlin was found guilty in federal court of bank robbery "by the use of a dangerous weapon." 18 U.S.C.A. § 2113(d). On appeal, McLaughlin argued that his unloaded gun did not qualify as a "dangerous weapon" under the federal bank robbery statute. The United States Supreme Court rejected the argument and upheld McLaughlin's conviction. The court said:

> Three reasons, each independently sufficient, support the conclusion that an unloaded gun is a "dangerous weapon." First, a gun is an article that is typically and characteristically dangerous; the use for which it is manufactured and sold is a dangerous one, and the law reasonably may presume that such an article is always dangerous even though it may not be armed at a particular time or place. In addition, the display of a gun instills fear in the average citizen; as a consequence, it creates an immediate danger that a violent response will ensue. Finally, a gun can cause harm when used as a bludgeon. 476 U.S. at 18.

McLaughlin v. United States, 476 U.S. 16, 106 S. Ct. 1677, 90 L.Ed.2d 15 (1986).

the Anti-Car Theft Act of 1992. Included in the new law is a section (to be codified as 18 U.S.C.A. § 2119) imposing severe penalties for anyone who "takes a motor vehicle that has been transported, shipped, or received in interstate or foreign commerce from the person or presence of another by force and violence or by intimidation, or attempt to do so."

The first trial under the new federal law was held in February, 1993, in the United States District Court in Orlando, Florida. Three young males were accused of stealing two vehicles and committing execution-style slayings of two young men and injuring a third in Central Florida in November 1992. The prosecution argued that the defendants committed the carjacking offense by stealing a car involved in interstate commerce, doing it by force, and using a firearm. Defense lawyers, on the other hand, argued that while the defendants may be guilty of some offenses under state law, they were not guilty of violating the new federal law on armed carjacking involving violence. A fourth defendant pleaded guilty and testified against the other three. After deliberating for six hours, a jury found the defendants guilty of conspiracy, two counts of armed carjacking involving death, and two counts of using a firearm during a felony. In April 1993, the three defendants were sentenced to life terms, plus 25 years. After their sentences were imposed in federal court, state prosecutors said they would prosecute the three for first-degree murder and seek the death penalty.

FORGERY AND UTTERING A FORGED INSTRUMENT

Blackstone defined common-law forgery as "the fraudulent making or alteration of a writing to the prejudice of another man's right." *State v. Murphy*, 24 A. 473 (R.I. 1892). The early cases reveal that such writings as wills, receipts, and physicians' certificates were subject to forgery. To convict a defendant of forgery under common law, it was essential to establish the accused's intent to defraud. *Levinson v. United States*, 47 F.2d 470 (6th Cir. 1931). Uttering a forged instrument was also a common-law offense, but one separate and distinct from forgery. *Utter*, a term of art synonymous with publishing, serves to distinguish the actual forgery from the act of passing a forged instrument to someone. See *State v. Singh*, 419 P.2d 403 (Ariz. App. 1966). As an indication of the lesser importance of commercial matters in early English society, the common law classified both forgery and uttering a forged instrument as misdemeanors. *State v. Murphy*, 24 A. 473 (R.I. 1892).

Statutory Expansion of Forgery Offenses

Unlike the common law, federal and state statutes generally classify forgery as a felony. Reflecting the importance of written and printed documentation in our modern economy, statutes in all American jurisdictions have extended the crime of forgery to almost every type of public or private legal instrument.

Federal Statutes. Under Federal law "[w]hoever, with intent to defraud, falsely makes, forges, counterfeits, or alters any obligation or other security of the United States" commits the crime of forgery. 18 U.S.C.A. § 471. Federal courts have stated that the manifest purpose of these laws is to protect all currency and obligations of the United States, *United States v. LeMon*, 622 F.2d 1022 (10th Cir. 1980), and that the prosecution must prove not only the passing, but also the defendant's "intent to pass the bad money." *United States v. Lorenzo*, 570 F.2d 294, 299 (9th Cir. 1978).

A number of other federal statutes relate to forgery and the counterfeiting of stamps, money orders, public records, and court documents. See 18 U.S.C.A. §§ 472–509. Additionally, many prosecutions are brought under 18 U.S.C.A. § 495, which makes it unlawful to forge and utter forged United States Treasury checks. To convict someone under this statute, the government must establish the defendant's specific fraudulent intent. *United States v. Sullivan*, 406 F.2d 180 (2d Cir. 1969).

State Statutes. Most states have substantially adopted the common-law definition of forgery, but have expanded the number of instruments that can be forged to include a lengthy list of public and private documents. For example, the Arizona Criminal Code makes forgery a felony and provides that

> A. A person commits forgery if, with intent to defraud, such person:
> 1. Falsely makes, completes or alters a written instrument; or
> 2. Knowingly possesses a forged instrument; or
> 3. Offers or presents, whether accepted or not, a forged instrument or one which contains false information.
>
> Ariz. Rev. Stat. § 13–2002.

Under this section, the offenses of forgery and uttering have been coupled under the term *forgery*, but the distinction as separate offenses must still be observed since the elements of the offenses are not the same and the proof required may differ. *State v. Reyes*, 458 P.2d 960 (Ariz. 1969). Thus under Arizona law the crime of forgery has three elements: (1) signing the name of another person; (2) intending to defraud; and (3) knowing that there is no authority to sign. *State v. Nettz*, 560 P.2d 814 (Ariz. App. 1977). Uttering, on the other hand, is the passing or publishing of a false, altered, or counterfeited paper or document. *State v. Reyes*, 458 P.2d 960 (Ariz. 1969). Proof of the intent to defraud is essential to obtain a conviction of forgery, *State v. Maxwell*, 445 P.2d 837 (Ariz. 1968), but such intent may be inferred from circumstances in which the false instrument is executed or issued. *State v. Gomez*, 553 P.2d 1233 (Ariz. App. 1976). Note that based on the wording of the statute proscribing forgery, a conviction of "attempt to pass" is a conviction of forgery, not of an attempt. *Ponds v. State*, 438 P.2d 423 (Ariz. App. 1968) (see Chapter 5).

Common Examples of Forgery and Uttering a Forged Instrument. Among the more common examples of forgery in our contemporary society are

- Signing another's name to an application for a driver's license
- Printing bogus tickets to a concert or sports event
- Signing another's name to a check on his or her bank account without authority
- Altering the amount of a check or note
- Signing another's name without authority to a certificate transferring shares of stock

- Signing a deed transferring someone's real estate
- Making an unauthorized change in the legal description of property being conveyed under a deed
- Altering the grades or credits on a college transcript

Uttering a forged instrument commonly occurs when a person knowingly delivers a forged check to someone in exchange for cash or merchandise, or knowingly sells bogus tickets for an event to others, or submits a deed with forged signatures for official recording.

Falsification of computerized records such as college credits and financial records poses new challenges to laws proscribing forgery. The increasing use of computers gives rise to the need for new applications of statutes proscribing forgery and uttering a forged instrument.

WORTHLESS CHECKS; CREDIT CARD FRAUD

As commercial banking developed, the passing of "bad checks" became a serious problem. A person who writes a worthless check on his or her bank account does not commit a forgery. In early cases some courts referred to issuance of checks without funds in the bank as use of a "false token." These cases were prosecuted under statutes making it unlawful to use false pretenses to obtain property. See, for example, *People v. Donaldson,* 11 P. 681 (Cal. 1886).

States have now enacted a variety of statutes making it unlawful to issue checks with insufficient funds to cover payment. Earlier statutes often provided that in order to be guilty of false pretenses for issuing a worthless check, a person had to fraudulently obtain goods. This proved to be an impracticable method to control issuance of checks by depositors who misgauged their checking account balances. The widespread use of commercial and personal banking led legislatures to create "worthless check" statutes to cope with the problem. These statutes usually classify such an offense as a misdemeanor, and legislatures have increasingly opted to allow offenders to make restitution of losses caused by worthless checks.

For example, the Texas law that makes issuance of bad checks a misdemeanor stipulates

> (a) A person commits an offense if he issues or passes a check or similar sight order for the payment of money knowing that the issuer does not have sufficient funds in or on deposit with the bank or other drawee for the payment in full of the check or order as well as all other checks or orders outstanding at the time of issuance. Vernon's Tex. Penal Code Ann., § 32.41(a).

The Texas Penal Code presumes the issuer knows that there are insufficient funds if he or she had no account with the bank or other drawee when the check was issued, or if payment is refused by the bank on presentation within thirty days after issue and the person who wrote the check failed to pay the holder in full within ten days after receiving notice of such refusal. Vernon's Tex. Penal Code Ann., § 32.41(b)(1–2). A person charged with an offense under Section 32.41 is permitted to make restitution under certain conditions. Vernon's Tex. Penal Code Ann., § 32.41(e).

CASE IN POINT

Forgery

The state prosecuted defendant Donald E. Hicks for forgery. At trial the evidence revealed that on August 4, 1984, defendant Hicks went to see Edmond Brown to make a payment on a debt. Hicks told Brown that he could pay him $100 on his debt if Brown could cash a two-party check for him. Hicks presented Brown with a check for $349 made out to Hicks on the account of Gott, Young, and Bogle, P.A., a Wichita law firm. The check was signed "Gott Young." The defendant told Brown that the check was a partial payment of a settlement of a claim stemming from an automobile accident. Hicks assured Brown that the check was good and endorsed it over to him. Brown accepted the check and returned $249 to Hicks. When the check was returned by the bank, Brown contacted the law firm. He was told that there was no one by the name of "Gott Young" at the firm, and that the firm had never represented Hicks. He further learned that some twenty-five checks from the firm's petty cash account were missing. Hicks was found guilty by a jury and his conviction was affirmed on appeal.

State v. Hicks, 714 P.2d 105 (Kan. App. 1986).

Credit Card Fraud

A credit card is issued to a named individual to provide its holder with a line of credit so that purchases may conveniently be made on credit. The person to whom the card is issued assumes the obligation to pay for goods or services delivered or rendered to that person or to the authorized bearer of the card. As previously noted, a person who makes a purchase through use of a stolen or otherwise fraudulently obtained credit card may be found guilty of theft under most modern larceny and theft statutes. Credit cards, however, are now in such widespread use that many states have enacted laws creating specific offenses for their improper use.

Pennsylvania has enacted such a statute, which is similar to Section 224.6 of the Model Penal Code:

> Section 4106. Credit cards
> (a) Offense defined—A person commits an offense if he:
> (1) uses a credit card for the purpose of obtaining property or service with knowledge that:
> (i) the card is stolen, forged or fictitious;
> (ii) the card belongs to another person who has not authorized its use;
> (iii) the card has been revoked or canceled; or
> (iv) for any other reason his use of the card is unauthorized by the issuer or the person to whom issued; or
> (2) makes, sells, gives, or otherwise transfers to another, or offers or advertises, or aids and abets any other person to use a credit card with the knowledge or reason to believe that it will be used to obtain property or services without payment of the lawful charges therefor; or

(3) publishes a credit card or code of an existing, canceled, revoked, expired, or nonexistent credit card, or the numbering or coding which is employed in the issuance of credit cards, with knowledge or reason to believe that it will be used to avoid the payment for any property or services. Purdon's Penn. Stat. Ann. § 4106(a).

Section 4106(c) of the above statute makes violation either a third-degree felony, a misdemeanor, or a summary offense, depending on the value of the property or service illegally secured or sought to be secured. Section 4106(d) provides that it is a defense if the actor can prove the intent and ability to meet all obligations to the issuer arising out of his or her use of the credit card.

HABITATION OFFENSES

Two felonies developed at common law reflect the value of privacy and the need to protect the security of a person's dwelling. The offenses of burglary and arson gave credence to the old English saying, "A man's home is his castle." These offenses were created to protect not only the dwelling house but also the buildings within the "curtilage," an enclosed area around the dwelling that typically included the cookhouse and other outbuildings. In England the enclosure had to be by a stone fence or wall; however, this custom has not been established in the United States. *State v. Bugg,* 72 P. 236 (Kan. 1903).

Both burglary and arson became felonies in the United States. Modern statutes have greatly broadened the scope of the common-law crimes of burglary and arson and extended the protection of the criminal law far beyond the traditional concept of offenses against habitation. Nevertheless, to understand their historic development it is helpful to classify them as offenses against habitation.

Burglary at Common Law

According to Blackstone, common-law burglary consisted of (1) breaking and entering of (2) a dwelling of another (3) during the nighttime (4) with intent to commit a felony therein. *State v. Ward,* 86 So. 552 (La. 1920). The "breaking" at common law could be either "actual" or "constructive." An actual breaking could be merely technical such as pushing open a door or opening a window. See *Cooper v. State,* 90 So. 693 (Fla. 1922). An entry gained through fraud or deception was considered a "constructive" breaking. *Commonwealth v. Lowrey,* 32 N.E. 940 (Mass. 1893). Even the slightest entry was deemed sufficient; for instance, a hand, a foot, or even a finger within the dwelling was regarded as a sufficient entry. See *Commonwealth v. Glover,* 111 Mass. 395 (1873). Proof of the defendant's intent to commit a felony was essential: A breaking and entering did not constitute burglary at common law unless the perpetrator had a specific intent to commit a felony (e.g., murder, rape, or larceny); it was not necessary, however, to prove that any felony was committed. *Hayes v. Commonwealth,* 188 S.W. 415 (Ky. 1916). *Dwelling* was defined as the house or place of habitation used by the occupier or member of the family "as a place to sleep in." See *Ex parte Vincent,* 26 Ala. 145

(1855). Finally, to constitute burglary at common law it was essential that the offense be committed at nighttime, generally defined as the period between sunset and sunrise. *Bowser v. State*, 110 A. 854 (Md. 1920).

Statutory Revisions of Burglary

Many states have enacted statutes proscribing breaking and entering, thereby placing a new label on the common-law crime of burglary. At a minimum these statutes expand the offense of burglary beyond dwelling houses and eliminate the requirement that the offense take place in the nighttime. Most retain the common-law requirement that the accused break and enter with intent to commit a felony. Many states, however, have also included the language "or theft." Even where the offense is still labeled burglary, legislatures have made significant changes in the common-law definition. In addition to eliminating the nighttime requirement, they have broadened the offense to include buildings and structures of all types. Today, most criminal codes include vehicles, aircraft, and vessels either in the definition of burglary or by a separate statute. Finally, modern statutes frequently provide that a person who enters a structure with consent, but who remains therein with intent to commit a felony, may be found guilty of burglary notwithstanding an original lawful entry. An example of this would be someone intentionally remaining in a department store intending to commit an offense therein after the store closes for the day.

Michigan law illustrates a modern statutory approach and specifies:

> Any person who shall break and enter with intent to commit any felony, or any larceny therein, any tent, hotel, office, store, shop, warehouse, barn, granary, factory or other building, structure, boat or ship, railroad car or any private apartment in any of such buildings or any unoccupied dwelling house, shall be guilty of a felony. Mich. Comp. Laws Ann. § 750.110.

The Michigan statute states that if the dwelling is occupied, the offender shall be punished more severely. Mich. Comp. Laws Ann. § 750.110. Another Michigan statute makes it an offense for a person to enter without breaking into any of the structures or vehicles enumerated in the breaking and entering statute. Mich. Comp. Laws Ann. § 750.111.

Possession of Burglar's Tools

Michigan, like most states, makes possession of burglar's tools a felony if the possessor has the intent to use the tools for burglarious purposes. Michigan law provides:

> Any person who shall knowingly have in his possession any nitroglycerine, or other explosive, thermite, engine, machine, tool or implement, device, chemical or substance, adapted and designed for cutting or burning through, forcing or breaking open any building, room, vault, safe or other depository, in order to steal therefrom any money or other property, knowing the same to be adapted and designed for the purpose aforesaid, with intent to use or employ the same for the purpose aforesaid, shall be guilty of a felony. Mich. Comp. Laws Ann. § 750.116.

CASE IN POINT

EVIDENCE SUFFICIENT TO ESTABLISH BURGLARY

On the morning of October 18, 1981, Philadelphia police were called to Cramer's Kiddy Shop. Entering the store, they heard footsteps on the roof. They went up to the second floor, where they discovered a two-foot hole in a wall with access to the roof. One of the officers went through the hole and found himself covered with plaster dust. He then observed two males climbing down an exterior wall. One of them was apprehended. His hands were dirty and his clothes were covered with plaster dust. In the alley behind the store, police located several items of children's clothing that had been taken from the store along with a crowbar. Patrick Carpenter, who was apprehended, was found guilty of burglary and other offenses. On appeal, Carpenter argued that the evidence was insufficient to warrant a conviction for burglary. The appellate court rejected the contention and upheld defendant's conviction.

Commonwealth v. Carpenter, 479 A.2d 603 (Pa. Super. 1984).

Many years ago, the Michigan Supreme Court emphasized that to obtain a conviction the state must prove the accused knowingly had possession of burglar's tools, knew the tools could be used for a criminal purpose, and intended to use them for such purpose. *People v. Jefferson,* 126 N.W. 829 (Mich. 1910).

Arson at Common Law

Like burglary, arson was a felony at common law designed to protect the security of the dwelling place. The crime consisted of (1) the willful and malicious burning (2) of a dwelling (3) of another. *State v. Long,* 90 S.E.2d 739 (N.C. 1956). There was no requirement that the dwelling be destroyed or even that it be damaged to a significant degree. In fact, a mere charring was sufficient, *People v. Oliff,* 197 N.E. 777 (Ill. 1935), but scorching or smoke damage did not constitute arson at common law. *Woolsey v. State,* 17 S.W. 546 (Tex. 1891). The common law defined the term *dwelling* as in burglary. Consequently, the burning of buildings within the curtilage constituted arson.

The language "willful and malicious" makes it appear that arson was a specific-intent crime, but it was not. Rather, the term *malice* was construed to mean deliberately and without justification or excuse. *State v. Pisano,* 141 A. 660 (Conn. 1928). The common law regarded arson as a general-intent crime with the required malice being presumed from an intentional burning of someone's dwelling. However, it was not arson at common law to set fire to one's own home. *State v. Young,* 36 So. 19 (Ala. 1904). Yet, some early English cases indicate that under circumstances where burning one's own house posed a danger to others that "houseburning" was a misdemeanor offense.

CASE IN POINT

PROVING THE CRIME OF ARSON

Early on the morning of September 23, 1981, a fire destroyed a log cabin belonging to Henry Xavier Kennedy. Investigators determined the fire was incendiary in origin. A hot plate with its switch in the "on" position was found in the most heavily burned area of the cabin. Investigators also determined that kerosene poured around the area of the hot plate had accelerated the fire.

Five days before the fire, Kennedy had renewed a $40,000 insurance policy on the cabin. Evidence was also presented that Kennedy's building business was slow. Kennedy introduced evidence of an alibi from midnight until 4:00 A.M. Although the fire was reported at 3:42 A.M., investigators testified that the incendiary device could have been set before midnight.

Kennedy was convicted of arson and his conviction was upheld on appeal.

Kennedy v. State, 323 S.E.2d 169 (Ga. App. 1984).

Statutory Revision of Arson

Modern statutes have extended the offense of arson to include the intentional burning of buildings, structures, and vehicles of all types. Frequently, this even includes a person's own property. A number of states have enacted statutes that provide that use of explosives to damage a structure constitutes arson. As in burglary, the modern offense of arson is designed to protect many forms of property. Therefore, arson can no longer be considered strictly a habitation offense. By categorizing arson, legislatures can make appropriate distinctions and provide penalties accordingly.

Michigan law embraces four categories of arson. One section provides:

> Any person who wilfully or maliciously burns any dwelling house, either occupied or unoccupied, or the contents thereof, whether owned by himself or another, or any building within the curtilage of such dwelling house, or the contents thereof, shall be guilty of a felony. Mich. Comp. Laws Ann. § 750.72.

Section 750.73 makes it a lesser felony for anyone to willfully or maliciously burn any building or other real property, or contents thereof, while Section 750.74 makes it a misdemeanor to willfully and maliciously burn personal property worth less than $50 and a felony if the value is greater. In contrast to Michigan, many state statutes broaden the scope of the offense by referring to "damage caused by fire" rather than "burning." And in contrast to the common law, under many modern statutes proof of damage by smoke or scorching is sufficient to constitute arson. See, for example, *State v. McVeigh,* 516 P.2d 918 (Kan. 1973).

The Michigan Compiled Laws also address insurance fraud and provide:

> Any person who shall wilfully burn any building or personal property which shall be at the time insured against loss or damage by fire with intent to injure and defraud the insurer, whether such person be the owner of the property or not, shall be guilty of a felony. Mich. Comp. Laws Ann. § 750.75.

For a fire to be "wilfully" set by the accused requires that the defendant commit such act stubbornly and for an unlawful purpose. Mere proof of carelessness or accident is not sufficient to establish guilt. *People v. McCarty,* 6 N.W.2d 919 (Mich. 1942). Most jurisdictions have enacted statutes making it a crime to burn any property with the intent to defraud an insurance company, usually requiring the prosecution to prove the defendant's specific intent to defraud.

MALICIOUS MISCHIEF

A mere trespass to land or personal property was not a crime at common law unless it was committed forcibly or maliciously. *State v. Wheeler,* 3 Vt. 344 (1830). It was however, a common-law misdemeanor called "malicious mischief" for a person to damage another's real or personal property. *State v. Watts,* 2 S.W. 342 (Ark. 1866). Modern statutes usually define the offense much as did the common law, often referring to the offense as "vandalism" and imposing penalties based on the extent of damage inflicted on the victim's property. For example, the California Penal Code states:

> (a) Every person who maliciously (1) defaces with paint or any other liquid, (2) damages or (3) destroys any real or personal property not his or her own, in cases otherwise than those specified by state law, is guilty of vandalism. West's Ann. Cal. Penal Code § 594.

The California statute sets the penalty based on the amount of defacement, damage, or destruction.

EXTORTION

In describing common-law extortion, Blackstone said it was "the taking by color of an office of money or other thing of value, that is not due, before it is due, or more than is due." See *State v. Cooper,* 113 S.W. 1048 (Tenn. 1908). Under most modern statutes extortion has been extended beyond acts by public officers.

The California law provides:

> Extortion is the obtaining of property from another, with his consent, or the obtaining of an official act of a public officer, induced by a wrongful use of force or fear, or under color of official right. West's Ann. Cal. Penal Code § 518.

It further stipulates:

> Fear, such as will constitute extortion, may be induced by a threat, either:
> 1. To do an unlawful injury to the person or property of the individual threatened or of a third person; or,
> 2. To accuse the individual threatened, or any relative of his, or member of his family, of any crime; or,
> 3. To expose, or to impute to him or them any deformity, disgrace or crime, or,
> 4. To expose any secret affecting him or them. West's Ann. Cal. Penal Code § 519.

In many instances the statutory offense of extortion has become synonymous with the common understanding of "blackmail." In fact, a federal statute, 18 U.S.C.A. §§ 875–876, that forbids sending extortion threats by mail is sometimes called "the blackmail statute."

Defenses to Crimes Involving Property

The common-law offenses of larceny and robbery were specific-intent crimes. This intent requirement has been carried over in statutes proscribing theft, either comprehensively or in various descriptive crimes, but the intent requirement in modern robbery statutes varies. Therefore, in a prosecution for theft a defendant may raise the defense of mistake of fact, but this does not necessarily follow when defending a charge of robbery (see Chapter 13). This means that a defendant who took items of property from another person in the good-faith belief that they belonged to the taker may have a defense. A classic example: Sherry leaves a coat on a coat rack and later Mary does also. The jackets are similar and Sherry mistakenly walks away with Mary's jacket. The problem becomes more acute if Mary has left a wallet in her jacket with hundreds of dollars of currency in it. These mistakes happen and furnish the justification for requiring the prosecution to prove a defendant's specific intent in theft offenses. Have you ever opened the door of a car like yours in a shopping center parking lot, thinking the car was your own?

In some theft prosecutions, mistake of law has been held to be a defense. This is limited to situations where there are exceedingly technical questions concerning ownership rights (see Chapter 13).

In a prosecution for forgery, an accused can defend by proving that he or she was authorized to sign another's name. Since forgery is a specific-intent crime, a mistake of fact can constitute a defense (see Chapter 13).

Burglary is generally a specific-intent crime. Thus, a mistake of fact can constitute a defense. For example, an intoxicated person who enters a "row-house" identical to his or her own may have a defense. And, of course, the requirement that the prosecution prove "an intent to commit a felony" would make it difficult to prove that a person who took refuge from a storm on the porch of an unoccupied dwelling did so with intent to commit a felony therein (see Chapter 13). Arson, on the other hand, is usually a general-intent crime. This imposes a limitation on defenses beyond consent, in which a person intentionally commits the proscribed acts. Since statutes proscribing the commission of arson with the intent to defraud an insurer usually require proof of the defendant's specific intent to defraud, the lack of such intent can be shown in defense.

Conclusion

Most statutory property crimes parallel the basic common-law scheme, but have been broadened to meet the demands of our changing society. While the common-law crimes against property and habitation provide a good starting point for legislating against offenses involving property, there is a need for continuing statutory revision to consolidate the laws proscribing certain property offenses that have proliferated over the years.

Statutes that proscribe various forms of theft and forgery need to be updated, particularly in light of computer and credit card crimes, which increasingly create serious problems in both the public and private sectors. Definitions must be reviewed to assure adequate protection against those who willfully take computer data or access computer systems without authority. Consumers are no longer willing to acquiesce in outmoded doctrines such as *caveat emptor.* Thus, laws concerning representations made in commercial transactions assume a role of importance in today's society. Consumer fraud, intentional false advertising, credit card fraud, and a variety of other scams need to be specifically proscribed or included in omnibus definitions of theft and forgery statutes.

The laws proscribing burglary and arson must protect more than homes. These offenses pose serious threats to lives and property, regardless of whether they are committed in a residential or business property, whether the structure involved is private or public, and whether it is a vehicle, vessel, building, or other structure. These offenses have moved from being crimes against habitation to being crimes against property. Modern statutes tend to make these offenses crimes against persons as well. With the almost universal dependence on insurance to protect against casualty losses, the need for a close look at statutes proscribing insurance fraud is also essential.

QUESTIONS FOR THOUGHT AND DISCUSSION

1. A. H. Hacker is a skilled computer operator at a business office. Through stealthful operation of his computer, he successfully obtains a list of names and addresses of a competitor's customers without the knowledge or consent of the competitor. For what offense would Hacker most likely be prosecuted in your state?

2. What advantages do you see in a state adopting a comprehensive theft statute?

3. Lefty Lightfingers steals a ham with a price tag of $19.50 from the meat counter in a supermarket. As he leaves the store, he is approached by a security guard. Lightfingers injures the security guard in his attempts to leave with the ham he has stolen. In your state, would Lightfingers be charged with petit theft, grand theft, or robbery? Explain.

4. Should the offense of forgery be divided into degrees based on the importance of the forged documents? If so, what criteria would you propose for the various degrees of the crime?

5. Sally Spendthrift has an established bank account at a local bank. She gives a check to a merchant for purchase of a new stereo. Her bank returns the check to the merchant because Ms. Spendthrift's account has insufficient funds to cover payment. Do you think Ms. Spendthrift should face criminal charges or simply be required to compensate the bank and anyone who suffered a loss?

6. Considering the various types of structures protected by burglary statutes, how would you classify burglary from the standpoint of ranking the most serious categories to the least serious categories?

7. Is it more important for theft offenses than robbery to be classified as specific-intent crimes? Why?

8. What provisions would you include in a model statute making arson a crime? Would you provide for separate degrees of the offense?

9. Give some examples of actions that would probably fall within the conduct proscribed by (a) extortion and (b) vandalism or malicious mischief statutes.

10. What offense would a person commit who destroyed or damaged data in someone's computer? If a person electronically accessed another's computer without permission, would this constitute a criminal offense?

CASES

STATE V. RICHARD

Supreme Court of Nebraska, 1984.
216 Neb. 832, 346 N.W.2d 399.

[This case deals with the offense of shoplifting.]

PER CURIAM.

Defendant was convicted in the county court for Scotts Bluff County of violation of Scottsbluff city ordinance § 13–201, which provided in part: "It is hereby declared unlawful for any person within the city to steal any money, goods or chattels of any kind whatever." Defendant appealed to the district court, in which his conviction and fine of $100 were affirmed. Defendant appeals to this court. For the reasons hereinafter stated we reverse and dismiss.

The evidence on behalf of the State showed that defendant entered Alexander's Super Market on March 25, 1983, between 7 and 8 A.M. He examined the bacon displayed for sale, picked up a 1-pound package, and walked by the meat counter. Alexander's meat manager followed defendant, and by demonstration at trial showed that defendant thrust his hand into his coat, went toward the express lane, and "didn't have the bacon [in his hand] anymore." The meat manager told the checker to call "service 50," which indicated that "shoplifting" was going on.

Other Alexander employees then came up, and the meat manager saw nothing further. On cross-examination the meat manager testified that he followed and watched defendant "[b]ecause he looked suspicious, in that when he picked up the bacon he moved his head from side to side."

The manager of Alexander's testified that he responded to the "service 50" call and first saw defendant halfway down one of the aisles, approached him and talked to him about the bacon, and defendant took the pound of bacon from his coat. The bacon was priced at $1.89. This witness could not remember whether defendant told him that he was going to pay for the bacon, but did remember that defendant handed the bacon to the witness and walked out of the store after the confrontation.

A Scottsbluff policeman testified that the manager of the store told the police officer that defendant told them he was going to pay for the bacon, gave the bacon back, informed the store personnel that "they were not going to hold him for the police," and left.

Defendant testified that he had examined different types of bacon, selected one pound, did not put it in his coat, was stopped by the store personnel, showed them his wallet with "seventy-some" dollars in it, offered to pay, and when that offer was refused told the store personnel that he was not trying to steal the bacon; and said "either you're going to take my money or . . . I'm going to walk back, . . . I'm going to put it down, I'm going to walk out of here."

It is clear from the evidence considered in the light most favorable to the State that the bacon was not removed from the store by defendant. Counsel for the parties agree that to constitute the crime of "stealing" there must be a taking and "asportation" with intent to steal. The State contends that in a self-service store, "The elements of a taking and asportation are satisfied where the evidence shows that the property was taken from the owner and was concealed or put in a convenient place for removal. The fact that the possession was brief or that the person was detected before the goods could be removed from the owner's premises is immaterial." . . .

We cannot agree. With the changes in merchandising and the enactment of new and different statutes affecting a shopper's conduct, we have gone beyond the law cited by the State that to take an article feloniously is accomplished by simply laying hold of, grasping, or seizing it *animo furandi,* with the hands or otherwise, and that the very least removal of it by the thief from the place where found is an asportation or carrying away. . . . To constitute larceny the object stolen must be removed from the premises of the owner, with intent to steal, before the larceny is complete. In so stating we reiterate what we said in *State v. Hauck,* 190 Neb. 534, 537, 209 N.W.2d 580, 583 (1973): "The determination of what constitutes a taking and carrying away of property with the intent to permanently deprive the owner of possession and whether that taking is with or without the consent of the owner involves issues of intent which are often difficult of determination. Where merchandise in a store is involved, those issues are vitally affected if the store is operated on a self-service basis. The cases appear to be in agreement that in a self-service store, where customers select and pick up articles to be paid for at the checkout counter, the mere picking up of an article in the display area does not constitute asportation." . . . In *Durphy v. United States*, 235 A.2d 326, 327 (D.C. 1967), the court stated that "the normal procedure in this type of market is for customers to circulate through the sales area, taking from the shelves any items they wish to buy but not paying for their selections until they pass through the check-out counter. . . . The fact that appellant placed the goods in a shopping bag provided no valid reason for the trial court to infer a criminal intent or a possession clearly adverse to the interest of the store."

Our holding is not to be read that defendant's conduct might not have warranted conviction on other charges, such as attempted stealing (Neb. Rev. Stat. § 28–201 (Reissue 1979), or violation of Neb. Rev. Stat. § 28–551.01(1) (Cum. Supp. 1982), which provides that a person commits the crime of theft by shoplifting when, with intent to appropriate property without paying for it, he "(a) Conceals or takes possession of the goods or merchandise of any store or retail establishment."

In this difficult area of the law regarding self-service stores, precision in charging and proving offenses will result in clarity in determining what conduct is, or is not, criminal.

Reversed and dismissed.

JONES v. COMMONWEALTH

Court of Appeals of Virginia, 1992.
13 Va. App. 566, 414 S.E.2d 193.

[In this case the Virginia Court of Appeals considers the sufficiency of the evidence to support the appellant's conviction for robbery.]

BRAY, Judge.

Jerry Earl Jones (defendant) was convicted in a jury trial of robbery and sentenced in accordance with the verdict to twenty years imprisonment. He contends that the evidence was insufficient to sustain the verdict. We disagree and affirm the conviction.

The evidence disclosed that, on the morning of March 17, 1989, Deputy John Stanton (Stanton) of the Williamsburg Sheriff's Department was transporting defendant from the "Richmond Penitentiary" to Williamsburg. Defendant was manacled in "leg chains and . . . a waist chain that ha[d] a handcuff attached to each side." Stanton was the operator of the "unmarked" vehicle, defendant was seated in the rear and no "divider" separated the two.

In route, defendant suddenly stated, "Sheriff, don't make me blow your damn brains out." Stanton was "startled" and "scared" and "jerked" his "head to the right to see what was going on." He observed defendant with "an object . . . something metal that appeared to be the barrel of a pistol," which Stanton "assumed it was." The vehicle was then travelling "approximately 65 [mph]," and Stanton lost control for "10 or 15 seconds," until it came to rest in the grassy median.

Stanton immediately began to "look and feel for [his] gun," which was missing and had been "in [his] holster at the time . . . the car went out of control." Unarmed, the deputy "was fearful for [his] life" and, when defendant demanded that Stanton "get the car back on the road," he "decided . . . that [he] wasn't going with" defendant. In an effort to "wreck" the car and "bail out," Stanton "cut . . . toward the guardrail" and "jumped out on the grass." Defendant, however, "got to the wheel and got it straightened out" and escaped in the vehicle.

The car was discovered in downtown Richmond later the same day with its two radio antennae and several hubcaps removed and in the truck. A "fake gun" was found on the rear seat. Defendant was arrested shortly thereafter on a Richmond street and Stanton's stolen pistol was found in the "waistband" of his trousers. He was indicted on March 20, 1989. . . .

. . . When the sufficiency of the evidence is challenged on appeal, it is well established that we must view the evidence in the light most favorable to the Commonwealth, granting to it all reasonable inferences fairly deducible therefrom. The conviction will be disturbed only if plainly wrong or without evidence to support it. . . .

The elements of robbery, a common law offense in Virginia, include a "taking, with intent to steal, of the personal property of another, from his person or in his presence, against his will, by violence or intimidation" which precedes or is "concomitant with the taking." . . .

Defendant threatened Stanton's life while brandishing an object which appeared to be a weapon. As a result, Stanton was fearful and surrendered the vehicle to defendant. Defendant then escaped with both the automobile and Stanton's pistol, apparently taken by defendant while Stanton was in extremity. These circumstances amply support a robbery conviction.

Accordingly, the judgment of conviction is affirmed.

STATE V. GOMEZ

Court of Appeals of Arizona, 1976.
27 Ariz. App. 248, 553 P.2d 1233.

[This case involves the crimes of forgery and embezzlement.]

KRUCKER, Judge.

This is an appeal from convictions of forgery, A.R.S. 13–421, and theft by embezzlement, A.R.S. 13–682, and concurrent sentences thereon of not less than eight nor more than ten years on the forgery charge and not less than eight nor more than ten years on the embezzlement charge. . . .

The pertinent facts are as follows. On June 3, 1975, Emma Cisneros purchased a 1964 Volkswagen van bus from one Chris Powers. A certificate of title was conveyed to Ms. Cisneros and testimony revealed that Gerald Wager, a notary public, notarized the signature of Chris Powers, which assigned the title to Ms. Cisneros.

The record reflects that Ms. Cisneros came in contact with appellant, Bobby Gomez, while dining at the Coronado Inn in Nogales on the evening of June 7, 1975. Appellant expressed interest in purchasing the 1964 VW microbus for $500, predicated upon a one-hour test drive. Ms. Cisneros agreed and when appellant failed to return after one and a half hours, she left the restaurant. For the next three months she was unsuccessful in her attempts to locate either the vehicle or appellant.

On September 17, 1975, Ms. Cisneros observed her VW microbus at the Diaz Garage in Nogales, Arizona. Mr. Diaz, a mechanic, testified that in mid-June, 1975, the vehicle was delivered for repairs to his garage in Mexico by Mr. Rodolfo Gomez, appellant's uncle. Although the record is not completely clear, apparently at a later date Diaz contacted Gomez to inform him that the repairs were complete. Diaz was directed to bring the microbus to the garage in Nogales, Arizona, which was owned by his uncle. The vehicle was delivered at noon on September 17, 1975.

After observing the microbus, Ms. Cisneros removed the ignition keys and told Mr. Diaz to send the person who claimed the van to her office at the Wager Insurance Agency in Nogales, Arizona. That same day appellant appeared at the Wager Insurance Agency to pick up the keys to the vehicle. Upon Ms. Cisneros' refusal to give up the keys, appellant left the agency but later returned with the certificate of title. Claiming that he did not want to have anything else to do with the car, Gomez gave the title to Ms. Cisneros.

The name and address of Ms. Cisneros had been removed from the certificate and replaced with the name and address of Bobby Gomez. Testimony revealed that the document was on the sun visor of the microbus when it was loaned to appellant on June 7, 1975.

On October 22, 1975, a preliminary hearing was held in the Santa Cruz County Justice Court. On January 14, 1976, verdicts of guilty were returned against appellant after a trial by jury on the aforementioned counts. . . .

Sufficiency of the Evidence

Appellant's . . . contention on appeal is that the State failed to present sufficient evidence to convict him of the crime of forgery. A.R.S. 13–421 (A) (1). Specifically, he complains that there was no showing that he actually did forge his name upon the document in question or of the requisite intent to defraud.

We have held that intent to defraud is an essential element of forgery. . . . However, intent to defraud may be, and often must be, inferred from the circumstances in which the false instrument is executed or issued. . . .

We do not require direct evidence of appellant physically obscuring or obliterating Ms. Cisneros' name and address with liquid paper and inserting his own. To do so would place a virtually impossible burden on the State. It is not within the best interests of justice to grant a special status to covert activities by rendering immune from prosecution those individuals performing actions outside the public view.

In the case at bench, a certificate of title was transferred to Ms. Cisneros and the signature of the transferor, Chris Powers, was notarized. Ms. Cisneros testified that the title was inside the microbus when appellant took the vehicle on June 7, 1975. She further testified that she next saw this document on September 17, 1975, when appellant produced it from his wallet at her place of work and returned it to her. Her name and address, which has appeared on the document, were replaced by that of appellant.

We have no difficulty in concluding that the circumstances of the disappearance and recovery of the vehicle, along with appellant's physical possession of the altered document, provided sufficient evidence to support the jury's determination that appellant altered the document with intent to defraud or aided and abetted the alteration with the same intent.

Appellant also contends that the State never showed "that the appellant ever embezzled anything" in violation of A.R.S. 13–682. We have stated that the gist of the crime of embezzlement is a breach of trust. . . . The elements necessary to establish embezzlement are a trust relation, possession or control of property by virtue of the trust relation, and a fraudulent appropriation of the property to a use or purpose not in the due and lawful execution of the trust. . . .

We believe there is ample evidence to support appellant's conviction of embezzlement. The record reflects that during a discussion of the possibility of appellant's purchase of Ms. Cisneros' VW microbus, appellant requested possession and control of the vehicle for the purpose of a test drive and stated that he would return "in about an hour or so." Ms. Cisneros waited for approximately one and a half hours before leaving the restaurant where she had met appellant. From early June until the discovery of the van in mid-September she attempted to locate both appellant and the vehicle.

The foregoing certainly reflects that possession and control of the microbus was entrusted to appellant for the express and limited purpose of a one-hour test drive as a condition of purchase. The vehicle was never returned and at no time did appellant tender payment for it or notify Ms. Cisneros of its whereabouts. Instead, from June 7 until its discovery on September 17, the microbus was apparently converted to appellant's own use. . . . The requisite intent is inferred from the circumstances. . . .

Affirmed.

STATE v. FELDT

Supreme Court of Montana, 1989.
239 Mont. 398, 781 P.2d 255.

[Charles Matthew Feldt was convicted of burglary and theft and was sentenced to concurrent five-year prison terms for each offense. In this case the Montana Supreme Court considers an appeal of the burglary conviction.]

SHEEHY, Justice.

. . . The issue on appeal is stated as follows: (1) Whether the trial court erred in finding that the defendant entered his employer's premises "unlawfully," thereby committing burglary under 45–6–204(1), MCA.

On the morning of April 27, 1987, the manager of T.C. Foods, a convenience store in Great Falls, Montana, was called to the store by the morning clerk. Upon arrival, the manager found a set of keys in the door, subsequently determined to have been issued to defendant, Feldt, an employee at T.C. Foods. The manager discovered $1,459 was missing from the safe. In addition, the manager found a note posted on the cash register which stated, "I know you trusted me, but I couldn't handle it at home. I am sorry. If you want, you can try and get the money out of my car or bike. Chuck."

On April 28, 1987, the defendant turned himself in to the Great Falls police department. He gave the police a bag containing $1,219 at the time of his surrender. He confessed to entering the store after hours by means of his keys, taking the money and leaving the note on the cash register.

At trial, the manager testified that all employees were given keys to the store and access to the store safe. The defendant testified that he was required to open and close the store and he was permitted access to the store's safe. According to both the manager and the defendant, the manager allowed employees to enter the store after business hours for any proper purposes. The evidence fails to disclose, from the State or from the defendant, that when the store key was delivered to Feldt, any limitation, written or oral, was placed upon his use of it, or upon his access to the safe. . . .

Section 45–6–204(1), MCA, defines burglary as follows:

> "A person commits the offense of burglary if he knowingly enters or remains unlawfully in an occupied structure with the purpose to commit an offense therein. . . ."

"Enters or remains unlawfully" is defined in 45–6–201, MCA, which reads in pertinent part:

> "A person enters or remains unlawfully . . . when he is not licensed, invited, or otherwise privileged to do so."

This Court in *State v. Starkweather* . . . [1931] held that an entry made by one who is licensed or privileged to be on the premises is not unlawful under the burglary statute. The Court in *Starkweather* stated: "There is no breaking in or entering a house or room and therefore, no burglary, if the person who enters has a right to do so." . . . To constitute a burglary the nature of the entry must itself be a trespass. . . .

This Court in *Starkweather* focused on whether there was a limitation upon the defendant's right to enter a pool hall. In *Starkweather,* the Court found no limitation on the defendant's right to enter the pool hall. This case turns on the same issue, that is whether there is any limitation on Feldt's right to enter T.C. Foods. The defendant Feldt was given permission to enter T.C. Foods where he was employed. As an employee of T.C. Foods, the manager gave Feldt a set of keys to enter the store and provided Feldt with access to the safe. In issuing the keys, the manager provided Feldt with authority to enter the premises at any time. The record reveals no limitations to the defendant's right to enter the store. However, the manager did testify at trial that Feldt could only enter the store after it was closed for proper purposes. Despite the manager's testimony, Feldt could enter T.C. Foods at any time day or night.

Under this Court's holding in *Starkweather,* and 45–6–204 and 45–6–201, MCA, the defendant can not be convicted of burglary. He lawfully entered the building after closing hours with keys provided by the manager of T.C. Foods. Feldt did not trespass when he entered T.C. Foods. His keys granted him authority to enter T.C. Foods after hours.

The State argues that Feldt abused his privilege to enter T.C. Foods after hours, when he entered for the improper purpose to steal the money from the safe. The State further contends that Feldt's improper entry into T.C. Foods after hours transforms his original permissible entry into a trespass that can form the basis of a burglary charge.... While Feldt acted improperly in taking the money from the safe, his entry into T.C. Foods was authorized by management. Feldt was properly charged and convicted for theft, but the State failed to meet the "unlawful entry" element of the burglary statute and this Court's previous holding under *Starkweather.*

Finally, the State argues that the requirement of a trespassory entry under *Starkweather* is no longer accurate under the new burglary statute. We find little merit in the State's argument, since the Criminal Code Commission specifically endorsed the Court's holding in *Starkweather* in rewriting the burglary statute....

The defendant had access to T.C. Foods and did not "enter or remain unlawfully" as defined in 45–6–201, MCA. Since there was no unlawful entry, the defendant's actions do not constitute a burglary as defined in 45–6–204, MCA. We reverse the burglary conviction. The theft conviction was not appealed. The sentence imposed upon Feldt for the District Court is modified to strike therefrom the penalty assessed for burglary, and as modified, the sentence is affirmed.

HARRISON, WEBER, and HUNT, JJ., concur.

GULBRANDSON, Justice, dissenting.

I respectfully dissent. The trial judge ... found [that] T.C. Foods store was closed for business when the defendant entered said store and took the money. Defendant did not have permission to enter the store at that time and he did not have permission to take the money.

In my view, there is sufficient evidence in the record to affirm the conviction for burglary. The manager of T.C. Foods store had personally hired the defendant and knew the defendant's work schedule. At trial, the manager testified as follows:

Q. Now, the Defendant, Charles Matthew Feldt, even though he is an employee of your store, did he have your permission to enter the store after hours?
A. No.
Q. And, if the Defendant was not working a shift on Sunday night before you arrive at the store Monday morning, then technically, isn't it correct, if at all, that an employee in his position would not have permission to go back and turn the coffee off or anything like that?
A. Right.
Q. Because he wouldn't have been working that shift, isn't that my understanding?
A. Yes.
Q. So, he really can't have any permission at all to go into the T.C. Foods between the times you closed on Sunday and you opened on Monday, isn't that my understanding of it?
A. Yes.
Q. He didn't have permission to go into the store for any purpose such as turning the alarm on, or turning the coffee off, maybe to lock a door, things like that. Isn't that my understanding of the situation?
A. Yes.

Testimony at trial established that the defendant had not worked on the Sunday preceding the incident, and he was not scheduled to work Monday, the day of the incident. The defendant testified personally as follows:

Q. Now you had nobody's permission to go into the store at that time; isn't that correct?
A. Not at that time.

The foregoing testimony, in my view, supports the trial judge's finding that defendant did not have permission to enter the store at that time. The record as a whole supports the trial judge's verdict that the defendant was guilty of burglary....

McDONOUGH, J., concurs.

TURNAGE, Chief Justice, concurring....

FOX V. STATE

Court of Appeals of Indiana, 1979.
179 Ind. App. 267, 384 N.E.2d 1159.

[This case deals with the crime of arson.]

SHIELDS, Judge.
Appellants were tried by a jury and convicted of first degree arson. . . . The statute under which appellants were charged and convicted is I.C. 35–16–1–1, which provides, in pertinent part:

> Any person who wilfully and maliciously sets fire to or burns or causes the setting of fire to or burning of . . . any kitchen, shop, barn, stable, garage or other outhouse, or other building that is part or parcel of any dwelling house . . .

Although no Indiana case has defined the phrase "part or parcel of any dwelling house," many other jurisdictions have done so. At common law, an outhouse which was a "parcel of" a dwelling house was one "used in connection therewith and situated within the curtilage." . . .

"Curtilage" has been defined as:

> . . . the space of ground adjoining the dwelling house used in connection therewith in the conduct of family affairs and for carrying on domestic purposes, usually including the buildings occupied in connection with the dwelling house. It is the propinquity to a dwelling and the use in connection with it for family purposes which is to be regarded. . . .

As the authorities indicate, it is the proximity to the dwelling and the use in connection therewith for family purposes and the carrying on of domestic employment that are of major importance in determining whether an area or building is to be considered within the "curtilage" (i.e., part or parcel) of the dwelling house. This comports with the view that first degree arson is an offense against the security of habitation, rather than property. . . .

In the case at bar, the evidence viewed most favorably to the State shows that the burned building was a barn that had been converted into a combination garage-work area-recreation room. The building, located 80 to 100 feet from the dwelling house, was insulated and panelled and housed a furnace, telephone, and stereo. The Mowerys (owners of the property) often kept vehicles in the building, and Mr. Mowery also had a work area in the building. The building had been used on several occasions for parties and the Mowery's daughter and her friends often used the building to play music and dance.

The usage of the building as an addition to their dwelling house, i.e., "for family purposes and the carrying on of domestic employment," and its proximity to the dwelling house, persuade us that it was within the "curtilage," i.e., that the building burned was "part or parcel" of the Mowery dwelling house. . . .

Appellants challenge the sufficiency of the evidence to establish their identity as the perpetrators of the arson at Mowerys' building. When reviewing the sufficiency of the evidence, this Court considers the evidence most favorable to the verdict together with all reasonable inferences which may be drawn from that evidence. If there is substantial evidence of probative value to support each element of the offense, the judgment will be affirmed. . . . Furthermore, this Court does not judge the credibility of witnesses nor weigh the evidence. . . .

In the case at bar, the evidence most favorable to the state reveals that the five appellants were seen together from approximately 2:30 to 3:00 A.M. visiting several bars in Marion, Grant County, Indiana, and driving a dirty, goldish-green 1968 Oldsmobile, registered to [defendant] Fox, which reportedly had "extremely loud mufflers." The appellants were imbibing in spirits at the Swing Bar when, somewhere around 3:00 A.M., Marion police officers were called to the bar twice to quell disturbances and, on the later occasion, also to close the bar. On the former occasion the bar was surrounded by police and [defendant] York was heard to say, "Isn't there some kind of charge against police harassment?" During this first visit Captain Mowery (Mowery), the owner of the property that was burned, "broke up" what appeared to be a verbal confrontation between Fox and another patron. As Fox was walking back to his table he stated "That's cool, Mowery. That's cool." During the second police visit to the bar, after Mowery announced that the bar was closed, Fox leaned over as he passed Mowery on the way out and said, "I'll see you later, Mowery," following which a verbal exchange of words occurred between Fox and Mowery. About the same time this confrontation occurred, [defendant] Havens said, "F_____ the pigs. We don't have to listen to this s_____ . Let's get out of here."

While the Swing Bar was being closed, Officer Ellis, en route back to his squad car, noticed suspicious-looking tools on the rear floor board of Fox's Oldsmobile. Mowery, upon being informed of these tools, ordered the vehicle to be kept under surveillance. Appellants left the Swing Bar and proceeded to the Kewpie Bar. While at the Kewpie Bar, [defendant] Perry left the table where all five appellants had been sitting, came back a few minutes later and stated, "Everything's okay. They're scattered." Fox then said, "Well, let's go then," telling an inquirer who was asking to go with them, "... we are just going to take care of a little business." After departing from the Kewpie Bar, appellants stopped at Stoller's Tavern and purchased a fifth of whiskey and six 6 oz. (sic) bottles of Coca Cola. Appellants were last seen, prior to the fire at Mowery's, parking the Oldsmobile behind a house in Marion at about 3:25 A.M., at which time surveillance of the vehicle was withdrawn. The vehicle was gone when Officer Stevens checked back at 3:50 A.M.

Carol Mowery (wife of Captain Mowery) was awakened by the dog's barking sometime between 3:30 and 4:00 A.M. After hearing a car idling for some time, she went downstairs and looked out the window and saw two people in a car parked by the barn and three others milling about by the barn. Immediately thereafter she saw flames shoot out of the cab of the stake-bed truck parked outside, next to the barn. She then saw the subjects get into the car and drive off. Some minutes later she called the police (testimony revealed that the call was received at 4:12 A.M.) and her brother-in-law, Clifford Mowery, who was a fireman. In a matter of minutes Clifford arrived and went out to the barn with Mrs. Mowery where they discovered that, in addition to the truck being on fire, the floor mat of the Corvette parked inside the barn and a wall and part of the ceiling of the barn were also aflame. Mrs. Mowery could not identify or describe any of the persons she saw except to say that she assumed they were males by the way they were dressed, and that one of them was very tall and large. She described the car she saw parked beside the barn as a dirty, greenish-gold Oldsmobile which had a noisy exhaust.

After the fire, the greenish-gold Oldsmobile was observed driving through Van Buren, Grant County, Indiana, which is located approximately seven miles east of Mowery's house. Marshall Marley and Officer Campbell pursued the vehicle and stopped it approximately three-fourths of a mile east of Van Buren at about 5:27 A.M. They arrested the occupants of the car, [defendants] Perry, Kapp, and Havens, on a preliminary charge of arson. The automobile was impounded. Mrs. Mowery later identified it as the car she saw by the barn the morning of the fire when an officer took her to a garage where it was parked with "several cars ... and some trucks and stuff."

Deputy Sheriff Cook pursued a gold, 1967 Buick through Marion sometime between 4:00 and 4:45 A.M. The Buick was subsequently found to have been stolen from Van Buren sometime earlier that night. Cook identified [defendants] Fox and York as the individuals who abandoned the vehicle and fled on foot.

Sheriff Ash, while looking around the burned area, found a 7 oz. (sic) coke bottle which smelled as if it had contained whiskey or alcohol. He further observed a bootprint in the snow beside the barn. Kapp's boots were subsequently brought to the scene and an impression of one of them was made in the snow beside this print. Photographs of the bootprint, as well as Kapp's boots, were admitted into evidence and the similarities were pointed out by the Sheriff. There was no evidence as to the presence of any inflammables on the scene. Fireman Mowery testified that in his opinion the fires were not accidental.

Assuming, arguendo, that this evidence is sufficient to prove that appellants were the five individuals Mrs. Mowery observed at the scene, there is still a link missing in the chain of circumstantial evidence which the State has woven around appellants: that is who were the two individuals Mrs. Mowery observed that remained in the car, and were these two individuals accessories to the commission of the arson? The State has proven that two individuals remained in the car while three other individuals were perpetrating the crime. Thus, in order to sustain the convictions of these two individuals, it must be shown that they were accessories to the arson.

The general rule is that mere presence at the scene of the crime is not sufficient to allow an inference of participation. . . . However, we acknowledge that presence, coupled with other circumstances, may be sufficient. Thus, evidence of companionship with one engaged in a crime, a course of conduct before and after the offense, and failure to oppose the crime when imposed with a duty to do so, without active participation in the commission of the crime, are circumstances which may be considered in determining whether aiding and abetting may be inferred. . . . However, an inference from such evidence, to be reasonable, must be coupled with evidence of knowledge or evidence from which knowledge may be reasonably inferred, that the criminal conduct is contemplated, in progress or completed.

Thus, the State must show that the ones alleged to aid or abet were aware of and consented to the activity condemned by law, . . . although it need not necessarily prove a pre-conceived plan. . . . In the case at bar, there was no evidence that could show the two individuals in the car had any knowledge that the arson was planned or committed. There was no evidence of their location in the car, or of any motion by them. While the testimony relating to the appellants' activities in the Kewpie Bar might indicate a criminal design in the making, can one infer from this evidence that they were scheming to commit an arson? This may raise a suspicion that appellants may have known of a criminal design to commit an arson, however, mere suspicion that appellants were aware of a criminal design is not enough. . . . The evidence adduced at trial is insufficient to sustain the convictions of the two individuals who were inside the car while the arson was being committed.

This leads to a further problem, being the lack of evidence indicating which of the appellants were inside the car. The only evidence indicating which of the appellants were outside the car was Kapp's bootprint found at the scene. The evidence is, therefore, sufficient to sustain Kapp's conviction as a principal. With respect to the other four appellants, however, we must reach a different result. Because there is insufficient evidence to sustain the convictions of the two individuals that were inside the car, and since there is no evidence indicating who those individuals were, how can we, as an appellate court, pick and choose which of the four remaining appellants were inside that car? The answer is: We cannot. It is fundamental to our system of law that guilt is individual. . . . Here, that means there must be sufficient evidence to support a finding, as to each appellant, that he was either a principal or an accessory to the arson as charged. The evidence was insufficient in this regard; thus, we are constrained to hold that the evidence was not sufficient to sustain the convictions of Fox, Havens, York, and Perry. . . .

Next, we consider Kapp's argument that the evidence is insufficient to establish a willful and malicious burning. Kapp properly cites *Ellis v. State,* (1969) 252 Ind. 472, 250 N.E.2d 364, as authority for the proposition that the law of Indiana presumes that a fire accidentally resulted from some providential cause, rather than from a criminal cause, unless the evidence proves otherwise. We do not agree, however, that the evidence was insufficient to overcome the State's burden of proving that the fire was not the result of natural causes.

As the Supreme Court noted in *Ellis,* there is rarely direct evidence of the actual lighting of a fire by an arsonist; rather, the evidence of arson is usually circumstantial. Such evidence is often of a negative character; that is, the criminal agency is shown by the absence of circumstances, conditions, and surroundings indicating that the fire resulted from an accidental cause. . . .

In the instant case, three persons were observed milling about a building late at night on property where they had no right to be. Immediately after one individual was observed standing beside it, flames shot out of the stake-bed truck. Furthermore, fires were subsequently discovered in two other separate locations. All this evidence, taken together, supports the inference that the fires were set "wilfully and maliciously." . . .

MILLER, J., concurs with opinion. [omitted.]
BUCHANAN, C. J., dissents with opinion. [omitted.]

STATE v. TONNISEN

Superior Court of New Jersey, Appellate Division, 1966.
92 N.J. Super. 452, 224 A.2d 21.

[This case involves the offense of malicious mischief.]

The opinion of the court was delivered by SULLIVAN, S.J.A.D.

After a trial by jury, defendant was convicted of malicious mischief. The statute involved is N.J.S. 2A:122–1, N.J.S.A., which provides:

> Any person who willfully or maliciously destroys, damages, injures or spoils any real or personal property of another, either of a public or private nature, for which no punishment is otherwise provided by statute, is guilty of a misdemeanor.

The State produced evidence that the employees of the Peter J. Schweitzer Plant were on strike and some of the employees were on a picket line across the entrance to the plant. Defendant was one of the employees at or near the plant entrance at the time of the incident in question.

A tank trailer truck loaded with caustic soda arrived at the plant entrance but was blocked by the pickets. A police officer on duty proceeded to clear a path for the truck through the picket line. Defendant was then seen by the officer and other persons to go over to the side of the truck and stick his hand in between the tractor and the trailer. When he withdrew his hand there was grease on it. The officer attempted to tell the driver "to hold it" but before his warning could be heard, the tractor pulled ahead and separated from the trailer which fell down on the road causing the bottom of the tank to crack and the contents thereof to begin to leak out on the road. Examination of the vehicle showed that the safety mechanism of the coupling between the tractor and trailer had been pulled. The dollar amount of the damage resulting from the incident was not shown by the State.

Defendant, who testified in his own defense, denied that he had put his hand "anywheres in the vicinity of the coupling between the truck and the trailer."

On this appeal defendant argues that the State failed to prove criminal willfullness or malice on defendant's part. We disagree. These elements are rarely if ever susceptible of direct proof. In the usual case they are inferred from the totality of the State's case. Here we find ample credible evidence from which a jury could have found that beyond a reasonable doubt defendant pulled the safety mechanism and did so willfully or maliciously within the intent of the statute. . . .

Affirmed.

CHAPTER 8

OFFENSES AGAINST PUBLIC MORALITY

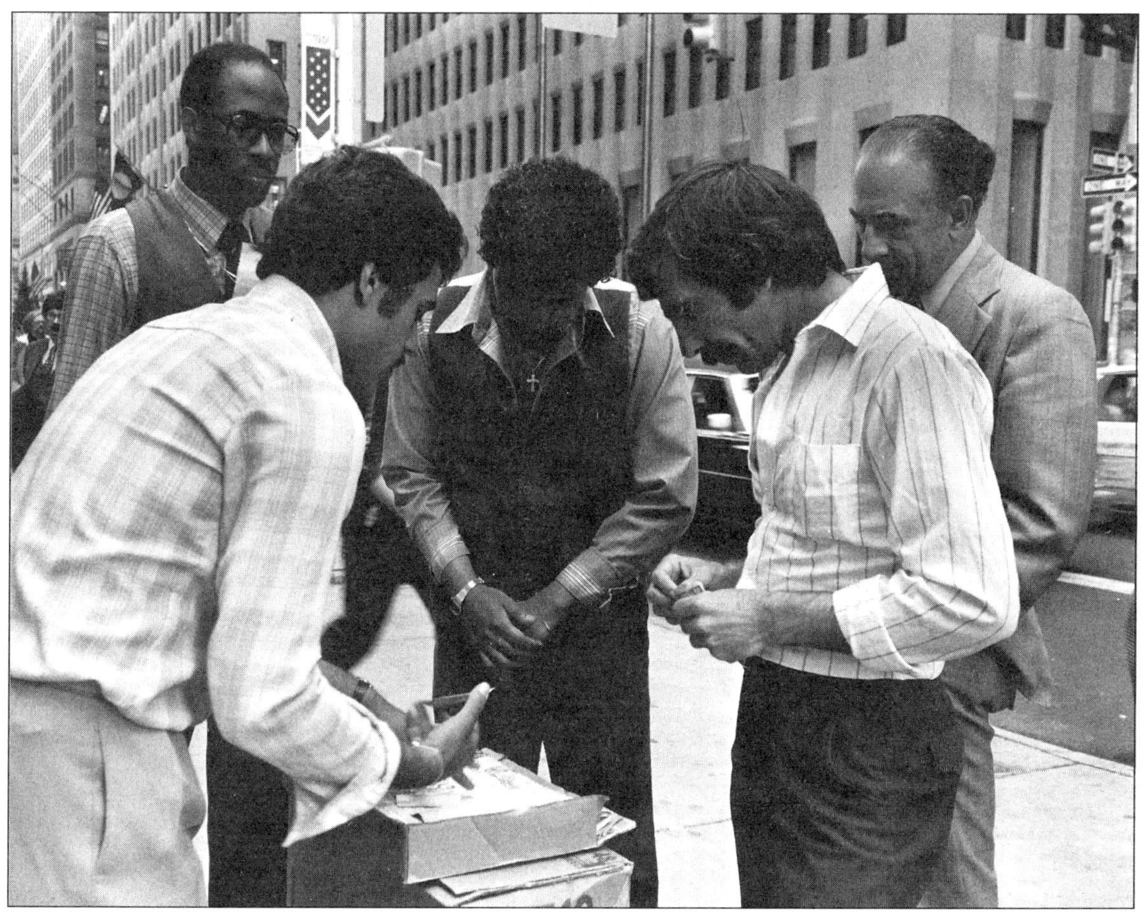

CHAPTER OUTLINE

Introduction
Criminal Prohibitions on Sexual Conduct
Indecent Exposure
Obscenity
Gambling
Conclusion

Cases
Bowers v. Hardwick
Austin v. State
Barnes v. Glen Theatre, Inc.
Radey v. State
United States v. Pinelli

INTRODUCTION

In this chapter we discuss a number of crimes traditionally classified as offenses against public morality. Many deal with sexual conduct—fornication and adultery, seduction, incest, bigamy, sodomy, prostitution, indecent exposure—and in a sense, obscenity and profanity. In this chapter we also examine gambling offenses. Offenses involving alcohol and drugs, while they may be viewed as crimes against morality, can also be seen as offenses against the public order and safety. Accordingly, they are dealt with in Chapter 9.

The Common-Law Background

The common law of crimes developed largely because of society's demands for security of persons and property, the need to maintain public order, and the judges' perceptions of society's concepts of morality. Many ideas of morality were based on the Bible and church doctrine; others were simply the product of the shared experiences of the people. These concepts became the foundation for the criminal laws in this country in the prerevolutionary days, when early settlers tended to equate sin with crime. Later, as legislative bodies defined crimes, the statutes more closely reflected the moral standards of the new American society. Eventually, the equation of crime with sin gave way to a more secular approach to crime.

Religious Influences

The contemporary criminal law still reflects to a great extent the morality of the Bible and church doctrine. In fact, it has been said that organized religion is the greatest single moral force in our society. Conflicts sometimes surface because this pluralistic nation has a constitutional prohibition against the establishment of religion and a guarantee of the free exercise thereof. Therefore, questions arise concerning whether a law with a religious origin can be enforced without offending these basic constitutional guarantees. The short answer is that most criminal laws that proscribe behavior forbidden by the Bible have also been found to serve a recognized secular purpose. Obviously, certain moral principles must be enforced for the protection of society. No one suggests that murder should not be regarded as criminal simply because of the biblical injunction, "Thou shall not kill." Historically, some of our ancestors imposed severe criminal sanctions for taking the name of the Lord in vain. Yet, few today who regard such an act as a serious sin would support criminal sanctions for violation of this commandment.

Is Morality a Legitimate Basis for Legislation?

An essential characteristic of a sovereign state is "police power," the power to legislate in pursuit of public health, safety, welfare, and morality. More than a century ago the United States Supreme Court assumed that regulation of morality was among the purposes of government when it stated:

> Whatever differences of opinion may exist as to the extent and boundaries of the police power, and however difficult it may be to render a satisfactory definition of it, there seems to be no doubt that it does extend to . . . the preservation of good order and the public morals. *Boston Beer Co. v. Massachusetts,* 97 U.S. (7 Otto) 25, 33, 24 L.Ed. 989 (1878).

Constitutional Limitations

In the United States, legislative bodies have broad authority to define conduct as criminal and to set the punishment to be meted out to violators. Of course, there are restrictions. As noted in Chapter 3, the U.S. Constitution and the constitutions of every state impose limitations on government efforts to criminalize certain forms of conduct. For example, in *Griswold v. Connecticut,* 381 U.S. 479, 85 S.Ct. 1678, 14 L.Ed.2d 510 (1965), the U.S. Supreme Court struck down a state law that made it a crime for all persons, even married couples, to use birth control devices. The Court said that the law violated the right of privacy that inheres in the Bill of Rights and is imposed on the states via the Fourteenth Amendment. Some would argue that this right of privacy ought to be interpreted to prohibit government from "legislating morality" altogether. The Supreme Court, however, has never accepted this view. Writing for the Court in *Bowers v. Hardwick,* 478 U.S. 186, 106 S.Ct. 2841, 92 L.Ed.2d 140 (1986), Justice Byron White observed that "the law . . . is constantly based on notions of morality, and if all laws representing essentially moral choices are to be invalidated . . ., the courts will be very busy indeed." 478 U.S. at 196, 106 S.Ct. at 2846, 92 L.Ed. at 149.

Police Power and the Social Consensus

It has long been assumed that legislative bodies have the authority to criminalize conduct they determine to be contrary to the health, safety, and morals of the people, as long as such prohibitions do not infringe rights protected by the state and federal constitutions. The problem is primarily one of legislative perception of the standards that society requires and is willing to accept. Historically, enforcement of the criminal law has largely depended on community acceptance of certain conduct being forbidden by law. But public opinion about law changes. A societal consensus resulted in a constitutional amendment in 1919 prohibiting the sale of intoxicating liquors. It proved unworkable, and after a strong consensus developed to repeal prohibition, the amendment was repealed in 1933. See U.S. Const. Amendments XVIII & XXI.

Today, there are varying attitudes as to whether certain forms of conduct should be illegal. For example, public opinion is divided on the need for laws making it a crime to engage in certain forms of gambling. Consequently, the criminal prohibitions against gambling vary considerably throughout the United States. Since the sexual revolution of the 1960s there has been an erosion of the consensus supporting laws prohibiting sexual activities between consenting adults. This decline in consensus has led many legislatures to revise their criminal codes to remove prohibitions against certain sexual conduct. As in the case of gambling laws, statutes governing sexual conduct now vary from state to state.

CRIMINAL PROHIBITIONS ON SEXUAL CONDUCT

Debate concerning offenses against public morality usually centers primarily on the statutory prohibitions against fornication, adultery, seduction, sodomy, prostitution, and, to a lesser degree, incest. Many people today believe that such behavior is, or at least ought to be, private in character and thus beyond the reach of the criminal law. In contrast, many still subscribe to the classical conservative view that such prohibitions are necessary to maintain a proper moral climate.

Fornication and Adultery

Fornication is sexual intercourse between unmarried persons. Adultery is generally defined as sexual intercourse between a male and female, at least one of whom is married to someone else. Fornication and adultery were regarded as offenses against morality and were punishable in the ecclesiastical courts in England. Neither was a common-law crime unless committed openly. In such instances the act was prosecuted as a public nuisance. *Richey v. State*, 87 N.E. 1032 (Ind. 1909). While these offenses have a biblical basis, there is a threefold legal rationale for proscribing such conduct: (1) to avoid disharmony in family relationships; (2) to prevent illegitimate births; and (3) to prevent the spread of sexually transmitted diseases.

Minnesota law addresses the subject of sex crimes in the traditional manner. Its criminal code provides: "When any man and single woman have sexual intercourse with each other, each is guilty of fornication, which is a misdemeanor." Minn. Stat. Ann. § 609.34. The Minnesota Supreme Court has said that the term *fornication* has a definite, well-understood meaning, and a single clandestine act of intercourse constitutes fornication in the usual acceptation of the term. *State v. Gieseke*, 147 N.W. 663 (Minn. 1914). In respect to adultery, a Minnesota statute provides: "When a married woman has sexual intercourse with a man other than her husband, whether married or not, both are guilty of adultery." Minn. Stat. Ann. § 609.36(1). The statute, however, stipulates that it is a defense to violation thereof "if the marital status of the woman was not known to the defendant at the time of the act of adultery." Minn. Stat. Ann. § 609.36(3).

These offenses, especially fornication, are rarely prosecuted today. Violations may be widespread, but they generally occur under the most private of circumstances. Consequently, complaints about these sexual encounters are seldom reported to the authorities. Furthermore, where the conduct is the subject of a complaint by a participant, it may fall under the classification of sexual battery offenses (see Chapter 6).

Seduction

Seduction was not a crime at a common law; hence, it exists only by statute. *Young v. Young*, 184 So. 187 (Ala. 1938). Statutes defining seduction vary somewhat, but in general the essence of the offense is that a male obtains sexual intercourse with a virtuous female on the unfulfilled promise of marriage. Many states have repealed their seduction statutes. Where such laws still exist, they generally provide that the female victim must be of previous chaste character

CASE IN POINT

SEDUCTION

A young man in Kentucky maintained that he was willing to marry the woman he seduced, but his parents would not consent so he could not secure a license. He was convicted of seduction, and he appealed. The appellate court upheld his conviction and sentence but was willing to give him another chance. The court directed the local judge to inform the defendant that he would be permitted to obtain a license without his parents' consent. The court then ruled: "If, upon such advice, the accused renews his statement of willingness to marry, the court will order that consent of the accused's parents be dispensed with, and that upon the marriage the judgment of conviction be suspended. Otherwise, the conviction will stand."

Combs v. Commonwealth, 283 S.W. 2d 714, 715 (Ky. 1955).

(i.e., one who has not voluntarily lost her virginity outside the bonds of wedlock), and that the male's promise to marry must be absolute and precede the act of intercourse. *State v. Wells,* 188 S.E. 326 (N.C. 1936). Statutes often stipulate that the offense can be committed only by a male of marriageable age. See, for example, *State v. Creed,* 88 S.E. 511 (N.C. 1916).

Today criminal prosecutions for seduction are rare. Historically, they served a significant role in persuading a recalcitrant suitor to marry the woman he seduced or face criminal proceedings.

Incest

Incest is sexual intercourse within or outside the bonds of marriage between persons related within certain prohibited degrees. *Haller v. State,* 232 S.W. 2d 829 (Ark. 1950). Incest was not a crime at common law but was punishable by the ecclesiastical courts. *State v. Tucker,* 93 N.E. 3 (Ind. 1910).

There are strong religious and moral taboos against incest. Furthermore, it has been almost universally believed that incest not only disrupts family relationships but also leads to genetically defective offspring. For these reasons, all states prohibit marriage or sexual relations between certain close relatives.

In *State v. Tucker,* the Indiana Supreme Court explained the background of incest as an offense in the United States by stating:

> [I]ncest has been forbidden to some extent by general custom, from the earliest times, and by peoples very little advanced in civilization. It is generally agreed that marriages between persons in the direct lineal line of consanguinity, and also between brother and sister, are unlawful as against the law of nature, independent of any church canon or statutory prohibition. This inflexible rule arises from the institution of the family, the basis of civilized society; and, the rights, duties, habits, and affections, flowing from that relation. Family intermarriage and domestic licentiousness would inevitably confuse parental filial duties and affections, and corrupt the moral sentiments of mankind. *State v. Tucker,* 93 N.E. 3 (Ind. 1910).

Statutes that prohibit intermarriage or sexual relations between persons within certain degrees of kinship usually refer to relationship by consanguinity (i.e., blood relationships). Typically, Florida law provides:

> Whoever knowingly marries or has sexual intercourse with a person to whom he is related by lineal consanguinity, or a brother, sister, uncle, aunt, nephew, or niece, commits incest, which constitutes a felony of the third degree. West's Fla. Stat. Ann. § 826.04.

Statutes do not usually distinguish between relationships of half-blood and full-blood. Some, however, go further than the Florida statute and classify close relationships between persons related by affinity (i.e., marriage), as well as relationships by the blood line, as incestuous. For example, Section 22–22–19.1 of the South Dakota Codified Laws provides: "Any person, fourteen years of age or older, who knowingly engages in sexual contact with another person, other than his spouse, if that person is under the age of twenty-one and is within the degree of consanguinity or affinity within which marriages are by the laws of this state declared void . . . is guilty of a felony."

To prove incest, the prosecution is usually only required to prove the defendant's knowledge of the relationship; the act of sexual intercourse in violation of the statute then satisfies the intent requirement.

Bigamy

Like most sexual offenses, bigamy was originally a canonical offense punishable by the ecclesiastical courts in England; later it became a common-law offense. See *People v. Martin,* 205 P. 121 (Cal. 1922). All American jurisdictions prohibit bigamy (i.e., marriage between two persons when one is already legally married to another). Usually these statutes require the prosecution to prove that the defendant had knowledge of the prior marital status of the person whom he or she married. Since everyone is presumed to know the consequences of his or her acts, no further intent need be shown.

Before the turn of the century, arguments were advanced that polygamy—the practice of one person being married to several spouses at the same time—was a religious practice protected by the First Amendment. These contentions were soundly rejected by the United States Supreme Court when it held that a religious belief cannot be made a justification for commission of an overt act made criminal by the state. *Reynolds v. United States,* 98 U.S. (8 Otto) 145, 25 L.Ed. 244 (1878).

Sodomy

The word *sodomy* is derived from the biblical account of Sodom, the city that was destroyed because of its vices. Sodomy consists of committing acts that were once commonly referred to as "crimes against nature." Sodomy was originally an ecclesiastical offense, but became a felony in the later stages of the common law. In his *Commentaries on the Laws of England,* Blackstone described sodomy as an offense "the very mention of which is a disgrace to human nature" and "a crime not fit to be named." In general, the offense includes oral and/or anal sex between humans and sexual intercourse between humans and animals (the latter is often termed "bestiality"). Until 1961, all states had statutes outlawing sodomy.

Today, less than half the states retain this offense, and enforcement is rare. When a person is prosecuted for sodomy, it is generally as an incident to a charge of rape or sexual battery. When sodomy is nonconsensual, it is considered a crime against a person, not as an offense against morality.

In the mid-1980s, sodomy became the subject of public discussion when a federal appeals court in Georgia struck down that state's sodomy law on the ground that it violated the constitutional right of privacy. The decision came in a civil case brought by an adult male who was arrested (but not prosecuted) for committing sodomy with another adult male in the privacy of his bedroom. In a 5–4 decision, the U.S. Supreme Court overturned the ruling and upheld Georgia's sodomy law. *Bowers v. Hardwick,* 478 U.S. 186, 106 S.Ct. 2841, 92 L.Ed.2d 140 (1986). Writing for the Court in *Hardwick,* Justice White concluded that the Constitution did not confer "a fundamental right to homosexuals to engage in acts of consensual sodomy." 478 U.S. at 192, 106 S.Ct. at 2844, 92 L.Ed.2d at 146. Dissenting, Justice Blackmun, joined by three other members of the Court, insisted that the case was not about the right to engage in homosexual sodomy, but, rather, about "the right to be let alone." 478 U.S. at 199, 106 S.Ct. at 2848, 92 L.Ed.2d at 151. Indeed, the Court's decision left open the question of whether sodomy laws would be enforceable against acts of heterosexual sodomy, whether within or without the bounds of marriage.

As an apparent moral statement, the *Hardwick* decision engendered considerable controversy. But the impact of the decision has been, and will continue to be, quite limited. First, as just noted, many jurisdictions have repealed their prohibitions against sodomy. Second, because most acts of sodomy are performed in private by consenting adults, they tend to be beyond the effective reach of the criminal law.

As noted in Chapter 3, a state constitution may afford more protection to its citizens than does the federal constitution. A recent judicial opinion based on the right of privacy illustrates this point. The Texas Court of Appeals held that the Texas statute criminalizing private sexual relations between consenting adults of the same sex violated the right of privacy guaranteed by the Texas Constitution. The court rejected the state's contention that the law implemented public morality, and further observed that there was no indication that the legislature intended the statute to be a disease-prevention measure. *State v. Morales,* 826 S.W.2d 201 (Tex. Cr. App. 1992).

Kentucky's sodomy statute makes it an offense for persons of the same sex to have consensual oral or anal sex. Observing that, "We need not sympathize, agree with, or even understand the sexual preference of homosexuals in order to recognize their right to equal treatment before the bar of criminal justice," the Kentucky Supreme Court also struck down the sodomy law on the ground that it violated privacy provisions of its state constitution. The court recognized the U.S. Supreme Court's decision in *Bowers v. Hardwick,* but noted that in *Bowers* the Supreme Court did not address the issue of equal protection because, unlike the Kentucky statute, the Georgia law before it applied to both heterosexual and homosexual sodomy. *Wasson v. State,* 842 S.W. 2d 487 (Ky. 1992).

Prostitution

Although prostitution was not a crime at common law, *Commonwealth v. King,* 372 N.E.2d 196 (Mass. 1977), statutes proscribing prostitution have been part of the

CASE IN POINT

Invalidity of Sodomy Law Under the New York Constitution

Ronald Onofre was charged with violating New York's consensual sodomy statute. Before his trial, Onofre moved for a dismissal of the indictment on the ground that enforcement of the statute invaded his constitutional right to privacy. After the motion was denied, Onofre admitted to having had "deviate sexual intercourse" with another male and was convicted. On appeal, the Appellate Division reversed the conviction and declared the sodomy law unconstitutional. The New York Court of Appeals affirmed, saying that the constitutional right of privacy included the freedom "to seek sexual gratification from what at least once was commonly regarded as 'deviant' conduct, so long as the decisions [to engage in such conduct] are voluntarily made by adults. . . ."

People v. Onofre, 415 N.E.2d 936, 940 (N.Y. 1980).

laws directed against public immorality since the early history of the United States. A prostitute is a person who indulges in indiscriminate sexual activity for hire. Today prostitution is illegal in all states except Nevada, where it exists by local option in some counties, although it is strictly regulated by law. See Nev. Rev. Stat. 201.380, 201.430, 201.440. Historically, statutes prohibiting prostitution have been directed at females who have sexual intercourse with males for compensation, but in recent years, as prostitution by males has increased, enforcement has come to be directed at males as well.

Previously, enforcement was directed almost exclusively at the prostitute. Newer statutes, however, provide for conviction of customers as well as prostitutes. This is appropriate because all participants in an offense should share the responsibility for their acts. Indeed, if the statutes are not so construed, they may be vulnerable to constitutional attack as a denial of equal protection of the law.

Lawmakers have officially deplored the existence of prostitution, and law enforcement authorities have long linked the activity with vice, narcotics offenses, and the exploitation of women. In addition to making prostitution an offense, most states make it an offense to solicit for a prostitute or to live off the earnings of a person engaged in prostitution. Statutes also commonly declare brothels and houses of prostitution as public nuisances.

Texas statutes provide that a person who offers or agrees to engage, or engages in sexual conduct for a fee, or who solicits another in a public place to engage in such conduct commits the misdemeanor offense of prostitution. Vernon's Tex. Penal Code Ann. § 43.02. Texas also makes promotion of prostitution a misdemeanor offense, Vernon's Tex. Penal Code Ann. §§ 43.03–43.04, and makes it a serious felony for a person to cause another by force, threat, or fraud to commit prostitution or to cause by any means a person younger than seventeen years to commit prostitution. Vernon's Tex. Penal Code Ann. § 43.05.

Prostitution has been dealt with primarily at the state and local level, but the federal government has also shown an interest in coping with the problem. The Mann Act, 18 U.S.C.A. § 2421 *et seq.*, prohibits interstate transportation of an individual for purposes of prostitution or with the intent to compel an individual to become a prostitute or to engage in any other immoral practice. The Supreme Court has held that the act applies to transporting persons for immoral purposes even if commercial vice is not involved. *Cleveland v. United States*, 329 U.S. 14, 67 S. Ct. 13, 91 L.Ed. 12 (1946).

Criticism of Laws Regulating Sexual Conduct

Considerable criticism is leveled at laws that proscribe sexual conduct between consenting adults. Those who advocate the repeal of statutes making fornication, adultery, and seduction crimes argue that sexual conduct between consenting adults is essentially a matter of private moral concern. They believe such behavior should be left to the discretion of the participants. Furthermore, they contend that the resources needed to fight serious crime should not be wasted in attempts to apprehend violators of sexual mores. Moreover, they argue that since laws against these activities are largely unenforced, they lend themselves to charges of arbitrary enforcement against persons whose lifestyles are socially unacceptable. Finally, many critics contend that the very fact that these laws are not enforced breeds disrespect and encourages violation of laws that society regards as essential.

There is considerably less support for repeal of laws forbidding incest. Some who do advocate the repeal of these laws advance the same arguments as for decriminalizing fornication, adultery, and seduction. Additionally, many who see incest as a genuine concern urge that government should approach the problem through counseling and by furnishing psychiatric assistance to transgressors, rather than making incest a penal offense.

TABLE 8.1 PROSTITUTION ARRESTS IN THE UNITED STATES, 1990, BY AGE AND SEX

Age	**Arrests**	**Percent***
Under 18	1281	1%
18–24	26,262	29%
25–29	25,875	28%
30–34	18,981	21%
35–39	9,703	11%
40–64	8,496	9%
65 and over	495	1%
Sex	**Arrests**	**Percent***
Male	32,770	36%
Female	58,323	64%
Total	91,093	100%

Note: Percentages have been rounded to nearest whole number.
Source: *Sourcebook of Criminal Justice Statistics 1991*, U.S. Department of Justice, Bureau of Justice Statistics, Washington, D.C.: USGPO, 1992.

Those who oppose the prostitution laws now extant in the United States point to the fact that the so-called oldest profession has survived many centuries of condemnation and yet exists as a cultural institution. Thus, they argue, it fulfills a socially desirable function because it furnishes an outlet for certain sexual impulses and tends to lessen the incidence of forcible sexual attacks on women. In addition to the need to conserve scarce resources to fight serious crime and the futility of trying to eradicate an ingrained institution, reformers contend that legalization of prostitution would lead to needed regulation. This, they point out, could provide for medical inspections to diminish the spread of sexually transmitted diseases. Finally, many critics of the present laws concerning prostitution contend that legalization would allow the police to wrest control of this activity from the grips of organized crime, and prohibit more effectively many of the vices that now accompany prostitution.

Bigamy and polygamy are still practiced in some areas. Given the fact that such marriages are considered null and void, some argue criminalizing such conduct is unnecessary. There is, however, no great movement to abolish such laws, and, in truth, any such effort would probably be to little avail.

The Prognosis for Reform

The repeal of laws prohibiting fornication is not a priority item for legislators. However, when criminal codes are revised, such laws often disappear. In our monogamous society, laws proscribing adultery will most likely remain as a public statement on morality, but for the reasons indicated, they will be largely unenforced. Seduction has been for the most part relegated to civil suits for breach of promise to marry, but even this type of action has been outlawed in many jurisdictions.

The practice of incest among those related by consanguinity is widely condemned in Western civilization, and laws forbidding it will undoubtedly remain. There is an area for limited reform. As noted, certain statutes forbid marriage among certain persons related by affinity. To the extent that incest statutes prohibit such practices as a brother marrying his deceased brother's wife, a change would be inoffensive to most and welcomed by many. In some cultures, such a practice is regarded as an obligation.

Monogamy is an ingrained institution in contemporary American culture, and it seems safe to predict that scattered efforts to revise laws prohibiting bigamy will continue to fall on deaf ears of legislators.

The prognosis on prostitution is a difficult one. One certainty is that increasingly, buyers as well as sellers of sexual services will be prosecuted. Despite the cries for reform, any decriminalization of prostitution will most likely be in selected locations only, and will confine activities to prescribed areas. The inherent privacy of the scene of offenses makes it very difficult to apprehend prostitutes and their customers. Therefore, enforcement is better directed to prosecution of those who are the procurers of prostitutes and solicitors for their services and not merely to those who render their services.

INDECENT EXPOSURE

At common law, it was a misdemeanor for persons to intentionally expose their "private parts" in a public place. *Noblett v. Commonwealth,* 72 S.E. 2d 241 (Va.

1952). Today, statutes and local ordinances in most jurisdictions make it a misdemeanor to expose one's private parts to the view of another under offensive circumstances. A number of state courts have upheld laws criminalizing indecent exposure against a variety of constitutional challenges. See, for example, *Keller v. State,* 738 P. 2d 186 (Okl. Crim. App. 1987), *cert. denied,* 484 U.S. 940, 108 S. Ct. 323, 98 L.Ed.2d 351 (1987); *State v. Ludwig,* 468 So.2d 1151 (La. 1985). Such laws, however, have been generally interpreted not to prohibit public exposure of the buttocks. See, for example, *Duvallon v. District of Columbia,* 515 A.2d 724 (D.C. App. 1986).

Frequently the offense of indecent exposure is termed "lewd and lascivious conduct." Because a person may expose himself or herself either accidentally or of necessity, laws generally provide that indecent exposure must be done willfully and in an offensive manner. See, for example, *People v. Randall,* 711 P.2d 689 (Colo. 1985). Often statutes require that offensive exposure must be in the "presence" of another person. Interpreting the term *presence,* the Florida Supreme Court has ruled that the term "encompasses sensory awareness as well as physical proximity." Consequently, the court reversed the conviction of a man who admitted to masturbating in the presence of his thirteen-month-old child. In the court's view, the child did not have "sensory awareness" of the act in question. *State v. Werner,* 609 So.2d 585 (Fla. 1992).

Nude Dancing in Places of Public Accommodation

Is nude dancing for entertainment in a bar or theater a form of indecent exposure? Or is it a form of expression protected by the First Amendment? In *Barnes v. Glen Theatre,* 501 U.S. ___, 111 S.Ct. 2456, 115 L.Ed.2d 504 (1991), the U.S. Supreme Court upheld an Indiana law that prohibited totally nude dancing. Writing for a plurality of justices, Chief Justice Rehnquist observed that "the governmental interest served by the text of the prohibition is societal disapproval of nudity in public places and among strangers." 501 U.S. at ___, 111 S.Ct. at 2463, 115 L.Ed.2d at 515. In Rehnquist's view, "Indiana's requirement that the dancers wear at least pasties and a G-string is modest, and the bare minimum necessary to achieve the state's purpose." 501 U.S. at ___, 111 S.Ct. at 2463, 115 L.Ed.2d at 515.

CASE IN POINT

INDECENT EXPOSURE

A man exposing himself in a second-story apartment in New Orleans was seen from below by persons in the apartment parking lot. He was prosecuted for indecent exposure under a statute that had been interpreted as criminalizing indecent exposure if it was viewable from any location open to the public. In upholding his conviction, the Louisiana Supreme Court noted that the parking lot from which the victims observed the man exposing himself was not enclosed, nor was it posted as private property, and was open to any visitors to the apartment complex.

State v. Clark, 372 So.2d 1218 (La. 1979).

Nudity and Seminudity on Public Beaches

Historically, public nudity has been taboo in Western societies. Yet only a few states have imposed outright bans. Many states maintain that public nudity on beaches and other recreational areas violates laws proscribing lewd and lascivious conduct or indecent exposure. For example, in Florida, where public beaches are popular attractions, signs are commonly posted notifying beachgoers that nude sunbathing is a violation of Florida Statute Section 877.03. Actually, that law prohibits "such acts as are of a nature to corrupt the public morals, or outrage the sense of public decency, or affect the peace and quiet of persons who may witness them." Arrests under this provision are not common, and the Florida appellate courts have yet to address the question of whether this section actually prohibits nude sunbathing. Meanwhile, Miami Beach and other Florida cities that attract large numbers of tourists have set aside specified areas where topless or nude sunbathing is permitted. Currently some local governing bodies in Florida are debating whether abbreviated types of beach attire, such as "thong bikinis," should be permitted on public beaches. Whether nude sunbathing should be permitted in public areas is moving to the forefront as such organizations as the American Sunbathing Association seek to expand recreational opportunities for those who perceive current societal restrictions on nudity as excessively repressive.

OBSCENITY

At common law, vulgar and obscene language and indecent public exhibitions were considered public nuisances, punishable as misdemeanors. See *State v. Miller,* 112 S.E.2d 472 (W. Va. 1960). Historically, federal and state governments in the United States passed laws banning various forms of obscenity. By the late 1800s, Congress had made it an offense to mail any "obscene, lewd or lascivious paper or writing" and provided that the word *obscene* should be given fully as broad a significance as it had at common law. *Knowles v. United States,* 170 F. 409 (8th Cir. 1909). The states also passed laws making sale or distribution of obscene materials a crime. Typically, Section 6567 of the Connecticut General Statutes (1949 Revision) provided that "Buying, selling, giving or showing any obscene, indecent or impure book, paper or picture is a crime." Likewise, most municipalities adopted ordinances proscribing various forms of obscenity.

Statutes and ordinances making obscenity an offense seldom defined it. Thus, they were vulnerable to contentions that they were vague and did not provide an ascertainable standard of guilt. As questions arose, the courts tended to define obscenity as sexual or erotic speech or conduct. The word *obscene* came to mean something offensive to the senses, that is, repulsive, disgusting, foul, or filthy. See *Williams v. State,* 94 So. 882 (Miss. 1923).

The Emerging Constitutional Standards

As mass communications developed, laws banning obscene speech, materials, and performances became subject to scrutiny under the First Amendment. The Supreme Court's first direct encounter with regulating obscenity came in *Roth v.*

United States, 354 U.S. 476, 77 S.Ct. 1304, 1 L.Ed.2d 1498 (1957). Roth was found guilty of sending erotic materials through the mail, and his conviction was affirmed on appeal. The Supreme Court granted review and announced that the dispositive issue was "whether obscenity is utterance within the area of protected speech and press." The Court held that obscenity was not constitutionally protected; rather, the Court viewed it as "utterly without redeeming social importance." After observing that "sex and obscenity are not synonymous," Justice Brennan, writing for the Court, said the test for determining obscenity was "whether to the average person applying contemporary community standards, the dominant theme of the material taken as a whole, appeals to the prurient interest."

By the late 1950s, there was a flood of erotic materials on the market. Whether particular materials were obscene had become an increasingly important issue. *Roth* effectively made the definition of obscenity a matter of federal constitutional law. It also evidenced the Court's concern for First Amendment freedoms and for protecting the free flow of expression from local interpretations of what constituted obscenity. Because of the problems in determining whether materials were obscene under the *Roth* standards, law enforcement officers experienced great difficulty in enforcing obscenity laws.

From 1957 to 1973, the Supreme Court granted review of a number of lower court decisions determining that particular books, plays, and movies were obscene, often explicating due process guidelines to be followed by lower courts in determining what constitutes obscenity. During this period the Court found the French film, "The Lovers," not to be obscene, and implied that national standards would govern in determining whether materials were obscene. There Justice Stewart, in expressing the view that obscenity is limited to "hard-core pornography," made his oft-quoted remark on obscenity, "I know it when I see it." *Jacobellis v. Ohio,* 378 U.S. 184, 197, 84 S. Ct. 1676, 1683, 12 L.Ed.2d 793 (1964) (Stewart, J. concurring).

As the 1970s approached, observers speculated that the Supreme Court was taking a more liberal approach. In *Stanley v. Georgia,* 394 U.S. 557, 89 S. Ct. 1243, 22 L.Ed.2d 542 (1969), the Court reviewed a defendant's conviction for violating a statute making knowing possession of obscene materials a crime. In *Stanley,* the police had seized materials (which the Court assumed to be obscene) from the defendant's home. In reversing the defendant's conviction, the Court held that "the State may no more prohibit mere possession of obscene matter on the ground that it may lead to antisocial conduct than it may prohibit possession of chemistry books on the ground that they may lead to the manufacture of homemade spirits." *Stanley,* 394 U.S. at 567, 89 S.Ct. at 1248, 22 L.Ed.2d at 551. Some read *Stanley* as an indication the Court was relaxing its standards on regulating obscenity. They were mistaken.

The Intractable Obscenity Problem

When the Supreme Court decided the seminal case of *Miller v. California,* 413 U.S. 15, 93 S.Ct. 2607, 37 L.Ed.2d 419 (1973), it referred to it as "one of a group of 'obscenity-pornography' cases" involving what Justice Harlan has called "the 'intractable obscenity problem'." 413 U.S. at 16, 93 S. Ct. at 2610, 37 L.Ed.2d at 426.

In *Miller,* the defendant had mailed unsolicited material containing explicit sexual drawings in violation of a California law. A jury found him guilty and an appellate court upheld the judgment without opinion. At the outset, Chief Justice Burger reiterated that obscene materials were unprotected by the Constitution. Then the Court made two revisions in its interpretations in *Roth*. First, the Court defined *community* in order to permit local juries to base their judgments on local and not national standards. Then the Court redefined the standards for determining obscenity, saying that the

> basic guidelines for the trier of fact must be: (1) whether "the average person, applying contemporary community standards" would find that the work, taken as a whole, appeals to the prurient interest; (b) whether the work depicts or describes, in a patently offensive way, sexual conduct specifically defined by the applicable state law; and (c) whether the work, taken as a whole, lacks serious literary, artistic, political, or scientific value. 413 U.S. at 24, 93 S.Ct. 2614, 37 L.Ed.2d at 431.

Finally, the Court expressly rejected any requirement that the challenged materials be found to be "utterly without redeeming social importance." 413 U.S. at 24, 93 S.Ct. at 2614, 37 L.Ed.2d at 431.

The Court gave examples of "patently offensive" by saying it meant "representations or descriptions of ultimate sexual acts, normal or perverted, actual or simulated . . . representations or descriptions of masturbation, excretory functions, and lewd exhibition of genitals." 413 U.S. at 25, 93 S.Ct. at 2615, 327 L.Ed.2d at 431. The Court made it clear that no one would be subject to prosecution unless the materials alleged to be obscene described patently offensive "hard-core" sexual conduct.

In a companion case, *Paris Adult Theatre I v. Slaton,* 413 U.S. 49, 93 S.Ct. 2628, 37 L.Ed.2d 446 (1973), the Court observed that the states have a right to "maintain a decent society" and may challenge obscene material even if it is shown only to consenting adults.

These decisions indicated an increasing concern over the issue of obscenity and allowed local juries to make judgments based on more explicit standards. They also tended to eliminate the practice of using expert witnesses to testify on such issues as contemporary community standards and whether materials were "utterly without redeeming social value."

Significant Post-*Miller* Developments

Miller may have clarified the tests for obscenity, but it did not satisfy those who sought to ban pornographic materials. For example, "Carnal Knowledge," a very successful movie in the early 1970s, was held not obscene under the *Miller* test. There were scenes in which "ultimate sexual acts" were understood to be taking place; however, the camera did not focus on the bodies of the actors nor was there any exhibition of genitals during such scenes. The Court said that the film was not a "portrayal of hard core sexual conduct for its own sake, and for the ensuing commercial gain" and did not depict sexual conduct in a patently offensive way. *Jenkins v. Georgia,* 418 U.S. 153, 161, 94 S. Ct. 2750, 2755, 41 L.Ed.2d 642, 650 (1974).

The 1980s witnessed two significant developments in the laws concerning obscenity. First, in *New York v. Ferber,* 458 U.S. 747, 102 S.Ct. 3348, 73 L.Ed.2d 1113

(1982), a unanimous Supreme Court held that child pornography, like obscenity, is unprotected by the First Amendment to the Constitution. The Court upheld a New York law prohibiting persons from distributing materials that depict children engaging in lewd sex. The Court found such laws valid even if the material does not appeal to the prurient interest of the average person and is not portrayed in a patently offensive manner. The Court found a compelling state interest in protecting the well-being of children and perceived no value in permitting performances and photo reproductions of children engaged in lewd sexual conduct.

The second significant development was a refinement of the Court's decision in *Miller.* In *Pope v. Illinois,* 481 U.S. 497, 107 S.Ct. 1918, 95 L.Ed.2d 439 (1987), the Court said that application of "contemporary community standards" is appropriate in evaluating the first two prongs of the *Miller* test for obscenity, that is, the work's appeal to the prurient interest and its patent offensiveness. However, the Court concluded that the third prong concerning the work's value cannot be tested by "community standards." The Court said the third prong must be determined on an objective basis, with the proper inquiry being

> not whether an ordinary member of any given community would find serious literary, artistic, political, or scientific value in allegedly obscene material, but whether a reasonable person would find such value in the material, taken as a whole. 481 U.S. at 500, 107 S.Ct. at 1921, 95 L.Ed.2d at 445.

State and Local Regulation of Obscenity

States, of course, may interpret their own constitutions to allow greater freedom of expression than is allowed under the current federal constitutional interpretations. In that vein, in 1987 the Oregon Supreme Court said:

> In this state any person can write, print, read, say, show or sell anything to a consenting adult even though that expression may be generally or universally condemned as "obscene." *State v. Henry,* 732 P.2d 9, 18 (Or. 1987).

Some states classify violations of their obscenity statutes by degree. For example, in New York, a person is guilty of obscenity in the third degree when, knowing its content and character, he or she:

1. Promotes, or possesses with intent to promote, any obscene material; or
2. Produces, presents or directs an obscene performance or participates in a portion thereof which is obscene or which contributes to its obscenity. McKinney's N.Y. Penal Law § 235.05.

A person is guilty of obscenity in the second degree "when he commits the crime of obscenity in the third degree ... and has been previously convicted of obscenity in the third degree." McKinney's N.Y. Penal Law § 235.06. A person is guilty of obscenity in the first degree "when, knowing its content and character, he wholesale promotes or possesses with intent to wholesale promote, any obscene material." McKinney's N.Y. Penal Law § 235.07. New York law makes third-degree obscenity a misdemeanor, while second- or first-degree obscenity is a felony.

States generally set higher penalties for exposing juveniles to pictures or shows where obscenity or even pornography is involved. In New York, disseminating indecent material to minors is a felony. McKinney's N.Y. Penal Law § 235.22.

Defenses to Charges of Obscenity

New York law provides a defense for those charged with obscenity if they can establish that the allegedly obscene material was disseminated to or performed for an audience of persons having scientific, educational, governmental, or other similar justification for possessing or viewing the material. McKinney's N.Y. Penal Law § 235.15. Moreover, it is a defense for disseminating indecent material to minors if the defendant had reasonable cause to believe that the minor involved was seventeen years old or older and exhibited official documentation to the defendant to establish that fact. McKinney's N.Y. Penal Law § 235.22. This latter provision was undoubtedly inserted to protect theater personnel from conviction on a strict liability basis.

Problems of Enforcement

Police and prosecutors often experience difficulty in determining what is to be considered obscene based on "contemporary community standards." Juries in most instances now determine the issue of obscenity simply by reviewing the material. As a result, it is not unusual for a given work to be determined obscene by a jury in one locality and not obscene by another jury in a different locality. For example, the rock musical stage production, "Hair," was found not to be obscene by a federal court in Georgia. *Southeastern Promotions, Ltd. v. Atlanta*, 334 F.Supp. 634 (N.D. Ga. 1971). The following year, it was found to be obscene by another federal court in Tennessee, but this decision was reversed by the Supreme Court. *Southeastern Promotions, Inc. v. Conrad*, 341 F.Supp. 465 (E.D. Tenn. 1972), *aff'd.*, 486 F.2d 894 (6th Cir. 1973), *rev'd.*, 420 U.S. 546, 95 S.Ct. 1239, 43 L.Ed.2d 448 (1975).

Legal problems incident to searches and seizures of allegedly obscene materials can be very technical. Since books, movies, and even live performances are presumptively protected by the First Amendment, the Supreme Court has held that police must obtain a search warrant prior to searches and seizures of such materials. *Roaden v. Kentucky*, 413 U.S. 496, 93 S. Ct. 2796, 37 L.Ed.2d 757 (1973). The Court has explained, however, that the Fourth Amendment does not prohibit undercover police officers from purchasing allegedly obscene materials because such a purchase would not constitute a "seizure." *Maryland v. Macon*, 472 U.S. 463, 105 S. Ct. 2778, 86 L.Ed.2d 370 (1985).

Likewise, courts are constantly being called upon to interpret the application of obscenity laws. In 1977, in *State v. Anonymous*, 377 A.2d 1342 (Conn. Super. 1977), the court considered a case of a high-school boy who, while riding on a school bus, extended his middle finger toward a highway trooper. He was charged under a statute making it an offense for a person to make an obscene gesture in a public place "with intent to cause inconvenience, annoyance or alarm or recklessly creating a risk thereof." 377 A.2d at 1343. The court found

CASE IN POINT

OBSCENITY

In the first federal appeals court decision applying the *Miller v. California* obscenity test to a musical composition, the Eleventh Circuit Court of Appeals ruled that the recording "As Nasty as They Wanna Be" by 2 Live Crew was not obscene. The Eleventh Circuit ruled that, even assuming the work was "patently offensive" and appealed to a "prurient interest," the trial judge erred in concluding, simply on the basis of his own listening to a tape recording, that the work lacked "serious artistic value."

Luke Records, Inc. v. Navarro, 960 F.2d 134 (11th Cir. 1992).

that the student was not guilty of violating the statute. To be obscene, the court said, an expression "must be in a significant way erotic." 377 A.2d at 1343 (citing *Cohen v. California,* 403 U.S. 15, 91 S. Ct. 1780, 29 L.Ed.2d 284 (1971)).

Profanity

Many states and local communities have statutes and ordinances making it an offense to use loud and profane language in public places. In recent years there have been challenges to the constitutionality of these measures. In some cases courts have struck down such laws for vagueness. In other instances courts have upheld their validity but ruled that such laws can be applied only where the defendant's language consisted of "fighting words" or the defendant's conduct threatened a breach of the peace (see Chapter 11).

GAMBLING

Traditionally, to gamble has meant to risk money on an event, chance, or contingency in the hope of realizing a gain. See *State v. Stripling,* 21 So. 409 (Ala. 1897). The common law did not regard gambling as an offense. *Bowden v. Nugent,* 226 P. 549 (Ariz. 1924). However, many of the new American states, either by constitution or statute, made all or certain forms of gambling illegal. Today federal laws and a variety of state statutes and local ordinances prohibit gambling. Laws regulating gambling come under the "police power" of the state, and the United States Supreme Court has recognized that there is no constitutional right to gamble. *Lewis v. United States,* 348 U.S. 419, 75 S.Ct. 415, 99 L.Ed. 475 (1955).

Bingo, craps, baccarat, poker, raffles, bookmaking, and slot machines are just a few common forms of gambling. Gambling also includes betting on sports events and card games. Many forms of gambling are legal; therefore, when considering gambling, we must separate the legal from the illegal. For example, those who pay something of value, that is, "a legal consideration," to take a chance to win a prize in a lottery are gambling. In many jurisdictions this is a criminal offense. Yet in several states lotteries are not only legal, they are an important source of public revenue. In effect, it is unregulated gambling that is illegal. A common form of unregulated gambling is "numbers." To play, you place a bet on a number with the hope that it will correspond to a preselected number. The "numbers racket" is widespread and, along with prostitution, is a major source of income for organized crime.

What Constitutes Gambling?

Retail stores conduct a variety of promotional schemes; local carnivals and fairs offer opportunities to play a variety of games for prizes. When are they gambling and when are they games of skill? And if games of skill, are they exempt from laws prohibiting gambling? Some statutes regulating gambling provide the answer. In other instances, courts may be called on to determine whether a particular activity offends a statutory prohibition against gambling. It is generally agreed that to constitute gambling, the activity must include these three elements: (1) a consideration, (2) a prize, and (3) a chance.

Most statutes prohibiting gambling are interpreted to exclude athletics or other contests in which participants pit their physical or mental skills against one another for a prize. Courts tend to be practical in their interpretations. For example, an Ohio appellate court found that a pinball machine that allowed the outcome of its operation to be determined largely by the skill of the user was not "a game of chance," and the pinball operators were not in violation of the Ohio gambling statute. *Progress Vending, Inc. v. Department of Liquor Control,* 394 N.E.2d 324 (Ohio App. 1978).

Statutory Regulation of Gambling

A federal statute called the Travel Act, 18 U.S.C.A. § 1952, prohibits interstate travel in aid of gambling. The act is not aimed at local criminal activity; its purpose is rather to attack crime that has a definite interstate aspect. *United States v. O'Dell,* 671 F.2d 191 (6th Cir. 1982).

Many states proscribe gambling broadly much the same as Florida law, which provides:

> Whoever plays or engages in any game at cards, keno, roulette, faro or other game of chance, at any place, by any device whatever, for money or other thing of value, shall be guilty of a misdemeanor of the second degree. West's Fla. Stat. Ann. § 849.08.

Typically, the Florida law creates exceptions for retail merchandising promotions. West's Fla. Stat. Ann. § 849.09. It also permits charitable, nonprofit, and veterans' organizations to conduct "bingo," a game in which players pay for the use of one or more bingo cards, numbers are drawn by chance, and prizes are awarded. West's Fla. Stat. Ann. §§ 849.093 and 849.0935. Where gambling is prohibited, states customarily make it unlawful to possess gambling devices and provide for their confiscation. See, for example, West's Fla. Stat. Ann. §§ 849.231, 849.232.

TABLE 8.2 LEGALIZED GAMBLING BY STATE

State	Gambling Allowed
Alabama	Pari-mutuel betting, bingo, tribal gaming
Alaska	Bingo only
Arizona	Pari-mutuel betting, lottery, bingo, tribal gaming
Arkansas	Pari-mutuel betting only
California	Pari-mutuel betting, lottery, card rooms, bingo, tribal gaming
Colorado	Pari-mutuel betting, lottery, casinos, bingo, tribal gaming
Connecticut	Pari-mutuel betting, lottery, bingo, tribal gaming, jai alai
Delaware	Pari-mutuel betting, lottery, bingo
District of Columbia	Lottery, bingo
Florida	Pari-mutuel betting, lottery, bingo, tribal gaming, jai alai
Georgia	Bingo
Hawaii	None
Idaho	Pari-mutuel betting, lottery, tribal gaming
Illinois	Pari-mutuel betting, lottery, bingo, riverboat casinos
Indiana	Lottery, bingo
Iowa	Pari-mutuel betting, lottery, riverboat casinos, bingo, tribal gaming
Kansas	Pari-mutuel betting, lottery, bingo, tribal gaming
Kentucky	Pari-mutuel betting, lottery, bingo
Louisiana	Pari-mutuel betting, lottery, bingo, tribal gaming; one casino (New Orleans)
Maine	Pari-mutuel betting, lottery, bingo
Maryland	Pari-mutuel betting, lottery, casinos, bingo
Massachusetts	Pari-mutuel betting, lottery, bingo
Michigan	Pari-mutuel betting, lottery, bingo, tribal gaming
Minnesota	Pari-mutuel betting, lottery, bingo, tribal gaming
Mississippi	Bingo, riverboat casinos
Missouri	Lottery, bingo, tribal gaming
Montana	Lottery, bingo, casinos, pari-mutuel betting, tribal gaming
Nebraska	Lottery, bingo, pari-mutuel betting, jai alai
Nevada	Bingo, casinos, pari-mutuel betting, sports betting
New Hampshire	Lottery, bingo, pari-mutuel betting
New Jersey	Lottery, bingo, pari-mutuel betting, casino gambling (Atlantic City only)
New Mexico	Bingo, pari-mutuel betting, tribal gaming
New York	Lottery, bingo, pari-mutuel betting, tribal gaming
North Carolina	Bingo, jai alai
North Dakota	Bingo, pari-mutuel betting, tribal gaming
Ohio	Lottery, bingo, pari-mutuel betting
Oklahoma	Bingo, pari-mutuel betting, tribal gaming
Oregon	Lottery, bingo, pari-mutuel betting, jai alai, tribal gaming
Pennsylvania	Lottery, bingo, pari-mutuel betting
Rhode Island	Lottery, bingo, pari-mutuel betting
South Carolina	Bingo, jai alai
South Dakota	Lottery, bingo, pari-mutuel betting, tribal gaming
Tennessee	Pari-mutuel betting
Texas	Bingo, pari-mutuel betting
Utah	None
Vermont	Lottery, bingo, pari-mutuel betting
Virginia	Lottery, bingo, pari-mutuel betting
Washington	Lottery, bingo, pari-mutuel betting, tribal gaming
West Virginia	Lottery, bingo, pari-mutuel betting
Wisconsin	Lottery, bingo, pari-mutuel betting, tribal gaming
Wyoming	Bingo, pari-mutuel betting

CASE IN POINT

What Constitutes an Illegal Gaming Machine?

The Michigan Liquor Control Commission imposed a $250 fine on the Sanford Eagles Club for having a "video poker" machine on its premises. The machine had five windows, and when a quarter was deposited, a playing card appeared in each window. Essentially, the contestant played a game of five-card draw against the machine. A "winner" could gain credits entitling the player to free replays based on a random "reshuffling" of the cards. After administrative and judicial hearings, the Court of Appeals held that the machine was not an illegal gaming device, since there was no monetary payoff. The Michigan Supreme Court reversed. The Court based its decision on a provision of the statute addressing gambling devices that exempted mechanical amusement devices that reward a player with replays as long as the device is not allowed to accumulate more than fourteen replays at one time. Because the video poker machine at issue in this case permitted the player to accumulate more than fourteen replays, it did not fall within the statutory exemption.

Automatic Music and Vending Corp. v. Liquor Control Comm., 396 N.W. 204 (Mich. 1986).

Prosecutorial Problems; Defenses

The problems encountered in enforcing prostitution and sexual laws are also obstacles to enforcing gambling statutes. Due to the consensual nature of gambling, apprehension of violators largely depends on the use of informants by police. Procedures for obtaining search and arrest warrants are technical and require close adherence to Fourth Amendment standards.

The prosecution, of course, must prove all elements of the offense. In most instances, this requires proof of a consideration, a prize, and a chance; however, some statutes have eliminated the requirement of a consideration. If the statute prohibiting gambling makes intent an element of the offense, the prosecution must prove the defendant's intent; otherwise, it is sufficient merely to prove the act of gambling.

Texas law makes it an offense to bet on results of games, contests, political nominations, or elections or to play games with cards and dice. See Vernon's Tex. Penal Code Ann. § 47.02(a). The state legislature has taken a pragmatic approach by providing that it is a defense to prosecution under that section of the statute if

> (1) the actor engaged in gambling in a private place; (2) no person received any economic benefit other than personal winnings; and (3) except for the advantage of skill or luck, the risks of losing and the chances of winning were the same for all participants. Vernon's Tex. Penal Code Ann. § 47.02(b).

In some instances a defendant charged with gambling may succeed in establishing entrapment, a defense discussed in Chapter 13.

The Paradox of Gambling Laws

The law on gambling seems paradoxical. Some laws authorize nonprofit organizations to conduct certain forms of gambling forbidden to others. In some states people can legally bet at dog tracks and horse tracks, yet may still be prosecuted for betting in their own homes on the World Series or the Kentucky Derby. Many reformers contend that present laws are ineffective to suppress gambling. Instead, they claim these laws actually lend support to the activities of organized crime.

Certain forms of legalized gambling, particularly state lotteries and state-franchised dog and horse tracks, have become increasingly acceptable. Yet unregulated forms of gambling will most likely continue to be prohibited in most instances. In any event, if inroads are to be made in controlling unregulated gambling, enforcement efforts must be directed primarily toward gambling activity that is under control of organized crime syndicates.

CONCLUSION

In addition to defining crimes against persons and property and establishing rules necessary to preserve public order, the law proscribes certain forms of conduct simply because they offend societal morality. Chief among these prohibitions are the laws prohibiting certain forms of sexual activity, public indecency, obscenity, profanity, and gambling. Offenses involving the use of alcohol and drugs, while sometimes categorized as offenses against public morality, also may be seen as threats to the public order, safety, and peace. They are therefore dealt with in a separate chapter.

Most offenses against morality, it should be remembered, are ecclesiastical in origin. Many now question whether the criminal law ought to be a vehicle for enforcing moral standards that originated from religious sources. However, the courts have not rejected morality as a proper basis for the criminal law. Clearly, the fact that a form of conduct was or is proscribed by one or more religious traditions is not a sufficient basis for criminalizing that activity. But if an act violates societal consensus, even if that consensus derives from religious traditions, it may be legitimately prohibited by the criminal law. As societal consensus changes, as it surely has with respect to sexual activities, pornography, and gambling, the prohibitions of the criminal law must, and do, change as well. Thus the offenses against public morality constitute a particularly dynamic area of the criminal law.

QUESTIONS FOR THOUGHT AND DISCUSSION

1. Is there a rational basis for the law to extend the crime of incest to prohibit intermarriage between persons related by affinity?
2. Should it be a defense to a charge of bigamy that both persons in the alleged bigamous union are adherents to a religious faith that sanctions polygamy?
3. Can the criminalization of sexual conduct such as prostitution and sodomy be reconciled with the constitutional right of privacy discussed in Chapter 3?

4. Would prostitution be more or less inimical to the public health, welfare, and morality if it were legalized and regulated?
5. Tanya Thong has been convicted of indecent exposure stemming from an incident in which she appeared topless on a public beach. On appeal, Thong argues that the indecent exposure statute amounts to unconstitutional sex discrimination because it prohibits women, but not men, from baring their breasts in public. Does Thong have a good argument?
6. Is it more desirable to regulate obscenity by criminalizing it or by using zoning to restrict its dissemination to certain locations?
7. How are laws proscribing obscenity susceptible to overbreadth and vagueness challenges discussed in Chapter 3?
8. What, if any, constitutional objections could be raised against a city ordinance making it a criminal offense "to use profane language in a public place"?
9. What forms of gambling are legal and illegal in your state? Are there any particular games that fall into a grey area between permitted and prohibited activity? Is church bingo legal in your state?
10. Gerald N. runs a video game arcade. One of his most popular games is called "Video Blackjack." Essentially, the game is a computerized form of blackjack in which the contestant plays against the computer. The cost of playing the game is 50 cents. If the contestant wins the game, he or she is issued a token that may used to play any other game in the arcade. Suppose your state gambling statute prohibits all "games involving valuable consideration, chance and a possible prize." If you were the public prosecutor, would you be concerned about the legality of this game?

CASES

BOWERS V. HARDWICK

Supreme Court of the United States, 1986.
478 U.S. 186, 106 S.Ct. 2841, 92 L.Ed.2d 140.

[In this case the Supreme Court considers a challenge to the constitutionality of a Georgia sodomy law as applied to homosexual conduct.]

Justice WHITE delivered the opinion of the Court.

In August 1982, respondent was charged with violating the Georgia statute criminalizing sodomy by committing that act with another adult male in the bedroom of respondent's home. After a preliminary hearing, the District Attorney decided not to present the matter to grand jury unless further evidence developed.

Respondent then brought suit in the Federal District Court, challenging the constitutionality of the statute insofar as it criminalized consensual sodomy. He asserted that he was a practicing homosexual, that the Georgia sodomy statute, as administered by the defendants, placed him in imminent danger of arrest, and that the statute for several reasons violates the Federal Constitution. The District Court granted the defendants' motion to dismiss. . . .

A divided panel of the Court of Appeals for the Eleventh Circuit reversed. . . . Relying on our decisions in *Griswold v. Connecticut* . . . [1965], *Eisenstadt v. Baird* . . . [1972], *Stanley v. Georgia* . . . [1969], and *Roe v. Wade* . . . [1969], the court went on to hold that the Georgia statute violated respondent's fundamental rights because his homosexual activity is a private and intimate association that is beyond the reach of the state regulation by reason of the Ninth Amendment and the Due Process Clause of the Fourteenth Amendment. The case was remanded for trial, at which, to prevail, the State would have to prove that the statute is supported by a compelling interest and is the most narrowly drawn means of achieving that end.

Because other Courts of Appeals have arrived at judgments contrary to that of the Eleventh Circuit in this case, we granted the State's petition for certiorari. . . .

This case does not require a judgment on whether laws against sodomy between consenting adults in general, or between homosexuals in particular, are wise or desirable. It raises no question about the right or propriety of state legislative decisions to repeal their laws that criminalize homosexual sodomy, or of state court decisions invalidating those laws on state constitutional grounds. The issue presented is whether the Federal Constitution confers a fundamental right upon homosexuals to engage in sodomy and hence invalidates the laws of the many States that still make such conduct illegal and have done so for a very long time. . . .

We first register our disagreement with the Court of Appeals . . . that the Court's prior cases have construed the Constitution to confer a right of privacy that extends to homosexual sodomy and for all intents and purposes have decided this case. . . .

Accepting the decisions in these cases and the above description of them, we think it evident that none of the rights announced in those cases bears any resemblance to the claimed constitutional right of homosexuals to engage in acts of sodomy, that is asserted in this case. No connection between family, marriage, or procreation on the one hand and homosexual activity on the other has been demonstrated, either by the Court of Appeals or by respondent. Moreover, any claim that these cases nevertheless stand for the proposition that any kind of private sexual conduct between consenting adults is constitutionally insulated from state proscription is insupportable. . . .

Precedent aside, however, respondent would have us announce, as the Court of Appeals did, a fundamental right to engage in homosexual sodomy. This we are quite unwilling to do. . . .

. . . Sodomy was a criminal offense at common law and was forbidden by the laws of the original thirteen States when they ratified the Bill of Rights. In 1868, when the Fourteenth Amendment was ratified, all but 5 of the 37 States in the Union had criminal sodomy laws. In fact, until 1961, all States outlawed sodomy, and today, 24 States and the District of Columbia continue to provide criminal penalties for sodomy performed in private and between consenting adults.... Against this background, to claim that a right to engage in such conduct is "deeply rooted in this Nation's history and tradition" or "implicit in the concept of ordered liberty" is, at best, facetious....

Nor are we inclined to take a more expansive view of our authority to discover new fundamental rights imbedded in the Due Process Clause. The Court is most vulnerable and comes nearest to illegitimacy when it deals with judge-made constitutional law having little or no recognizable roots in the language or design of the Constitution....

Respondent, however, asserts that the result should be different where the homosexual conduct occurs in the privacy of the home.... Plainly enough, otherwise illegal conduct is not always immunized whenever it occurs in the home. Victimless crimes, such as the possession and use of illegal drugs, do not escape the law where they are committed at home.... And if respondent's submission is limited to the voluntary sexual conduct between consenting adults, it would be difficult, except by fiat, to limit the claimed right to homosexual conduct while leaving exposed to prosecution adultery, incest, and other sexual crimes even though they are committed in the home. We are unwilling to start down that road.

Even if the conduct at issue here is not a fundamental right, respondent asserts that there must be a rational basis for the law and there is none in this case other than the presumed belief of a majority of the electorate in Georgia that homosexual sodomy is immoral and unacceptable. This is said to be an inadequate rationale to support the law. The law, however, is constantly based on notions of morality; and if all laws representing essentially moral choices are to be invalidated under the Due Process Clause, the courts will be very busy indeed. Even respondent makes no such claim, but insists that majority sentiments about the morality of homosexuality should be declared inadequate. We do not agree, and are unpersuaded that the sodomy laws of some 25 States should be invalidated on this basis....

Accordingly, the judgment of the Court of Appeals is reversed.

Chief Justice BURGER, concurring.

I join the Court's opinion, but I write separately to underscore my view that in constitutional terms there is no such thing as a fundamental right to commit homosexual sodomy.

As the Court notes, ... the proscriptions against sodomy have very "ancient roots." Decisions of individuals relating to homosexual conduct have been subject to state intervention throughout the history of Western Civilization. Condemnation of those practices is firmly rooted in Judeao-Christian moral and ethical standards. Homosexual sodomy was a capital crime under Roman law.... During the English Reformation when powers of the ecclesiastical courts were transferred to the King's Courts, the first English statute criminalizing sodomy was passed.... Blackstone described "the infamous crime against nature" as an offense of "deeper malignity" than rape, an heinous act "the very mention of which is a disgrace to human nature," and "a crime not fit to be named."... The common law of England, including its prohibition of sodomy, became the received law of Georgia and the other Colonies. In 1816 the Georgia Legislature passed the statute at issue here, and that statute has been continuously in force in one form or another since that time. To hold that the act of homosexual sodomy is somehow protected as a fundamental right would be to cast aside millennia of moral teaching....

Justice POWELL, concurring....

Justice BLACKMUN, with whom Justice BRENNAN, Justice MARSHALL, and Justice STEVENS join, dissenting.

... The Court concludes today that none of our prior cases dealing with various decisions that individuals are entitled to make free of governmental interference "bears any resemblance to the claimed constitutional right of homosexuals to engage in acts of sodomy that is asserted in this case."... We protect ... rights not because they contribute, in some direct and material way, to the general public welfare, but because they form so central a part of an individual's life. "[T]he concept of privacy embodies the 'moral fact that a person belongs to himself and not others nor to society as a whole.' "...

The behavior for which Hardwick faces prosecution occurred in his own home, a place to which the Fourth Amendment attaches special significance. The Court's treatment of this aspect of this case is symptomatic of its overall refusal to consider the broad principles that have informed our treatment of privacy in specific cases. Just as the right to privacy is more than the mere aggregation of a number of entitlements to engage in specific behavior, so too, protecting the physical integrity of the home is more than merely a means of protecting specific activities that often take place there.... [T]he essence of a Fourth Amendment violation is "not the breaking of [a person's] doors, and the rummaging of his drawers," but rather is "the invasion of his indefeasible right of personal security, personal liberty and private property."...

... [T]he right of an individual to conduct intimate relationships in the intimacy of his or her own home seems to me to be the heart of the Constitution's protection of privacy....

Justice STEVENS, with whom Justice BRENNAN and Justice MARSHALL join, dissenting....

AUSTIN V. STATE

Court of Appeals of Texas, 1990.
794 S.W.2d 408.

[In this case, a Texas appellate court determines whether there was sufficient evidence to support the appellant's conviction for prostitution.]

JOHN F. ONION, Jr., Assigned Justice.

This is an appeal from a conviction for prostitution. Tex. Pen. Code Ann. § 43.02(a)(1) (1989). At the conclusion of the bench trial, the trial court assessed appellant's punishment at sixty (60) days confinement in the county jail, and at a fine of $200.00. The imposition of the sentence was suspended, and the appellant was placed on probation of 180 days subject to certain conditions of probation....

... [A]ppellant contends the evidence was insufficient to support her conviction. The elements of the offense under § 43.03(a)(1) are:

(1) A person
(2) knowingly
(3) offers or agrees to engage in sexual conduct
(4) in return for a fee payable to the actor....

The complaint and information in the instant case alleged in pertinent part that the appellant on or about April 30, 1988, "did then and there knowingly agree to engage in sexual conduct for a fee, to wit: the said Kimberli Austin agreed to have sexual intercourse with J. Hutto for a fee."

Thus, the State had the burden to prove beyond a reasonable doubt that (1) Kimberli Austin (2) did knowingly (3) agree to engage in sexual conduct, to wit: sexual intercourse with J. Hutto (4) for a fee.

In the instant bench trial there was only one witness—Officer John Hutto of the Austin Police Department. He related that on April 20, 1988, he and other officers were in the process of investigating massage parlors and modeling studios; that on that date he went to the Satin Spa in Travis County. Hutto entered a living room area where there was a male and two females. The male told Hutto to select one of the females, and Hutto selected the appellant Austin. She led him down a hall to a room where there was a sign or signs as to the prices for "Basic Body Rub" and "Swedish Deep Muscle Rub." The appellant informed Hutto the "Basic Rub" was a "fingertip" massage, and the "Swedish Deep Muscle Rub" was a "more thorough and stimulating rub." The highest cost of the former was $60.00 for 60 minutes, and the highest cost of the latter was $130.00 for 60 minutes. Hutto, a veteran of several years with the Austin Police Department, had experience with the terminology and understood that "Swedish Deep Muscle Rub" was "a catch phrase" or "key words" for prostitution. Hutto gave appellant $140.00 for the highest price "Swedish" rub. Appellant left the room and returned with his change of $10.00. They both then disrobed. The nude appellant laid face down on the bed and asked Hutto to massage her back, which he did for ten minutes. Then the appellant gave Hutto massage on his back, legs, and buttocks for ten minutes. Appellant then asked Hutto if he would "like to end the session." He pretended not to understand, protesting that he had only been there twenty minutes, and had paid for an hour. Appellant repeated her inquiry. Hutto then asked if they ended the session could he "get more than just a rub." Appellant said "yes," and Hutto inquired whether he needed to pay her more money or give her a tip. Appellant replied "no, it's all taken care of."

The record then reflects on redirect examination:

A. And after she said it was taken care of I asked her what I could get. And she asked me what did I want. And I told her a blow job or maybe a f____k. And she said "Choose one. It's one or the other."

Q. Was that—was either the blow job or the f____k included in the $130.00?

A. That was my understanding. Because she said that it was taken care of when I asked her if I needed to pay more. . . .

A. Well, we agreed on sexual intercourse and she—she—I asked her if she had some protection I could use, and she said "Yes" and got a condom out of her purse.

Q. Did the defendant agree to engage in sexual conduct with you for a fee?

A. Yes.

Q. And specifically what was that sexual conduct?

A. Sexual intercourse.

The trial judge in a bench trial is the sole trier of the facts, the credibility of the witnesses and the weight to be given to their testimony, and may accept any part of or all the testimony given by the witnesses. . . .

Reconciliation of conflicts and inconsistent testimony is for the trier of fact. . . . The trier of fact may believe or disbelieve all or any part of a witness' testimony, and may accept one part of a witness' testimony and reject the remainder. . . . Conflicts will not call for reversal if there is enough credible testimony to support the conviction. . . .

And certainly the credibility of a witness is a matter for the trier of fact rather than for the Court of Appeals. . . .

The standard for review of the sufficiency of evidence is where, viewing the evidence in the light most favorable to the judgment of the court (in a bench trial), any rational trier of fact could have found the essential elements of the crime charged beyond a reasonable doubt. . . . The standard remains the same for direct and circumstantial evidence cases. . . .

Appellant agrees that the prosecution established all the elements of the offense except one. Appellant acknowledges the proof showed she agreed to engage in sexual intercourse, but argues the evidence does not show that she did so "for a fee." She contends the $130.00 "session" ended before she agreed to the sexual intercourse, that she "was no longer being compensated for her personal services, and that she made no effort to obtain compensation for any sexual activity." The State counters that the evidence showed that Hutto agreed to end the 20-minute "session" only after he determined from the appellant that he could get "more than a rub" and that it was "all taken care of," and that the parties agreed to sexual intercourse. There was certainly evidence to this effect, and the trial court was the trier of the facts.". . .

The judgment is affirmed.

POWERS, Justice, dissenting.

. . . I believe the evidence insufficent to establish . . . that Austin "knowingly" agreed to sexual intercourse for a fee. . . .

In the present case, there was no initial agreement for conduct on Austin's part that was explicitly sexual. Instead, the officer paid $130 for a "massage" described as a "Swedish Deep Muscle Rub." If that meant sexual conduct, it was only by innuendo or suspicion. "Swedish Deep Muscle Rub" was ambiguous at best as to what it meant; nominally at least it was a "massage." Thus, the evidence does not show, *without more,* a link between the fee paid by the officer and Austin's subsequent agreement for sexual relations, reached *after* the the fee was paid and the massage begun. . . .

BARNES v. GLEN THEATRE, INC.

Supreme Court of the United States, 1991.
501 U.S. ___, 111 S.Ct. 2456, 115 L.Ed.2d 504.

[Two South Bend, Indiana, establishments that featured all-nude dancing brought suit in the United States District Court for the Northern District of Indiana, seeking an injunction against enforcement of an Indiana statute prohibiting complete nudity in public places. The District Court dismissed the case, concluding that "the type of dancing these plaintiffs wish to perform is not expressive activity protected by the Constitution of the United States." On appeal, the Seventh Circuit reversed, holding that the nude dancing at issue was "expressive conduct protected by the First Amendment." The Supreme Court granted certiorari.]

Chief Justice REHNQUIST . . . [announced the judgment of the Court].

. . . The Kitty Kat Lounge, Inc. (Kitty Kat) is located in the city of South Bend. It sells alcoholic beverages and presents "go-go dancing." Its proprietor desires to present "totally nude dancing," but an applicable Indiana statute regulating public nudity requires that the dancers wear "pasties" and a "G-string" when they dance. . . .

Respondent Glen Theatre, Inc. is an Indiana corporation with a place of business in South Bend. Its primary business is supplying so-called adult entertainment through written and printed materials, movie showings, and live entertainment at the "bookstore" consists of nude and seminude performances and showings of the female body through glass panels. Customers sit in a booth and insert coins into a timing mechanism that permits them to observe the live nude and seminude dancers for a period of time. . . .

Several of our cases contain language suggesting that nude dancing of the kind involved here is expressive conduct protected by the First Amendment. . . .

Indiana, of course, has not banned nude dancing as such, but has proscribed public nudity across the board. The Supreme Court of Indiana has construed the Indiana statute to preclude nudity in what are essentially places of public accommodation such as the Glen Theatre and the Kitty Kat Lounge. In such places, respondents point out, minors are excluded and there are no non-consenting viewers. Respondents contend that while the state may license establishments such as the ones involved here, and limit the geographical area in which they do business, it may not in any way limit the performance of the dances within them without violating the First Amendment. The petitioner contends, on the other hand, that Indiana's restriction on nude dancing is a valid "time, place or manner" restriction. . . .

The "time, place, or manner" test was developed for evaluating restriction on expression taking place on the public property which had been dedicated as a "public forum," . . . although we have on at least one occasion applied it to conduct occurring on private property. . . . . . . [T]his test has been interpreted to embody much the same standards as those set forth in *United States v. O'Brien* . . . (1968), and we turn, therefore, to the rule enunciated in *O'Brien*.. . .

> . . . [W]hen 'speech' and 'nonspeech' elements are combined in the same course of conduct, a sufficiently important governmental interest in regulating the nonspeech element can justify incidental limitation on First Amendment freedoms. . . . [W]e think it clear that a government regulation is sufficiently justified if it is within the constitutional power of the Government; if it furthers an important or substantial governmental interest; if the governmental interest is unrelated to the suppression of free expression; and if the incidental restriction on alleged First Amendment freedoms is no greater than essential to the furtherance of that interest. . . .

Applying the . . . test enunciated above, we find that Indiana's public indecency statute is justified despite its incidental limitations on some expressive activity. The public indecency statute is clearly within the constitutional power of the State and furthers substantial governmental interests. It is impossible to discern, other than from the test of the statute, exactly what governmental interest the Indiana legislators had in mind when they enacted this statute, for Indiana does not record legislative history, and the state's highest court has not shed additional light on the statute's purpose. Nonetheless, the statute's purpose of protecting societal order and morality is clear from its text and history. Public indecency statutes of this sort are of ancient origin, and presently exist in at least 47 States. Public indecency, including nudity, was a criminal offense at common law, and this Court recognized the common-law roots of the offense of "gross and open indecency" in *Winters v. New York* . . . (1948). Public nudity was considered an act *malum en se*.. . .

This public indecency statute follows a long line of earlier Indiana statutes banning all public nudity. The history of Indiana's public indecency statute shows that it predates barroom nude dancing and was enacted as a general prohibition. . . .

This and other public indecency statutes were designed to protect morals and public order. The traditional police power of the States is defined as the authority to provide for the public health, safety, and morals, and we have upheld such a basis for legislation. . . .

Thus, the public indecency statute furthers a substantial government interest in protecting order and morality. This interest is unrelated to the suppression of free expression. Some may view restricting nudity on moral grounds as necessarily related to expression. We disagree. It can be argued, of course, that almost limitless types of conduct—including appearing in the nude in public—are "expressive," and in one sense of the word this is true. People who go about in the nude in public may be expressing something about themselves by so doing. But the court rejected this expansive notion of "expressive conduct" in *O'Brien,* saying

> We cannot accept the view that an apparently limitless variety of conduct can be labeled 'speech' whenever the person engaging in the conduct intends thereby to express an idea. . . .

Respondents contend that even though prohibiting nudity in public generally may not be related to suppressing expression, prohibiting the performance of nude dancing is related to expression because the state seeks to prevent its erotic message. Therefore, they reason that the application of the Indiana statute to the nude dancing in this case violates the First Amendment, because it fails the third part of the *O'Brien* test, viz: the governmental interest must be unrelated to the suppression of free expression.

But we do not think that when Indiana applies its statute to the nude dancing in these nightclubs it is proscribing nudity because of the erotic message conveyed by the dancers. Presumably numerous other erotic performances are presented at these establishments and similar clubs without any interference from the state, so long as the performers wore a scant amount of clothing. Likewise the requirement that the dancers don pasties and a G-string does not deprive the dance of whatever erotic message it conveys; it simply makes the message slightly less graphic. The perceived evil that Indiana seeks to address is not erotic dancing, but public nudity. The appearance of people of all shapes, sizes and ages in the nude at a beach, for example, would convey little if any erotic message, yet the state still seeks to prevent it. Public nudity is the evil the state seeks to prevent, whether or not it is combined with expressive activity. . . .

The fourth part of the *O'Brien* test requires that the incidental restriction on First Amendment freedom be no greater than is essential to the furtherance of the governmental interest. As indicated in the discussion above, the governmental interest served by the text of the prohibition is societal disapproval of nudity in public places and among strangers. The statutory prohibition is not a means to some greater end, but and end in itself. It is without cavil that the public indecency statute is "narrowly tailored"; Indiana's requirement that the dancers wear at least pasties and a G-string is modest, and the bare minimum necessary to achieve the state's purpose.

The judgment of the Court of Appeals accordingly is . . . reversed.

Justice SCALIA, concurring in the judgment. . . .

Justice SOUTER, concurring in the judgment. . . .

Justice WHITE, with whom Justice MARSHALL, Justice BLACKMUN, and Justice STEVENS join, dissenting.

. . . The purpose of forbidding people from appearing nude in parks, beaches, hot dog stands, and like public places is to protect others from offense. But that could not possibly be the purpose of preventing nude dancing in theaters and barrooms since the viewers are exclusively consenting adults who pay money to see these dances. The purpose of the proscription in these contexts is to protect the viewers from what the State believes is the harmful message that nude dancing communicates. . . .

That the performances in the Kitty Kat Lounge may not be high art, to say the least, and may not appeal to the Court, is hardly an excuse for distorting and ignoring settled doctrine. The Court's assessment of the artistic merits of nude dancing performances should not be the determining factor in deciding this case. In the words of Justice Harlan, "it is largely because governmental officials cannot make principled decisions in this area that the Constitution leaves matters of taste and style so largely to the individual." . . . "[W]hile the entertainment afforded by a nude ballet at Lincoln Center to those who can pay the price may differ vastly in content (as viewed by judges) or in quality (as viewed by critics), it may not differ in substance from the dance viewed by the person who . . . wants some 'entertainment' with his beer or shot of rye." . . .

. . . Accordingly, I would affirm the judgment of the Court of Appeals, and dissent from this Court's judgment.

RADEY V. STATE

Court of Appeals of Ohio, 1989.
54 Ohio App. 3d 18, 560 N.E. 2d 247.

[In this case, an Ohio appellate court discusses the operational definition of obscenity. The appellant was charged with pandering obscenity in violation of Ohio law. He was tried before a jury and convicted.]

REECE, Judge.

Defendant-appellant, Richard A. Radey, was arrested by members of the Medina Police Department after he had sold ten greeting cards to two Medina police officers. . . . All of the cards have photographic depictions that are either sexually suggestive or explicit. . . . The photographs often show nude male or female figures and in most cases show one or the other's genitals. In none of the cards is penetration, however slight, depicted. Nor is there a showing of contact between a mouth or tongue and a penis, vagina or anus. . . .

This court is obligated to make an independent, *de novo* judgment as to whether the material involved is constitutionally protected. . . .

In *Miller [v. California* (1973)], the Supreme Court set forth the current test for determining whether challenged materials are obscene. *Miller* stated the test for judging whether material is obscene as follows:

"The basic guidelines for the trier of fact must be: (a) whether 'the average person, applying contemporary community standards' would find that the work, taken as a whole, appeals to the prurient interest . . ., (b) whether the work depicts or describes, in a patently offensive way, sexual conduct specifically defined by the applicable state law; and (c) whether the work, taken as a whole, lacks serious literary, artistic, political, or scientific value. . . .

In *Pope v. Illinois* . . . (1987), the Supreme Court reiterated that parts (a) and (b) of the *Miller* tripartite test should be determined with reference to contemporary community standards. The court held that the proper inquiry for part (c) is whether a reasonable person would find value in the material taken as a whole.

The Supreme Court has characterized the second part of the *Miller* test as a two-step inquiry. . . . The threshold or substantive question is whether the materials depicted "hard core" sexual conduct. The second part of the test is whether, as a matter of fact, the materials were patently offensive under contemporary community standards. Moreover, *Miller* requires that this court review the jury finding under part (c). . . .

Radey was charged with pandering obscenity under R.C. 2907.32(A)(2), which stated (134 Ohio Laws, Part II, 1866, 1915):

"(A) No person, with knowledge of the character of the material or performance involved, shall do any of the following: "(2) Exhibit or advertise for sale or dissemination, or sell or publicly disseminate or display any obscene material[.]"

"Obscene" is defined in R.C. 2907.01(F):

"(F) When considered as a whole, and judged with reference to ordinary adults or, if it is designed for sexual deviates or other specially susceptible group, judged with reference to that group, any material or performance is 'obscene' if any of the following apply:
"(1) Its dominant appeal is to prurient interests:
"(2) Its dominant tendency is to arouse lust by displaying or depicting sexual activity, masturbation, sexual excitement, or nudity in a way that tends to represent human beings as mere objects of sexual appetite;
"(3) Its dominant tendency is to arouse lust by displaying or depicting bestiality or extreme or bizarre violence, cruelty, or brutality;
"(4) Its dominant tendency is to appeal to scatological interest by displaying or depicting human bodily functions of elimination in a way that inspires disgust or revulsion in persons with ordinary sensibilities, without serving any genuine scientific, educational, sociological, moral, or artistic purpose;
"(5) It contains a series of displays or descriptions of sexual activity, masturbation, sexual excitement, nudity, bestiality, extreme or bizarre violence, cruelty, or brutality, or human bodily functions of elimination, the cumulative effect of which is a dominant tendency to appeal to prurient or scatological interest, when the appeal to such an interest is primarily for its own sake or for commercial exploitation, rather than primarily for a genuine scientific, educational, sociological, moral, or artistic purpose."

The Supreme Court of Ohio has found R.C. 2907.01(f) to be constitutional when read *in pari materia* with the *Miller* guidelines. . . . Therefore, the *Miller* test for defining obscenity was incorporated into the statute by an authoritative state court construction specifically sanctioned by *Miller*. . . . Therefore, when the Ohio statutes are read to incorporate the guidelines prescribed in *Miller*, the material:

(a) must depict conduct which is expressly set forth by the definition of "sexual conduct" in R.C. 2907.01(A); and (b) the sexual conduct depicted must be "obscene," as defined in R.C. 2907.01(F)(1) to (5); and (c) the material must meet the three guidelines of *Miller*.

In this case, the purchased articles are not obscene as a matter of law. The items do not, in and of themselves, describe or depict "hard core sexual conduct" as defined in the Ohio statutes and as required by *Miller*. . . .

Accordingly, . . . the judgment of conviction is reversed and appellant is discharged.

UNITED STATES v. PINELLI

United States Court of Appeals, Tenth Circuit, 1989.
890 F.2d 1461.

[In this case, the U.S. Court of Appeals for the Tenth Circuit reviews the sufficiency of the evidence against seven defendants convicted of several federal offenses related to gambling activities.]

PHILLIPS, District Judge, sitting by designation.

This gambling prosecution stems from a thirty-five (35) count indictment returned by a federal grand jury sitting in Colorado on February 5, 1986. The indictment charged fourteen defendants, including the seven appellants here, with violating several federal criminal statutes. The pertinent statutes on appeal are 18 U.S.C. § 1955 (operating an illegal gambling business in violation of the laws of Colorado, involving five or more persons, with gross wagers in excess of $2,000 on any single day), 18 U.S.C. § 1952 (interstate use of a telephone to facilitate the gambling business); 26 U.S.C. § 7201 (income tax evasion), 26 U.S.C. § 7262 (failure to pay gambling occupation tax), and 26 U.S.C. § 7203 (failure to file requisite tax forms).

Four defendants entered pleas of guilty prior to trial. Three defendants were acquitted on all charges by the jury. The remaining seven defendants, appellants here, suffered convictions on the counts. . . .

Appellants have raised numerous issues on appeal. . . . We find that there was abundant evidence from which a reasonable jury could find the defendants guilty of the offense for which they were convicted, and further find no reversible error in the record of this case. Accordingly, we affirm the convictions of all seven appellants. . . .

In a challenge based upon the sufficiency of the evidence, we must affirm the judgment of conviction if there is record evidence which would allow a rational trier-of-fact to find the appellants guilty of the crimes charged in the indictment. . . . Moreover, this Court must view the evidence in the light most favorable to the government. . . . Viewed in that light, we conclude that the evidence, both direct and circumstantial, satisfies the test.

The government's evidence at trial focused on appellant's gambling activities from September through December, 1984. The evidence consisted of the testimony of thirty-six (36) witnesses, including numerous bettor witnesses, the introduction of several hundred tape recordings of telephone conversations intercepted pursuant to court-authorized electronic surveillance, documentary evidence seized pursuant to search warrants executed on December 9, 1984 after the termination of the wiretap, and expert testimony by an FBI agent on the roles played by the various defendants in the gambling operation.

The electronic surveillance in this case was active for approximately twenty-four days in November and December, 1984. The government's wiretap evidence and seized records in this case indicated the gambling business in question accepted wagers in excess of $2,300,000 in November and December, 1984. . . .

Special Agent William Holmes of the Federal Bureau of Investigation testified as an expert witness for the government as to the roles of each of the participants in the gambling activity in question. His opinions were based on review of the electronic surveillance and search evidence. . . . He did not rely on and was not privy to the testimony of the bettor witnesses. . . . At the outset of his testimony, Holmes explained some basic gambling terminology which will be helpful in explaining the roles of each of the appellants.

Holmes described the "point spread" or "line" as having the purpose of attracting equal amounts of betting on each side of a contest. Bookmakers change the line on a particular game to attract betting on the other team. A line of "Denver minus six" means Denver is favored by six points and to win a bet on Denver, Denver must win by seven or more points. The term "vig" or "vigorish" represents a ten percent commission charged to losing bets, which compensates the bookmaker for the privilege of placing bets. In other words, a $100 losing bet would require payment of $110, which payment includes a $10 "vig." According to Holmes, a bookmaker theoretically strives to accept the same amount of bets on each side of a contest, or balance his books, and take the "vig" as profit.

Agent Holmes explained the concept of "lay-off wagering" as that which allows a bookmaker "to get rid of wagers that he feels he is not financially able to handle and reduce the risk of great financial loss by having to pay off on large sums of money." . . . The following example of lay-off wagering was provided by Holmes during his testimony: Suppose Bookmaker X has wagers of $1,500 on team A and $1,000 on team B. Bookmaker X would lay-off the $500 excess on team A with Bookmaker Y. If team A wins, Bookmaker X would collect $1,000 from those who bet on team B, plus the 10% vig for a total of $1,100. Bookmaker X would collect his $500 lay-off wager from Bookmaker Y, which would make the total amount collected $1,600. From this amount, he would have to pay his bettors who had bet $1,500 on team A. Bookmaker X would thus make a profit of $100 without risking any of his own money. If Bookmaker X had not laid-off his excess wagers and team A had won, then he would have collected $1,100 from the losers ($1,100 + 10% vig) and had to pay out $1,500 to the winners for a net loss of $400. . . . As will be shown, the concept of lay-off wagering played a central role in the successful prosecution of appellants.

Viewing the evidence in the light most favorable to the government, as we must, a brief summary of the evidence pertaining to each appellant is set forth below. . . . [The Court summarizes the evidence against all seven appellants. Only the summaries pertaining to Phil Pinelli and David Pinelli are retained here.]

. . . The evidence introduced by the government established that defendant Phil Pinelli was in the business of accepting wagers on sporting events. Specifically, the evidence indicated that Phil Pinelli accepted over $800,000 in wagers during November and December, 1984. . . .

Evidence consisted of taped conversations between Phil Pinelli and his brother David Pinelli demonstrated a mutuality of risk between the two brothers in their wagering activities, . . . and indicated the brothers had mutual financial interests. . . . Further, wiretapped telephone conversations demonstrated that Phil Pinelli accepted wagers from, and placed wagers with, other bookmakers.

For instance, from taped conversations introduced by the government it was evident that Phil Pinelli accepted wagers from another bookmaker, Aaron Mosko, and placed bets by telephone with Ralph Lackey. . . . In particular, the government introduced a taped conversation between Aaron Mosko and Phil Pinelli in which Mosko told Pinelli that he "needed" certain amounts on various games. . . . In another telephone conversation introduced by the government between Pinelli and a person identified as "Doc," Pinelli told Doc that he had "about five or six bookmakers and they unload their, like Aaron and them guys, they load all their shit on me."

The evidence introduced by the government also indicated that Phil Pinelli kept his gambling records in such a way as to obfuscate their true meaning. For instance, a review of seized records indicates that none of his accounts were identified by recognizable names, but rather by entries such as "K" and "PB.". . . Moreover, the government introduced a taped conversation between Pinelli and Aaron Mosko in which Pinelli explained to Mosko that he kept his books in a certain manner so "if they ever pick up my book, they'll say twenty to twenty, you know, they can't say what they are.". . . Phil Pinelli received line formation for his gambling activities by placing telephone calls to Las Vegas. . . .

FBI Agent Holmes testified that in his opinion Phil Pinelli was in the business of accepting sports wagering activity and David Pinelli was his partner and assisted Phil in accepting wagers, setting line, and deciding lay-off policy. . .

Tape recorded conversations between the two brothers demonstrated the mutuality of financial interests between the two. . . . For instance, in one conversation the Pinellis discussed what they collectively had on Denver and how much they wanted to "lay-off.". . . In another conversation David and Phil Pinelli went over the day's wagering activity. . . .

Agent Holmes described David Pinelli as a partner of Phil Pinelli in his gambling business who assisted Phil in accepting wagers, setting line, and deciding lay-off policy. . . .

Central to appellants' challenge to the sufficiency of the evidence is their claim that the government did not prove the jurisdictional elements of 18 U.S.C. § 1955. Section 1955 makes it a crime to operate an illegal gambling business in violation of the laws of the State of Colorado involving five or more persons which was in substantially continuous operation in excess of thirty days, or which had gross wagers in excess of $2,000 on any single day. Here, the multiple telephone calls on particular days, as well as the coordination among appellants which was evident in many conversations, together with the generated revenues, which were substantially in excess of $2,000 per day, amply provide a basis for the jury's findings.

The remaining charges may be briefly summarized. Title 18 U.S.C. § 1952 prohibits interstate telephone calls which facilitate a gambling business. Title 26 U.S. § 7203 makes it a misdemeanor for willful attempts to evade the 2% excise tax on wagers accepted. Title 26 U.S.C. § 7203 makes it a misdemeanor for willful failure to file a tax return, while 26 U.S.C. § 7262 is a misdemeanor offense arising out of the failure to pay the gambling occupation tax.

We are convinced that the evidence collectively, both direct and circumstantial, when viewed in the light most favorable to the government, satisfies each of the essential elements of Section 1955 and the other counts of conviction, and demonstrates appellants' participation in a substantial and continuous bookmaking business conducted by multiple bookmakers and others linked through lay-off wagering, exchange and the use of line formation and ancillary activities.

JUDGMENT AFFIRMED.

DRUG AND ALCOHOL OFFENSES

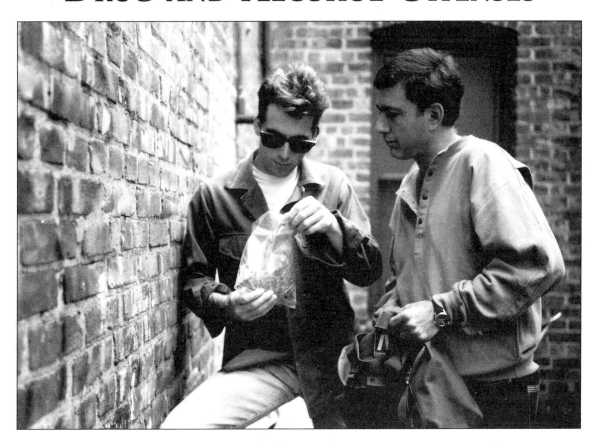

CHAPTER OUTLINE

Introduction
Drug Offenses
Intoxication Offenses
Conclusion

Cases
Robinson v. California
Embry v. State
Powell v. Texas
People v. Randolph

INTRODUCTION

In this chapter we examine a number of offenses involving the misuse of drugs and alcohol. Because the English common law had little to say about the abuse of alcohol, and nothing to say about illicit drugs, these offenses are based on statutory enactments. These enactments reflect the modern awareness of the adverse social consequences of drug and alcohol abuse. While drug and alcohol offenses may be, and often are, classified as crimes against public morality, they are sufficiently distinctive in character and frequent in their occurrence to warrant separate treatment in a study of criminal law.

DRUG OFFENSES

The misuse of drugs is among the oldest vices in society. Drug abuse not only involves moral questions but also creates dramatic economic, social, and health problems. Illegal trafficking in drugs has led to commission of many violent crimes as well as to instances of official corruption. And many violent crimes are committed by people under the influence of illicit drugs. The Bureau of Justice Statistics reports that "a quarter of jail inmates, a third of State prisoners, and two-fifths of youths in long-term, State-operated facilities admit that they were under the influence of an illegal drug at the time of their offense" (U.S. Department of Justice, Bureau of Justice Statistics, *Drug and Crime Facts*, 1991, p. 3).

In the 1980s, the focus of the drug problem was the widespread use of cocaine and, in particular, "crack," an inexpensive form of cocaine that is ingested through smoking. The prevalence of cocaine and the destructive consequences of its use led political leaders to declare a "war on drugs" in the late 1980s. While the national war on drugs has not been completely successful, there is evidence that it has had a positive impact. In 1985, 13.1 percent of high school seniors reported that they had used cocaine within the last twelve months; by 1990 the figure had declined to 5.3 percent (U.S. Department of Justice, Bureau of Justice Statistics, *Drug and Crime Facts*, 1991, p. 17).

Some commentators, believing that the national "war on drugs" has failed, have argued for the legalization of drugs like marijuana, cocaine, and heroin. These commentators would prefer to see use of these drugs legalized, although highly regulated, with increased efforts directed toward educational and treatment programs. Most people disagree with this perspective, however. A 1990 Gallup Poll found that a substantial majority of Americans believed that legalization would make matters worse, not better (see Table 9.1).

Federal Laws

In the United States, the 1960s saw a resurgence of drug abuse, a problem that had caused great concern in the early twentieth century when it was legal to market products containing opium and cocaine. As attention focused on the illegal use of drugs as a national problem, Congress enacted the Comprehensive Drug Abuse Prevention and Control Act of 1970. 21 U.S.C.A. § 811 *et seq*. The act, commonly referred to as the Controlled Substance Act, establishes schedules listing controlled substances according to their potential for abuse. Penalties for

TABLE 9.1 PUBLIC PERCEPTIONS OF THE LIKELY EFFECTS OF LEGALIZING DRUGS, 1990

Legalization would increase:	% Agreeing:
Drug use in the public schools	65
The number of drug addicts	67
The number of drug overdoses	63
Drug-related crime	52

Source: Gallup Poll, 1990, reported in Bureau of Justice Statistics, U.S. Department of Justice, *Drug and Crime Facts, 1991,* p. 21.

offenses involving the manufacture, sale, distribution, and possession depend on the substance involved, 21 U.S.C.A. § 841, with provision for registered practitioners to dispense narcotics for approved purposes. 21 U.S.C.A. § 823.

In 1972, the Uniform Controlled Substances Act was drafted by the Commissioners on Uniform Laws. Its purpose was to achieve uniformity among state and federal laws. The majority of states have now adopted the uniform act, often with some minor modifications. Like the federal statute, the uniform act classifies controlled substances according to their potential for abuse. For example, opiates are included in Schedule I because they are unsafe for use even under medical treatment, while Schedule II includes drugs that have a high potential for abuse but may be medically acceptable under certain conditions. The remaining schedules include controlled substances that have lesser potential for abuse and dependency. The range includes such well-known controlled substances as cocaine, amphetamines, tranquilizers, and barbiturates.

State Statutes

All states make the *manufacture, sale, and possession* of controlled substances illegal. Offenses involving drugs that have a high potential for abuse (e.g., heroin and cocaine) are usually very serious felonies. Although it is constitutionally permissible to enact such laws, states may not criminalize the mere *status* of being addicted to such drugs without running afoul of the Cruel and Unusual Punishments Clause of the Eighth Amendment to the U.S. Constitution. *Robinson v. California,* 370 U.S. 660, 82 S.Ct. 1417, 8 L.Ed.2d 758 (1962).

The Nebraska statute is fairly typical of state drug laws. It stipulates that:

> (1) Except as authorized by the Uniform Controlled Substances Act, it shall be unlawful for any person knowingly or intentionally: (a) To manufacture, distribute, deliver, dispense, or possess with intent to manufacture, distribute, deliver, or dispense a controlled substance. . . .
> (2) [omitted]
> (3) A person knowingly or intentionally possessing a controlled substance, except marijuana, unless such substance was obtained directly or pursuant to a valid prescription or order from a practitioner while acting in the course of his or her professional practice, or except as otherwise authorized by the act, shall be guilty of a class IV felony.
> Rev. Stat. Neb. § 28–416 (1)(2)(3) (1989).

Offenses involving the mere *possession* of less harmful substances are often classified as lesser-degree felonies or, where a very small quantity of marijuana is involved, are frequently classified as misdmeanors. For example, in Nebraska, possession of more than one ounce but less than one pound of marijuana is a misdemeanor; possession of more than one pound is a felony. Rev. Stat. Neb. § 28–416 (6)(7) (1989).

During the 1970s a number of states decriminalized their antimarijuana laws by removing the threat of a jail sentence for possession offenses. In Nebraska, for example, possession of less than one ounce of marijuana is considered an "infraction" for which a first-time offender may be fined no more than one hundred dollars and made to attend a drug education course. Rev. Stat. Neb. § 28–416 (8)(a) (1989).

The impetus of the drive to decriminalize marijuana has diminished, and from 1978 to the present further attempts at decriminalization have been unsuccessful. Despite the attempts at enforcement, marijuana remains widely available and provides an example of the difficulty in enforcing a law that has less than universal public support. Nevertheless, courts have generally declined to reassess legislative judgments in this area, and statutes making it a criminal offense to possess marijuana have withstood numerous constitutional challenges. See, for example, *State v. Smith,* 610 P.2d 869 (Wash. 1980); *People v. Riddle,* 237 N.W.2d 491 (Mich. App. 1975).

One notable exception to the state courts' general deference to legislative prohibitions of marijuana possession is *Ravin v. State,* 537 P.2d 494 (Alaska 1975), where the Alaska Supreme Court ruled that possession of small quantities of marijuana by an adult for personal use in the home was protected by that state's constitutional right of privacy. This decision was effectively overturned, however, by a 1991 amendment to the state constitution.

Prohibition of Drug Paraphernalia; Forfeiture of Property

Possession of paraphernalia associated with illicit drug use is also commonly a criminal offense. Controlled substances and illegal paraphernalia are declared contraband and are subject to confiscation. Likewise, vehicles and aircraft involved in trafficking of controlled substances may be seized and declared forfeited under various federal and state statutes. See, for example, 21 U.S.C.A. § 881. In addition, in 1984 Congress enacted a law providing for forfeiture of real estate used in illegal drug trafficking. 21 U.S.C.A. § 881(h). However, in *United States v. A Parcel of Land,* 507 U.S. ____, 113 S.Ct. 1126, 122 L.Ed.2d 469 (1993), the Supreme Court ruled that, although proceeds traceable to an unlawful drug transaction are subject to forfeiture, an owner's lack of knowledge that her home had been purchased with proceeds of illegal drug transactions constitutes a defense to a forfeiture proceeding under federal law. Moreover, the Court has set a theoretical limit on the amount of property that may be seized by government through forfeiture. In *Austin v. United States,* 509 U.S. ____, 113 S.Ct. 289, 125 L.Ed.2d 488 (1993), the Court remanded for reconsideration a case where the federal government seized a business and a mobile home from a man who sold two grams of cocaine to an undercover agent. The Court ruled that forfeitures, although they are not technically criminal proceedings, are subject to the Excessive Fines Clause of the Eighth Amendment.

Problems of Enforcement

Federal and state laws on controlled substances mirror one another in many respects. Federal enforcement is usually directed against major interstate or international drug traffickers; states usually concentrate on those who possess or distribute controlled substances. Many drug-trafficking violations of federal law involve prosecution for conspiracy. Unlike many state laws, the federal law on conspiracy to violate the Controlled Substance Act does not require proof of an overt act. 21 U.S.C.A. § 846; *United States v. Wilson,* 657 F.2d 755 (5th Cir. 1981).

Because those involved in narcotics transactions are usually willing participants, enforcement often depends on use of confidential informants by police. Obtaining search warrants and making arrests based on probable cause often present difficult Fourth Amendment problems, some of which are discussed in Chapters 14 and 15.

Prosecutorial Problems

The level of intent that the prosecution must establish in contraband cases can vary according to the particular statutory offense (see Chapter 4). However, courts have generally held that statutes making possession, distribution, or trafficking in contraband unlawful require the prosecution to prove only the defendant's general intent. See, for example, *State v. Williams,* 352 So. 2d 1295 (La. 1977); *State v. Bender,* 579 P.2d 796 (N.M. 1978).

In drug possession cases, a critical problem is proving that the defendant was in possession of a controlled substance. The prosecution may prove either *actual* or *constructive* possession of contraband to satisfy the possession requirement. Proof of actual possession is established upon proof that the contraband was found on the accused's person or that the accused was in exclusive possession of the premises or vehicle where the contraband was discovered. However, where the accused is not in actual possession, or where the accused and another person jointly occupy a dwelling or automobile where contraband is discovered, the prosecution must attempt to prove what the law calls constructive possession.

A person has constructive possession of contraband if he or she has ownership, dominion, or control over the contraband itself, or over the premises in which it is concealed. *United States v. Schubel,* 912 F.2d 952 (8th Cir. 1990). The prosecution usually attempts to establish constructive possession by evidence of incriminating statements and circumstances from which the defendant's ability to control the contraband may be inferred. This can pose a formidable difficulty.

Defenses

Defendants on trial for drug offenses sometimes assert that they were entrapped by the police, a defense discussed in Chapter 13. More frequently, defense counsel attempt to suppress the contraband seized by police on the ground that it was obtained in violation of the Fourth Amendment prohibition against unreasonable searches and seizures (see Chapter 2). In some instances, a

CASE IN POINT

IS COCAINE POSSESSION A CRIME OF MORAL TURPITUDE?

Jimmy Major was arrested and charged with distribution of crack cocaine. At trial, Major took the stand to testify that he "had nothing to do " with illegal drugs or drug dealing. On cross-examination, the prosecutor asked Major whether he had ever used or possessed crack cocaine, to which Major replied in the negative. To impeach Major's credibility, the prosecutor then introduced evidence of Major's prior conviction for simple possession of cocaine. Major was convicted and appealed. The South Carolina Supreme Court was asked to decide whether evidence of the prior simple possession conviction was properly admitted at trial. Under South Carolina law, the question was whether simple possession of cocaine was a crime of moral turpitude. If so, the prior conviction could be used to impeach the credibility of Major's testimony as to his own good character with respect to involvement with drug dealing.

In 1987 the South Carolina Supreme Court had held that the crime of possession of cocaine was not a crime of moral turpitude since it involved "primarily self-destructive behavior." *State v. Ball,* 354 S.E. 2d 906, 908 (S.C. 1987). In *Ball,* the Court noted that "[i]n determining whether a crime is one involving moral turpitude, the Court focuses primarily on the duty to society and fellow men which is breached by the commission of the crime." 354 S.E. 2d at 908.

In Major's case, the Court reversed its prior holding in *Ball,* saying in part:

> We retain the test articulated in *Ball* for determining whether a crime qualifies as one of "moral turpitude," but we overrule *Ball* because of its holding regarding cocaine possession. The drug "cocaine" has torn at the very fabric of our nation. Families have been ripped apart, minds have been ruined, and lives have been lost. It is common knowledge that the drug is highly addictive and potentially fatal. The addictive nature of the drug, combined with its expense, has caused our prisons to swell with those who have been motivated to support their drug habit through criminal acts. In some areas of the world, entire governments have been undermined by the cocaine industry. As stated by Chief Justice Gregory in his dissent in *Ball,* "[o]ne who possesses this controlled substance, even for his own use, fosters the prosperity of the lucrative and destructive industry of illicit cocaine manufacture and trafficking." *Ball,* 354, S.E.2d at 909. (Gregory, C.J. dissenting). Because of our present "war on drugs," and because any involvement with cocaine contributes to the destruction of ordered society, we hold that mere possession of cocaine is a crime of moral turpitude.

State v. Major, 391 S.E.2d 235 (S.C. 1990).

defendant presents an expert witness to contest the type of contraband introduced in evidence, and frequently defendants challenge the chain of custody of the contraband from the time it was seized until the time it was introduced into evidence. Since the gravity of the offense is often based on the amount of contraband seized, defendants sometimes challenge the weight of the contraband

CASE IN POINT

CONSTRUCTIVE POSSESSION OF DRUGS

After Minneapolis police obtained a tip that crack cocaine was being sold out of cars parked in front of a certain duplex, an officer observed a blue Cadillac parked in front of the building. A female later identified as the defendant, Nina Knox, made several trips between the car and the duplex. At one point she drove the car from the scene, but returned shortly and sat in the car for a period of time as a number of men approached the car and walked away after brief encounters. The officer, who was experienced in dealing with drug offenses, believed the activities he witnessed to be drug transactions, although he was unable to observe money and drugs being exchanged. Knox was arrested, and a search of the car produced 14.3 grams of crack cocaine and $2,200 in cash. A search of Knox's purse produced a large amount of money and food stamps. Knox was convicted in federal court of possession with intent to distribute a controlled substance.

On appeal, Knox challenged the sufficiency of the evidence, arguing that it failed to establish that she was in physical control of the cocaine and was intending to sell it. The U.S. Court of Appeals rejected Knox's contention, holding that there was sufficient evidence for the trial court to conclude that she was in constructive possession of the cocaine and intended to distribute it. The court concluded that the evidence supported a finding that Knox had exercised "dominion over the premises in which the contraband [was] concealed," since she was observed driving the car, sitting in the car, and entering it on several occasions. The court further concluded that intent to distribute could be inferred from the fact that sizable amounts of cash and cocaine were found at the scene. Knox's conviction was affirmed.

United States v. Knox, 888 F.2d 585 (8th Cir. 1989).

being introduced into evidence. Finally, in cases where defendants are charged with possession with intent to deliver drugs within a certain proximity of a school, which is a separate and more serious offense in many states, defendants often challenge the measurement of the distance between the school and the location where the defendant was alleged to be when the offense occurred.

In a number of cases, courts have rejected such defenses as economic coercion and duress (see Chapter 13), and several state courts have refused to allow a defendant to claim that possession or use of illicit substances was a "medical necessity." See, for example, *Spillers v. State,* 245 S.E.2d 54 (Ga. App. 1978). However, in 1991 a Florida appellate court reversed a trial court decision refusing to allow evidence in support of such a defense. In *Jenks v. State,* 582 So.2d 676 (Fla. App. 1991), a husband had contracted acquired immune deficiency syndrome (AIDS) through a blood transfusion; his wife acquired it from him. Both were charged with possession and cultivation of marijuana. They claimed their actions were for their own relief, and they presented medical experts who testified that no other drug treatment was available to effectively eliminate the nausea they suffered from AIDS. Observing that the evil to be avoided was more heinous than the unlawful act perpetrated to avoid it, the appellate court directed the lower court to permit the defendants to assert the defense of medical necessity.

Intoxication Offenses

By the turn of the twentieth century, alcohol had come to be perceived by a substantial segment of the population as an evil that had to be eradicated. In response to growing, but far from unanimous, public sentiment, Congress enacted the Eighteenth Amendment, which was ratified in 1919. This amendment, widely referred to as "Prohibition," made unlawful the "manufacture, sale, or transportation of intoxicating liquors" within the United States. The national prohibition of alcohol was widely violated and contributed greatly to the development of organized crime syndicates in this country. Ultimately, Prohibition was repealed by the Twenty-First Amendment, ratified in 1933. However, under the Twenty-First Amendment, state and local governments retain the authority to ban or regulate the manufacture, sale, and use of alcohol within their borders. Indeed, while the sale of alcohol is widespread today, there are still a number of so-called dry counties throughout the United States, mainly in the South and Midwest, where the sale of all or some alcoholic beverages is prohibited. While no state has chosen to ban the sale of alcohol altogether, all states regulate alcoholic beverages and retain a number of alcohol-related offenses.

Two offenses of statutory origin in the United States are directed at those who consume excessive amounts of alcoholic beverages. They are public drunkenness and driving while under the influence of intoxicants. These are sometimes regarded as offenses against public morality, but they are primarily designed to protect the safety of the public, as well as of the offender.

Public Drunkenness Laws

Laws and ordinances making public drunkenness an offense have long been enforced by all jurisdictions, with most states and municipalities simply providing that whoever shall become intoxicated from the voluntary use of intoxicating liquors shall be punished. The offense merely involves the accused being found in a public place in a state of intoxication and usually has been classified as a minor misdemeanor. A common police practice has been to take offenders into custody and release them once they have "sobered up." Some have referred to this practice as a "revolving door."

Trends in Public Drunkenness Cases

There is a growing awareness that alcoholism is a disease, and many have urged that the criminal law is an inappropriate mechanism to deal with it. Additionally, some reformers have contended that criminalizing the public presence of an intoxicated person is contrary to the Eighth Amendment's prohibition of cruel and unusual punishments. The Supreme Court, however, has declined to accept such a view. Instead, in *Powell v. Texas*, 392 U.S. 514, 88 S. Ct. 2145, 20 L.Ed.2d

CASE IN POINT

SUFFICIENCY OF EVIDENCE TO SUSTAIN DWI CONVICTION

After investigating the scene of a one-vehicle accident in which a driver had evidently lost control of his truck, Deputy Sheriff Michael Redmond went to the hospital where the driver had been taken. The deputy later testified that the driver had no apparent injuries, but that his speech was slurred and there was a strong odor of alcohol about him. The driver was subjected to a blood test that revealed a high level of alcohol in the blood, but the results of this test were barred from trial due to evidentiary problems. The defendant, Paul T. Ryan, was nevertheless convicted of driving while intoxicated. On appeal, Ryan challenged the sufficiency of the evidence presented against him. The appellate court sustained the conviction, however, saying: "A careful review of the record convinces us, without considering the result of the blood test, that there is substantial evidence to sustain appellant's conviction."

Ryan v. State, 786 S.W. 2d 835, 837 (Ark. App. 1990).

1254 (1968), it upheld a public intoxication law. In effect, the Court ruled that the defendant Powell was not being punished for his status as an alcoholic, but rather for his presence in a public place in an inebriated condition.

In recent years some states have enacted statutes directing police officers to take persons found intoxicated in public places to treatment facilities rather than to incarcerate them. Consistent with this approach, many statutes now criminalize only "disorderly intoxication." This newer offense involves the offender being intoxicated in public and endangering the safety of others, not merely being in a state of intoxication in public. See, for example, West's Fla. Stat. Ann. § 856.011.

Driving While under the Influence of Alcohol or Drugs

The carnage on the American highways attests to the urgent need for states to take stern measures to keep drunk drivers off the road, and all states have enacted laws attempting to accomplish this goal. The "classical" offense in this area is driving while intoxicated (DWI), or more accurately, operating a motor vehicle while intoxicated. In the 1960s and 1970s, many jurisdictions expanded the offense to prohibit driving while under the influence of intoxicating liquors or drugs (DUI). DWI and DUI laws sometimes allowed a defendant to avoid conviction due to the ambiguity of his or her subjective behavior. In response to this problem, most states have modified their statutes to prohibit driving with an unlawful blood-alcohol level (DUBAL), which is defined as 0.10 percent or more alcohol in the bloodstream. By 1993, eight states had adopted an even stricter standard, prohibiting a 0.08 percent blood alcohol level. This is illustrated by Section 23152 of the California Vehicle Code, which states:

TABLE 9.2 DWI, DUI, AND DUBAL ARRESTS IN THE UNITED STATES, 1972–1990

Year	Arrests (nearest thousand)
1972	604,000
1973	654,000
1974	617,000
1975	909,000
1976	838,000
1977	1,104,000
1978	1,205,000
1979	1,232,000
1980	1,304,000
1981	1,422,000
1982	1,405,000
1983	1,613,000
1984	1,347,000
1985	1,503,000
1986	1,459,000
1987	1,410,000
1988	1,294,000
1989	1,333,000
1990	1,391,000

Source: Source: U.S. Department of Justice, *Criminal Justice Sourcebook, 1991,* p. 468.

(a) It is unlawful for any person who is under the influence of an alcoholic beverage or any drug, or under the combined influence of an alcoholic beverage and any drug, to drive a vehicle.
(b) It is unlawful for any person who has 0.08 percent or more, by weight, of alcohol in his or her blood to drive a vehicle.
West's Cal. Ann. Vehicle Code § 23152 (a) (b).

The California Supreme Court has upheld this statute against constitutional attack, stating that it is a rational exercise of the state's police power, provides adequate notice of the conduct proscribed, and is not void for vagueness. *Burg v. Municipal Court,* 673 P.2d 732 (Cal. 1983), *cert. denied,* 466 U.S. 967, 104 S. Ct. 2337, 80 L.Ed. 2d 812 (1984). Several other state courts have upheld similar statutes against a variety of constitutional attacks.

Prosecution and Defense of DWI, DUI, and DUBAL Charges

To obtain a conviction for DWI, DUI or DUBAL, the prosecution must first establish that the defendant charged with driving while intoxicated or driving under the influence was operating the vehicle. This may be accomplished by eyewitness or circumstantial evidence. Next the prosecution must establish the intoxication. Statutes, it should be noted, often refer to intoxication occurring as a result of alcohol or from ingestion of contraband substances. Intoxication is often a difficult state to articulate. Therefore, police often use such field sobriety techniques as the touching-finger-to-nose, walking-the-line, counting backwards, and similar tests to corroborate their testimony concerning the defendant's condition at the time of arrest.

In *Berkemer v. McCarty*, 468 U.S. 420, 104 S.Ct. 3138, 82 L.Ed.2d 317 (1984), the U.S. Supreme Court held that an officer's roadside questioning of an administration of a field sobriety test to an individual stopped for irregular driving was not a "custodial interrogation" that required giving the suspect the *Miranda* warnings. The Court cautioned, however, that the *Miranda* warnings apply once the suspect is under arrest.

There is evidence that field sobriety tests may be somewhat unreliable, and courts are beginning to scrutinize cases that rely solely on field sobriety tests without supporting chemical testing of the blood, urine, or breath of the suspect. Still, most courts permit persons to be convicted of DUI without chemical tests, especially when multiple sobriety tests have been performed by more than one officer.

Increasingly, police videotape suspects' performance on field sobriety tests and make audio tape recordings of suspects' speech. Many police agencies today have mobile blood-alcohol testing units ("Batmobiles") equipped with breathalyzer testing machines, videotape equipment, and voice recorders. These vans, available at the call of the arresting officer, give the police the opportunity to promptly collect evidence at or near the scene of the arrest.

While generally regarded as superior to field sobriety tests from an evidentiary standpoint, chemical tests are not wholly devoid of problems. When prosecutors rely solely on chemical evidence, defense counsel often challenge the reliability and validity of chemical testing equipment and the operator's level of competence. Ideally, to obtain a conviction, a prosecutor would like to have evidence that the defendant was driving abnormally, that he or she smelled of alcohol, exhibited slurred speech, failed a battery of field sobriety tests administered by several officers, and registered an impermissibly high blood-alcohol level on one or more chemical tests performed by a trained technician. Of course, in the real world of law enforcement, such thorough evidence is seldom obtained.

Implied Consent Statutes

To facilitate chemical testing in DWI, DUI, and DUBAL cases, California and most other jurisdictions have enacted "implied consent" statutes. Under these laws, a person who drives a motor vehicle is deemed to have given consent to a urine test for drugs and to blood, breath, or urine testing to determine blood-alcohol content. The testing is made incident to a lawful arrest of a driver. See, for example, West's Ann. Cal. Vehicle Code § 23157. The Supreme Court has upheld the validity of the Massachusetts Implied Consent law providing for suspension of the driver's license of a person who refuses to take a breathalyzer test. *Mackey v. Montrym*, 443 U.S. 1, 99 S. Ct. 2612, 61 L.Ed.2d 321 (1979).

CONCLUSION

The widespread abuse of drugs and alcohol is a serious social problem with many undesirable consequences. Society has responded to this problem largely through the criminal justice system. There are those, however, who believe that criminalizing drug possession is undesirable public policy. Yet, in the 1990s, the public appears to be strongly committed to maintaining, if not increasing, the criminal sanctions against the manufacture, sale, and possession of drugs. It is equally committed to strengthening criminal penalties and stepping up enforcement with respect to drunk driving. For the foreseeable future, these undesirable behaviors will remain criminal offenses and, accordingly, major problems for police, prosecutors, and prison officials.

QUESTIONS FOR THOUGHT AND DISCUSSION

1. Is it sensible to maintain the criminal prohibitions against illicit drugs, or should these substances be legalized, carefully regulated, and their abuse dealt with through other means?
2. What are the typical difficulties facing prosecutors seeking convictions in drug possession cases?
3. Why, according to the Supreme Court in *Robinson v. California*, may a person not be held criminally liable for being addicted to illicit narcotics?
4. Should chronic alcoholism be a defense to intoxication offenses such as public drunkenness or driving under the influence?
5. Is requiring a person suspected of driving while intoxicated to submit to a blood-alcohol test a violation of the Fifth Amendment prohibition against compulsory self-incrimination?
6. During the late afternoon, police were called to quell a disturbance at a motel where the management had reported some disorderly conduct and apparent drug use. Outside the motel, the police observed Henry Egad standing by a tree. About eighteen inches from Egad's feet, the police discovered a matchbox on the ground. Their examination revealed that the matchbox contained a substance that later proved to be PCP, an illegal drug. Police placed Egad under arrest and charged him with possession of a controlled substance. Based on these facts alone, do you think the prosecutor can establish that Egad was in possession of the PCP?

CASES

ROBINSON V. CALIFORNIA

Supreme Court of the United States, 1962.
370 U.S. 660, 82 S.Ct. 1417, 8 L.Ed. 2d 758.

[Robinson was convicted in a California court of violating a state statute that made it a criminal offense to "be addicted to the use of narcotics." In this appeal to the U.S. Supreme Court, Robinson challenges the constitutionality of that statute, as it had been interpreted by the California courts, as violative of the Cruel and Unusual Punishments Clause of the Eighth Amendment to the U.S. Constitution.]

Mr. Justice STEWART delivered the opinion of the Court.

... This statute ... is not one which punishes a person for the use of narcotics, for their purchase, sale or possession, or for anti-social or disorderly behavior resulting from their administration. It is not a law which even purports to provide or require medical treatment. Rather, we deal with a statute which makes the "status" of narcotic addiction a criminal offense, for which the offender may be prosecuted "at any time before he reforms." California has said that a person can be continuously guilty of this offense, whether or not he has ever used or possessed any narcotics within the state, and whether or not he has been guilty of any anti-social behavior there.

It is unlikely that any state at this moment in history would attempt to make it a criminal offense for a person to be mentally ill, or a leper, or to be afflicted with a venereal disease. A state might determine that the general health and welfare require that the victims of these and other human afflictions be dealt with by compulsory treatment, involving quarantine, confinement, or sequestration. But, in the light of contemporary human knowledge, a law which made a criminal offense of such a disease would doubtless be universally thought to be an infliction of cruel and unusual punishment in violation of the eighth and 14th amendments.

We cannot but consider the statute before us as of the same category. In this Court counsel for the state recognized that narcotic addiction is an illness. Indeed, it is apparently an illness which may be contracted innocently or involuntarily. We hold that a state law which imprisons a person thus afflicted as a criminal, even though he has never touched any narcotic drug within the state or been guilty of any irregular behavior there, inflicts a cruel and unusual punishment in violation of the 14th amendment. To be sure, imprisonment for 90 days is not, in the abstract, a punishment which is either cruel or unusual. But the question cannot be considered in the abstract. Even one day in prison would be a cruel and unusual punishment for the "crime" of having a common cold.

We are not unmindful that the vicious evils of the narcotics traffic have occasioned the grave concern of government. There are, as we have said, countless fronts on which those evils may be legitimately attacked. We deal in this case only within an individual provision of a particularized local law as it has so far been interpreted by the California courts.

Reversed.

Mr. Justice FRANKFURTER took no part in the consideration or decision of this case.

Mr. Justice DOUGLAS, concurring.

... [T]he addict is a sick person. He may, of course, be confined for treatment or for the protection of society. Cruel and unusual punishment results not from confinement, but from convicting the addict of a crime. A prosecution for addiction, with its resulting stigma and irreparable damage to the good name of the accused, cannot be justified as a means of protecting society, where a civil commitment would do as well.

Mr. Justice CLARK, dissenting....

Mr. Justice WHITE, dissenting....

EMBRY V. STATE

Supreme Court of Arkansas, 1990.
302 Ark. 608, 792 S.W.2d 318.

[In this case, the Arkansas Supreme Court considers the sufficiency of the evidence to support the convictions of two individuals for possession of illegal drugs with intent to deliver.]

TURNER, Justice.

Sammie Lee Embry and John Wesley Phillips, a.k.a. Ibraheem Shabazz, were each convicted of possession of cocaine with intent to deliver and possession of marijuana with intent to deliver. Embry was sentenced to 20 years on the cocaine charge and five years on the marijuana charge. Phillips was found to be an habitual offender, previously convicted of four or more felonies and was thus sentenced to life imprisonment on the cocaine charge and to 20 years on the marijuana charge. Both defendants appeal the convictions. We find the appeal of Embry to be meritorious and reverse and dismiss his convictions. Phillips's appeal, however, is without merit, and we therefore affirm.

Embry and Patricia Booker had an off-and-on relationship; consequently, Embry spent considerable amounts of time at Booker's residence at 1414 May Avenue in Fort Smith. Embry, who was the father of Booker's child, kept clothing at Booker's house and frequently stayed there.

Law enforcement authorities placed the house under surveillance as a probable outlet for drugs and gave identifiable currency to a confidential informant who was to make a drug buy at that address. When the informant returned, he delivered a quantity of crack cocaine to the authorities. The police obtained a search warrant, and at 2:50 P.M. the officers conducted a search of the Booker residence. They found illicit controlled substances and arrested Booker, Phillips, and others at the scene. Embry was not at the house at the time of the search and arrests. About an hour later, after leaving work, he arrived at the residence and was taken into custody. . . .

It is well established that the state need not prove the accused had actual possession of a controlled substance; constructive possession is sufficient. . . . Constructive possession, which is the control or right to control the contraband, can be implied where the contraband is found in a place immediately and exclusively accessible to the accused and subject to his control. . . .

Where there is joint occupancy of the premises where the contraband is seized, some additional factor must be found to link the accused to the contraband. . . . In such instances, the state must prove that the accused exercised care, control, and management over the contraband and also that the accused knew that the matter possessed was contraband. . . .

The appellant Embry was not present when the house was entered and searched and had no controlled substance on his person at the time of the arrest. He had no ownership interest in the house or furnishings, though he was a frequent (if not full-time) occupant and kept personal clothing there. It cannot be said that he had a superior or an equal right to the control of the house. He made no effort to dispose of any incriminating matter and made no incriminating statement. . . .

. . . [Embry] possessed no contraband, and the state failed to prove that he constructively possessed either the marijuana or cocaine found at the residence. His conviction must therefore be reversed.

Considering next the challenge by the appellant Phillips/Shabazz to the sufficiency of the evidence, the record reveals an entirely different scenario under the same facts. Though Phillips had no possessory interest in the house or furnishings, he had sold marijuana, according to testimony, and another substance thought to be cocaine inside the Booker house and at the front door; he was present at the time of the search and attempted to flee from the officer entering the front door; then, when confronted by officers entering through the back door, he tossed away a cigarette package later determined to contain marijuana cigarettes. During the search, the officers discovered a .25 caliber semi-automatic pistol in a closet which had been brought to the Booker house by Phillips and was later found to belong to Phillips's girlfriend.

All of the recited evidence was sufficient to support the jury's finding of guilt. . . .

POWELL V. TEXAS

Supreme Court of the United States, 1968.
392 U.S. 514, 88 S. Ct. 2145, 20 L.Ed.2d 1254.

[In this case the U.S. Supreme Court considers whether it is cruel and unusual punishment under the Eighth Amendment to convict a person suffering from chronic alcoholism of the crime of public drunkenness.]

Mr. Justice MARSHALL announced the judgment of the Court and delivered an opinion in which The CHIEF JUSTICE, Mr. Justice BLACK, and Mr. Justice HARLAN join.

In late December 1966, appellant [Leroy Powell] was arrested and charged with being found in a state of intoxication in a public place. . . .

. . .[Powell's] counsel urged that appellant was "afflicted with the disease of chronic alcoholism," that "his appearance in public [while drunk was] not of his own volition," and therefore that to punish him criminally for that conduct would be cruel and unusual, in violation of the Eighth and Fourteenth Amendments to the Untied States Constitution.

The trial judge in the county court, sitting without a jury, made certain findings of fact, but ruled as a matter of law that chronic alcoholism was not a defense to the charge. He found appellant guilty, and fined him $50. . . .

Appellant . . . seeks to come within the application of the Cruel and Unusual Punishment Clause announced in *Robinson v. California* . . . (1962), which . . . held . . . that "a state statute which imprisons a person thus afflicted [with narcotic addition] as a criminal, even though he has never touched any narcotic drug within the State or been guilty of any irregular behavior there, inflicts a cruel and unusual punishment." . . .

On its face the present case does not fall within that holding, since appellant was convicted, not for being a chronic alcoholic, but for being in public while drunk on a particular occasion. The State of Texas thus has not sought to punish a mere status, as California did in *Robinson,* nor has it attempted to regulate appellant's criminal sanction for public behavior which may create substantial health and safety hazards, both for appellant and for members of the general public, and which offends the moral and aesthetic sensibilities of a large segment of the community. This seems a far cry from convicting one for being an addict, being a chronic alcoholic, being "mentally ill, or a leper." . . .

. . .[T]he most troubling aspects of this case, were *Robinson* to be extended to meet it, would be the scope and content of what could only be a constitutional doctrine of criminal responsibility. In dissent it is urged that the decision could be limited to conduct which is "a characteristic and involuntary part of the pattern of the disease as it afflicts" the particular individual, and that "[i]t is not foreseeable" that it would be applied "in the case of offenses such as driving a car while intoxicated, assault, theft, or robbery." . . . That is limitation by fiat. In the first place, nothing in the logic of the dissent would limit its application to chronic alcoholics. If Leroy Powell cannot be convicted of public intoxication, it is difficult to see how a State can convict an individual for murder, if that individual, while exhibiting normal behavior in all other respects, suffers from a "compulsion" to kill, which is an "exceedingly strong influence," but "not completely overpowering." Even if we limit our consideration to chronic alcoholics, it would seem impossible to confine the principle within the arbitrary bounds which the dissent seems to envision.

It is not difficult to imagine a case involving psychiatric testimony to the effect that an individual suffers from some aggressive neurosis which he is able to control when sober; that very little alcohol suffices to remove the inhibitions which normally contain these aggressions, with the result that the individual engages in assaultive behavior without becoming actually intoxicated; and that the individual suffers from a very strong desire to drink, which is an "exceedingly strong influence" but "not completely overpowering." Without being untrue to the rationale of this case, should the principles advanced in dissent be accepted here, the Court could not avoid holding such an individual constitutionally unaccountable for his assaultive behavior.

Traditional common-law concepts of personal accountability and essential considerations of federalism lead us to disagree with appellant. We are unable to conclude, on the state of this record or on the current state of medical knowledge, that chronic alcoholics in general, and Leroy Powell in particular, suffer from such an irresistible compulsion to drink and to get drunk in public that they are utterly unable to control their performance of either or both of these acts and thus cannot be deterred at all from public intoxication. And in any event this Court has never articulated a general constitutional doctrine of *mens rea*.

We cannot cast aside the centuries-long evolution of the collection of interlocking and overlapping concepts which the common law has utilized to assess the moral accountability of an individual for his antisocial deeds. The doctrines of *actus reus, mens rea,* insanity, mistake, justification, and duress have historically provided the tools for a constantly shifting adjustment of the tension between the medical views of the nature of man. This process of adjustment has always been thought to be the province of the States.

Nothing could be less fruitful than for this Court to be impelled into defining some sort of insanity test in constitutional terms. . . . It is simply not yet the time to write into the Constitution formulas cast in terms whose meaning, let alone relevance, is not yet clear either to doctors or to lawyers.

Affirmed.

Mr. Justice BLACK, whom Mr. Justice HARLAN joins, concurring. . . .

Mr. Justice WHITE, concurring in the result.

. . . I cannot say that the chronic alcoholic who proves his disease and a compulsion to drink is shielded from conviction when he has knowingly failed to take feasible precautions against committing a criminal act, here the act of going to or remaining in a public place. On such facts the alcoholic is like a person with smallpox, who could be convicted for being on the street but not for being ill, or, like the epileptic, who would be punished for driving a car but not for his disease. . . .

Mr. Justice FORTAS, with whom Mr. Justice DOUGLAS, Mr. Justice BRENNAN, and Mr. Justice STEWART join, dissenting.

In the present case, appellant is charged with a crime composed of two elements—being intoxicated and being found in a public place while in that condition. The crime, so defined, differs from that in *Robinson*. The statute covers more than a mere status. But the essential constitutional defect here is the same as in *Robinson,* for in both cases the particular defendant was accused of being in a condition which he had no capacity to change or avoid. The trial judge sitting as trier of fact found, upon the medical and other relevant testimony, that Powell is a "chronic alcoholic." He defined appellant's "chronic alcoholism" as "a disease which destroys the afflicted person's will power to resist the constant, excessive consumption of alcohol." He also found that "a chronic alcoholic does not appear in public by his own volition but under a compulsion symptomatic of the disease of chronic alcoholism." I read these findings to mean that appellant was powerless to avoid drinking; that having taken his first drink, he had "an uncontrollable compulsion to drink" to the point of intoxication; and that, once intoxicated, he could not prevent himself from appearing in public places. . . .

The findings in this case . . . compel the conclusion that the infliction upon appellant of a criminal penalty for being intoxicated in a public place would be "cruel and inhuman punishment" within the prohibition of the Eighth Amendment. This conclusion follows because appellant is a "chronic alcoholic" who, according to the trier of fact, cannot resist the "constant excessive consumption of alcohol" and does not appear in public by his own volition but under a "compulsion" which is part of his condition.

I would reverse the judgment below.

PEOPLE v. RANDOLPH

Appellate Department, Superior Court of Ventura County, California, 1989.
262 Cal.Rptr. 378.

[Kerry Don Randolph was charged with violating the California Vehicle Code Section 23152, subdivision (a), driving while under the influence of alcohol, and section 23152, subdivison (b), driving with 0.10 percent or more of alcohol in his blood. He admitted a prior similar conviction. Randolph was convicted by a jury and sentenced to probation. He appealed, challenging the sufficiency of the evidence introduced against him at trial.]

OSBORNE, Judge.

...We have reviewed the detailed 31-page engrossed settled statement on appeal to determine whether it discloses substantial evidence such that any reasonable trier of fact could find appellant guilty beyond a reasonable doubt.

At the trial the witnesses were an experienced traffic officer and an experienced criminalist.

1. *Testimony of the Officer:*

The officer testified to the driving, arrest, and tests. At 11:55 P.M., the officer saw two cars southbound on Victoria Avenue on the Santa Clara River bridge. He later ascertained that appellant was driving the first car. The first car hit its brakes, causing the second to come nearly to a complete stop. Appellant then accelerated, began drifting over the double line, slowed down, and accelerated again. At the next curve, both cars slowed, and the second tried to pass appellant on the right shoulder. Appellant abruptly cut the second car off to the right. There could have been a collision. The second car then tried to pass on the left, and appellant pulled into the oncoming lane and cut off the second car again. The officer stopped both cars.

He approached the first car. Appellant... began yelling that someone had been tailgating him. After appellant calmed down, he was cooperative. The officer smelled the odor of an alcoholic beverage on his breath, and noted appellant's eyes were bloodshot and glassy.

Appellant said he had two burritos to eat at 6 P.M., and drank from 9 to 10:15 that evening at a party. He said he felt the effects of the alcohol "a little bit."

The officer had appellant perform several field sobriety tests. Appellant's performance on some was unremarkable.

The officer asked appellant to select one leg and stand on it for 15 seconds. Defendant held his leg up one second, put his foot down, lifted it for a second, put it down, stood staring into space, lifted it for two seconds, put it down, then lifted it for about ten seconds while hopping on his foot, eventually losing his balance.

Defendant was instructed to walk heel-to-toe nine steps out and seven steps back. Appellant walked seven steps heel-to-toe, then stated, "Oh, yeah, you wanted me to walk nine." He then took three more steps which were not heel-to-toe, turned and walked back eight steps heel-to-toe.

The officer instructed appellant to write numbers backwards from 99 to 69. He transposed two numbers.

After being arrested, appellant selected a breath test which was administered to him at the Ventura County jail by the officer. The officer used a checklist as he had in administering the test 150 to 200 times before. The tests were taken at 12:31 and 12:33 A.M. the day after appellant was stopped. The results were 0.10 and 0.10 percent.

In the opinion of the officer, appellant was under the influence of alcohol.

2. *Testimony of the Criminalist:*

The criminalist testified to his education and experience, the license held by the laboratory, the operation of the Intoxilyzer, and the training of the officer to operate the Intoxilyzer.

If a subject gives an adequate deep-lung air sample, the Intoxilyzer will record an accurate blood-alcohol percent. If the subject provides an inadequate sample, the result shown on the machine will be lower than the subject's actual blood-alcohol percent. The relationship between blood-alcohol and breath-alcohol is good, that is, usually within 0.01 percent, in a healthy subject in the elimination phase.

As a person's alcohol level increases, the probability of causing an accident increases. Mental factors, including judgment and the ability to gather and process information, are affected. The ability to concentrate on a task and one's attitude toward driving change. Inhibitions are one of the first things affected. If the alcohol level gets high enough, balance and coordination are affected. One can be under the influence of alcohol for driving at 0.05 BAL. All persons are impaired and cannot drive safely at 0.10 BAL. Drunk people have more alcohol in their systems than people who are merely impaired. From 0.15 BAL and up, where the physical impairment is more obvious, you see staggering and slurred speech as opposed to just the mental factors. Given defendant's weight, he explained the relationship between blood-alcohol concentration and how much alcohol he must have drunk. Alcohol is metabolized at a "pretty predictable rate" of 0.015 percent per hour.

The manufacturer of the Intoxilyzer states the machine's accuracy is better than plus or minus 0.01 percent.

Because the statute is expressed in terms of blood-alcohol level, breath-alcohol results must be converted to equivalent blood-alcohol results. The ratio between breath alcohol and blood alcohol varies to some degree among individuals. The state requires breath testing machines, such as the Intoxilyzer, to be constructed to use a specified conversion ratio. He referred to the writings of Dr. DeBowski, an expert whose opinion is that the actual ratio for approximately 85 percent of the population is such that a breath test underestimates the actual blood-alcohol level by 0.01 percent. . . .

The jury had evidence of appellant's driving, his performance on field sobriety tests, his behavior, his breath test results, and the time elapsed from drinking and driving to the breath tests. A reasonable trier of fact could have found beyond a reasonable doubt that appellant drove a vehicle while having a blood-alcohol level of 0.10 percent or more. There was sufficient evidence to sustain the conviction. . . .

Finding no error, the judgment is affirmed.

JONES, P.J., and LANE, J., concur.

CHAPTER 10

OFFENSES AGAINST PUBLIC HEALTH AND THE ENVIRONMENT

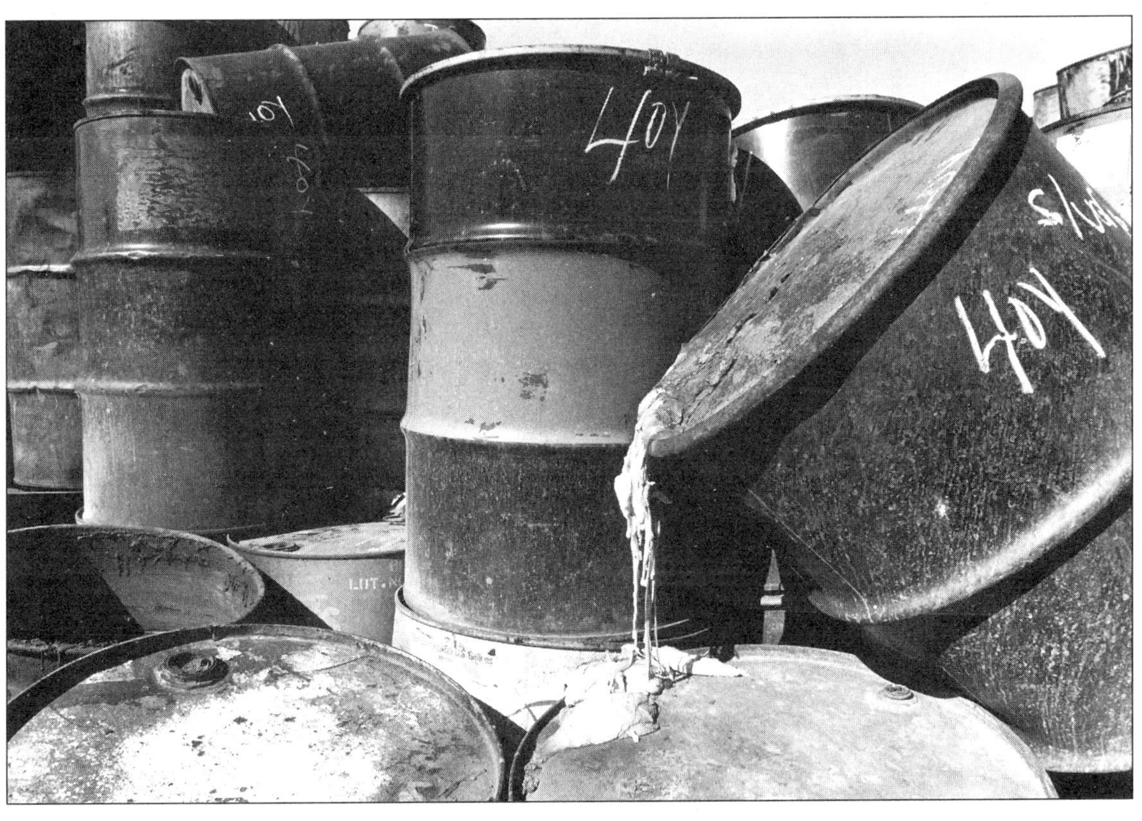

CHAPTER OUTLINE

Introduction

Although developed judicially, common-law crimes were revised and expanded by legislative bodies to meet the needs of our evolving society. In contrast, crimes against the public health and the environment originated directly from federal and state legislatures in response to the needs of a changing society. Many offenses relating to public health developed during the industrial revolution as a result of the widespread distribution of food, drugs, and cosmetics and the need to control communicable diseases. By the early 1900s municipalities perceived the need for zoning to control nuisances and to regulate land use. Since the middle of this century, pollution of the ground, water, and air has been recognized as a major threat to the health and welfare of the people and, indeed, to the ecological balance of the earth.

Enforcement of regulations in these fields is accomplished largely through regulatory agencies and measures imposing civil liability. Nevertheless, legislatures have found it necessary to impose criminal sanctions to effectively enforce standards and to deter violators. While not faced with the severe environmental problems of our age, the common law did regard wildlife, game, and fish as resources to be preserved. Accordingly, state and federal governments have enacted regulations and imposed criminal sanctions on poachers to protect these resources for the benefit of the public.

In contrast to the typical common-law crimes, many offenses against the public health and environment consist of an offender's neglect to comply with required standards or failure to take action required by law. These offenses are *mala prohibita,* and statutes criminalizing conduct in these areas generally contemplate a lower level of intent, frequently imposing a standard of strict liability. For example, in *State v. Budd Co.,* 425 N.E.2d 935 (Ohio App. 1980), the defendant was convicted under a state law that made it a criminal offense to dispose of garbage or other pollutants in any ditch, pond, stream, or other watercourse. On appeal, the court rejected the appellant's argument that it was necessary for the state to prove his criminal intent. The court observed that the statute did not require proof of intent, and that "the destruction of wildlife through pollution, will occur whenever the waterways are intentionally or accidentally polluted." 425 N.E.2d at 938.

Public Health Regulation

The authority of government to enact laws to protect the public health is a basic function of the "police power." Statutes delegating to public health agencies the power to declare quarantines, and later to require inoculations to control communicable diseases, were among the earliest application of this police power. At the turn of the century, the Supreme Court reviewed a defendant's sentence to pay a fine for refusing to be vaccinated for smallpox as required by a Cambridge, Massachusetts ordinance. The defendant argued that a compulsory vaccination law invaded his liberty secured by the Constitution. Rejecting this contention, the Court observed that "persons and property are subjected to all kinds of restraints and burdens in order to secure the general comfort, health, and prosperity of the state." *Jacobson v. Massachusetts,* 197 U.S. 11, 26, 25 S.Ct. 358, 361, 49 L.Ed. 643, 650 (1905).

Today numerous federal, state, and local laws address health concerns, providing criminal penalties for serious violations. Modern statutes address a variety of contemporary problems. For example, the California Health and Safety Code in Section 3198 provides that "any person infected with a venereal disease in an infectious state who knows of such condition and who marries or has sexual intercourse, is guilty of a misdemeanor." In *Reynolds v. McNichols,* 488 F.2d 1378 (10th Cir. 1973), a federal appeals court upheld a Denver, Colorado, "hold and treat" ordinance authorizing detention and treatment, if necessary, of a woman arrested for prostitution who was reasonably suspected of having a venereal disease. Indeed, many states now have statutes providing criminal penalties for health care professionals who fail to report communicable diseases. See, for example, West's Colo. Stat. Ann. §§ 25–4–402–408.

A California appellate court recently held that under a "special needs" doctrine, the state, without individualized suspicion, may require that a person convicted of prostitution be tested for acquired immune deficiency syndrome (AIDS). *Love v. Superior Court,* 276 Cal. Rptr. 660 (Cal. App. 1990). Florida has enacted laws criminalizing intentional sexual transmission of HIV without a partner's consent, and making it a felony for a person who is HIV-positive to donate blood or organs. West's Fla. Stat. Ann. §§ 381.004; 384.24. In Nevada a licensed prostitute who practices with knowledge of a positive HIV test result is guilty of a felony. Nev. Rev. Stat. § 201.358.

Most public health laws that impose criminal penalties frequently do not include any intent requirement. In those instances the government need only prove the defendant violated the statute. Offenses of this type are known as "strict-liability offenses," a concept discussed in Chapter 4.

The Federal Pure Food, Drug, and Cosmetics Act

Congress first enacted legislation to prevent the importation of adulterated drugs and medicines in 1848. Today, numerous federal acts relate to foods and drugs, but the basic Food, Drug, and Cosmetic Act dates back to 1906. It was comprehensively amended in 1938, and subsequently amended many times. 21 U.S.C.A. §§ 301–391. The present law prohibits traffic in food, drugs, and cosmetics being prepared or handled under unsanitary circumstances or under conditions that render them injurious to health. Included in its broad sweep are prohibitions against misbranding and adulteration of food, drugs, and cosmetics, as well as requirements for truthful labeling. The act provides substantial fines and imprisonment for violators. Among other prohibitions, Section 331 proscribes:

> (k) The alteration, mutilation, destruction, obliteration, or removal of the whole or any part of the labeling of, or the doing of any other act with respect to, a food, drug, device, or cosmetic, if such act is done while such article is held for sale (whether or not the first sale) after shipment in interstate commerce and results in such article being adulterated or misbranded.

Section 453 (g) states that a food shall be deemed to be adulterated:

> (3) if it consists in whole or in part of any filthy, putrid, or decomposed substance . . . or [if it is] otherwise unfit for food; [or] (4) if it has been prepared, packed, or held under insanitary conditions whereby it may have become contaminated with filth, or whereby it may have been rendered injurious to health. . . .

Like most public health laws, food and drug laws fall in the category of regulatory offenses. Therefore, unless the statute criminalizing conduct or failure to act requires an intent element, criminal liability can attach without proof of the defendant's intent. *United States v. Park,* 421 U.S. 658, 670, 95 S.Ct. 1903, 1910, 44 L.Ed.2d 489, 500 (1975).

Criminal Liability of "Responsible Corporate Officers"

Food, drugs, and cosmetics are usually produced and distributed by corporate enterprises. To effectively enforce regulatory laws imposing criminal sanctions in these areas, government agencies must be able to affix responsibility on individuals in supervisory positions as well as on corporate entities. The Supreme Court first recognized the concept of a "responsible corporate officer" in *United States v. Dotterweich,* 320 U.S. 277, 64 S.Ct. 134, 88 L.Ed. 48 (1943), but prior to 1975 there were conflicting federal court decisions on whether a corporate officer who failed to take measures to prevent violations of the food and drug laws from occurring could be held criminally liable. Noting a conflict in decisions among the courts of appeal, the Supreme Court addressed the standard of liability of corporate officers under the Pure Food, Drug, and Cosmetic Act in *United States v. Park, supra.* There, a national retail food chain and its president and chief executive officer were charged with causing food shipped in interstate commerce to be held in a building accessible to rodents and exposed to contamination. The food chain pled guilty, but its president contested the charges against him. He contended that while he retained authority over corporate affairs, he delegated "normal operating duties," including sanitation, to lower-level personnel. In rejecting his contention as a basis of nonliability, the Court held that the prosecution establishes a *prima facie* case of the guilt of the accused when it establishes that "the defendant had, by reason of his position in the corporation, responsibility and authority either to prevent in the first instance or promptly to correct, the violation complained of, and that he failed to do so." 421 U.S. at 673, 95 S.Ct. at 1912, 44 L.Ed.2d at 502.

Criticism of "Strict Liability" Public Health Laws

Many legal scholars condemn the imposition of strict liability in regulatory offenses, such as food, drug, and health laws. They contend that it brands as criminals people who are without moral fault. Arguing against making violation of such laws punishable by incarceration, critics suggest decriminalization, liability predicated on a negligence standard rather than on strict liability, or punishment by only a monetary fine. These criticisms notwithstanding, Congress has determined that the interest of society requires a high standard of care and has been unwilling to eliminate either the strict-liability standard or incarceration. As previously noted, the courts hold that a corporate agent who bears a responsible relationship to the operation of the enterprise, and has power to take measures necessary to ensure compliance, can be found guilty of violating such regulatory statutes.

CASE IN POINT

RESPONSIBILITY FOLLOWS AUTHORITY

Dean Starr, secretary-treasurer of Cheney Brothers Food Corporation, was convicted of violating the Federal Food, Drug, and Cosmetic Act, 21U.S.C.A. §§ 301–391, for allowing contamination of food stored in a company warehouse over which he had operational responsibility. After an inspector from the Food and Drug Administration (FDA) pointed out the problem, the janitor for the warehouse was instructed to make corrections, but no action was taken. A month later, a second inspection by the FDA disclosed that the problem had not been corrected.

On appeal, Starr contended that he was not responsible because the janitor in charge had failed to comply with instructions to clean up the warehouse. The court rejected his argument, noting that Mr. Starr was aware of the problem after the first inspection and had ample time to remedy the situation. In affirming his conviction, the court also observed that supervisory officers have a duty to anticipate the shortcomings of their delegees.

United States v. Starr, 535 F.2d 512 (9th Cir. 1976).

PLANNING AND ZONING ACTIVITIES

Although sometimes used interchangeably, the terms, *zoning* and *planning* are not synonymous. Zoning is concerned primarily with the use and regulation of buildings and structures, whereas planning is a broader term embracing the systematic and orderly development of a community. *State ex rel. Kearns v. Ohio Power Co.,* 127 N.E.2d 394, 399 (Ohio 1955). In *Village of Euclid, Ohio v. Ambler Realty Co.,* 272 U.S. 365, 47 S.Ct. 114, 71 L.Ed. 303 (1926), the Supreme Court first upheld the concept of comprehensive zoning, which allows local governments to divide areas of the community and to designate the permitted and prohibited land uses in the respective districts. Since then zoning has become both widespread and sophisticated. Building codes are generally encompassed within the overall local zoning requirements. Today, comprehensive planning guides the development of a community, and that planning is implemented to a large degree by local zoning ordinances (their enactment usually preceded by studies and recommendations of professional consultants). Additionally, local citizens are enlisted to sit on planning and zoning boards that make recommendations to the governing body. Any comprehensive zoning ordinance must provide for a board of adjustment to act in a quasi-judicial capacity. The board must have the power to grant variances where strict enforcement of an ordinance would cause an undue hardship to property owners. It may also be empowered to approve special exceptions based on the landowner's compliance with specified criteria.

As with other regulatory measures, enforcement of local zoning codes is accomplished administratively in most instances. Failing this, local governments resort to civil court actions, commonly seeking injunctive relief against violators. Most zoning ordinances classify violations as misdemeanors and provide for a fine and a jail term upon conviction. Zoning ordinances, like most health regulations, generally do not include an intent requirement. Prosecution of violators is usually undertaken only as a last resort. But once a state or local government commences prosecution of a defendant for violation of a zoning ordinance, it must meet all burdens placed on the prosecution in criminal proceedings. *People v. St. Agatha Home for Children*, 389 N.E.2d 1098 (N.Y. 1979).

The Scope of Federal and State Environmental Laws

Numerous federal statutes and agencies play a part in regulation and enforcement of the laws affecting our environment. Among the older agencies are the Army Corps of Engineers, the Coast Guard, and the Departments of the Interior, Commerce, Transportation, and Justice. A newer agency, the Environmental Protection Agency (EPA), acts under authority of some twenty-nine major congressional enactments and has significant responsibilities in numerous areas including hazardous wastes, toxic substances, and noise pollution. State environmental agencies became active in the 1970s, and planning and coordinating councils now function at state, regional, and local levels. They play an important part in environmental regulation through establishment of pollution controls, water management programs, waste water, and solid-waste disposal programs.

Environmental regulation at the federal and state levels has become a vast undertaking, but until recently government agencies have relied almost exclusively on civil penalties as an enforcement tool. The concept changed in the 1980s, when criminal enforcement of environmental laws became prominent, particularly in instances of egregious violations involving hazardous waste disposal, water pollution, and air pollution. These enforcement policies were in effect long before the *Exxon Valdez* supertanker spilled millions of gallons of crude oil in Alaskan waters in 1989, destroying wildlife and despoiling beaches.

Some environmental crimes only require proof that the defendant committed a proscribed act or failed to comply with a required standard. In prosecutions of these strict-liability offenses, the government may establish the defendant's guilt in a manner similar to prosecuting many crimes against the public health. Other statutes require the government to establish the defendant's "negligent" conduct or a "willful" or "knowing" violation, and many court decisions in environmental prosecutions turn on whether the evidence is sufficient to meet the required statutory standard.

Major Federal Environmental Legislation Providing Criminal Sanctions

Congress enacted its first major environmental law, the Rivers and Harbors Act, in 1899. 33 U.S.C.A. §§ 401–467. This act makes it a misdemeanor to discharge

CASE IN POINT

THE *EXXON VALDEZ* PROSECUTION

In March 1989, the supertanker *Exxon Valdez* ran aground and ruptured, spilling more than 240,000 barrels of oil into Alaska's Prince William Sound and wreaking havoc on the natural environment. Subsequently, the federal government brought criminal charges against the Exxon Shipping Co. and its parent, Exxon Corporation, under the Clean Water Act and several other federal environmental statutes. In October 1991, one week before the case was scheduled to go to trial, Exxon accepted a plea bargain under which it agreed to pay $25 million in federal fines and another $100 million in restitution, split between the federal and state governments. The $125 million fine was the largest environmental criminal fine in U.S. history.

Source: Stephen Raucher, "Raising the Stakes for Environmental Polluters: The Exxon Valdez Criminal Prosecution." *Ecology Law Quarterly* 147 (1993).

refuse into the navigable waters of the United States. Notwithstanding the act's provisions for criminal enforcement, the federal government traditionally sought enforcement through the civil courts. In recent years, the following acts of Congress have provided significant means to enforce criminal violations of environmental laws and regulations:

- *Clean Air Amendments of 1970,* 42 U.S.C.A. §§ 7401–7642
- *Federal Water Pollution Control Act of 1972* (Clean Water Act), 33 U.S.C.A. §§ 1251–1387
- *Resource Conservation and Recovery Act of 1976* (RCRA), 42 U.S.C.A. §§ 6901–6992
- *Toxic Substances Control Act of 1976* (TSCA), 15 U.S.C.A. §§ 2601–2671
- *Comprehensive Environmental Response, Compensation and Liability Act of 1980* (CERCLA), 42 U.S.C.A. §§ 9601–9675

The Clean Air Act (CLA)

The Clean Air Act sets federal standards designed to enhance the quality of the air by deterring air polluters. In 1977, Congress passed a series of amendments establishing stricter standards for air quality. As amended, the act provides criminal sanctions for violation of any provisions for which civil penalties apply, and for any person who knowingly makes any false representation in a document filed under the act. Enforcement may be delegated to the states pursuant to the State Implementation Plan (SIP), 42 U.S.C.A. § 7410, but the states are not required to enact minimum criminal provisions to receive EPA approval of their implementation plans. Indeed, while some states track the substantial federal penalties in their own statutes, most provide for lesser penalties and some do not include imprisonment as a sanction. For example, in Oklahoma a violation of its Clean Air Act provides for a fine of $500, imprisonment for a year, or both 63 Okl.

Stats. Ann. § 1–1802(L), whereas a first offender who violates the air pollution laws in Maryland is subject to a fine of $25,000 to $50,000 per day of violation. Code of Md. § 2–609.1(b)(2)(i).

Two reasons have been advanced for the relatively few criminal prosecutions in respect to air pollution as compared to prosecutions for violations of hazardous waste and water pollution laws. First, the cost of criminal enforcement in this area apparently is great, and second, the problems of enforcement are made exceedingly difficult for states because pollution of the air is a less stationary category of pollution.

The Federal Water Pollution Control Act of 1972 (Clean Water Act)

The Federal Water Pollution Control Act of 1972 (Clean Water Act), 33 U.S.C.A. §§ 1251–1270, is designed to control water pollution and regulate industrial and other discharges into navigable waters. Although the Clean Water Act is enforced primarily through civil means, criminal sanctions have been imposed for "willful" or "negligent" violations of certain provisions concerning permits and the making of false statements. Amendments in 1987 eliminated the "willful" requirement and imposed more stringent penalties for negligent violations and even more severe penalties for knowing violations of the act's criminal provisions. 33 U.S.C.A. § 1319(c).

A majority of the states have programs approved by the EPA. While states vary somewhat in their approaches, many provide penalties similar to those in the federal act for either willful or negligent violations of water pollution provisions.

Courts tend to construe the penal provisions of the Clean Water Act broadly, and generally hold supervisory personnel vested with authority to a high standard of compliance. The trend in the federal courts seems to be to hold responsible corporate officers criminally liable in environmental offenses despite their lack of "consciousness of wrongdoing." See, for example, *United States v. Brittain,* 931 F.2d 1413, 1419 (10th Cir. 1991).

The Resource Conservation and Recovery Act (RCRA)

Enactment of RCRA in 1976 was a significant step in environmental control. Its objective is to encourage the states—through grants, technical assistance, and advice—to establish standards and provide for civil and criminal enforcement of state regulations. The EPA sets minimum standards requiring the states to enact criminal penalties against any person who knowingly stores or transports any hazardous waste to an unpermitted facility, or who treats such waste without a permit or makes false representations to secure a permit. All states have enacted criminal statutes pursuant to the criteria specified in RCRA.

RCRA proscribes a comprehensive list of illegal actions and imposes criminal penalties on any person who:

1. knowingly transports or causes to be transported any hazardous waste to an unpermitted facility, 42 U.S.C.A. § 6928(d)(1);

CASE IN POINT

CRIMINAL PROSECUTION UNDER THE CLEAN WATER ACT

David W. Boldt was Chemical Engineering Manager for Astro Circuit Corporation, a Massachusetts company that manufactured circuit boards using an electroplating process. Boldt's duties included supervising the company's pretreatment process, a part of the pollution control system. He was charged with six counts of violating the Clean Water Act. He was convicted on two counts: one for knowingly aiding and abetting the discharge of pollutants into a municipal sewer in 1987, when the copper level in Astro's effluent greatly exceeded the federal standards; another for ordering a subordinate in 1988 to dump 3,100 gallons of partially treated industrial waste water containing excessive metals into the municipal sewer. At trial Boldt asserted the defense of impossibility to the first incident, arguing he was only a mid-level manager who was not responsible for the discharge. Boldt acknowledged responsibility for the second discharge, but pleaded the defense of necessity, arguing it was necessary to authorize the discharge to avoid a worse harm.

In upholding both convictions, the appellate court observed that the evidence showed that pollution control was part of Boldt's area of responsibility and that, as to the 1987 violation, he was aware of the practice of bypassing the pollution control system and had condoned it on the occasion at issue. As to the 1988 incident, the court found the evidence undisputed that Boldt directly ordered his subordinate to dump the copper waste water, a conclusion bolstered by his subordinate's testimony that Boldt attempted to cover up the incident. Finally, the appellate court observed that the record of the trial disclosed that the president of Astro testified that Boldt was authorized to shut down the plant.

United States v. Boldt, 929 F.2d 35 (1st Cir. 1991).

2. knowingly treats, stores, or disposes of any hazardous waste without a permit, in knowing violation of any material condition or requirement of the interim status regulations, 42 U.S.C.A. § 6928(d)(2)(A)-(C); or one who
3. knowingly omits material information or makes any false statement or representation in any record or document required to be maintained under the regulations or submitted to the [EPA] or any state which is authorized to run RCRA programs, 42 U.S.C.A. § 6928(d)(3).

In addition, Section 6928(e) makes it a criminal offense to knowingly place another person in imminent danger of death or serious bodily injury in conjunction with the transportation, storage, or disposal of hazardous wastes.

RCRA has become an important tool for enforcement and one prosecutors frequently rely on in prosecuting persons who illegally dispose of hazardous wastes. In *United States v. Johnson & Towers, Inc.*, 741 F.2d 662, 664 (3d Cir. 1984), the court held that the term *person* in RCRA Section 6928(d) includes employees as well as owners and operators, and that proof of the knowledge element required may be inferred as to those individuals holding responsible corporate positions.

In prosecutions under RCRA, did Congress intend that it would be necessary for the government to prove that a defendant knew the waste material being stored or transported was listed as a hazardous waste? In *United States v. Hayes International Corp.*, 786 F.2d 1499, 1503 (11th Cir. 1986), the court affirmed a conviction under Section 6928(d)(1) for unlawfully transporting hazardous waste materials to a nonpermitted facility and ruled that neither a lack of knowledge that paint waste was a hazardous material, nor ignorance of the permit requirement, was a defense. Conviction for the treatment, storage, or disposal of hazardous waste without an RCRA permit has been more problematic. In *United States v. Hoflin*, 880 F.2d 1033, 1038 (9th Cir. 1989), the court held that the government is not required to prove the defendant's knowledge of the lack of a permit in order to secure a conviction in either transport or storage cases, but nevertheless a person who does not know that the waste materials he or she is disposing of is hazardous cannot be guilty of violating Section 6928(d)(2)(a).

One of the most serious cases brought under the RCRA involved Section 6928(e), which makes it a criminal violation to knowingly place employees "in imminent danger of death or serious bodily injury." *United States v. Protex Industries, Inc.*, 874 F.2d 740, 742 (10th Cir. 1989), involved a company that operated a drum recycling facility and in connection with its business purchased drums that previously contained toxic chemicals. The evidence revealed that the company's safety provisions were inadequate to protect its employees and that, as a result, certain company employees suffered from solvent poisoning and exhibited serious maladies. The court upheld a conviction of Protex for placing employees in an industrial environment without sufficient protection against exposure to toxic chemicals.

The Toxic Substances Control Act (TSCA)

The Toxic Substances Control Act of 1976 authorizes the EPA to require testing and to prohibit the manufacture, distribution, or use of certain chemical substances that present an unreasonable risk of injury to health or the environment, and to regulate their disposal. Although the act depends primarily on civil penalties, a person who "knowingly" or "willfully" fails to maintain records or submit reports as required violates the criminal provisions of the act. 15 U.S.C.A. §§ 2614; 2615(b). In 1982, the court upheld the conviction of Robert Earl Ward, Jr., the chairman of the board of Ward Transformer Company, on eight counts of the unlawful disposal of toxic substances (PCB-containing oils from used transformers) and willfully aiding and abetting the unlawful disposal of toxic substances. The evidence at trial revealed that while the defendant himself did not dispose of the toxic substances, the company's employees performed the task while he was kept advised of the progress. *United States v. Ward*, 676 F. 2d 94 (4th Cir. 1982).

The Comprehensive Environmental Response, Compensation, and Liability Act (CERCLA)

In 1980 Congress enacted the Comprehensive Environmental Response, Compensation, and Liability Act (CERCLA), commonly known as the Superfund

Law. Its purpose is to finance cleanup and provide for civil suits by citizens. As revised in 1986, the act requires notice to federal and state agencies of any "release" of a "reportable quantity" of a listed hazardous substance. *Release* is broadly defined, and *reportable quantity* is related to each of the several hundred "hazardous substances." CERCLA also provides for EPA to promulgate regulations for the collection and disposal of solid wastes. The act imposes criminal sanctions against those who fail to report as required, or who destroy or falsify records. 42 U.S.C.A. § 9603(d)(2).

Standard of Liability of Corporate Officers

As previously noted, many of the violations in the public health area are caused by corporate entities; therefore, courts often focus on whether an accused by reason of his or her position in the corporate enterprise had sufficient responsibility and authority to either prevent or correct the violation charged. The same legal doctrine of law is being applied by the courts in respect to environmental crimes. In fact, Congress has adopted the "responsible corporate officer" doctrine in the Clean Air Act, 42 U.S.C.A. § 7413(c)(3) and the Clean Water Act, 33 U.S.C.A. § 1319(c)(3)(6). And the doctrine has been upheld in CERCLA cases by federal appeals courts. For example, in *United States v. Carr,* 880 F.2d 1550 (2d Cir. 1989), the court rejected a maintenance supervisor's argument that he could not be guilty because he was a relatively low-level employee. The court explained that CERCLA imposes criminal responsibility on a person "even of relatively low rank" who acts in a supervisory capacity and is "in a position to detect, prevent, and abate a release of hazardous substances." 880 F.2d at 1554. Thus, it is becoming clear that a responsible corporate officer not only cannot avoid criminal liability by delegating tasks to others but also must remedy any violations that occur. At the state level, corporate executives have been charged with criminally negligent homicide and manslaughter where employees' deaths have resulted from the improper use of hazardous substances. See, for example, *People v. Hegedus,* 443 N.W.2d 127 (Mich. 1989); *State ex rel. Cornellier v. Black,* 425 N.W.2d 21 (Wis. App. 1988).

Environmental Laws Lack Uniformity

Disparate environmental standards, enforcement policies, and sanctions in the areas of water and air pollution and disposal of hazardous wastes can lead to "shopping" by industry to secure locations that will enable them to be more competitive by not having to comply with stringent environmental standards. Significant differences exist among the fifty states in the standards of proof required and in the sanctions imposed for criminal violations of hazardous waste, water pollution, and air pollution laws.

Compare the differences between the statutory language in the Kentucky and Vermont offenses set out in Table 10.1. What level of proof should be required for establishing a defendant's guilt under the "knowingly" standard of the Kentucky laws? Would a different standard of proof be required under Vermont's laws concerning hazardous wastes and air pollution?

TABLE 10.1 Kentucky and Vermont Environmental Laws Imposing Criminal Penalties Concerning Hazardous Wastes, Water Pollution, and Air Pollution

---

Kentucky Revised Statutes Annotated

HAZARDOUS WASTES

Unlawful acts: Knowingly engaging in the generation, treatment, storage, transportation, or disposal of hazardous wastes in violation of this chapter, or contrary to a permit, order, or administrative regulation issued or promulgated under the chapter; or knowingly making a false statement, representation, or certification in an application for, or form pertaining to, a permit, or in a notice or report required by the terms and conditions of an issued permit. Ky. Rev. Stat. Ann. § 224.99–010(6).

Penalties: Felony; imprisonment between one and five years or a fine up to $25,000 per day of violation, or both. § 224.99–010(6).

WATER POLLUTION

Unlawful acts: Knowingly, or with criminal negligence, violating any of the following:
§ 224.70–110 (water pollution)
§ 224.73–120 (monitoring and reporting)
§ 244.40–100 (waste disposal)
§ 244.50–545 (oil pollution)
§ 224.40–305 (unpermitted waste disposal facilities)
Any determination, permit, administrative regulation, or order of the Cabinet promulgated pursuant to those sections which have become final; or knowingly providing false information in any document filed or required to be maintained under this chapter; or knowingly rendering inaccurate any monitoring device or method required to be maintained. § 294.99–010(4).

Penalties: Misdemeanor; imprisonment up to one year or a fine between $1,000 and $15,000 per day of violation, or both. § 294.99–010(4).

AIR POLLUTION

Unlawful acts: Knowingly, or with criminal negligence, violating § 224 (monitoring and reporting) or 244.330 (air pollution), or any determination, permit, administrative regulation, or order of the Cabinet promulgated pursuant to those sections which have become final; or knowingly providing false information in any document filed or required to be maintained under this chapter, or knowingly rendering inaccurate any monitoring device or method required to be maintained. § 294.99–010(4).

Penalties: Misdemeanor; imprisonment up to one year or a fine between $1,000 and $15,000 per day of violation, or both. § 294.99–010(4).

Vermont Statutes Annotated

HAZARDOUS WASTES

Unlawful acts: Violating any provision of the waste management chapter (transportation, storage, disposal, or treatment of hazardous waste: permit and manifest requirements), rules promulgated therein, or terms or conditions of any order of certification. Vt. Stat. Ann., Title 10, § 6612(a) (1991).

Penalties: Imprisonment up to six months or a fine up to $25,000 per day of violation, or both. Title 10, § 6612(a).

WATER POLLUTION

Unlawful acts: Violating any provision of the water pollution control subchapter, or failing, neglecting, or refusing to obey or comply with any order or the terms of any permit issued under this subchapter. Title 10, § 1275(a).

Penalties: Imprisonment up to six months or a fine up to $25,000 per day of violation, or both. Title 10, § 1275(a).

Unlawful acts: Knowingly making any false statement, representation, or certification in any document filed or required to be maintained under the water pollution control subchapter, or by any permit, rule, regulation, or order issued thereunder; or falsifying, tampering with, or knowingly rendering inaccurate any monitoring device or method required to be maintained under this subchapter, or by any permit, rule, regulation, or order issued thereunder. Title 10, §1275(b).

Penalties: Imprisonment up to six months or a fine up to $10,000 or both. § 1275(b).

AIR POLLUTION

Unlawful acts: Violating a provision of the air pollution control chapter (discharge of air contaminants without a permit or in violation of pollution standards) except § 563 and § 567 (relating to motor vehicles and confidential records), or any rule issued thereunder. Title 10, § 568. *Penalties:* Fine up to $2,000 per violation. Title 10, § 568.

Unfortunately, fines imposed on violators of environmental laws are too often looked upon as "costs of doing business," because in reality these costs may be passed on to the ultimate consumer. The threat of imprisonment, on the other hand, is one cost that cannot be passed on to a consumer, and it is therefore a powerful deterrent to those who would pollute the environment. As states become more aggressive in the prosecution of environmental crimes, more uniformity of criminal sanctions will undoubtedly develop, much as it has in the more common criminal offenses.

Noise Pollution

Congress enacted the Quiet Communities Act of 1978, 42 U.S.C.A. §§ 4901–4918, to protect the environment against noise pollution, which has come to be perceived as a growing danger to health and welfare of the population. Sections 4909 and 4910 provide criminal penalties for those who "knowingly" or "wilfully" import, manufacture, or distribute products that fail to comply with noise standards specified in the statute. The act recognizes, however, that the primary responsibility for protecting communities against noise pollution lies with state and local governments.

Historically, local governments have adopted ordinances that prohibit excessive noise. In the twentieth century, ordinances have reflected concern over amplified sound equipment. The Ithaca, New York, law is fairly typical:

> No person shall play, operate or use, or cause to be played operated or used, any mechanical instrument, radio or wireless, speaker or horn, or any other instrument, device or thing in the city so as to disturb the peace and quiet of any neighborhood. The Code of Ordinances of the City of Ithaca, N.Y., Art. 16, § 16–12, subdivision (b).

Ordinances of this type may be applied to prohibit the use of loud stereo equipment in an apartment building where residents live in close quarters, or to disband loud late-night parties that are disturbing neighbors. Such an ordinance might be enforced against a person whose car stereo is played so loudly as to be an annoyance or even a safety hazard.

Antismoking Legislation

As society has become more aware of the ill effects of smoking and, in particular, the hazards of "second-hand smoke," governments have moved to restrict smoking in public buildings and places of public accommodation and transportation. Perhaps the best known example is the Federal Aviation Administration regulation prohibiting smoking altogether on domestic passenger airline flights. Most antismoking regulations carry minor civil penalties analogous to parking tickets. However, some jurisdictions have experimented with criminal sanctions. For example, a Minnesota statute provides that "[n]o person shall smoke in a public place or at a public meeting except in designated smoking areas." Minn. S.A. § 144.414. Section 144.417 provides that "[a]ny person who violates section 144.414 is guilty of a petty misdemeanor." As people become more aware of the dangers of "passive smoking," the use of criminal sanctions against smokers is apt to increase.

Fish and Game Laws

Since the early common law, fish and game have been viewed as animals *ferae naturae,* meaning that the state as sovereign owns them in trust for the people. *Bayside Fish Flour Co. v. Gentry,* 297 U.S. 422, 56 S.Ct. 513, 80 L. Ed. 772 (1936). As trustee, the state has the duty to preserve and protect wildlife by regulating fishing in public and private streams and controlling the taking of game. *Shively v. Bowlby,* 152 U.S. 1, 14 S.Ct. 548, 38 L.Ed. 331 (1894). Owners of private property retain a qualified interest, so those seeking to take fish or game from the confines of their property must secure their permission.

While it is generally within the jurisdiction of the states to regulate wildlife, fish, and game, it is settled law that the federal government has jurisdiction to enact statutes to carry out treaties in regard to migratory birds. The jealous regard that the states have over wildlife within their borders led Missouri to challenge the constitutionality of the Migratory Bird Conservation Act, a statute passed by Congress to enforce the provisions of the Migratory Bird Treaty entered into by the United States in 1916. Missouri claimed the federal statute infringed rights reserved to the states by the Tenth Amendment to the United States Constitution. The Supreme Court rejected that challenge, thereby settling the issue of federal control. The Court held that Article II, Section 2 of the Constitution grants the president the power to make treaties, and Article I, Section 8 gives Congress the power to enact legislation to enforce those treaties. *Missouri v. Holland,* 252 U.S. 416, 40 S.Ct. 382, 64 L.Ed. 641 (1920). Of course, the federal government retains jurisdiction to protect all wildlife, game, and fish within national game preserves. *Hunt v. United States,* 278 U.S. 96, 49 S.Ct. 38, 73 L. Ed. 200 (1928). Enforcement of the Migratory Bird Act (MBA), 16 U.S.C.A. §§ 703–712, remains a viable part of the federal environmental enforcement program. Following conflicting court decisions on whether the penal provisions of MBA imposed *strict liability* for both misdemeanor and felony violations, Congress inserted the word *knowingly* into the section of the Act providing criminal sanctions, thus requiring the prosecution to prove the defendant's *mens rea* as well as *actus reus* to establish a violation (see Chapter 4).

Modern efforts of the federal government to preserve the environment through protection of wildlife is illustrated by the Federal Endangered Species Act of 1973, 16 U.S.C.A. §§ 1531–1544. This act is designed to conserve ecosystems by preserving wildlife, fish and plants. And while enforcement is largely through civil penalties, criminal liability is imposed against any person who *knowingly* violates regulations issued under the act. 16 U.S.C.A. § 1540(b). In *United States v. Billie,* 667 F.Supp. 1485 (S.D. Fla. 1987), the defendant was charged with killing a Florida panther, an endangered species. He argued that the prosecution had to prove his specific intent; that is, that he knew the animal he shot was a Florida panther, as opposed to a species of panther not on the list of "endangered species." The U.S. District Court rejected his argument and held that the government "need prove only that the defendant acted with general intent when he shot the animal in question." 667 F.Supp. at 1493. The court discussed the fact that the defendant was charged with violating a regulatory statute enacted to conserve and protect endangered species, and that its purposes would be eviscerated if the government had to prove that a hunter who killed an animal recognized the particular subspecies as being protected under the act. 667 F.Supp. at 1492–93.

Legislatures may make it a strict-liability offense to take or possess fish and game in violation of regulations, *Cummings v. Commonwealth,* 255 S.W. 2d 997 (Ky. 1953). Most states have done so, usually imposing strict liability for taking quantities of game or fish in excess of permitted allowances and for hunting and fishing during closed seasons. But it can be quite difficult to determine whether a given law that imposes a criminal penalty for violating a fishing or game regulation is a strict-liability statute. If a wildlife penal statute includes words incorporating a *mens rea* requirement, it is clear that the prosecution must prove the defendant's intent as well as the *actus reus.* While it is difficult to generalize, if a wildlife penal law does not explicitly require intent by including such words as *willfully* or *knowingly,* only proof of the *actus reus* of the offense is required. The courts have tended to make an exception to this general rule where the offense is of a more serious criminal character (e.g., smuggling and chemical trafficking), or where the offense is designated as a felony or carries a severe punishment.

In *State v. Rice,* 626 P.2d 104 (Alaska 1981), the court considered a game regulation that lacked any requirement for criminal intent. As noted, this type of regulation is generally treated much like a traffic law. The Alaska Supreme Court took a different approach, saying that "strict liability is an exception to the rule which requires criminal intent" and criminal statutes will be "strictly construed to require some degree of *mens rea* absent a clear legislative intent to the contrary." 626 P.2d at 108.

Statutes also commonly make it a strict-liability offense to use improper types of fishing nets, to hunt with artificial lights, and to shoot over baited fields. In addition, they provide for forfeiture of illegal equipment used to hunt or fish in violation of laws. See, for example, *State v. Billiot,* 229 So.2d 72 (La. 1969), where the Louisiana Supreme Court upheld the forfeiture of seines and other devices used in trawling for shrimp during a closed season.

Irrespective of whether a penal statute imposes strict liability or proof of intent, the prosecution is not required to establish that a person accused of fishing in a closed season actually caught fish, *State v. Parker,* 167 A. 854, 855 (Me. 1933), nor is it a defense that a hunter has failed to kill any game. *Key v. State,* 384 S.W.2d 22 (Tenn. 1964).

CONCLUSION

Imposing strict criminal liability on responsible corporate officers has proven to be successful in deterring violations of laws protecting the purity and safety of food and drugs. Moreover, the concept of strict liability is firm in respect to traditional public health statutes. Strict liability is also applied to transgressors of wildlife regulations, although—whenever a violation rises to the level of a felony—courts are inclined to require proof of the defendant's intent before upholding a conviction that visits serious consequences on the offender.

Until recently governmental agencies relied almost exclusively on civil penalties to punish violators of environmental laws, but the regulatory climate is changing. During the 1990s, we will continue to witness an increased reliance by federal and state authorities on criminal sanctions, often with greatly increased penalties. As this trend continues, legislatures (or, in their absence, courts of law) will most likely include a *mens rea* requirement in regulatory statutes that subject violators to severe punishment.

Noise pollution and smoking in public places are being increasingly viewed by society as detrimental. It is reasonable to expect that criminal sanctions—which, after all, mirror societal norms—will be increasingly applied to these problems.

QUESTIONS FOR THOUGHT AND DISCUSSION

1. Are criminal sanctions essential to the effective enforcement of food, drug, and cosmetic laws?
2. Should the term *responsible corporate officer* be explicitly defined by statute, or should courts make this determination on a case-by-case basis?
3. Does your community impose criminal penalties for violations of zoning regulations? If so, are violations treated as strict-liability offenses?
4. Should efforts be made to formulate a model state code of environmental regulations?
5. Should smoking be prohibited in all public places? If so, should violations be treated as civil or criminal infractions?
6. Do you think hunting and fishing violations should be decriminalized and treated as civil infractions in the way that many states treat traffic offenses?
7. Should environmental crimes that carry major penalties be strict-liability offenses, or should prosecutors be required to prove that a defendant "knowingly" or "willfully" committed an offense?

CASE

UNITED STATES v. SELLERS

United States Court of Appeals, Fifth Circuit, 1991.
926 F.2d 410.

[In this case, the U.S. Court of Appeals for the Fifth Circuit reviews a criminal conviction under the Resource Conservation and Recovery Act. The appellant, James Ralph Sellers, was convicted of sixteen counts of knowingly and willfully disposing of a hazardous waste without obtaining a permit, as required by RCRA.]

KING, Circuit Judge:

On March 5, 1989, residents in rural Jones County, Mississippi discovered sixteen 55-gallon drums of hazardous paint waste on an embankment of the Camp Branch Creek, which flows into the Leaf River. These drums were later determined to contain paint waste and methylethylketone (M.E.K.), a paint solvent, and one of the drums was found to be leaking. Sellers was indicted on October 16, 1989 on sixteen counts of violating 42 U.S.C. § 6928(d)(2)(A) for disposing of sixteen drums of hazardous waste without a permit on or about March 4 or 5, 1989. Sellers was tried January 8 through 11, 1990 in front of a jury. On the issue of guilt or innocence, the jury heard testimony from 14 government witnesses and two defense witnesses. The government witnesses testified about the discovery of the drums, the circumstances surrounding the waste's origin in Port Violet, Louisiana, and the fact that Sellers had been paid $45 per drum to dispose of the waste. In addition, the government called James William Ward (Ward), who testified that he had assisted Sellers in loading the 55-gallon drums in Louisiana and transporting them to Jones County, Mississippi where Ward and Sellers unloaded them. Ward testified that Sellers did not tell him what was in the drums, but did tell Ward that it was flammable. Subsequently, Ward voluntarily came forward and told the police about his involvement in dumping the drums. Testimony by other witnesses established that Sellers did not have a permit as required for disposing of hazardous waste, nor did he take the waste to a licensed disposal area. The government's last witness in its case in chief, Douglas E. Bourgeois (Bourgeois), was allowed to testify over Seller's objection. Bourgeois testified that he had a conversation with Sellers in late April or sometime in May in which Sellers stated that he had been hauling waste chemicals and discarding them in a rural area outside Petal, Mississippi. During the conversation, Sellers referred to M.E.K, which he knew was a solvent used primarily to clean paint equipment.

The crux of Sellers's defense was that he denied dumping the paint waste in question. He testified that it was Ward alone who had dumped the drums into Camp Branch Creek, although he admitted that his family owned property in Jones County near the site of the dumping.

After deliberation, the jury found Sellers guilty of all sixteen counts of the indictment. On March 14, 1990, Sellers was sentenced to 41 months imprisonment on each count, with the sentences to run concurrently. In addition, Sellers was sentenced to three years of supervised release and was ordered to make restitution to the State of Mississippi of $6,130.70, the amount required to clean up the hazardous waste site. Sellers also received a special assessment of $800. Sellers filed a timely notice of appeal.

II

On appeal, Sellers contends that the district court erred 1) by admitting testimony that he contends is inadmissible under Fed.R.Evid. 403 and 404(b), [and] 2) by failing to give the jury a requested charge regarding the knowledge required to violate § 6928. . . .

A. Admission of Testimony

Sellers first contends that the district court erred by admitting the testimony of Bourgeois. Sellers claims that Bourgeois testified that sometime in late April or May, 1989 Sellers stated that he was, at that time, hauling chemicals and dumping them outside of Petal, Mississippi. Sellers argues that this evidence was inadmissible under Fed.R.Evid. 403 and 404(b).

. . .[T]his testimony is admissible either as an admission, or for the permissible purpose of establishing the extent of Sellers's knowledge of his acts. Thus, Sellers's argument is without merit.

B. Jury Charge

Sellers next contends that the district court erred in refusing to give a jury instruction requested by Sellers. . . .

The district court gave the following instructions:

> In order to establish the offenses charged in the indictment, the Government must prove each one of the following elements by proof beyond a reasonable doubt.
>
> First. That the Defendant knowingly disposed of, or commanded and caused others to dispose of, wastes as charged in the indictment.
>
> Second. That the Defendant knew what the wastes were.
>
> Third. That the wastes were listed or identified or characterized by the United States Environmental Protection Agency, known as E.P.A., as a hazardous waste pursuant to the Resource Conservation and Recovery Act.
>
> And Fourth. That the Defendant had not obtained a permit from either the E.P.A. or the State of Mississippi authorizing the disposal under the Resource Conservation and Recovery Act.
>
> Although the Government must prove that the waste disposed of was listed or identified or characterized by the E.P.A. as a hazardous waste, the Government is not required to prove that the Defendant knew that the waste was a hazardous waste within the meaning of the regulations. In other words, the Government need only prove that the Defendant knew what the waste was; that is, paint and paint solvent waste, along with the other essential elements the Court has previously given you.
>
> However, the Government is not required to establish that the waste in question actually entered the environment, was emitted into the air, or discharged into water. It is sufficient for the Government to prove that the hazardous waste was placed into or on the land in such a manner that it could enter the environment, the air, or water, including ground water.
>
> The term hazardous waste, as used in the R.C.R.A. statute, includes any refuse and other discarded or abandoned material, including solid, liquid or semi-solid material resulting from industrial or commercial operations and community activities, which because of its quantity, concentration, or physical chemical or infectious characteristics may; A, cause or significantly contribute to an increase in serious, irreversible, or incapacitating and reversible illness; or B, pose a substantial presence or potential hazard to human health or the environment if improperly treated, stored, transported, or disposed of, or otherwise managed, and which has been identified or listed as a hazardous waste by the United States Environmental Protection Agency.

In his objections to the district court's proposed jury charge, Sellers requested that the district court give the following instruction:

> Second: that the Defendant knew or reasonably should have known that the substance was waste;
>
> Or alternatively:
>
> that the Defendant knew or reasonably should have known that the substance was waste and that the waste could be harmful to persons or the environment if . . . improperly disposed of.

The applicable statute [R.C.R.A.] . . . provides criminal penalties for "[a]ny person who . . . knowingly treats, stores, or disposes of any hazardous waste identified or listed under this subchapter . . . without a permit under this subchapter. . . ."

On appeal, Sellers argues that the jury charge should have required the government to prove that Sellers knew that the paint waste could be hazardous or harmful to persons or the environment. Sellers argues that a "reading of the statute involved . . . leads to the conclusion that Congress intended to punish only knowing violations."

In the Supreme Court case of *United States v. International Minerals & Chem. Corp.* [1971], the defendant corporation challenged its conviction for violating I.C.C. regulations while shipping sulfuric acid in interstate commerce.... It claimed that, because it was unaware of the regulations, it could not have "knowingly" violated them as required under 18 U.S.C. § 834(f). The Supreme Court determined that although Congress required some *mens rea* by its use of the word "knowingly" in the statute, knowledge of the regulation was not part of this *mens rea* requirement. Rather, "knowingly" was intended to apply to mistakes of fact such as if "a person thinking in good faith that he was shipping distilled water" actually shipped dangerous acid.... The Court stated that if "[p]encils, dental floss [and] paper clips] were regulated, knowledge of the regulations would have to be an element of the offense because of substantial due process questions."... However, "where ... dangerous or deleterious devices or products or obnoxious waste materials are involved, the probability of regulation is so great that anyone who is aware that he is in possession of them or dealing with them must be presumed to be aware of the regulation."... Thus, when a person knowingly possesses an instrumentality which by its nature is potentially dangerous, he is imputed with the knowledge that it may be regulated by public health legislation....

There is support for Sellers's argument as it relates to § 6928 in the opinions of several other circuits.... We need not reach this issue, however, because we have concluded that it is being raised for the first time on appeal and we find that the district court's failure to give a more complete instruction was not plain error.

At trial, Sellers requested an instruction that the government must prove that "the Defendant knew or reasonably should have known that the substance was waste." This instruction was not necessary as the district court's instruction explicitly required the government to prove that "the Defendants knew what the wastes were ... paint and paint solvent waste."

In the alternative, Sellers requested that the trial court instruct the jury that "the Defendant knew or reasonably should have known that the substance was waste and that the waste could be harmful to persons or the environment if ... improperly disposed of." Although the district judge did not give his reason for rejecting this instruction, it is clear that this instruction is incorrect. There is no requirement that the defendant must know that the waste would be harmful "if improperly disposed of." Under Seller's construction, arguably he would not be liable if he disposed of the harmful waste in what he considered to be proper containers. Because this alternative instruction suggested by Sellers is legally deficient, the district court was correct in rejecting it.

Focusing only on the first half of this second requested instruction, Sellers argues on appeal that the district court erred by not giving an instruction that the government must prove that the defendant knew that the waste was hazardous or dangerous....

Assuming, *arguendo,* that the district court should have charged the jury that the government was required to prove that the defendant knew that the substance he disposed of was potentially hazardous or dangerous to persons or the environment, in the present case the omission was not plain error. It is clear that paint and paint solvent waste, by its very nature, is potentially dangerous to the environment and to persons. Thus it should have come as no surprise to Sellers that the disposal of that waste is regulated. The evidence presented at trial established that Sellers knew that the waste he was disposing included M.E.K., a paint solvent, and that this substance was extremely flammable. There can be no doubt that Sellers knew that the substance he was disposing of was potentially dangerous to human beings and the environment and that regulations, therefore, would exist governing the manner of its disposal. Under these circumstances, we cannot say that the jury charge as a whole constituted "plain error." Therefore, we find no ground for reversal....

Based on the foregoing, we affirm the conviction and sentence imposed on James Ralph Sellers by the district court.

AFFIRMED.

CHAPTER 11

Offenses Against Public Order and Safety

CHAPTER OUTLINE

Introduction
The Common-Law Background
Breaches of the Peace
Constitutional Limitations on Defining Breaches of the Peace
Vagrancy
Traffic Violations
Weapons Offenses
Conclusion

Cases

State v. Mast
Commonwealth v. Young
Feiner v. New York
Papachristou v. City of Jacksonville
State v. Young
United States v. Evans

INTRODUCTION

Without question, government has a fundamental obligation to protect the public order and safety, much as it has to protect public health and the environment. The criminal law is one way government performs this function—by criminalizing acts that threaten society's interests in order and safety. This category of offenses includes breaches of the peace such as unlawful assembly, riot, and disorderly conduct. It also includes vagrancy and loitering, which are designed to control persons whose conduct society considers threatening or undesirable. All of the aforementioned crimes are based on English common law.

In this chapter, we also briefly discuss traffic violations and weapons offenses, which, while unknown to the common law, exist by virtue of modern legislation aimed at protecting the public safety.

THE COMMON-LAW BACKGROUND

As with most basic criminal offenses, the crimes against public order and safety are rooted in the common law. The common law recognized the right of the people to assemble peaceably for lawful purposes. Nevertheless, the maintenance of public order was given a high priority. To maintain order, the common law developed three misdemeanors: unlawful assembly, rout, and riot. If three or more persons met together with the intention of cooperating to disturb the public peace through the doing of an unlawful act, their gathering was considered an unlawful assembly. If they took steps to achieve their purpose, it was a rout; and if they actually executed their plans, they committed a riot. *State v. Wooldridge*, 40 S.E.2d 899 (W. Va. 1946). Vagrancy was also an offense at common law originally designed to control the economics of the populace by punishing idleness. *Fenster v. Leary*, 229 N.E.2d 426 (N.Y. 1967).

BREACHES OF THE PEACE

In the United States, the responsibility for maintaining public order and peace rests primarily with state and local governments, although the federal government has a significant role as well. A variety of state statutes and local ordinances prohibit unlawful assemblies, riots, and disorderly conduct. Control of unlawful assemblies and riots is aimed at group behavior, while laws proscribing disorderly conduct are aimed at both group and individual behavior. Through enforcement of laws prohibiting disorderly conduct, state and local governments attempt to prevent such undesirable conduct as violent and tumultuous behavior, offensive language and gestures, actions impeding movement of persons on public sidewalks and roads, and disturbances of lawfully conducted meetings.

Unlawful Assembly and Riot

Most states have enacted statutes proscribing unlawful assemblies and riots. For example, the Indiana Code defines *unlawful assembly* as "an assembly of five or more persons whose common object is to commit an unlawful act, or a lawful act by unlawful means." West's Ann. Ind. Code 35–45–1–1. It further defines *tumultuous conduct* as "conduct that results in, or is likely to result in, serious bodily injury to a person or substantial damage to property." West's Ann. Ind. Code 35–45–1–1. Under the Indiana Code, a person who is a "member of an unlawful assembly who recklessly, knowingly, or intentionally engages in tumultuous conduct commits rioting." Under Indiana law, the offense is punishable as a misdemeanor unless committed while armed with a deadly weapon, in which case it becomes a felony. West's Ann. Ind. Code 35–45–1–2.

Historically federal statutes have made it a crime to riot. However, the controversy over the Vietnam War, racial unrest, poverty, and a host of other social ills during the 1960s became catalysts for riotous behavior beyond proportions experienced for many years. To better cope with riots, Congress enacted the Federal Anti-Riot Act of 1968. The act was designed to punish riotous acts occurring in interstate travel or involving the use of interstate facilities. The act makes it unlawful for:

> Whoever travels in interstate or foreign commerce or uses any facility of interstate or foreign commerce, including, but not limited to, the mail, telegraph, telephone, radio, or television, with intent—
> (A) to incite a riot; or
> (B) to organize, promote, encourage, participate in, or carry on a riot; or
> (C) to commit any act of violence in furtherance of a riot; or
> (D) to aid or abet any person in inciting or participating in or carrying on a riot or committing any act of violence in furtherance of a riot;
> and who either during the course of any such travel or use or thereafter performs or attempts to perform any other overt act for any purpose specified in subparagraph (A), (B), (C), or (D) of this paragraph. 18 U.S.C.A. § 2101(a)(1).

The act comprehensively defines *riot* by stating:

> [T]he term "riot" means a public disturbance involving (1) an act or acts of violence by one or more persons part of an assemblage of three or more persons, which act or acts shall constitute a clear and present danger of, or shall result in, damage or injury to the property of any other person or to the person of any other individual or (2) a threat or threats of the commission of an act or acts of violence by one or more persons part of an assemblage of three or more persons having, individually or collectively, the ability of immediate execution of such threat or threats, where the performance of the threatened act or acts of violence would constitute a clear and present danger of, or would result in, damage or injury to the property of any other person or to the person of any other individual. 18 U.S.C.A. § 2102(a).

It defines *to incite a riot* by explaining:

> [T]he term "to incite a riot," or "to organize, promote, encourage, participate in, or carry on a riot," includes, but is not limited to, urging or instigating other persons to riot, but shall not be deemed to mean the mere oral or written (1) advocacy of ideas

or (2) expression of belief, not involving advocacy of any act or acts of violence or assertion of the rightness of, or the right to commit, any such act or acts. 18 U.S.C.A. § 2102(b).

In 1972 the United States Court of Appeals for the seventh circuit held that the Anti-Riot Act is not unconstitutionally vague or overbroad in relation to the First Amendment. *United States v. Dellinger,* 472 F.2d 340 (7th Cir. 1972), cert. denied, 410 U.S. 970, 93 S.Ct. 1443, 35 L.Ed.2d 706 (1973).

Disorderly Conduct

Closely related to statutes prohibiting unlawful assembly and riot are laws making disorderly conduct an offense. The Indiana Code concisely, yet comprehensively, proscribes disorderly conduct by providing:

> A person who recklessly, knowingly or intentionally: (1) engages in fighting or in tumultuous conduct; (2) makes unreasonable noise and continues to do so after being asked to stop; (3) disrupts a lawful assembly of persons; commits disorderly conduct.... West's Ann. Ind. Code § 35–45–1–3.

In *Cavazos v. State,* 455 N.E.2d 618 (Ind. App. 1983), an Indiana appellate court said that the application of the disorderly conduct statute to speech must be limited to unprotected classes of expression (e.g., obscenity, fighting words, public nuisance, and incitement to imminent lawless action). Thus, the court found that a defendant calling a police officer an "asshole" and continuing to debate with him about the arrest of her brother was insufficient to support her conviction for disorderly conduct. The court reasoned that the defendant's words to the police officer did not constitute any of the named unprotected classes of speech. Subsequently, another Indiana Court declared that the words *engages in* in the statute require present, completed conduct likely to injure persons. *Gebhard v. State,* 484 N.E.2d 45 (Ind. App. 1985).

Statutes and ordinances similar to those in Indiana are found in virtually every state. Some state statutes and local ordinances go further and prohibit the use of indecent or profane language. Many laws of this type have met the fate of an ordinance in Baton Rouge, Louisiana, that made it unlawful for any person to use "indecent, vile, profane or blasphemous language on or near the streets, alleys, sidewalks, or other places of public resort." That ordinance was declared unconstitutional as a violation of the First Amendment protection of free speech. *Baton Rouge v. Ewing,* 308 So.2d 776 (La. 1975).

Constitutional Limitations on Defining Breaches of the Peace

The United States Supreme Court has rendered a number of opinions with respect to First Amendment limitations on laws proscribing disorderly conduct and other breaches of the peace. In 1942 the Court stated:

> There are certain well-defined and narrowly limited classes of speech, the prevention and punishment of which has never been thought to raise a Constitutional problem.

> These include the lewd and obscene, the profane, the libelous, and the insulting or "fighting" words—those which by their very utterance inflict or tend to incite an immediate breach of the peace. *Chaplinsky v. New Hampshire,* 315 U.S. 568, 571–572, 62 S.Ct. 766, 769, 86 L.Ed. 1031, 1035 (1942).

The principles announced in *Chaplinsky* have proven difficult to apply. Some seven years after *Chaplinsky,* the Court overturned a conviction of a priest who was charged with breach of the peace after he gave a speech filled with racial and political epithets. His remarks resulted in a riotous crowd gathering outside the meeting hall where he spoke. At trial, the judge defined breach of the peace to include speech which "stirs the public to anger, invites a dispute, brings about a condition of unrest or creates a disturbance." The Supreme Court reversed, holding that a conviction for breach of the peace for conduct as defined by the trial judge violated the First Amendment. *Terminiello v. City of Chicago,* 337 U.S. 1, 69 S.Ct. 894, 93 L.Ed. 1131 (1949).

As noted earlier, the 1960s was an extremely turbulent decade. In a not uncommon scene, on the morning of March 2, 1961, a large group of black students congregated on the lawn of the statehouse in Columbia, South Carolina, to protest the state's segregation laws. Speeches were made; songs were sung. The students responded by clapping and stamping their feet. A large crowd of onlookers gathered nearby. Nobody among the crowd caused or threatened any trouble, and there was no obstruction of pedestrian or vehicular traffic. A contingent of thirty or more police officers was present to meet any foreseeable possibility of disorder. After refusing to obey a police order to disperse, many of the students were arrested and found guity of breach of the peace. In reversing their convictions, the United States Supreme Court said:

CASE IN POINT

APPLICATION OF A RIOT STATUTE

A young black girl was shot and seriously wounded by a white male who claimed she was picking peaches from his trees. The man was arrested but soon released on bail. After his release, a large crowd from the black community gathered and began demonstrating and demanding the man be jailed. As a result of his participation in the demonstration, defendant Miller was charged with violating a state law proscribing riots, the constitutionality of which had been previously upheld by the state supreme court. Miller was convicted and appealed.

On appeal, Miller admitted that he had exhorted the crowd to "take the Mayor's Million-Dollar-Mall" and that in his exhortations he had used such terms as "killer cops." He argued that his conviction should be overturned because his conduct amounted to no more than constitutionally protected "political hyperbole." The Supreme Court of Delaware rejected his contention and found that his conduct, even accepting his own version of the facts, was an incitement to lawless action that fell outside the category of "political hyperbole."

Miller v. State, 374 A.2d 271 (Del. 1977).

> These petitioners were convicted of an offense as to be, in the words of the South Carolina Supreme Court, "not susceptible of exact definition." And they were convicted upon evidence which showed no more than that the opinions which they were peaceably expressing were sufficiently opposed to the views of the majority of the community to attract a crowd and necessitate police protection. . . .
>
> The Fourteenth Amendment does not permit a State to make criminal the peaceful expression of unpopular views. *Edwards v. South Carolina,* 372 U.S. 229, 237, 83 S.Ct. 680, 684, 9 L.Ed.2d 697, 703 (1963).

It is instructive to compare and contrast *Edwards* with a case in the 1970s in which the Supreme Court upheld a conviction for disorderly conduct arising out of a confrontation between a police officer and a student protestor. After conducting a political demonstration, a number of students got into their cars and formed an entourage. A police officer stopped one of the vehicles after noting that its license plate had expired. The other cars in the group also pulled over. One of the students approached the officer to find out what was wrong. After explaining the situation, the officer asked the student to leave. Upon refusing to do so, the student was arrested for violating Section 437.016(1)(f) of the Kentucky Revised Statutes, which provided that a person was guilty of disorderly conduct, "if, with intent to cause public inconvenience, annoyance or alarm, or recklessly creating a risk thereof," he "congregates with other persons in a public place and refuses to comply with a lawful order of the police to disperse." A conviction for disorderly conduct was upheld by the Kentucky Court of Appeals. *Colten v. Commonwealth,* 467 S.W.2d 374 (Ky. 1971). In refusing to set aside the action of the state court, the United States Supreme Court said:

> As the Kentucky statute was construed by the state court, . . . a crime is committed only where there is no bona fide intention to exercise a constitutional right—in which event, by definition, the statute infringes no protected speech or conduct—or where the interest so clearly outweighs the collective interest sought to be asserted that the latter must be deemed to be insubstantial. . . . Individuals may not be convicted under the Kentucky statute merely for expressing unpopular or annoying ideas. The statute comes into operation only when the individual's interest in expression, judged in the light of all relevant factors, is "minuscule" compared to a particular public interest in preventing that expression or conduct at that time and place. *Colten v. Kentucky,* 407 U.S. 104, 111, 92 S.Ct. 1953, 1958, 32 L.Ed.2d 584, 590 (1972).

The "Fighting Words" Doctrine

As the Supreme Court observed in *Chaplinsky v. New Hampshire, supra,* the utterance of "fighting words" is beyond protection of the First Amendment. But law enforcement officers and courts encounter difficult problems in determining whether given words in a given context fall within the definition of fighting words. In *Chaplinsky* the Supreme Court said that fighting words are those that: (1) inflict injury; (2) tend to create a breach of the peace; and (3) are not an essential part of the exposition of ideas. Thus, when a defendant is charged with verbal conduct in violating a statute or ordinance making the use of profane or obscene language disorderly conduct, the courts must determine the effects of the defendant's particular words in context of the situations. Some courts take the view that when profanities or obscenities are directed at a police officer that a different standard applies from those directed at the ordinary citizen. These courts reason that a police officer by training is taught not to react violently or to retaliate against persons who use such insulting language, and therefore they often refuse to convict defendants in such circumstances. See, for example, *State v. John W.*, 418 A. 2d 1097 (Me. 1980). Irrespective of the situation, the prosecution must establish that such verbal conduct tended to incite violence.

In analyzing statutes proscribing breaches of the peace, unlawful assemblies, riots, and disorderly conduct, we must keep in mind two essential principles. First, unless a statute contains specific definitions of terms, courts generally rely on common-law definitions to interpret its terms. *Commonwealth v. Duitch,* 67 A. 2d 821 (Pa. Super. 1949). Second, the statute must be interpreted and applied in a manner not to offend the First Amendment guarantees of speech, assembly, and religion.

"Hate Crimes"

In response to a growing trend of occurrences in which extremist groups expressed hatred or bigotry toward minorities, some jurisdictions enacted measures prohibiting "hate crimes." One such law was enacted by the city of St. Paul, Minnesota. The St. Paul Bias-Motivated Crime Ordinance, St. Paul, Minn. Legis. Code § 292.02 (1990), provided:

> Whoever places on public or private property a symbol, object, appellation, characterization or graffiti, including, but not limited to, a burning cross or Nazi swastika, which one knows or has reasonable grounds to know arouses anger, alarm or resentment in others on the basis of race, color, creed, religion or gender commits disorderly conduct and shall be guilty of a misdemeanor.

In construing the ordinance, the Minnesota Supreme Court held that it prohibited only "fighting words," that is, those utterances outside the protections of the First Amendment. *In re Welfare of R.A.V.*, 464 N.W. 2d 507 (Minn. 1991). In a much-publicized 1992 decision, the U.S. Supreme Court declared the ordinance unconstitutional. *R.A.V. v. City of St.Paul,* 505 U.S. ___, 112 S.Ct. 2538, 120 L.Ed.2d 305 (1992). Writing for the Court, Justice Antonin Scalia stated: "Even assuming, *arguendo,* that all of the expression reached by the ordinance is proscribable under the 'fighting words' doctrine, we nonetheless conclude that the ordinance is facially unconstutional in that it prohibits otherwise permitted speech solely on the basis of the subjects the speech addresses." 505 U.S. at 112 S.Ct. at 2542, 120 L.Ed.2d at 316.

The Court's decision in *R.A.V.* raised serious questions as to whether hate crimes legislation can be made to conform with constitutional standards. Remember, however, that states and communities have a number of legal means at their disposal in combating hate crimes. For example, an individual who burns a cross on someone else's front lawn may be charged with criminal trespass and possibly with malicious mischief or vandalism (see Chapter 7).

In contrast to its 1992 decision in *R.A.V.*, the Supreme Court in 1993 upheld a Wisconsin statute that increases the severity of punishment if a crime victim is chosen on the basis of race or other designated characteristics. In *Wisconsin v. Mitchell*, 1993, WL 195271 (U.S. Wis.), 508 U.S. ___, 113 S.Ct. 2194, 124 L.Ed.2d 436 (1993) the Court ruled unanimously that increasing punishment because the defendant targeted the victim on the basis of his race does not infringe the defendant's freedom of conscience protected by the First Amendment. The Court distinguished the case from *R.A.V.*, noting that the Wisconsin statute was aimed at conduct, while the St. Paul ordinance invalidated in *R.A.V.* was aimed squarely at expression.

VAGRANCY

Elites in feudal England placed great emphasis on able-bodied serfs performing labor and not straying from their assigned tasks. This was motivated by both the need for laborers and the desire to prevent idle persons from becoming public charges. Even with the breakup of feudal estates, England found it necessary to prevent workers from moving from one area to another in search of improved working conditions. Thus, to regulate the economics of the populace, the common law developed the misdemeanor offense of vagrancy. The offense comprised three elements: (1) being without visible means of support; (2) being without employment; and (3) being able to work but refusing to do so. *Fenster v. Leary*, 229 N.E.2d 426 (N.Y. 1967).

Eventually the emphasis shifted from merely punishing idleness toward the prevention of crime as England enacted statutes defining vagrancy. The objective then became to protect the people and their property from persons considered potential criminals or simply regarded as undesirables. Thus, by the time the American colonists settled in their new environment, the concept of punishing vagrants had become firmly implanted, and the colonists found it to be a desirable way to prevent idleness and to outlaw conduct offensive to their social mores.

The American Approach to Vagrancy

During the 1800s virtually all American states and most cities enacted statutes and ordinances punishing a wide variety of conduct as vagrancy. Statutory language was intentionally rather vague, presumably to allow police broad discretion to arrest persons they deemed undesirable to the community. Vagrancy laws not only proscribed such acts as disorderly conduct, begging, and loitering; they also criminalized the condition of being poor, idle, of bad reputation, or simply "wandering around without any lawful purpose." By making a person's status an offense, these laws ran counter to the historic concept that a crime consisted of the commission of an unlawful act or the failure to perform a required act. Frequently, vagrancy laws were directed against persons without the means to contest their validity or to challenge the application of such laws to them. Enforcement of vagrancy laws resulted in numerous persons being taken into custody, although many were released shortly thereafter on the condition that they move on to another area.

While there was considerable criticism of these practices, there was little incentive for lawyers to attack the constitutionality of these laws, since the United States Supreme Court had sanctioned them in 1837 by saying:

> We think it [is] as competent and as necessary for a state to provide precautionary measures against the moral pestilence of paupers, vagabonds, and possibly convicts; as it is to guard against . . . physical pestilence. . . . *City of New York v. Miln,* 36 U.S. (11 Pet.) 102, 142, 9 L.Ed. 648, 664 (1837).

In the 1900s arrests and convictions for vagrancy were common, yet comparatively few of the convictions were appealed. During the first half of the century, appellate courts issued opinions upholding convictions in a variety of circumstances. For example, in Minnesota a defendant's conviction was affirmed for wandering about the streets with no place of abode and without giving a good account of himself. *State v. Woods,* 163 N.W. 518 (Minn. 1917). In an instance in Virginia, an appellate court held that a defendant's conduct in consorting with gamblers and idlers constituted the offense of vagrancy. *Morgan v. Commonwealth,* 191 S.E. 791 (Va. 1937). Even a defendant's conduct as part of "a group of 4 or 5 suspicious men" at a saloon was, under the particular circumstances, held to be vagrancy. *State v. Carroll,* 30 A.2d 54 (N.J. 1943), *aff'd,* 33 A.2d 907 (1943).

The wide range of vaguely-proscribed conduct in vagrancy laws made them susceptible of arbitrary enforcement by law enforcement agencies. In their efforts to prevent crime and to control the so-called undesirable, these laws became somewhat of a catch-all of the criminal justice system. Police commonly used them as a basis to arrest a suspect, who was then held pending investigation, or as a method of getting the suspect to confess. Vagrancy laws also furnished a convenient basis for police to justify a search incident to arrest as an exception to the warrant requirement of the Fourth Amendment.

By the 1950s the vagrancy laws were being enforced primarily against loafers, alcoholics, derelicts, and tramps when they left the environs of "skid row" and ventured into the more "respectable" neighborhoods, where residents found their presence offensive. By 1960 the constitutionality of the vagrancy laws was frequently being challenged on grounds that they were vague, violated due process of law requirements, and exceeded the police power of the states. Such challenges were rejected by state and federal courts, with the courts generally upholding the right of the legislature to define what constitutes being a vagrant. See, for example, *State v. Finrow,* 405 P.2d 600 (Wash. 1965). During the 1960s, however, a number of statutes defining a vagrant as a person "without visible means of support" or who "wanders around the streets at late hours" or who "fails to give account of himself" were declared unconstitutional. In *Fenster v. Leary,* 229 N.E. 2d 426 (N.Y. 1967), New York's highest court declared a statute that defined as vagrants "persons who, not having visible means to maintain themselves, live without employment" was unconstitutional on due process grounds and constituted an overreaching of police power. The court said that the law "provides punishment for a person's conduct which in no way impinges on the rights of others." 229 N.E.2d at 428.

The Death Knell of Vagrancy Laws

In 1972, the United States Supreme Court issued an opinion that was to have a profound effect on the enforcement of vagrancy laws in the United States. *Papachristou v. City of Jacksonville,* 405 U.S. 156, 92 S.Ct. 839, 31 L.Ed.2d 110 (1972).

CASE IN POINT

SEARCH INCIDENT TO ARREST FOR VAGRANCY

At about midnight on February 17, 1968, Lloyd Powell and several companions entered the Bonanza Liquor Store in San Bernadino, California. An altercation developed between Powell and the manager over Powell's alleged attempt to steal a bottle of wine. In the ensuing struggle, Powell shot and killed the manager's wife. Ten hours later, a police officer in Henderson, Nevada, arrested Powell under the local vagrancy ordinance. In a search incident to the arrest, the officer discovered a .38-caliber revolver with six spent cartridges in the cylinder. Laboratory analysis determined that the weapon was used in the murder of the liquor store owner's wife. Powell was convicted of second-degree murder and sentenced to prison. Although the Henderson, Nevada, vagrancy ordinance was later declared unconstitutional by a federal court, the use of the evidence against Powell, and his conviction for murder, were ultimately sustained.

Stone v. Powell, 428 U.S. 465, 96 S.Ct 3037, 49 L.Ed.2d 1067 (1976).

In Jacksonville, Florida, eight defendants were convicted under a municipal ordinance that broadly defined vagrancy and levied criminal penalties of up to 90 days imprisonment, a $500.00 fine, or both on violators. The ordinance included language common to many of the statutes and ordinances extant at the time. It provided:

> Rogues and vagabonds, or dissolute persons who go about begging, common gamblers, persons who use juggling or unlawful games or plays, common drunkards, common night walkers, thieves, pilferers or pickpockets, traders in stolen property, lewd, wanton and lascivious persons, keepers of gambling places, common railers and brawlers, persons wandering or strolling around from place to place without any lawful purpose or object, habitual loafers, disorderly persons, persons neglecting all lawful business and habitually spending their time by frequenting houses of ill fame, gaming houses, or places where alcoholic beverages are sold or served, persons able to work but habitually living upon the earnings of their wives or minor children shall be deemed vagrants. . . . Quoted in *Papachristou,* 405 U.S. at 158–159, n. 1, 92 S.Ct. at 840, 31 L.Ed.2d at 112.

Speaking for a unanimous Supreme Court, Justice William O. Douglas said that the Jacksonville ordinance was void for vagueness, both in the sense that it "fails to give a person of ordinary intelligence fair notice that his contemplated conduct is forbidden by the statute and because it encourages arbitrary and erratic arrests and convictions." 405 U.S. at 162, 92 S.Ct. at 843, 31 L.Ed.2d at 115. On the same date, the Court vacated the convictions of several other defendants who had been convicted of vagrancy in a state court under a Florida Statute (Section

856.02) that defined vagrancy similar to the Jacksonville ordinance. *Smith v. Florida*, 405 U.S. 172, 92 S.Ct. 848, 31 L.Ed.2d 122 (1972).

Loitering

The widespread invalidation of vagrancy laws resulted in legislative bodies enacting new laws to control specifically defined behavior that states and local communities found unacceptable. In lieu of proscribing "wandering around without any apparent purpose" legislatures used language to control such activities as "loitering on school grounds without legitimate reason." And instead of proscribing the status of being a "common gambler," they made it unlawful to "loiter in a public place for the purpose of gambling." Thus, by no longer criminalizing a person's *status* and by specifying the circumstances under which a person would be in violation of the law, the new approach sought to give credence to constitutional principles while still providing the police with the tools they needed to prevent crime.

The new approach to proscribing loitering is exemplified by the New York state law that provides:

> A person is guilty of loitering when he:
>
> 1. Loiters, remains or wanders about in a public place for the purpose of begging [held unconstitutional on the ground that it violated the First Amendment in *Loper v. N.Y. City Police Dept.*, 999 F.2d 699 (2nd. Cir. 1993)]; or
> 2. Loiters or remains in a public place for the purpose of gambling with cards, dice or other gambling paraphernalia; or
> 3. Loiters or remains in a public place for the purpose of engaging, or soliciting another person to engage, in deviate sexual intercourse or other sexual behavior of a deviate nature [invalidated in *People v. Uplinger*, 447 N.E.2d 62 (N.Y. 1983), on the ground that there is no requirement that the proscribed conduct be offensive or annoying to others]; or
> 4. Being masked or in any manner disguised by unusual attire or facial alteration, loiters, remains or congregates in a public place with other persons so masked or disguised, or knowingly permits or aids persons so masked or disguised to congregate in a public place; except that such conduct is not unlawful when it occurs in connection with a masquerade party or like entertainment if, when such entertainment is held in a city which has promulgated regulations in connection with such affairs, permission is first obtained from the police or other appropriate authorities; or
> 5. Loiters or remains in or about school grounds, a college or university building or grounds, not having any reason or relationship involving custody of or responsibility for a pupil or student, or any other specific, legitimate reason for being there, and not having written permission from anyone authorized to grant the same; or
> 6. Loiters or remains in any transportation facility, unless specifically authorized to do so, for the purpose of soliciting or engaging in any business, trade or commercial transactions involving the sale of merchandise or services, or for the purpose of entertaining persons by singing, dancing or playing any musical instrument; or

> 7. Loiters or remains in any transportation facility, or is found sleeping therein, and is unable to give a satisfactory explanation of his presence [held unconstitutional in *People v. Bright*, 520 N.E.2d 1355 (N.Y. 1988), on the ground that it required the suspect to prove "satisfactory explanation of his presence" to avoid arrest].
>
> McKinney's N.Y. Penal Law § 240.35.

As noted above, several provisions of this statute have been declared unconstitutional. But the statute, in the main, remains operative.

On the other hand, some states and municipalities continued to proscribe vagrancy but in a much narrower manner than did the Jacksonville ordinance invalidated by the Supreme Court. For example, Section 207.030 of the Nevada Revised Statutes enumerates specific acts that constitute vagrancy. These prohibited acts include solicitation or engaging in lewd acts in public, loitering on private property of others in the nighttime or upon the streets, and refusing to identify or account for one's presence when requested by a peace officer if the surrounding circumstances indicate that the public safety demands identification.

In 1976 the Georgia legislature enacted a comprehensive law defining loitering and prowling. It provides:

> (a) A person commits the offense of loitering or prowling when he is in a place at a time or in a manner not usual for law-abiding individuals under circumstances that warrant a justifiable and reasonable alarm or immediate concern for the safety of persons or property in the vicinity.
>
> (b) Among the circumstances which may be considered in determining whether alarm is warranted is the fact that the person takes flight upon the appearance of a law enforcement officer, refuses to identify himself, or manifestly endeavors to conceal himself or any object. Unless flight by the person or other circumstances make it impracticable, a law enforcement officer shall, prior to any arrest for an offense under this Code section, afford the person an opportunity to dispel any alarm or immediate concern which would otherwise be warranted by requesting the person to identify himself and explain his presence and conduct. No person shall be convicted of an offense under this Code section if the law enforcement officer failed to comply with the foregoing procedure or if it appears at trial that the explanation given by the person was true and would have dispelled the alarm or immediate concern.
>
> (c) A person committing the offense of loitering or prowling shall be guilty of a misdemeanor.
>
> Official Ga. Code Ann. § 16–11–36.

In *Bell v. State*, 313 S.E.2d 678 (Ga. 1984), a defendant was charged with violating the new Georgia loitering and prowling statute after a police officer observed him and a companion in downtown Atlanta near midnight. The two men were squeezing their bodies between the wall and a locked gate of a parking garage in order to exit the garage. When the officer attempted to question them, the companion ran but defendant Bell remained. After Bell's companion was apprehended and the officer gave them an opportunity to explain their presence, the defendant told the officer he was taking a shortcut through the garage. Knowing that this path did not amount to a shortcut, but instead required far greater effort on the part of the defendant, the officer placed him under arrest. Bell was convicted of violating the new Georgia loitering and prowling law.

On appeal to the Georgia Supreme Court, the defendant relied on a prior state supreme court decision striking down a municipal loitering ordinance that provided no guidelines by which "a citizen who desired to conform his conduct to [the law] would be [able] to discern whether he risked criminal responsibility." *Bullock v. City of Dallas*, 281 S.E.2d 613, 615 (Ga. 1981). The ordinance invalidated in *Bullock* provided that:

> No person shall remain or loiter upon any premises to which the public has access, including but not limited to such places as business and shopping area parking lots, where the person's presence upon such premises is unrelated to the normal activity, use or business for which such premises are made available to the public. Dallas City Ordinance § 5–112(a).

In *Bell* the Georgia Supreme Court found the defendant's reliance on its earlier decision in *Bullock* misplaced. The court concluded that unlike the Dallas ordinance, the new Georgia loitering statute was not void for vagueness, since it applies only where peace and order are threatened or where the safety of persons or property is jeopardized. Moreover, the new law sufficiently advises persons of ordinary intelligence of the conduct that is prohibited. Thus the court affirmed Bell's conviction. It did, however, caution that the legislature intended for trial courts to determine whether the defendant's explanation is true and should reasonably have dispelled the arresting officer's concern for the safety of persons or property in the area.

TRAFFIC VIOLATIONS

States, and often municipalities, have adopted laws defining a wide range of motor vehicle violations. These are generally strict-liability offenses; therefore, there is generally no requirement to prove criminal intent to find a defendant guilty of a traffic violation (see Chapter 4). Among other offenses, these laws proscribe speeding; failing to yield the right-of-way; failing to observe traffic officers, signs and signals; driving without required equipment; etc. During the 1970s and 1980s, states adopted a number of "model" laws, so that traffic offenses are highly uniform across the states. This uniformity is both necessary and desirable given the mobility of today's populace and the volume of traffic on the nation's highways.

When a driver is stopped for a traffic violation, police may observe conduct or evidence that gives rise to probable cause to conduct a search or make an arrest. Frequently drugs, alcohol, and weapons are discovered by police officers stopping automobiles for routine traffic violations.

Decriminalization of Traffic Offenses

Historically, traffic offenders were treated like persons committing other misdemeanors; they were arrested and required to post bond in order to avoid confinement pending the adjudication of their case. Since the 1960s most states and municipalities have decriminalized minor traffic offenses, which means that these offenses are now considered "civil infractions" rather than misdemeanors.

Consequently, offenders are now commonly issued citations or "tickets" instead of being subject to arrest. Offenders may avoid a court appearance by simply paying a fine according to a predetermined schedule of fines. Of course, offenders may elect to contest the charge by appearing in the appropriate court, often a municipal or "traffic court." In addition to fines, most states assess "points" against a driver for traffic violations, and an accumulation of points can lead to suspension or revocation of a driver's license. The decriminalization of routine traffic offenses has proved to be an expeditious and efficient means of maintaining discipline and order on the public thoroughfares. However, under most traffic codes, the more serious motor vehicle offenses, such as driving while intoxicated, eluding a police officer, and reckless driving, are still defined as misdemeanors and offenders are subject to arrest.

WEAPONS OFFENSES

The Second Amendment to the United States Constitution provides that "a well regulated Militia, being necessary to the security of a free state, the right of the people to keep and bear Arms, shall not be infringed." Nevertheless, there are numerous state and federal statutory prohibitions against the manufacture, sale, possession, and use of firearms and other weapons. For example, federal law prohibits the sale, possession, and use of machine guns. The Supreme Court has said that federal gun control laws do not violate the Second Amendment, because the amendment only protects the keeping and bearing of arms in the context of a well-regulated militia. See *United States v. Miller,* 307 U.S. 174, 59 S.Ct. 816, 83 L.Ed. 1206 (1939); *Lewis v. United States,* 445 U.S. 55, 100 S.Ct. 915, 63 L.Ed.2d 198 (1980).

The Illinois weapons statute, see Ill. Rev. Stat. Ann. Ch. 38, § 24, is fairly typical of state laws proscribing the unlawful use of weapons. Section 24–1 prohibits the manufacture, sale, and possession of various types of weapons that have no value either for hunting, archery, or marksmanship; or for the protection of a person's home from intruders. Explosives, gaseous devices, machine guns, and gun silencers are among the particular weapons banned. The law also prohibits carrying a wide variety of weapons, including "stun guns," "dangerous knives," "billy clubs," etc., with the intent of unlawfully using the weapon against another.

The Illinois statute also prohibits the manufacture, sale, transfer, possession, or discharge of metal-piercing bullets or bullets represented to be metal-piercing. §§ 24–2.1, 24–2.2, 24–3.2. In addition, the law proscribes the unlawful sale or delivery of firearms on any school premises, § 24–3.3, carrying concealed weapons, § 24–1.4, or carrying weapons while a person's face is masked or hooded so as to conceal a person's identity. § 24–1.9.

Like most states, Illinois exempts police officers and various other public officials, as well as licensed private investigators and security personnel, from the statutory prohibitions regarding possession and use of firearms. Ill. Rev. Stat. Ann. § 24–2.

Concealed Weapons

States commonly enact statutes making it unlawful to carry a concealed weapon. Most define *concealed* as a weapon being carried on or about a person in such a manner as to conceal it from the ordinary sight of another person. It follows that a defendant was properly convicted of carrying a concealed weapon in her purse when it was disclosed by a metal detector at a courthouse. *Schaaf v. Commonwealth,* 258 S.E.2d 574 (Va. 1979). But more often, litigation involves less than absolute concealment. For example, a Georgia appellate court ruled that even though the handle of a pistol tucked in a defendant's pants was visible to some extent through a slit in his shirt, the weapon was concealed. *Marshall v. State,* 200 S.E.2d 902 (Ga. App. 1973). Similarly, in *People v. Charron,* 220 N.W.2d 216 (Mich. App. 1974), a Michigan appellate court held that a knife slightly protruding from a defendant's rear pocket was a concealed weapon.

Many concealed-weapons statutes also make it an offense to carry a concealed weapon in a vehicle, and in numerous cases courts have been called upon to rule on the application of these laws. For example, in one case a defendant reached into his automobile and withdrew a revolver from a shelf behind the driver's seat. In affirming the defendant's conviction, the Wisconsin Supreme Court said, "[i]f the weapon is hidden from ordinary observation, it is concealed." The court noted that "absolute invisibility to other persons" was not "indispensable to concealment." The question was: "Was [the weapon] carried so as not to be discernible by ordinary observation?" *Mularkey v. State,* 230 N.W. 76, 77 (Wis. 1930). More recently, an Illinois appellate court observed that "[i]t is well settled . . . that a weapon is 'concealed' . . . even though there is some notice of its presence to an alert police officer who can see part of the gun when he approaches the vehicle." *People v. Williams,* 350 N.E. 2d 81, 83 (Ill. App. 1976).

CASE IN POINT

UNLAWFUL POSSESSION OF A FIREARM

South Carolina law provides that it is unlawful for any person to carry a pistol about his or her person, regardless of whether the pistol is concealed. S.C. Code § 16–23–20. The statute provides twelve exceptions to the prohibition. Barry Clarke was convicted of violating the statute after he was stopped for a traffic violation and the police officer noticed a gun in a holster next to the driver's seat. On appeal, Clarke argued that the burden of proof should have been on the prosecution to show that he did not qualify under any of the twelve exceptions to the prohibition. The South Carolina Supreme Court disagreed, saying that "[t]he general rule, when dealing statutory crimes to which there are exceptions, is that the defendant 'has the burden of excusing or justifying his act; and hence the burden may be on him to bring himself within an exception in the statute or to prove the issuance of a license or permit.' "

State v. Clarke, 396 S.E. 2d 827 (S.C. 1990).

CONCLUSION

Offenses against public order and safety present a picture of the dynamic development of the common law in a constitutional democracy. The need to maintain order, protect the public safety, and prevent crime are high-priority items on the agenda of any organized society. Yet, the United States Constitution mandates that government maintain a delicate balance between these interests and the rights of the citizens. Of particular relevance to offenses against public order are the protections of the First Amendment.

In studying offenses against public order and safety, indeed the criminal law generally, we should realize that the law must be viewed from a sociological, political, and philosophical perspective and not merely as a set of objective rules of conduct. The offenses against public order have been shaped to a great extent by social change and political events. They have also been sculpted by the values of freedom of speech and assembly that are held within the broader legal and political culture.

QUESTIONS FOR THOUGHT AND DISCUSSION

1. Why has it been necessary for American courts to interpret laws proscribing breach of peace and vagrancy more strictly than did the English common-law courts?

2. How does the Federal Anti-Riot Act seek to prevent the definition of "to incite a riot" from being applied in such a way as to violate First Amendment guarantees of freedom of expression?

3. Is the language of the Indiana Code that proscribes disorderly conduct sufficiently precise to meet the constitutional standard of giving a person of ordinary intelligence fair notice of what conduct is forbidden?

4. Consider the following hypothetical case: Members of the American Nazi Party announced a demonstration to be held in Pleasant Ridge, a predominantly Jewish suburb of Metropolis. The Pleasant Ridge city council quickly adopted an ordinance requiring groups planning demonstrations to obtain a permit from the police department. Under the ordinance, to hold a demonstration without a permit was a misdemeanor, punishable by a $1,000 fine and 60 days in jail. The Nazis applied for a permit and were denied on the grounds that their presence in Pleasant Ridge constituted a "clear and present danger to the public order." The Nazis held their demonstration anyway. Approximately one hundred demonstrators congregated on the city square. Many were dressed in Nazi uniforms; others carried banners emblazoned with swastikas, and others held signs on which were printed anti-Semitic slogans. Pleasant Ridge police arrived at the scene and asked the demonstrators to disperse. When they refused, police arrested a number of demonstrators; others ran to avoid arrest. The leader of the Nazi group, Eisenfaust, was convicted of a number of offenses, including violation of the new ordinance. On appeal, Eisenfaust is challenging the constitutionality of the ordinance. In your opinion, does he have a case?

5. Why did the English common-law concept of making vagrancy a crime take root in America? What purposes did it serve in the early history of the United States?

6. How did the Jacksonville, Florida, vagrancy ordinance invalidated by the Supreme Court in the *Papachristou* case offend the Constitution of the United States? Have

the reforms in vagrancy laws at the state and local levels sufficiently removed the threat of criminalizing a person's status? Are they now written with the precision necessary to protect citizens from arbitrary enforcement of the law?

7. Why have the courts refused to interpret the Second Amendment protection of the "right to keep and bear arms" to prohibit gun control legislation?
8. Why are most traffic violations strict-liability offenses?
9. Have traffic offenses been decriminalized in your state? To what extent? What procedures are available to contest a traffic ticket?

CASES

State v. Mast

Missouri Court of Appeals, 1986.
713 S.W.2d 601.

[This case involves the offenses of unlawful assembly and refusal to disperse.]

DOWD, Judge.

Defendant, Steve Mast, appeals his jury conviction on Count I, unlawful assembly in violation of § 574.040 RSMo (1979), a Class B misdemeanor, and on Count II, refusal to disperse from an unlawful assembly, in violation of Sec. 574.060 RSMo (1979), a Class C misdemeanor. On Count I, defendant was sentenced to a fine of $250.00 plus costs. On count II, defendant was sentenced to two days in jail plus a fine of $100.00 plus costs. The information was filed in Lewis County, and after a change in venue, a jury trial was held in the Knox County Circuit Court. Defendant appeals from these convictions.

On appeal, defendant contends the evidence was insufficient to support the convictions and it was therefore error not to grant his motions for judgments of acquittal.

In testing the sufficiency of the evidence by a motion for judgment of acquittal, the evidence must be viewed in the light most favorable to the state, assuming the evidence of the state and every reasonable inference therefrom to be true, and the evidence and inferences to the contrary are disregarded. . . .

On October 31, 1984, Halloween night, defendant, a student at Northeast Missouri State College in Kirksville, drove to the town of Maywood so that he could participate in the traditional Halloween gathering with his friends. Defendant was aware of Maywood's reputation for "anything goes on Halloween." He had been in Maywood on Halloween in past years, and arrived in Maywood around 5:45 P.M. with a friend, Donnie Martin. Defendant was dressed in his ROTC army fatigues and his face was covered with a black substance. Defendant had a bundle of bottle rockets in his possession and Donnie Martin carried a can of spray paint in his back pocket.

After arriving in Maywood, defendant and Donnie Martin socialized with some friends in front of a general store. Jerry Callow, the deputy sheriff, and Steve Waters, the special deputy appointed for Halloween night, warned defendant and his friends "to keep it down and keep it within reason." At that time, the officers explained to them that seven or more gathered constituted an illegal assembly, but as long as they were not doing anything but having fun, then the officers had no objections. Moreover, Waters informed defendant that it was not illegal to possess bottle rockets, but it was illegal to fire the bottle rockets. Additionally, he confiscated Donnie Martin's can of spray paint because of previous acts of vandalism.

Throughout the course of the night, different unlawful activities transpired such as: bottle rockets were set off in close vicinity to the general store's gas pumps and in the direction of the police car; Mr. Seals' house was egged and a stop sign was placed on his front porch; fire bombs and M-80s were set off; and eggs, bottle rockets, and a beer bottle were all thrown in the direction of the officers and their patrol car. In fact, Officer Callow was struck by an egg.

All of the above occurrences are not attributable to the defendant, but in the course of the evening the officers saw the defendant set off one bottle rocket away from the crowd and the buildings. The officers had difficulty identifying and determining the members of the crowd who were taking part in the unlawful activities. At one point in the evening, Deputy Callow told the crowd that they were getting unruly and committing unlawful acts, and consequently he "asked them to break it up." In response to his request, the crowd divided up into groups of four or five, but these groups did not separate far from each other and proceeded to call the officers names. After the officers departed, the crowd regrouped and continued to set off bottle rockets and fire bombs and throw eggs. Shortly after

10:30 P.M., the two officers turned on the red lights of their patrol car, drove up to the scattering crowd and made some arrests. Waters saw defendant in the middle of the crowd, immediately prior to this time, but he did not see defendant after the arrests.

This is the first appellate attack on the present unlawful assembly statute (§ 574.040 (RSMo 1978). This statute provides in part:

> 1. A person commits the crime of unlawful assembly if he knowingly assembles with six or more other persons and agrees with such persons to violate any of the criminal laws of this state or of the United States with force or violence.

A presumption exists "that the intent of the legislature in enacting a statute is to serve the best interests and welfare of the citizenry at large." . . . This presumption must take into consideration the fact that the legislature did not intend to effect an unreasonable, oppressive or absurd result. . . . Consequently, when interpreting § 574.040, we must determine the legislature's intent from what can be necessarily implied from the language it employed, because the legislature did not expressly state its intention. By identifying the general purposes for enacting a statute and by identifying the problem sought to be remedied, we can ascertain legislative intent. . . .

Since § 574.040 was enacted, no Missouri case has interpreted this statute. However, other jurisdictions have addressed this issue interpreting similar statutes. The court in *Lair v. State*, 316 P.2d 225, 234 (Okla. Crim. App. 1957), defined an unlawful assembly as being an assembly which consists of three or more persons assembled to do an unlawful act or who being assembled, attempt to do a lawful act in a violent or unlawful manner to the terror and the disturbance of the public in general. . . . To constitute the offense of unlawful assembly, the participants must have a common purpose and act in concert. The intent or purpose necessary to render an assembly unlawful need not exist from the onset, but may be formed either before or at the time of the assembly. . . .

An unlawful assembly causes a disturbance of the public order so that it is reasonable for rational, firm and courageous persons in the neighborhood of the assembly to believe the assembly will cause injury to persons or damage to property and will interfere with the rights of others by committing disorderly acts. . . . The intent with which such persons assemble is the very offense of unlawful assembly in that this intent is reflected by the participants' acts, conduct and language. . . . The purpose of unlawful assembly statutes is to discourage assemblies which interfere with the rights of others and endanger the public peace and excite fear and alarm among the people.

Even though a person does not individually commit a violent act which poses a clear and present danger of violence, this individual can be guilty of unlawful assembly. . . . The statutory denunciation applies to the assembly at large. Consequently, each member of an assembly need not individually commit unlawful acts to render the assembly unlawful, but a person can become a member of an unlawful assembly by not disassociating himself from the group assembled and by knowingly joining or remaining with the group assembled after it has become unlawful. . . . Whether a person acted knowingly and whether the necessary intent existed, are both questions of fact for the jury. . . .

> If it were necessary that each member of an unlawful assembly commit an unlawful act, before that member could be convicted then there would be no necessity to make participation in the unlawful assembly a crime. The independent unlawful act would itself be grounds for prosecution. . . . In short every person who is present and cognizant of the unlawful acts being committed by the other members of the assembly can be found guilty of being unlawfully assembled.

When applying the foregoing principles to the facts in this case, we must view the evidence in a manner most favorable to the state. At its inception, the gathering in Maywood on Halloween night was a lawful assembly, however as the night progressed, the participants' purpose in assembling changed. Undoubtedly, the assembly was disturbing the public peace and interfering with the rights of others. The persons in the neighborhood of the assembly had cause to fear the assembly would inflict damage to property and would commit disorderly acts. Throughout the evening, fire bombs, bottle rockets, M-80s, and eggs were being thrown at houses and people. Both Waters and Callow saw defendant fire a bottle rocket which is an unlawful act, according to the deputies. Defendant is no less guilty because he fired only one bottle rocket. Additionally, defendant drove his car across Mr. Seals' lawn.

Moreover, defendant had been in Maywood on previous Halloweens, and so he was aware of the type of activities that take place there on Halloween. Therefore, it is evident that defendant knew the purpose of the gathering on Halloween night. To be convicted of unlawful assembly, defendant did not have to participate or encourage every harmful act which occurred that night. For that matter defendant need not have actually committed an unlawful act. His presence alone in the unlawful assembly was enough for conviction, because he knowingly assembled with the other members, and he was under a duty to disassociate himself from the group after other members of the group committed unlawful acts.

Defendant would have us construe the statutory section in such a manner so as to vitiate the purpose of the statute. We will favor a construction that avoids this unjust and unreasonable result. Defendant contends that no agreement existed between the group members, and consequently, he could not be guilty of participating in an unlawful assembly. Such a narrow reading of the statute would defeat its purpose and create an absurd result by making it almost impossible to satisfy the elements of an unlawful assembly. Even though the group assembled did not expressly, verbally agree, their common unlawful purpose was expressed by their overt acts. Therefore, the members of the assembly intended to and in fact participated in an unlawful assembly. The assembly members' acts, conduct and language indicated their adoption of the unlawful conduct of the other members assembled. Moreover, defendant performed an unlawful act himself so his guilt is not established by his presence alone.

> The common law offense of unlawful assembly is defined as follows: To constitute an offense it must appear that there was common intent of persons assembled to attain purpose, . . . by commission of acts of intimidation and disorder likely to produce danger to peace of neighborhood, and actually tending to inspire courageous persons with well-grounded fear of serious breaches of public peace. . . .

The purpose of an unlawful assembly statute is to penalize the members of assemblies when their conduct causes a disturbance or damage. . . . The members must meet and form a common purpose to violate any of the criminal laws, but they do not have to actually violate the law. . . . The state has a strong and legitimate interest in protecting against criminal acts of force or violence in order to preserve public tranquility and other rights belonging to the public in general. "In furtherance of this interest, it must be able to 'nip in the bud' riots and may, therefore, regulate and proscribe unlawful assemblies." . . . The gathering in Maywood on Halloween originally was a lawful one, but as the night progressed, the members of the assembly acted with common intent to attain a purpose which interfered with the rights of others by committing disorderly and unlawful acts. Based on the foregoing principles, we hold there was substantial evidence to support the conviction of unlawful assembly. Point one is denied.

Defendant's second point on appeal is that the trial court erred in denying his motion for judgment of acquittal on the charge of refusal to disperse because the evidence was manifestly insufficient to sustain a conviction. Taking the evidence in the light most favorable to the state, the evidence was sufficient to show that on Halloween night an unlawful assembly had gathered in Maywood, and defendant had been lawfully warned to disperse. After hearing the warning, the defendant did as requested, but after a short period of time, he returned to the gathering. This evidence is sufficient to sustain his conviction for failure to disperse. Missouri's refusal to disperse statute states:

> 1. A person commits the crime of refusal to disperse if, being present at the scene of an unlawful assembly, or at the scene of a riot, he knowingly fails or refuses to obey the lawful command of a law enforcement officer to depart from the scene of such unlawful assembly or riot. . . .

Whether a person knowingly fails or refuses to obey the dispersal order is a question of fact for the jury. To be guilty of the charge of refusal to disperse, a person must be at the scene of an unlawful assembly and know of the command to disperse, and still refuse to obey. The evidence favorable to the state showed that defendant heard Callow order the crowd to disperse by telling it "to break it up." In response to this command, the gathering broke up into groups of four and five and then proceeded to regroup shortly thereafter. By regrouping, defendant in effect refused to obey the lawful command of Callow to depart from the scene of the unlawful assembly.

Defendant alleges that the warning given was inadequate because it did not expressly order the crowd to go home or to leave town. § 574.060 does not require a warning to expressly designate a location where the crowd is to disperse. A person who "knowingly fails or refuses to obey the lawful command of a law enforcement officer to disperse from the scene of the such unlawful assembly," is guilty of this crime.... The warning could be reasonably understood to mean that the crowd was to leave the area. The failure of the warning to describe the area to be vacated has nothing to do with the defendant's failure to comply. After Callow warned the crowd to break it up, the crowd regrouped, thus suggesting that the crowd would have disregarded the warning in any event.

Words are to be interpreted according to their plain and ordinary meaning which is the commonly accepted dictionary definition. "Break up" is defined as "to disrupt the continuity or flow or to bring to an end." ... A person of reasonable intelligence would understand the words "break it up" to mean that he is supposed to depart from the area. In total disregard and in defiance of the command, defendant remained in the area in question. By his inaction, defendant was not complying with the command to disperse. Defendant's second point on appeal, therefore, is denied.

For the foregoing reasons, the judgment of the trial court is affirmed.

REINHARD and CRIST, JJ., concur.

COMMONWEALTH V. YOUNG

Superior Court of Pennsylvania, 1988.
370 Pa. Super. 42, 535 A.2d 1141.

[This decision examines the offense of disorderly conduct.]

HESTER, Judge.

On September 24, 1986, appellant was found guilty of the summary offense of disorderly conduct by a district justice. On appeal to the Court of Common Pleas of Erie County, he was again found guilty of the same offense following a *de novo* hearing held on December 4, 1986. This appeal followed the January 8, 1987 judgment of sentence of thirty days imprisonment, a fine, and costs. We affirm.

The evidence introduced at trial establishes the following. On August 28, 1986, at approximately 2:45 A.M., appellant and Quincy Barnes were on the campus at Behrend College. They went to Perry Hall, a co-ed dormitory. The women's section of the dormitory consists of two floors on the right side of the building. The two sides are separated by a lobby. To enter the right side, which is locked, a non-resident must be accompanied by a resident with a key. The first-floor women's restroom, located in the middle of the hall, serves approximately fifty dormitory residents and has six stalls containing toilets, six shower stalls, and sinks.

An unidentified resident admitted appellant and Barnes into the first floor women's section, and accompanied them to the room of a dormitory resident the two men knew. They visited briefly with that resident, and on their way out of the dormitory, the two men walked into the women's restroom. Appellant walked over to the stall, which did not lock, opened the door and said: "Hey baby, what you doing." ... The woman screamed, pulled up her pants and chased the men out of the dormitory. She testified that she was extremely frightened by the incident as she was not sure of the men's intentions when they opened the stall door.

In his defense, appellant testified that while he had gone to Perry Hall and visited with the resident he knew, he did not enter the restroom.

He argues that the evidence was insufficient to support his conviction for disorderly conduct. The test we apply in this situation is as follows:

> In testing the sufficiency of the evidence, we must view the evidence in a light most favorable to the Commonwealth as the verdict winner and draw all reasonable inferences upon which the fact finder could have properly based its verdict. . . . A determination must be made as to whether there exists sufficient evidence to enable the trier of fact to find, beyond a reasonable doubt, every element of the crime for which the appellant has been convicted. . . .

Disorderly conduct is defined in relevant part as follows:

> § 5503. **Disorderly Conduct**
> **(a)** Offense defined.—A person is guilty of disorderly conduct if, with intent to cause public inconvenience, annoyance or alarm, or recklessly creating a risk thereof, he: . . . creates a hazardous or physically offensive condition by any act which serves no legitimate purpose of the actor. . . .
> **(c)** Definition.—As used in this section the word "public" means affecting or likely to affect persons in a place to which the public or a substantial group has access; among the places included are highways, transport facilities, schools, prisons, apartment houses, places of business or amusement, any neighborhood, or any premises which are open to the public.

We reject appellant's argument that since his conduct affected only a single individual, he did not have the *mens rea* to cause "public" inconvenience, annoyance or alarm as defined by the statute. The statute specifically states that "recklessly creating a risk" of public annoyance or alarm is sufficient. The evidence viewed in the light most favorable to the Commonwealth establishes that appellant deliberately entered a women's public restroom without justification.

Under the statutory definition, the restroom was a public place. The term includes a place to which the public *or* a "substantial group" has access. . . . The restroom serves the fifty women who reside in the dormitory. Moreover, any female visitor can freely gain access to the area. Thus, the restroom is accessible to a substantial group. The size of the restroom supports this conclusion: it has six toilet stalls and six shower stalls, which is larger than public restrooms in most department stores and restaurants. There are some limitations on access in that a nonresident must be admitted to the general area by a resident. However, this does not alter the fact that a substantial group has access. Apartment houses, defined by the statute as public, are similarly restricted.

When appellant entered the public restroom, he recklessly created a *risk* of public annoyance or alarm. The fortuitous fact that only one individual was in the area does not vitiate the risk he created. Any number of women, in various states of undress, could have been using the showers, sinks and toilets in the area.

We have held that one who exhibits disorderly behavior in a public place is guilty of disorderly conduct even if that behavior is directed at a single individual. . . .

Appellant did not know the victim and was not searching for her. In this context, she was a member of the general public, and appellant deliberately entered the women's restroom solely to find *anyone* in her position or in a similarly embarrassing situation. He thereby created a risk of public annoyance or alarm, even if only one individual was alarmed and annoyed.

Further, the evidence establishes that appellant's conduct created a physically offensive condition to the victim. She was performing a private bodily function. She feared that appellant and his companion were going to assault her. Any reasonable woman in her situation would have been offended by appellant's actions. . . .

In *Commonwealth v. Greene*, 410 Pa. 111, 115–16, 189 A.2d 141, 144 (1963) which is still authoritative on this subject, Justice Musmanno noted that: "In Pennsylvania the crime of disorderly conduct embraces activity which disturbs the peace and dignity of a community." Justice Musmanno emphasized that the touchstone of disorderly conduct is an activity that does not form "an integral part of the movement of a civilized community." . . . Appellant's behavior fits those descriptions.

Viewing the evidence in the light most favorable to the Commonwealth and drawing all reasonable inferences therefrom, we believe that District Justice Peter Nakoski and Judge Shad Connelly of the Court of Common Pleas of Erie County correctly found appellant guilty of disorderly conduct. We therefore affirm the judgment of sentence.

BECK, J., files a dissenting opinion. . . .

FEINER V. NEW YORK

Supreme Court of the United States, 1951.
340 U.S. 315, 71 S. Ct. 303, 95 L.Ed. 295.

[In this classic case, the U.S. Supreme Court considers the First Amendment implications of a conviction for disorderly conduct.]

Mr. Chief Justice VINSON delivered the opinion of the Court.

Petitioner was convicted of the offense of disorderly conduct, a misdemeanor under the New York penal laws, in the Court of Special Sessions of the City of Syracuse and was sentenced to thirty days in the county penitentiary. The conviction was affirmed by the Onondaga County Court and the New York Court of Appeals. . . . The case is here on certiorari, . . . petitioner having claimed that the conviction is in violation of his right of free speech under the Fourteenth Amendment. . . .

On the evening of March 8, 1949, petitioner Irving Feiner was addressing an open-air meeting at the corner of South McBride and Harrison Streets in the City of Syracuse. At approximately 6:30 P.M., the police received a telephone complaint concerning the meeting, and two officers were detailed to investigate. One of these officers went to the scene immediately, the other arriving some twelve minutes later. They found a crowd of about seventy-five or eighty people, both Negro and white, filling the sidewalk and spreading out into the street. Petitioner, standing on a large wooden box on the sidewalk, was addressing the crowd through a loud-speaker system attached to an automobile. Although the purpose of his speech was to urge his listeners to attend a meeting to be held that night in the Syracuse Hotel, in its course he was making derogatory remarks concerning President Truman, the American Legion, the Mayor of Syracuse, and other local political officials.

The police officers made no effort to interfere with petitioner's speech, but were first concerned with the effect of the crowd on both pedestrian and vehicular traffic. They observed the situation from the opposite side of the street, noting that some pedestrians were forced to walk in the street to avoid the crowd. Since traffic was passing at the time, the officers attempted to get the people listening to petitioner back on the sidewalk. The crowd was restless and there was some pushing, shoving and milling around. One of the officers telephoned the police station from a nearby store, and then both policemen crossed the street and mingled with the crowd without any intention of arresting the speaker.

At this time, petitioner was speaking in a "loud, high-pitched voice." He gave the impression that he was endeavoring to arouse the Negro people against the whites, urging that they rise up in arms and fight for equal rights. The statements before such a mixed audience "stirred up a little excitement." Some of the onlookers made remarks to the police about their inability to handle the crowd and at least one threatened violence if the police did not act. There were others who appeared to be favoring petitioner's arguments. Because of the feeling that existed in the crowd both for and against the speaker, the officers finally "stepped in to prevent it from resulting in a fight." One of the officers approached the petitioner, not for the purpose of arresting him, but to get him to break up the crowd. He asked petitioner to get down off the box, but the latter refused to accede to his request and continued talking. The officer waited for a minute and then demanded that he cease talking. Although the officer had thus twice requested petitioner to stop over the course of several minutes, petitioner not only ignored him but continued talking. During all this time, the crowd was pressing closer around petitioner and the officer. Finally, the officer told petitioner he was under arrest and ordered him to get down from the box, reaching up to grab him. Petitioner stepped down, announcing over the microphone that "the law has arrived, and I suppose they will take over now." In all, the officer had asked petitioner to get down off the box three times over a space of four or five minutes. Petitioner had been speaking for over a half hour.

On these facts, petitioner was specifically charged with . . . [disorderly conduct]. The bill of particulars, demanded by petitioner and furnished by the State, gave in detail the facts upon which the prosecution relied to support the charge of disorderly conduct. Paragraph C is particularly pertinent here: "By ignoring and refusing to heed and obey reasonable police orders issued at the time and place mentioned in the Information to regulate and control said crowd and to prevent a breach or breaches of the peace and to prevent injury to pedestrians attempting to use said walk, and being forced into the highway adjacent to the place in question, and prevent injury to the public generally."

We are not faced here with blind condonation by a state court of arbitrary police action. Petitioner was accorded a full, fair trial. The trial judge heard testimony supporting and contradicting the judgment of the police officers that a clear danger of disorder was threatened. After weighing this contradictory evidence, the trial judge reached the conclusion that the police officers were justified in taking action to prevent a breach of the peace. The exercise of the police officers' proper discretionary power to prevent a breach of the peace was thus approved by the trial court and later by two courts on review. The courts below recognized petitioner's right to hold a street meeting at this locality, to make use of loud-speaking equipment in giving his speech, and to make derogatory remarks concerning public officials and the American Legion. They found that the officers in making the arrest were motivated solely by a proper concern for the preservation of order and protection of the general welfare, and that there was no evidence which could lend color to a claim that the acts of the police were a cover for suppression of petitioner's views and opinions. Petitioner was thus neither arrested nor convicted for the making or the content of his speech. Rather, it was the reaction which it actually engendered.

The language of *Cantwell v. Connecticut* . . . is appropriate here. "The offense known as breach of the peace embraces a great variety of conduct destroying or menacing public order and tranquility. It includes not only violent acts but acts and words likely to produce violence in others. No one would have the hardihood to suggest that the principle of freedom of speech sanctions incitement to riot or that religious liberty connotes the privilege to exhort others to physical attack upon those belonging to another sect. When clear and present danger of riot, disorder, interference with traffic upon the public streets, or other immediate threat to public safety, peace, or order, appears, the power of the State to prevent or punish is obvious." . . . The findings of the New York courts as to the condition of the crowd and the refusal of petitioner to obey the police requests, supported as they are by the record of this case, are persuasive that the conviction of petitioner for violation of public peace, order and authority does not exceed the bounds of proper state police action. This Court respects, as it must, the interest of the community in maintaining peace and order on its streets. . . . We cannot say that the preservation of that interest here encroaches on the constitutional rights of this petitioner.

We are well aware that the ordinary murmurings and objections of a hostile audience cannot be allowed to silence a speaker, and are also mindful of the possible danger of giving overzealous police officials complete discretion to break up otherwise lawful public meetings. "A State may not unduly suppress free communication of views, religious or other, under the guise of conserving desirable conditions." . . .

But we are not faced here with such a situation. It is one thing to say that the police cannot be used as an instrument for the suppression of unpopular views, and another to say that, when as here the speaker passes the bounds of argument or persuasion and undertakes incitement to riot, they are powerless to prevent a breach of the peace. Nor in this case can we condemn the considered judgment of three New York courts approving the means which the police, faced with a crisis, used in the exercise of their power and duty to preserve peace and order. The findings of the state courts as to the existing situation and the imminence of greater disorder coupled with petitioner's deliberate defiance of the police officers convince us that we should not reverse this conviction in the name of free speech.

Affirmed.

Mr. Justice FRANKFURTER concurs in the result.

Mr. Justice BLACK, dissenting. . . .

Mr. Justice DOUGLAS, with whom Mr. Justice MINTON concurs, dissenting.

. . . Public assemblies and public speech occupy an important role in American life. One high function of the police is to protect these lawful gatherings so that the speakers may exercise their constitutional rights. When unpopular causes are sponsored from the public platform, there will commonly be mutterings and unrest and heckling from the crowd. When a speaker mounts a platform it is not unusual to find him resorting to exaggeration, to vilification of ideas and men, to the making of false charges. But those extravagances . . . do not justify penalizing the speaker by depriving him of the platform or by punishing him for his conduct.

A speaker may not, of course, incite a riot any more than he may incite a breach of the peace by the use of "fighting words." . . . But this record shows no such extremes. It shows an unsympathetic audience and the threat of one man to haul the speaker from the stage. It is against that kind of threat that speakers need police protection. If they do not receive it and instead the police throw their weight on the side of those who would break up the meetings, the police become the new censors of speech. Police censorship has all the vices of the censorship from city halls which we have repeatedly struck down. . . .

PAPACHRISTOU V. CITY OF JACKSONVILLE

Supreme Court of the United States, 1972.
405 U.S. 156, 92 S. Ct. 839, 31 L.Ed.2d 110.

[In this seminal case, the U.S. Supreme Court considers the constitutionality of a local vagrancy ordinance.]

Mr. Justice DOUGLAS delivered the opinion of the Court.

This case involves eight defendants who were convicted in a Florida municipal court of violating a Jacksonville, Florida, vagrancy ordinance. Their convictions were affirmed by the Florida Circuit Court in a consolidated appeal, and their petition for certiorari was denied by the District Court of Appeal. . . . The case is here on a petition for certiorari, which we granted. . . . For reasons which will appear, we reverse.

At issue are five consolidated cases. Margaret Papachristou, Betty Calloway, Eugene Eddie Melton, and Leonard Johnson were all arrested early on a Sunday morning, and charged with vagrancy—"prowling by auto."

Jimmy Lee Smith and Milton Henry were charged with vagrancy—"vagabonds."

Henry Edward Heath and a codefendant were arrested for vagrancy—"loitering" and "common thief."

Thomas Owen Campbell was charged with vagrancy—"common thief."

Hugh Brown was charged with vagrancy—"disorderly loitering on street" and "disorderly conduct—resisting arrest with violence."

The facts are stipulated. Papachristou and Calloway are white females. Melton and Johnson are black males. Papachristou was enrolled in a job-training program sponsored by the State Employment Service at Florida Junior College in Jacksonville. Calloway was a typing and shorthand teacher at a state mental institution located near Jacksonville. She was the owner of the automobile in which the four defendants were arrested. Melton was a Vietnam war veteran who had been released from the Navy after nine months in a veterans' hospital. On the date of his arrest he was a part-time computer helper while attending college as a full-time student in Jacksonville. Johnson was a tow-motor operator in a grocery chain warehouse and was a lifelong resident of Jacksonville.

At the time of their arrest the four of them were riding in Calloway's car on the main thoroughfare in Jacksonville. They had left a restaurant owned by Johnson's uncle where they had eaten and were on their way to a nightclub. The arresting officers denied that the racial mixture in the car played any part in the decision to make the arrest. The arrest, they said, was made because the defendants had stopped near a used-car lot which had been broken into several times. There was, however, no evidence of any breaking and entering on the night in question.

Of these four charged with "prowling by auto" none had been previously arrested except Papachristou who had once been convicted of a municipal offense.

Jimmy Lee Smith and Milton Henry (who is not a petitioner) were arrested between 9 and 10 A.M. on a weekday in downtown Jacksonville, while waiting for a friend who was to lend them a car so they could apply for a job at a produce company. Smith was a part-time produce worker and part-time organizer for a Negro political group. He had a common-law wife and three children supported by him and his wife. He had been arrested several times but convicted only once. Smith's companion, Henry, was an 18-year-old high school student with no previous record of arrest.

This morning it was cold, and Smith had no jacket, so they went briefly into a dry cleaning shop to wait, but left when requested to do so. They thereafter walked back and forth two or three times over a two-block stretch looking for their friend. The store owners, who apparently were wary of Smith and his companion, summoned two police officers who searched the men and found neither had a weapon. But they were arrested because the officers said they had no identification and because the officers did not believe their story.

Heath and a codefendant were arrested for "loitering" and for "common thief." Both were residents of Jacksonville, Heath having lived there all his life and being employed at an automobile body shop. Heath had previously been arrested but his codefendant has no arrest record. Heath and his companion were arrested when they drove up to a residence shared by Heath's girl friend and some other girls. Some police officers were already there in the process of arresting another man. When Heath and his companion started backing out of the driveway, the officers signaled to them to stop and asked them to get out of the car, which they did. Thereupon they and the automobile were searched. Although no contraband or incriminating evidence was found, they were both arrested, Heath being charged with being a "common thief" because he was reputed to be a thief. The codefendant was charged with "loitering" because he was standing in the driveway, an act which the officers admitted was done only at their command.

Campbell was arrested as he reached his home very early one morning and was charged with "common thief." He was stopped by officers because he was traveling at a high rate of speed, yet no speeding charge was placed against him.

Brown was arrested when he was observed leaving a downtown Jacksonville hotel by a police officer seated in a cruiser. The police testified he was reputed to be a thief, narcotics pusher, and generally opprobrious character. The officer called Brown over to the car, intending at that time to arrest him unless he had a good explanation for being on the street. Brown walked over to the police cruiser, as commanded, and the officer began to search him, apparently preparatory to placing him in the car. In the process of the search he came on two small packets which were later found to contain heroin. When the officer touched the pocket where the packets were, Brown began to resist. He was charged with "disorderly loitering on street" and "disorderly conduct—resisting arrest with violence." While he was also charged with a narcotics violation, that charge was nolled.

Jacksonville's ordinance and Florida's statute were "derived from early English law," . . . and employ "archaic language" in their definitions of vagrants. . . . The history is an oftentold tale. The breakup of feudal estates in England led to labor shortages which in turn resulted in the Statutes of Laborers, designed to stabilize the labor force by prohibiting increases in wages and prohibiting the movement of workers from their home areas in search of improved conditions. Later vagrancy laws became criminal aspects of the poor laws. The series of laws passed in England on the subject became increasingly severe. But "the theory of the Elizabethan poor laws no longer fits the facts." ... The conditions which spawned these laws may be gone, but the archaic classifications remain.

This ordinance is void for vagueness, both in the sense that it "fails to give a person of ordinary intelligence fair notice that his contemplated conduct is forbidden by the statute," ... and because it encourages arbitrary and erratic arrests and convictions....

Living under a rule of law entails various suppositions, one of which is that "[all persons] are entitled to be informed as to what the State commands or forbids." ...

The poor among us, the minorities, the average householder are ... not alerted to the regulatory schemes of vagrancy laws; and we assume they would have no understanding of their meaning and impact if they read them. Nor are they protected from being caught in the vagrancy net by the necessity of having a specific intent to commit an unlawful act....

The Jacksonville ordinance makes criminal activities which by modern standards are normally innocent. "Nightwalking" is one. Florida construes the ordinance not to make criminal one night's wandering, ... only the "habitual" wanderer or, as the ordinance describes it, "common night walkers." We know, however, from experience that sleepless people often walk at night, perhaps hopeful that sleep-inducing relaxation will result.

Luis Munoz-Marin, former Governor of Puerto Rico, commented once that "loafing" was a national virtue in his Commonwealth and that it should be encouraged. It is, however, a crime in Jacksonville.

"[P]ersons able to work but habitually living upon the earnings of their wives or minor children"—like habitually living "without visible means of support"—might implicate unemployed pillars of the community who have married rich wives.

"[P]ersons able to work but habitually living upon the earnings of their wives or minor children" may also embrace unemployed people out of the labor market, by reason of a recession or disemployed by reason of technological or so-called structural displacements.

Persons "wandering or strolling" from place to place have been extolled by Walt Whitman and Vachel Lindsay. The qualification "without any lawful purpose or object" may be a trap for innocent acts. Persons "neglecting all lawful business and habitually spending their time by frequenting ... places where alcoholic beverages are sold or served" would literally embrace many members of golf clubs and city clubs.

Walkers and strollers and wanderers may be going to or coming from a burglary. Loafers or loiterers may be "casing" a place for a holdup. Letting one's wife support him is an intra-family matter, and normally of no concern to the police. Yet it may, of course, be the setting for numerous crimes.

The difficulty is that these activities are historically part of the amenities of life as we have known them. They are not mentioned in the Constitution or in the Bill of Rights. These unwritten amenities have been in part responsible for giving our people the feeling of independence and self-confidence, the feeling of creativity. These amenities have dignified the right of dissent and have honored the right to be nonconformists and the right to defy submissiveness. They have encouraged lives of high spirits rather than hushed, suffocating silence....

This aspect of the vagrancy ordinance before us is suggested by what this Court said in 1876 about a broad criminal statute enacted by Congress: "It would certainly be dangerous if the legislature could set a net large enough to catch all possible offenders, and leave it to the courts to step inside and say who could be rightfully detained, and who should be set at large." ...

Another aspect of the ordinance's vagueness appears when we focus, not on the lack of notice given a potential offender, but on the effect of the unfettered discretion it places in the hands of the Jacksonville police. Caleb Foote, an early student of this subject, has called the vagrancy-type law as offering "punishment by analogy." ... Such crimes, though long common in Russia, are not compatible with our constitutional system. We allow our police to make arrests only on "probable cause," a Fourth and

Fourteenth Amendment standard applicable to the States as well as to the Federal Government. Arresting a person on suspicion, like arresting a person for investigation, is foreign to our system, even when the arrest is for past criminality. Future criminality, however, is the common justification for the presence of vagrancy statutes. . . . Florida has, indeed, construed her vagrancy statute "as necessary regulations," inter alia, "to deter vagabondage and prevent crimes."

A direction by a legislature to the police to arrest all "suspicious" persons would not pass constitutional muster. A vagrancy prosecution may be merely the cloak for a conviction which could not be obtained on the real but undisclosed grounds for the arrest. . . .

Those generally implicated by the imprecise terms of the ordinance—poor people, nonconformists, dissenters, idlers—may be required to comport themselves according to the lifestyle deemed appropriate by the Jacksonville police and the courts. Where, as here, there are no standards governing the exercise of the discretion granted by the ordinance, the scheme permits and encourages an arbitrary and discriminatory enforcement of the law. It furnishes a convenient tool for "harsh and discriminatory enforcement by local prosecuting officials, against particular groups deemed to merit their displeasure." . . .

A presumption that people who might walk or loaf or loiter or stroll or frequent houses where liquor is sold or who are supported by their wives or who look suspicious to the police are to become future criminals is too precarious for a rule of law. The implicit presumption in these generalized vagrancy standards—that crime is being nipped in the bud—is too extravagant to deserve extended treatment. Of course, vagrancy statutes are useful to the police. Of course, they are nets making easy the roundup of so called undesirables. But the rule of law implies equality and justice in its application. Vagrancy laws of the Jacksonville type teach that the scales of justice are so tipped even-handed administration of the law is not possible. The rule of law, evenly applied to minorities as well as majorities, to the poor as well as the rich, is the great mucilage that holds society together.

The Jacksonville ordinance cannot be squared with our constitutional standards and is plainly unconstitutional.

Reversed.

Mr. Justice POWELL and Mr. Justice REHNQUIST took no part in the consideration or decision of this case.

STATE v. YOUNG

Court of Appeals of Ohio, 1988.
50 Ohio App. 3d 17, 552 N.E.2d 226.

[Kevin W. Young was convicted of violating Ohio R.C. 4511.44 by failing to yield to approaching traffic. In this appeal to the Ohio Court of Appeals, Young claims the trial judge erred in interpreting the statute under which he was convicted].

McCORMAC, Judge.

. . . On April 10, 1987, defendant was driving southbound on U.S. Route 33 through Nelsonville when he noted a traffic jam caused by an accident. To avoid the traffic jam, Young pulled into a private driveway leading to the Nelsonville Sewage Treatment Plant and turned around.

At this point, U.S. Route 33 has three lanes—a southbound, a northbound, and a center lane, which is a turning lane only.

Young wanted to turn north onto U.S. 33. He waited in the private driveway until a car in the southbound lane of U.S. 33 motioned for him to go. Young drove across the southbound lane before he turned north. He testified that he looked to see if there was any traffic coming but he could not see anything until he got to the center lane because his vision was blocked by stopped traffic.

Officer Waggoner was traveling southbound on U.S. 33 in the center turn lane going thirty miles an hour. He testified that he was trying to get to a car accident and that he could not travel in the normal lane because it was backed up. Officer Waggoner had on his warning lights, but not his siren. He testified that he was trying to turn on his siren, which is located on the floor. When he looked up, Young's car was across the center lane. The two cars collided.

Defendant argues that the trial court erred in interpreting R.C. 4511.44 to require motorists to yield the right-of-way to illegally operated oncoming traffic.

R.C. 4511.44 specifies that a driver entering or crossing a highway from any place other than another roadway shall "yield the right-of-way to all traffic approaching on the roadway to be entered or crossed." R.C. 4511.01(UU) states that:

> " 'Right of way' means the right of a vehicle . . . to proceed uninterruptedly in a lawful manner in the direction in which it or he is moving in preference to another vehicle . . . approaching from a different direction into its or his path."

This definition of right-of-way must be used in conjunction with R.C. 4511.44. . . . Thus, in order to find a defendant guilty of the criminal violation of R.C. 4511.44, it is necessary to find that defendant failed to yield to a vehicle proceeding uninterruptedly in a lawful manner because those are the elements of the offense. It is not sufficient simply to find that defendant was negligent, careless or at fault, partially or totally, in causing the accident.

The issue then is whether the police officer proceeding in the turn-only lane at thirty miles an hour displaying warning lights, but not using his siren, was proceeding in a lawful manner. That question must be answered in the negative. An operator of a public safety vehicle may drive in a turn-only lane lawfully only if he uses at least one flashing, rotating, or oscillating light visible under normal atmospheric conditions from a condition of five hundred feet from the front of the vehicle and he gives an audible signal by siren, exhaust whistle, or bell. . . . The evidence is clear that the police officer failed to give an audible signal and that, therefore, he lost his preferential status as the driver of an emergency vehicle by operating his vehicle unlawfully. . . . Moreover, there was not due regard for the safety of all persons and property on the highway when the police officer drove thirty miles an hour in a turn-only lane, particularly when he failed to use his siren.

Appellant's assignment of error is sustained. The judgment of the trial court is reversed, and the cause is remanded to the trial court with instructions to enter final judgment for defendant.

Judgment reversed and cause remanded.

GREY, P.J., and STEPHENSON, J., concur.

UNITED STATES V. EVANS

United States Court of Appeals, Ninth Circuit, 1991.
928 F.2d 858.

[In this case, the Ninth Circuit Court of Appeals considers the constitutionality of the federal statute that prohibits possession of unregistered machine guns, 26 U.S.C. Sec. 5861(d) (1982). The appellant, Creed M. Evans, was convicted in U.S. District Court of making false statements to the Bureau of Alcohol, Tobacco, and Firearms. In his appeal, Evans argues that the mere possession of machine guns is not sufficiently related to interstate commerce to permit Congress to make it a criminal offense.]

WIGGINS, Circuit Judge:

. . . Evans contends that Congress lacks the power to prohibit the mere possession of unregistered machine guns without requiring proof of a nexus with interstate commerce. The general standard by which a statute that is said to violate the Commerce Clause is to be measured is firmly established. Although we independently review the validity of an act that is said to violate the Commerce Clause, . . . our review is conducted in a highly deferential manner. We consider whether a reasonable Congress could find that the class of activity regulated affects interstate commerce. . . . Congress need not make specific findings of fact to support its conclusion that a class of activity affects interstate commerce. . . . However, if Congress does make such findings, they carry great weight in this court's analysis. . . .

The statutes at issue in this case easily meet this standard. Congress specifically found that at least 750,000 people had been killed in the United States by firearms between the turn of the century and the time of the Act's enactment. It was thus reasonable for Congress to conclude that the possession of firearms affects the national economy, if only through the insurance industry. Since Evans does not contend that any specific Constitutional rights are implicated, this rather tenuous nexus between the activity regulated and interstate commerce is sufficient. . . .

We AFFIRM the judgement of the District Court.

CHAPTER 12

Offenses Against Justice and Public Administration

CHAPTER OUTLINE

Introduction
The Common-Law Background
Bribery
Perjury
Obstruction of Justice
Resisting Arrest
Compounding a Crime
Escape
Criminal Contempt
Conclusion

Cases

State v. Gustafson
United States v. Scott
People v. Gettings
State v. Ring
State v. Blanton

Introduction

We are shocked to read headlines that tell of public officials convicted of corruption and bribery. Likewise, we question the effectiveness of the judicial process when we learn that perjured testimony has sent an innocent person to prison. And, we are frightened by the television announcement that a dangerous criminal has escaped and is at large. Incidents like this remind us of the fallibility of our criminal justice system. We would like to believe that such events are sensational because they are so unusual. Unfortunately, they are all too common. Yet, we must realize that as our nation has become more densely populated, urbanized, and technological, our relationships have become less personal. These and other factors have resulted in an increased need for the criminal law to serve as a deterrent, and where necessary, as a means to punish those who breach the public trust and those who corrupt the orderly processes of government and the justice system by their actions.

The Common-Law Background

Common-law judges found it essential to create certain offenses to maintain the integrity of the law and the administration of justice. Principally, these offenses were bribery, perjury and subornation of perjury, obstruction of justice, compounding a crime, and escape. At common law, these offenses were misdemeanors. Additionally the common law developed the concept of criminal contempt to enable judges to maintain the dignity and authority of the courts and the respect due judicial officers.

As the administration of justice became more sophisticated, these offenses were codified and, in many instances, classified as felonies by federal and state jurisdictions. Criminal contempt, while not a crime in the technical sense, is now regarded as a crime for virtually all purposes. These traditional common-law offenses have been expanded and augmented by a variety of modern statutes.

Bribery

The concept of bribery dates back to biblical times. From early in religious history it was regarded as sinful to attempt to influence the judge with a gift, because the judge represented the divine. Thus, when the common law developed the crime of bribery, it sought to penalize only persons whose actions were designed to improperly influence those identified with the administration of justice. Later, it was considered bribery for anyone to give or receive anything of value or any valuable service or promise with the intent to influence any public officer in the discharge of a legal duty. See *People v. Patillo,* 54 N.E.2d 548 (Ill. 1944).

The Modern Statutory Offense of Bribery

Today, federal statutes proscribe bribery of public officers and witnesses as well as jurors and government employees and functionaries. 18 U.S.C.A. § 201. State statutes generally define bribery in broad terms and frequently address specific situations as well. The trend has been to enlarge the common-law approach by extending the offense to new categories of persons and conduct and by making the punishment more severe. The broad statutory definition of bribery is illustrated by the Florida law that provides:

> "Bribery" means corruptly to give, offer, or promise to any public servant, or, if a public servant, corruptly to request, solicit, accept, or agree to accept for himself or another, any pecuniary or other benefit with an intent or purpose to influence the performance of any act or omission which the person believes to be, or the public servant represents as being, within the official discretion of a public servant, in violation of a public duty, or in performance of a public duty. Fla. Stat. Ann. § 838.015(1).

Courts generally construe such terms as *public servant* and *benefit* broadly, to accomplish the intended legislative purpose of statutes defining bribery. The quoted statute makes explicit that the person bribed need not have authority to accomplish the act sought or represented. Irrespective of statutes, courts generally hold that where the act intended to be influenced is connected with a person's public duty, it is immaterial whether the person bribed has the authority to do a specific act. See, for example, *State v. Hendricks,* 186 P.2d 943 (Ariz. 1947).

The Range of Bribery Offenses

Acts sought to be accomplished by bribes cover a wide range of conduct. Common examples include obtaining the release or acquittal of an arrestee, securing an award of a government contract, and even obtaining a favorable vote by a legislator on a pending bill. Although we commonly think of money being offered or requested as a bribe, a variety of other things are offered, sought, or exchanged. These not only include tangible items, but also sometimes extend to price advantages, use of vehicles, vacation homes, and even sexual favors.

The Burden of the Prosecution

The gist of the crime of bribery is the unlawful offer or agreement to do something under color of office. Ordinarily, the prosecution must prove not only the offer or agreement or the request or acceptance of a benefit but also that the defendant had a false or corrupt intent. One of the difficulties encountered in prosecuting a bribery charge is establishing the corrupt intent element. For example, it can be extremely difficult to prove that a person received employment or was granted a contract as a result of a bribe. The difficulty is compounded because not infrequently bribes are disguised as gifts or even as political or charitable contributions.

Offenses Extending the Concept of Bribery

Many states have enacted statutes to extend the offense of bribery to encompass conduct of persons other than public officials and employees. These states have classified certain corrupt business practices as "commercial bribery." The New

CASE IN POINT

Bribery: What Constitutes a *Thing of Value?*

Defendant was convicted of bribery under an Alabama statute that provided that it was bribery for any public official to accept "any gift, gratuity, or other thing of value." On appeal, defendant argued that "sexual intercourse, or the promise of sexual intercourse, or the promise of other sexual favors or relationship" did not meet the test of being a "thing of value" under the bribery statute. The Alabama Court of Criminal Appeals rejected the defendant's contention, saying, "The word 'thing' does not necessarily mean a substance. . . . [I]t includes an act, or action."

McDonald v. State, 329 So.2d 583 (Ala. Crim. App. 1975), *cert. quashed,* 329 So.2d 596 (Ala. 1976), *cert. denied,* 429 U.S. 834, 97 S. Ct. 99, 50 L.Ed.2d 99 (1976).

Jersey law making commercial bribery a crime is comprehensive and, as amended in 1986, provides:

> Section 2C:21–10:
> a. A person commits a crime if he solicits, accepts or agrees to accept any benefit as consideration for knowingly violating or agreeing to violate a duty of fidelity to which he is subject as:
> (1). An agent, partner or employee of another;
> (2). A trustee, guardian, or other fiduciary;
> (3). A lawyer, physician, accountant, appraiser, or other professional adviser or informant;
> (4). An officer, director, manager or other participant in the direction of the affairs of an incorporated or unincorporated association;
> (5). A labor official, including any duly appointed representative of a labor organization or any duly appointed trustee or representative of an employee welfare trust fund; or
> (6). An arbitrator or other purportedly disinterested adjudicator or referee.
> b. A person who holds himself out to the public as being engaged in the business of making disinterested selection, appraisal, or criticism of commodities, real properties or services commits a crime if he solicits, accepts or agrees to accept any benefit to influence his selection, appraisal or criticism.
> c. A person commits a crime if he confers, or offers or agrees to confer, any benefit the acceptance of which would be criminal under this section.
> N.J. Stat. Ann. § 2C:21–10.

Under the New Jersey statute the benefit offered, conferred, agreed to be conferred, solicited, accepted, or agreed to determines the degree of the crime and the penalty.

Most states now have made it a criminal offense to offer anything of value to a participant or official in an amateur or professional athletic contest to vary his or her performance, or for a participant or official in a sports event to accept a bribe under such circumstances. See, for example, Iowa Code Ann. § 722.3; *State v. Di Paglia,* 71 N.W.2d 601 (Iowa 1955).

Defenses to the Crime of Bribery

Of course, the fact that an offer to bribe is not legally enforceable is no defense. The only recognized defense to a charge of bribery, other than denial, is entrapment. See *State v. Harrington,* 332 So.2d 764 (La. 1976). The defense of entrapment is discussed in Chapter 13.

PERJURY

Like bribery, the crime of perjury has its roots in biblical times. The Mosaic Code included an admonition against the bearing of false witness. At common law perjury came to consist of willfully giving under oath in a judicial proceeding false testimony material to the issue. *Commonwealth v. Hinkle,* 197 S.W. 455 (Ky. 1917). Because of the narrow scope of the offense, it was eventually supplemented by the common-law offense of false swearing, a crime committed when an oath was taken in other than a judicial proceeding.

Elements of the Offense of Perjury

These common-law offenses have been codified by federal law, 18 U.S.C.A. § 1621, that provides:

> Whoever (1) having taken an oath before a competent tribunal, officer, or person, in any case in which a law of the United States authorizes an oath to be administered, that he will testify, declare, depose, or certify truly, or that any written testimony, declaration, deposition, or certificate by him subscribed, is true, willfully and contrary to such oath states or subscribes any material matter which he does not believe to be true; or (2) in any declaration, certificate, verification, or statement under penalty of perjury as permitted under section 1746 of title 28, United States Code, willfully subscribes as true any material matter which he does not believe to be true; is guilty of perjury. . . .

All states have laws making perjury a criminal offense. For example, the California perjury statute provides that a person who has taken an oath to tell the truth and who "wilfully and contrary to such oath, states as true any material matter which he knows to be false" is guilty of perjury. West's Ann. Cal. Penal Code § 118. While Section 118 relates to oaths in administrative and judicial proceedings, Section 118 (a) makes it perjury for a person to give a false affidavit to be used in those proceedings. As in other jurisdictions, additional California statutes make it unlawful for anyone to give a false statement under oath in various applications, certificates, and reports.

The Burden of the Prosecution

To convict a defendant of perjury, the prosecution must establish that the defendant took an oath to tell the truth and knowingly made a false statement of fact. Statutes usually permit anyone with scruples against taking an oath to affirm that a statement is true. In either event, a person cannot be lawfully convicted of perjury unless there is proof that he or she was administered the oath by or made an affirmation before someone with legal authority. *Whitaker v. Commonwealth,* 367 S.W.2d 831 (Ky. 1963). Furthermore, the defendant's statement must have been material. This means that the testimony given by the defendant must have been capable of influencing the tribunal on the issues before it. *United States v. Jackson,* 640 F.2d 614 (8th Cir. 1981), *cert. denied,* 454 U.S. 1057, 102 S. Ct. 605, 70 L.Ed.2d 594 (1981), The vast majority of jurisdictions hold that the question of materiality in a prosecution for perjury is an issue to be decided by the judge. In 1992, the New Jersey Supreme Court disagreed. That court held unconstitutional a portion of the state's perjury statute that directed this issue be determined by the court. The court reasoned that since materiality is an element of the crime of perjury, the Constitution requires that the jury must determine that element of the crime, as others, beyond a reasonable doubt. *State v. Anderson,* 603 A.2d 928 (N.J. 1992).

Some statutes that define perjury require the prosecution to prove that the defendant's statement was made with the "intent to deceive." See, for example, Vernon's Tex. Penal Code Ann. § 37.02(a). Irrespective of statutory requirements, most jurisdictions require the prosecution to prove that the defendant's false statement was made "willfully and corruptly," because at common law perjury was a specific-intent crime. Requiring the prosecution to prove the defendant's specific intent generally eliminates the likelihood of a defendant being convicted for simply having made a careless or offhanded statement.

Perjury is frequently said to be one of the most difficult crimes to prove. The inherent difficulty of convicting a defendant of this offense is exacerbated by the "two witness rule" that prevails in most jurisdictions. Under this rule the prosecution must prove the falsity of a defendant's statements either by two witnesses or by one witness and corroborating documents or circumstances. See, for example, McKinney's N.Y. Penal Law § 210.50.

Perjury by Contradictory Statements

Early American cases followed the common-law principle that a defendant could not be convicted of perjury based on having made two contradictory statements unless the prosecution established which one of the statements was false. *Paytes v. State,* 191 S.W. 975 (Tenn. 1917). This rule of law has now been largely eliminated by statutes that make it unnecessary for the prosecution to establish which of two contradictory statements is false to obtain a conviction. See, for example, McKinney's N.Y. Penal Law § 210.20; West's Fla. Stat. Ann. § 837.021(3).

Subornation of Perjury

At common law subornation of perjury consisted of instigating or procuring another person to commit perjury. *State v. Chambers,* 104 S.E. 670 (N.C. 1920). Subornation of perjury is now generally defined by statutes much as it was at common law. To convict a defendant of the offense, the prosecution must first establish that the defendant induced another to testify falsely and that an actual perjury has been committed. *State v. Devers,* 272 A.2d 794 (Md. 1971), *cert. denied,* 404 U.S. 824, 92 S. Ct. 50, 30 L.Ed.2d 52 (1971). Thus, the Tennessee Supreme Court upheld a subornation of perjury conviction of an attorney for counseling

CASE IN POINT

PERJURY: THE TRUTH MUST BE UNEQUIVOCAL

A police officer was convicted of committing perjury on the basis of his denial of having received money from certain persons while in performance of his police duties. On appeal, he argued that his answer, "No sir. Not for my duties," to the prosecutor's question whether he received any money from any persons while on official duty as a Chicago policeman was literally true and therefore formed no basis for his conviction. The United States Court of Appeals, Seventh Circuit, rejected his contention. The court explained his initial response, "No sir," was directly responsive and false, so that his nonresponsive attempted hedge that followed was not effective.

United States v. Nickels, 502 F.2d 1173 (7th Cir. 1974), *cert. denied,* 426 U.S. 911, 96 S. Ct. 2237, 48 L.Ed.2d 837 (1976).

four men charged with illegally selling whiskey to commit perjury. The attorney was prosecuted, however, only after his four clients were convicted. *Grant v. State,* 374 S.W.2d 391 (Tenn. 1964).

Defenses to the Crime of Perjury

Truth, of course, is a complete defense to a charge of perjury; therefore, a defendant who while under oath gives an answer that is "literally accurate, technically responsive or legally truthful" cannot lawfully be convicted of perjury. *United States v. Wall,* 371 F.2d 398, 400 (6th Cir. 1967).

After making a false statement under oath, a witness sometimes recants and tells the truth. If this recantation occurs before the original tribunal where the testimony was given, some state courts hold it to be a defense. For example, New York courts have held that recantation is a defense, provided it occurs promptly, before the body conducting the inquiry (e.g., a grand jury) has been deceived or any prejudice has occurred, and before the defendant's perjury has most likely become known to the authorities. *People v. Ezaugi,* 141 N.E.2d 580 (N.Y. 1957). On the other hand, many courts take the position that a subsequent recantation, even on cross-examination, is no defense to a charge that a witness has made a perjurious statement. See, for example, *State v. Phillips,* 259 P.2d 185 (Kan. 1953).

Federal law provides for a recantation defense to a prosecution for perjury if the perjured testimony has not substantially affected the proceedings, or it has not become manifest that such falsity has been or will be exposed. 18 U.S.C.A. § 1623(d). To avail of the defense, a defendant must unequivocally repudiate his or her prior testimony. *United States v. Tobias,* 863 F.2d 685 (9th Cir. 1988).

OBSTRUCTION OF JUSTICE

At common law it was a crime to commit an act obstructing or tending to obstruct public justice. See *Baker v. State,* 178 S.E.2d 278 (Ga. App. 1970), *cert.*

denied, 401 U.S. 1012, 91 S. Ct. 1265, 28 L.Ed.2d 549 (1971). Likewise, the perversion of governmental administration was a common-law offense. *Commonwealth v. McKarski,* 222 A.2d 411 (Pa. Super. 1966).

Modern Statutory Development

Several federal statutes make it unlawful to obstruct federal officials in execution of writs and other court processes; to tamper with or retaliate against witnesses, informants, and victims; or to obstruct criminal investigations. Additional federal statutes proscribe interference with governmental proceedings, court orders, jurors, and court officers. See 18 U.S.C.A. §§ 1501–1515.

Postal laws make it an offense to willfully and knowingly obstruct or retard the passage of the mail. 18 U.S.C.A. § 1701. Thus, in *United States v. Upshaw,* 895 F.2d 109 (3d Cir. 1990), a federal appeals court upheld a defendant's conviction for obstructing mail where a postal truck driver took home a package after he signed out from work.

All jurisdictions have statutes proscribing interference with officers in the performance of their duties. Some statutes define obstruction to embrace many forms of conduct. Common examples include making it unlawful to give false information to an officer with the intent to interfere with the officer's lawful performance of duties; to impersonate an officer; to intimidate a victim or witness; and to tamper with a juror or with physical evidence to be offered in official proceedings. Many states have comprehensive statutes making it an offense to refuse to render assistance to law enforcement officers or to prevent, hinder, or delay the discovery or apprehension of persons sought by law enforcement.

The Citizen's Duty to Assist Law Enforcement Officers

Citizens have a duty to come to the assistance of law enforcement officers upon request. Rather typical of the statutory mandates in this area is the Ohio law that states:

> No person shall negligently fail or refuse to aid a law enforcement officer, when called upon for assistance in preventing or halting the commission of an offense, or in apprehending or detaining an offender, when such aid can be given without a substantial risk of physical harm to the person giving it. Ohio Rev. Code Ann. § 2921.23(a).

RESISTING ARREST

All jurisdictions make it unlawful for a person to resist arrest. The common law did not permit a person to resist a lawful arrest by an authorized officer of the law. It did, however, permit a person to use force to resist an unlawful arrest. *United States v. Heliczer,* 373 F.2d 241 (2d Cir. 1967), *cert. denied,* 388 U.S. 917, 87 S.Ct. 2133, 18 L.Ed.2d 1359 (1967). Until recently this rule of law was applied in most American jurisdictions, but the functioning of the rule in modern society brought about the need to change it. The legality of an arrest may frequently be a close question, and since officers will normally overcome resistance with necessary force, there is a great danger of escalating violence between the officer and the arrestee. Thus, courts have been reexamining this common-law doctrine and holding that there is no longer authority to use physical force to resist an arrest by a police officer, whether such arrest is legal or illegal. See *Miller v. State*, 462 P.2d 421 (Alaska 1969).

Legislatures, too, have reexamined the issue of using physical force in resisting arrest. In 1980, the New York legislature amended its penal law to provide:

> A person may not use physical force to resist an arrest, whether authorized or unauthorized, which is being effected or attempted by a police officer or peace officer when it would reasonably appear that the latter is a police officer or peace officer. McKinney's N.Y. Penal Law § 35.27.

Oregon law provides: "A person commits the crime of resisting arrest if the person intentionally resists a person known by the person to be a peace officer in making an arrest." Or. Rev. Stat. § 162.315(1). In *State v. Wright*, 799 P.2d 642 (Or. 1990), the Oregon Supreme Court held that a person may not lawfully resist arrest, even if the arresting officer lacked the legal authority to make the arrest, provided that the officer was acting under color of official authority. Additionally, the court observed that if a police officer uses excessive force in making an arrest, the arrestee may use only such physical force as is reasonably necessary to defend against such excessive force.

The modern statutory and judicial revisions to the common-law approach make sense. It is not too great a burden today for a person who believes himself or herself unlawfully arrested to submit to the officer and seek legal remedies in court. Unlike the conditions that existed when the common law developed the rule permitting an arrestee to use force, legal counsel is readily available today. Moreover, today's detention facilities do not resemble the crude dungeons where arrestees were incarcerated for lengthy periods prior to arraignment under the English common law. The abandonment of the common-law rule is another example of a rule of law ceasing to exist when the rationale for it has ceased to exist.

COMPOUNDING A CRIME

At common law a person who accepted money or something else of value in exchange for agreeing not to prosecute a felony was guilty of compounding a felony. *State v. Hodge*, 55 S.E. 626 (N.C. 1906). Likewise, the common law considered it a misdemeanor to compound a misdemeanor, if the misdemeanor was an offense against public justice and dangerous to society. *State v. Carver*, 39 A. 973 (N.H. 1898). To conceal a felony was also a common-law offense known as misprision of felony. This latter offense was justified by the person's common-law duty to inform authorities about any felony of which that person had knowledge. *Commonwealth v. Lopes*, 61 N.E.2d 849 (Mass. 1945).

The Modern Statutory Approach

The legal theory underlying making it an offense to compound a crime is that it debases justice to allow an offender to bargain to escape the consequences of his or her crime. Most states have enacted statutes making it a crime to compound a felony, but some have expanded the common-law rule by making it a crime to compound any offense. To illustrate, New Hampshire law provides that a person is guilty of a misdemeanor who:

> 1. Solicits, accepts, or agrees to accept any benefit as consideration for his refraining from initiating or aiding in a criminal prosecution; or
> 2. Confers, offers, or agrees to confer any benefit upon another as consideration for such person refraining from initiating or aiding in a criminal prosecution.
> 3. It is an affirmative defense that the value of the benefit did not exceed an amount which the actor believed to be due as restitution or indemnification for the loss caused, or to be caused by the offense. N.H. Rev. Stat. Ann. § 642:5.

Most states have not made misprision of felony a statutory crime, probably relying on enforcement of statutes making it an offense to become an accessory after the fact to an offense (see Chapter 4). The federal criminal code, however, specifically makes misprision of felony a crime, the gist of the offense being concealment and not merely the failure to report a felony. 18 U.S.C.A. § 4.

A Common Scenario of Compounding a Crime

The offense of compounding a crime often appears where a crime victim whose goods have been stolen agrees with the thief to take back the goods in exchange for not prosecuting. Such an action would ordinarily constitute an offense by the victim. But the New Hampshire statute makes it an affirmative defense that the value of the benefit did not exceed that which the actor believed due as restitution for a loss. In some instances courts will approve dismissal of a prosecution upon an agreement for restitution to the victim, but persons should not reach such an agreement without prior court approval.

ESCAPE

At common law a person who departed from lawful custody committed the crime of escape. Where the prisoner used force, the offense came to be known as prison break. Finally, a person who forcibly freed another from lawful custody was guilty of the offense of rescue. See *State v. Sutton,* 84 N.E. 824 (Ind. 1908).

Modern Statutory Approaches to Escape

Statutes proscribing escape are generally broad enough to embrace all three of the common-law offenses relating to escape. Often the punishment is more severe when force has been used. Federal statutes prohibit a person who has been lawfully arrested or confined from escaping or attempting to escape from custody, 18 U.S.C.A. § 751, or from rescuing or attempting to rescue a federal prisoner, 18 U.S.C.A. § 752. Most state statutes define escape in rather simple terms. For example, Texas law provides that a person commits the offense of escape "if he escapes from custody when he is: (1) under arrest for, charged with, or convicted of an offense; or (2) in custody pursuant to a lawful order of court." Vernon's Tex. Penal Code Ann. § 38.07.

The Elements of the Offense of Escape

The gist of the offense of escape is the prisoner's departure from lawful custody. Lawful custody is generally presumed once the prosecutor establishes that the escapee was confined to an institution specified by law. In other instances it may be essential for the prosecutor to establish proof of lawful custody; however, those who escape from a jail, juvenile detention home, penal institution, or reformatory are usually presumed to have been in lawful custody. Likewise, a person who fails to return to detention following a temporary release or furlough generally falls within the ambit of escape statutes.

Of course, if a statute requires specific intent, the prosecution must establish this before a conviction can be lawfully obtained. Absent an explicit statutory requirement, courts are divided on the issue of whether the prosecution must prove the defendant's specific intent to avoid lawful confinement. The Supreme Court has held that under the federal statute, the government need only prove that the escapee knew that his or her actions would result in leaving confinement without permission. *United States v. Bailey*, 444 U.S. 394, 100 S. Ct. 624, 62 L.Ed.2d 575 (1980).

State appellate courts have split on whether the prosecution must prove that the escapee intended to leave or be absent from lawful custody. Recognizing that a slim majority of jurisdictions hold that intent is not an element of the crime, a Florida appellate court in 1975 held that the state must prove that a defendant intended to leave or be absent from lawful custody, despite the lack of such a statutory requirement in Florida law. In justifying its position the court raised some interesting "horribles" under which a defendant charged with escape could be improperly convicted if the state were not required to establish the escapee's specific intent to avoid lawful confinement. In one scenario the court hypothesized that a road gang member had fallen asleep under a tree and was left behind by a negligent guard. The prisoner awakened only to find the guards and work detail had returned to the prison. Because of such possibilities the court opted for what it considered the better view of requiring the prosecution to establish the defendant's specific intent. *Helton v. State*, 311 So.2d 381 (Fla. App. 1975).

Defenses to the Charge of Escape

It occasionally occurs that an innocent person has been unlawfully confined. Nevertheless, if custody was lawful, the fact that a person was innocent is not generally recognized as a defense to a charge of escape. See *Woods v. Commonwealth*, 152 S.W.2d 997 (Ky. 1941). Of course, a person who escapes can always assert the defense of unlawful confinement or custody. *State v. Dickson*, 288 N.W.2d 48 (Neb. 1980).

In 1980 the United States Supreme Court recognized the defense of necessity as being valid in the context of the crime of escape. To sustain the defense, the Court said a prisoner must demonstrate (1) that because of an imminent threat of harm, escape was the prisoner's only reasonable alternative; and (2) that the prisoner made a bona fide effort to surrender or return to custody as soon as the duress or necessity lost its coercive force. *United States v. Bailey,* 444 U.S. 394, 100 S.Ct. 624, 62 L.Ed.2d 575 (1980).

Legislatures generally respond to public opinion, and improvement of prison conditions is not a high priority for most voters. Since courts tend to focus on issues where the legislative process affords no relief, they will undoubtedly continue to give attention to complaints concerning prison conditions. As they do, prisoners will most likely seek to extend the defense of necessity to justify an escape based on the inadequacy of prison conditions. Some have already argued that the denial of needed medical care should be recognized as a defense to escape. Until now courts have generally refused to accept such a defense. See, for example, *Commonwealth v. Stanley,* 446 A.2d 583 (Pa. 1982).

The guidelines established by the court in *Lovercamp* have been favorably received by other appellate courts. See, for example, *People v. Unger,* 338 N.E.2d 442 (Ill. App. 1975), *aff'd.,* 362 N.E.2d 319 (Ill. 1977); *State v. Alcantaro,* 407 So.2d 922 (Fla. App. 1981), *rev. denied,* 413 So.2d 875 (Fla. 1982).

CRIMINAL CONTEMPT

Early in the history of the common law, judges began to exercise the power to punish persons whose conduct interfered with the orderly functioning of the courts in the administration of justice. Federal and state courts exercise the power to hold an offender—sometimes called a "contemnor"—in either civil or criminal contempt.

Civil contempt is beyond the scope of this text. Suffice it to say it is a sanction imposed to coerce a recalcitrant person to obey a court order. For example, a court may hold someone in civil contempt for failing to pay court-ordered support for dependents.

The power of the federal courts to hold persons in criminal contempt is recognized by statute. 21 U.S.C.A. § 401. However, even in the absence of statutory recognition, the courts are deemed to have broad inherent powers to hold persons in contempt. See, for example, *Martin v. Waters,* 259 S.E.2d 153 (Ga. App. 1979); *United States v. Wendy,* 575 F.2d 1025 (2d Cir. 1978).

The Purpose of Imposing Criminal Contempt

A court imposes criminal contempt to punish an offender whose deliberate conduct is calculated to obstruct or embarrass the court or to degrade a judicial officer in the role of administering justice. Intent is always an element in criminal contempt proceedings.

CASE IN POINT

ESCAPE: A LIMITED DEFENSE OF DURESS OR NECESSITY

During the 1970s there was considerable focus on the conditions of our prisons. This is illustrated by a landmark California decision in 1974. Defendant Marsha Lovercamp was attacked by other inmates demanding sex. Prison authorities failed to provide Lovercamp with adequate protection and she escaped. She was found guilty of escape, but an appellate court awarded her a new trial because the trial judge had denied her the opportunity to submit evidence of her plight as a justification for her escape. In reversing Lovercamp's conviction, the appellate court enumerated guidelines for asserting the defense of duress or necessity in these situations. The court opined that a limited defense is available if the following conditions exist:

(1) The prisoner is faced with a specific threat of death, forcible sexual attack or substantial bodily injury in the immediate future;
(2) There is no time for a complaint to the authorities or there exists a history of futile complaints which make any result from such complaints illusory;
(3) There is no time or opportunity to resort to the courts;
(4) There is no evidence of force or violence used toward prison personnel or other "innocent" persons in the escape; and
(5) The prisoner immediately reports to the proper authorities when he has attained a position of safety from the immediate threat.

People v. Lovercamp, 118 Cal. Rptr. 110 (Cal. App. 1974).

Criminal contempt is classified as either direct or indirect. Direct contempt is contemptuous behavior committed in the presence of the court. Disruption of the examination of a witness or an assault on a judge or juror are examples of direct contempt. Indirect contempt, sometimes called constructive contempt, occurs outside the court's presence. An illustration of indirect contempt would be a juror discussing the facts of a case with a news reporter at a lunch break before the trial of a case has been completed.

Is Criminal Contempt a Crime?

Until the 1960s there was considerable division of thinking on this subject. In 1968 the United States Supreme Court in *Bloom v. Illinois,* 391 U.S. 194, 88 S. Ct. 1477, 20 L.Ed.2d 522 (1968), held that criminal contempt is a crime in the ordinary sense and may be punished by fine, imprisonment, or both. A person charged with criminal contempt is presumed innocent and must be afforded the procedural and substantive benefits of due process of law. Consequently, a contemnor must be proven guilty beyond a reasonable doubt before being held in criminal contempt. In some states, criminal contempt has been made a statutory crime. See, for example, McKinney's N.Y. Penal Law § 215.50–51.

Direct and Indirect Criminal Contempt

Direct criminal contempt proceedings are usually handled summarily. The judge must inform the contemnor of the accusation and ask if he or she can show any cause to preclude the court from entering a judgment of contempt. The court then proceeds to enter its judgment accordingly. Courts justify the summary character of these proceedings because the contemptuous act has occurred in the presence of the judge.

The process is more formal in indirect contempt proceedings. The judge is required to issue a written order to the contemnor to show cause as to why he or she should not be held in contempt of court. The order must set forth the essential facts of the charge and allow the contemnor a reasonable time to prepare a defense. The judge tries all issues of law and fact, but the contemnor has the right to counsel, to compulsory process to secure witnesses, and to refuse to testify.

United States Supreme Court decisions have established basic due process rights that must be accorded contemnors in these proceedings. Of course, if there are statutes or court rules in a particular jurisdiction that prescribe the method of processing criminal contempt, the judge must not deviate from those rules to the prejudice of the contemnor's rights. In any contempt proceeding, if the contemnor is to be sentenced to a term of imprisonment for more than six months, he or she is entitled to a jury trial. *Baldwin v. New York,* 399 U.S. 66, 90 S. Ct. 1886, 26 L.Ed.2d 437 (1970).

Legislative Contempt

Legislative bodies also have the power to punish by contempt those persons whose deliberate acts impede legislative activities. Some states have enacted statutes to cover specific instances of criminal contempt in respect to legislative functions. New York, for example, makes it criminal contempt of the legislature for a person who has been subpoenaed to refuse to attend, be sworn, answer proper questions, or produce proper evidence. McKinney's N.Y. Penal Law § 215.60.

CASE IN POINT

DIRECT CRIMINAL CONTEMPT

Defendant William Carr was convicted of armed robbery and sentenced to serve from four to eight years in prison. When the judge pronounced the sentence, Carr proceeded to punch the prosecutor in the nose. The trial judge found Carr in direct criminal contempt of court and sentenced him to serve an additional six months in prison. In addition to appealing his conviction, Carr also contested his sentence for contempt. In rejecting his challenge, the Appellate Court of Illinois observed, "[i]t would be frivolous to argue that to punch an assistant state attorney in open court was not direct contempt."

People v. Carr, 278 N.E.2d 839 (Ill. App. 1971).

CASE IN POINT

LEGISLATIVE CONTEMPT

An outstanding example of a legislative body acting on its own to hold a person in contempt was the highly publicized and emotionally charged case involving James E. Groppi, a former priest. In September 1969, Father Groppi attracted national attention when he led a group of protesters who allegedly seized a Wisconsin legislative chamber. Groppi was arrested, held in contempt, and sentenced to jail by the Wisconsin legislature. The resolution holding him in contempt was adopted by the legislature without first giving Groppi any notice or an opportunity to respond by way of a defense or to present any matters in extenuation or mitigation. For these reasons, the United States Supreme Court reversed his conviction.

Groppi v. Leslie, 404 U.S. 496, 92 S. Ct. 582, 30 L.Ed.2d 632 (1972).

Courts have been zealous in assuring that legislative bodies afford contemnors due process of law before adjudging them to be in contempt. See, for example, *Watkins v. United States,* 354 U.S. 178, 77 S. Ct. 1173, 1 L.Ed.2d 1273 (1957). In practice, the Congress and state legislative bodies frequently make citations for contempt and then turn the matter over to the courts to handle.

CONCLUSION

The fair and impartial administration of justice and the orderly processes of democratic government depend on the honesty and integrity of those who occupy positions of authority. Hence, the basic common-law offenses described in this chapter have endured over the centuries. The offense of bribery seeks to avoid corruption of those in positions of trust, while the crime of perjury seeks to maintain the integrity of the judicial system and agencies of government.

To safeguard the security and effectiveness of law enforcement personnel, all jurisdictions make it a crime to resist arrest, even if the arrest is later declared to be unlawful. Since society must assure confinement of those it has chosen to incarcerate, it is essential to maintain the offense of escape. However, with increased awareness of inhumane prison conditions and the rights of prisoners, courts have recognized necessity as a defense to a charge of escape. The abandonment of the common-law principle that allowed a person to forcibly resist an unlawful arrest, and the recognition of the necessity defense in the law of escape, both demonstrate the dynamic nature of the criminal law in response to societal change.

Finally, to maintain the effectiveness and the dignity of the judicial and legislative processes, courts and legislatures must have the authority to hold persons in contempt, although that authority must be exercised with due regard for the constitutional rights of contemnors.

QUESTIONS FOR THOUGHT AND DISCUSSION

1. Why have contemporary legislative bodies expanded the scope of bribery and extended it to cover classes of persons beyond public officials?
2. How does the requirement that the prosecution prove a defendant's specific intent to deceive protect citizens from unwarranted prosecutions for perjury?
3. Contrast the common-law rule allowing a person to resist an unlawful arrest with the modern trend of requiring citizens to submit to unlawful arrests by police officers. Which approach makes more sense in modern society?
4. Is a state statute that makes it a criminal offense "to hinder or delay a law enforcement officer in the performance of his or her duties" likely to be held void for vagueness under the tests outlined in Chapter 3?
5. Would a person who accepts the return of stolen goods from a thief without agreeing to refrain from filing a criminal complaint be guilty of compounding a crime?
6. Despite the wording of most statutes proscribing the offense of escape, courts increasingly require the prosecution to prove the defendant's specific intent to avoid lawful confinement. Are courts justified in imposing such a requirement on the statutory law?
7. Have courts aided society by allowing escapees from prison to defend their actions on the basis of intolerable prison conditions? Are such conditions likely to be remedied by the legislative process?
8. Can you describe some specific acts that a trial judge could justifiably consider to be direct contempts of court?
9. Why does the law require more formal proceedings in cases of indirect contempt than in cases of direct criminal contempt?

CASES

STATE V. GUSTAFSON

Court of Appeals of Minnesota, 1986.
396 N.W.2d 583.

[The appellant, Gustafson, was convicted of bribery and conspiracy to commit perjury.]

FOLEY, Judge.

. . . On October 2, 1984 appellant was on a motorcycle talking to someone in a parked car. After ignoring several requests by a police officer to move the motorcycle, which was obstructing traffic, appellant was given a citation. Appellant was placed in the rear of the squad car after failing to have identification and giving a false name; he was patted down pursuant to police department rules. The police officer felt a hard object inside appellant's leather jacket and pulled out a beeper. Two plastic bags were also seized from the jacket; one containing a white powdery substance, the other containing folded pieces of paper. Money totalling $1,330 was also taken from appellant. The bags were later tested and found to contain cocaine. Appellant was charged with possession of cocaine and was released from jail. Upon his release, he picked up a vest and gloves, part of the property taken the night of the arrest. The leather coat, beeper and money were held for evidence. Appellant never claimed that the leather coat or gloves were not his.

Appellant's cocaine possession trial was scheduled for March 12, 1985. In mid-February 1985, appellant called an acquaintance, Andrew Beggs, and offered to give him a car worth $200 to $300 if Beggs would tell appellant's lawyer, Joe Kaminsky, that Beggs owned the leather jacket. Appellant told Beggs that his brother had done something similar and had gotten away with it.

Appellant later told Beggs that if he [Gustafson] were convicted he would go to jail. Appellant explained the circumstances surrounding his arrest and told Beggs to say that he had won the cocaine in a pool game. Appellant then drove Beggs to a street in North Minneapolis to show him the car he had promised, gave Beggs the keys and assured him that he would provide title to the vehicle "in time." Appellant further told Beggs that since Beggs had a clean record the most he would get was probation.

A few days later appellant drove Beggs to Kaminsky's office where Beggs told Kaminsky the jacket and cocaine were his. When Kaminsky asked Beggs where the jacket was, he responded that he had it for the past two weeks. Kaminsky then informed Beggs that the police still had the jacket.

Appellant told Beggs that another witness was needed to corroborate the story since Beggs had mistakenly claimed possession of the jacket. Appellant then asked Brian Guyant to claim that he had observed Beggs give appellant the jacket. Guyant agreed and met with Beggs to make their stories consistent. A few days later, Beggs met with appellant, appellant's girlfriend and appellant's mother to discuss the story again. Beggs took notes at the meeting.

Beggs and Guyant went to Kaminsky's office on March 11, 1985. Minneapolis Police Officer Wayne Brademan and Hennepin County Attorney's Office Investigator Paul Stanton were also present at the meeting. Beggs was asked to identify the jacket but had difficulty locating the pocket in which the cocaine was found. Stanton testified that Beggs seemed nervous and confused. Beggs testified that Brademan and Stanton laughed when he could not find the inside pocket and he suspected that they did not believe his story that he had loaned appellant the jacket when appellant was about to test drive a motorcycle he had planned to purchase. Beggs was arrested. A search of his pockets produced a marijuana cigarette and two sheets of paper containing notes relating to the story he had just told.

After Beggs was in jail for three hours, he called Stanton and the next day said that he had lied about the cocaine and ownership of the jacket. Beggs explained that appellant had asked him to take the rap and gave a statement. The investigators then decided to set up a taped conversation between

Beggs and appellant to determine who actually owned the cocaine. Beggs was released from jail and a "body bug" was placed on his back. Beggs was also given a phony complaint which stated that he was charged with possession of cocaine and possession of cocaine with intent to sell.

Beggs met appellant at a North Minneapolis home owned by Beggs' brother. Stanton and another police officer were in the basement during this meeting. In the tape recording, appellant makes numerous incriminating statements.

During the conversation, appellant referred to the cocaine as "my stash." He did not disagree when Beggs referred to their fabricated story nor did he disagree when Beggs said that Kaminsky knew he was lying. Appellant did show concern over the crib sheets found in Beggs' pocket, however, and reassured Beggs that at most he would serve 30 days in the workhouse. Appellant disagreed with the description of the seized cocaine in the phony complaint being in a baggie and said it was in a zip lock bag and also said that he had "two white papers" and "three rocks." When Beggs asked for title to the car, appellant said that he forgot it. Subsequently, appellant's brother and Guyant brought the title card to Beggs who then turned it over to the investigators.

On April 18, 1985 a complaint was filed charging appellant with one count of conspiracy to commit perjury and one count of bribery. Both complaints (cocaine possession and conspiracy to commit perjury/bribery) were set for trial and were severed at appellant's request. At the first trial for cocaine possession, appellant did not testify. He was eventually acquitted.

At the second trial, appellant testified in his own defense, claiming that Beggs gave him the jacket and gloves to wear and denying ownership of the cocaine found in the jacket. Appellant stated that he did not tell anyone earlier that the jacket and cocaine belonged to Beggs because he was not a "snitch." He further testified that he sold the car to Beggs for $100 and that Beggs still owed him $50. Appellant was convicted of bribery and conspiracy to commit perjury and this appeal followed. . . .

We . . . conclude that the evidence was sufficient for the jury to convict appellant of bribery and conspiracy to commit perjury. Beggs' testimony was amply corroborated by evidence that appellant gave Beggs a car, by the crib notes found on Beggs at his arrest and by appellant's statements during the taped conversation. . . .

United States v. Scott

United States Court of Appeals, Eighth Circuit, 1982.
682 F.2d 695.

[This case deals with perjury by contradictory statements. The appellant, Teresa Ann Scott, was convicted in the U.S. District Court for the Western District of Missouri of three counts of making inconsistent material declarations while under oath.]

MCMILLAN, Circuit Judge.

. . . On July 20, 1980, FBI Agent Robert Callahan went to Scott's residence to question her about the November 1979 robbery of the Blue Valley Federal Savings & Loan (Blue Valley) and the January 1980 robbery of the Rockhill Federal Savings Loan (Rockhill). Scott was not at home so Callahan left a message for her to contact him. The following Monday, July 14, Scott voluntarily went to the FBI office located in Kansas City, Missouri, and met with Agents Callahan and Parnell Miles. Callahan told Scott that he had a government witness who was going to testify in such a way as to implicate Scott in numerous crimes if she did not cooperate in the FBI's investigation of the robberies. Scott agreed and examined three bank surveillance photographs taken during the two robberies. Scott identified Bobby McNeal, her present boyfriend, and George Brown, a former boyfriend, as the individuals in the Blue Valley photograph and McNeal and Olie

Ealom, her half-brother, as the individuals in the Rockhill photographs.

At some point Scott made statements implicating herself as an accessory to the robberies. An understanding was reached whereby Scott would not be indicted in exchange for her cooperation with the government. On December 30, 1980, Scott was deposed in connection with the government's case against McNeal for the Blue Valley robbery. She was shown the same bank surveillance photographs, exhibits C, D, and E, and again identified the individuals in exhibit C, the Blue Valley robbery, as Brown and McNeal and the individuals in exhibit E, the Rockhill robbery, as Ealom and McNeal. The face of the person identified as McNeal was not identifiable in the photographs. However, Scott stated that the striped coat worn by that person during both robberies belonged to her and that she had lent it to McNeal on the morning of the Blue Valley robbery. In addition, exhibit D was a front shot of that person and showed that he was made up to appear as a woman during the Blue Valley robbery. Scott stated that she had applied McNeal's makeup on the morning of the Blue Valley robbery.

On January 20, 1981, Scott was called to testify at McNeal's trial. On direct examination she was again shown exhibits C, D, and E. However, she testified that she could not identify the striped coat worn by one of the individuals in exhibit C, that she could not identify the individual in exhibit D whom she had previously identified as McNeal, and that she could not identify the individuals in exhibit E whom she had previously identified as McNeal and Ealom. The jury found McNeal not guilty and shortly thereafter the government dismissed its case against McNeal and Ealom for the Rockhill robbery.

The government subsequently charged Scott with three counts of making irreconcilably contradictory declarations under oath in violation of 18 U.S.C. § 1623. At her trial Scott testified that her deposition testimony was false and that she had recanted at McNeal's trial. Scott also testified that the reason she lied during the deposition was Callahan's threat that she could be sent to prison and lose custody of her children if she did not cooperate with the investigation. Scott further testified that before she made the July 20, 1980, statement to Callahan he had told her that he already knew the identities of the individuals in the bank surveillance photographs and also knew that the striped coat belonged to Scott. On cross-examination Scott admitted that she had visited McNeal at the Wyandotte County Jail on January 14, 1981, signed the deposition on January 15, and visited McNeal again on January 16. The jury found Scott guilty on all three counts.

On appeal Scott first argues that her prosecution was barred by the "recant" provision of 18 U.S.C. § 1623(d) which provides:

> Where, in the same continuous court or grand jury proceeding in which a declaration is made, the person making the declaration admits such declaration to be false, such admission shall bar prosecution under this section if, at the time the admission is made the declaration has not substantially affected the proceeding, or it has not become manifest that such falsity has been or will be exposed.

Alternatively, Scott argues that, in light of this section, there was insufficient evidence to support her conviction. We reject these arguments.

Scott did not raise the recantation argument by pretrial motion. Rather, she attempted to convince the jury that her deposition testimony was false and that she had recanted at McNeal's trial. The recantation section of the statute was included in the jury instructions and referred to in her counsel's closing argument. Because Scott chose to submit the issue to the jury the question before us is whether there is substantial evidence, taking the view most favorable to the government to support the verdict. See *Glasser v. United States,* 315 U.S. 60, 80, 62 S.Ct., 457, 469, 86 L.Ed. 680 (1942). Viewed in this light, the evidence shows that the government agreed not to indict Scott as an accomplice in the robberies in exchange for her testimony at McNeal's trial, that her deposition testimony was consistent with earlier statements made to the FBI and finally, that she was romantically involved with McNeal and visited him the day before and after signing the deposition. The jury could reasonably have found from the evidence that Scott was truthful in the deposition and lied at McNeal's trial.

Scott next argues that neither the indictment nor the jury instruction defining the elements of the offense included all the essential elements of the offense. Specifically, Scott asserts that the ancillary nature of her deposition had to be alleged in the indictment and that the instruction should have required the jury to make a finding that the deposition was an ancillary proceeding. There is no merit to this argument.

Title 18 U.S.C. § 1623 applies to inconsistent declarations made "in any proceeding before or ancillary to any court or grand jury of the United States." The term "ancillary" proceedings has been construed to include depositions and exclude "statements given in less formal contexts than depositions." *Dunn v. United States,* 442 U.S. 100, 111, 99S.Ct. 2190, 2196, 60 L.Ed.2d 743 (1979). Therefore, the terms "deposition" and "ancillary proceeding" are synonymous under the statute and requiring the indictment to specifically allege the ancillary nature of the deposition or requiring the jury to find that a deposition is an ancillary proceeding would be redundant. . . .

The judgment of the district court is affirmed.

PEOPLE V. GETTINGS

Appellate Court of Illinois, Third District, 1983.
116 Ill.App. 3d 657, 72 Ill. Dec. 419, 452 N.E.2d 672.

[The defendant, Jimmy L. Gettings, challenges his conviction and sentence on three counts of perjury which followed his jury trial in the circuit court of Tazewell County, Illinois.]

BARRY, Justice:

. . . This cause had its origin in defendant's failure to pay sheriff's fees for two small claims actions. The State's Attorney of Tazewell County brought suits to recover amounts of $50 and $38, respectively, plus costs, and judgments were obtained against defendant. Thereafter, the State's Attorney filed a Citation to Discover Assets, and on July 24, 1980, at the hearing pursuant to the Citation, defendant stated that he did not own any real estate, that he did not own any vehicles, and that no one owed him any money.

He was later indicted on four counts of perjury, and was tried on the first three counts. The indictment alleged that defendant committed the offense of perjury by stating under oath in a civil proceeding a false statement which he did not believe to be true in that he stated (count I) that he did not own any real estate, (count II) that he did not own a vehicle, and (count III) that no one owed him any money. Defendant was tried before a jury and found guilty on all three counts, but upon appeal, his convictions were set aside and the cause remanded for a new trial because of certain remarks by a witness and by the prosecutor which this court found to be inflammatory and prejudicial. . . .

After introducing evidence establishing that at the July 24, 1980, hearing on the Citation to Discover Assets, defendant had denied ownership of real property, had denied ownership of any vehicles, and had stated that no one owed him any money, the State presented additional evidence showing that on July 24, 1980, defendant had title to 1.5 acres of land in Peoria County, that he had title to a 1971 Ford pickup truck, and that he had written a letter on July 22 notifying a customer that he had filed liens against the customer's property and that he would be charged 1½ per cent interest per month until the $122.25 judgment and costs were paid.

Defendant presented no evidence in his own behalf although he exercised his peremptory jury challenges, cross-examined several witnesses, and made a competent closing argument to the jury. The jury returned verdicts of guilty on all three counts, and after receiving updated presentencing reports, the trial court sentenced defendant to 90 days in jail with credit for time served, a fine of $2,000, and 30 months probation with no credit for time previously served while the appeal was pending. Defendant has again appealed from his conviction and sentence.

Defendant first contends that the indictment was insufficient as a matter of law to state an offense because it did not contain an allegation that defendant had knowledge of the falsity of the statements at the time they were made. . . .

We conclude that the indictment in the case before us was sufficient to state the offense of perjury.

Next, defendant contends that the trial court erred in failing to instruct the jury that an essential element of the crime of perjury is defendant's knowledge of the falsity of the statements he made. Without objection from defendant, the court gave IPI Crim. No. 22.01, which states:

> "A person commits the offense of perjury when he, under oath or affirmation, makes a false statement and at the time he makes the statement he believes it is not true."

Thus, the court instructed the jury as to the elements of the crime as defined by the statute, and such instruction is not error. . . .

Defendant also contends that the state's evidence did not prove him guilty beyond a reasonable doubt because the questions which were the basis for the charge asked for conclusions or belief and because the State did not establish that defendant had knowledge of the falsity of his answers. The questions to which defendant answered "no" were: "Do you own any real estate?" "Do you own any vehicles?" "Does anyone owe you any money?"

We cannot say that these questions asked for conclusions or mere opinion; they were straight forward, factual questions. Considering the evidence establishing that defendant did at that time own real estate and a truck, and that he was actively trying to collect a judgment owed to him, the jury could quite properly infer that defendant believed his answers to be false at the time he gave them. We hold, therefore, that defendant was proved guilty beyond a reasonable doubt. . . .

Accordingly, we affirm the judgment of conviction and the sentence imposed by the circuit court of Tazewell County.

Affirmed.

STOUDER, P. J., and ALLOY, J., concur.

STATE V. RING

Supreme Court of Maine, 1978.
387 A.2d 241.

[This case involves the offense of attempted escape.]

PER CURIAM.

Appellants Donald Ring and Ricky Waugh bring this appeal from judgments entered following a jury trial in the Knox County Superior Court. Appellants were tried jointly for attempted escape . . . from the Maine State Prison.

Appellants assert two issues on appeal. They . . . challenge the sufficiency of the evidence to demonstrate that there were the overt acts or intent necessary to constitute the offense of attempted escape. . . .

We deny the appeal.

The record shows that on July 28, 1976, the date of the alleged attempted escape, both appellants were incarcerated in the Maine State Prison where they were serving sentences imposed for prior crimes. They had no official permission to be absent on that day. A prison guard testified at trial that he had seen appellants walking together in the prison yard around 1:00 P.M. One appellant was observed carrying an unconcealed "rope" and a hammer.

When it later appeared that neither appellant had showed up for the 4:00 P.M. cell count, a search of the prison was undertaken. Eventually both appellants were discovered in the "steam cage," a dark, enclosed unused portion of the prison. Subsequent searches revealed the presence of the "rope" and hammer hidden in crevices in the room.

Appellant Ring chose to testify on his own behalf. He basically contended that he and some other inmates had been drinking "homebrew" and had decided to hide in the steam cage so that their intoxication would not be discovered. While this story was corroborated by another inmate, the bag out of which appellants had been drinking was never discovered. Appellant Waugh decided not to testify.

Appellants first contend that the evidence was insufficient to prove that they intended to escape.

They further claim that the evidence demonstrated, at most, mere preparation for an escape, not the requisite overt act.

We disagree.

As appellants contend, intent to "leave[s] official custody" or to "fail[s] to return to official custody following temporary leave" must be proven in order to establish a violation.... Moreover, appellants are correct when they argue that in proving an "attempt," the State must prove more than mere preparation; it must prove "a positive action ... directed towards the execution of the crime." ...

Our task in assessing the sufficiency of the evidence on these two points, however, is not to retry the case or to substitute our impressions of the facts for those of the jurors. Our function is merely to ascertain if the jury was warranted in finding for the State.... A witness' credibility is a jury matter....

The jury here was justified in rejecting the testimony that appellants were in the "steam cage" solely to avoid detection of their intoxication. The fact of being hidden and the fact of their possession of "rope" and a hammer would have demonstrated to the jury that appellants had an intent to escape and that they had taken actions "directed toward the execution of the crime." This was a justified finding despite the fact that the actual escape might have been difficult to execute under the facts presented in this case....

The entry must be:

Appeal denied.

Judgments affirmed.

DELAHANTY, J., did not sit.

STATE V. BLANTON

Superior Court of New Jersey, Appellate Division, 1979.
166 N.J. Super. 62, 398 A.2d 1328.

[This case involves the offenses of assault and battery upon a police officer, "atrocious assault and battery," and resisting arrest.]

CONFORD, P. J. A. D., Retired (temporarily assigned).

These are consolidated appeals by defendant Elijah Blanton, Sr. ("Elijah") and his son, John Blanton ("John"). Elijah was convicted of assault and battery upon a police officer and John of atrocious assault and battery and resisting arrest. The events giving rise to the charges resulting in these convictions occurred in the course of a disturbance on May 28, 1976 at a playground near a low-income housing project in Long Branch.

The police were originally dispatched to the playground after Elijah's wife called to report an argument between another of her sons and a third person she thought to be in possession of a gun. No gun was found. However, Elijah was carrying on in a loud manner, yelling at and chasing children and arguing with the purported possessor of the gun. There was other testimony that Elijah was simply trying to restore peace to the area. The police soon withdrew from the scene.

Within a short time the police returned to the scene on the order of a superior officer to arrest Elijah if he was found to be causing trouble. The return of the police developed into a melee either witnessed or participated in by a large number of people, mostly juveniles. According to the State's evidence, Officers Wettermark and Brown accosted Elijah and informed him he was under arrest. He pulled away from them, and sticks and other objects were thrown at the officers, Officer Wettermark being struck by some of them. Officer Brown embraced Elijah in a full nelson and in return was bitten by Elijah on his arm. This action was the basis of the charge against Elijah of assault and battery against a police officer.

The charges against John arose out of the attempt of Officer DeFillipo to go to the aid of the officers seeking to arrest Elijah. DeFillipo testified that as he approached the officers and Elijah he noticed an individual wearing an orange tee shirt to his right at a distance of between six and ten feet and immediately thereafter sustained a blow to the top of his head. The man in the orange shirt was John. DeFillipo at once turned around and confronted John, the latter looking directly at him, about three feet away. John had a stick or pipe in his hand of a cylindrical shape and about 2 ½ feet long. There were no other people in the immediate area. John turned and ran toward his apartment with DeFillipo and Officer Richards in pursuit, the former yelling, "I want him. He hit me." John ran into one door and out another, whereupon he was tackled by one of the officers. There was testimony that John was resisting the officers' efforts to subdue him, "moving his arms about" and attempting to arise from the ground. DeFillipo was bleeding profusely from his scalp. There was other testimony that prior to the assault on Officer DeFillipo John had run into Officer May and had struck him on the arm with a stick and then continued running. However, he was acquitted of a separate charge of assault on Officer May.

John's testimonial version of the events was that he was in the playground practicing for a state championship relay meet to be held the next day and that he was in possession of a relay baton about 12 inches long. When the police came upon the scene they began spraying mace. John saw his father surrounded by police officers and others and asked the officers to let his father alone. One of the officers angrily reached for his gun and John ran away in fear, alleging, before an objection by the State was sustained, that he recalled a former local incident involving the shooting of a juvenile by police. He did not strike anyone but remembered bumping into someone while running away. No one told him he was under arrest at any time. He was assaulted by the police after he emerged from his home. . . .

Defendant [John Blanton] argues that the trial judge's instructions to the jury with respect to the charge of resisting arrest were defective because they permitted the jury to conclude that John's flight from the pursuing officers constituted guilt of the offense of resisting arrest. The specific portion of the charge to the jury objected to consisted of the instruction that among the elements of the crime required to be proven by the State was one that defendant "did know that he was under arrest or that the officer was attempting to arrest him and . . . that with that knowledge the defendant John Blanton intentionally sought to avoid or frustrate that arrest."

Our examination of the relevant authorities satisfies us that there was no error in the charge even if the jurors could understand therefrom that flight from a police officer with knowledge by the fugitive that the officer was attempting to arrest him and with the purpose of avoiding or frustrating that arrest, constituted guilt of the common-law offense of resisting arrest.

Resisting arrest is an integral part of the common-law crime of "obstruction of or resistance to a public officer in the performance of his duties." . . . [T]he use of actual force is not always necessary to constitute the offense so long as there is some overt act of obstruction. . . . In many jurisdictions this crime has been codified, and the statutes have generally been construed as permitting a determination of guilt without a finding of the use of force or violence against the officer. . . . The California cases hold that flight from an officer seeking to arrest is sufficient to constitute evidence of a violation of a statute punishing a person who willfully resists, delays or obstructs a public officer in the discharge of any duty of his office. . . .

In formulating § 2C:29–2 of The New Jersey Penal Code . . . the New Jersey Criminal Law Revision Commission stated: "We reject the MPC [Model Penal Code] view that mere nonsubmission should not be an offense, believing an affirmative policy of submission to be appropriate as now seems to be our law." . . . The cited section of the Code, both as proposed and adopted, provides for guilt of resisting arrest if the person "purposely prevents a law enforcement officer from effecting a lawful arrest." Such offenses are divided into two categories, one being a crime of the fourth degree and the other a disorderly persons offense. Guilt of the former arises if the person uses or threatens to use physical force or violence against the officer or another, or uses any other means to create a substantial risk of causing physical injury to the officer or another. It thus appears that while mere flight from an intending arresting officer may, depending upon other circumstances, be regarded under the new statute as only a disorderly persons offense, the general offense of resisting arrest may be found to have been committed short of use of force or risk of causing injury so long as the accused has purposely sought to prevent the police officer from effecting an arrest. Our view of the common law . . . is, accordingly, that flight knowingly intended to prevent a police officer from effecting an arrest of the fugitive constitutes guilt of the common-law crime of resisting arrest.

The circumstances given in evidence clearly permitted the jury to find that John knew the police were seeking to arrest him. Office DeFillipo testified that while pursuing John he yelled out, "I want him. He hit me." John admitted, in effect, that he was seeking to elude the police, although his explanation of his flight was consistent with innocence of the crime of assault. Nevertheless, knowing that a uniformed police officer was seeking to apprehend him, it was his duty to submit and not resist. . . .

We consequently find no error in the trial judge's instructions to the jury in the respect complained of. . . .

CHAPTER 13

Criminal Responsibility and Defenses

CHAPTER OUTLINE

Cases

Introduction

As the English common law developed, the concept of criminal responsibility became a significant consideration. As it did, various defenses to criminal conduct emerged. Incapacity to commit a crime because of infancy or insanity and, under some circumstances, as a result of intoxication, came to be recognized as defenses. Self-defense, defense of others, and defense of habitation and other property were also recognized as defenses. Moreover, the common law allowed a defendant to assert ignorance or mistake of fact that occurred honestly as an excuse for having committed a criminal act. Alibi, necessity, duress, and—under limited circumstances—consent were recognized as defenses.

Essentially these defenses have been recognized in the various jurisdictions in the United States, although they have been modified over the years. The Fifth Amendment to the United States Constitution and corresponding provisions of the state constitutions furnish defendants two additional defenses: immunity and double jeopardy. Legislatures initiated the concept of a statute of limitations on the prosecution of most crimes, and through judicial development, entrapment has become a recognized defense where improper governmental conduct has induced an otherwise innocent person to commit a crime.

In previous chapters, we have mentioned some defenses applicable to specific substantive crimes. We revisit some of those defenses in this chapter, further examining the scope of common-law, constitutional, and statutory defenses to criminal charges.

Defenses in General

For purposes of analysis and study, defenses to crimes may be conveniently divided into six categories: (1) those asserting lack of capacity (infancy, intoxication, insanity, automatism); (2) those justifying use of force (self-defense, defense of others, defense of property and habitation, and defense of using force to resist an arrest); (3) those alleging a mistake of fact or of law; (4) those assailing governmental conduct (entrapment, selective prosecution); (5) those relying on constitutional or statutory rights (immunity, double jeopardy, statutes of limitation); and (6) those claiming alibi, duress, necessity, and consent.

Defendants who plead not guilty to a criminal charge may not only rely on their general denial, they may offer any defense (sometimes called a negative defense) not required to be specifically pled. A defendant merely has the burden of raising some evidence of a negative defense; however, in some instances the prosecution's own evidence may raise the issue. Once such evidence is produced, the prosecution has the burden to overcome it. For example, Henry Homeowner is charged with manslaughter of a person who forced entry into his home one night after Homeowner had gone to bed. Homeowner claims to have acted in self-defense by using deadly force to defend his homeplace. If any evidence discloses that he acted in self-defense, then to establish that Homeowner is guilty of manslaughter, the prosecution must prove that he did not act reasonably.

A defense that must be specifically pled is classified as an affirmative defense, that is, one that does not negate any element of the crime, but rather consists of new matters relied upon as an excuse or justification for the defendant's otherwise illegal conduct. To illustrate, Larry Boatman is charged with burglary of a vacant beach cottage. He pleads not guilty, raising the affirmative defense of necessity. He argues that while he entered the cottage with the intent to take food from within, it was an act of necessity because he and his starving companions were shipwrecked in a desolate area without other means of obtaining food or drinking water. Ordinarily, a defendant has the burden to prove the matters offered as an affirmative defense. Therefore, it is up to Boatman to prove by the preponderance (greater weight) of the evidence that he acted out of necessity.

The prosecution is always required to prove the defendant guilty beyond any reasonable doubt. Nevertheless, a state may constitutionally place the burden on a defendant to establish an affirmative defense as long as that defense is not one that negates any element of the crime the prosecution must prove to convict the defendant. *Patterson v. New York,* 432 U.S. 197, 97 S.Ct. 2319, 53 L.Ed.2d 281 (1977). Defenses authorized by statute are sometimes styled as affirmative defenses, but merely labeling a defense an affirmative defense is not sufficient. Courts must look to the substance to make certain an affirmative defense is one that excuses or justifies conduct that would otherwise lead to criminal responsibility, and not one that negates any element of the crime.

DEFENSES ASSERTING LACK OF CAPACITY TO COMMIT A CRIME

There are four defenses asserting the lack of capacity to commit a crime: infancy, intoxication, insanity and automatism.

Infancy

The common law regarded a child under age 7 as incapable of forming criminal intent. This gave rise to a conclusive presumption of incapacity for a child under age 7. This presumption of incapacity was rebuttable regarding a child over 7 but under 14, with the prosecution having the burden to demonstrate that a child under 14 was capable of comprehending the wrongdoing involved in commission of an offense. Children over age 14 were treated as adults. *Commonwealth v. Cavalier,* 131 A. 229 (Pa. 1925).

The rationale for these common-law presumptions was that young children require protection from the harshness of the adversary processes of the law. Some jurisdictions have abolished these presumptions because legislatures have provided that children under certain ages, usually 16 to 18, are subject to the jurisdiction of the juvenile courts, where the procedures are tailored toward less mature offenders. In establishing juvenile courts, the legislatures frequently intend to eliminate the common-law presumption of incapacity of infants. See *People v. Miller,* 334 N.E.2d 421 (Ill. App. 1975), for the court's perception of legislative intent under Illinois law. Under federal law, a juvenile is a person who has not attained age 18 at the time of the commission of an offense, 18 U.S.C.A. § 5031.

Starting with Illinois in 1899, all states developed juvenile court systems. These courts traditionally handled juvenile offenders separately from adults in nonadversarial proceedings. The theory was that the state acted as *parens patriae,* taking a clinical and rehabilitative, rather than an adversarial or punitive, approach to youthful offenders. Nevertheless, the system suffered from many deficiencies such as inadequate staffing and substandard facilities, and the results were disappointing. Many youthful offenders were not rehabilitated, nor were they afforded even the most basic constitutional rights accorded adults in the criminal justice system. In the words of the United States Supreme Court, "the child receives the worst of both worlds: that he gets neither the protections accorded to adults nor the solicitous care and regenerative treatment postulated for children." *Kent v. United States,* 383 U.S. 541, 556, 86 S. Ct. 1045, 1054, 16 L. Ed. 2d 84, 94 (1966).

Intoxication

Intoxication may result from ingestion of alcohol or drugs. The common law did not excuse a person who voluntarily became intoxicated from responsibility for criminal conduct. *State v. Yarborough,* 18 P. 474 (Kan. 1888). In an early English case, the court approved a death sentence for a homicide committed by an extremely intoxicated defendant. *Reniger v. Fogossa,* 75 Eng. Rep. 1 (1550).

In considering intoxication today, we must first distinguish voluntary from involuntary intoxication. In most jurisdictions, voluntary intoxication may be considered in determining whether a defendant can formulate the *specific* intent required to be established in such crimes as larceny, burglary, and premeditated murder. See, for example, *State v. Brooks,* 436 P.2d 91 (Mont. 1967). A few courts will not even permit a jury to consider voluntary intoxication on the issue of specific intent. See, for example, *State v. Hegwood,* 558 S.W.2d 378 (Mo. App. 1977). All courts have rejected the defense of voluntary intoxication to charges in general-intent crimes. See, for example, *United States v. Hanson,* 618 F.2d 1261 (8th Cir. 1980), *cert. denied,* 449 U.S. 854, 101 S. Ct. 148, 66 L.Ed.2d 67 (1980) (assault on a federal officer); *Commonwealth v. Bridge,* 435 A.2d 151 (Pa. 1981) (voluntary manslaughter); *State v. Keaten,* 390 A.2d 1043 (Me. 1978) (gross sexual misconduct). These decisions are grounded on public policy concerns of not excusing conduct by those who voluntarily impair their own judgment.

Involuntary intoxication rarely occurs, but when it does, it relieves the criminality of an act committed under its influence if, as a result of intoxication, the defendant no longer knows right from wrong. *State v. Mriglot,* 564 P.2d 784 (Wash. 1977). A person may become involuntarily intoxicated by fraudulent contrivance or through trickery or fraud of another person. See, for example, *Johnson v. Commonwealth,* 115 S.E. 673 (Va. 1923), or through inadvertent ingestion of medicine. See *People v. Carlo,* 361 N.Y.S.2d 168 (N.Y. App. Div. 1974). The New Hampshire Supreme Court summarized the law in this area when it declared:

> Generally the defense of involuntary intoxication will only be considered when it is shown that the intoxication was the product of external pressures such as fraud,

force, or coercion, or when intoxication resulted from a medical prescription. *State v. Plummer,* 374 A.2d 431, 435 (N.H. 1977).

Intoxication as a defense to criminal liability has been codified in some jurisdictions. Section 939.42 of the Wisconsin Statutes summarizes the general law in stating:

> An intoxicated or a drugged condition of the actor is a defense only if such condition:
> (1) Is involuntarily produced and renders the actor incapable of distinguishing between right and wrong in regard to the alleged criminal act at the time the act is committed; or
> (2) Negatives the existence of a state of mind essential to the crime *except as provided in* § 939.24(3). Wis. Stat. Ann. § 939.42.

The Wisconsin legislature inserted the italicized exception in 1987 to assure that a voluntarily produced intoxicated or drugged condition is not a defense to liability for criminal recklessness.

Wisconsin courts have said that to establish the defense of *involuntary* intoxication, the accused must show the inability to tell right from wrong at time of the offense; to establish *voluntary* intoxication, the defendant must show that the defendant's condition negated the existence of the state of mind necessary to commit the crime. *State v. Repp,* 342 N.W.2d 771 (Wis. App. 1983), *aff'd.* 362 N.W.2d 415 (Wis. 1985).

Insanity

All persons are presumed sane unless previously adjudicated insane. Even a person who has been adjudicated legally insane may still be found guilty of a criminal act if it was committed during a lucid interval. Insanity is a legal concept and is defined differently in various jurisdictions in the United States. A person who meets the requirements of the definition as of the time of commission of an offense may rely upon the defense of insanity as an excuse for a crime. Trial will be either continued or canceled for a defendant whose mental condition renders him or her incapable of understanding the nature of the charges, the range of potential penalties, and the nature of the adversary process. In this section we address insanity at the time of commission of an offense and describe the background of the insanity defense, current standards for asserting the defense, and some contemporary developments in this area.

Few cases have caused as great a concern over the functioning of the criminal justice system as the verdict of "not guilty by reason of insanity" in the federal court trial of John Hinckley for the 1981 shooting of President Ronald Reagan, his press secretary, and two law officers. The defense of insanity has never been popular with the public. It has sometimes been called "a rich man's defense," because defendants who invoke it frequently expend considerable financial resources to present psychiatric testimony. The Hinckley verdict motivated Congress and several state legislatures to review the status of insanity defenses.

The concept of mental responsibility has its historic roots in Anglo-American law, for as pointed out in Chapter 4 the common-law crimes included a mental element, the *mens rea*. Nevertheless, the common law was slow to develop any standard for a mental condition that would excuse a person from criminal responsibility. By the eighteenth century some English courts applied what has sometimes been called a "wild beast" test. For example, one English judge opined that

> a man . . . totally deprived of his understanding and memory, . . . and doth not know what he is doing, no more than an infant, than a brute, or a wild beast . . . is never the object of punishment. *Rex v. Arnold,* 16 Howell's State Trials 695 (Eng. 1724).

The M'Naghten Rule. Little progress occurred in the development of the defense of insanity until 1843, when an event in England caused even greater consternation than the American reaction to the Hinckley verdict. Suffering from delusions that he was being persecuted by government officials, Daniel M'Naghten decided to kill Sir Robert Peel, the British Home Secretary. (Peel was the founder of the British Police System, hence the term *bobbies* is still applied to British law officers.) From outside Peel's home, M'Naghten saw Peel's secretary, Edward Drummond, leave the house. Believing Drummond to be Peel, M'Naghten shot and killed him.

At trial, M'Naghten's barristers argued that he was insane at the time of the shooting and therefore should be found not guilty. The jury agreed. Enraged by the verdict, Queen Victoria insisted that the law provide a yardstick for the defense of insanity. The House of Lords responded, and the test they developed is still referred to as the *M'Naghten rule.* It provides that

> it must be clearly proved that, at the time of committing the act, the party accused was labouring under such a defect of reason, from disease of the mind, as not to know the nature and quality of the act he was doing; or, if he did know it, that he did not know what he was doing was wrong. *M'Naghten's Case,* 8 Eng. Rep. 718 (1843).

The *M'Naghten* rule became the test for insanity used in both federal and state courts in the United States. As psychology and psychiatry developed new theories of mental capacity, critics attacked the *M'Naghten* rule as being based solely on cognition (i.e., a process of the intellect) and ignoring a person's emotions. In response, some courts accepted the "irresistible impulse" test that stressed volition (i.e., self-control) as a supplement to the *M'Naghten* rule. See *Parsons v. State,* 2 So. 854 (Ala. 1887). This allowed a person who knew an act was wrong but who acted under an uncontrollable desire or the duress of mental disease to be excused from a criminal act.

The Durham Test. Another test for insanity evolved from *Durham v. United States,* where the United States Court of Appeals for the District of Columbia held that an accused is not criminally responsible if that person's unlawful act was "the product of mental disease or defect." 214 F.2d 862, 876 (D.C. Cir. 1954). The *Durham* standard was applauded by many psychiatrists, but it gained little judicial support outside of the District of Columbia. It was eventually discarded even there. *United States v. Brawner,* 471 F.2d 969 (D.C. Cir. 1972).

The ALI Standard. In 1962, the American Law Institute (ALI), an association of distinguished lawyers and judges, proposed a new standard combining both cognitive and volitional capacities as a test for insanity. It is sometimes referred to as the *substantial capacity* test and says:

> A person is not responsible for criminal conduct if at the time of such conduct, as a result of mental disease or defect, a person lacks substantial capacity either to appreciate the wrongfulness of his conduct or to conform his conduct to the requirements of the law.

The ALI test was adopted by most federal courts and has sometimes been referred to as the *Freeman* rule, stemming from an endorsement of the test by the United States Court of Appeals for the Second Circuit in *United States v. Freeman,* 357 F.2d 606 (2d Cir. 1966). It was this substantial capacity concept that was applied in the Hinckley case.

State courts, however, divided in their approaches to the defense of insanity. Many opted to follow the new ALI test; the remainder adhered to the basic *M'Naghten* "right from wrong" test. Under the ALI criteria a showing of substantial impairment of a person's mental faculties is enough to meet the test of insanity. In contrast, to establish insanity under a strict *M'Naghten* approach, there must be a showing of total incapacity, and evidence that does not tend to prove or disprove the defendant's ability to distinguish right from wrong is irrelevant.

New Federal Standard. Dissatisfied with the ALI test, Congress decided to eliminate the volitional prong in the federal test for insanity and to revert substantially to the *M'Naghten* rule when it enacted the Insanity Defense Reform Act of 1984. This act provides that in federal courts:

> It is an affirmative defense to a prosecution under any Federal statute that, at the time of the commission of the acts constituting the offense, the defendant, as a result of a severe mental disease or defect, was unable to appreciate the nature and quality or the wrongfulness of his acts. Mental disease or defect does not otherwise constitute a defense. 18 U.S.C.A. § 17(a).

Additionally, the act stipulates "The defendant has the burden of proving the defense of insanity by clear and convincing evidence." 18 U.S.C.A. § 17(b). The *clear and convincing* standard is higher than the usual civil evidentiary standard of *preponderance of the evidence* but somewhat lower than the standard of *beyond a reasonable doubt,* which is the evidentiary standard required for criminal convictions. While there has been some controversy concerning the legitimacy of placing the burden of proof of insanity on the defendant, the United States Supreme Court has held that this type of "burden shifting" does not violate the defendant's right of due process of law under the federal Constitution. *Patterson v. New York,* 432 U.S. 197, 97 S. Ct. 2319, 53 L.Ed.2d 281 (1977). Moreover, two federal appellate court decisions in 1986 affirmed the constitutionality of this "burden shifting" under the 1984 federal act. *United States v. Freeman,* 804 F.2d 1574 (11th Cir. 1986); *United States v. Amos,* 803 F.2d 419 (8th Cir. 1986).

Effect of the Insanity Defense Reform Act on Use of Psychiatric Evidence to Negate Specific Intent

Under the Insanity Defense Reform Act, psychiatric evidence of impaired volitional control is inadmissible to support an insanity defense. After passage of the new law, a question arose as to whether Congress also intended to prohibit the use of psychiatric evidence to negate a defendant's specific intent to commit an offense. In 1990, the United States Court of Appeals for the Eleventh Circuit addressed the issue observing that "[b]oth Congress and the courts have recognized the crucial distinction between evidence of psychological impairment that supports an 'affirmative defense,' and psychological evidence that negates an element of the offense charged." The court ruled that the language of the new federal act does not bar the use of psychiatric evidence to negate specific intent where that level of intent is an element of the offense charged by the government. *United States v. Cameron,* 907 F.2d 1051, 1063 (11th Cir. 1990).

Contemporary State Developments. Although Congress has now placed the burden to prove their defense on defendants who plead insanity in federal courts, state courts are divided on who bears the burden of proof. In some states where insanity is classified as an affirmative defense, the defendant bears the burden of proof of insanity, usually by a "preponderance of the evidence." See, for example, *Clark v. State,* 588 P.2d 1027 (Nev. 1979). In other states, when a defendant pleads insanity and introduces some evidence of insanity, the state must then establish the defendant's sanity, usually by proof "beyond a reasonable doubt," the standard required for establishing a defendant's guilt. See, for example, *Parkin v. State,* 238 So.2d 817 (Fla. 1970). When the issue of insanity is raised, courts permit laypersons as well as expert witnesses to testify on the issue of the defendant's insanity.

Unlike a defendant who is simply found not guilty, a defendant who is found not guilty by reason of insanity is exposed to institutionalization and may, in some circumstances, be committed to a mental institution. *Jones v. United States,* 463 U.S. 354, 103 S. Ct. 3043, 77 L.Ed.2d 694 (1983). This is generally accomplished subsequent to the verdict by the trial judge, who determines whether protection of the public requires that the defendant be confined.

Guilty, but . . . . On the premise that a person should not be found not guilty on basis of insanity, some states have recently resorted to verdicts of "guilty but mentally ill" in cases where the defendant's insanity has been established. For example, in *People v. Sorna,* the court explained that this category of verdict deals with situations "where a defendant's mental illness does not deprive him of substantial capacity sufficient to satisfy the insanity test but does warrant treatment in addition to incarceration." 276 N.W.2d 892, 896 (Mich. App. 1979).

Automatism

Older cases treat defendants who claim that their unlawful acts were committed because of an involuntary condition such as somnambulism (i.e., sleepwalking) within the context of the insanity defense. Newer cases tend to classify such involuntary actions as automatism and view them as a basis for an affirmative defense independent from insanity. See, for example, *Fulcher v. State,* 633 P.2d 142 (Wyo. 1981). One reason cited in *Fulcher* for regarding automatism as a separate defense is that there are generally no follow-up consequences such as institutionalization, which usually occurs in an acquittal by reason of insanity.

CASE IN POINT

INSANITY DEFENSE

Joy Ann Robey was charged with involuntary manslaughter and child abuse in connection with the death of her 10-month-old daughter, Christina. At trial, Robey admitted to beating the child severely and repeatedly over a two-month period but pleaded not guilty by reason of insanity. The trial court found that the defendant was temporarily insane each time she beat the child, but that she returned to sanity thereafter. Accordingly, the defendant could not be held criminally liable for the beatings but was responsible for her failure to seek medical care for her child. Robey was convicted of involuntary manslaughter and child abuse and sentenced to three concurrent ten-year terms in prison. Her conviction was upheld on appeal over her contention that the trial court erred in holding her criminally responsible after acknowledging that she was insane at the time of the beatings.

Robey v. State, 456 A.2d 953 (Md. App. 1983).

DEFENSES JUSTIFYING THE USE OF FORCE

The use of force may be a defense to a criminal charge that the defendant caused injury or death to another. Therefore, the defense of justifiable use of force may be applicable to the assaultive and homicidal offenses.

As a starting point, the use of "deadly force" (i.e., force likely to cause death or serious bodily injury) must be distinguished from the use of "nondeadly force." In general, the use of deadly force in self-defense requires that the person using such force: (1) be in a place where he or she has a right to be; (2) act without fault; and (3) act in reasonable fear or apprehension of death or great bodily harm. *Lilly v. State,* 506 N.E.2d 23 (Ind. 1987). In evaluating whether the use of deadly force is reasonable, courts consider numerous factors. Among these are the respective size, age, and physical abilities of the parties, whether the attacker is armed, and the attacker's reputation for violence. Ordinarily, a person may use whatever nondeadly force that appears reasonably necessary under the circumstances. *State v. Clay,* 256 S.E.2d 176 (N.C. 1979).

Self-Defense

Defendants frequently admit the commission of acts that constitute an assaultive or homicidal offense, but assert having acted in self-defense. Once a defendant raises the issue of self-defense, it becomes incumbent on the prosecution to prove beyond a reasonable doubt that the defendant did not act in self-defense. *Wash v. State,* 456 N.E.2d 1009 (Ind. 1983). There exist variations in the law on the permitted degree of force that can be used in self-defense, but the test of reasonableness appears common to all views. In determining the lawfulness of force used in self-defense, courts first look to see if the force used by the aggressor was unlawful. If so, the defender must show there was a necessity to use force for self-protection and that the degree of force used by the defender was reasonable considering the parties and circumstances.

At common law a person attacked had a duty "to retreat to the wall" before using deadly force in self-defense. *State v. Sipes,* 209 N.W. 458 (Iowa 1926). In *Scott v. State,* 34 So. 2d 718 (Miss. 1948), the court explained that to justify the slaying of another in self-defense at common law there must have been *actual* danger of loss of life or suffering of great bodily harm, but that the American approach has been that the danger *need not be actual but must be reasonably apparent and imminent.*

A majority of courts reject the common-law doctrine of requiring a person to retreat to the greatest extent possible before meeting force with force. Rather, they say that a person attacked or threatened may stand his or her ground and use any force reasonably necessary to prevent harm. Courts that take this view often state it in positive terms, as did the Oklahoma Court of Criminal Appeals when citing one of its 1912 precedents. It said: "The law in Oklahoma is clear: There is no duty to retreat if one is threatened with bodily harm." *Neal v. State,* 597 P.2d 334, 337 (Okl. Crim. App. 1979).

A substantial minority of courts, however, have adopted the principle that a person who can safely retreat must do so before using deadly force. As the Tennessee Supreme Court has stated:

> The law of excusable homicide requires that the defendant must have employed all means reasonably in his power, consistent with his own safety, to avoid danger and avert the necessity of taking another's life. This requirement includes the duty to retreat if, and, to the extent, that it can be done in safety. *State v. Kennamore,* 604 S.W.2d 856, 860 (Tenn. 1980).

Courts that follow the "retreat" rule have generally adopted the principle that a person does not have to retreat in his or her own dwelling. *State v. Bennett,* 105 N.W. 324 (Iowa 1905).

The Wisconsin Statutes codify the general law on use of force in self-defense by providing:

> A person is privileged to threaten or intentionally use force against another for the purpose of preventing or terminating what he reasonably believes to be an unlawful interference with his person by such other person. The actor may intentionally use only such force or threat thereof as he reasonably believes is necessary to prevent or terminate the interference. He may not intentionally use force which is intended or likely to cause death or great bodily harm unless he reasonably believes that such force is necessary to prevent imminent death or great bodily harm to himself. Wis. Stat. Ann. § 939.48(1).

The use of deadly force presents the greatest issue in self-defense. As noted earlier, deadly force may be used only where it reasonably appears necessary to use such force to prevent death or serious injury. In considering whether a defendant is justified in using deadly force, the law has traditionally applied an *objective* test. See, for example, *State v. Bess,* 247 A.2d 669 (N.J. 1968). Today, however, there is a conflict in the law and some courts apply a *subjective* standard of reasonableness to determine if circumstances are sufficient to induce in the defendant an honest and reasonable belief that force must be used. See, for example, *State v. Wanrow,* 559 P.2d 548 (Wash. 1977). The objective test requires the jury to place itself in the shoes of a hypothetical "reasonable and prudent person," whereas the subjective test permits a jury "to place itself in the defendant's own shoes."

Much of the impetus for courts applying the subjective test to determine whether the use of deadly force is reasonable has resulted from cases where women charged with committing assaultive or homicidal offenses against men have defended their use of force. In the leading case just cited (*State v. Wanrow*), Yvonne Wanrow, a woman on crutches, was convicted of second-degree murder and first-degree assault in her fatal shooting of a large, intoxicated man who refused to leave her home. In reversing her convictions, the Washington Supreme Court held that the trial judge erred by giving instructions to the jury that did not make it clear that Ms. Wanrow's actions were to be judged against her own *subjective* impressions and not those which the jury might determine to be objectively reasonable. The Court added:

> In our society women suffer from a conspicuous lack of access to training in and the means of developing those skills necessary to effectively repel a male assailant without resorting to the use of deadly weapons.

The Battered Woman Syndrome (BWS); the Battered Child Syndrome (BCS): Expanding the Concept of Self-Defense

Beyond the subjective standard of self-defense, in recent years the concept of self-defense by women has been expanded where a woman claims to have been continually battered by a man. The "battered spouse syndrome" soon became the "battered woman syndrome" (BWS). It describes a pattern of psychological and behavioral symptoms of women living with males in a battering relationship. Some jurisdictions now permit a female in that situation who is charged with assaulting or killing a man to show that even though she did not face immediate harm, her plea of self-defense should be recognized because her actions were her response to constant battering by the man with whom she lived.

Relatively little decisional law from the higher courts has developed in this area; however, in 1989 a California appellate court held that when a woman kills her batterer and pleads self-defense, expert testimony about BWS is admissible to explain how her particular experiences as a battered woman affected her perceptions of danger and her honest belief in its imminence. *People v. Aris,* 264 Cal. Rptr. 167 (Cal. App. 1989).

Following the same rationale, if there is evidence that a child has been abused continually over an extended period, there is a movement now to assert the "battered child syndrome" (BCS) in defense of a child accused of assaulting or killing a parent. Texas law now allows such evidence, including expert testimony, in cases involving children who kill their parents. Vernon's Tex. Pen. Code Ann. § 19.03. Many prosecutors claim the use of BCS is undermining the law of self-defense, yet there are experts who claim that a child's perceptions of the need to use force are shaped by his or her experience of constant abuse by a parent. They argue that when juries hear such evidence they may be persuaded that a child acted in self-defense and not out of retribution.

In the state of Washington, a boy who killed his stepfather was convicted of second-degree murder and two counts of second-degree assault. At his trial, the court held that evidence of the battered child syndrome could not, as a matter of law, support a finding of self-defense because there was no "imminent threat" to the defendant. In a much-discussed opinion the appellate court held this was error. "Neither law nor logic suggest any reason to limit to women recognition of the impact a battering relationship may have on the victim's actions or perceptions. . . . the rationale underlying the admissibility of testimony regarding the battered women syndrome is at least as compelling, if not more so, when applied to children." *State v. Janes,* 822 P.2d 1238, 1243 (Wash. App. 1992).

Defense of Others

At common law a defender had the right to use reasonable force to prevent commission of a felony or to protect members of the household who were endangered, a principle that was codified in many jurisdictions. See, for example, *State v. Fair,* 211 A.2d 359 (N.J. 1965). The trend in American jurisdictions is to allow a person "to stand in the shoes of the victim" and to use such reasonable force as is necessary to defend anyone, irrespective of relationship, from harm. As the court noted in *State v. Grier,* "What one may do for himself, he may do for another." 609 S.W.2d 201, 203 (Mo. App. 1980). Today a number of states have statutes that permit a person to assert force on behalf of another. To illustrate, the Wisconsin Statute provides:

> A person is privileged to defend a third person from real or apparent unlawful interference by another under the same conditions and by the same means as those under and by which he is privileged to defend himself from real or apparent unlawful interference, provided that he reasonably believes that the facts are such that the third person would be privileged to act in self-defense and that his intervention is necessary for the protection of the third person. Wis. Stat. Ann. § 939.48(4).

Like the quoted Wisconsin statute, many statutes limit a person's right to defend another individual from harm to those persons who "reasonably believe" that force is necessary to protect another. Some courts take a more restrictive view and hold that an intervenor is justified in using force to defend another only if the party being defended would have been justified in using the same force in self-defense. Of course, under either standard, the right to go to the defense of another does not authorize a person to resort to retaliatory force.

Defense of Property

The right to defend your property is more limited than the right to defend your homeplace or yourself. The common law allowed a person in lawful possession of property to use reasonable, but not deadly, force to protect it. *Russell v. State,* 122 So. 683 (Ala. 1929). Today, the use of force to protect a person's property is often defined by statute. Typically, Iowa law provides that "[a] person is justified in the use of reasonable force to prevent or terminate criminal interference with his or her possession or other right to property." Iowa Code Ann. § 704.4. The quoted statutory language generally represents contemporary decisional law even in absence of a statute.

Some older court decisions hold that a person may oppose force with force, even to the extent of taking a life in defense of his or her person, family, or property against a person attempting to commit a violent felony such as murder, robbery, or rape. These decisions, however, focus on preventing a dangerous felony rather than simply on the protection or recapture of property. The prevailing view of the courts is that, in the absence of the felonious use of force by an aggressor, a person must not inflict deadly harm simply for the protection or recapture of property. *State v. McCombs,* 253 S.E.2d 906 (N.C. 1979). The reason for this is that the law places higher value on preserving the life of the wrongdoer than on protection of someone's property.

One method of defending property has been through the use of a mechanical device commonly known as a "spring gun" that is set to go off when someone trips a wire or opens a door. In the earlier history of the country these devices were used on farms, in unoccupied structures, and sometimes set in a residence at night to wound or kill an intruder. Some early court decisions said that use of a spring gun that resulted in the death of an intruder into a person's home was justified in instances where a homeowner, if present, would have been authorized to use deadly force.

Today, if someone is killed or injured as a result of a spring gun or similar mechanical device, the party who set it (and anyone who caused it to be set) generally will be held criminally responsible for any resulting death or injury. This is true even if the intruder's conduct would ordinarily cause a party to believe that the intrusion threatened death or serious bodily injury, conditions that might justify the use of deadly force. The Model Penal Code takes the position that a device for protection of property may be used only if it "is not designed to cause or known to create a substantial risk of causing death or serious bodily harm." M.P.C. § 3.06(5).

Even courts in jurisdictions that have not adopted the MPC take a harsh view of the use of such mechanical devices, reasoning that to allow persons to

CASE IN POINT

THE LAW OF SELF-DEFENSE

Defendant Ernest Young was distributing religious literature on the street when he was approached by George Coleman, who began to harass and swear at him. Later Coleman again accosted Young, this time at a table in a fast-food restaurant. Coleman began swearing at Young and grabbed his arm. Young pulled out a handgun and shot Coleman three times, killing him. Young was charged with and tried for murder. Notwithstanding his plea of self-defense, the jury returned a verdict of guilty of voluntary manslaughter. The appellate court reviewing the conviction said: "The jury heard appellant's story and it determined that he acted in the heat of the moment rather than in self-defense. There is ample evidence to support its verdict." The defendant's conviction was affirmed.

Young v. State, 451 N.E.2d 91 (Ind. App. 1983).

use them can imperil the lives of innocent persons such as firefighters, police officers, and even children at play. Finally, some courts point to another reason: While a deadly mechanical device acts without mercy or discretion, yet there is always the possibility that a human being protecting property would avoid taking a human life or injuring someone. See *People v. Ceballos*, 526 P.2d 241 (Cal. 1974).

Defense of Habitation

The common law placed great emphasis on the security of a person's dwelling and permitted the use of deadly force against an intruder. *Russell v. State*, 122 So. 683 (Ala. 1929). This historical view was chronicled by the Illinois Supreme Court in *People v. Eatman*, when it observed:

> As a matter of history the defense of habitation has been the most favored branch of self-defense from the earliest times. Lord Coke, in his Commentaries, says: "A man's home is his castle—for where shall a man be safe if it be not in his house?" 91 N.E.2d 387, 390 (Ill. 1950).

Referring to a person's defense of habitation, the *Eatman* court opined that "he may use all of the force apparently necessary to repel any invasion of his home." 91 N.E. 2d at 390. This is sometimes referred to as the "castle doctrine." While a householder may, under some circumstances, be justified in using deadly force, the householder would not be justified in taking a life to repel a mere trespass.

In *State v. McCombs, supra*, the North Carolina Supreme Court said that the use of deadly force is generally justified to prevent a forcible entry into the habitation by such circumstances as threats or where the occupant reasonably apprehends death or great bodily harm to self or other occupant or reasonably believes the assailant intends to commit a felony. This general principle is subject to some statutory and decisional variations.

The courts have generally applied the castle doctrine against trespassers, but they have divided on whether this doctrine applies to co-occupants or others legally on the premises. Older cases hold that a person need not retreat when assailed by a co-occupant—see, for example, *People v. Tomlins*, 107 N.E. 496 (N.Y. 1914)—but many newer decisions hold that when an assailant and the victim are both legal occupants of the same home, the castle doctrine does not apply. For example, in *State v. Bobbitt*, 415 So.2d 724 (Fla. 1982), the Florida Supreme Court refused to apply the doctrine where both spouses were legally occupying the same home.

Defense to Being Arrested

At common law a person had the right to use such force as reasonably necessary, short of killing, to resist an unlawful arrest. *Regina v. Tooley*, 92 Eng. Rep. 349 (1710). The common-law rule developed at a time when bail was largely unavailable, arraignments were delayed for months until a royal judge arrived,

CASE IN POINT

DEFENSE OF HABITATION

Defendant Raines was charged with murder in connection with the death of Ricky Stinson. Stinson was the passenger in a car driven by James Neese. The evidence showed that Neese had threatened to kill Raines, and that Neese had driven past Raines's trailer and fired some shots out the window of his car. Raines was not home at the time, but when he returned his live-in companion, Sharon Quates, told him what had happened. A few minutes later they heard a car approaching and went outside. Quates identified the car as the same one from which the shots had been fired. As the car drove away, Raines fired five shots from a semiautomatic rifle. Quates testified that Raines said that "he'd just shoot the tire out and stop it and we'd go get the law and find out who it was." However, one of the bullets struck Ricky Stinson in the head, killing him. Despite his plea that he acted in self-defense and defense of his habitation, Raines was convicted of manslaughter.

The conviction was upheld on appeal, the appellate court saying that "although Raines may well have been in fear of danger when the . . . car approached, such fear alone did not justify his firing at the car as it drove down the public road past his trailer." The court further observed: "One assaulted in his house need not flee therefrom. But his house is his castle only for the purposes of defense. It cannot be turned into an arsenal for the purpose of offensive effort against the lives of others."

Raines v. State, 455 So.2d 967, 972–3 (Ala. Crim. App. 1984).

and conditions in English jails were deplorable. Until recently most American courts have followed the English view. See, for example, *State v. Small,* 169 N.W. 116 (Iowa 1918). In some states a person may still forcibly resist an unlawful arrest.

As pointed out in Chapter 12, the rationale for the rule has substantially eroded. Increasingly, legislatures and courts recognize that resisting an arrest exposes both the officer and the arrestee to escalating violence. Moreover, defendants are now promptly arraigned, and counsel is generally available to debate the legality of an arrest in court. See *United States v. Ferrone,* 438 F.2d 381 (3d Cir. 1971), *cert. denied,* 402 U.S. 1008, 91 S. Ct. 2188, 29 L.Ed.2d 430 (1971); *State v. Ramsdell,* 285 A.2d 399 (R.I. 1971).

Use of Force by Police

Most states have statutes or police regulations that specify the degree of force that may be used to apprehend violators. Officers are usually permitted to use such force as is reasonably necessary to effect an arrest. In practice, deadly force is seldom used by modern police forces; yet many states have statutes that authorize the use of deadly force by police in apprehending felons.

In 1974 a Memphis, Tennessee, police officer shot and killed an unarmed 15-year-old-boy who fled from the scene of a reported burglary. The officer acted pursuant to a state law that permitted use of deadly force in such an instance. Civil litigation ensued and, in 1985, the United States Supreme Court ruled that the use of deadly force to apprehend a suspect is a seizure governed by the Fourth Amendment requirement of reasonableness. The Court held unconstitutional the statute that permitted an officer to use all necessary means to effect an arrest if the suspect flees or forcibly resists. The decision effectively limits an officer's use of deadly force to instances where it is necessary to prevent the escape of an arrestee who, the officer has probable cause to believe, poses a significant threat of death or serious injury to the officer or others. *Tennessee v. Garner*, 471 U.S. 1, 105 S. Ct. 1694, 85 L.Ed.2d 1 (1985).

A law enforcement officer who injures or kills a person or damages someone's property is sometimes charged with a criminal offense. An officer who kills or injures while in line of duty may assert the defense of having performed a public function. As long as the officer acted reasonably and not in violation of the Fourth Amendment, a statute or valid police regulations, the defense is established.

DEFENSES BASED ON MISTAKE

There are two defenses based on a defendant's mistake: mistake of law and mistake of fact.

Mistake of Law

One of the best-known maxims of the law is that "ignorance of the law is no excuse." It is obvious that the safety and welfare of society demand that persons not be excused from commission of criminal acts on the basis of their claims of not knowing that they committed crimes. See, for example, *Hoover v. State*, 59 Ala. 57 (1877). While this is the generally accepted view, in some instances a defendant's honest, but mistaken, view of the law may be accepted as a defense. One example is where such a mistake negates the specific-intent element of a crime. Thus, a mistake of law may be asserted as a defense in a larceny case where there is a technical question of who has legal title to an asset. *State v. Abbey*, 474 P.2d 62 (Ariz. App. 1970). Likewise, a defendant's good-faith, but mistaken, trust in the validity of a divorce has been held to be a defense to a charge of bigamy. *Long v. State*, 65 A.2d 489 (Del. 1949).

The Illinois Criminal Code lists four exceptions to the general rule that a person's ignorance of the law does not excuse unlawful conduct: It provides:

> A person's reasonable belief that certain conduct does not constitute a criminal offense is a defense if:
>
> (1) The offense is defined by an administrative regulation which is not known to him and has not been published or otherwise made reasonably available to him, and he could not have acquired such knowledge by the exercise of due diligence pursuant to facts known to him; or
>
> (2) He acts in reliance upon a statute which later is determined to be invalid; or
>
> (3) He acts in reliance upon an order or opinion of an Illinois Appellate or Supreme Court, or a United States appellate court later overruled or reversed; or

CASE IN POINT

WHEN A PENALTY IS IMPOSED FOR FAILURE TO ACT, REASONABLE NOTICE OF A LOCAL ORDINANCE MAY BE REQUIRED

A Los Angeles, California, ordinance made it unlawful for any "convicted persons" to remain in the city for more than five days without registering with the police; or if they lived outside of the city, to enter the city on five or more occasions during a thirty-day period without registering. Virginia Lambert, a convicted felon, was found guilty of failing to register, fined $250, and placed on probation for three years.

On appeal to the United States Supreme Court, Lambert's conviction was reversed. Writing for the Court, Justice Douglas observed: "Enshrined in our concept of due process is the requirement of notice. Notice is sometimes essential so that the citizen has the chance to defend charges. . . . Notice is required in a myriad of situations where a penalty or forfeiture might be suffered from mere failure to act."

Lambert v. California, 355 U.S. 225, 78 S.Ct 240, 2 L.Ed.2d 228 (1957).

(4) He acts in reliance upon an official interpretation of the statute, regulation or order defining the offense, made by a public officer or agency legally authorized to interpret such statute. Smith-Hurd Ann. 720 ILCS 5/4-8(b).

Citing the preceding exceptions, the Illinois Supreme Court held that a taxpayer who contended that she reasonably believed that she would be subject only to civil penalties, not to criminal sanctions, for failure to file an occupational tax return, did not present a "mistake of law" defense. *People v. Sevilla*, 547 N.E.2d 117 (Ill. 1989).

In *United States v. Moore*, 627 F.2d 830 (7th Cir. 1980), *cert. denied*, 450 U.S. 916, 101 S. Ct. 1360, 67 L.Ed.2d 342 (1981), the court said, "[T]he mistake of law defense is extremely limited and the mistake must be objectively reasonable." 627 F.2d at 833. Furthermore, courts have long made it clear that a dishonest pretense of ignorance of the law will never be recognized by a court as a defense. *State v. Carroll*, 60 S.W. 1087 (Mo. 1901).

A defendant may always raise the unconstitutionality of a statute as a defense to a prosecution for its violation. But a person who violates a statute thinking it unconstitutional does so at his or her peril; for courts have said that a person's belief that a statute is unconstitutional, even if based on advice of counsel, does not constitute a valid defense for violating the law. *State v. Thorstad*, 261 N.W.2d 899 (N.D. 1978), *cert. denied*, 436 U.S. 906, 98 S. Ct. 2237, 56 L.Ed.2d 404 (1978).

Mistake of Fact

In contrast to the ancient common-law maxim that "ignorance of the law is no excuse," at common law ignorance or mistake of fact, guarded by an honest purpose, afforded a defendant a sufficient excuse for a supposed criminal act. *Farrell v. State,* 32 Ohio St. 456 (1877). American courts have agreed, but have generally said that a mistake of fact will not be recognized as a defense to a general-intent crime unless the mistake is a reasonable one for a person to make under the circumstances. However, even an unreasonable mistake may be asserted as a defense to a crime that requires a specific intent. The decisions in recent years have indicated that a mistake of fact may be a defense as long as it negatives the existence of the mental state essential to the crime charged. See, for example, *State v. Fuentes,* 577 P.2d 452 (N.M. App. 1978), *cert. denied,* 577 P.2d 1256 (N.M. 1978).

Some jurisdictions have codified the mistake-of-fact defense. In Indiana, for example, mistake of fact is an affirmative defense by statute:

> It is a defense that the person who engaged in the prohibited conduct was reasonably mistaken about a matter of fact if the mistake negates the culpability required for commission of the offense. West's Ind. Code Ann. § 35–41–3–7.

In strict-liability offenses, the defense of mistake of fact is unavailing since these offenses are not based on intent (see Chapter 4). In pointing out that this view represents the weight of authority, the Montana Supreme Court held that ignorance or even a *bona fide* belief that a minor was of legal age did not constitute a defense to prosecution for selling intoxicating liquor to a minor, unless expressly made so by the statute. *State v. Parr,* 283 P.2d 1086 (Mont. 1955). Likewise, as pointed out in Chapter 4, since having consensual sexual relations with a minor is generally considered a strict-liability offense, a mistake of fact as to a minor's age is generally not a defense to a charge of statutory rape. Even if a court finds that a statutory rape statute requires proof of a general criminal intent to convict, a defendant's reasonable mistake of fact concerning a female's age is generally not available as a defense. *State v. Stiffler,* 788 P.2d 220 (Idaho 1990). However, in 1964 the California Supreme Court departed from this almost universally accepted rule and held that an accused's good-faith, reasonable belief that a female had reached the age of consent would be a defense to statutory rape. *People v. Hernandez,* 393 P.2d 673 (Cal. 1964).

In the past few years, in cases of statutory rape, some trial courts have heard arguments based on a minor's right to privacy. The contention is that since a minor female can consent to an abortion, she should be able to consent to sexual intercourse. Although this argument has generally fallen on deaf ears, some trial judges have questioned the need to continue to employ a strict-liability standard in consensual sexual relationships where the female is a minor and appears and represents herself as an adult.

DEFENSES BASED ON CONSTITUTIONAL AND STATUTORY AUTHORITY

The guarantees of the Bill of Rights give rise to two constitutional defenses: immunity and double jeopardy. In addition, a defense may be based on a so-called "statute of limitations."

Immunity—A Constitutional Defense

Everyone is familiar with the scenario of the witness who invokes the constitutional privilege against self-incrimination based on the Fifth Amendment to the Constitution that provides that "[N]o person . . . shall be compelled in any criminal case to be a witness against himself." The privilege against self-incrimination is applicable to the states through the Fourteenth Amendment, *Malloy v. Hogan*, 378 U.S. 1, 84 S. Ct. 1489, 12 L.Ed.2d 653 (1964), although states have similar protections in their constitutions.

The privilege against self-incrimination guaranteed by the federal Constitution is a personal one that applies only to natural persons and not corporations. *United States v. White*, 322 U.S. 694, 64 S. Ct. 1248, 88 L.Ed. 1542 (1944). A strict reading of the clause would limit the privilege to testimony given in a criminal trial. The Supreme Court, however, has held that an individual may refuse "to answer official questions put to him in any . . . proceeding, civil or criminal, formal or informal, where the answers might incriminate him in future criminal proceedings." *Lefkowitz v. Turley*, 414 U.S. 70, 77, 94 S. Ct. 316, 322, 38 L.Ed.2d 274, 281 (1973). A classic example is the privilege of suspects in police custody to invoke their *Miranda* rights, a subject we discuss in Chapter 15.

Use Immunity. Frequently, when a witness invokes the Fifth Amendment and refuses to testify, the court is requested to compel the requested testimony. This may be accomplished by conferring on the witness *immunity*, which is a grant of amnesty to protect the witness from prosecution through the use of compelled testimony. A witness compelled to give incriminating testimony thus receives *use immunity* (i.e., the testimony given cannot be used against the witness). This form of immunity is co-extensive with the scope of the privilege against self-incrimination and meets the demands of the Constitution. *Kastigar v. United States*, 406 U.S. 441, 92 S. Ct. 1653, 32 L.Ed.2d 212 (1972).

Transactional Immunity. In some states a witness who testifies under a grant of immunity is given *transactional immunity*, a broader protection than required under the federal Constitution. Transactional immunity protects a witness from prosecution for any activity mentioned in the witness's testimony. A recent example of requiring broader protection occurred in 1993 when the Alaska Supreme Court ruled that its state constitution requires that witnesses who are compelled to testify be given the more-protective transactional immunity from prosecution, not just use or derivative immunity as required by the federal constitution. *State v. Gonzalez*, 853 P.2d 526 (Alaska 1993).

As noted in Chapter 16, a defendant may assert the defense of immunity by a pretrial motion. Despite a grant of immunity, a witness may be prosecuted for making material false statements under oath. *United States v. Apfelbaum*, 445 U.S. 115, 100 S. Ct. 948, 63 L.Ed.2d 250 (1980) (see Chapter 12).

Contractual Immunity. Sometimes a witness is granted *contractual immunity* by a prosecutor with approval of the court. The purpose is to induce a suspect to testify against someone and thereby enable the prosecution to obtain a conviction not otherwise obtainable because of constitutional protection against self-incrimination. This type of immunity is rarely granted if other available evidence will lead to a conviction. The authority to grant immunity in federal courts is vested in the United States Attorney with approval of the Attorney General or certain authorized assistants. 18 U.S.C.A. § 6003. At the state level such authority is generally vested in the chief prosecuting officer (i.e., the district or state attorney).

Diplomatic Immunity. Another form of immunity is called diplomatic immunity. Under international law, a person who has diplomatic status and serves as a part of a diplomatic mission, as well as members of the diplomat's staff and household, is immune from arrest and prosecution.

Double Jeopardy: Another Constitutional Defense

The concept of forbidding retrial of a defendant who has been found not guilty developed from the common law. *Ex parte Lange*, 85 U.S. (18 Wall.) 163, 21 L.Ed. 872 (1873). The Fifth Amendment to the United States Constitution embodied the principle by stating "[N]or shall any person be subject for the same offence to be twice put in jeopardy of life or limb." This language in the Fifth Amendment is referred to as the *double jeopardy* clause. It was made applicable to the states through the Fourteenth Amendment in *Benton v. Maryland*, 395 U.S. 784, 89 S. Ct. 2056, 23 L.Ed.2d 707 (1969). Even before that all states provided essentially the same protection through their constitutions, statutes, or judicial decisions recognizing common-law principles.

Justice Black expressed the rationale underlying the double jeopardy clause when he wrote:

> The underlying idea, one that is deeply ingrained in at least the Anglo-American system of jurisprudence, is that the State with all its resources and power should not be allowed to make repeated attempts to convict an individual for an alleged offense, thereby subjecting him to embarrassment, expense and ordeal and compelling him to live in a continuing state of anxiety and insecurity, as well as enhancing the possibility that even though innocent he may be found guilty. *Green v. United States*, 355 U.S. 184, 187–188, 78 S. Ct. 221, 223, 2 L.Ed.2d 199, 204 (1957).

Jeopardy attaches once the jury is sworn in, *Crist v. Bretz*, 437 U.S. 28, 98 S. Ct. 2156, 57 L.Ed.2d 24 (1978), or when the first witness is sworn in to testify in a nonjury trial. *Serfass v. United States*, 420 U.S. 377, 95 S. Ct. 1055, 43 L.Ed.2d 265 (1975). As we note in Chapter 16, the defense of double jeopardy may be asserted by pretrial motion.

The double jeopardy clause forbids a second prosecution for the same offense after a defendant has been acquitted. *Ball v. United States*, 163 U.S. 662, 16 S. Ct. 1192, 41 L.Ed. 300 (1896). In recent years this principle has been applied even after a conviction. *United States v. Wilson*, 420 U.S. 332, 95 S. Ct. 1013, 43 L.Ed.2d 232 (1975). But, if a defendant appeals a conviction and prevails, it is not double jeopardy for the prosecution to retry the defendant unless the appellate court has ruled that there was insufficient evidence to sustain the conviction. *Burks v. United States*, 437 U.S. 1, 98 S. Ct. 2141, 57 L.Ed.2d 1 (1978). Note the distinction between a conviction reversed by a higher court on basis of *insufficient* evidence and a defendant's conviction being vacated and a new trial ordered based on the *weight* of the evidence. In the latter case, a retrial of the defendant would not constitute double jeopardy. *Tibbs v. Florida,* 457 U.S. 31, 102 S. Ct. 2211, 72 L.Ed.2d 652 (1982). Nor is it double jeopardy to retry a defendant if the trial court, at the defendant's request, has declared a mistrial. *Oregon v. Kennedy,* 456 U.S. 667, 102 S. Ct. 2083, 72 L.Ed.2d 416 (1982). If, however, the government moves for a mistrial and the defendant objects, the prosecution must establish a "manifest necessity" for the mistrial in order for a retrial to be permitted. An example of a manifest necessity might be a highly improper opening statement by the defendant's counsel. *Arizona v. Washington,* 434 U.S. 497, 98 S. Ct. 824, 54 L.Ed.2d 717 (1978).

Some offenses are crimes against both the federal and state governments. The policy, and in some instances state law, forbids a second prosecution once an offender has been prosecuted in a different jurisdiction. Nevertheless, under our federal system the double jeopardy clause does not preclude a prosecution by both the federal and state governments, since separate sovereigns are involved. *Bartkus v. Illinois,* 359 U.S. 121, 79 S. Ct. 676, 3 L.Ed.2d 684 (1959). Yet, this principle does not allow two courts within a state to try an accused for the same offense. Therefore, a person who has been prosecuted in a city or county court cannot be tried again in any court in the state for the same offense. *Waller v. Florida,* 397 U.S. 387, 90 S. Ct. 1184, 25 L.Ed.2d 435 (1970). In addition to protecting against a second prosecution for the same offense after conviction or acquittal, the double jeopardy clause protects against multiple punishments for the same offense. *North Carolina v. Pearce,* 395 U.S. 711, 89 S.Ct. 2072, 23 L.Ed.2d 656 (1969). The Constitution, however, does not define *same offense.* In 1932 the Supreme Court said:

> The applicable rule is that, where the same act or transaction constitutes a violation of two distinct statutory provisions, the test to be applied to determine whether there are two offenses or only one is whether each provision requires proof of an additional fact which the other does not. *Blockburger v. United States,* 284 U.S. 299, 304, 52 S. Ct. 180, 182, 76 L.Ed. 306, 309 (1932).

The *Blockburger* test compares the elements of the crimes in question. It is a tool of interpretation and creates a presumption of legislative intent, but it is not designed to contravene such intent. Rather, the Supreme Court has said that it is the "legislative intent" if clear that determines the scope of what constitutes "same offenses." *Missouri v. Hunter,* 459 U.S. 359, 103 S. Ct. 673, 74 L.Ed.2d 535 (1983); *Albernaz v. United States,* 450 U.S. 333, 101 S. Ct. 1137, 67 L.Ed.2d 275 (1981). In 1980, the Supreme Court reviewed a case where the defendant was first convicted of failing to slow down to avoid an accident with his car and later charged with manslaughter arising from the same incident. After reciting the "elements" test in *Blockburger,* the Court stated that "if in the pending manslaughter prosection Illinois relies on and proves a failure to slow to avoid an accident as the reckless act necessary to prove manslaughter, Vitale [the defendant] would have a substantial claim of double jeopardy under the Fifth and Fourteenth Amendments of the United States Constitution" *Illinois v. Vitale,* 447 U.S. 410, 420, 100 S.Ct. 2260, 2267, 65 L.Ed.2d 228, 238 (1980).

The *Blockburger* test examines the *elements,* not the *facts.* Since the Supreme Court's decision in *Vitale,* not all courts have regarded *Blockburger* as the exclusive method of determining whether successive prosecutions violate the principle of double jeopardy. Indeed, some courts look also to the evidence to be presented to prove those crimes. For example, the Connecticut Supreme Court citing *Vitale* held that prosecution of a defendant for operating a vehicle under the influence of intoxicants after prior acquittal for manslaughter with a motor vehicle while intoxicated was barred by principle of double jeopardy. Even though the offenses were not the same under the *Blockburger* test, the same evidence offered to prove a violation of the offense charged in the first prosecution was to be the sole evidence offered to prove an element of the offense charged in the second prosecution. Thus, the court held the second prosecution barred by the principle of double jeopardy. *State v. Lonergan*, 566 A.2d 677 (Conn. 1989). Other courts continue to determine the issue of double jeopardy by applying the *Blockburger* test. See, for example, *Butler v. State*, 816 S.W.2d 124 (Tex. App. 1991).

In *Grady v. Corbin*, 495 U.S. 508, 110 S.Ct. 2084, 109 L.Ed.2d 548 (1990), the Supreme Court continued to follow the approach in *Illinois v. Vitale, supra,* saying that "if to establish an essential element of an offense charged in that prosecution, the government will prove conduct that constitutes an offense for which the defendant has already been prosecuted," a second prosecution may not be had. 495 U.S. at 510, 110 S.Ct. at 2087, 109 L.Ed.2d at ___. This became known as the "same evidence" test and barred a second prosecution based on the same conduct by the defendant that was at issue in the first prosecution. In June 1993, however, in *United States v. Dixon*, 509 U.S. ___, 113 S.Ct. 2849, 125 L.Ed.2d 556 (1993), by a 5-4 margin, the Court overruled *Grady v. Corbin* replacing the "same evidence" test for double jeopardy analysis by a return to the "same elements" test from *Blockburger v. United States*, which bars punishment for offenses that have the same elements, or when one offense includes or is included in another offense. In *Dixon* the Court also ruled that a criminal contempt conviction represents a "jeopardy" that triggers the bar against a second prosecution for the same offense.

In a high-profile case in 1992, four Los Angeles police officers were tried by jury in a California state court on charges arising out of the beating of Rodney King, an African-American motorist stopped by the police for traffic infractions. The event was videotaped by an onlooker and televised nationally. The jury's verdict finding them not guilty was followed by considerable outrage and large-scale destructive rioting in Los Angeles. Despite their acquittal, the federal government brought new charges against the officers for violating King's civil rights. Their pleas that the new federal charges were barred by the double jeopardy clause of the Fifth Amendment were rejected by the United States District Court, and in April 1993 two of the four officers were convicted after a jury trial.

As noted earlier, the dual sovereignty of the federal government and the states allow separate trials of a defendant for the same offense. In the past this has not been a major problem, since it has been governmental policy not to cause duplicate prosecutions. Some deviations from this policy have occurred in recent years. In response to increasing attempts to try defendants in state and federal courts on similar charges, the American Bar Association has announced it is forming a task force to study the double jeopardy issue.

Statutes of Limitation

A statute of limitations is a legislative enactment that places a time limit on the prosecution of a crime. Common law placed no time limits on prosecution, but the federal government and almost all states have prescribed certain time limits for prosecution of most offenses. These statutes seldom place time limits on prosecutions for murder and other very serious offenses.

There are two primary public policy reasons for enacting statutes of limitations on the prosecution of crimes. First, it is generally accepted that a person should not be under threat of prosecution for too long a period. Second, after a prolonged period, proof is either unavailable or, if available, perhaps not credible.

Under most statutes of limitations the period for prosecution begins when a crime is committed, and not when it is discovered. The period ends when an arrest warrant is issued, an indictment is returned, or an information is filed. The period of limitations is interrupted while a perpetrator is a fugitive or conceals one's self from authorities. This cessation of the statute of limitations is often referred to as a "tolling" of the statutory period.

Federal statutes of limitations provide a five-year limitation on prosecution of noncapital crimes. 18 U.S.C.A. § 3282 *et seq*. While limitations periods vary among the states, the Ohio law appears representative. It provides:

> Except as otherwise provided in this section, a prosecution shall be barred unless it is commenced within the following periods after an offense is committed:
>
> (1) For a felony other than aggravated murder or murder, six years;
> (2) For a misdemeanor other than a minor misdemeanor, two years;
> (3) For a minor misdemeanor, six months. Page's Ohio Rev. Code Ann. § 2901.13(A).

There is a conflict among the various jurisdictions as to whether a statute of limitations in a criminal action is an affirmative defense. An affirmative defense that is not pled is deemed waived. Therefore, where courts consider a defendant's assertion that a prosecution is barred by the statute of limitations to be an affirmative defense, the running of the statutory period would not necessarily bar the prosecution. Other courts follow the rule that if the state's information or indictment discloses that the prosecution is initiated beyond the period allowed by the applicable statute of limitations, the prosecution is barred. In this latter instance, a convicted defendant could raise on appeal the issue of the statute of limitations having barred prosecution of the offense.

Defenses Based on Government Conduct

There are two defenses based on improper government conduct: entrapment and selective prosecution. These defenses are grounded in the constitutional requirements of due process and equal protection of the law.

Entrapment

Law enforcement officers may provide an opportunity for a predisposed person to commit a crime, but they are not permitted to "manufacture" crime by implanting criminal ideas into innocent minds. Therefore, a person who has been induced to commit an offense under these latter circumstances may plead the defense of entrapment. The defense of entrapment is often asserted by a defendant who claims entrapment as a result of inducement by an undercover police officer or a confidential police informant. It is not available to a defendant who has been entrapped by a person not associated with the government or police. See *Henderson v. United States,* 237 F.2d 169 (5th Cir. 1956).

Entrapment was not a defense under the common law, but it has long been recognized in federal and state courts in the United States. In 1980, the Tennessee Supreme Court acknowledged that Tennessee was the only state in the Union that did not allow entrapment as a defense and proceeded to remedy the situation by declaring, "From this day forward entrapment is a defense to a Tennessee criminal prosecution." *State v. Jones,* 598 S.W.2d 209, 212 (Tenn. 1980).

In a landmark case arising during prohibition days, the United States Supreme Court held that a federal officer had entrapped a defendant by using improper inducements to cause him to buy illegal liquor for the officer. The Court opined that entrapment occurs when criminal conduct involved is "the product of the creative activity of [law enforcement officers]." *Sorrells v. United States,* 287 U.S. 435, 451, 53 S. Ct. 210, 216, 77 L.Ed. 413, 422 (1932).

In *Sorrells,* the majority of the justices viewed entrapment as whether the defendant's criminal intent originated in the mind of the officer or whether the defendant was predisposed to commit the offense. This focus on the predisposition of the defendant has come to be known as the "subjective test" of entrapment. A minority of justices in *Sorrells* would have applied what is now known as the "objective test." Under this view, the court would simply determine whether the police methods were so improper as likely to induce or ensnare a person into committing a crime. The objective test is obviously designed to prohibit police methods that pose a substantial risk of inducing people to commit crimes.

In the past, the majority of federal and state courts have followed the subjective view, and a person who pled entrapment was held to have admitted commission of the offense. See, for example, *United States v. Sedigh,* 658 F.2d 1010 (5th Cir. 1981), *cert. denied,* 455 U.S. 921, 102 S. Ct. 1279, 71 L.Ed.2d 462 (1982); *State v. Amodei,* 563 P.2d 440 (Kan. 1977). A jury would then determine whether the defendant committed the crime because of predisposition, or whether the defendant was improperly induced to do so by the police. To sustain the defense of entrapment, it is usually sufficient for the defendant to show that the police used methods of persuasion likely to cause a normally law-abiding person to commit the offense. See, for example, *State v. Mullen,* 216 N.W. 2d 375 (Iowa 1974); but see *United States v. Demma,* 523 F.2d 981 (9th Cir. 1975), holding that a defendant may assert entrapment without being required to concede commission of the crime or any element thereof.

Where courts follow the objective view, the judge, not the jury, determines whether the police methods were so improper as to constitute entrapment. See, for example, *People v. D'Angelo,* 257 N.W.2d 655 (Mich. 1977). Some federal courts have simply said that where police conduct is outrageous, it becomes a question of law for the judge to determine if governmental misconduct is so shocking as to be a due process of law violation. See, for example, *United States v. Wylie,* 625 F.2d 1371 (9th Cir. 1980), *cert. denied,* 449 U.S. 1080, 101 S. Ct. 863, 66 L.Ed.2d 804

(1981). In courts that strictly follow the objective view, the defendant's predisposition to commit an offense is irrelevant.

Recent decisions indicate that the subjective and objective tests can coexist. Some state courts now first determine whether a defendant who pleads entrapment has been ensnared by outrageous police methods. If so, the judge dismisses the charges against the ensnared defendant. If not, the court then allows the defendant to attempt to establish the defense of entrapment by proving improper inducement. The prosecution usually counters with evidence showing the defendant's prior criminal activity and ready acquiescence in committing the crime charged. The court then instructs the jury to determine whether the defendant committed the crime because of his or her predisposition or through inducement by the police. At least two states have adopted this general approach. *Cruz v. State*, 465 So.2d 516 (Fla. 1985), *cert. denied*, 473 U.S. 905, 105 S. Ct. 3527, 87 L.Ed.2d 652 (1985); *State v. Talbot*, 364 A.2d 9 (N.J. 1976).

Two principal reasons account for the increased assertion of the defense of entrapment in recent years. First, a large number of violations of narcotics laws have been prosecuted on the basis of undercover police activity and evidence given by confidential police informants. Second, there has been increased attention to prosecuting corruption involving government officials. Perhaps the most highly publicized cases in recent years resulted from the 1980 Abscam operation, in which Federal Bureau of Investigation (FBI) agents posed as wealthy Arab businessmen and attempted to buy influence from members of Congress. Despite their claims of entrapment, several members of Congress were found guilty of offenses involving misuse of office. See, for example, *United States v. Jenrette*, 744 F.2d 817 (D.C. Cir. 1984), *cert. denied*, 471 U.S. 1099, 105 S. Ct. 2321, 85 L.Ed.2d 840 (1985).

In 1987, Keith Jacobson was indicted for violating the Child Protection Act of 1984, 18 U.S.C.A. § 2252(a)(2)(A), which criminalizes the knowing receipt through the mails of a "visual depiction [that] involves the use of a minor engaging in sexually explicit conduct." At trial Jacobson contended the government entrapped him into committing the crime. A jury found him guilty, and his conviction was affirmed by the Court of Appeals. The United States Supreme Court granted review.

In evaluating the evidence at Jacobson's trial, the Supreme Court found that while it was still legal to so, Jacobson ordered some magazines containing photos of nude boys. After Congress enacted the Child Protection Act making this illegal, two government agencies sent mail to Jacobson through fictitious organizations to explore his willingness to break the law. He was literally bombarded with solicitations, which included communications decrying censorship and questioning the legitimacy and constitutionality of the government's efforts to restrict availability of sexually explicit materials. He finally responded to an undercover solicitation to order child pornography and was arrested after a controlled delivery of the explicit sexual materials.

After pointing out that for 26 months the government agents had made Jacobson the target of repeated mailings, the Court held that the prosecution failed, as a matter of law, to produce evidence that Jacobson was predisposed, independent of the government's acts, to violate the law. Adding that government agents may not implant a criminal design in an innocent person's mind and

CASE IN POINT

ENTRAPMENT AS A MATTER OF LAW

Law enforcement officers told a female that she might not be prosecuted for possession of cocaine if she would become a confidential informant. She agreed and met with the defendant, James Banks, a suspected drug dealer, on two nights. The meetings included "kissing and hugging," after which she told defendant James Banks that if he "could get her something [they] would get together for the weekend, fool around and party." Defendant obtained some cocaine for her and as a result he was arrested. The trial judge dismissed the charges because the uncontested facts established that the officers used a method with a substantial risk of persuading or inducing the defendant to commit a criminal offense.

The state appealed the dismissal. The appellate court affirmed, observing: "When law enforcement agencies utilize confidential informants who use sex, or the express or implied promise thereof, to obtain contraband the defendant did not already possess, there is no way for the courts or anyone else to determine whether such inducement served only to uncover an existing propensity or created a new one. This violates the threshold objective test."

State v. Banks, 499 So.2d 894 (Fla. App. 1986).

then induce commission of a crime, the Court reversed his conviction, observing that Congress had not intended for government officials to instigate crime by luring persons otherwise innocent to commit offenses. *Jacobson v. United States,* 503 U.S. 540, 112 S.Ct. 1535, 118 L.Ed.2d 174 (1992).

While the Court's decision is not grounded on constitutional principles, it not only affects federal enforcement activities, it signals state enforcement authorities not to play on the weaknesses of innocent parties and beguile them into committing crimes.

Selective Prosecution

Selective enforcement of the criminal law is not itself a constitutional violation, and therefore, without more, it does not constitute a defense. *Oyler v. Boles,* 368 U.S. 448, 82 S. Ct. 501, 7 L.Ed.2d 446 (1962). There are many cases rejecting the defense of selective prosecution. To prevail, a defendant must ordinarily demonstrate that other similarly situated persons have not been prosecuted for similar conduct, and that the defendant's selection for prosecution was based on some impermissible ground such as race, religion, or exercise of the First Amendment rights of free speech. *United States v. Arias,* 575 F.2d 253 (9th Cir. 1978), *cert. denied,* 439 U.S. 868, 99 S. Ct. 196, 58 L.Ed.2d 179 (1978).

DEFENSES BASED ON ALIBI, DURESS, NECESSITY, AND CONSENT

Individuals prosecuted for crimes often defend themselves by invoking an alibi—a claim that it was impossible for the defendant to have committed the

CASE IN POINT

REJECTING THE DEFENSE OF SELECTIVE PROSECUTION

In 1982, David Alan Wayte was indicted for willfully failing to register under the Military Selective Service Act. Wayte sought dismissal of the indictment on the ground of selective prosecution. He contended that he and the others being prosecuted had been singled out of an estimated 674,000 nonregistrants because they had voiced opposition to the Selective Service requirements. The district court dismissed the indictment on the ground that the government had failed to rebut Wayte's *prima facie* showing of selective prosecution. The case was eventually heard by the United States Supreme Court. The Court held that the government's passive enforcement policy, under which it prosecuted only those nonregistrants who reported themselves or were reported by others, did not violate the First or Fifth Amendments to the Constitution.

Wayte v. United States, 470 U.S. 598, 105 S. Ct. 1524, 84 L.Ed.2d 547 (1985).

crime because he or she was somewhere else at the time the crime was committed. Less common, but equally well-established, are defenses based on duress, necessity, and consent.

Alibi

Alibi means "elsewhere," and the defense of alibi may be interposed by a defendant who claims to have been at a place other than where the crime allegedly occurred. A criminal defendant who relies on an alibi as a defense does not deny that a crime was committed. Rather, he or she denies the ability to have perpetrated such crime because of having been elsewhere at the time.

As recently pointed out by the Colorado Supreme Court, most jurisdictions that have addressed the issue have concluded that an alibi is not an affirmative defense. *People v. Huckleberry*, 768 P.2d 1235 (Colo. 1989). A few, however, characterize the defense as an affirmative one requiring proof of alibi by the defendant. Generally, a defendant who asserts an affirmative defense essentially admits the conduct charged and seeks to excuse or justify it. One who claims an alibi does not so admit. Therefore, it seems logical not to classify alibi as an affirmative defense. As explained by the Missouri Supreme Court:

> The theory of alibi is that the fact of defendant's presence elsewhere is essentially inconsistent with his presence at the place where the alleged offense was committed and, therefore, defendant could not have personally participated. Although the defense is not an affirmative one, the fact of defendant's presence elsewhere is an affirmative fact logically operating to negative his presence at the time and place. *State v. Armstead*, 283 S.W.2d 577, 581 (Mo. 1955).

Statutes or court rules commonly require that to assert alibi as a defense, a defendant must notify the prosecution in advance of trial and furnish the names of witnesses the defendant intends to use to support the alibi. The Supreme

Court has said that this requirement does not violate the defendant's right to due process of law. *Williams v. Florida,* 399 U.S. 78, 90 S.Ct. 1893, 26 L.Ed. 2d 446 (1970). However, in 1973 the Court held that when the state requires such information, the prosecution must make similar disclosures to the defendant concerning refutation of the evidence the defendant furnishes. *Wardius v. Oregon,* 412 U.S. 470, 93 S.Ct. 2208, 37 L.Ed.2d 82 (1973). Alibi notice statutes and court rules now commonly require disclosure by both defense and the prosecution.

Duress

The common law recognized that duress can be a defense to criminal charges if the coercion exerted involved the use of threats of harm that were "present, imminent and pending" and "of such nature as to include well grounded apprehensions of death or serious bodily harm if the act was not done." Nevertheless, no form of duress, even the threat of imminent death, was sufficient to excuse the intentional killing of an innocent human being. *State v. Toscano,* 378 A.2d 755 (N.J. 1977). American courts have generally followed this approach, with both federal and state courts having made it clear that threats of future harm are not sufficient to constitute duress. See, for example, *United States v. Agard,* 605 F.2d 665 (2d Cir. 1979); *State v. Clay,* 264 N.W. 77 (Iowa 1935).

The defense of duress, sometimes referred to as coercion, compulsion, or duress, is recognized today either by statute or decisional law. Duress has been asserted most frequently by defendants who have committed robberies and thefts and by prisoners who have escaped from custody. Some courts look upon duress as negating an element of the offense charged and classify it as a negative defense. See *People v. Graham,* 129 Cal. Rptr. 31 (Cal. App. 1976). Other courts classify duress as an affirmative defense and require the defendant to prove the defense by the greater weight of the evidence.

There was a common-law presumption that if a wife committed a felony other than murder or treason in her husband's presence, she did so under coercion of her husband. *Morton v. State,* 209 S.W. 644 (Tenn. 1919). The presumption has little significance in modern America and has been abolished in some jurisdictions either by statute, see, for example, Wis. Stat. Ann. § 939.46(2), or by judicial decision. See *People v. Statley,* 206 P.2d 76 (Cal. App. 1949). Despite these precedents, in November 1992 a California appellate court announced a new development in the law of duress. The court held that evidence of the battered woman syndrome (BWS) is admissible to support a woman's defense that she committed robbery offenses because she was afraid the man she lived with would kill her if she did not do as he demanded. *People v. Romero,* 13 Cal. Rptr. 2d 332 (Cal. App. 1992). The court compared the situation to California decisions allowing evidence of BWS when a woman is accused of killing a man she lives with who batters her. (See previous discussion of self-defense in this chapter).

In *People v. Merhige,* 180 N.W. 418 (Mich. 1920), the defendant, a cab driver, transported passengers to a bank, knowing they planned to commit a robbery. It was established at trial that the passengers held a gun to the defendant's head and that he believed he would be killed if he attempted to escape or render his cab inoperable. On basis of the defendant having acted under duress, the Michigan Supreme Court reversed the cab driver's conviction.

Perhaps one of the most dramatic instances where a defendant claimed to have acted under coercion or duress had its beginning on February 4, 1974. On that date members of a radical group known as the Symbionese Liberation Army (SLA) kidnapped Patricia Hearst, a young woman living in California. After being taken captive, Ms. Hearst became involved in the SLA activities and was charged with participating in an armed robbery and other offenses while in captivity. When finally liberated from her captors, Ms. Hearst was tried in a federal district court in San Francisco, California. Among her defenses, she asserted coercion and duress. The Hearst trial was highlighted by considerable psychiatric evidence of "brainwashing" and compulsion. The judge instructed the jury that duress or coercion may provide a legal excuse, but that a compulsion must be present and immediate, carry a well-founded fear of death or bodily injury, and offer no possible escape from such compulsion. Nevertheless, the jury rejected the defense asserted, and convicted and sentenced Ms. Hearst to prison in March 1976. She was later granted executive clemency by President Jimmy Carter.

Prisoners who escape custody frequently plead duress. As pointed out in Chapter 12, the requirement for establishing duress as a defense to escape requires the defendant to show that a *bona fide* effort was made to surrender or return to custody as soon as the claimed duress has ended or lost its coercive force. See *United States v. Bailey,* 444 U.S. 394, 100 S. Ct. 624, 62 L.Ed.2d 575 (1980).

There is a conflict among jurisdictions whether a threat against persons other than the defendant is a sufficient basis for a defendant to invoke the defense of duress. Kansas allows a person to plead duress as a defense to crimes other than murder where the threat is against one's spouse, parent, brother, or sister. Kansas Stat. Ann. § 21–3209. Some courts have adhered to this view irrespective of statute; others have concluded that threats against other persons are not sufficient to constitute duress. For example, in *Jackson v. State,* 504 S.W.2d 488 (Tex. Crim. App. 1974), the court said that since the statute defining duress did not include threats concerning third parties, the court would not permit threats against members of the defendant's family to be considered as a basis to assert the defense of duress.

CASE IN POINT

REJECTING ECONOMIC DURESS AS A DEFENSE

Defendant was arrested on board a boat in the Gulf of Mexico just off the coast of Florida and was charged with trafficking in cannabis in excess of ten thousand pounds. He pled not guilty and asserted the defense of duress. At trial the defendant and his wife testified that economic reasons forced him to participate in trafficking in cannabis by piloting the boat. The trial judge declined to instruct the jury on duress, and the defendant was convicted. On appeal, the court affirmed the conviction and said that such claim of economic coercion was insufficient to call for a jury instruction on duress.

Corujo v. State, 424 So.2d 43 (Fla. App. 1982), *rev. denied,* 434 So.2d 886 (Fla. 1983).

Necessity

In the defense of duress, the situation has its source in the actions of others. In the defense of necessity, forces beyond the actor's control are said to have required a person's choice of the lesser of two evils. Early common-law cases recognized that "a man may break the words of the law . . . through necessity." *Regina v. Fogossa,* 75 Eng. Rep. 1 (1550). Contemporary American judicial authorities hold that if there is a reasonable legal alternative to violating the law, the defense of necessity fails.

Suppose several people are shipwrecked on a cold night. One person swims to shore, breaks into an unoccupied beach cottage, and takes food and blankets to assist the injured until help can be secured. Prosecution in such an event would be unlikely, but if prosecuted, the defendant would properly plead the defense of necessity.

In recent years a number of defendants have attempted to justify actions involving "civil disobedience" on the ground of necessity in instances where they have forcefully asserted their personal or political beliefs. These attempts to employ the defense of necessity have generally been unsuccessful.

One of the most dramatic acts of civil disobedience occurred in 1980 when a group of antinuclear activists entered a factory in Pennsylvania, damaged components of nuclear bombs, and poured human blood on the premises. An appellate court approved of the defendants entering a defense of necessity; however, the Pennsylvania Supreme Court reversed the decision. *Commonwealth v. Berrigan,* 501 A.2d 226 (Pa. 1985). A number of further attempts to plead the necessity defense by antinuclear activists have also failed.

In most but not all cases, the necessity defense has been unavailing to defendants espousing other social and political causes. In one instance, several defendants were charged with criminal trespass when they refused to leave an abortion clinic in Anchorage, Alaska. They claimed their actions were necessary to avert the imminent peril to human life that would result from abortions being performed. They were convicted, and on appeal they argued the trial court erred in refusing to instruct the jury on their claim of necessity as a defense. In rejecting their contention, the Alaska Supreme Court outlined three requirements that must be met by a person who pleads the defense of necessity:

> 1) The act charged must have been done to prevent a significant evil; 2) there must have been no adequate alternative; 3) the harm caused must not have been disproportionate to the harm avoided. *Cleveland v. Municipality of Anchorage,* 631 P.2d 1073, 1078 (Alaska 1981).

Not all social and political protesters have been unsuccessful in pleading the defense of necessity. It was widely reported in the press in April 1987 that Amy Carter, a 19-year-old college student, and fourteen co-defendants charged with trespassing and disorderly conduct in Northampton, Massachusetts, successfully employed the defense of necessity. The defendants were peace activists who claimed their actions were legitimate protests against misleading recruiting and other allegedly illegal activities by the Central Intelligence Agency (CIA) on college campuses. A jury found the defendants not guilty.

An issue is surfacing as to whether to allow a defense of "medical necessity." You may recall that in Chapter 9 concerning offenses involving drugs and alcohol, we noted that several state courts have refused to allow a defendant charged with possession or use of contraband substances to assert the defense of medical necessity. Nevertheless, in 1991 a Florida court of appeal allowed a husband and wife who contracted acquired immune deficiency syndrome (AIDS) to assert that defense to charges of possession and cultivation of marijuana. *Jenks v. State*, 582 So.2d 676 (Fla. App. 1991).

A Wisconsin statute codifies the defense of necessity by providing:

> Pressure of natural physical forces which causes the actor reasonably to believe that his or her act is the only means of preventing imminent public disaster, or imminent death or great bodily harm to the actor or another and which causes him or her so to act, is a defense to a prosecution for any crime based on that act, except that if the prosecution is for first-degree intentional homicide, the degree of the crime is reduced to second-degree intentional homicide. Wis. Stat. Ann. § 939.47.

Consent

Since a victim may not excuse a criminal act, historically courts have said that consent is not a defense to a criminal prosecution. *State v. West*, 57 S.W. 1071 (Mo. 1900). But there are exceptions to this general statement. For example, where lack of consent is an element of the offense, consent may be a defense. This may be true in a prosecution for rape where competent adults freely consent before having sexual relations. In certain contact sports, such as football and boxing, consent is implied and may be a defense to reasonable instances of physical contact that may otherwise be regarded as batteries. Of course, a valid consent presupposes that it is given by a person legally competent to do so and is not induced by force, duress, or deception.

SOME ATTEMPTED DEFENSES

Although they are rarely successful, defendants sometimes employ novel and innovative defenses. Some of the more interesting recent attempted defenses involve the victim's negligence, religious beliefs and practices, premenstrual syndrome, compulsive gambling, post-traumatic stress disorder, "junk food" defense and television intoxication.

Victim's Negligence

Federal and state courts hold that a victim's negligence, credulity, or wrongdoing are not defenses to a prosecution. *United States v. Kreimer*, 609 F.2d 126 (5th Cir. 1980); *State v. Lunz*, 273 N.W.2d 767 (Wis. 1979). Likewise, since a crime is an offense against society as well as the victim, it follows that a victim's forgiveness or condonation does not relieve an actor of criminal responsibility.

Religious Beliefs and Practices

Contentions by defendants that they have been commanded by God or the Scriptures to commit illegal acts have long been rejected by the courts. See *Hotema v. United States,* 186 U.S. 413, 22 S. Ct. 895, 46 L.Ed. 1225 (1902). Moreover, laws prohibiting religious rites that endanger the lives, health, or safety of the participants or others are customarily upheld by the courts. This is illustrated by the Kentucky Court of Appeals' decision in *Lawson v. Commonwealth,* 164 S.W.2d 972 (Ky. 1942). There, despite the defendants' contentions that their constitutional guarantees of freedom of religion were violated, the court upheld the constitutionality of a statute making it a misdemeanor for anyone to handle snakes or reptiles in connection with any religious service.

Courts have traditionally upheld the right of parents to raise their children by their own religious beliefs, ruling that the state's interest must give way to the parents' religious beliefs that preclude medical treatment when the child's life is not immediately imperiled. *In re Green,* 292 A.2d 387 (Pa. 1972). Nevertheless, the courts have held that where a child's life is imperiled the parents have an affirmative duty to provide medical care that will protect a child's life. Thus, an appellate court upheld a conviction of parents for manslaughter when it found that a child's death was directly caused by the parents' failure to secure needed medical care for their child. *Commonwealth v. Barnhart,* 497 A.2d 616 (Pa. Super. 1985), *appeal denied,* 538 A.2d 874 (Pa. 1988).

In about half of the states, child abuse and criminal neglect statutes permit parents to choose "spiritual means or prayer" as a response to illness without regard to a child's medical condition. Thus, in *State v. McKown,* 461 N.W.2d 720 (Minn. App. 1990), the court upheld dismissal of manslaughter charges against a parent and stepparent who relied on spiritual means and failed to secure medical treatment for an 11-year-old boy who died as a result of serious medical problems resulting from diabetes.

The need to furnish medical care to children poses a problem of balancing the parents' interests in bringing up their offspring in accordance with their religious beliefs against the interest of the state in preservation of life. In January 1988, the press reported that the American Academy of Pediatrics urged repeal of laws allowing parents to reject medical treatment for their children on religious grounds. The academy pointed out that about three-fourths of the states have laws that permit some rejection of medical care on religious or philosophical grounds. The academy noted, however, that courts frequently have intervened to order certain treatments for minors.

Premenstrual Syndrome

Premenstrual syndrome (PMS) refers to certain physiological changes that occur in some women, usually in the days close to onset of menstruation. This results from hormonal imbalance and may cause serious depression and irritability. In some cases medical treatment is required. Some argue that a woman so affected should be allowed to assert PMS as a defense to criminal conduct, since some physicians say that PMS directly affects behavior. Nevertheless, PMS has not been accepted as a defense in the United States. In England it has been recognized as a basis to mitigate punishment.

Compulsive Gambling

Evidence of compulsive gambling is generally not considered as a defense unless it rises to the level of insanity. For example, a defendant was convicted of entering a bank with intent to commit larceny and robbery. On appeal, he argued that the trial court erred in instructing the jury that "as a matter of law pathological gambling disorder is not a disease or defect within the meaning of the American Law Institute test for insanity." The United States Court of Appeals, while still applying the former ALI standard, rejected his contention. *United States v. Gould,* 741 F.2d 45 (4th Cir. 1984).

Post-traumatic Stress Disorder (PTSD)

Post-traumatic stress disorder (PTSD) commonly refers to the unique stresses suffered during combat, often manifesting such symptoms as flashbacks, outbursts of anger, and blocked-out memories. After World War I, these conditions were usually referred to as *shell shock.* Following World War II, the term *combat fatigue* was often used to describe such anxiety disorders. Present generations have heard these conditions described as the "Vietnam veteran stress syndrome." Because of the bizarre type of warfare that service personnel endured in Vietnam, the unpopularity of the war, availability of drugs, and the difficulties encountered in adjusting to civilian life, many veterans suffered severe psychological reactions. Whether the stress of the combat operations in the recent Desert Storm operation will cause any widespread traumatic symptoms remains to be seen.

While not a legal defense in itself, in some instances PTSD may affect a defendant's understanding to the point of allowing a plea of insanity. More frequently, PTSD will be introduced as evidence bearing on a defendant's intent, or offered at a sentencing hearing in an effort to mitigate punishment.

The "Junk Food" Defense

Dan White, a former city supervisor, shot and killed the mayor of San Francisco in 1978. Following this he killed another supervisor who was a leader of the local gay community. In defense to charges of first-degree murder, White's counsel sought to establish that his client was depressed by having gorged himself on junk foods. White was convicted of manslaughter instead of murder, giving some credence to reports that the jury may have accepted White's defense. Since this was jury action, it set no precedent to establish any such defense.

Television Intoxication

A novel defense was presented to a trial court in Miami, Florida, in 1978. An adolescent boy was tried for the first-degree murder of an elderly woman. He attempted to establish insanity on the basis of psychiatric testimony concerning the effects of "involuntary subliminal television intoxication." The trial court rejected his claim. An appellate court, stating that the trial judge correctly limited the evidence to the requirements of the *M'Naghten* rule, found no difficulty in upholding the trial court's decision. *Zamora v. State,* 361 So.2d 776 (Fla. App. 1978), *cert. denied,* 372 So.2d 472 (Fla. 1979).

CONCLUSION

Consistent with the historic common-law concept of *mens rea* as an essential element of a crime, infants and insane persons are not held criminally responsible for their acts. Today, courts still encounter difficulties in affixing the legal responsibility of juveniles. Despite our vastly increased knowledge of genetics and mental capacity, courts and legislatures continue to struggle with the definition of insanity and the problem of how to handle those persons adjudged insane. Likewise, with the rise in the use of alcohol and drugs, the problem of intoxication as a defense plagues the judicial system.

A person's right to use reasonable force in self-defense and defense of property and habitation has always been regarded as basic in Anglo-American jurisprudence; yet in modern society it becomes increasingly difficult to determine the extent of force that may be used in other situations. The use of chokeholds by police and the use of force by parents and by guardians and teachers who serve *in loco parentis* present difficult questions. To what extent should police be permitted to use force in making arrests? When does the legitimate use of disciplinary force cease and child abuse begin? And what about the battered woman who seeks to justify her use of force against a charge of homicide or assault on the man she lives with?

Mistake of fact and mistake of law are merely expository of the common-sense foundation of the criminal law. They are a part of the civilized application of law. So too are the defenses of necessity and duress, but these defenses must be viewed in the context of our ever-changing socioeconomic environment.

A number of defenses have developed because of our constitutional system. Immunity, double jeopardy, and the right to a speedy trial have evolved with the continuing constitutional development of individual rights. The statute of limitations defense emerged from our penchant for definiteness and our distrust of prosecutions resting on stale testimony. Our inherent distaste for "frame-ups" and outrageous conduct by the police have caused entrapment to become a viable defense to admitted criminal conduct.

The concepts of criminal responsibility and of criminal defenses will continue to evolve in response to our increased knowledge of human behavior and society's balance of the rights of the individual against its legitimate demand for protection.

QUESTIONS FOR THOUGHT AND DISCUSSION

1. In general, courts permit intoxication evidence only to the extent that it negates the *mens rea of* a specific-intent crime. Should evidence of voluntary intoxication be allowed for both general-intent and specific-intent crimes? Alternatively, should courts bar such evidence for *both* general intent and specific-intent crimes? What position has been taken by the courts of your state?

2. What is the test for insanity in your state? Who has the burden of proof once the defendant introduces some evidence of insanity? Do you think the test in your state adequately protects (a) the public, and (b) the defendant's rights?

3. While taking his nightly walk, Charley Goodneighbor saw Joe Macho commit a battery on Charlene Loverly, a 14-year-old girl. Goodneighbor came to Charlene's defense and struck Macho so hard it fractured his skull. The police arrested both Macho and Goodneighbor. Goodneighbor explained to the police that he came to Charlene's aid to prevent her from being injured by Macho. What factors will the prosecutor probably consider in determining whether to file charges against Goodneighbor?

4. Harvey Homeowner, a "black belt" in karate, arrives at his home to find an intruder fleeing from the garage. Homeowner pursues the intruder across the front yard and catches him in the street. An exchange of blows renders the intruder unconscious. A medical examination reveals substantial brain damage to the intruder as a result of the blows inflicted by Homeowner. In a prosecution for aggravated battery, can Homeowner successfully assert as a defense his use of force to protect his habitation?

5. Sally Shopper drives a 1992 grey Honda Accord. She parks it in a shopping center lot while she shops. Two hours later, Sally enters a car parked nearby that is almost identical to hers. As she drives away the owner spots her and demands that a nearby police officer stop her. Just as the officer approaches her, Sally realizes that she is in someone else's vehicle. Had she looked at the vehicle more carefully, she would have observed that it had a license tag from a different state and some unique bumper stickers. On complaint of the owner, the officer arrests Sally and charges her with theft. What is Sally likely to assert in her defense?

6. A poor man steals food from a convenience market. When prosecuted for theft, he pleads the defense of necessity. The prosecutor urges the trial judge to strike the defense on the ground that the defendant could have qualified for assistance from local welfare organizations. Should the defendant be allowed to present his defense to the jury? Do you think he has a credible defense? Why or why not?

7. A defendant was found guilty of having forcible sexual intercourse with a 15-year-old female of previous chaste character. He is charged, convicted, and sentenced for violating two statutes: (a) common-law rape involving force and lack of consent, and (b) statutory rape involving intercourse with a minor of previous chaste character. On appeal, the defendant contends that his sentence violates the double jeopardy clause of the Fifth Amendment. What arguments is his counsel likely to present to the appellate court? What should be the appellate court's decision?

8. The police suspect Mary Jane Narky of having sold marijuana at the Sibanac Bar. An undercover agent approaches her and asks her to go out with him. After a movie, the agent says that he would like to buy some marijuana for his close friend. At first Mary Jane makes no response. They make another date and after a very pleasant evening together, the undercover agent pleads with Mary Jane to help him find marijuana for his friend. She agrees, and the next day she delivers a quantity of the contraband to the agent, who gives her $200. As he concludes

his purchase, the undercover agent arrests Mary Jane and chargers her with the sale of contraband. Mary Jane's attorney pleads entrapment at her trial. Do you think her defense will be successful? Why or why not?

9. Why did the United States Supreme Court in *Tennessee v. Garner* (1985) invalidate a state law permitting police officers to use deadly force to apprehend fleeing felons? Under *Garner*, when is a police officer justified in using deadly force? What impact has the *Garner* decision had on law enforcement?

10. Boris Bottlemore has just finished celebrating his new job promotion by consuming ten double shots of bourbon in a bar near his home. He staggers from the bar to his home, which is one of twenty identical row houses on his block. In his inebriated state, Boris mistakes his neighbor's home for his own. Finding the door unlocked, he enters and promptly raids the refrigerator. He then collapses on a couch in the living room and passes out. The next morning, Patty Purebred, who has just moved into the home, is shocked to find a stranger sleeping in her living room and her refrigerator standing open, with food strewn across the kitchen floor. She telephones the police, who arrive and take Bottlemore into custody, charging him with burglary. What defense(s) is (are) available to Bottlemore? How would you assess his chances before a jury?

11. Should the courts recognize battered woman syndrome (BWS) as a defense to assaultive and homicidal crimes by a woman living with a man who continually batters her? What position does your state take on this issue?

CASES

MOON V. STATE

Supreme Court of Indiana, 1981.
275 Ind. 651, 419 N.E.2d 740.

[This case raises the issue of intoxication as a defense to a charge of attempted robbery.]

HUNTER, Justice.

The defendant, James C. Moon, was convicted in a bench trial of attempted robbery, a class A felony, Ind.Code § 35–42–5–1 (Burns 1979 Repl.), and carrying a handgun without a license, a class D felony, Ind.Code § 35–23–4.1–18(c) (Burns 1979 Repl.). He was sentenced to concurrent terms of twenty years for the class A felony and two years for the class D felony. Moon presents the following issues for our review:

1. Whether the evidence was sufficient to sustain his conviction; and
2. Whether the judgment of the trial court was contrary to law.

The evidence indicates that during the evening of November 7, 1979, the defendant and a machete-bearing accomplice entered the Brookside Market at 2129 Brookside Avenue in Indianapolis. The defendant, who was carrying a revolver, fired a shot at the ceiling and demanded money from the cashier. Startled by the shot, a patron near the cash register bolted down an aisle toward the rear of the store. The machete-bearing accomplice gave chase.

Their path carried them toward a window, largely veiled from public view, which connected the owner's living quarters to the store. Through the window the owner had been observing the developments. As the two men neared the window, the owner saw the accomplice raise the machete to swing it at the patron. At that point the owner pushed the window open and fired five shots at the accomplice.

Wounded by the gunfire, the accomplice dropped the machete and, together with the defendant, fled the premises. In the aftermath, it was discovered that one of the bullets fired by the owner had ricocheted and hit the cashier in the leg.

I

Defendant contends that the evidence is insufficient to sustain his conviction for attempted robbery as a class A felony. That contention is predicated on the fact that the "bodily injury" necessary to elevate attempted robbery to a felony of class A status, Ind. Code § 35–42–5–1 (Burns 1979 Repl.) was inflicted by a bullet fired by the owner of the Brookside Market. Since neither he nor his accomplice fired the shot which injured the cashier, defendant maintains there is no evidence to establish his liability for class A attempted robbery.

We disagree. The responsibility for any bodily injury which occurs during the commission or attempted commission of a robbery rests on the perpetrators of the crime, regardless of who inflicts the injury, so long as it is a natural and probable consequence of the events and circumstances surrounding the robbery or attempt. . . . Here, the defendant and his accomplice walked into a grocery store armed with a revolver and machete. They fired a shot into the air, demanded money, and swung a machete at a store patron. The bodily injury which ultimately occurred, albeit caused by the gunfire of the store owner, was a natural consequence of the conduct of the defendant and his accomplice in attempting the robbery. Accordingly, the evidence was sufficient to sustain the defendant's conviction for attempted robbery as a class A felony.

Defendant also argues that the evidence was insufficient to support the conclusion that he was capable of forming the specific intent to attempt the robbery. He predicates his defense of intoxication on his testimony and pretrial statements that he had ingested extensive amounts of drugs prior to the robbery attempt and remembered nothing about it.

Voluntary intoxication is no defense in a criminal proceeding unless it is shown that the defendant was so intoxicated as to be incapable of forming the requisite intent. . . .

Testimony of witness at the robbery scene indicates that the defendant was the person who fired the shot at the ceiling, demanded the cashier turn over the money, and ordered a patron not to interfere in the robbery. The record also reveals that once the store owner began shooting, the defendant had the presence of mind and physical capacity to flee the Brookside Market, drive the getaway car, and flee on foot from police pursuit after abandoning the vehicle. Based on this evidence, the fact-finder could reasonably conclude that the defendant was not so intoxicated that he was incapable of forming the requisite intent.

II

Defendant's contention that the judgment of the trial court is contrary to law is predicated on the argument the court erred in permitting a witness to be questioned about the defendant's prior criminal history. The record reveals, however, that defendant neither objected to the questioning at trial nor challenged it in his motion to correct errors. Consequently, the allegation of error has not been preserved for our review. . . .

For all the foregoing reasons, there was no trial court error and the judgment of the trial court should be affirmed.

Judgment Affirmed.

GIVEN, C. J., and PRENTICE and PIVARNIK, JJ., concur.

DeBRULER, J., concurs in result.

UNITED STATES V. FREEMAN

United States Court of Appeals, Eleventh Circuit, 1986.
804 F.2d 1574.

[This case examines the insanity defense and the Insanity Defense Reform Act of 1984.]

HILL, Circuit Judge.

Appellant Dwayne Freeman challenges his conviction of bank robbery under 18 U.S.C. § 2113(b), (d) (1982). At trial, the facts surrounding the robbery and the defendant's guilt were never at issue. Freeman merely contests the trial court's determination that [he] was sane at the time of the offense. Freeman bases his appeal on two grounds. First, he challenges the constitutionality of the Insanity Defense Reform Act of 1984, Pub.L.No. 98–473, § 402, 98 Stat. 1837, 2057 (codified at 18 U.S.C. § 20 (Supp. 1986); Fed.R.Evid. 704(b). Second, Freeman asserts that as a matter of law, he has established his insanity by clear and convincing evidence. We reject both of the defendant's arguments.

The Insanity Defense Reform Act produced three principal changes to the insanity defense in federal courts. First, the definition of insanity was restricted so that a valid defense only exists where the defendant was "unable to appreciate the nature of the wrongfulness of his acts" at the time of the offense. The amendment thus eliminated the volitional prong of the defense; prior to the Act, a defendant could assert a valid defense if he were unable to appreciate the nature of his act *or* unable to conform his conduct to the law. . . . The second change produced by the Act resulted in a shifting of the burden of proof from the government to the defendant. Prior to the Act, the government was required to prove beyond a reasonable doubt that the defendant was sane at the time of the offense. . . . Under the current act, the defendant must prove his insanity by clear and convincing evidence. . . . The third change prohibits experts for either the government or defendant from testifying as to the ultimate issue of the accused's sanity. . . .

The defendant's principal contention concerning the constitutionality of the act pertains to the burden of proof being placed on the defendant. . . . *Davis v. United States*, 160 U.S. 469, 16 S. Ct. 353, 40 L.Ed. 499 (1895), established that the prosecution must prove the defendant's sanity beyond a reasonable doubt in federal cases. The Supreme Court, however, has pointed out that *Davis* is not a constitutional ruling, but an exercise of the Supreme Court's supervisory power over prosecutions in federal court. *Leland v. Oregon*, 343 U.S. 790, 72 S. Ct. 1002, 96 L.Ed. 1302 (1952); *Patterson v. New York*, 432 U.S. 197, 97 S. Ct. 2319, 53 L.Ed.2d 281 (1977).

In *Leland*, the Court held that a state could constitutionally require a defendant to prove insanity beyond a reasonable doubt. . . . The Supreme court . . . has repeatedly reaffirmed the *Leland* holding. . . .

At oral argument, Freeman attempted to distinguish *Leland* by urging this court to adopt stricter constitutional standards for federal courts than that required for state courts under *Leland*. The only suggestion we can find indicating that federal courts may discover stricter constitutional requirements for federal criminal trials than state criminal trials is *United States v. Mitchell*, 725 F.2d 832, 835 n. 5 (2d Cir. 1983). To the extent that *Mitchell* goes beyond observing that the Bill of Rights were only partially incorporated by the fourteenth amendment, we disagree with it. No logical basis exists to distinguish between a state legislature's constitutional power to require a defendant to prove insanity and the United States Congress' power to require defendant to prove insanity. The United States Constitution does not draw meaningless distinctions. Therefore, *Leland* compels a holding that the aspect of the Insanity Reform Act of 1984 requiring a defendant to prove insanity by clear and convincing evidence is constitutional.

Additionally, we hold that the Act's restriction against opinion testimony as to the ultimate issue of insanity does not restrict the defendant in the preparation of his defense in violation of the Fifth Amendment. . . . The defendant is not prohibited from introducing evidence which would assist the jury in making this determination. Furthermore, the restriction . . . is applicable to the government, as well as the defendant. There is no constitutional violation. . . .

Freeman additionally contends that he has established his insanity by clear and convincing evidence. [At trial,] Dwayne Freeman asserted that he was an enthusiastic volunteer for the "Save the Children" campaign to feed starving children in drought-stricken Ethiopia. Freeman's evidence was that he degenerated to the point of obsession. He then became depressed about not raising enough money for the children. On February 26, 1985, Freeman robbed a bank, allegedly to obtain money for the Ethiopia fund.

The district court found that the defendant had failed to prove by clear and convincing evidence that he was unable to appreciate the nature and quality of his acts at the time of the offense. . . .

A psychiatric team from the federal institute at Springfield, Missouri did conclude that Freeman was suffering from severe mental illness and was manic depressive or possibly schizophrenic. Additionally, Freeman presented evidence showing that he had been hearing noises and was experiencing severe depression prior to the robbery. Ample evidence exists, however, indicating that Freeman knew his conduct was wrongful. The evidence shows Freeman changed his clothes after robbing the bank to avoid identification. Freeman employed a mask, handgun and satchel to execute the robbery and avoid apprehension. He informed bank personnel that if the police were called, he would come back and kill everyone. When spotted by the police, Freeman ran to avoid apprehension. Finally, Freeman's probation officer observed Freeman's demeanor as being entirely appropriate following his arrest. The district court's decision was not clearly erroneous.

We therefore AFFIRM the district court's decision.

STATE V. FREEMAN

Supreme Court of Iowa, 1990.
450 N.W.2d 826.

[In this case, the Iowa Supreme Court considers the defense of mistake of fact in the context of a conviction for "delivering a simulated controlled substance."]

MCGIVERIN, Chief Justice.

The facts of this case are not disputed. The defendant, Robert Eric Freeman, agreed to sell a controlled substance, cocaine, to Keith Hatcher. Unfortunately for Freeman, Hatcher was cooperating with the government. Hatcher gave Freeman $200, and Freeman gave Hatcher approximately two grams of what was supposed to be cocaine. To everyone's surprise, the "cocaine" turned out to be acetaminophen. Acetaminophen is not a controlled substance.

Freeman was convicted at a bench trial of delivering a simulated controlled substance with respect to a substance represented to be cocaine, in violation of Iowa Code section 204.410(2)(a) (1987). The sole question presented by Freeman's appeal is whether he can be convicted of delivering a simulated controlled substance when, in fact, he believed he was delivering and intended to deliver cocaine.

Our review is to determine whether any error of law occurred. Iowa R.App.P. 4. Finding no error, we affirm the conviction.

I. The statutory framework.

Iowa Code section 204.410(2) provides, in relevant part:

> [I]t is unlawful for a person to create, deliver, or possess with intent to deliver ... a simulated controlled substance....

The term "simulated controlled substance" is defined by Iowa Code section 204.10(27):

> "Simulated controlled substance" means a substance which is not a controlled substance but which is expressly represented to be a controlled substance, or a substance which is not a controlled substance but which is impliedly represented to be a controlled substance and which because of its nature, packaging, or appearance would lead a reasonable person to believe it to be a controlled substance.

Violation of section 204.401(2) with respect to a simulated controlled substance represented to be cocaine is a class "C" felony....

II. Scienter and the offense of delivery of a simulated controlled substance.

Our cases indicate that knowledge of the nature of the substance delivered is an imputed element of section 204.401(1) offenses.... Proof of such knowledge has been required to separate those persons who innocently commit the overt acts of the offense from those persons who commit the overt acts of the offense with scienter, or criminal intent.... In general, only the latter are criminally responsible for their acts....

The Iowa Code prohibits delivery of controlled substances and imitation controlled substances, as well as delivery of counterfeit substances, in language nearly identical to that prohibiting delivery of simulated controlled substances.... The distinctions between these statutory classifications are not relevant to this case.

Seizing upon the similarity of the statutory prohibitions, Freeman argues that he cannot be convicted of delivering a simulated controlled substance because he mistakenly believed he was delivering and intended to deliver an actual controlled substance.

We disagree. Freeman's construction of section 204.401(2) would convert the offense of delivery of a simulated controlled substance into one requiring knowing misrepresentation of the nature of the substance delivered. The statute clearly does not require knowing misrepresentation of the nature of the substance delivered.

Reading sections 204.401(2) and 204.10(27) together shows that the gist of this offense is knowing representation of a substance to be a controlled substance and delivery of a noncontrolled substance rather than knowing misrepresentation and delivery. As one court explained under similar circumstances, statutes like section 204.401(2) are designed "to discourage anyone from engaging or appearing to engage in the narcotics traffic rather than to define the contractual rights of the pusher and his victim. . . ."

Freeman's mistaken belief regarding the substance he delivered cannot save him from conviction. Mistake of fact is a defense to a crime of scienter or criminal intent only where the mistake precludes the existence of the mental state necessary to commit the crime. . . . In this case, Freeman would not be innocent of wrongdoing had the situation been as he supposed; rather he would be guilty of delivering a controlled substance. His mistake is no defense. The scienter required to hold him criminally responsible for committing the overt acts of the charged offense is present regardless of the mistake. Freeman knowingly represented to Hatcher that the substance he delivered was cocaine.

In conclusion, we hold that a person who delivers a substance that is not a controlled substance, but who knowingly represents the substance to be a controlled substance, commits the offense of delivery of a simulated controlled substance regardless of whether the person believed that the substance was controlled or not controlled. . . .

Affirmed.

PEOPLE V. GREENE

Appellate Court of Illinois, 1987.
160 Ill. App. 3d 1089, 112 Ill. Dec. 483, 513 N.E.2d 1092.

[This case examines, among other things, self-defense as a defense to a homicide charge.]

Justice MANNING delivered the opinion of the court.

Defendant, James Greene, was charged by indictment with the murder of Rickey Baldwin. Following a bench trial in the circuit court of Cook County, the defendant was found guilty of murder (Ill. Rev.Stat.1985, ch. 38, par. 9–1), and sentenced to 27 years imprisonment. . . . Defendant contends in his appeal that: (1) the trial court erred by restricting cross-examination of one of the State's witnesses; (2) he was not proved guilty of murder beyond a reasonable doubt; (3) the evidence justified at the most a conviction for voluntary manslaughter; and (4) the sentence of 27 years imprisonment was excessive.

Hugh Adams testified that during the early morning hours on July 29, 1983, he was standing outside of the Ida B. Wells housing project at 39th and Langley Avenue when he saw the victims, Rickey Baldwin ("Rickey Dog") and Marcus Thompson ("Morocco") leave the building located at 706 East 39th Street. Baldwin (hereinafter referred to as the victim) was carrying a ten-speed bicycle. He called out to Adams and Adams walked towards him and Thompson. At this time Adams noticed the defendant standing near the side of the 706 East 39th Street building. He saw the defendant reach into his pants, pull out a gun and fire one shot at the group.

Adams yelled, "break" and they all ran in different directions. After Adams ran across the street, he turned and saw defendant chase the victim. When the victim tripped over a chain and tried to flee, defendant shot him in the back. The defendant then put the gun in the front of his pants, ran towards Adams and proceeded to the housing project.

Marcus Thompson testified that on July 29, 1983, during the early morning hours he was on the eighth floor of the 706 East 39th Street building when the victim left his girlfriend's apartment. Thompson told the victim that he had seen the defendant earlier in the building. The victim pulled a 30-inch chain from his ten-speed bicycle and the two of them walked down the back stairs and left the building together. The victim was a member of the Black P. Stone Rangers gang and defendant was a member of the Gangster Goon Squad, a rival gang.

After they exited the building, the victim called Hugh Adams, who began walking towards them, and it was at this time that the defendant shot at the group. The victim, Adams and Thompson ran in different directions. The defendant chased only the victim. Thompson testified that he heard a second shot fired but he did not actually see the defendant shoot the victim, nor did he see a chain beside the victim after he had been shot.

Thompson heard no verbal exchange between defendant and victim before the former fired the weapon nor did he observe the victim physically threaten defendant with a chain.

The defendant, James Greene, testified that he did not intentionally try to kill the victim. However, when the victim, Adams and Thompson began walking towards him, he was "scared" and "panicked" because of a prior encounter with the victim. Specifically, on September 17, 1982, the victim and some of his friends followed defendant after he left a store at 38th and Cottage Grove. Defendant was shot by someone in the victim's group. The defendant was hospitalized for six months as a result of the gunshot wound. Also, the bullet was never removed because it was too close to his heart. The defendant added that a relative of the victim came to the hospital and told defendant that he "better not say nothing." Although the defendant did not at that time tell the police who had shot him, he had told his brother that "Rickey Dog" shot him.

The defendant further testified that on July 29, 1983, at midnight, he visited his girlfriend on the 8th floor of the 706 East 39th Street building. When he arrived on the eighth floor, the victim and Thompson were there, but defendant did not speak to them. When defendant left his girlfriend's apartment at 1:30 A.M. the victim and Thompson faced the front of the building. Defendant added that he went down the back stairs to avoid them but walked "through the building" and exited from the front entrance.

Defendant proceeded to the corner, turned and heard either the victim or Thompson "drop a bicycle." He observed the victim, who had a "chain wrapped double around his hand," and Thompson approached him. Thompson then called Hugh Adams who was across the street. Thompson, Adams and the victim then walked toward the defendant who pulled out a gun and fired a shot. When the three men fled, defendant pursued the victim, whom defendant shot from a distance of 10 to 15 feet while the victim was running away.

Detective Henry Sigler was assigned to investigate the death of Rickey Baldwin. Defendant was arrested on January 3, 1984, and signed a written confession on January 4, 1984, which stated that after the victim tripped over a small chain fence the defendant shot him in the back. The statement was stipulated to at trial. Additionally, there was a stipulation regarding a report submitted by the Cook County Medical Examiner's Office which performed a postmortem examination on the victim. Dr. Eupil Choi would testify "that Rickey Baldwin died of a bullet wound of the back with penetrations in the aorta and the lung, with internal bleeding."

At the close of all the evidence, the court found the defendant guilty of murder, and sentenced him to 27 years imprisonment. Subsequently, defense counsel filed a written motion for a new trial and a motion to reduce the sentence. Both motions were denied by the trial court and the defendant filed this appeal.

The defendant contends that the trial court erred by barring the defense from cross-examination one of the State's occurrence witnesses concerning that witness' recent arrest for possession of a controlled substance and the factual matrix surrounding the victim's and witness' plea of guilty to a charge of felony theft in May of 1983. . . .

The defendant . . . contends that the weight of the evidence showed that he acted in self-defense when he shot the victim and that his conviction for murder should be reversed. Alternatively, the defendant argues that his murder conviction should be reduced to voluntary manslaughter since he had a reasonable belief that he was acting in self-defense. Whether a homicide is murder or manslaughter, or whether it is justified as self-defense, is a question to be determined by the trier of fact. . . .

The defendant relies upon the following factors to support his contention that he acted in self-defense. The victim was: (1) a convicted felon; (2) a member of a rival gang; (3) armed with a chain; (4) older than the defendant; (5) accompanied by two companions while the defendant was alone; and (6) the victim had accompanied other individuals, one of whom had shot the defendant the previous year.

The general rule regarding justifiable use of force provides:

> A person is justified in the use of force against another when and to the extent that he reasonably believes that such conduct is necessary to defend himself or another against such other's imminent use of unlawful force. However, he is justified in the use of force which is intended or likely to cause death or great bodily harm only if he reasonably believes that such force is necessary to prevent imminent death or great bodily harm to himself or another, or the commission of a forceable felony. . . .

The use of force in defense of the person is justified where (1) that force is threatened against the person; (2) the person threatened is not the aggressor; (3) the danger of harm is imminent; (4) the force threatened is unlawful; and (5) the person threatened must actually believe that a danger exists, that the use of force is necessary and that such beliefs are reasonable. . . .

The issue of self-defense is an affirmative defense based upon satisfaction of the above elements. . . . This defense is raised only if the defendant presents some evidence regarding each element. . . . Once the issue is raised, the State must prove beyond a reasonable doubt that the defendant did not act in self-defense. . . .

This issue of self-defense is determined by the trier of fact. If the trier of fact has determined that the State has negated beyond a reasonable doubt any one of the elements justifying the use of force, then the State has carried its burden of proof. . . . The trier of fact's decision on the issue of self-defense will not be disturbed on review unless the decision is so improbable or unsatisfactory as to raise a reasonable doubt of the defendant's guilt. . . .

The State argues that in the instant case there was no evidence to support self-defense. We agree. The defendant became the aggressor when he fired a warning shot at the three individuals approaching him who withdrew when defendant fired the weapon. Defendant then proceeded to chase only the victim and shot him in the back. Therefore, he can not claim that he was in imminent fear of death or great bodily harm. If the defendant is the aggressor, the use of deadly force is justified only if:

> (1) Such force is so great that he reasonably believes that he is in imminent danger of death or great bodily harm, and that he has exhausted every reasonable means to escape such danger other than the use of force which is likely to cause death or great bodily harm to the assailant; or (2) In good faith, he withdraws from physical contact with the assailant and indicates clearly to the assailant that he desires to withdraw and terminate the use of force. . . .

The defendant as the aggressor never attempted to escape the danger, if such danger existed. Moreover, he never withdrew nor terminated the use of force. In fact, he accelerated his use of force by pursuing the victim and firing a second shot, although the victim had retreated.

A reading of the record fails to reveal any evidence which tends to show that force was threatened against the defendant. Although it is undisputed that the victim was carrying a 30-inch chain, there is no evidence that the victim used the chain to threaten the defendant. Moreover, by the defendant's own testimony he admitted to shooting the victim in the back from a distance of 10 feet.

Even if the victim had been the initial aggressor, the right of self-defense does not permit the pursuit and killing in retaliation or revenge of an initial aggressor after he retreats. . . .

Clearly, the evidence supports the trial court's decision to reject defendant's claim of self-defense. After a review of the record, we must conclude that the trial court's decision was not so improbable or unsatisfactory as to suggest reasonable doubt of the defendant's guilt.

Alternatively, the defendant contends that the evidence supports a finding of voluntary manslaughter. A person commits voluntary manslaughter if he kills an individual without lawful justification under a sudden and intense passion resulting from serious provocation, or if he intentionally or knowingly kills an individual believing the circumstances would justify or exonerate the killing, but his belief is unreasonable. . . .

The record in the instant case revealed that the defendant did not act under a "sudden and intense passion resulting from serious provocation." Defendant testified that no verbal exchange occurred between the defendant and victim nor did the victim physically threaten him with the chain. The defendant deliberately chased and shot the victim after the latter fell.

In regards to the defendant's unreasonable belief that the circumstances would justify the killing, defendant points out that he was "scared" and "panicked" when Thompson, Adams and the victim began to walk towards him. However, we fail to see how the defendant could have been in fear of harm from these individuals when they ran after the first shot was fired. We believe that the evidence supports a finding that the defendant had no subjective belief that the force he used was necessary, which is consistent with the finding of murder, not voluntary manslaughter.

A person commits murder if he either intends to kill or do great bodily harm to that individual or another or if he knows that such acts create a strong probability of death or great bodily harm. . . . It is not necessary to prove that the defendant had the intent to commit murder, only that he voluntarily and willfully committed an act, the natural consequences of which was to cause death or great bodily harm. . . . Although the defendant asserts that he did not intentionally kill the victim, he knew or should have known that the natural and probable consequences of shooting the victim in the back would cause death or do great bodily harm.

The reviewing court's power to reduce a murder conviction to manslaughter . . . should be cautiously exercised. . . . Based on the facts of this case we will not substitute our judgment for that of the trier of fact. We find no reason to disturb the trial court's finding upon review. . . .

JUDGMENT AFFIRMED.

CAMPBELL and O'CONNOR, JJ., concurring.

CRUZ V. STATE

Supreme Court of Florida, 1985.
465 So.2d 516.

[This case examines the defense of entrapment.]

EHRLICH, Justice.

This case is before us on appeal from a decision of the Second District Court of Appeal, *State v. Cruz,* 426 So.2d 1308 (Fla. 2d DCA 1983). The decision directly and expressly conflicts with *State v. Casper,* 417 So.2d 263 (Fla. 1st DCA), review denied, 418 So.2d 1280 (Fla. 1982). We take jurisdiction pursuant to article V. section 3(b)(3), Florida Constitution. We disapprove the district court's decision.

Tampa police undertook a decoy operation in a high-crime area. An officer posed as an inebriated indigent, smelling of alcohol and pretending to drink wine from a bottle. The officer leaned against a building near an alleyway, his face to the wall. Plainly displayed from a rear pants pocket was $150 in currency, paper-clipped together. Defendant Cruz and a woman happened upon the scene as passersby some time after 10 P.M. Cruz approached the decoy officer, may have attempted to say something to him, then continued on his way. Ten to fifteen minutes later, the defendant and his companion returned to the scene and Cruz took the money from the decoy's pocket without harming him in any way. Officers then arrested Cruz as he walked from the scene. The decoy situation did not involve the same modus operandi as any of the unsolved crimes which had occurred in the area. Police were not seeking a particular individual, nor were they aware of any prior criminal acts by the defendant.

Cruz was charged by information with grand theft. Pursuant to Florida Rule of Criminal Procedure 3.190(c)(4), Cruz moved to dismiss the information, arguing that the arrest constituted entrapment as a matter of law. The trial court granted the motion to dismiss on the authority of *State v. Casper*. . . . On appeal, the Second District court of appeal reversed, acknowledging its decision was in conflict with Casper.

The entrapment defense arises from a recognition that sometimes police activity will induce an otherwise innocent individual to commit the criminal act the police activity seeks to produce. . . .

The entrapment defense . . . normally focuses on the predisposition of the defendant. We adopted this view in *State v. Dickinson*, 370 So.2d 762 (Fla. 1979). The First District, in *State v. Casper*, . . . focused on predisposition when it found the "drunken bum"decoy at issue here to constitute entrapment as a matter of law. In *Casper*, Jacksonville police set up a decoy situation legally indistinguishable from the scenario in this case. The *Casper* court held that the state must prove the defendant was predisposed to steal from the decoy and that predisposition can be found under four circumstances: (1) the defendant has prior convictions for similar crimes; (2) the defendant has a reputation for committing similar crimes; (3) police have a reasonable suspicion the defendant was engaged in similar crimes; or (4) the defendant showed ready acquiescence to commit the crime suggested by police. . . . The *Casper* court found no evidence of the first two elements in that case. The third element is irrelevant in the type of random expedition at issue here. The question thus boiled down to whether Casper "readily acquiesced" to the criminal scenario. The *Casper* court found that an otherwise unpredisposed passerby who chose to take the money did not acquiesce, but "succumbed to temptation . . . to the lure of the bait." . . . The *Casper* court therefore distinguished between "succumbing to temptation" and "readily acquiescing," and found that this is a question of law: where a trial judge finds the defendant succumbed to temptation, the matter shall not be put to a jury.

The Second District, in the case now before us, rejected this position. The *Cruz* court found that such a judgment is one for the jury to make. "[W]here, as here, a defendant's intent or state of mind (i.e., predisposition) is an issue, that issue should not be decided on a motion to dismiss. . . . Petitioner would have this court hold that where the only evidence of predisposition is the commission of the crime the police scenario was designed to elicit, there is an insufficient showing of predisposition, as a matter of law. We do not agree.

We agree with the Second District that the question of predisposition will always be a question of fact for the jury. However, we also believe that the First District's concern for entrapment scenarios in which the innocent will succumb to temptation is well founded. To protect against such abuse, we turn to another aspect of entrapment.

Entrapment is a potentially dangerous tool given to police to fight crime. "Society is at war with the criminal classes, and courts have uniformly held that in waging this warfare the forces of prevention and detection may use traps, decoys, and deception to obtain evidence of crime." . . . "The appropriate object of this permitted activity, frequently essential to the enforcement of the law, is to reveal the criminal design; to expose the illicit traffic, the prohibited publication, the fraudulent use of the mails, the illegal conspiracy, or other offenses, and thus to disclose the would-be violators of the law. A different question is presented when the criminal design originates with the officials of the Government, and they implant in the mind of an innocent person the disposition to commit the alleged offense and induce its commission in order that they may prosecute." . . . "Such a gross abuse of authority given for the purpose of detecting and punishing crime, and not for the making of criminals, deserves the severest condemnation, but the question whether it precludes prosecution or affords a ground of defense, and, if so, upon what theory, has given rise to conflicting opinions." . . .

To guide the trial courts, we propound the following threshold test of an entrapment defense: Entrapment has not occurred as a matter of law where police activity (1) has as its end the interruption of a specific ongoing criminal activity; and (2) utilizes means reasonably tailored to apprehend those involved in the ongoing criminal activity.

The first prong of this test addresses the problem of police "virtue testing," that is, police activity seeking to prosecute crime where no such crime exists but for the police activity engendering the crime. As Justice Roberts wrote . . . , "society is at war with the criminal classes." . . . Police must fight this war, not engage in the manufacture of new hostilities.

The second prong of the threshold test addresses the problem of inappropriate techniques. Considerations in deciding whether police activity is permissible under this prong include whether a government agent "induces or encourages another person to engage in conduct constituting such offense by either: (a) making knowingly false representations designed to induce the belief that such conduct is not prohibited: or (b) employing methods of persuasion or inducement which create a substantial risk that such an offense will be committed by persons other than those who are ready to commit it." ...

Applying this test to the case before us, we find that the drunken bum decoy operation fails. In Cruz's motion to dismiss, one of the undisputed facts was that "none of the unsolved crimes occurring near this location involved the same modus operandi as the simulated situation created by the officers." ... The record thus implies police were apparently attempting to interrupt some kind of ongoing criminal activity. However, the record does not show what specific activity was targeted. This lack of focus is sufficient for the scenario to fail the first prong of the test. However, even if the police were seeking to catch persons who had been "rolling" drunks in the area, the criminal scenario here, with $150 (paper-clipped to ensure more than $100 was taken, making the offense a felony) enticingly protruding from the back pocket of a person seemingly incapable of noticing its removal, carries with it the "substantial risk that such an offense will be committed by persons other than those who are ready to commit it." ... This sufficiently addresses the *Casper* court's proper recognition that entrapment has occurred where "the decoy simply provided the opportunity to commit a crime to anyone who succumbed to the lure of the bait." ... This test also recognizes, as the *Cruz* court did, that the considerations inherent in our threshold test are not properly addressed in the context of the predisposition element of the second, subjective test.

For the reasons discussed, we hold that the police activity in the instant case constituted entrapment as a matter of law under the threshold test adopted here. Accordingly, we quash the district court decision.

It is so ordered. . . .

ALDERMAN, Justice, dissenting. . . .

CHAPTER 14

The Dynamics of the Criminal Law

CHAPTER OUTLINE

Introduction
Issues Involving the Exercise of Constitutional Rights
Elements of Crime—Criminal Intent
Inchoate Crimes
Offenses Against Persons
Crimes Against Property and Habitation
Offenses Against Morality
Drugs and Alcohol Offenses
Offenses Against Public Health and the Environment
Offenses Against Public Order and Safety
Offenses Against Justice and Public Administration
Criminal Responsibility and Defenses
The 1994 Federal Crime Bill
Conclusion

Cases
United States v. Lopez

INTRODUCTION

As we noted in Chapter 1, law is a formal means of social control. In the criminal law the standards for defining offenses to protect persons and property and society's interests in peace, order, safety, and decency are dynamic. From its early common-law heritage, the development of the substantive criminal law in America has closely followed the progress of society, generally reflecting its changing norms. This closing chapter focuses on some significant recent developments and trends in the continuing definition of substantive crimes. The chapter begins with an examination of current criminal law issues involving the exercise of constitutional rights. It closes with a brief analysis of the landmark federal Crime Bill of 1994.

ISSUES INVOLVING THE EXERCISE OF CONSTITUTIONAL RIGHTS

Section 5 of the Fourteenth Amendment to the U.S. Constitution authorizes Congress to enact "appropriate legislation" to protect citizens in the enjoyment of civil rights and liberties. In recent years Congress has invoked this power by enacting laws aimed at the protection of religious properties and the exercise of abortion rights.

Protection of Religious Properties

In 1988 Congress made it a federal crime to vandalize religious property or otherwise interfere with any person's free exercise of religion. 18 U.S.C.A. § 247. Since the law was enacted, despite thousands of instances of vandalism against churches, synagogues, and other religious properties, federal prosecutions have been extremely rare. This has led some to question the federal government's seriousness about the problem.

Access to Abortion and the Right to Oppose Legalized Abortion

Few questions today have greater philosophical, religious, ethical, medical, and political saliency than the issue of abortion. The Supreme Court's seminal decision *Roe v. Wade*, 419 U.S. 113, 93 S.Ct. 705, 35 L.Ed.2d 147 (1973)—declaring that the constitutional right to privacy includes a right to abortion—remains basically intact. Seemingly irreconcilable views on the subject of abortion exist, however, and the issue continues to spawn legislative and judicial attention. The continuing clashes between demonstrators resulting in injuries and even death have caused some states to respond by restricting the proximity of demonstrators to clinics. In *Madsen v. Women's Health Center*, 512 U.S. ____, 114 S.Ct. 2516, 129 L.Ed.2d 593 (1994), the U.S. Supreme Court attempted to balance the constitutional rights of those seeking access to abortion clinics against the First Amendment rights of the protesters. In a 6–3 decision, the Court upheld the basic provisions of a state court injunction intended to keep disruptive protesters from blocking access to the clinics.

On May 26, 1994, President Clinton signed the "Freedom of Access to Clinic Entrances Act" (FACE), 18 U.S.C.A. § 248. The new federal law was prompted by the 1993 killing of an abortion doctor outside a Pensacola clinic, as well as by numerous episodes around the country in which persons working at or seeking access to abortion clinics had been harassed and threatened by antiabortion activists. The new Act provides civil and criminal remedies against

> whoever by force or threat of force or physical obstruction, intentionally injures, intimidates or interferes with or attempts to injure, intimidate or interfere with any person because that person is or has been, or in order to intimidate such person or any other person or any class of persons from obtaining or providing reproductive health services. 18 U.S.C.A. § 248.

An initial interpretation by a U.S. District Court for the Eastern District of Virginia in June 1994 held that the new Act was within the power delegated to Congress under the Commerce Clause of the U.S. Constitution. Further, the court declared that the Act does not violate the freedoms of speech and religion protected by the First Amendment. *American Life League, Inc. v. Reno,* 855 F.Supp. 137 (E.D. Va. 1994).

In October 1994, Paul Hill, a former minister, became the first person in the nation to be found guilty of violating FACE, the new federal law, by his shotgun slayings of a physician and his escort outside an abortion clinic in Pensacola, Florida. On December 2, 1994, Hill received two life prison terms for the federal violations. Hill was subsequently tried in state court on charges of murder and attempted murder arising out of the event at the clinic. After the state court trial judge denied Hill the right to assert "justifiable homicide" as a defense, a jury in Pensacola, Florida found him guilty of first-degree (premeditated) murder. On December 7, 1994, after the jury recommended the death penalty, the state court sentenced Hill to die in the electric chair. The court appointed a public defender to assist Hill, who had represented himself at trial, with the mandatory appeal to the Florida Supreme Court.

ELEMENTS OF CRIMES—CRIMINAL INTENT

As noted in Chapter 4, criminal intent, or *mens rea,* is an essential element of most crimes. In 1993, state courts continued to refine the doctrine of transferred intent. In 1994, the U.S. Supreme Court scrutinized statutory offenses outside the field of public health that did not include an explicit intent requirement.

The Doctrine of Transferred Intent

The doctrine of transferred intent links the perpetrator's mental state toward an intended victim with the resulting harm to another person who inadvertently becomes the victim. In the classic illustration, A aims a gun at B intending to kill B. A misses and instead kills C. A's mental state directed against B is said to be transferred to C, the unintended victim (see Chapter 4). The purpose of the doctrine of transferred intent is to prevent a defendant who has committed all the elements of a crime from escaping responsibility for that crime.

In *Ford v. State*, 625 A.2d 984 (Md. 1993), Maryland's highest court recognized that the doctrine of transferred intent applies to both general- and specific-intent crimes, but the court distinguished its applicability to two types of specific-intent offenses. The first requires a specific intent to cause somebody a specific type of harm, and the doctrine is applicable. The second includes only those offenses that, by statutory definition, require a specific intent to cause a *specific type of harm to a specific person* (i.e., where the statute requires that the defendant's intent be directed toward the actual victim). Thus, if a defendant charged with attempted murder shot at but missed the intended victim, the defendant may still be convicted of attempted murder. In such an instance the defendant's *premeditated intent* to kill a specific victim would not apply to an unintended victim who was killed. Of course, a killing of an unintended victim resulting from such an event could be prosecuted as a homicidal crime, but not one that required the defendant's specific intent to murder. A similar rationale was adopted earlier by a California appellate court. See *People v. Birreuta,* 208 Cal. Rptr. 635 (Cal. App. 1984).

Strict Liability

The so-called strict liability offenses are those in which the prosecution is not required to prove the defendant's criminal intent. In Chapter 10 we point out that statutes regulating the public health are generally strict liability laws, and the prosecution is not required to establish a violator's intent. But in dealing with statutory crimes outside the ambit of "regulatory" laws, courts often take a different view. Recent federal decisions illustrate how this concept has come under increased scrutiny by the courts.

In *United States v. Garrett*, 984 F.2d 1402 (5th Cir. 1993), a federal appeals court reviewed a defendant's conviction for violation of a federal law making it a misdemeanor to board an aircraft with a concealed weapon. The federal statute, 49 U.S.C.A. App. § 1472(l)(1), is silent on the question of *mens rea.* Nevertheless, the court presumed that some degree of mental element was appropriate and applied a "defendant should have known" standard that requires the prosecution to prove the defendant had at least a minimal level of intent to commit an unlawful act.

In 1994, the U.S. Supreme Court issued two significant opinions rejecting the applicability of strict liability concepts to federal criminal statutes. The first of these cases involved a defendant, Waldemar Ratzlaf, who sought to pay a Nevada casino a gambling debt with $100,000 cash. When he was informed that the casino would have to report to state and federal authorities all cash payments in excess of $10,000, he structured his payments by delivering a series of $9,500 cashier's checks to the casino. Ratzlaf was charged with violating the provisions of 31 U.S.C.A. §§ 5322 & 5324 that make it a crime to willfully violate certain "antistructuring" provisions. At Ratzlaf's trial, the judge instructed the jury that the government only had to prove Ratzlaf's knowledge of the reporting requirement and his intent to evade that requirement, not that Ratzlaf knew that structuring was unlawful. The Ninth Circuit Court of Appeals affirmed his conviction. *United States v. Ratzlaf*, 976 F.2d 1280 (9th Cir. 1992).

In January 1994, the U.S. Supreme Court in a 5–4 decision reversed Ratzlaf's conviction and held that to obtain a conviction under the federal statute the government must prove that the defendant knew that his conduct was unlawful. *Ratzlaf v. United States,* 510 U.S. ___, 114 S.Ct. 655, 126 L.Ed.2d 615 (1994). In the Court's majority opinion, Justice Ginsburg recognized the common practice of taxpayers "structuring" their affairs to take advantage of revenue laws. She wrote:

> [W]e are unpersuaded by the argument that structuring is so obviously "evil" or inherently "bad" that the "willfulness" requirement is satisfied irrespective of the defendant's knowledge of the illegality of structuring. 114 S.Ct. at 662.

A dissenting justice pointed out that "the majority's interpretation of the anti-structuring provision is at odds with . . . the fundamental principle that knowledge of illegality is not required for a criminal act." 114 S.Ct. at 670.

Following this, in May 1994, the Supreme Court reversed the conviction of Harold E. Staples for unlawful possession of an unregistered firearm, an offense under 26 U.S.C.A. § 586(d). *Staples v. United States,* 511 U.S. ___, 114 S.Ct. 1793, 128 L.Ed.2d 608 (1994). Section 586(d) is also silent as to any requirement that the government must prove the accused's intent in order to establish a violation. Over Staples' objection, the trial judge instructed the jury as follows:

> The Government need not prove the defendant knows he's dealing with a weapon possessing every last characteristic [which subjects it] to the regulation. It would be enough to prove he knows that he is dealing with a dangerous device of a type as would alert one to the likelihood of regulation. 114 S.Ct. at 1796.

The Supreme Court disapproved of the trial judge's instructions and rejected the argument that the Act was a public welfare statute and therefore did not possess a *mens rea* element. Instead, the Court held that it was incumbent on the Government to prove beyond a reasonable doubt that the defendant knew that the weapon he possessed was defined as a machine-gun under the statute. In doing so, the Court distinguished the criminal charges against Staples from the strict liability "public welfare" and "regulatory" offenses, and observed that the silence on the part of Congress in respect to imposing an intent requirement did not suggest a purpose to dispense with the established common-law rule of requiring some degree of *mens rea* in criminal statutes.

INCHOATE CRIMES

In Chapter 5 we discuss the elements that must be established in the inchoate crimes of attempt, solicitation, and conspiracy. Statutes defining the offenses of attempt and conspiracy commonly refer to a requirement to establish a "substantial step" or "overt act" as an element of each offense.

The Meaning of "Substantial Step" in the Context of Attempt and Conspiracy

In March 1994, in *State v. Dent,* 869 P.2d 392 (1994), the Supreme Court of Washington handed down an opinion articulating the difference between the *actus reus* requirement in the crimes of attempt and conspiracy. Washington statutes include definitions of these two inchoate offenses. *Attempt* is defined as follows:

> A person is guilty of an attempt to commit crime if, with intent to commit a specific crime, he does any act *which is a substantial step toward the commission of that crime.* RCW 9A.28.020(1).

In contrast, *conspiracy* is defined as follows:

> A person is guilty of criminal conspiracy when, with intent that conduct constituting crime be performed, he agrees with one or more persons to engage in or cause the performance of such conduct, and any one of them *takes a substantial step in pursuance of such agreement.* RCW 9A.28.040(1).

The Washington Supreme Court observed that the two crimes differ in the nature of the conduct sought to be prohibited and in the significance of the "substantial step" requirement (known as the "overt act" requirement in some jurisdictions) in each context. "A substantial step," the court noted, "is required in the context of attempt to prevent the imposition of punishment based on intent alone." But the court explained that the purpose of the substantial step or overt act requirement is different in the context of conspiracy. "The purpose of the 'substantial step' requirement is, therefore, to manifest that the conspiracy is at work, and is neither a project still resting solely in the minds of the conspirators nor a fully completed operation no longer in existence." 869 P.2d at 397. For these reasons the court concluded that the state's conspiracy statute requires only an act that is "a 'substantial step' in pursuance of [the] agreement" as opposed to the attempt statute which requires "a substantial step toward the commission of [the] crime." 869 P.2d at 398.

Offenses Against Persons

Offenses against persons include a wide variety of crimes. Reflecting rapid social change, the law in this area is highly dynamic, especially with regard to abortion, suicide, sexual battery, "stalking," and child abuse. The last several years have seen important legal developments with respect to each of these issues.

Homicide

As noted in Chapter 6, the prosecution carries a number of burdens in homicide cases. At common law, the requirement that a fetus be "born alive" precluded a conviction for homicide of the fetus when the accused took the life of a mother who was pregnant with a "viable" fetus (one capable of living outside the mother's womb). To override this doctrine some states, including California, have enacted statutes that define murder to include the unlawful killing of a fetus.

In 1994, the California Supreme Court reviewed a decision where the defendant claimed that because a fetus could have been legally aborted under the ruling in *Roe v. Wade*, 419 U.S. 113, 93 S.Ct. 705, 35 L.Ed.2d 147 (1973), he could not be prosecuted the murder of the mother's fetus. In rejecting the defendant's contention, the court held that as long as a mother's privacy interests in seeking to terminate a pregnancy are not at stake, "the legislature may determine whether, and at what point, it should protect life inside a mother's womb from homicide." The court indicated that as long as a fetus has progressed beyond its embryonic stage of the first seven or eight weeks, a third-party killing of the fetus with malice aforethought is "murder." Thus the court rejected the defendant's contention that the fetus must be viable before an accused can be convicted of a crime for destroying the fetus. A dissenting judge would have construed the term *fetus* in the statute to mean a viable fetus. *People v. Davis*, 872 P.2d 591 (Cal. 1994).

Another obstacle to prosecuting homicide offenses has been the common-law "one year and a day" rule that prohibits holding a person responsible for a victim's death if more than a year and a day intervenes between the time the injury is inflicted and the victim's death. In recent years, several states have either legislatively or judicially abolished this archaic and inflexible rule. Despite this trend, in 1994 a federal appellate court reversed a conviction for murder committed on a United States military reservation where more than one year and a day intervened from the date of assault and the victim's death. The court felt constrained to apply the common-law rule made applicable in federal prosecution for murder in an 1891 decision by the United States Supreme Court. *United States v. Chase*, 18 F.3d 1166 (4th Cir. 1994).

Assisted Suicide

A Michigan trial court held that Dr. Jack Kevorkian could not be found guilty of a homicidal act for having assisted a terminally ill patient to commit suicide. However, on May 10, 1994, in a two-to-one decision, the Michigan Court of Appeals reversed that holding and ruled that Michigan's murder statute applied to Dr. Kevorkian's conduct of assisting victims in voluntarily committing suicide. The court's holding came despite the fact that the act of committing suicide was not a criminal act and regardless of Dr. Kevorkian's status as a physician. The dissenting judge pointed out that neither suicide nor attempted suicide is a crime in Michigan and observed, "It is logically incomprehensible that a person can be charged with a capital crime for aiding and abetting a *lawful* act." *People v. Kevorkian*, 517 N.W.2d 293, 298 (Mich. App. 1994). On December 13, 1994, the Michigan Supreme Court upheld the state's statutory ban on assisted suicide, saying there is no constitutional right to assisted suicide. The court ruled in four consolidated cases, three of which involved criminal charges against Dr. Kevorkian. In its ruling the court observed that while suicide is not murder, "assisting suicide is its own species of crime." 527 N.W.2d 714, 739 (Mich., Dec. 13, 1994). On April 24, 1995, the U.S. Supreme Court declined to consider a challenge by Dr. Kevorkian and others to the Michigan Supreme Court's ruling in December 1994 that the Constitution does not protect any right to assisted suicide.

As noted in Chapter 6, a Michigan law banning assisted suicide that took effect on April 1, 1993, set a fifteen-month period to allow the legislature to address the problem in more depth. News reports said that on November 25, 1994, Dr. Kevorkian assisted in the suicide of his twenty-first "patient" or "victim," depending on how one views the issue. While prosecutors were determining whether to charge Kevorkian, a question was raised as to whether the temporary law had expired. On December 7, 1994, the Michigan Senate passed a bill making permanent the state's temporary ban on assisted suicide. The bill was sent to be voted on by the Michigan House of Representatives.

A proposal to allow physician-assisted suicide was defeated by California voters in 1992. However, on November 8, 1994, voters in Oregon adopted (by a narrow margin) a law providing for physician-assisted suicide for terminally ill patients. Unlike the California proposal that was defeated, the Oregon law provides that the patient must ask for the lethal dose three times, including once in writing. Thereafter, the patient must get a second doctor's opinion and wait fifteen days before being assisted to die. Several physicians, terminally ill patients and residential care facilities challenged the law on various constitutional grounds. The day before it was to take effect, a federal district court in Oregon enjoined its implementation. The court ruled the measure adopted by the voters violated the plaintiffs' freedom of association and religion, and offended the concepts of due process and equal protection of the law. *Lee v. Oregon,* 869 F.Supp. 1491 (D. Or. 1994).

Before the federal court in Oregon ruled in *Lee v. Oregon,* a U.S. District Court in Seattle, Washington had ruled that a Washington state statute that classifies assisted suicide as a felony was unconstitutional. *Compassion in Dying v. State,* 850 F. Supp 1454 (W.D. Wash. 1994). But on March 9, 1995, the U.S. Court of Appeals for the Ninth Circuit, in a 2-1 decision, reversed the district court's decision in *Compassion.* In apparently the highest federal court to rule on the issue of assisted suicide, the Ninth Circuit termed assisted suicide as "antithetical to the defense of human life." Further, the court said: "The district court declared the statute unconstitutional on its face without adequate consideration of Washington's interest that, individually and convergently, outweigh any alleged liberty of suicide."

Sexual Battery

The element of force or a victim's "fear of immediate bodily injury" remains in statutory definitions of intentional sexual battery (rape). The trend has been for courts to find that psychological and emotional stress can constitute the required force where a female has unequivocally denied access to a male seeking sexual intercourse. For example, in *People v. Iniquez,* 872 P.2d 1183 (Cal. 1994), at issue was whether the evidence supported the jury's verdict finding that a victim of a sexual assault had suffered fear of immediate bodily injury, as required by a state statute. On the eve of her wedding the defendant approached the victim as she slept on the floor of a friend's house. He admitted that he removed the victim's pants, fondled her buttocks, and had sexual intercourse with her. And while he acknowledged that she did not consent, he argued, and an intermediate state appellate court agreed, that his conviction should be reversed because there was no evidence of any force nor was the female in fear of immediate bodily injury. On review the California Supreme Court pointed to the fact that the defendant's weight was twice that of the victim's, and that his actions caused the victim's serenity to be violated as she slept. The court further explained that simply because the victim did not say, "I am afraid, please stop," did not negate the fact that she was paralyzed in fear when she submitted, and the jury could have concluded from the evidence that the victim responded simply out of fear. Thus, the California Supreme Court reversed the action taken by the intermediate appellate court and affirmed the defendant's conviction.

A Pennsylvania decision in May 1994 that strictly construed the force requirement in a rape statute attracted widespread media contention. The Pennsylvania Supreme Court reviewed a conviction under a statute defining rape as a serious felony whenever a person engages in sexual intercourse "by forcible compulsion." At trial the female victim had testified that the defendant had at no time threatened her, that his hands did not restrain her in any manner during the actual penetration, and while she stated "no" throughout the encounter, that the weight of his body on top of her was the only force applied. The court recognized the victim's repeated negative assertions as relevant to the issue of consent, but held that the testimony at trial simply failed to prove that the defendant made the female complainant engage in sexual intercourse by forcible compulsion as required by the statute. The court reversed the defendant's conviction for rape but reinstated his conviction for indecent assault. *Commonwealth v. Berkowitz,* 641 A.2d 1161 (Pa., 1994). Some women's groups loudly decried the result of the court's ruling.

As reported in Chapter 6, in May 1993 a Texas jury implicitly rejected a defendant's claim that by asking a male attacker to wear a condom, the female had consented to sexual intercourse; hence he was not guilty of rape. The defendant's contention did not go completely unnoticed. In 1994 the Florida Legislature amended Florida Statutes, Section 794.022, to add:

> An offender's use of a prophylactic device, or a victim's request that an offender use a prophylactic device, is not, by itself, relevant to either the issue of whether or not the offense was committed or the issue of whether or not the victim consented.

Florida Statutes, Section 800.04, makes a sexual relationship with a person under age 16 a felony and provides that neither the victim's lack of chastity nor the victim's consent is a defense. In 1989, the Florida Supreme Court in *In re T.W.,* 551 So.2d 1186 (Fla. 1989), held that the right of privacy provision in Florida's constitution prohibits the legislature from requiring a parent's consent when a minor seeks an abortion. In an attempt to extend that ruling, a defendant convicted of violating Section 800.04 asked the Florida Supreme Court to hold that statute unconstitutional on the ground that it intrudes on the right of a minor to exercise consent to sexual intercourse. In rejecting that contention, the court observed:

> The rights of privacy that have been granted to minors to not vitiate the legislature's efforts and authority to protect minors from conduct of others. . . . Florida has an obligation and a compelling interest in protecting children from sexual activity and exploitation before their minds and bodies have sufficiently matured to make it appropriate, safe and healthy for them. *Jones v. State,* 640 So.2d 1084, 1087 (Fla. 1994).

Stalking

As of 1993, thirty-one states had adopted laws prohibiting "stalking." Stalking laws are designed to punish those who repeatedly follow or harass another. Many of these new statutes require that the stalker first make a "credible threat" against another person. This proved to be an impediment to prosecution, so by late 1994 newer statutes were redefining "credible threat" to include a "pattern of conduct" of actions that includes behavior directed toward the victim or the victim's immediate family or close associates. Additionally, states have been modifying the requirement that stalkers must have the apparent ability to carry out a threat. Instead, new statutory language frequently requires only that a stalker intend "to place a person in reasonable fear for his or her safety."

Can there be stalking by computer? Recently law enforcement authorities have received complaints from women who are being "stalked by computer." This usually involves relentless electronic communications by obsessive admirers designed to torment their victims. With the volume of messages being sent by computer, it is likely that legislatures may soon address computer stalking.

Child Abuse

In *Commonwealth v. Welch,* 864 S.W.2d 280 (Ky. 1993), the Kentucky Supreme Court held that its child abuse statute [KRS 508.110], which criminalizes abuse of "another person of whom [the offender] has actual custody" which "places him in a situation that may cause him serious physical injury" does not apply to a mother whose baby suffered injuries as a result of the mother's ingestion of drugs during her pregnancy. In reaching its decision, the court cited decisions from other courts including the Florida Supreme Court's opinion in *Johnson v. State,* 602 So.2d 1288 (Fla. 1992). In *Johnson v. State,* the court held that cocaine passing through a baby's umbilical cord after birth, but before the cord was cut, did not violate a Florida law making it a crime for an adult to deliver a controlled substance to a minor.

In addition to prohibiting intentional acts of child abuse, statutes frequently make it a criminal offense to "negligently subject a child to endangerment." Because crime definitions must be strictly construed, some courts have found it necessary to admonish the prosecution to make a strong showing of criminal negligence rather than to simply establish the level of negligence required in tort cases such as automobile accidents. See, for example, *Santillanes v. State,* 849 P.2d 358 (N.M. 1993).

CRIMES AGAINST PROPERTY AND HABITATION

In addition to discussing the well-known offenses involving property, in Chapter 7 we mention how the pervasive use of computers has given rise to a variety of new crimes. In turn, legislative bodies have responded by enacting new statutory offenses to cope with the various aspects of computer crime. To cope with the rise in the number of carjackings throughout the nation, states have now followed the lead of the federal government by enacting laws making carjacking a serious felony.

Computer Crimes

A 1994 decision from New York's highest court illustrates how prosecution of computer crimes can involve some very technical aspects. Robert Versaggi was found guilty of computer tampering for intentionally altering two computer programs designed to provide uninterrupted telephone service to the Eastman Kodak corporate offices. The New York computer crime statute did not define the word *alter.* In attempting to reverse his conviction, Versaggi argued that he was not guilty of altering the computer programs because he did not change them; rather, he merely activated existing instructions that commanded the computer to shut down. The court, however, agreed with the prosecution that the defendant's conduct did constitute tampering within the meaning of the statute because it effectively "altered" the computer programs by interrupting the telephone service to Kodak's two office facilities. *People v. Versaggi,* 629 N.E. 2d 1034 (N.Y. 1994).

Carjacking

"Carjacking" is the violent theft of an automobile from the presence of a driver and/or passengers. In the early 1990s, the public became alarmed about the dramatic rise in carjacking. In 1992, Congress enacted 18 U.S.C.A. § 2119, which makes it a federal crime to steal any vehicle "transported, shipped or received in interstate commerce" while possessing a firearm during the commission of the offense. The act is thus based, like many modern federal criminal laws, on Congress' broad power to regulate interstate commerce. See U.S. Const., Art. I, Sec. 8. In 1993, a federal district judge in Nashville, Tennessee, invalidated the carjacking law, declaring that Congress had no constitutional authority to make carjacking a federal crime. *United States v. Cortner,* 834 F.Supp 242 (M.D. Tenn. 1993). Judge Thomas A. Wiseman, Jr. suggested that in deference to Congress, the courts had stretched the Commerce Clause "beyond the wildest imagination of the Framers and beyond any rational interpretation of the language itself," and noted that "Congress has had a recent penchant for passing a federal criminal statute on any well publicized criminal activity." 834 F.Supp. at 244.

In *United States v. Johnson,* 22 F.3d 106 (6th Cir. 1994), the United States Court of Appeals for the Sixth Circuit overruled Judge Wiseman and upheld the constitutionality of the carjacking statute. The court found the law to be well within Congress' power over interstate commerce and noted the numerous instances in which Congress had invoked the Commerce Clause to prohibit criminal activity. The Sixth Circuit also rejected the argument that the new federal statute only covers cars "moving in interstate commerce" at the time of the carjacking. Instead it found that the Act applies even if a car has "come to rest" in a state as long as, at some point, the car was in interstate commerce.

In 1993, the FBI devoted thirteen agents and spent $1.5 million to investigate some 290 carjackings across the country. Considering that nearly 29,000 carjackings were reported nationwide in 1992, the effectiveness of the new federal carjacking statute appears limited. Carjacking thus appears to be a problem primarily for state and local law enforcement authorities. Through recent legislative action, carjacking has become an offense in most states. Rather typical is the amendment to the Michigan Penal Code enacted by the 1994 session of the Michigan Legislature, which is codified as M.C.L.A. § 750.529a:

> A person who by force or violence, or by threat of force or violence, or by putting in fear robs, steals, or takes a motor vehicle . . . from another person, in the presence of that person or the presence of a passenger or in the presence of any other person in lawful possession of the motor vehicle, is guilty of carjacking, a felony.

OFFENSES AGAINST MORALITY

In the past few years, the public and the courts have shown concern for two moral issues: gambling and obscenity. Voters in several states have taken the lead in deciding whether to legalize certain forms of gambling. In the obscenity area, courts have focused on the issue of child pornography.

Gambling

In Chapter 8, Table 8.2 itemizes the extent to which gambling is allowed in the states. By popular initiative in the November 1994 election, the voters in Missouri approved slot machines for riverboats, and in New Mexico they approved video gambling and a lottery. However, voters in Colorado, Florida, Massachusetts, Rhode Island, Wyoming, and the Navajo Reservation rejected casino gambling.

Obscenity

Chapter 8 includes a discussion of the Supreme Court's seminal obscenity decision, *Miller v. California,* 413 U.S. 15, 93 S.Ct. 2607, 37 L.Ed.2d 419 (1973), which defined *community* to permit local juries to base their judgments as to whether materials are obscene on local rather than national standards. In July 1994, a California couple, Robert and Carleen Thomas, were found guilty in federal court in Memphis, Tennessee, of transmitting obscene computer images through interstate phone lines. They were, however, acquitted of engaging in child pornography. The defendants argued that they were held to the high community standards of Tennessee, while the community standards of California would have permitted their activity. Their contention brings into question the applicability of the local community standards announced in *Miller* to material that is transmitted via the "information superhighway."

Child Pornography

In 1982, a unanimous Supreme Court ruled that child pornography laws are not to be judged by the standards that govern obscenity (see Chapter 8). A federal statute, 18 U.S.C.A. § 2252(a)(2), makes it a crime to knowingly transport or ship materials depicting minors engaging in sexually explicit conduct. The problem has been whether it is essential for the government to prove that an accused knows the nature of the child pornography. In *United States v. X-Citement Video, Inc.,* 982 F.2d 1285 (9th Cir. 1992), a Los Angeles porn shop owner was convicted for distributing sexually explicit videotapes after it was established that the actress featured in the tapes had been underage when she made many of the films. The U.S. Court of Appeals for the Ninth Circuit reversed the defendant's conviction and struck down the federal child pornography statute on the ground that it violated the First Amendment. The court noted that the statute defining the offense did not require proof that the defendant knew the porn star was underage.

In November 1994, the Supreme Court overturned the Ninth Circuit's decision. Although the federal statute does not explicitly require the government to prove the defendant's knowledge that materials were pornographic, the Court interpreted the law as if it does. Nevertheless, the Court reinstated the defendant's conviction because it found the government had provided sufficient evidence to establish that the defendant knew the pornographic materials in question involved an underage female. *United States v. X-Citement Video, Inc.,* U.S. ___, 115 S.Ct. 464, 130 L.Ed.2d 372 (1994). Justices Scalia and Thomas dissented, with Justice Scalia saying the Court's decision put "in place a relatively toothless child-pornography law that Congress did not enact." 115 S.Ct. at 476. The dissenters likened the requirements under the federal law to the strict liability requirement in statutory rape laws. They opined that a defendant should be held liable irrespective of knowing if the performer was underage.

DRUG AND ALCOHOL OFFENSES

Although state and federal drug laws have become increasingly punitive, the federal courts are limiting government efforts to prosecute laundering of drug money and government seizures of property used in drug crimes.

Forfeiture of Property

Frequently, federal and state governments have seized property belonging to defendants found guilty of drug offenses. After James Daniel Good pled guilty to a drug offense, the United States sought forfeiture of his house and land. Without prior notice or hearing to Good, the federal magistrate authorized the government to seize Good's property. In *United States v. Good Real Property,* 510 U.S. ___, 114 S.Ct. 492, 126 L.Ed.2d 490 (1993), the Supreme Court ruled that the government is constitutionally prohibited from seizing real property, in the absence of exigent circumstances, without first notifying and affording the owner a hearing.

Money Laundering

Bobby McDougold, a former Green Beret sergeant who was wounded in Vietnam, was convicted of "money laundering," an offense under 18 U.S.C.A. § 1956. McDougold had purchased a 1990 Beretta for cash given to him by a friend who was a known drug dealer. In reviewing his conviction, the federal appellate court noted that there was no documentary evidence and no direct testimony that the defendant knew the money he received was "drug money." Rather, the government's evidence showed only that the money came from drug dealers who were friends of the defendant. Finally, the court pointed out that even if the defendant knew that the $10,000 he used to purchase an automobile was drug money, there was insufficient evidence to show that he knew of its source. Accordingly, the U.S. Court of Appeals reversed his conviction. *United States v. McDougold,* 990 F.2d 259 (6th Cir. 1993).

OFFENSES AGAINST PUBLIC HEALTH AND THE ENVIRONMENT

On January 14, 1994, the Environmental Protection Agency (EPA) released a memo from its Office of Criminal Enforcement announcing the factors to be used in determining when violations of federal environmental laws merit criminal enforcement. The two general conditions that are to guide selection of cases for criminal prosecution are the significance of environmental harm and culpability of the violator's conduct. But the EPA emphasized that the decision whether to pursue prosecution is left to the Environmental Crimes Section of the Department of Justice.

The *Exxon Valdez* Case

In Chapter 10 we mention that the fine imposed against the Exxon Corporation under the Clean Water Act and several other federal environmental statutes was the largest environmental criminal fine in U.S. history. In March 1994 Joseph Hazlewood, the captain of the super tanker Exxon Valdez, was convicted of "negligent discharge of oil," a misdemeanor under Alaska law. The court sentenced Hazlewood to 90 days in jail and $100 fine, but suspended the sentence on condition that he perform 100 hours of community service and pay $50,000 in restitution. Hazlewood's conviction was reviewed by the Alaska Court of Appeals and the Supreme Court of Alaska.

The Court of Appeals reversed the conviction, on the ground that no source of evidence was available to prosecute him independent of a report given by him to the U.S. Coast Guard as required by the Federal Water Pollution Control Act (33 U.S.C.A. § 1321). The federal act provides that any person in charge of a vessel [must] notify the government immediately of "any discharge of oil or a hazardous substance from such vessel." In reversing Hazlewood's conviction, the court pointed out that the statute further provides that "such notification shall not be used against any such person in any criminal case." *Hazlewood v. State*, 836 P.2d 943 (Alaska App. 1992).

On December 3, 1993, the Alaska Supreme Court remanded the case to the Court of Appeals directing it to determine if the evidence relied on by the state in prosecution of Hazlewood would have been discovered without reference to his immunized statements. *State v. Hazlewood*, 866 P.2d 827 (Alaska 1993).

The Meaning of "Point Source" in the Clean Water Act

Defendant Geronimo Villegas, vice president of Plaza Health Laboratories, was convicted of discharging vials of human blood (pollutants) into the Hudson River in violation of the Clean Water Act (33 U.S.C.A. §§ 1311 & 1319(c)(2)). In appealing his conviction, Villegas argued that the discharge of pollutants from a "point source" as defined in 33 U.S.C.A. § 1362(14) does not include discharges resulting from individual acts, thus the element of the crime of "knowingly discharging pollutants from a 'point source' " was not established. Rather, he contended the term *point source* was placed in the federal statute to target industrial and municipal polluters. He argued that, despite the heinous character of the acts involved, the statute does not include discharges that result from individual human acts. A federal court of appeals agreed, saying that *point source* as used in the Clean Water Act refers to municipal and industrial discharges. In reversing the defendant's conviction, the court said:

> We find no suggestion in the act itself or in the history of its passage that Congress intended to impose criminal liability on an individual for the myriad, random acts of

> human waste disposal, for example a passerby who flings a candy wrapper in the Hudson River or a urinating swimmer. *United States v. Plaza Health Laboratories, Inc.*, 3 F.3d 643, 647 (2nd Cir. 1993).

A dissenting judge thought the defendant's activity functioned as a "discrete conveyance" and that Congress worded the statute to bar corporate officers such as Villegas from disposing of corporate wastes into navigable waters by hand as well as by pipe. 3 F.3d at 650, 656.

OFFENSES AGAINST PUBLIC ORDER AND SAFETY

The last few years have seen a number of legislative and judicial developments relative to access to abortion clinics, gun control, hate crimes, and loitering. All of these come under the rubric of public order and safety.

Interference with Access to Abortion Clinics

As we noted earlier, the new federal Freedom of Access to Clinic Entrances Act (FACE), 18 U.S.C.A. § 248, provides for criminal sanctions against persons who use force or intimidation to interfere with access to abortion clinics. Federal courts are also permitted to use injunctions to prohibit antiabortion protesters from blocking access to clinics. State courts may also use injunctions to protect the public order and safety when antiabortion demonstrations threaten to become violent. See, for example, *Madsen v. Women's Health Center*, 512 U.S. ___, 114 S.Ct. 2516, 129 L.Ed.2d 593 (1994).

Gun Control

In the early 1990s, Congress enacted two important gun control statutes. The Gun-Free School Zones Act of 1990, 18 U.S.C.A. § 922, made it unlawful for any individual knowingly to possess a firearm in a school zone, regardless of whether the school is in session. The 1993 Brady Bill, also codified at 18 U.S.C.A. § 922, requires a five-working-day waiting period for the purchase of a handgun. And the 1994 Crime Bill bans the manufacture, transfer, or possession of certain firearms classified as "assault weapons." 18 U.S.C.A. § 922(v)(1). Legal challenges to the Brady Bill are underway, and anti-gun-control groups are gearing up to challenge the ban on assault weapons contained in the 1994 Crime Bill.

In the Gun-Free School Zones Act of 1990, Congress made it a federal offense "for any individual knowingly to possess a firearm at a place that the individual knows, or has reasonable cause to believe, is a school zone." 18 U.S.C. § 922(q)(1)(A). In adopting this prohibition, Congress relied on its broad powers to regulate interstate commerce. See U.S. Const., Art. I, § 8. In April 1995, the U.S. Supreme Court declared this prohibition exceeded Congress' authority to regulate interstate commerce. Writing for the Court, Chief Justice Rehnquist observed that "[t]he Act neither regulates a commercial activity nor contains a requirement that the possession be connected in any way to interstate commerce." United States v. Lopez, ___ U.S. ___, 115 S.Ct. 1624, 131 L.Ed.2d 626 (1995). The *Lopez* decision, while it marks the outer limits of Congressional authority under the Commerce Clause, does not greatly affect the criminal law as it relates to firearms. More than forty States already have laws criminalizing the possession of firearms on or near school grounds. See, e.g., Alaska Stat. Ann. §§ 11.61.195(a)(2)(A), 11.61.220(a)(4)(A) (Supp. 1994); Cal. Penal Code Ann. § 626.9 (West Supp. 1994); Mass. Gen. Laws § 269:10(j) (1992); N. J. Stat. Ann. § 2C:39-5(e) (West Supp. 1994); Va. Code Ann. § 18.2-308.1 (1988); Wis. Stat. § 948.605 (1991–1992). It is likely that the rest of the states will adopt such a prohibition now that the Supreme Court has prevented Congress from enacting a national proscription.

Loitering

After the Supreme Court sounded the death knell to vagrancy laws in *Papachristou v. City of Jacksonville,* 405 U.S. 156, 92 S.Ct. 839, 31 L.Ed.2d 110 (1972) (see Chapter 11), a new generation of laws making loitering a crime came on the scene. These new laws are narrower and often focus on preventing such crimes as prostitution and drug dealing. Courts scrutinize such ordinances carefully because they often prohibit or restrict constitutionally protected activities.

One such ordinance enacted by Akron, Ohio, made it an offense to loiter "for the purpose of engaging in drug-related activity." The ordinance then listed eleven factors that may be considered in determining whether such purpose is manifested. The Ohio Supreme Court found the ordinance to be unconstitutionally vague under both the federal and state constitutions. The court faulted the ordinance for not giving persons of ordinary intelligence a reasonable opportunity to know what conduct was prohibited. Moreover, the court held that the enumerated factors to be considered (e.g., looking like a drug user, being in an area known for unlawful drug use, etc.) could well be innocent and constitutionally protected conduct. Finally, the court pointed out that the ordinance was flawed because it delegated matters to enforcement authorities without providing necessary objective standards. *Akron v. Rowland,* 618 N.E.2d 138 (Ohio 1993).

Ordinances with a more narrow scope have been upheld by the courts as not being impermissibly vague. Nevertheless, any ordinance that proscribes loitering without clearly defining the activities prohibited and without providing objective guidelines for enforcement is vulnerable to constitutional objections.

Hate Crimes

In *State v. Sheldon,* 629 A.2d 753 (Md. 1993), Maryland's highest court upheld a lower court's dismissal of charges under a statute making it a felony to "burn or cause to be burned any cross or other religious symbol upon any private or public property within the state without the express consent of the owner of such property." Although the court termed the open and deliberate burning of religious symbols "odious to thoughtful members of our society," nonetheless it determined that the burning of religious symbols represents expression that falls within the permissible bounds of the First Amendment to the U.S. Constitution. The court concluded:

> Those who wish to burn crosses and other religious symbols may do so free of this regulation, but not free of other criminal statutes, or of the public disrepute and countervailing opinion which will ultimately provide the most persuasive rejoinder to such acts. 629 A.2d at 763.

OFFENSES AGAINST JUSTICE AND PUBLIC ADMINISTRATION

In discussing perjury, we point out in Chapter 12 that the inherent difficulty in proving the crime of perjury is exacerbated by the "two witness rule" that prevails in most jurisdictions. In *United States v. Chaplin,* 25 F.3d 1373 (7th Cir. 1994), a U.S. Court of Appeals traced the common-law history of the two-witness rule. The court explained that the historic rationale for this common-law rule was that on a charge of perjury the accused's oath was always in effect in evidence and that, if only one witness was offered to establish the defendant's perjury, there would be merely one oath against another. While the rule has been frequently characterized as an anachronism that does not reflect the needs of modern jury trials, nevertheless, the U.S. Supreme Court in *Weiler v. United States,* 323 U.S. 606, 65 S.Ct. 548, 89 L.Ed. 495 (1945), declined to abandon the rule in federal prosecutions.

In *Chaplin, supra,* the federal appeals court explained that the two-witness rule may be satisfied by the testimony of one witness and presentation of sufficient corroborating evidence. The court set out two criteria for proving perjury:

> (1) falsity of testimony must be established by more than the uncorroborated testimony of one witness, and (2) circumstantial evidence, no matter how persuasive, will not by itself support a conviction for perjury. 25 F.3d at 1377.

CRIMINAL RESPONSIBILITY AND DEFENSES

The trend is to restrict the use of insanity, necessity, and duress as defenses. At the same time, courts have attempted to clarify the applicability of the defense of double jeopardy and to define their positions on the availability of entrapment as a defense. An accused is granted considerable leeway in presenting defensive matters in court, although attempted defenses often present excuses from individual responsibility beyond those allowed by well-settled rules of law. In addition to the novel defenses evaluated in Chapter 13, a host of "excuses and abuses" have recently appeared in the courts by defendants who claim "victim status."

The Insanity Defense

In 1979, the Montana legislature abolished the defense of insanity. Idaho and Utah followed Montana's lead. In *State v. Cowan,* 861 P.2d 884 (Mont. 1993), the Montana Supreme Court held that a state law abolishing the insanity defense did not violate the federal constitution. The defendant, asserting a constitutional right to plead the defense of insanity, asked the U.S. Supreme Court to review his case. In March 1994, the Court refused to review the *Cowan* decision. *Cowan v. Montana,* ____ U.S. ____, 114 S.Ct. 1371, 128 L.Ed.2d 48 (1994). While the Court declined to definitely settle the issue, its action suggests that the federal constitution does not require that states allow a defendant to plead insanity.

On April 4, 1995, a federal jury found Francisco Martin Duran guilty of attempting to assassinate President Bill Clinton. Duran's counsel conceded at trial that Duran was guilty of some weapons charges and damaging federal property, however, they argued that he was a paranoid schizophrenic who was shooting at the White House as a symbol of a government he hated. Unlike the trial where John Hinckley was found "not guilty by reason of insanity" for the 1981 shooting former President Ronald Reagan, the new federal standard for insanity applied in Duran's trial (see Chapter 13). After deliberating about five hours, the jury rejected Duran's plea of insanity and found Duran guilty on the charge of attempting to assassinate the President as well as several other weapons, assault, and damaging of federal property counts.

Self-Defense

It has always been the law that a person charged with a homicidal crime may plead self-defense. Historically self-defense has required that the accused *objectively* believed that his or her actions were necessary for safety. Therefore, most courts have held a defendant who pleads self-defense to the standard of the hypothetical "reasonable person." However, as we pointed out in Chapter 13, some courts now apply a *subjective* test that permits a jury "to place itself in the defendant's own shoes." This latter concept has recently become known as "imperfect self-defense." It holds that an accused is required only to entertain a *subjective* belief of the necessity to take another person's life in self-defense.

Now the issue has surfaced whether imperfect self-defense can be raised by a defendant charged with a nonhomicidal crime. In *Richmond v. State,* 623 A.2d 630 (Md. 1993), Maryland's highest court reviewed a defendant's convictions for battery and for maliciously wounding another with intention to disable the victim. Richmond argued that the trial court should have allowed him to rely on imperfect self-defense, as is permitted in a homicide prosecution. This reliance, Richmond argued, should negate the specific intent of the offense. The court disagreed and held that the defense of imperfect self-defense is limited to criminal homicide and its shadow forms, such as attempted murder.

Double Jeopardy

In 1994 the United States Supreme Court handed down two significant rulings on double jeopardy. First, it invalidated "a dangerous drug tax" imposed on a party already convicted of possession of illegal drugs. The Court ruled that the added tax amounted to double jeopardy in violation of the Fifth and Fourteenth Amendments to the U.S. Constitution. *Montana v. Kurth Ranch,* 511 U.S. ___, 114 S.Ct. 1937, 128 L.Ed.2d 767 (1994). Following this, in *Schiro v. Farley,* 510 U.S. ___, 114 S.Ct. 783, 127 L.Ed.2d 47 (1994), the Court made it clear that the sentencing phase of a criminal trial is not a subsequent prosecution for purposes of the Double Jeopardy Clause of the Constitution. Thus, it held that a defendant cannot rely on double jeopardy as a defense to sentencing imposed in a bifurcated trial where the sentencing aspect is not considered until after a jury finds a defendant guilty. This method of bifurcated trials has become common in capital cases in states that impose the death penalty.

Statutes of Limitations

Statutes of limitations are generally not made applicable to charges of murder. This fact was dramatized in February 1994, when Byron De La Beckwith was convicted for the June 1963 murder of Medgar Evers. Evers was secretary for the National Association for the Advancement of Colored People, and his death galvanized support for the enactment of civil rights laws in the 1960s. Two trials in 1964 where Beckwith was charged with homicide ended in deadlocked juries. But after extended litigation, and a lapse of more than thirty years since the victim's death, a Mississippi jury found Beckwith guilty of killing Evers.

Entrapment

The Supreme Court's 1992 decision in *Jacobson v. United States,* 503 U.S. ____, 112 S.Ct. 1535, 118 L.Ed.2d 174 (1992), reported in Chapter 13, signaled to lower federal tribunals that Congress had not intended government officials to instigate crime by luring persons into criminal activity. Following the lead in *Jacobson,* in January 1994, the U.S. Court of Appeals for the Seventh Circuit rendered an *en banc* decision on the issue of the government's burden when the defense pleads entrapment. The court held that the government must prove that the defendant was not only "willing" to commit the offense charged, but also that he or she was "ready" to commit the offense in absence of official encouragement. *United States v. Hollingsworth,* 9 F.3d 593 (7th Cir. 1994).

In 1993 and 1994, defendants continued to assert the defense of entrapment in state courts, especially in narcotics cases. In the 1980s some state courts began to follow the objective view of entrapment where the judge, not the jury, determines whether police methods were so improper as to constitute entrapment as a matter of law. If so, the defendant's predisposition to commit an offense is irrelevant, and the court dismisses the charge.

In 1993 the Wyoming Supreme Court aligned itself with those states that have declined to adopt the objective theory of entrapment. Nevertheless, that court indicated that the defense of "outrageous government conduct" remains available, but can be relied on only in circumstances where police conduct is violative of fundamental fairness and shocking to the universal sense of justice mandated by the Due Process Clause of the Fifth and Fourteenth Amendments to the U.S. Constitution. *Rivera v. State,* 846 P.2d 1 (Wyo. 1993).

Necessity

Courts continue to say that a defendant cannot, on the ground of necessity, justify preventing a person from performing a lawful act. Thus appellate courts have uniformly declined to recognize a defense of necessity (see Chapter 13) asserted by those who commit trespass on or who unlawfully occupy abortion clinics. See, for example, *State v. Bowers,* 498 N.W.2d 202 (S.D. 1993).

Duress

On November 7, 1994, the U.S. Court of Appeals for the Fifth Circuit aligned itself with other federal appellate courts in holding that evidence of "battered woman's syndrome" is not relevant to establish the defense of duress. The court explained that duress is based on objective requirements. To succeed, the coercive force of the threat must be sufficient that a person of ordinary firmness would succumb, and there must be no reasonable alternative to violating the law. The court viewed evidence of battered woman's syndrome as being a claim of subjective vulnerability. It held that expert testimony dealing with the defendant's subjective perceptions stemming from the battered woman syndrome to have been properly excluded as evidence. *United States v. Willis*, 38 F.3d 170 (5th Cir. 1994).

Nontraditional Defenses

In additional to the novel attempted defenses mentioned in Chapter 13, claims of "urban survival syndrome," "black rage," "pornographic intoxication," and "multiple personalities" have been asserted as defenses, usually without success. Some observers claim that the assertion of these "creative defenses" is a response to the trend of legislatively imposed mandatory sentences and statutes decreeing a "three strikes and you're out" punishment. Others look upon these claims as simply evidencing a lack of personal accountability. They often blame the proffering of these defenses on television dramas and radio talk shows.

These novel defenses may lead to an occasional acquittal. It must be remembered that where a novel defense is presented and either a court declares a mistrial or the defendant is found not guilty, the matters offered defensively are not evaluated by appellate courts. Hence, such defenses seldom gain recognition from the courts.

In 1993, California charged Erik and Lyle Menendez, ages 18 and 21, respectively, with the murder of their parents. The defendants admitted killing their parents but claimed that they had been victims of abuse. Two trials in Los Angeles ended in mistrials because jurors could not agree on a verdict. In contrast, in November 1994, a jury in Butler, Pennsylvania, found Michael Ricksgers guilty of first-degree murder despite his claim that he suffered from sleep apnea. Defense lawyers unsuccessfully argued that the defendant's sleep disorder—which causes snoring, gagging, and odd movements—led him to shoot his wife.

In 1994, Lorena Bobbit was charged with severing her husband's penis, a fact that was not in controversy. She relied on the defense of insanity but in a novel way. She told a story about her husband's alleged cruel and abusive behavior toward her and attempted to establish herself as a victim, and a jury in Manses, Virginia acquitted her. Some observers have characterized her acquittal as a jury nullification rather than a true finding of "not guilty by reason of insanity."

THE 1994 FEDERAL CRIME BILL

After heated debate Congress enacted, and in September 1994 President Clinton signed, the "Violent Crime Control and Law Enforcement Act of 1994" (commonly referred to as "the federal Crime Bill"). This new legislation attempts to deal with root causes of crime through prevention programs, by supplying federal funds to augment state and local law enforcement capabilities, and by making provisions to build or expand state prisons. The new Act also provides grants for numerous educational and training projects for criminal justice functionaries and for assistance to crime victims.

Much of the debate surrounding enactment of the new Crime Bill concerned the various social programs that Congress designed to prevent crime and provisions restricting the manufacture, transfer, and possession of certain "assault" weapons. In addition, Congress established the death penalty for various categories of serious federal offenses, added several new federal crimes, and increased the punishment authorized for numerous federal offenses. The substantive offenses created or modified by the new legislation concern violations of federal laws, including crimes committed on federal property, and offenses involving interstate activities.

Domestic Violence

By creating an offense of "interstate domestic violence," the new Act should greatly assist in the prosecution of those who injure spouses or intimate partners and then move away to protect themselves. Section 40221 of the Act inserts a new chapter (entitled Domestic Violence) after Chapter 110 in 18 U.S.C.A., making it a crime for a person who

> travels across a State line or enters or leaves Indian country with the intent to injure, harass, or intimidate that person's spouse or intimate partner, and who, in the course of or as a result of such travel, intentionally commits a crime of violence and thereby causes bodily injury to such spouse or intimate partner.

or

> who causes a spouse or intimate partner to cross a State line or to enter or leave Indian country by force, coercion, duress, or fraud and, in the course or as a result of that conduct, intentionally commits a crime of violence and thereby causes bodily injury to such spouse or intimate partner.

This section also makes criminal crossing, or forcing a spouse or intimate partner to cross, a state line with the intent to engage in conduct "that violates the portion of a protection order that involves protection against credible threats of violence, repeated harassment, or bodily injury to the person or persons for whom the protection order was issued." Christopher Bailey was charged under the new federal domestic violence law with crossing a state line to assault his spouse. In the first conviction under the new Act, on May 23, 1995, Bailey was found guilty in Charleston, West Virginia for assaulting his spouse and driving her around West Virginia and Kentucky until he finally carried her into an emergency room.

"Substantial Bodily Injury" Redefined

Section 170201 amends 18 U.S.C.A. § 113 concerning assaults against persons who have not attained 16 years of age, and redefines the term *substantial bodily injury* to include "a temporary but substantial disfigurement; or a temporary but substantial loss or impairment of the function of any bodily member, organ, or mental faculty."

New Provisions Concerning Violence

Section 60019 adds new offenses to Title 18, Chapter 111 of U.S.C.A. concerning violence against maritime navigation and at international airports, and the use of weapons of mass destruction. Section 60008 amends Title 18, Chapter 2 of U.S.C.A. and is aimed at "drive-by shootings" by making it an offense to fire a weapon into a group of two or more persons in an attempt to escape detection of a major drug offense.

Child Pornography

Section 160001 adds new provisions concerning production of sexually explicit depictions of a minor for importation into the United States. In Section 160002, Congress requests states to enact legislation prohibiting the production, distribution, receipt, or simple possession of materials depicting a person under age 18 engaging in sexually explicit conduct. And in Section 160003, Congress declares its intent in enacting laws concerning child pornography. The section says that depiction of a minor engaging in "sexually explicit conduct" is prohibited if a person photographs the minor in such a way as to exhibit the child in a lascivious manner.

Computer and "White Collar" Crime

Section 290001, known as "The Computer Abuse Amendments Act of 1994," updates 18 U.S.C.A. § 1030(a)(5) by strengthening existing federal law on computer crime.

Section 320601 addresses amendments to white-collar crime. It amends Title 18, Chapter 41 of U.S.C.A. by criminalizing the receipt, possession, concealment, or disposition of the proceeds of extortion or ransom money.

Section 320902 amends Title 18, Chapter 31 of U.S.C.A. to proscribe the theft or concealment of theft of major artworks from museums and specifies a twenty-year statute of limitations on prosecutions.

Effect of the New Federal Crime Bill

The new federal Crime Bill was enacted by Congress only after serious debate, however, as noted, that debate focused largely on issues other than the creation of new substantive crimes. Despite the creation of new offenses, the new legislation may have a minimal effect on criminal prosecutions because, as pointed out in Chapter 2, over ninety percent of criminal prosecutions in the United States are handled at the state level for violations of state criminal laws. Nevertheless, by increasing penalties, providing for mandatory sentences, and adding the death penalty for numerous federal crimes (§ 60003), the new law makes a strong statement of national policy. Moreover, enactment of the provisions concerning interstate violence against spouses and intimate partners fills an existing void in the criminal law. Other sections fill in some "gaps" in the federal criminal law. Finally, Section 320935, which amends the Federal Rules of Evidence to allow federal prosecutors to use "evidence of the defendant's commission of [other] sexual offenses" in sexual assault and child molestation cases, may also serve as an example to the states.

Most federal criminal laws are found in Title 18 of the U.S. Code, entitled "Crimes and Criminal Procedure," but many are scattered throughout the entire Code. Some terms used in those laws have meanings that vary according to the particular offense. For example, the term *willful* has been interpreted differently in its use in various statutes defining federal offenses. Although the new federal Crime Bill has been viewed by some observers as a major achievement, many lawyers and judges are disappointed that Congress failed to take the opportunity to revise and consolidate all federal criminal laws. While revision and consolidation do not appear to be imminent, by mid-1995 political observers were predicting that the new Republican-controlled Congress would enact amendments to the Crime Bill.

CONCLUSION

In this chapter, we have identified some of the more important recent developments and trends in the substantive criminal law. The creation of new crimes, the reinterpretation of existing laws to cope with societal changes, and the assertion of new defenses all point to the highly dynamic nature of the criminal law.

QUESTIONS FOR THOUGHT AND DISCUSSION

1. Should assisted suicide be a crime? If so, should it be tantamount to aiding and abetting murder? If not, what protections should be put in place to prevent abuse?
2. Compare and contrast *People v. Iniquez* (Cal. 1994) and *Commonwealth v. Berkowitz* (Pa. 1994), two sexual battery decisions discussed in this chapter. Which expresses a more reasonable view on how the "force" element is established in a rape prosecution?
3. Historically, a defendant who pleads self-defense has been held to the objective standard of a "reasonable person." Some courts now apply a subjective test that allows the jury "to place itself in the defendant's own shoes." Which approach do you find more plausible? Why?
4. Do television and radio "talk shows" that present bizarre stories of abuse and victimization predispose prospective jurors to accept defenses in which defendants claim to have been victimized by society or by other individuals?
5. What prompted Congress to enact the prohibitions against interstate domestic violence contained in the 1994 federal Crime Bill? What specific acts are prohibited by the statute?

CASES

UNITED STATES V. LOPEZ

Supreme Court of the United States, 1995
___ U.S. ___, 115 S.Ct. 1624, 131 L.Ed.2d 626

Chief Justice REHNQUIST delivered the opinion of the Court.

In the Gun-Free School Zones Act of 1990, Congress made it a federal offense "for any individual knowingly to possess a firearm at a place that the individual knows, or has reasonable cause to believe, is a school zone." * * * The Act neither regulates a commercial activity nor contains a requirement that the possession be connected in any way to interstate commerce. We hold that the Act exceeds the authority of Congress "[t]o regulate Commerce.

On March 10, 1992, respondent, who was then a 12th-grade student, arrived at Edison High School in San Antonio, Texas, carrying a concealed .38 caliber handgun and five bullets. Acting upon an anonymous tip, school authorities confronted respondent, who admitted that he was carrying the weapon. He was arrested and charged under Texas law with firearm possession on school premises. * * * The next day, the state charges were dismissed after federal agents charged respondent by complaint with violating the Gun-Free School Zones Act of 1990. * * *

A federal grand jury indicted respondent on one count of knowing possession of a firearm at a school zone . . . Respondent moved to dismiss his federal indictment on the ground that § 922(q) "is unconstitutional as it is beyond the power of Congress to legislate control over our public schools." The District Court denied the motion, concluding that [the challenged statute] "is a constitutional exercise of Congress' well-defined power to regulate activities in and affecting commerce, and the 'business' of elementary, middle and high schools . . . affects interstate commerce." * * * Respondent waived his right to a jury trial. The District Court conducted a bench trial, found him guilty . . . and sentenced him to six months' imprisonment and two years' supervised release.

On appeal, respondent challenged his conviction based on his claim that [the challenged statute] exceeded Congress' power to legislate under the Commerce Clause. The Court of Appeals for the Fifth Circuit agreed and reversed respondent's conviction. It held that, in light of what it characterized as insufficient congressional findings and legislative history, "section 922(q), in the full reach of its terms, is invalid as beyond the power of Congress under the Commerce Clause." * * * Because of the importance of the issue, we granted certiorari, * * * and we now affirm. . . .

. . . [W]e have identified three broad categories of activity that Congress may regulate under its commerce power. * * * First, Congress may regulate the use of the channels of interstate commerce. * * * Second, Congress is empowered to regulate and protect the instrumentalities of interstate commerce, or persons or things in interstate commerce, even though the threat may come only from intrastate activities. * * * For example, the destruction of an aircraft or . . . thefts from interstate shipments. Finally, Congress' commerce authority includes the power to regulate those activities having a substantial relation to interstate commerce, i.e., those activities that substantially affect interstate commerce. * * *

Within this final category, admittedly, our case law has not been clear whether an activity must "affect" or "substantially affect" interstate commerce in order to be within Congress' power to regulate it under the Commerce Clause. * * * We conclude, consistent with the great weight of our case law, that the proper test requires an analysis of whether the regulated activity "substantially affects" interstate commerce.

We now turn to consider the power of Congress, in the light of this framework, to enact [the challenged statute]. The first two categories of authority may be quickly disposed of: [the challenged statute] is not a regulation of the use of the channels of interstate commerce, nor is it an attempt to prohibit the interstate transportation of a commodity through the channels of commerce; nor can [the challenged statute] be justified as a regulation by which Congress has sought to protect an instrumentality of interstate commerce or a thing in interstate commerce. Thus, if [the challenged statute] is to be sustained, it must be under the third category as a regulation of an activity that substantially affects interstate commerce. . . .

. . . [The challenged statute] is a criminal statute that by its terms has nothing to do with "commerce" or any sort of economic enterprise, however broadly one might define those terms. [It] is not an essential part of a larger regulation of economic activity, in which the regulatory scheme could be undercut unless the intrastate activity were regulated. It cannot, therefore, be sustained under our cases upholding regulations of activities that arise out of or are connected with a commercial transaction, which viewed in the aggregate, substantially affects interstate commerce. . . .

The Government's essential contention, *in fine*, is that we may determine here that [the challenged statute] is valid because possession of a firearm in a local school zone does indeed substantially affect interstate commerce. * * * The Government argues that possession of a firearm in a school zone may result in violent crime and that violent crime can be expected to affect the functioning of the national economy in two ways. First, the costs of violent crime are substantial, and, through the mechanism of insurance, those costs are spread throughout the population. * * * Second, violent crime reduces the willingness of individuals to travel to areas within the country that are perceived to be unsafe. * * * The Government also argues that the presence of guns in schools poses a substantial threat to the educational process by threatening the learning environment. A handicapped educational process, in turn, will result in a less productive citizenry. That, in turn, would have an adverse effect on the Nation's economic well-being. As a result, the Government argues that Congress could rationally have concluded that [the challenged statute] substantially affects interstate commerce.

We pause to consider the implications of the Government's arguments. The Government admits, under its "costs of crime" reasoning, that Congress could regulate not only all violent crime, but all activities that might lead to violent crime, regardless of how tenuously they relate to interstate commerce. * * * Similarly, under the Government's "national productivity" reasoning, Congress could regulate any activity that it found was related to the economic productivity of individual citizens: family law (including marriage, divorce, and child custody), for example. Under the theories that the Government presents in support of [the challenged statute], it is difficult to perceive any limitation on federal power, even in areas such as criminal law enforcement or education where States historically have been sovereign. Thus, if we were to accept the Government's arguments, we are hard-pressed to posit any activity by an individual that Congress is without power to regulate. . . .

To uphold the Government's contentions here, we would have to pile inference upon inference in a manner that would bid fair to convert congressional authority under the Commerce Clause to a general police power of the sort retained by the States. Admittedly, some of our prior cases have taken long steps down that road, giving great deference to congressional action. * * * The broad language in these opinions has suggested the possibility of additional expansion, but we decline here to proceed any further. To do so would require us to conclude that the Constitution's enumeration of powers does not presuppose something not enumerated, * * * and that there never will be a distinction between what is truly national and what is truly local. This we are unwilling to do.

For the foregoing reasons the judgment of the Court of Appeals is Affirmed.

Justice KENNEDY, with whom Justice O'CONNOR joins, concurring. . . .

Justice THOMAS, concurring. . . .

Justice STEVENS, dissenting.

. . . Guns are both articles of commerce and articles that can be used to restrain commerce. Their possession is the consequence, either directly or indirectly, of commercial activity. In my judgment, Congress' power to regulate commerce in firearms includes the power to prohibit possession of guns at any location because of their potentially harmful use; it necessarily follows that Congress may also prohibit their possession in particular markets. The market for the possession of handguns by school-age children is, distressingly, substantial. Whether or not the national interest in eliminating that market would have justified federal legislation in 1789, it surely does today.

Justice SOUTER, dissenting. . . .

Justice BREYER, with whom Justice STEVENS, Justice SOUTER, and Justice GINSBURG join, dissenting.

The issue in this case is whether the Commerce Clause authorizes Congress to enact a statute that makes it a crime to possess a gun in, or near, a school. * * * In my view, the statute falls well within the scope of the commerce power as this Court has understood that power over the last half-century.

In reaching this conclusion, I apply three basic principles of Commerce Clause interpretation. First, the power to "regulate Commerce . . . among the several States" * * * encompasses the power to regulate local activities insofar as they significantly affect interstate commerce. . . . Second, in determining whether a local activity will likely have a significant effect upon interstate commerce, a court must consider, not the effect of an individual act (a single instance of gun possession), but rather the cumulative effect of all similar instances (i.e., the effect of all guns possessed in or near schools). . . . Third, the Constitution requires us to judge the connection between a regulated activity and interstate commerce, not directly, but at one remove. Courts must give Congress a degree of leeway in determining the existence of a significant factual connection between the regulated activity and interstate commerce-both because the Constitution delegates the commerce power directly to Congress and because the determination requires an empirical judgment of a kind that a legislature is more likely than a court to make with accuracy. The traditional words "rational basis" capture this leeway. * * * Thus, the specific question before us, as the Court recognizes, is not whether the "regulated activity sufficiently affected interstate commerce" but, rather, whether Congress could have had "a rational basis" for so concluding. . . .

. . . [W]e must ask whether Congress could have had a rational basis for finding a significant (or substantial) connection between gun-related school violence and interstate commerce. Or, to put the question in the language of the explicit finding that Congress made when it amended this law in 1994: Could Congress rationally have found that "violent crime in school zones," through its effect on the "quality of education," significantly (or substantially) affects "interstate" or "foreign commerce"? * * * As long as one views the commerce connection, not as a "technical legal conception," but as "a practical one," * * * the answer to this question must be yes. Numerous reports and studies-generated both inside and outside government-make clear that Congress could reasonably have found the empirical connection that its law, implicitly or explicitly, asserts. . . .

For one thing, reports, hearings, and other readily available literature make clear that the problem of guns in and around schools is widespread and extremely serious. These materials report, for example, that four percent of American high school students (and six percent of inner-city high school students) carry a gun to school at least occasionally, * * * that 12 percent of urban high school students have had guns fired at them, * * * that 20 percent of those students have been threatened with guns, * * * and that, in any 6-month period, several hundred thousand schoolchildren are victims of violent crimes in or near their schools. * * * And, they report that this widespread violence in schools throughout the Nation significantly interferes with the quality of education in those schools. * * * Based on reports such as these, Congress obviously could have thought that guns and learning are mutually exclusive. * * * And, Congress could therefore have found a substantial educational problem—teachers unable to teach, students unable to learn—and concluded that guns near schools contribute substantially to the size and scope of that problem.

Having found that guns in schools significantly undermine the quality of education in our Nation's classrooms, Congress could also have found, given the effect of education upon interstate and foreign commerce, that gun-related violence in and around schools is a commercial, as well as a human, problem. Education, although far more than a matter of economics, has long been inextricably intertwined with the Nation's economy. . . .

The economic links I have just sketched seem fairly obvious. Why then is it not equally obvious, in light of those links, that a widespread, serious, and substantial physical threat to teaching and learning also substantially threatens the commerce to which that teaching and learning is inextricably tied? That is to say, guns in the hands of six percent of inner-city high school students and gun-related violence throughout a city's schools must threaten the trade and commerce that those schools support. The only question, then, is whether the latter threat is (to use the majority's terminology) "substantial." And, the evidence of (1) the extent of the gun-related violence problem, * * * (2) the extent of the resulting negative effect on classroom learning, * * * and (3) the extent of the consequent negative commercial effects, * * * when taken together, indicate a threat to trade and commerce that is "substantial." At the very least, Congress could rationally have concluded that the links are "substantial."

Specifically, Congress could have found that gun-related violence near the classroom poses a serious economic threat (1) to consequently inadequately educated workers who must endure low paying jobs, * * * and (2) to communities and businesses that might (in today's "information society") otherwise gain, from a well-educated work force, an important commercial advantage, * * * of a kind that location near a railhead or harbor provided in the past. . . .

In sum, to find this legislation within the scope of the Commerce Clause would permit "Congress . . . to act in terms of economic . . . realities." * * * It would interpret the Clause as this Court has traditionally interpreted it, with the exception of one wrong turn subsequently corrected. * * * Upholding this legislation would do no more than simply recognize that Congress had a "rational basis" for finding a significant connection between guns in or near schools and (through their effect on education) the interstate and foreign commerce they threaten. For these reasons, I would reverse the judgment of the Court of Appeals. . . .

APPENDICES

APPENDIX A

RICO: AN ASSAULT ON ORGANIZED CRIME

After the ratification in 1919 of the Eighteenth Amendment outlawing the manufacture, sale, and distribution of alcoholic beverages, organized crime gained a strong foothold in the United States. During the Prohibition Era, organizations operating outside the law trafficked in liquor and were involved in prostitution. Despite the repeal of that amendment in 1933, these crime syndicates continued their activities and expanded into loansharking, gambling, narcotics, and extortion. They infiltrated legitimate businesses and conducted widespread illegal operations through complex business structures.

As discussed in the text, the common-law development of crime definitions focused on particular acts of individual wrongdoing and on inchoate activities. Congress and the state legislatures generally followed this "transactional" approach in defining statutory crimes, but these crime definitions did not cover ongoing criminal activity by organized groups. In addition, traditional methods of law enforcement and criminal prosecution proved ineffective to cope with the activities of organized crime.

In 1967, the President's Commission on Law Enforcement and the Administration of Justice issued a comprehensive report on the dimensions of crime in the United States. This led to congressional findings that organized crime had weakened the stability of the nation's economy through infiltration of legitimate businesses and labor unions and threatened to subvert and corrupt our democratic processes. In response, Congress enacted the Organized Crime Control Act of 1970, Title 9 of which was entitled "Racketeer Influenced and Corrupt Organizations." The act is commonly referred to by the acronym "RICO." In congressional debates Senator McClelland, who conducted investigations leading to passage of the new act, pointed out that Title 9 "[p]rohibits infiltration of legitimate organizations by racketeers . . . where interstate commerce is affected." 116 Cong. Rec. 585 (1970).

RICO created new crimes and a new approach to criminal prosecution. First, it makes it a crime for any person "who has received any income derived, directly or indirectly, from a pattern of racketeering activity or through collection of an unlawful debt . . . to use or invest [in] any enterprise which is engaged in interstate or foreign commerce." 18 U.S.C.A. § 1962(a). Second, it makes it unlawful for any such person to participate, directly or indirectly, in the conduct of the enterprise's affairs through a "pattern of racketeering." 18 U.S.C.A. § 1962(b). Third, it makes it criminal for any person "employed by or associated with any enterprise engaged in, or the activities of which affect, interstate or foreign commerce, to conduct or participate, directly or indirectly, in the conduct of such enterprise's affairs through a pattern of racketeering activity or collection of unlawful debt." 18 U.S.C.A. § 1962(c). Finally, it prohibits conspiracies to violate any of these proscriptions. 18 U.S.C.A. § 1962(d).

In addition to substantial fines, imprisonment for not more than twenty years, or both, the act provides for forfeiture to the United States of any interest acquired or maintained in violation of Section 1962. 18 U.S.C.A. § 1963(a). Recognizing that law enforcement agencies cannot handle the task completely, the act provides for an award of treble damages plus costs and attorney fees in civil actions instituted by persons who suffer losses as a result of RICO violations. 18 U.S.C.A. § 1964(c). Since RICO does not contain its own statute of limitations, the general five-year statute of limitations for noncapital federal offenses applies. *United States v. Bethea,* 672 F.2d 407 (5th Cir. 1982).

The scope of the act is expansive. It broadly defines *racketeering activity* to include a variety of federal offenses and nine state crimes that are characteristically felonies. 18 U.S.C.A. § 1961(1). To establish a "pattern of racketeering activity" requires proof of at least two of these acts of racketeering having occurred within a period of ten years, excluding any period of imprisonment. 18 U.S.C.A. § 1961(5). These acts are frequently referred to by the courts as "predicate acts" and any combination of two or more can constitute a pattern of racketeering. To obtain a conviction under RICO, the government must establish the defendant's involvement in a "pattern of racketeering or collection of an unlawful debt." See, for example, *United States v. Dozier,* 672 F.2d 531 (5th Cir.), *cert. denied,* 459 U.S. 943, 103 S. Ct. 256, 74 L.Ed.2d 200 (1982). The fact that there is but one objective underlying separate acts of racketeering does not diminish the applicability of RICO to those actions. *United States v. Starnes,* 644 F.2d 673 (7th Cir.), *cert. denied,* 454 U.S. 826, 102 S. Ct. 116, 70 L.Ed.2d 101 (1981). There is no requirement that a state conviction be obtained before a state offense can be used as a predicate act of the racketeering activity charged. *United States v. Malatesta,* 583 F.2d 748 (5th Cir. 1978), *cert. denied,* 440 U.S. 962, 99 S. Ct. 1508, 59 L.Ed.2d 777 (1979).

RICO also defines *enterprise* broadly to include "any individual, partnership, corporation, association, or other legal entity, and any union or group of individuals associated in fact although not a legal entity." 18 U.S.C.A. § 1961(4). The Supreme Court has said that the term encompasses both legitimate and illegitimate enterprises. *United States v. Turkette,* 452 U.S. 576, 101 S. Ct. 2524, 69 L.Ed.2d 246 (1981). Lower federal courts have held the term includes both private and public entities such as corporations, banks, and decedents' estates, as well as state agencies, police departments, traffic courts, and prostitution rings.

RICO does not criminalize the status of a person for being a racketeer—it criminalizes a person's conduct of an enterprise through a pattern of racketeering. *United States v. Phillips,* 664 F.2d 971 (5th Cir. 1981), *cert. denied,* 457 U.S. 1136, 102 S. Ct. 2965, 73 L.Ed.2d 1354 (1982). Therefore, when a jury finds that a defendant has committed the predicate acts, it must still find that these acts were committed in connection with a pattern of racketeering or collection of an unlawful debt. A RICO violation involves a separate criminal proceeding. Therefore, the Double Jeopardy Clause of the United States Constitution does not prohibit the government from prosecuting a defendant for a RICO charge where the defendant has been previously prosecuted for a substantive offense used as one of the predicate crimes. *United States. v. Smith,* 574 F.2d 308 (5th Cir.), *cert. denied,* 439 U.S. 931, 99 S. Ct. 321, 58 L.Ed.2d 325 (1978).

The following three cases illustrate some RICO prosecutions:

- Former police officers were charged with violating RICO by accepting bribes to protect individuals involved in gambling and vice. *United States v. Brown,* 555 F.2d 407 (5th Cir. 1977), *cert. denied,* 435 U.S. 904, 98 S. Ct. 1448, 55 L.Ed.2d 494 (1978).
- Defendants were convicted of operating an illegal gambling business and conspiring to obstruct state law enforcement. *United States v. Zemek,* 634 F.2d 1159 (9th Cir. 1980).
- Several members of the Outlaws Motorcycle Club were prosecuted for a RICO violation based on narcotics and prostitution offenses. *United States v. Watchmaker,* 761 F.2d 1459 (11th Cir. 1985), *cert. denied,* 474 U.S. 1100, 106 S. Ct. 879, 88 L.Ed.2d 917 (1986).

Some RICO prosecutions have involved well-known political figures. For example, Maryland governor Marvin Mandel was prosecuted on charges of mail fraud and four other RICO counts. *United States v. Mandel,* 415 F. Supp. 997 (D. Md. 1976).

RICO was conceived as a weapon for prosecution of organized crime. Prosecutors have long experienced difficulty in securing convictions of organized crime leaders for violating specific criminal statutes. In part this occurs because the evidence of a specific statutory violation may be unconvincing to a judge or jury. The reaction of a judge or jury is likely to be different when the prosecution parades before the court evidence of a series of violations that reveals a pattern of criminal behavior.

RICO can be an effective tool in the hands of prosecutors in their fight against crime syndicates. Yet membership in organized crime is not a necessary element for a conviction under RICO. Unlike criminal statutes that historically have been narrowly construed, Congress provided that RICO is to be liberally interpreted to effectuate its remedial purposes. The liberal construction of the enterprise requirement and the fact that the pattern requirement of racketeering activity is cast in numerical terms has caused some critics to contend that RICO is a "catch-all" statute that gives prosecutors too much discretion to expand the range of indictable offenses.

RICO has been extended beyond its original purpose to target such nonorganized crime as the white-collar criminal and the corrupt government official. Thus, through RICO a prosecutor can circumvent statutes of limitation and inflict multiple punishments for the same offenses. Despite criticism, RICO is firmly established as a weapon in the arsenal available to federal prosecutors to combat racketeering and corruption, both private and public, whether organized or not.

RICO has become available to many state prosecutors as most of the states have adopted RICO-type statutes. Some closely parallel the federal act; others have varying provisions concerning prohibited acts, sanctions, forfeitures of property, and the procedures involved.

Because it departs from the traditional transactional approach to criminal law, RICO is a controversial concept. Yet, given RICO's obvious utility in combatting organized crime, white-collar crime, and political corruption, theoretical reservations about RICO are not apt to find a sympathetic ear among legislators and judges.

CASE

United States v. Gambino

United States Court of Appeals, Second Circuit, 1977.
566 F.2d 414,

[The appellants, Gambino and Conti, were convicted of a number of offenses including violations of the federal RICO statute.]

GURFEIN, Circuit Judge.

. . . The appellants contend that there was insufficient evidence to prove a conspiracy to acquire and maintain control of the private sanitation industry in the Coop City area of the Bronx through a pattern of racketeering activity. They argue that there was insufficient evidence to warrant a conviction under Count Four, which charged that Gambino and Conti used threats and violence in order to collect an extension of credit for Peter Darminio. Specifically, they point to an alleged lack of corroboration of Darminio's testimony.

The general outline of the case indicates that Gambino and Conti had controlled certain stops for private garbage collection in the Bronx but were unable to get a carting license from the City. They arranged for Terminal Sanitation, a licensed private sanitation firm, owned by Peter and Anthony Darminio, to collect at all of the stops which Gambino had previously acquired in the Bronx. The Darminios were required to kick back to Gambino one-third of all the moneys they received from servicing the stops.

[The trial court] . . . found that Gambino and Conti maintained control of garbage collection in Coop City and other areas of the Bronx by threatening to kill competitors and by administering beatings. This activity included an assault on an undercover agent of the FBI who was posing as a cart man and who had solicited a stop in Coop City. [The trial court] also found that Gambino engaged in extensive loansharking activities, lending a total of $90,000 to Peter and Anthony Darminio in 1970 and 1971 and $75,000 to Peter in 1972. These loans were collected by Gambino and Conti through the use of threats and violence.

The court carefully reviewed the evidence. Ralph Torres, an employee of Gambino and Conti, was found to be a credible witness by . . . [the trial court]. Although the credibility of Peter Darminio was in question, his testimony concerning the defendant's extortionate extensions of credit was corroborated by an exhibit in evidence bearing Gambino's handwriting, headed with the word "Peter" and containing a column of figures and certain calculations. [The trial court] . . . further found that Conti, who was collecting the payments, threatened and beat Darminio from time to time when he was late in making payments.

In July of 1973 one Bernard Ettinger, who had sold Terminal to the Darminios in 1968 and who had not been paid in full in connection with the sale, complained in writing to the New York City Department of Consumer Affairs, requesting that the Department see to it that the Darminios fulfilled their obligations to him before the department approved any sale of stops registered to Terminal. Shortly thereafter, Conti visited Ettinger at his office, slapped Mr. Ettinger on the face, and told him that he had better not complain to the department.

On an earlier occasion when Ettinger had threatened to foreclose on Anthony Darminio's home, on which he held a mortgage, Mr. and Mrs. Darminio had asked Mr. Gambino for assistance, and Gambino replied, "Don't worry about it. I'll send Carlo Conti to straighten it out." In 1974, Ettinger pressed Darminio for payment, which was then a balance of $90,000. A meeting was arranged. Gambino came with Darminio. Gambino said that if Ettinger would settle, Darminio could sell some stops and there would be some stops left over so that Peter Darminio could continue his route. Ettinger agreed to settle for $40,000. One Joseph Perillo, who was also present at the meeting, indicated that he was prepared to purchase some stops from Terminal but did not have money with him for a down payment.

Gambino gave Perillo $5,000, which Perillo, in turn, gave to Ettinger. The court found Ettinger to be a highly credible witness.

In November 1975, Terminal entered into a contract with P & S Sanitation, a newly organized company, to take over Terminal's stops. The court found that Gambino was active in P & S.

In the Fall of 1976, the FBI incorporated American Automated Refuse & Waste Removal, Inc., and set up an office in the Bronx. They bought trucks and a winch, the winch being shipped from Texas, and arranged to dump the garbage in New Jersey. They then began soliciting garbage collection accounts, including Harry's Service Station which they knew was being serviced by P & S Sanitation. On December 1, 1976, Harry's entered into an agreement with American Automated, the Government company. American Automated arranged to drop off a container at Harry's to store garbage which would be collected by Automated. Shortly thereafter, Conti telephoned American Automated and came to the office. He threatened to kill the person seated at the desk, who called himself Wayne Dacon but who was in fact an agent of the FBI named Walter Wayne Orrell. Conti's statement to Orrell included a threat to throw the agent out of the window. This conversation was tape-recorded and the tape was received in evidence. Conti indicated that anything new that opened up in Coop City was his. There were two places on the tape where a crunching sound was audible. Agent Orrell testified that Conti punched him. The evidence established that Conti acted frequently at the behest of Gambino, that both men conspired to acquire and maintain control of the private sanitation industry in Coop City and other areas of the Bronx through a pattern of racketeering activity and they in fact carried out the purpose of the conspiracy, that both men obstructed commerce by extorting payments from Terminal Sanitation and its principals, and that Conti attempted to obstruct commerce by assaulting and threatening to kill persons associated with American Automated, Inc.

These findings ... cannot lightly be set aside. Nor do we see any reason for so doing. We hold that there was sufficient evidence to sustain the conviction. . . .

The judgment of conviction of each appellant is affirmed in respects. . . .

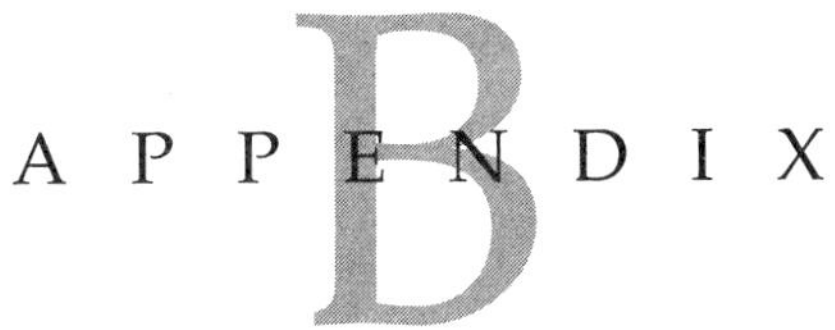

Access to the Law through Legal Research

The Nature of Legal Research

Successful legal research requires a systematic method of finding the law applicable to a particular problem or set of facts. Before beginning research it is helpful, if not essential, for the criminal justice professional or student to have a basic understanding of the law and the legal system.

After assembling the relevant facts and completing a preliminary analysis of the problem, the researcher must find the applicable constitutional and statutory materials and then search for authoritative interpretations of the law. Interpretations are usually found in appellate court decisions construing the particular constitutional provision or statute in analogous situations. These judicial decisions are referred to as "cases in point." Legislative and judicial sources of the law are referred to as "primary sources" because they are authoritative.

A variety of other legal materials, called "secondary sources," are available to the researcher. These consist of legal encyclopedias, textbooks by scholars and practitioners, law reviews published by law schools and journals, and periodicals published by various legal organizations. These secondary sources are extremely helpful to the researcher, especially to one unfamiliar with the law in a given area.

Primary Legal Sources

Federal and state constitutions are often the beginning points in legal research in the criminal justice area, since they provide the framework for our government and guarantee certain basic rights to the accused. As explained in this text, the rights of an accused are protected by several provisions of the federal Constitution and the Bill of Rights. Most state constitutions afford criminal defendants similar protections. For instance, a person concerned about the legality of an arrest, search, or seizure would examine the relevant constitutional provisions and then seek to determine how the courts have construed the law in analogous situations.

Federal offenses are defined in statutes enacted by the United States Congress, and state offenses are defined in statutes enacted by state legislatures. Federal statutes (in sequence of their adoption) are published annually in the *United States Statutes at Large.* Most states have similar volumes, called session laws, that incorporate the laws enacted during a given session of the legislature. These federal and state laws are initially compiled in sequence of their adoption. Later they are merged into legal codes that systematically arrange the statutes by subject and provide an index. Of far greater assistance to the criminal justice researcher are commercially prepared codes that classify all federal and state laws of a general and permanent nature by subject and include reference materials and exhaustive indexes. These volumes are kept current by periodic supplements and revised volumes.

The United States Code Annotated

One popular compilation of the federal law widely used by lawyers, judges, and criminal justice professionals is the *United States Code Annotated.* "U.S.C.A.," as it is known, is published by West Publishing Company of St. Paul, Minnesota (the publisher of this text). The U.S.C.A. consists of fifty separate titles that conform to the text of the Official Code of the Laws of the United States. Title 18, for instance, is entitled "Crimes and Criminal Procedure" and is of particular interest to the criminal justice researcher. Each section of statutory law in U.S.C.A. is followed by a series of annotations consisting of court decisions interpreting the particular statute along with historical notes, cross-references, and other editorial features. If the researcher knows only the popular name of a federal statute, the corresponding U.S. Code title and section number can be found in the Popular Name Table. A sample page from the U.S.C.A. is included as Exhibit 1. A sample page from the Popular Name Table is included as Exhibit 2.

Annotated State Codes

Most states have annotated statutes published by either the state or a private publisher. For example, *West's Annotated California Codes* follows the same general format as the United States Code Annotated. A sample page is included as Exhibit 3. Annotated statutes are popular aids to legal research and can save the researcher valuable time in locating cases in point. They are especially effective tools for locating interpretations of criminal statutes.

The National Reporter System

Volumes containing appellate court decisions are referred to as "reporters." The National Reporter System® includes decisions from the United States Supreme Court, the lower federal courts, and the state appellate courts. Back reporters are now available both in West's Ultra Fiche and in bound-volumes editions.

Decisions of the United States Supreme Court are officially published in the United States Reports (abbreviated U.S.). Two private organizations also report these decisions in hard-cover volumes. The *Supreme Court Reporter* (abbreviated S. Ct.) is published by West, and *Lawyers Edition,* now in its second series (abbreviated L.Ed.2d), is published by the Lawyers Cooperative Publishing Company. References to judicial decisions found in the reporters are called "citations." United States Supreme Court decisions are often cited to all three publications: for example, *Miranda v. Arizona,* 384 U.S. 436, 86 S. Ct. 1602, 16 L.Ed.2d 694 (1966). A sample page from West's *Supreme Court Reporter* is included as Exhibit 4.

CHAPTER 87—PRISONS

Cross References

Escape and rescue, see section 751 et seq. of this title.

§ 1791. Traffic in contraband articles

Whoever, contrary to any rule or regulation promulgated by the Attorney General, introduces or attempts to introduce into or upon the grounds of any Federal penal or correctional institution or takes or attempts to take or send therefrom anything whatsoever, shall be imprisoned not more than ten years.

(June 25, 1948, c. 645, 62 Stat. 786.)

Historical and Revision Notes

Reviser's Note. Based on Title 18, U.S.C., 1940 ed., §§ 753j, 908 (May 14, 1930, c. 274, § 11, 46 Stat. 327; May 27, 1930, c. 339, § 8, 46 Stat. 390).

Section consolidates sections 753j and 908 of Title 18, U.S.C., 1940 ed. The section was broadened to include the taking or sending out of contraband from the institution. This was suggested by representatives of the Federal Bureau of Prisons and the Criminal Division of the Department of Justice. In other respects the section was rewritten without change of substance.

The words "narcotic", "drug", "weapon" and "contraband" were omitted, since the insertion of the words "contrary to any rule or regulation promulgated by the attorney general" preserves the intent of the original statutes.

Words "guilty of a felony" were deleted as unnecessary in view of definitive section 1 of this title. (See also reviser's note under section 550 of this title.)

Minor verbal changes also were made.

Cross References

Bureau of Prisons employees, power to arrest without warrant for violations of this section, see section 3050 of this title.

West's Federal Forms

Sentence and fine, see § 7531 et seq.

Code of Federal Regulations

Federal penal and correctional institutions, traffic in contraband articles, see 28 CFR 6.1.

Library References

Prisons ⚷17½.
C.J.S. Prisons § 22.

Notes of Decisions

Aiding and abetting 7
Admissibility of evidence 13
Articles prohibited 3
Assistance of counsel 11

585

EXHIBIT 1 United States Code Annotated Source: Reprinted with permission from 18 U.S.C.A. § 1791, Copyright © 1984 By West Publishing Co., 1-800-328-9352.

Crimes and Criminal Procedure—Continued

Oct. 28, 1992, Pub.L. 102–550, Title XIII, Subtitle A, § 1353, Title XV, Subtitle A, §§ 1504(c), 1512(a), (c), 1522(a), 1523(a), 1524, 1525(c)(1), 1526, 1527, 1528, 1530, 1531, 1533, 1534, 1536, Subtitle D, § 1543, Subtitle E, §§ 1552, 1553, 1554, 106 Stat. 3970, 4055, 4057, 4063, 4064, 4065, 4066, 4067, 4069, 4070, 4071 (Title 18, §§ 474, 474A, 504, 981, 982, 984, 986, 1510, 1905, 1956, 1957, 1960, 6001)

Oct. 28, 1992, Pub.L. 102–561, 106 Stat. 4233 (Title 18, § 2319)

Oct. 29, 1992, Pub.L. 102–572, Title I, § 103, Title VII, §§ 701, 703, 106 Stat. 4507, 4514, 4515 (Title 18, §§ 3143, 3154, 3401, 3603)

Criminal Appeals Act

Mar. 2, 1907, ch. 2564, 34 Stat. 1246 (See Title 18, § 3731)

Criminal Code

Mar. 4, 1909, ch. 321, 35 Stat. 1088 (See Title 18, chapters 1–15)

June 25, 1910, ch. 431, § 6, 36 Stat. 857 (See Title 18, §§ 1853, 1856)

Mar. 4, 1921, ch. 172, 41 Stat. 1444 (See Title 18, §§ 831–835)

Mar. 28, 1940, ch. 73, 54 Stat. 80 (See Title 18, § 1382)

Apr. 30, 1940, ch. 164, 54 Stat. 171 (See Title 18, § 1024)

June 6, 1940, ch. 241, 54 Stat. 234 (See Title 18, § 13)

June 11, 1940, ch. 323, 54 Stat. 304 (See Title 18, § 7)

Apr. 1, 1944, ch. 151, 58 Stat. 149 (See Title 18, § 491)

Sept. 27, 1944, ch. 425, 58 Stat. 752 (See Title 18, § 371)

June 8, 1945, ch. 178, 59 Stat. 234 (See Title 18, §§ 371, 1503, 1505)

Criminal Fine Enforcement Act of 1984

Pub.L. 98–596, Oct. 30, 1984, 98 Stat. 3134 (Title 18, §§ 1, 1 note, 3565, 3565 note, 3569, 3579, 3591 to 3599, 3611 note, 3621 to 3624, 3651, 3655, 4209, 4214; Title 18, F.R.Crim.Proc. Rules 12.2, 12.2 note)

Criminal Fine Improvements Act of 1987

Pub.L. 100–185, Dec. 11, 1987, 101 Stat. 1279 (Title 18, §§ 1 note, 18, 19, 3013, 3559, 3571, 3572, 3573, 3611, 3611 note, 3612, 3663; Title 28, § 604)

Criminal Justice Act Revision of 1984

Pub.L. 98–473, Title II, § 1901, Oct. 12, 1984, 98 Stat. 2185 (Title 18, § 3006A)

Criminal Justice Act Revision of 1986

Pub.L. 99–651, Title I, Nov. 14, 1986, 100 Stat. 3642 (Title 18, § 3006A)

Criminal Justice Act of 1964

Pub. L. 88–455, Aug. 20, 1964, 78 Stat. 552 (Title 18, § 3006A)

Criminal Law and Procedure Technical Amendments Act of 1986

Pub.L. 99–646, Nov. 10, 1986, 100 Stat. 3592 (Title 18, §§ 1 note, 3, 17, 18, 113, 115, 201, 201 note, 203, 203 note, 209, 219, 351, 373, 513, 524, 666, 1028, 1029, 1111, 1153, 1201, 1366, 1512, 1515, 1791, 1791 note, 1793, 1961, 1963, 2031, 2032, 2113, 2232, 2241, 2241 notes, 2242, 2243, 2244, 2245, 2315, 2320, 3050, 3076, 3141, 3142, 3143, 3143 note, 3144, 3146, 3147, 3148, 3150a, 3156, 3156 note, 3185, 3522, 3551 note, 3552, 3552 note, 3553, 3553 notes, 3556, 3561, 3561 note, 3563, 3563 notes, 3579, 3579 notes, 3583, 3583 note, 3603, 3603 note, 3624, 3624 note, 3671, 3671 note, 3672, 3672 note, 3673, 3673 note, 3681, 3682, 3731, 3742, 4044, 4045, 4082, 4203, 4204, 4208, 4209, 4210, 4214, 4217, 5003, 5037, 5037 note; Title 18, F.R.Crim.Proc. Rules 12.2, 29, 29 note, 32, 32 note, 32.1, 32.1 note; Title 21, §§ 802, 812, 845a, 875, 878, 881; Title 28, §§ 546, 992, 993, 994, 1921, 1921 note; Title 42, §§ 257, 300w–3, 300w–4, 9511, 10601, 10603, 10604)

Pub.L. 100–185, § 4(c), Dec. 11, 1987, 101 Stat. 1279 (Title 18, § 18)

Pub.L. 100–690, Title VII, §§ 7012 to 7014, Nov. 18, 1988, 102 Stat. 4395 (Title 18, §§ 18, 1961, 4217)

Criminal Victims Protection Act of 1990

Pub.L. 101–581, Nov. 15, 1990, 104 Stat. 2865 (Title 11, §§ 101 note, 523, 523 note, 1328)

Pub.L. 101–647, Title XXXI, Nov. 29, 1990, 104 Stat. 4916 (Title 11, §§ 101 note, 523, 523 note, 1328)

Critical Agricultural Materials Act

Pub.L. 95–592, Nov. 4, 1978, 92 Stat. 2529 (Title 7, §§ 178, 178a to 178n, 1314f); Pub.L. 98–284, May 16, 1984, 98 Stat. 184 (Title 7, §§ 178, 178 note, 178a to 178i, 178k to 178n)

Pub.L. 99–198, Title XIV, § 1439, Dec. 23, 1985, 99 Stat. 1559 (Title 7, § 178c)

Pub.L. 101–624, Title XVI, § 1601(e), Nov. 28, 1990, 104 Stat. 3704 (Title 7, § 178n)

EXHIBIT 2 Popular Name Table (from U.S.C.A) Source: Reprinted with permission from U.S.C.A. Popular Name Table, Copyright © 1992 By West Publishing Co., 1-800-328-9352.

warrant. People v. Golden (1971) 97 Cal.Rptr. 476, 20 C.A.3d 211.

4. Affidavits

"Oral" procedure is permitted only as to affidavit in support of search and warrant itself must be in writing. Bowyer v. Superior Court of Santa Cruz County (1974) 111 Cal.Rptr. 628, 37 C.A.3d 151, rehearing denied 112 Cal.Rptr. 266, 37 C.A.3d 151.

For an affidavit based on informant's hearsay statement to be legally sufficient to support issuance of a search warrant, two requirements must be met: (1) affidavit must allege the informant's statement in language that is factual rather than conclusionary and must establish that informant spoke with personal knowledge of the matters contained in such statement, and (2) the affidavit must contain some underlying factual information from which magistrate issuing the warrant can reasonably conclude that informant was credible or his information reliable. People v. Hamilton (1969) 77 Cal.Rptr. 785, 454 P.2d 681, 71 C.2d 176.

5. Arrest

An arrest without a warrant may not be made on a belief, founded on information received from a third person, that a misdemeanor is being committed. Ware v. Dunn (1947) 183 P.2d 128, 80 C.A.2d 936.

Arrest under warrant issued by justice of peace directed to any sheriff "in the state," where proper sheriff did receive warrant and executed it, and person arrested was not prejudiced, and was not ground for complaint by person arrested, notwithstanding under statutes warrant should have been directed to any sheriff "in the county". Elliott v. Haskins (1937) 67 P.2d 698, 20 C.A.2d 591.

6. Unreasonable searches

Alleged action of city police on specified occasions in blocking off designated portions of city and stopping all persons and automobiles entering or leaving the blocked off area and searching them without first obtaining a search warrant and without having probable cause for believing the searched individuals to have violated some law or that automobiles were carrying contraband, would be unconstitutional as being "unreasonable searches and seizures". Wirin v. Horrall (1948) 193 P.2d 470, 85 C.A.2d 497.

7. Admissibility of evidence

Rule excluding in criminal prosecutions evidence obtained through unlawful searches and seizures by police and governmental officers does not apply to evidence obtained by a private person, not employed by nor associated with a governmental unit. People v. Johnson (1957) 315 P.2d 468, 153 C.A.2d 870.

Evidence obtained in violation of constitutional guarantees against unreasonable searches and seizures is inadmissible. People v. Cahan (1955) 282 P.2d 905, 44 C.2d 434, 50 A.L.R.2d 513.

In a prosecution for burglary in the second degree, the fact that articles claimed to have been taken were seized from the person of accused without warrant in violation of Const.Art. 1, § 19 (repealed; see, now, Const.Art. 1, § 13) did not render their introduction in evidence error, although the court overruled the motion of accused to have the articles returned to him. People v. Watson (1922) 206 P. 648, 57 C.A. 85.

8. Federal and state warrants distinguished

Although a California municipal court judge is a "judge of a court of record" and thus authorized to issue federal warrants, the search warrant in question was clearly issued under state, not federal, authority, where it was issued by a California municipal judge on a California form, on the application of a California narcotics agent, and where there was no attempt to comply with the requirements of Fed. Rules of Cr.Proc. rule 41, 18 U.S.C.A. U. S. v. Radlick (C.A.1978) 581 F.2d 225.

§ 1524. Issuance; grounds; special master

(a) A search warrant may be issued upon any of the following grounds:

(1) When the property was stolen or embezzled.

(2) When the property or things were used as the means of committing a felony.

(3) When the property or things are in the possession of any person with the intent to use it as a means of committing a public of-

EXHIBIT 3 West's Annotated California Code Source: Reprinted with permission from *West's Annotated California Codes,* Vol. 51A, § 1524.

Since 1889 the decisions of the United States Courts of Appeals have been published in West's *Federal Reporter,* now in its second series (abbreviated F.2d). Decisions of federal district (trial) courts are published in *West's Federal Supplement* (abbreviated F. Supp.). A citation to a case in *Federal Reporter* will read, for example, *Newman v. United States,* 817 F.2d 635 (10th Cir. 1987). This refers to a 1987 case reported in volume 817, page 635 of the *Federal Reporter,* second series, decided by the United States Court of Appeals for the 10th Circuit. A citation to *United States v. Klopfenstine,* 673 F. Supp. 356 (W.D. Mo. 1987), refers to a 1987 federal district court decision from the western district of Missouri reported in volume 673, page 356 of the *Federal Supplement.*

Additional federal reporters publish the decisions from other federal courts (e.g., bankruptcy and military appeals), but the federal reporters referred to earlier are those most frequently used by criminal justice professionals.

The Regional Reporters

The decisions of the highest state courts (usually but not always called supreme courts) and the decisions of other state appellate courts (usually referred to as intermediate appellate courts) are found in seven regional reporters, West's *California Reporter,* and the *New York Supplement.* Regional reporters, with their abbreviation in parentheses, include decisions from the following states:

Atlantic Reporter: (A. and A.2d)	Maine, Vermont, New Hampshire, Connecticut, Rhode Island, Pennsylvania, New Jersey, Maryland, Delaware, and the District of Columbia
North Eastern Reporter: (N.E. and N.E.2d)	Illinois, Indiana, Massachusetts, New York (court of last resort only), and Ohio
North Western Reporter: (N.W. and N.W.2d)	North Dakota, South Dakota, Nebraska, Minnesota, Iowa, Michigan, and Wisconsin
Pacific Reporter: (P. and P.2d)	Washington, Oregon, California, Montana, Idaho, Nevada, Utah, Arizona, Wyoming, Colorado, New Mexico, Kansas, Oklahoma, Alaska, and Hawaii
Southern Reporter: (So. and So.2d)	Florida, Alabama, Mississippi, and Louisiana
South Eastern Reporter: (S.E. and S.E.2d)	Virginia, West Virginia, North Carolina, South Carolina, and Georgia
South Western Reporter: (S.W. and S.W.2d)	Texas, Missouri, Arkansas, Kentucky, and Tennessee

For many states (in addition to New York and California), West publishes separate volumes reporting the decisions as they appear in the regional reporters. *Pennsylvania Reporter* and *Texas Cases* are examples of this.

384 U.S. 436
Ernesto A. MIRANDA, Petitioner,
v.
STATE OF ARIZONA.

Michael VIGNERA, Petitioner,
v.
STATE OF NEW YORK.

Carl Calvin WESTOVER, Petitioner,
v.
UNITED STATES.

STATE OF CALIFORNIA, Petitioner,
v.
Roy Allen STEWART.

Nos. 759-761, 584.

Argued Feb. 28, March 1 and 2, 1966.

Decided June 13, 1966.

Rehearing Denied No. 584
Oct. 10, 1966.

See 87 S.Ct. 11.

Criminal prosecutions. The Superior Court, Maricopa County, Arizona, rendered judgment, and the Supreme Court of Arizona, 98 Ariz. 18, 401 P.2d 721, affirmed. The Supreme Court, Kings County, New York, rendered judgment, and the Supreme Court, Appellate Division, Second Department, 21 A.D.2d 752, 252 N.Y.S.2d 19, affirmed, as did the Court of Appeals of the State of New York at 15 N.Y.2d 970, 259 N.Y.S.2d 857, 207 N.E.2d 527. The United States District Court for the Northern District of California, Northern Division, rendered judgment, and the United States Court of Appeals for the Ninth Circuit, 342 F.2d 684, affirmed. The Superior Court, Los Angeles County, California, rendered judgment and the Supreme Court of California, 62 Cal.2d 571, 43 Cal. Rptr. 201, 400 P.2d 97, reversed. In the first three cases, defendants obtained certiorari, and the State of California obtained certiorari in the fourth case. The Supreme Court, Mr. Chief Justice Warren, held that statements obtained from defendants during incommunicado interrogation in police-dominated atmosphere, without full warning of constitutional rights, were inadmissible as having been obtained in violation of Fifth Amendment privilege against self-incrimination.

Judgments in first three cases reversed and judgment in fourth case affirmed.

Mr. Justice Harlan, Mr. Justice Stewart, and Mr. Justice White dissented; Mr. Justice Clark dissented in part.

1. Courts ⚿397½

Certiorari was granted in cases involving admissibility of defendants' statements to police to explore some facets of problems of applying privilege against self-incrimination to in-custody interrogation and to give concrete constitutional guidelines for law enforcement agencies and courts to follow.

2. Criminal Law ⚿393(1), 641.1

Constitutional rights to assistance of counsel and protection against self-incrimination were secured for ages to come and designed to approach immortality as nearly as human institutions can approach it. U.S.C.A.Const. Amends. 5, 6.

3. Criminal Law ⚿412.1(4)

Prosecution may not use statements, whether exculpatory or inculpatory, stemming from custodial interrogation of defendant unless it demonstrates use of procedural safeguards effective to secure privilege against self-incrimination. U.S.C.A.Const. Amend. 5.

4. Criminal Law ⚿412.1(4)

"Custodial interrogation", within rule limiting admissibility of statements stemming from such interrogation, means questioning initiated by law enforcement officers after person has been taken into custody or otherwise deprived of his freedom of action in any significant way. U.S.C.A.Const. Amend. 5.

See publication Words and Phrases for other judicial constructions and definitions.

EXHIBIT 4 Supreme Court Reporter Source: Reprinted with permission from 86 S. Ct. 1602.

The following examples of citation forms appear in some of the regional reporters:

- *State v. Hogan*, 480 So.2d 288 (La. 1985). This refers to a 1985 decision of the Louisiana Supreme Court found in volume 480, page 288 of the *Southern Reporter*, second series.
- *State v. Nungesser*, 269 N.W.2d 449 (Iowa 1978). This refers to a 1978 decision of the Iowa Supreme Court found in volume 269, page 449 of the *North Western Reporter*, second series.
- *Henry v. State*, 567 S.W.2d 7 (Tex. Cr. App. 1978). This refers to a 1978 decision of the Texas Court of Criminal appeals found in volume 567, page 7 of the *South Western Reporter*, second series.

A sample page from *Southern Reporter*, second series, is included as Exhibit 5.

Syllabi, Headnotes, and Key Numbers

The National Reporter System and the regional reporters contain not only the official text of each reported decision but also a brief summary of the decision, called the "syllabus," and one or more topically indexed "headnotes." These headnotes briefly describe the principles of law expounded by the court and are indexed by a series of topic "key numbers." West assigns these key numbers to specific points of decisional law. For instance, decisions dealing with first-degree murder are classified under the topic "homicide" and assigned a key number for each particular aspect of that crime. Thus a homicide case dealing with the intent requirement in first-degree murder may be classified as: "Homicide KEY NUMBER SYSTEM 9—Intent and design to effect death." Using this key number system, a researcher can locate headnotes of various appellate decisions on this aspect of homicide and is, in turn, led to relevant decisional law. In addition, each of these volumes contains a table of statutes construed in the cases reported in that volume, with reference to the American Bar Association's Standards for Criminal Justice.

United States Law Week

United States Law Week, published by the Bureau of National Affairs, Inc., Washington, D.C., presents a weekly survey of American law. *Law Week* includes all the latest decisions from the United States Supreme Court as well as significant current decisions from other federal and state courts.

Criminal Law Reporter

Published by the Bureau of National Affairs, Inc., Washington, D.C., the weekly *Criminal Law Reporter* reviews contemporary developments in the criminal law. It is an excellent source of commentaries on current state and federal court decisions in the criminal law area.

imprisonment. It is indeed unlikely that the enactment of art. 893.1 was designed to punish more severely those who commit negligent homicide than perpetrators of second degree murder, manslaughter, aggravated battery, etc.

In summary, therefore, we find as regards defendant's second assignment of error that the art. 893.1 enhancement is not constitutionally infirm as cruel, unusual and excessive punishment; that the absence of art. 894.1 sentence articulation in this case was harmless, there existing in this record sufficient factors to support this penalty which is well within the statutory range; that the two year penalty imposed in this case under § 14:95.2 is illegal; that art. 893.1 is applicable to all felonies, including those specially enumerated in § 14:95.2 and that therefore the art. 893.1 enhancement in this case is valid.

Decree

Accordingly, defendant's conviction is affirmed; his sentence is reversed and the case remanded for resentencing in accordance with the views expressed herein and according to law.

CONVICTION AFFIRMED; SENTENCE REVERSED; CASE REMANDED.

DIXON, C.J., and DENNIS, J., concur.

WATSON, J., dissents as to requiring notice.

STATE of Louisiana

v.

Patrick HOGAN.

No. 84–K–1847.

Supreme Court of Louisiana.

Dec. 2, 1985.

Defendant was convicted in the First Judicial District Court, Parish of Caddo, Charles R. Lindsay, J., of aggravated battery, and he appealed. The Court of Appeal, 454 So.2d 1235, affirmed, and defendant's petition for writ of review was granted. The Supreme Court, Calogero, J., held that: (1) sentence enhancement by reason of use of a firearm in commission of a felony was not constitutionally infirm as cruel, unusual and excessive; (2) existence of some mitigating factors did not preclude enhancement; (3) imposition of an additional two-year penalty for use of a gun while attempting commission of a specified felony was impermissible when not preceded by an appropriate notice; and (4) enhancement was not invalid, however, since minimum sentence mandated by use of firearm was applicable to all felonies.

Conviction affirmed, sentence reversed, and case remanded.

Dennis, J., concurred.

Watson, J., dissented as to requiring notice.

1. Criminal Law ⚷1206.1(1), 1213.2(1)

General sentencing enhancement statute [LSA-R.S. 14:34, 14:95; LSA-C.Cr.P. art. 893.1] applicable when a firearm is used in commission of a felony, does not impose cruel, unusual, and excessive punishment and is not constitutionally infirm on its face or as applied. U.S.C.A. Const. Amend. 8.

2. Criminal Law ⚷1213.8(7)

Imposition of mandatory minimum sentence under enhancement statute [LSA-R.S. 14:34, 14:95; LSA-C.Cr.P. art. 893.1]

EXHIBIT 5 Southern Reporter Source: Reprinted with permission from 480 So.2d 288.

The Digests

West also publishes Decennial Digests that topically index all the appellate court decisions from the state and federal courts. Digests are tools that enable the researcher to locate cases in point through topics and key numbers. Ten Decennial Digests have been published as of 1991, the most recent being the *Tenth Decennial Digest* (Part 1) that embraces federal and state appellate decisions from 1986–1991. A series of federal digests contains key number headnotes for decisions of the federal courts. The current series published by West is *Federal Practice Digest* 4th. In addition, separate digests are published for most states as well as for the Atlantic, North Western, Pacific, and South Eastern reporters. The index at the beginning of each topic identifies the various points of law by numerically arranged key numbers. In addition to the basic topic of criminal law, many topics in the field of criminal law are listed by specific crimes (e.g., homicide, forgery, bribery). Procedural topics such as arrest and search and seizure are also included. The digests contain a descriptive word index and a table of cases sorted by name, listing the key numbers corresponding to the decisions. Thus the researcher may find, by key number, reference topics that relate to the principles set out in the headnotes prepared for each judicial decision. A researcher who locates a topic and key number has access to all reported decisions on this point of law. Through use of these volumes, a researcher familiar with a case by name may use it to find a direct reference to a point of law. A sample page from the *Texas Digest*, second series, is reprinted as Exhibit 6.

Shepard's Citations

Shepard's Citations is a series published by Shepard's/McGraw-Hill, Inc., of Colorado Springs, Colorado. It provides the judicial history of cases by reference to the volume and page number of the cases in the particular reporters. By using the symbols explained in this work, the researcher can determine whether a particular decision has been affirmed, followed, distinguished, modified, or reversed by subsequent court decisions. Most attorneys "Shepardize" the cases they cite in their law briefs to support various principles of law. There is a separate set of *Shepard's Citations* for the United States Supreme Court reports, the federal appellate and district courts, for each regional reporter, and for each state that has an official reporter.

Secondary Legal Sources

Legal authorities other than constitutions, statutes, ordinances, regulations, and court decisions are called "secondary sources," yet they are essential tools in legal research. A basic necessity for any legal researcher's work is a good law dictionary. Several are published, and *Black's Law Dictionary®* (6th ed.) is one of the best known. *Black's* is available both in print and computer disk media. Beyond dictionaries, the most common secondary legal authorities are legal

6 Tex D 2d—155 **ARREST** ⟹63.3

For references to other topics, see Descriptive-Word Index

was observed in act of smoking a marihuana cigarette, for violation of narcotics laws, was legal. Code Cr.Proc.Tex.1925, arts. 212, 215; 26 U.S.C.A. §§ 2557(b) (1), 2593(a).
Rent v. U. S., 209 F.2d 893.

D.C.Tex. 1975. Arrest and subsequent detention of husband plaintiff by deputies without warrant was not unlawful where husband plaintiff appeared to be intoxicated in public place. 28 U.S.C.A. § 1343; 42 U.S.C.A. §§ 1983, 1985; U.S.C.A.Const. Amend. 4; Vernon's Ann.Tex.C.C.P. art. 14.01.
Lamb v. Cartwright, 393 F.Supp. 1081, affirmed 524 F.2d 238.

D.C.Tex. 1972. The "presence" of the officer, under Texas statute providing that a police officer may arrest an offender without a warrant for any offense committed in his "presence" or within his view, is satisfied if the violation occurs within reach of the officer's senses. Vernon's Ann.Tex.C.C.P. art. 14.01(b).
Taylor v. McDonald, 346 F.Supp. 390.

D.C.Tex. 1967. It is not the case that officer may arrest person committing felony in his presence irrespective of whose privacy officer must violate in order to place commission of felony in his presence.
Gonzales v. Beto, 266 F.Supp. 751, affirmed State of Tex. v. Gonzales, 388 F.2d 145.

Tex.Cr.App. 1981. Observation by police officer of the exchange of money between defendant and another person for tinfoil bindles coupled with officer's knowledge that heroin is normally packaged in tinfoil bindles was sufficient to provide probable cause to believe that an offense had been committed and, thus, defendant's warrantless arrest was valid under statute which allows peace officer to arrest an offender without a warrant "for any offense committed in his presence or within his view." Vernon's Ann.C.C.P. art. 14.01(b).
Boyd v. State, 621 S.W.2d 616.

Tex.Cr.App. 1981. Where defendant was observed in supermarket placing a steak and bottle of bath oil in her purse and observed leaving the store without paying for such items and was apprehended and placed in custody of city police officer who had been summoned by the manager, defendant's arrest was lawful. Vernon's Ann.C.C.P. art. 18.16.
Stewart v. State, 611 S.W.2d 434.

Tex.Cr.App. 1980. Peace officer need not determine whether material in question is in fact obscene in order to make a valid arrest for offense of commercially distributing obscene material; warrantless arrest is proper if there is probable cause to believe the publication commercially distributed in officer's presence or within his view was obscene. Vernon's Ann.C.C.P. art. 14.01(b); V.T.C.A., Penal Code § 43.21(1).
Carlock v. State, 609 S.W.2d 787.

Tex.Cr.App. 1980. Fact that defendants were in possession of a stolen gun several hours prior to their arrest was not a sufficient basis for the officers' conclusion that defendants were committing an offense within their presence so as to justify a warrantless arrest.
Green v. State, 594 S.W.2d 72.

Tex.Cr.App. 1979. Defendant had no reasonable expectation of privacy while sitting in a restaurant, so that, upon observing drug transaction in plain view from public vantage point outside the restaurant and recognizing it as offense, officers were authorized to make warrantless arrest. Vernon's Ann.C.C.P. art. 14.01.
Hamilton v. State, 590 S.W.2d 503.

Tex.Cr.App. 1979. Where defendants' vehicle was not stopped by any overt action on the part of off-duty police officers, who simply turned around and began to follow defendants' vehicle after spotting it traveling in the opposite direction and noting that defendants appeared to be smoking a marihuana cigarette, where it was only after defendants stopped at a traffic light that one officer was able to approach the vehicle and then noticed the odor of marihuana, and where it was at that point that the officer directed defendants to pull over to the side of the street and get out of their car, the arrest and subsequent search were reasonable under the circumstances. Vernon's Ann.C.C.P. art. 14.01(b).
Isam v. State, 582 S.W.2d 441.

Tex.Cr.App. 1979. Although detective did not view any of the reading matter of the magazine before making warrantless arrest of seller, the magazine's front and back covers, depicting an act of fellatio on a nude male and an act of cunnilingus on a nude female, gave the officer sufficient probable cause to reasonably believe that a violation of the obscenity statute had occurred in his presence and within his view justifying a warrantless arrest. V.T.C.A., Penal Code § 43.21(1); Vernon's Ann.C.C.P. art. 14.01(b).
Price v. State, 579 S.W.2d 492.

Tex.Cr.App. 1979. Though the scope of an investigation cannot exceed the purposes which justify initiating the investigation, if, while questioning a motorist regarding the operation of his vehicle, an officer sees evidence of a criminal violation in open view or in some other manner acquires probable cause with respect to a more serious charge, the officer may arrest for that offense and, incident thereto, conduct an additional search for physical evidence. Vernon's Ann.Civ.St. art.

see Vernon's Annotated Texas Statutes

EXHIBIT 6 Texas Digest 2d Source: Reprinted with permission from West's Texas Digest 2d, Vol. 6, Page 155. Copyright © 1982 By West Publishing Co., 1-800-328-9352.

encyclopedias. These are arranged alphabetically by subject and are used much like any standard encyclopedia.

There are two principal national encyclopedias of the law: *Corpus Juris Secundum* (C.J.S.), published by West, and *American Jurisprudence,* second edition (Am.Jur.2d), published by Lawyers Cooperative Publishing Company of Rochester, New York. A sample page from C.J.S. appears as Exhibit 7. Appellate courts frequently document propositions of law contained in their opinions by citations to these encyclopedias, as well as to cases in the reporters. Each of these encyclopedias is an excellent set of reference books; one significant difference is that the West publication cites more court decisions, while the Lawyers Cooperative publication limits its footnote references to the leading cases pertinent to the principles of law in the text. *Corpus Juris Secundum* includes valuable cross-references to West topic key numbers and other secondary sources, including forms. *American Jurisprudence 2d* includes valuable footnote references to another of the company's publications, *American Law Reports,* now in its fourth series. These volumes (cited as A.L.R.) include annotations to the decisional law on selected topics. For example, a 1987 annotation from A.L.R. entitled "Snowmobile Operation as D.W.I. or D.U.I." appears in 56 A.L.R. 4th 1092.

Both *Corpus Juris Secundum* and *American Jurisprudence 2d* are supplemented annually by cumulative pocket parts and are exceptionally well indexed. They serve as an excellent starting point for a researcher, because they provide a general overview of topics. For example, a person researching the defenses available to a defendant charged with forgery would find a good discussion of the law in this area in either of these encyclopedias. A citation to the text on defenses to forgery found in *Corpus Juris Secundum* would read: 37 C.J.S. Forgery § 41; in *American Jurisprudence 2d* it would read: 36 Am. Jur. 2d Forgery § 42.

In addition to these major national encyclopedias, some states have encyclopedias for the jurisprudence of their state, for example, *Pennsylvania Law Encyclopedia* and *Texas Jurisprudence.* Like the volumes of *Corpus Juris Secundum* and *American Jurisprudence 2d,* most encyclopedias of state law are annually supplemented with cumulative pocket parts.

Textbooks and other treatises on legal subjects often read much like encyclopedias. However, most address specific subjects in great depth. Two of the better known textbooks on law are Wharton's *Criminal Evidence,* published by Lawyers Cooperative; and LaFave and Scott, *Substantive Criminal Law,* published by West.

In addition, many leading law schools publish law reviews that contain articles, commentaries, and notes by academics, judges, lawyers, and law students who exhaustively research topics. A recent law review article in the criminal justice field, "Running Rampant: The Imposition of Sanctions and the Use of Force Against Fleeing Criminal Suspects," 80 Geo. L.J. 2175 (August 1992), refers to a scholarly article published in volume 80 at page 2175 of the Georgetown Law Journal.

An example of a professional publication is the *Criminal Law Bulletin,* published bimonthly by Warren, Gorham and Lamont, Inc. of Boston, Massachusetts. It contains many valuable articles of contemporary interest. For instance, "Stop and Frisk: The Triumph of Law Enforcement Over Private Rights" was published in the January–February 1988 issue. The American Bar Association and most state bar associations publish numerous professional articles in their religious beliefs.[38] The burden falls on prison officials to prove that the food available to a religious inmate is consistent with his dietary laws and provides adequate nourishment.[39] Thus, a prisoner who strictly adheres to Jewish dietary laws may be entitled to prepare his own meals during the Passover holiday,[40] and Muslim inmates may be entitled to a diet that provides them with adequate nourishment without requiring them to eat pork.[41]

However, where Muslim inmates are able to practice their religion conscientiously and still receive a sufficiently nutritious diet, the prison is not obligated to provide them with a special diet.[42]

Prison authorities are not required to supply a prisoner with a special religious diet where the prisoner's beliefs are not religious in nature.[43]

§ 95. Religious Names

Although under some authorities prisoners lose the right to change their names for religious purposes, other authorities generally preclude a categorical refusal to accord legal recognition to religious names adopted by incarcerated persons.

Library References

Prisons ⇔4(14).

Although it has been held that a common-law name change, even for religious purposes, is among the rights that inmates lose as inconsistent with their status as prisoners,[44] it has also been held that a state's categorical refusal to accord legal recognition to religious names adopted by incarcerated persons is not reasonably and substantially justified by considerations of prison discipline and order.[45]

Thus, the inmates' free exercise of religion may be burdened by prison officials who continue for all purposes to use the names under which the inmates were committed,[46] and it may be unlawful for the state to refuse to deliver mail addressed to the prisoner under his legal religious name.[47]

On the other hand, inmates are not entitled to have prison officials use their new names for all purposes.[48] For example, correctional authorities generally do not have to reorganize institutional records to reflect prisoners' legally adopted religious names.[49]

E. COMMUNICATIONS AND VISITING RIGHTS AND RESTRICTIONS

§ 96. Communications in General

Prison inmates have a right to communicate with people living in free society, but this right is not unfettered and may be limited by prison officials in order to promote legitimate institutional interests.

Library References

Prisons ⇔4(5, 6).

Prison inmates have a constitutional right to communicate with people living in free society.[50] However, this right is not absolute, and is subject

38. U.S.—Prushinowski v. Hambrick, D.C.N.C., 570 F.Supp. 863.

39. U.S.—Prushinowski v. Hambrick, D.C.N.C., 570 F.Supp. 863.

40. U.S.—Schlesinger v. Carlson, D.C.Pa., 489 F.Supp. 612.

41. U.S.—Masjid Muhammad-D.C.C. v. Keve, D.C.Del., 479 F.Supp. 1311.

42. U.S.—Masjid Muhammad-D.C.C. v. Keve, D.C.Del., 479 F.Supp. 1311.

43. U.S.—Africa v Commonwealth of Pennsylvania, C.A.Pa., 662 F.2d 1025, certiorari denied 102 S.Ct. 1756, 456 U.S. 908, 72 L.Ed.2d 165.

44. U.S.—Salahuddin v. Coughlin, D.C.N.Y., 591 F.Supp. 353.

45. U.S.—Barrett v. Commonwealth of Virginia, C.A.Va., 689 F.2d 498.

46. U.S.—Masjid Muhammad-D.C.C. v. Keve, D.C.Del., 479 F.Supp. 1311.

47. U.S.—Barrett v. Commonwealth of Virginia, C.A.Va., 689 F.2d 498.

Masjid Muhammad-D.C.C. v. Keve, D.C.Del., 479 F.Supp. 1311.

48. U.S.—Azeez v. Fairman, D.C.Ill., 604 F.Supp. 357—Masjid Muhammad-D.C.C. v. Keve, D.C.Del., 479 F.Supp. 1311.

49. U.S.—Barrett v. Commonwealth of Virginia, C.A.Va., 689 F.2d 498.

Azeez v. Fairman, D.C.Ill., 604 F.Supp. 357.

Failure to follow statutory mechanism

Inmates' constitutional rights were not violated by failure of prison officials to recognize their use of Muslim names in records of department of correctional services, where inmates had not followed statutory mechanism for name change.

U.S.—Salahuddin v. Coughlin, D.C.N.Y., 591 F.Supp. 353.

50. U.S.—Pell v. Procunier, Cal., 94 S.Ct. 2800, 417 U.S. 817, 41 L.Ed.2d 495.

Inmates of Allegheny County Jail v. Wecht, D.C.Pa., 565 F.Supp. 1278.

Friends and relatives

U.S.—Hutchings v. Corum, D.C.Mo., 501 F.Supp. 1276.

501

EXHIBIT 7 Corpus Juris Secundum Source: Reprinted with permission from Corpus Juris Secundum, Vol. 72, Prisons § 96, Pg. 501.

journals and reports. Some of these present contemporary views on the administration of justice.

The *Index to Legal Periodicals*, published by H. W. Wilson Company of the Bronx, New York, indexes articles from leading legal publications by subject and author. This valuable research tool is found in many law libraries and is kept current by periodic supplements.

Words and Phrases, another West publication, consists of numerous volumes alphabetically arranged in dictionary form. Hundreds of thousands of legal terms are defined with citations to appellate court decisions. The volumes are kept current by annual pocket part supplements. A sample page from *Words and Phrases* is reprinted as Exhibit 8.

Periodicals published by law schools, bar associations, and other professional organizations may be of considerable value both in doing research and in gaining a perspective on many contemporary problems in the criminal justice field. The federal government also publishes numerous studies of value to the criminal justice professional and student.

Computerized Legal Research

WESTLAW® is a computerized legal retrieval system that operates from a central computer system at the West headquarters in St. Paul, Minnesota. Stored there are the data bases for state and federal statutes, appellate decisions, attorney general opinions, and certain legal periodicals. For example, the law review article referred to earlier, "Running Rampant: The Imposition of Sanctions and the Use of Force Against Fleeing Criminal Suspects," 80 Geo. L.J. 2175 (August 1992), is available on WESTLAW in the GEOLJ database, and can be retrieved using the query **ci(80 +5 2175)**. WESTLAW can be accessed through a wide variety of computer equipment, including mainframe terminals, personal computers, and word processers. Subscribers have terminals and printers in their offices and enter queries into the system to begin research. A properly formulated query pinpoints the legal issue to be researched and instructs WESTLAW to retrieve all data relevant to the query.

WESTLAW has available a searching method that uses natural language, called WIN™, that allows queries to be entered in plain English. The statutes, cases, and other research results found on WESTLAW can be printed out on paper or downloaded onto computer disks, allowing the material to be incorporated into word processing documents. Computer-assisted legal research (CALR) is an increasingly useful supplement to traditional methods of legal research.

How to Research a Specific Point of Law

The following example demonstrates how a legal researcher might employ the research tools discussed earlier to find the law applicable to a given set of facts. Consider this hypothetical scenario: Mary Jones, a student at a Florida college, filed a complaint accusing Jay Grabbo of taking her purse while she was walking across campus. In her statement to the police, Jones was somewhat vague on whether Grabbo had used any force in taking the purse and whether she had

RESISTANCE—Cont'd

Where a contract for the purchase of defendant's stock in plaintiff corporation provided that defendant should not concern himself in the manufacture or sale of resistance or steel armature binding wire, sheet, or strip, such manufactures must be understood as some alloy of copper used in the manufacture of electric apparatus which does not conduct electricity as freely as pure copper, which is the best conductor, and hence is called "resistance, wire, sheet, or strip." Driver-Harris Wire Co. v. Driver, 62 A. 461, 463, 70 N.J.Eq. 34.

Breaking of glass bottles on roadway over which pneumatic-tired trucks, which were loaded with goods being removed from building by United States Marshal under writ of replevin, were required to pass, held criminal contempt of court, since "resistance" as used in contempt statute includes willful purpose and intent to prevent execution of process of court. Russell v. United States, C.C.A.Minn., 86 F.2d 389, 394, 109 A.L.R. 297.

RESIST HORSES, CATTLE AND LIVE STOCK

Under the statute which requires railroad companies to maintain fences sufficient to "resist horses, cattle and live stock," an instruction that a company was required to maintain one sufficient to "turn stock" was not improper; the quoted terms being synonmous. Deal v. St. Louis, I. M. & S. Ry. Co., 129 S.W. 50, 52, 144 Mo.App. 684.

Under Rev.St.1899, § 1105, Mo.St.Ann. § 4761, p. 2144, requiring a railroad company to construct and maintain fences sufficient to prevent stock getting on the track, an instruction in an action under such section for injuries to stock, which defined a lawful fence as one sufficient "to resist horses, cattle, swine, and like stock," was not erroneous for using the phrase "to resist"; such phrase not being as strong as the phrase "to prevent" in the statute. Hax v. Quincy, O. & K. C. R. Co., 100 S.W. 693, 695, 123 Mo.App. 172.

RESISTING AN OFFICER

To constitute the offense of "resisting an officer," under Act March 8, 1831, § 9, it is not necessary that the officer should be assaulted, beaten, or bruised. Woodworth v. State, 26 Ohio St. 196, 200.

RESISTING AN OFFICER—Cont'd

A justice of the peace being a conservator of the peace, under Const. art. 7, § 40, and being, under Crawford & Moses' Dig. § 2906, without authority to make an arrest himself, act of one in resisting an arrest by a justice does not constitute offense of "resisting an officer," in violation of section 2585 et seq. Herdison v. State, 265 S.W. 84, 86, 166 Ark. 33.

"Resist," as used in Code, § 4476, providing for the punishment of any person who shall knowingly and willfully obstruct, resist, or oppose any officer or other person duly authorized in serving or executing any lawful process, imports force. The words "obstruct," "resist," or "oppose" mean the same thing, and the word "oppose" would cover the meaning of the word "resist" or "obstruct." It does not mean to oppose or impede the process with which the officer is armed, or to defeat its execution, but that the officer himself shall be obstructed. Davis v. State, 76 Ga. 721, 722.

RESISTING AN OFFICER IN DISCHARGE OF HIS DUTY

Where police officers investigated defendant's premises to determine whether he was killing sheep or cattle in alleged violation of an ordinance and after failing to discover indications of such killing one of officers informed defendant that he was under arrest and attempted to put upon his hand a wrist chain and defendant resisted such action for three or four minutes and then submitted quietly, defendant's actions did not constitute "resisting an officer in discharge of his duty" since officers had no right to arrest defendant. City of Chicago v. Delich, 1st Dist. No. 20,686, 193 Ill.App. 72.

Where police officers investigated defendant's premises to determine whether he was killing sheep or cattle in alleged violation of an ordinance and after failing to discover indications of such killing one of officers informed defendant that he was under arrest and attempted to put upon his hand a wrist chain and defendant resisted such action for three or four minutes and then submitted quietly, action of wife who took some part in the altercation with the officers did not constitute "resisting an officer in discharge of his duty," since officers had no right to arrest defendant. City of Chicago v. Delich, 1st Dist., No. 20,687, 193 Ill. App. 74.

EXHIBIT 8 Words and Phrases Source: Reprinted with permission from Words and Phrases, Vol. 37, Pg. 612.

offered any resistance. She stated that she had recently purchased the purse for $59, and that it contained $42 in cash plus a few personal articles of little value. Further inquiry by the police revealed that Grabbo was unarmed and that Jones did try to hold on to the purse, but that Grabbo had yanked it from her.

Under Florida law, theft of Jones's purse would be petit theft if the total value was less than $300. West's Fla. Stat. Ann. § 812.014. This offense is a misdemeanor for which the maximum penalty is sixty days in jail and a $500 fine. West's Fla. Stats. Ann. § 775.082 and § 775.083. Unarmed robbery, on the other hand, is a second-degree felony that subjects the offender to a maximum fifteen years imprisonment and a fine of $10,000. West's Fla. Stats. Ann. § 812.13; § 775.082 & § 775.083. It is therefore very important to determine whether Grabbo should be charged with petit theft or robbery.

A researcher who needs to gain a general background on the offense of robbery and how it differs from theft may profitably consult one of the legal encyclopedias mentioned earlier. Someone with a general knowledge of criminal offenses may still need to review the offense of robbery from the standpoint of state law. If so, *Florida Jurisprudence 2d* or some similar text should be consulted.

Given a general knowledge of the crimes of theft and robbery, a likely starting point would be the state statutes. In this instance reference could be made to the official Florida Statutes. From a research standpoint it might be more productive to locate the statute proscribing robbery in the index to West's *Florida Statutes Annotated* and review the statute and the pertinent annotations in both the principal volume and the pocket part. The researcher would quickly find the offense of robbery defined in Section 812.13 and would then proceed to references noted under the topics of "force" and "resistance" following the text of the statute. These topics would identify pertinent Florida appellate decisions on these points. For example, the researcher would find a headnote to *Mims v. State,* 342 So.2d 116 (Fla. App. 1977), indicating that purse snatching is not robbery if no more force is used than is necessary to physically remove the property from a person who does not resist. If the victim does resist and that resistance is overcome by the force of the perpetrator, however, the crime of robbery is complete. Another reference points the researcher to *Goldsmith v. State,* 573 So.2d 445 (Fla. App. 1991), which held that the slight force used in snatching a $10 bill from a person's hand without touching the person was insufficient to constitute the crime of robbery, and instead constituted the crime of petit theft. Additional decisions refer to these and related points of law.

After locating these and other pertinent references, the researcher should go to the *Southern Reporter 2d* and read the located cases. After concluding the search, the researcher should "Shepardize" the decisions to determine if they have been subsequently commented on, distinguished, or even reversed.

The steps outlined here are basic and are designed to illustrate only the most rudimentary principles of gaining access to the criminal law on a particular subject. As previously indicated, another method may involve the use of digests with the key number system of research. Moreover, there will often be issues of interest still undecided by courts in a particular state. If so, then research into the statutes and court decisions of other states may be undertaken. Often the methodology and level of research pursued depend on the researcher's objective, knowledge of the subject and experience in conducting legal research.

Conclusion

An understanding of how to gain access to the primary and secondary sources of the criminal law is tremendously important. Nevertheless, familiarity with these resources and the basic methodology of legal research does not equate with the professional skill of the lawyer. Unlike the hypothetical scenario given earlier, many legal problems involve extremely complex factual and legal situations. Only persons professionally trained in the law can analyze the facts, discern the key issues, locate the relevant authorities, and make the critical legal judgments routinely called for in the administration of the criminal justice system.

The Constitution of the United States of America

We the People of the United States, in Order to form a more perfect Union, establish Justice, insure domestic Tranquility, provide for the common defence, promote the general Welfare, and secure the Blessings of Liberty to ourselves and our Posterity, do ordain and establish this Constitution for the United States of America.

ARTICLE I

Section 1 All legislative Powers herein granted shall be vested in a Congress of the United States, which shall consist of a Senate and House of Representatives.
Section 2 (1) The House of Representatives shall be composed of Members chosen every second Year by the People of the several States, and the Electors in each State shall have the Qualifications requisite for Electors of the most numerous Branch of the State Legislature.

(2) No Person shall be a Representative who shall not have attained to the age of twenty-five Years, and been seven Years a Citizen of the United States, and who shall not, when elected, be an Inhabitant of that State in which he shall be chosen.

(3) Representatives and direct Taxes shall be apportioned among the several States which may be included within this Union, according to their respective Numbers, which shall be determined by adding to the whole Number of free Persons, including those bound to Service for a Term of Years, and excluding Indians not taxed, three fifths of all other Persons. The actual Enumeration shall be made within three Years after the first Meeting of the Congress of the United States, and within every subsequent Term of ten Years, in such Manner as they shall by Law direct. The Number of Representatives shall not exceed one for every thirty Thousand, but each State shall have at Least one Representative; and until such enumeration shall be made, the State of New Hampshire shall be entitled to chuse three, Massachusetts eight, Rhode Island and Providence Plantations one, Connecticut five, New York six, New Jersey four, Pennsylvania eight, Delaware one, Maryland six, Virginia ten, North Carolina five, South Carolina five, and Georgia three.

(4) When vacancies happen in the Representation from any State, the Executive Authority thereof shall issue Writs of Election to fill such Vacancies.

(5) The House of Representatives shall chuse their Speaker and other Officers; and shall have the sole Power of Impeachment.

Section 3 (1) The Senate of the United States shall be composed of two Senators from each State, chosen by the Legislature thereof, for six Years; and each Senator shall have one Vote.

(2) Immediately after they shall be assembled in Consequence of the first Election, they shall be divided as equally as may be into three Classes. The Seats of the Senators of the first Class shall be vacated at the Expiration of the second Year, of the second Class at the Expiration of the fourth Year, and of the third Class at the Expiration of the sixth Year, so that one third may be chosen every second Year; and if Vacancies happen by Resignation, or otherwise, during the Recess of the Legislature of any State, the Executive thereof may make temporary Appointments until the next Meeting of the Legislature, which shall then fill such Vacancies.

(3) No Person shall be a Senator who shall not have attained, to the Age of thirty Years, and been nine Years a Citizen of the United States, and who shall not, when elected, be an Inhabitant of that State for which he shall be chosen.

(4) The Vice President of the United States shall be President of the Senate, but shall have no Vote, unless they be equally divided.

(5) The Senate shall chuse their other Officers, and also a President pro tempore, in the Absence of the Vice President, or when he shall exercise the Office of the President of the United States.

(6) The Senate shall have the sole Power to try all Impeachments. When sitting for that Purpose, they shall be on Oath or Affirmation. When the President of the United States is tried, the Chief Justice shall preside: And no Person shall be convicted without the Concurrence of two thirds of the Members present.

(7) Judgment in Cases of Impeachment shall not extend further than to removal from Office, and disqualification to hold and enjoy any Office of honor, Trust or Profit under the United States: but the Party convicted shall nevertheless be liable and subject to Indictment, Trial, Judgment and Punishment, according to Law.

Section 4 (1) The Times, Places and Manner of holding Elections for Senators and Representatives, shall be prescribed in each State by the Legislature thereof; but the Congress may at any time by Law make or alter such Regulations, except as to the Places of chusing Senators.

(2) The Congress shall assemble at least once in every Year, and such Meeting shall be on the first Monday in December, unless they shall by Law appoint a different Day.

Section 5 (1) Each House shall be the Judge of the Elections, Returns and Qualifications of its own Members, and a Majority of each shall constitute a Quorum to do Business; but a smaller Number may adjourn from day to day, and may be authorized to compel the Attendance of absent Members, in such Manner, and under such Penalties as each House may provide.

(2) Each House may determine the Rules of its Proceedings, punish its Members for disorderly Behaviour, and, with the Concurrence of two thirds, expel a Member.

(3) Each House shall keep a Journal of its Proceedings, and from time to time publish the same, excepting such Parts as may in their Judgment require Secrecy; and the Yeas and Nays of the Members of either House on any question shall, at the Desire of one fifth of those Present, be entered on the Journal.

(4) Neither House, during the Session of Congress, shall, without the Consent of the other, adjourn for more than three days, nor to any other Place than that in which the two Houses shall be sitting.

Section 6 (1) The Senators and Representatives shall receive a Compensation for their Services, to be ascertained by Law, and paid out of the Treasury of the United States. They shall in all Cases, except Treason, Felony and Breach of the Peace, be privileged from Arrest during their Attendance at the Session of their respective Houses, and in going to and returning from the same; and for any Speech or Debate in either House, they shall not be questioned in any other Place.

(2) No Senator or Representative shall, during the Time for which he was elected, be appointed to any civil Office under the Authority of the United States, which shall have been created, or the Emoluments whereof shall have been increased during such time; and no Person holding any Office under the United States, shall be a Member of either House during his Continuance in Office.

Section 7 (1) All Bills for raising Revenue shall originate in the House of Representatives; but the Senate may propose or concur with Amendments as on other Bills.

(2) Every Bill which shall have passed the House of Representatives and the Senate, shall, before it become a Law, be presented to the President of the United States; If he approve he shall sign it, but if not he shall return it, with his Objections to that House in which it shall have originated, who shall enter the Objections at large on their Journal, and proceed to reconsider it. If after such Reconsideration two thirds of that House shall agree to pass the Bill, it shall be sent, together with the Objections, to the other House, by which it shall likewise be reconsidered, and if approved by two thirds of that House, it shall become a Law. But in all such Cases the Votes of both Houses shall be determined by Yeas and Nays, and the Names of the Persons voting for and against the Bill shall be entered on the Journal of each House respectively. If any Bill shall not be returned by the President within ten Days (Sunday excepted) after it shall have been presented to him, the Same shall be a Law, in like Manner as if he had signed it, unless the Congress by their Adjournment prevent its Return, in which Case it shall not be a Law.

(3) Every Order, Resolution, or Vote to which the Concurrence of the Senate and House of Representatives may be necessary (except on a question of Adjournment) shall be presented to the President of the United States; and before the Same shall take Effect, shall be approved by him, or being disapproved by him, shall be repassed by two thirds of the Senate and House of Representatives, according to the Rules and Limitations prescribed in the Case of a Bill.

Section 8 (1) The Congress shall have Power To lay and collect Taxes, Duties, Imposts and Excises, to pay the Debts and provide for the common Defence and general Welfare of the United States; but all Duties, Imposts and Excises shall be uniform throughout the United States;

(2) To borrow Money on the credit of the United States;

(3) To regulate Commerce with foreign Nations, and among the several States, and with the Indian Tribes;

(4) To establish an uniform Rule of Naturalization, and uniform Laws on the subject of Bankruptcies throughout the United States;

(5) To coin Money, regulate the Value thereof, and of foreign Coin, and to fix the Standard of Weights and Measures;

(6) To provide for the Punishment of counterfeiting the Securities and current Coin of the United States;

(7) To establish Post Offices and post Roads;

(8) To promote the Progress of Science and useful Arts, by securing for limited Times to Authors and Inventors the exclusive Right to their respective Writings and Discoveries;

(9) To constitute Tribunals inferior to the supreme Court;

(10) To define and punish Piracies and Felonies committed on the high Seas, and Offenses against the Law of Nations;

(11) To declare War, grant Letters of Marque and Reprisal, and make Rules concerning Captures on Land and Water;

(12) To raise and support Armies, but no Appropriation of Money to that Use shall be for a longer Term than two Years;

(13) To provide and maintain a Navy;

(14) To make Rules for the Government and Regulation of the land and naval Forces;

(15) To provide for calling forth the Militia to execute the Laws of the Union, suppress Insurrections and repel Invasions;

(16) To provide for organizing, arming, and disciplining, the Militia, and for governing such Part of them as may be employed in the Service of the United States, reserving to the States respectively, the Appointment of the Officers, and the Authority of training the Militia according to the discipline prescribed by Congress;

(17) To exercise exclusive Legislation in all Cases whatsoever, over such District (not exceeding ten Miles square) as may, by Cession of particular States, and the Acceptance of Congress, become the Seat of the Government of the United States, and to exercise like Authority over all Places purchased by the Consent of the Legislature of the State in which the Same shall be, for the Erection of Forts, Magazines, Arsenals, dock-Yards, and other needful Buildings;—And

(18) To make all Laws which shall be necessary and proper for carrying into Execution the foregoing Powers, and all other Powers vested by this Constitution in the Government of the United States, or in any Department or Officer thereof.

Section 9 (1) The Migration or Importation of such Persons as any of the States now existing shall think proper to admit, shall not be prohibited by the Congress prior to the Year one thousand eight hundred and eight, but a Tax or Duty may be imposed on such Importation, not exceeding ten dollars for each Person.

(2) The Privilege of the Writ of Habeas Corpus shall not be suspended unless when in Cases of Rebellion or Invasion the public Safety may require it.

(3) No Bill of Attainder or ex post facto Law shall be passed.

(4) No Capitation, or other direct, Tax shall be laid, unless in Proportion to the Census or Enumeration herein before directed to be taken.

(5) No Tax or Duty shall be laid on Articles exported from any State.

(6) No Preference shall be given by any Regulation of Commerce or Revenue to the Ports of one State over those of another; nor shall Vessels bound to, or from, one State, be obliged to enter, clear or pay Duties in another.

(7) No Money shall be drawn from the Treasury, but in Consequence of Appropriations made by Law; and a regular Statement and Account of the Receipts and Expenditures of all public Money shall be published from time to time.

(8) No Title of Nobility shall be granted by the United States: And no Person holding any Office of Profit or Trust under them, shall, without the Consent of the Congress, accept of any present, Emolument, Office, or Title, of any kind whatever, from any King, Prince or foreign State.

Section 10 (1) No State shall enter into any Treaty, Alliance, or Confederation; grant Letters of Marque and Reprisal; coin Money; emit Bills of Credit; make any Thing but gold and silver Coin a Tender in Payment of Debts; pass any Bill of Attainder, ex post facto Law, or Law impairing the Obligation of Contracts, or grant any Title of Nobility.

(2) No State shall, without the Consent of Congress, lay any Imposts or Duties on Imports or Exports, except what may be absolutely necessary for executing its inspection Laws: and the net Produce of all Duties and Imposts, laid by any State on Imports or Exports, shall be for the Use of the Treasury of the United States; and all such Laws shall be subject to the Revision and Control of the Congress.

(3) No State shall, without the Consent of Congress, lay any Duty of Tonnage, keep Troops, or Ships of War in time of Peace, enter into any Agreement or Compact with another State, or with a foreign Power, or engage in War, unless actually invaded, or in such imminent Danger as will not admit of Delay.

ARTICLE II

Section 1 (1) The executive Power shall be vested in a President of the United States of America. He shall hold his Office during the Term of four Years, and, together with the Vice President, chosen for the same Term, be elected, as follows:

(2) Each State shall appoint, in such Manner as the Legislature thereof may direct, a Number of Electors, equal to the whole Number of Senators and Representatives to which the State may be entitled in the Congress: but no Senator or Representative, or Person holding an Office of Trust or Profit under the United States, shall be appointed an Elector.

The Electors shall meet in their respective States, and vote by Ballot for two Persons, of whom one at least shall not be an Inhabitant of the same State with themselves. And they shall make a List of all the Persons voted for, and of the Number of Votes for each; which List they shall sign and certify, and transmit sealed to the Seat of the Government of the United States, directed to the President of the Senate. The President of the Senate shall, in the presence of the Senate and House of Representatives, open all the Certificates, and the Votes shall then be counted. The Person having the greatest Number of Votes shall be the President, if such Number be a Majority of the whole Number of Electors appointed; and if there be more than one who have such Majority, and have an equal Number of Votes, then the House of Representatives shall immediately chuse by Ballot one of them for President; and if no Person have a Majority, then from the five highest on the List the said House shall in like Manner chuse the

President. But in chusing the President, the Votes shall be taken by States, the Representation from each State having one Vote; a quorum for this Purpose shall consist of a Member or Members from two thirds of the States, and a Majority of all the States shall be necessary to a Choice. In every Case, after the Choice of the President, the Person having the greatest Number of Votes of the Electors shall be the Vice President. But if there should remain two or more who have equal Votes, the Senate shall chuse from them by Ballot the Vice President.

(3) The Congress may determine the Time of chusing the Electors, and the Day on which they shall give their Votes; which Day shall be the same throughout the United States.

(4) No Person except a natural born Citizen, or a Citizen of the United States, at the time of the Adoption of this Constitution, shall be eligible to the Office of President; neither shall any Person be eligible to that Office who shall not have attained to the Age of thirty five Years, and been fourteen Years a Resident within the United States.

(5) In Case of the Removal of the President from Office, or of his Death, Resignation, or Inability to discharge the Powers and Duties of the said Office, the Same shall devolve on the Vice President, and the Congress may by Law provide for the Case of Removal, Death, Resignation or Inability, both of the President and Vice President, declaring what Officer shall then act as President, and such Officer shall act accordingly, until the Disability be removed, or a President shall be elected.

(6) The President shall, at stated Times, receive for his Services, a Compensation, which shall neither be increased nor diminished during the Period for which he shall have been elected, and he shall not receive within that Period any other Emolument from the United States, or any of them.

(7) Before he enter on the Execution of his Office, he shall take the following Oath or Affirmation:—"I do solemnly swear (or affirm) that I will faithfully execute the Office of President of the United States, and will to the best of my Ability, preserve, protect and defend the Constitution of the United States."

Section 2 (1) The President shall be Commander in Chief of the Army and Navy of the United States, and of the Militia of the several States, when called into the actual Service of the United States; he may require the Opinion, in writing, of the principal Officer in each of the executive Departments, upon any Subject relating to the Duties of their respective Offices, and he shall have Power to grant Reprieves and Pardons for Offenses against the United States, except in Cases of Impeachment.

(2) He shall have Power, by and with the Advice and Consent of the Senate, to make Treaties, provided two thirds of the Senators present concur; and he shall nominate, and by and with the Advice and Consent of the Senate, shall appoint Ambassadors, other public Ministers and Consuls, Judges of the supreme Court, and all other Officers of the United States, whose Appointments are not herein otherwise provided for, and which shall be established by Law: but the Congress may by Law vest the Appointment of such inferior Officers, as they think proper, in the President alone, in the Courts of Law, or in the Heads of Departments.

(3) The President shall have Power to fill up all Vacancies that may happen during the Recess of the Senate, by granting Commissions which shall expire at the End of their next Session.

Section 3 He shall from time to time give to the Congress Information of the State of the Union, and recommend to their Consideration such Measures as he shall judge necessary and expedient; he may, on extraordinary Occasions, convene both Houses, or either of them, and in Case of Disagreement between them, with Respect to the Time of Adjournment, he may adjourn them to such Time as he shall think proper; he shall receive Ambassadors and other public Ministers; he shall take Care that the Laws be faithfully executed, and shall Commission all the Officers of the United States.

Section 4 The President, Vice President and all Civil Officers of the United States, shall be removed from Office on Impeachment for, and Conviction of, Treason, Bribery, or other high Crimes and Misdemeanors.

ARTICLE III

Section 1 The judicial Power of the United States, shall be vested in one supreme Court, and in such inferior Courts as the Congress may from time to time ordain and establish. The Judges, both of the supreme and inferior Courts, shall hold their Offices during good Behaviour, and shall, at stated Times, receive for their Services, a Compensation, which shall not be diminished during their Continuance in Office.

Section 2 (1) The judicial Power shall extend to all Cases, in Law and Equity, arising under this Constitution, the Laws of the United States, and Treaties made, or which shall be made, under their Authority;—to all Cases affecting Ambassadors, other public Ministers and Consuls;—to all Cases of admiralty and maritime Jurisdiction;—to Controversies to which the United States shall be a party;—to Controversies between two or more States;—between a State and Citizens of another State;—between Citizens of different States;—between Citizens of the same State claiming Lands under Grants of different States, and between a State, or the Citizens thereof, and foreign States, Citizens or Subjects.

(2) In all Cases affecting Ambassadors, other public Ministers and Consuls, and those in which a State shall be Party, the supreme Court shall have original Jurisdiction. In all the other Cases before mentioned, the supreme Court shall have appellate Jurisdiction, both as to Law and Fact, with such Exceptions, and under such Regulations as the Congress shall make.

(3) The Trial of all Crimes, except in Cases of Impeachment, shall be by Jury; and such Trial shall be held in the State where the said Crimes shall have been committed; but when not committed within any State, the Trial shall be at such Place or Places as the Congress may by Law have directed.

Section 3 (1) Treason against the United States, shall consist only in levying War against them, or in adhering to their Enemies, giving them Aid and Comfort. No Person shall be convicted of Treason unless on the Testimony of two Witnesses to the same overt Act, or on Confession in open Court.

(2) The Congress shall have Power to declare the Punishment of Treason, but no Attainder of Treason shall work Corruption of Blood, or Forfeiture except during the Life of the Person attainted.

ARTICLE IV

Section 1 Full Faith and Credit shall be given in each State to the public Acts, Records, and judicial Proceedings of every other State. And the Congress may by general Laws prescribe the Manner in which such Acts, Records and Proceedings shall be proved, and the Effect thereof.

Section 2 (1) The Citizens of each State shall be entitled to all privileges and Immunities of Citizens in the several States.

(2) A Person charged in any State with Treason, Felony, or other Crime, who shall flee from Justice, and be found in another State, shall on Demand of the executive Authority of the State from which he fled, be delivered up, to be removed to the State having Jurisdiction of the Crime.

(3) No Person held to Service of Labour in one State, under the Laws thereof, escaping into another, shall, in Consequence of any Law or Regulation therein, be discharged from such Service or Labour, but shall be delivered up on Claim of the Party to whom such Service or Labour may be due.

Section 3 (1) New States may be admitted by the Congress into this Union; but no new State shall be formed or erected within the Jurisdiction of any other State; nor any State be formed by the Junction of two or more States, or Parts of States, without the Consent of the Legislatures of the States concerned as well as of the Congress.

(2) The Congress shall have power to dispose of and make all needful Rules and Regulations respecting the Territory or other Property belonging to the United States; and nothing in this Constitution shall be so construed as to Prejudice any Claims of the United States, or of any particular State.

Section 4 The United States shall guarantee to every State in this Union a Republican Form of Government, and shall protect each of them against Invasion; and on Application of the Legislature, or of the Executive (when the Legislature cannot be convened) against domestic Violence.

ARTICLE V

The Congress, whenever two thirds of both Houses shall deem it necessary, shall propose Amendments to this Constitution, or, on the Application of the Legislatures of two thirds of the several States, shall call a Convention for proposing Amendments, which, in either Case, shall be valid to all Intents and Purposes, as Part of this Constitution, when ratified by the Legislatures of three fourths of the several States, or by Conventions in three fourths thereof, as the one or the other Mode of Ratification may be proposed by the Congress; Provided that no Amendment which may be made prior to the Year One thousand eight hundred and eight shall in any Manner affect the first and fourth Clauses in the Ninth Section of the first Article; and that no State, without its Consent, shall be deprived of its equal Suffrage in the Senate.

ARTICLE VI

(1) All Debts contracted and Engagements entered into, before the Adoption of this Constitution, shall be as valid against the United States under this Constitution, as under the Confederation.

(2) This Constitution, and the Laws of the United States which shall be made in Pursuance thereof; and all Treaties made, or which shall be made, under the Authority of the United States, shall be the supreme Law of the Land; and the Judges in every State shall be bound thereby, any Thing in the Constitution or Laws of any State to the Contrary notwithstanding.

(3) The Senators and Representatives before mentioned, and the Members of the several State Legislatures, and all executive and judicial Officers, both of the United States and of the several States, shall be bound by Oath or Affirmation, to support this Constitution; but no religious Test shall ever be required as a Qualification to any Office or public Trust under the United States.

ARTICLE VII

The Ratification of the Conventions of nine States, shall be sufficient for the Establishment of this Constitution between the States so ratifying the Same.

ARTICLES IN ADDITION TO, AND AMENDMENT OF, THE CONSTITUTION OF THE UNITED STATES OF AMERICA, PROPOSED BY CONGRESS, AND RATIFIED BY THE SEVERAL STATES, PURSUANT TO THE FIFTH ARTICLE OF THE ORIGINAL CONSTITUTION

AMENDMENT I (1791)

Congress shall make no law respecting an establishment of religion, or prohibiting the free exercise thereof; or abridging the freedom of speech, or of the press; or the right of the people peaceably to assemble, and to petition the Government for a redress of grievances.

AMENDMENT II (1791)

A well regulated Militia, being necessary to the security of a free state, the right of the people to keep and bear Arms, shall not be infringed.

AMENDMENT III (1791)

No Soldier shall, in time of peace be quartered in any house, without the consent of the Owner, nor in time of war, but in a manner to be prescribed by law.

AMENDMENT IV (1791)

The right of the people to be secure in their persons, houses, papers, and effects, against unreasonable searches and seizures, shall not be violated, and no Warrants shall issue, but upon probable cause, supported by Oath or affirmation, and particularly describing the place to be searched, and the persons or things to be seized.

AMENDMENT V (1791)

No person shall be held to answer for a capital, or otherwise infamous crime, unless on a presentment or indictment of a Grand Jury, except in cases arising in the land or naval forces, or in the Militia, when in actual service in time of War or public danger; nor shall any person be subject for the same offence to be twice put in jeopardy of life or limb; nor shall be compelled in any criminal case to be a witness against himself, nor be deprived of life, liberty, or property, without due process of law; nor shall private property be taken for public use, without just compensation.

AMENDMENT VI (1791)

In all criminal prosecutions, the accused shall enjoy the right to a speedy and public trial, by an impartial jury of the State and district wherein the crime shall have been committed, which district shall have been previously ascertained by law, and to be informed of the nature and cause of the accusation; to be confronted with the witnesses against him; to have compulsory process for obtaining witnesses in his favor, and to have the Assistance of Counsel for his defence.

AMENDMENT VII (1791)

In Suits at common law, where the value in controversy shall exceed twenty dollars, the right of trial by jury shall be preserved, and no fact tried by a jury, shall be otherwise re-examined in any Court of the United States, than according to the rules of the common law.

AMENDMENT VIII (1791)

Excessive bail shall not be required, nor excessive fines imposed, nor cruel and unusual punishments inflicted.

AMENDMENT IX (1791)

The enumeration in the Constitution, of certain rights, shall not be construed to deny or disparage others retained by the people.

AMENDMENT X (1791)

The powers not delegated to the United States by the Constitution, nor prohibited by it to the States, are reserved to the States respectively, or to the people.

AMENDMENT XI (1798)

The Judicial power of the United States shall not be construed to extend to any suit in law or equity, commenced or prosecuted against one of the United States by Citizens of another State, or by Citizens or Subjects of any Foreign State.

AMENDMENT XII (1804)

The Electors shall meet in their respective states and vote by ballot for President and Vice-President, one of whom, at least, shall not be an inhabitant of the same state with themselves; they shall name in their ballots the person voted for as President, and in distinct ballots the person voted for as Vice-President, and they shall make distinct lists of all persons voted for as President, and of all persons voted for as Vice-President, and of the number of votes for each, which lists they shall sign and certify, and transmit sealed to the seat of the government of the United States, directed to the President of the Senate;—The President of the Senate shall, in the presence of the Senate and House of Representatives, open all the certificates and the votes shall then be counted;—The person having the greatest number of votes for President, shall be the President, if such number be a majority of the whole number of Electors appointed; and if no person have such majority, then from the persons having the highest numbers not exceeding three on the list of those voted for as President, the House of Representatives shall choose immediately, by ballot, the President. But in choosing the President, the votes shall be taken by states, the representation from each state having one vote; a quorum for this purpose shall consist of a member or members from two-thirds of the states, and a majority of all the states shall be necessary to a choice. And if the House of Representatives shall not choose a President whenever the right of choice shall devolve upon them, before the fourth day of March next following, then the Vice-President shall act as President, as in the case of the death or other constitutional disability of the President—The person having the greatest number of votes as Vice-President, shall be the Vice-President, if such number be a majority of the whole number of Electors appointed, and if no person have a majority, then from the two highest numbers on the list, the Senate shall choose the Vice-President; A quorum for the purpose shall consist of two-thirds of the whole number of Senators, and a majority of the whole number shall be necessary to a choice. But no person constitutionally ineligible to the office of President shall be eligible to that of Vice-President of the United States.

AMENDMENT XIII (1865)

Section 1 Neither slavery nor involuntary servitude, except as a punishment for crime whereof the party shall have been duly convicted, shall exist within the United States, or any place subject to their jurisdiction.
Section 2 Congress shall have power to enforce this article by appropriate legislation.

AMENDMENT XIV (1868)

Section 1 All persons born or naturalized in the United States and subject to the jurisdiction thereof, are citizens of the United States and of the State wherein they reside. No State shall make or enforce any law which shall abridge the privileges or immunities of citizens of the United States; nor shall any State deprive any person of life, liberty, or property, without due process of law; nor deny to any person within its jurisdiction the equal protection of the laws.
Section 2 Representatives shall be apportioned among the several States according to their respective numbers, counting the whole number of persons in each State, excluding Indians not taxed. But when the right to vote at any election for the choice of electors for President and Vice-President of the United States, Representatives in Congress, the Executive and Judicial officers of a State, or the

members of the Legislature thereof, is denied to any of the male inhabitants of such State, being twenty-one years of age, and citizens of the United States, or in any way abridged, except for participation in rebellion, or other crime, the basis of representation therein shall be reduced in the proportion which the number of such male citizens shall bear to the whole number of male citizens twenty-one years of age in such State.

Section 3 No person shall be a Senator or Representative in Congress, or elector of President and Vice-President, or hold any office, civil or military, under the United States, or under any State, who, having previously taken an oath, as a member of Congress, or as an officer of the United States, or as a member of any State legislature, or as an executive or judicial officer of any State, to support the Constitution of the United States, shall have engaged in insurrection or rebellion against the same, or given aid or comfort to the enemies thereof. But Congress may by a vote of two-thirds of each House, remove such disability.

Section 4 The validity of the public debt of the United States, authorized by law, including debts incurred for payment of pensions and bounties for services in suppressing insurrection or rebellion, shall not be questioned. But neither the United States nor any State shall assume or pay any debt or obligation incurred in aid of insurrection or rebellion against the United States, or any claim for the loss or emancipation of any slave; but all such debts, obligations and claims shall be held illegal and void.

Section 5 The Congress shall have power to enforce, by appropriate legislation, the provisions of this article.

AMENDMENT XV (1870)

Section 1 The right of citizens of the United States to vote shall not be denied or abridged by the United States or by any State on account of race, color, or previous condition of servitude.

Section 2 The Congress shall have power to enforce this article by appropriate legislation.

AMENDMENT XVI (1913)

The Congress shall have power to lay and collect taxes on incomes, from whatever source derived, without apportionment among the several States, and without regard to any census or enumeration.

AMENDMENT XVII (1913)

The Senate of the United States shall be composed of two Senators from each State, elected by the people thereof, for six years; and each Senator shall have one vote. The electors in each State shall have the qualifications requisite for electors of the most numerous branch of the State legislatures.

When vacancies happen in the representation of any State in the Senate, the executive authority of such State shall issue writs of election to fill such vacancies: *Provided,* That the legislature of any State may empower the executive thereof to make temporary appointments until the people fill the vacancies by election as the legislature may direct.

This amendment shall not be so construed as to affect the election or term of any Senator chosen before it becomes valid as part of the Constitution.

AMENDMENT XVIII (1919)

Section 1 After one year from the ratification of this article the manufacture, sale, or transportation of intoxicating liquors within, the importation thereof into, or the exportation thereof from the United States and all territory subject to the jurisdiction thereof for beverage purposes is hereby prohibited.
Section 2 The Congress and the several States shall have concurrent power to enforce this article by appropriate legislation.
Section 3 This article shall be inoperative unless it shall have been ratified as an amendment to the Constitution by the legislatures of the several States, as provided in the Constitution, within seven years from the date of the submission hereof to the States by the Congress.

AMENDMENT XIX (1920)

The right of citizens of the United States to vote shall not be denied or abridged by the United States or by any State on account of sex.

Congress shall have power to enforce this article by appropriate legislation.

AMENDMENT XX (1933)

Section 1 The terms of the President and Vice President shall end at noon on the 20th day of January, and the terms of Senators and Representatives at noon on the 3d day of January, of the years in which such terms would have ended if this article had not been ratified; and the terms of their successors shall then begin.
Section 2 The Congress shall assemble at least once in every year, and such meeting shall begin at noon on the 3d day of January, unless they shall by law appoint a different day.
Section 3 If, at the time fixed for the beginning of the term of the President, the President elect shall have died, the Vice President elect shall become President. If a President shall not have been chosen before the time fixed for the beginning of his term, or if the President elect shall have failed to qualify, then the Vice President elect shall act as President until a President shall have qualified; and the Congress may by law provide for the case wherein neither a President elect nor a Vice President elect shall have qualified, declaring who shall then act as President, or the manner in which one who is to act shall be selected, and such person shall act accordingly until a President or Vice President shall have qualified.
Section 4 The Congress may by law provide for the case of the death of any of the persons from whom the House of Representatives may choose a President whenever the right of choice shall have devolved upon them, and for the case of the death of any of the persons from whom the Senate may choose a Vice President whenever the right of choice shall have devolved upon them.
Section 5 Sections 1 and 2 shall take effect on the 15th day of October following the ratification of this article.

Section 6 This article shall be inoperative unless it shall have been ratified as an amendment to the Constitution by the legislatures of three-fourths of the several States within seven years from the date of its submission.

AMENDMENT XXI (1933)

Section 1 The eighteenth article of amendment to the Constitution of the United States is hereby repealed.
Section 2 The transportation or importation into any State, Territory or possession of the United States for delivery or use therein of intoxicating liquors, in violation of the laws thereof, is hereby prohibited.
Section 3 This article shall be inoperative unless it shall have been ratified as an amendment to the Constitution by conventions in the several States, as provided in the Constitution, within seven years from the date of the submission hereof to the States by the Congress.

AMENDMENT XXII (1951)

Section 1 No person shall be elected to the office of the President more than twice, and no person who has held the office of President, or acted as President, for more than two years of a term to which some other person was elected President shall be elected to the office of the President more than once. But this Article shall not apply to any person holding the office of President when this Article was proposed by the Congress, and shall not prevent any person who may be holding the office of President, or acting as President, during the term within which this Article becomes operative from holding the office of President or acting as President during the remainder of such term.
Section 2 This Article shall be inoperative unless it shall have been ratified as an amendment to the Constitution by the legislatures of three-fourths of the several States within seven years from the date of its submission to the States by the Congress.

AMENDMENT XXIII (1961)

Section 1 The District constituting the seat of Government of the United States shall appoint in such manner as the Congress may direct:

A number of electors of President and Vice President equal to the whole number of Senators and Representatives in Congress to which the District would be entitled if it were a State, but in no event more than the least populous State; they shall be in addition to those appointed by the States, but they shall be considered, for the purposes of the election of President and Vice President, to be electors appointed by a State; and they shall meet in the District and perform such duties as provided by the twelfth article of amendment.
Section 2 The Congress shall have power to enforce this article by appropriate legislation.

AMENDMENT XXIV (1964)

Section 1 The right of citizens of the United States to vote in any primary or other election for President or Vice President, for electors for President or Vice President, or for Senator or Representative in Congress, shall not be denied or abridged by the United States or any State by reason of failure to pay any poll tax or other tax.

Section 2 The Congress shall have power to enforce this article by appropriate legislation.

AMENDMENT XXV (1967)

Section 1 In case of the removal of the President from office or of his death or resignation, the Vice President shall become President.
Section 2 Whenever there is a vacancy in the office of the Vice President, the President shall nominate a Vice President who shall take office upon confirmation by a majority vote of both Houses of Congress.
Section 3 Whenever the President transmits to the President pro tempore of the Senate and the Speaker of the House of Representatives his written declaration that he is unable to discharge the powers and duties of his office, and until he transmits to them a written declaration to the contrary, such powers and duties shall be discharged by the Vice President as Acting President.
Section 4 Whenever the Vice President and a majority of either the principal officers of the executive departments or of such other body as Congress may by law provide, transmit to the President pro tempore of the Senate and the Speaker of the House of Representatives their written declaration that the President is unable to discharge the powers and duties of his office, the Vice President shall immediately assume the powers and duties of the office as Acting President.

Thereafter, when the President transmits to the President pro tempore of the Senate and the Speaker of the House of Representatives his written declaration that no inability exists, he shall resume the powers and duties of his office unless the Vice President and a majority of either the principal officers of the executive department or of such other body as Congress may by law provide, transmit within four days to the President pro tempore of the Senate and the Speaker of the House of Representatives their written declaration that the President is unable to discharge the powers and duties of his office. Thereupon Congress shall decide the issue, assembling within forty-eight hours for that purpose if not in session. If the Congress, within twenty-one days after receipt of the latter written declaration, or, if Congress is not in session, within twenty-one days after Congress is required to assemble, determines by two-thirds vote of both Houses that the President is unable to discharge the powers and duties of his office, the Vice President shall continue to discharge the same as Acting President; otherwise, the President shall resume the powers and duties of his office.

AMENDMENT XXVI (1971)

Section 1 The right of citizens of the United States, who are eighteen years of age or older, to vote shall not be denied or abridged by the United States or by any State on account of age.
Section 2 The Congress shall have power to enforce this article by appropriate legislation.

AMENDMENT XXVII (1992)

No law, varying the compensation for the services of Senators and Representatives, shall take effect until an election of Representatives have intervened.

GLOSSARY

abrogate To annul, destroy, or cancel.
accessory A person who aids in the commission of a crime.
accusatorial system A system of criminal justice where the prosecution bears the burden of proving the guilt of the accused.
actus reus A "wrongful act" that, combined with other necessary elements of crime, constitutes criminal liability.
adjudication The formal decision of a court in a given case.
adultery Voluntary sexual intercourse where at least one of the parties is married to someone other than the sexual partner.
adversary system A system of justice involving conflicting parties where the role of the judge is to remain neutral.
affiant A person who makes an affidavit.
affidavit A written document attesting to specific facts of which the affiant has knowledge, and sworn to by the affiant.
affirm To uphold, ratify, or approve.
affirmative defense Defense to a criminal charge where defendant bears the burden of proof. Examples include automatism, intoxication, coercion, and duress.
aggravating circumstances Factors attending the commission of a crime that make the crime or its consequences worse.
aiding and abetting Assisting in or otherwise facilitating the commission of a crime.
alibi Defense to a criminal charge that places the defendant at some other place than the scene of the crime at the time the crime occurred.
allegation Assertion or claim made by a party to a legal action.
amendment A modification, addition, or deletion.
animus furundi Intent to steal or otherwise deprive an owner of property.
appeal Review by a higher court of a lower court decision.
appellant A person who takes an appeal to a higher court.
appellate jurisdiction The authority of a court to hear appeals from decisions of lower courts.
appellee A person against whom an appeal is taken.
arraignment An appearance before a court of law for the purpose of pleading to a criminal charge.
arrest To take someone into custody or otherwise deprive that person of freedom of movement.
arrestee A person who is arrested.
arson The crime of intentionally burning someone else's house or building—now commonly extended to other property as well.
asportation The carrying away of something: in kidnapping, the carrying away of the victim; in larceny, the carrying away of the victim's property.
assault The attempt or threat to inflict bodily injury upon another person.
asylum Sanctuary; a place of refuge.
attempt An intent to commit a crime coupled with an act taken toward committing the offense.
automatism A set of actions taken during a state of unconsciousness.

bail The conditional release of a person charged with a crime.
battery The unlawful use of force against another person that entails some injury or offensive touching.
bench trial A trial held before a judge without a jury present.
bench warrant An arrest warrant issued by a judge.
best evidence rule To prove the content of a writing, the original document or best facsimile must be produced.

bifurcated trial A capital trial with separate phases for determining guilt and punishment.
bigamy The crime of being married to more than one spouse at the same time.
bill of attainder A legislative act imposing punishment without trial upon persons deemed guilty of treason or felonies. (Prohibited by the U. S. Constitution.)
bona fide "In good faith"; without the attempt to defraud or deceive.
bounty hunter A person paid a fee or commission to capture a defendant who had fled a jurisdiction to escape punishment.
breach of the peace The crime of disturbing the public tranquility and order. A generic term encompassing disorderly conduct, riot, etc.
breaking Forceful, unlawful entry into a building or conveyance.
bribery The crime of offering, giving, requesting, solicitings or receiving something of value to influence a decision of a public official.
brief A document filed by a party to a lawsuit to convince the court of the merits of that party's case.
burden of proof The requirement to introduce evidence to prove an alleged fact or set of facts.
burglary At common law, the crime of breaking and entering a house with the intent to commit a felony therein. Under modern statutes, burglary frequently consists of breaking and entering a structure with the intent to commit any offense therein.

canonical Pertaining to the canons or laws of a church.
capias "That you take." A general term for various court orders requiring that some named person be taken into custody.
capital crime A crime for which death is a permissible punishment.
caption At common law, a taking or seizure.
carnal knowledge Sexual intercourse.
case law Law derived from judicial decisions.
castle doctrine "A man's home is his castle." At common law, the right to use whatever force is necessary to protect one's dwelling and its inhabitants from an unlawful entry or attack.
caveat emptor "Let the buyer beware." Common-law maxim requiring the consumer to judge the quality of a product before making a purchase.
certiorari Writ issued by an appellate court to grant discretionary review of a case decided by a lower court.
challenge for cause Objection to a prospective juror on some specified ground (e.g., a close relationship to a party to the case).
chilling effect A law or policy that discourages persons from exercising their rights.
circumstantial evidence Indirect evidence from which the existence of certain facts may be inferred.
civil action A lawsuit brought to enforce private rights and to remedy violations thereof.
clear and present danger doctrine In constitutional law, the doctrine that the First Amendment does not protect those forms of expression that pose a clear and present danger of bringing about some substantive evil that government has a right to prevent.
clemency A grant of mercy by an executive official commuting a sentence or pardoning a criminal.
code A systematic collection of laws.
collateral attack The attempt to defeat the outcome of a judicial proceeding by challenging it in a different proceeding or court.
common law A body of law that develops through judicial decisions, as distinct from legislative enactments. Originally developed by English courts of law.
community control A sentence imposed on a person found guilty of a crime that requires that the offender be placed in an individualized program of noninstitutional confinement.
community service A sentence requiring that the criminal perform some specific service to the community for some specified period of time.
commutation A form of clemency that lessens the punishment for a person convicted of a crime.
competency The state of being legally fit to give testimony or stand trial.
compounding a crime The crime of receiving something of value in exchange for an agreement not to file a criminal complaint.
compurgation A method of trial used before the thirteenth century whereby a person charged with a crime could be absolved by swearing to innocence and producing a number of other persons willing to swear that they believed the accused's declaration of innocence.
concurring opinion Opinion handed down by a judge that supports the judgment of the court but often based on different reasoning.
confidential informant (C.I.) An informant known to the police but whose identity is held in confidence.
consanguinity Kinship; the state of being related by blood.
consent Voluntarily yielding to the will or desire of another person.
conspiracy The crime of two or more persons agreeing or planning to commit a crime. The crime of conspiracy is distinct from the crime contemplated by the conspirators (the "target crime").

construction Interpretation

constructive breaking Where the law implies a breaking. For example, a person who gains entry into someone's house through fraud or deception may be said to have made a constructive breaking.

constructive possession Being in the position to effectively control something, even if it is not actually in one's possession.

contemnor A person found to be in contempt of court.

contempt of court Any action that embarrasses, hinders, obstructs, or is calculated to lessen the dignity of a court of law.

continuance Delay of a judicial proceeding on the motion of one of the parties.

contraband Any property that is inherently illegal to produce or possess.

controlled substance A drug designated by law as contraband.

conversion The unlawful assumption of the rights of ownership to someone else's property.

corporal punishment Punishment that inflicts pain or injury to a person's body.

corpus delicti "The body of the crime." The material thing upon which a crime has been committed (e.g., a burned-out building in a case of arson).

corroboration Evidence that strengthens evidence already given.

counsel A lawyer who represents a party.

counterfeiting The crime of producing or passing imitations, usually false money or other evidence of value (e.g., stamps or securities).

criminal Pertaining to crime; a person convicted of a crime.

criminal intent A necessary element of a crime—the evil intent associated with the commission of a crime.

criminal negligence A failure to exercise the degree of caution or care necessary to avoid being charged with a crime.

criminal procedure The rules of law governing the procedures by which crimes are investigated, prosecuted, adjudicated, and punished.

criminal syndicalism The crime of advocating violence as a means to accomplish political change.

criminology The study of the nature of, causes of, and means of dealing with crime.

culpability Guilt.

curtilage At common law, the enclosed space surrounding a dwelling house; in modern codes, this space has been extended to encompass other buildings.

deadly force The degree of force that may result in the death of the person against whom the force is applied.

death-qualified jury A trial jury composed of persons who do not entertain scruples against imposing a death sentence.

de facto "In fact"; as a matter of fact.

defendant A person charged with a crime or against whom a civil action has been initiated.

defense A defendant's stated reasons of law or fact as to why thed prosecution or plaintiff should not prevail.

definite sentence Criminal penalty set by law with no discretion for the judge or correctional officials to individualize punishment.

de jure "In law"; as a matter of law.

de minimis "Minimal."

demurrer A document challenging the legal sufficiency of a complaint or indictment.

deposition The recorded sworn testimony of a witness; not given in open court.

depraved mind A serious moral deficiency; the highest level of malice.

detention Holding someone in custody.

determinate sentence Variation on definite sentencing whereby a judge fixes the term of incarceration within statutory limits.

deterrence Prevention of criminal activity by punishing criminals so that others will not engage in such activity.

dicta Statements contained in a judicial opinion that are not essential to the resolution of the case and do not become legal precedents.

discretion The power of public officials to act in certain situations according to their own judgment rather than relying on set rules or procedures.

discretionary review Form of appellate court review of lower court decisions that is not mandatory but occurs at the discretion of the appellate court. *See also* certiorari.

dismissal A judicial order terminating a case.

disorderly conduct Illegal behavior that disturbs the public peace or order.

disposition The final settlement of a case.

dissenting opinion An opinion rendered by a judge disavowing or attacking the decision of a collegial court.

docket The set of cases pending before a court of law.

double jeopardy The condition of being tried twice for the same criminal offense.

drug courier profile A set of characteristics thought to typify persons engaged in drug smuggling.

DUBAL Driving with an unlawful blood alcohol level.

due process Procedural and substantive rights of citizens against government actions that threaten the denial of life, liberty, or property.

DUI The crime of driving under the influence of alcohol or drugs.
duress The use of illegal confinement or threats of harm to coerce someone to do something he or she would not do otherwise.
Durham test A test for determining insanity developed by the United States Court of Appeals for the District of Columbia Circuit in the case of Durham v. United States (1954). Under this test, a person is not criminally responsible for an unlawful act if it was the product of a mental disease or defect.
duty An obligation that a person has by law or contract.
DWI The crime of driving while intoxicated.

ecclesiastical Pertaining to religious laws or institutions.
embezzlement The crime of using a position of trust or authority to transfer or convert the money or property of another to oneself.
en banc "In the bench." Refers to a session of a court, usually an appellate court, in which all judges assigned to the court participate.
entrapment The act of government agents in inducing someone to commit a crime that the person otherwise would not be disposed to commit.
escape Unlawfully fleeing to avoid arrest or confinement.
evidence Testimony, writings, or material objects offered in proof of an alleged fact or proposition.
evidentiary Pertaining to the rules of evidence or the evidence in a particular case.
exclusionary rule Judicial doctrine forbidding the use of evidence in a criminal trial where the evidence was obtained in violation of the defendant's constitutional rights.
exculpatory Tending to exonerate a person of allegations of wrongdoing.
exigent circumstances Situations that demand unusual or immediate action.
ex parte Refers to a proceeding in which only one party is involved or represented.
expert witness A witness called to testify to knowledge of technical matters based on particular training.
***ex post facto* law** A retroactive law that criminalizes actions that were innocent at the time they were taken or increases punishment for a criminal act after it was committed.
extortion The crime of obtaining money or property by threats of force or the inducement of fear.
extradition The surrender of a person by one jurisdiction to another for the purpose of criminal prosecution.

false arrest The tort or crime of unlawfully restraining a person.
false imprisonment *See* false arrest.
false pretenses The crime of obtaining money or property through misrepresentation.
felony A serious crime for which a person may be imprisoned for more than one year.
felony murder A homicide committed during the course of committing another felony (e.g., armed robbery).
"fighting words" doctrine The First Amendment doctrine that holds that certain utterances are not constitutionally protected as free speech if they are inherently likely to provoke a violent response from the audience.
flogging Whipping with a lash as a form of corporal punishment.
forfeiture Sacrifice of ownership or some right (usually property) as a penalty.
forgery The crime of making a false written instrument or materially altering a written instrument (e.g., a check, promissory note, or college transcript) with the intent to defraud.
fornication Sexual intercourse between unmarried persons; an offense in some jurisdictions.
fraud Intentional deception or distortion in order to gain something of value.
fundamental error In a judicial proceeding, an error that affects the substantial rights of the accused or is an affront to the integrity of the court.

gambling Operating or playing a game for money in the hope of gaining more than the amount played.
general intent The state of mind to do something prohibited by law without necessarily intending to accomplish the harm that results from the illegal act.
general warrant A search or arrest warrant that is not particular as to the person to be arrested or the property to be seized.
good-time credit Credit toward early release from prison based on good behavior during confinement (often referred to as "gain time").
graft Fraudulent acquisition of public funds for personal gain by a public official.
grand jury A group of citizens convened either to conduct an investigation or to determine if there is sufficient evidence to warrant prosecution of an accused.

habeas corpus "You have the body." A judicial writ requiring that a party be brought before a court. The primary function of *habeas corpus* is to release a person from unlawful confinement.

habitation Residence or dwelling place.
habitual offender statute A law that imposes an additional punishment on a criminal who has previously been convicted of crimes.
harmless error doctrine The doctrine that minor or harmless errors during a trial do not require reversal of the judgment by an appellate court.
hearing A proceeding, usually less formal than a trial, held to determine definite issues of fact or law.
hearsay evidence Statements made by someone other than a witness offered in evidence at a trial or hearing to prove the truth of the matter asserted. Normally inadmissible as evidence, but this is subject to exceptions.
holding The legal principle drawn from a judicial decision.
homicide The killing of a human being.
hot pursuit The right of police to cross jurisdictional lines to apprehend a suspect or criminal; also refers to Fourth Amendment doctrine allowing warrantless searches and arrests where police pursue a fleeing suspect into a protected area.
"hung jury" A trial jury unable to reach a verdict.
hypothetical question A question based on an assumed set of facts. Hypothetical questions may be asked of expert witnesses in criminal trials.

illegitimacy Condition of a child being born out of wedlock.
immunity Exemption from civil suit or prosecution. *See also* use immunity and transactional immunity.
impeachment A legislative act bringing a charge against a public official that, if proven in a legislative trial, will cause his or her removal from public office; impugning the credibility of a witness by introducing contradictory evidence or proving his or her bad character.
in camera In a judge's chambers.
incapacitation Making it impossible for someone to do something.
incapacity An inability, legal or actual, to act.
incarceration Imprisonment.
incest Sexual intercourse with a close blood relative or, in some cases, a person related by affinity.
inchoate offenses Offenses preparatory to committing other crimes. Inchoate offenses include attempt, conspiracy, and solicitation.
incite To provoke or set in motion.
inciting a riot The crime of instigating or provoking a riot.
inculpatory Tending to incriminate.
indefinite sentence Form of criminal sentencing whereby a judge imposes a term of incarceration within statutory parameters, and corrections officials determine actual time served through parole or other means.
indeterminate sentence Form of criminal sentencing where criminals are sentenced to prison for indeterminate periods until corrections officials determine that rehabilitation has been accomplished.
index crimes Offenses included in the F.B.I. Uniform Crime Reports: willful homicide, forcible rape, robbery, burglary, aggravated assault, grand larceny, and motor vehicle theft.
indictment A formal document handed down by a grand jury accusing one or more persons of the commission of a crime or crimes.
indigent Poor; unable to afford legal representation.
infancy The condition of being below the age of legal majority.
in forma pauperis "In the manner of a pauper." Waiver of filing costs and other fees associated with judicial proceedings to allow an indigent person to proceed.
information A document filed by a prosecutor charging one or more persons with commission of crime.
infra "Below."
initial appearance After arrest, the first appearance of the accused before a judge or magistrate.
injunction A court order prohibiting someone from doing some specified act or commanding someone to undo some wrong or injury.
in loco parentis "In the place of the parents."
inmate One who is confined in a jail or prison.
in re "In the matter of."
insanity A degree of mental illness that negates the legal capacity or responsibility of the affected person.
insanity defense A defense that seeks to exonerate the accused by showing that he or she was insane and thus not legally responsible.
intangible property Property with no tangible value, such as bonds, promissory notes, and stock certificates.
intent A state of mind in which a person seeks to accomplish a given result through a course of action.
inter alia "Among other things."
interrogation Questioning of a suspect by police or questioning of a witness by counsel.
interrogatories Written questions put to a witness.
intoxication Condition in which a person has impaired physical and/or mental capacities due to ingestion of drugs or alcohol.
invalidate Annul, negate, set aside.
ipso facto "By the mere fact"; by the fact itself.
irresistible impulse A desire that cannot be resisted due to impairment of the will by mental disease.

joinder Coupling two or more criminal prosecutions.
joyriding The temporary taking of an automobile without intent to permanently deprive the owner of same.
judgment The final and official decision of a court of law in a given case.
judicial review The power of courts of law to review governmental acts and declare them null and void if they are found to be unconstitutional.
jurisdiction The authority of a court to hear and decide certain categories of legal disputes. Jurisdiction relates to the authority of a court over the person, subject matter, and geographical area.
jurist A person who is skilled or well versed in the law; term often applied to lawyers and judges.
jury A group of citizens convened for the purpose of deciding factual questions relevant to a civil or criminal case.
justifiable homicide Killing another in self-defense or defense of others when there is serious danger of death or great bodily harm to self or others, or when authorized by law.
juvenile A person who has not yet attained the age of legal majority.
juvenile delinquency Condition of a juvenile who has violated criminal laws.

kidnapping The forcible abduction and carrying away of a person against that person's will.
kinship Relationship by blood.

larceny The unlawful taking of property with the intent of permanently depriving the owner of same.
legislation Law enacted by a lawmaking body.
legislature A lawmaking body such as the Congress of the United States or a state assembly.
lex non scripta "The unwritten law" or common law.
libel The tort of defamation through published writing or pictures.
loitering Standing around idly, "hanging around."

magistrate A judge with minor or limited authority.
Magna Charta The "Great Charter" signed by King John in 1215 guaranteeing the legal rights of English subjects. Generally considered the foundation of Anglo-American constitutionalism.
mala in se "Evil in itself." Refers to crimes like murder that are universally condemned.
mala prohibita "Prohibited evil." Refers to crimes that are wrong primarily because the law declares them to be wrong.
malice aforethought The mental predetermination to commit an illegal act.
malicious mischief The crime of willful destruction of the personal property of another.
mandate A command or order.
manslaughter The crime of unlawful killing of another person without malice.
material Important, relevant, necessary.
mayhem At common law, the crime of injuring someone so as to render that person less able to fight.
mens rea "Guilty mind," criminal intent.
***Miranda* warning** Based on the Supreme Court's decision in *Miranda v. Arizona* (1967), this warning is given by police to individuals who are taken into custody before they are interrogated. The warning informs persons in custody that they have the right to remain silent and to have a lawyer present during questioning, and that anything they say can and will be used against them in a court of law.
miscarriage of justice Decision of a court that is inconsistent with the substantial rights of a party to the case.
misdemeanor A minor offense usually punishable by fine or imprisonment for less than one year.
misprision of felony The crime of concealing a felony committed by another.
misrepresentation An untrue statement of fact made to deceive or mislead.
mistake of fact Unconscious ignorance of a fact or belief in the existence of something that does not exist.
mistake of law An erroneous opinion of legal principles applied to a set of facts.
mitigation Reduction or alleviation, usually of punishment.
M'Naghten Rule A classic test of criminal responsibility. Under this test, a person is not criminally responsible for an act if at the time of commission he or she was laboring under such a defect of reason or disease of the mind so as not to know the nature of the act or, if he or she did know the nature of the act, did not know it was wrong.
monogamy Having only one spouse, as distinct from bigamy or polygamy.
moot A point that no longer has any practical significance; academic.
motion An application to a court of law for the purpose of obtaining some particular order or ruling.
murder The unlawful killing of a person by another, with malice aforethought or premeditation.

necessity A condition that compels or requires a certain course of action.

negligence The failure to exercise ordinary care or caution.
nolo contendere "I will not contest it." A plea to a criminal charge that, although it is not an admission of guilt, generally has the same effect as a plea of guilty.
notary public A person empowered by law to administer oaths, to certify things as true, and to perform various minor official acts.
nuisance An unlawful or unreasonable use of a person's property that results in an injury to another or to the public.
nullen crimen, nulla poena, sine lege "There is no crime, there is no punishment, without law."

obiter dicta *See* dicta.
obscenity Sexually oriented material that is patently offensive, appeals to a prurient or unnatural interest in sex, and lacks serious scientific, artistic, or literary content.
obstruction of justice The crime of impeding or preventing law enforcement or the administration of justice.
omission The failure to do what the law requires a person to do.
opinion of the court The opinion summarizing the views of the majority of judges participating in a judicial decision.
oral argument Verbal presentation made to an appellate court in an attempt to persuade the court to affirm, reverse, or modify a lower court decision.
ordinance An enactment of a local governing body such as a city council or commission.
organized crime Syndicates involved in racketeering and other criminal activities.
original jurisdiction The authority of a court of law to hear a case in the first instance.
overbreadth doctrine First Amendment doctrine that holds that a law is invalid if it can be applied to punish people for engaging in constitutionally protected expression.
overrule To reverse or annul by subsequent action.

panel A set of jurors or judges assigned to hear a case.
pardon An executive action that mitigates or sets aside punishment for a crime.
parens patriae "The parent of the country." Refers to the role of the state as guardian of minors or other legally disabled persons.
parole Conditional release from jail or prison of a person who has served part of his or her sentence.
penal Of or pertaining to punishment.
penitentiary A prison.
penology The study or practice of prison management.
per curiam "By the court." A phrase used to distinguish an opinion rendered by the whole court rather than by an individual judge.
perjury The crime of lying under oath, as in a court of law.
per se "By itself"; in itself.
petition A formal written request addressed to a court of law.
petitioner A person who brings a petition before a court of law.
petit jury A trial jury, usually composed of either six or twelve persons.
petty (petit) offenses Minor crimes for which fines or short jail terms are the only prescribed modes of punishment.
***Pinkerton* Rule** Rule enunciated by the Supreme Court in *Pinkerton v. United States* (1946) holding that a member of a conspiracy is liable for all offenses committed in furtherance of the conspiracy.
PKPA The Parental Kidnapping Prevention Act, designed to prevent "child snatching" by noncustodial parents.
plaintiff A person who initiates a civil suit.
plea bargain An agreement between a defendant and a prosecutor whereby the defendant agrees to plead guilty in exchange for some concession (e.g., a reduction in the number of charges brought).
plurality opinion An opinion of an appellate court that is joined by more judges than have joined any concurring opinion, although not by a majority of judges in the court.
PMS Premenstrual syndrome.
police power The power of government to legislate to protect public health, safety, welfare, and morality.
polygamy Plural marriage; having more than one spouse.
pornography Material that appeals to the sexual impulse or appetite.
postconviction relief Term applied to various mechanisms a defendant may use to challenge a conviction after other routes of appeal have been exhausted.
precedent A judicial decision cited as authority controlling or influencing the outcome of a similar case.
prejudicial error An error at trial that substantially affects the interests of the accused.
preliminary hearing A hearing held to determine whether there is sufficient evidence to hold an accused for trial.
premeditation Deliberate decision or plan to commit a crime.

preponderance of evidence Evidence that has greater weight than countervailing evidence.
presentence investigation An investigation held before sentencing a convicted criminal to aid the court in determining the appropriate punishment.
presentence report A report containing the results of a presentence investigation.
presumption An assumption of a fact not yet proven.
presumption of innocence In a criminal trial, the accused is presumed innocent until proven guilty.
presumption of validity In constitutional law, a statute is generally presumed to be valid until it is demonstrated otherwise.
pretrial motion A request for a ruling or order before the commencement of a trial.
preventive detention Holding a suspect in custody before trial to prevent escape or other wrongdoing.
prima facie "On its face"; at first glance.
principal A perpetrator of, or aider and abettor in, the commission of a crime (as distinguished from an accessory).
probable cause A reasonable ground for belief in certain alleged facts.
probation Conditional release of a convicted criminal in lieu of incarceration.
probative Tending to prove the truth or falsehood of a proposition.
pro bono "For the good." Performing service without compensation.
procedural due process Set of procedures designed to ensure fairness in a judicial or administrative proceeding.
procedural law The law regulating governmental procedure (e.g., rules of criminal procedure).
profanity Irreverence toward sacred things.
proscribe To forbid; prohibit.
pro se On one's own behalf.
prosecution Initiation and conduct of a criminal case.
prosecutor Official empowered to initiate and conduct criminal charges.
prosecutrix A female prosecutor; a female victim who makes a criminal complaint.
***pro se* defense** Representing oneself in a criminal case.
prostitution The act of selling sexual favors.
proximate cause The cause that is nearest a given effect in a causal relationship.
prurient interest An excessive or unnatural interest in sex.
public defender An official responsible for defending indigent persons charged with crimes.
public law General classification of law consisting of constitutional law, administrative law, international law, and criminal law.

quash To vacate or annul.

rape shield law A law that protects the identity of a rape victim or prevents disclosure of a victim's sexual history.
real property Land and buildings permanently attached thereto.
reasonable doubt The doubt that a reasonable person might entertain in regard to the veracity of a proposition after hearing the evidence.
reasonable suspicion A reasonable person's suspicion that criminal activity is afoot.
recidivism Repeating criminal activity.
recognizance An obligation to appear in a court of law at a given time.
recusal A decision of a judge to withdraw from a given case, usually because of bias or personal interest.
regulation A rule or order prescribed by controlling authority.
rehabilitation Restoring someone or something to its former status.
relevant evidence Evidence tending to prove or disprove an alleged fact.
remand To send back.
remedy The means by which a right is enforced or a wrong is redressed.
repeal A legislative act removing a law from the statute books.
resisting arrest The crime of obstructing or opposing a police officer making an arrest.
res judicata "Things judged." Matters already decided by courts, not subject to relitigation.
respondent A person asked to respond to a lawsuit or writ.
restitution The act of compensating someone for losses suffered.
retribution Something demanded as payment.
retroactive Referring to things past.
reverse To set aside a decision on appeal.
revocation The withdrawal of some right or power (e.g., the revocation of parole).
riot A public disturbance involving acts of violence, usually by three or more persons.
robbery The crime of taking money or property from a person against that person's will by means of force.
rout At common law, disturbance of the peace similar to riot but without carrying out the intended purpose.

rule of four U.S. Supreme Court rule whereby the Court grants *certiorari* only on the agreement of at least four justices.

sanction Penalty or other mechanism of enforcement.

seduction The common-law crime of inducing a woman of previously chaste character to have sexual intercourse outside of wedlock on the promise of marriage.

self-defense The protection of one's person against an attack.

self-representation *See* pro se defense.

sentence The official pronouncement of punishment in a criminal case.

severance Separation of cases so that they can be tried separately.

sexual assault *See* sexual battery.

sexual battery In modern statutes, the unlawful oral, anal, or vaginal penetration by or union with the sexual organ of another.

sheriff The chief law enforcement officer of the county.

skip tracer A person who tracks down alleged offenders who have fled to avoid prosecution.

slander The tort of defaming someone's character through verbal statements.

sodomy Oral or anal sex between persons, or sex between a person and an animal (the latter commonly referred to as bestiality).

solicitation The inchoate offense of requesting or encouraging someone to engage in illegal conduct.

specific intent The mental purpose to accomplish a specific act prohibited by law.

stare decisis The doctrine of deciding cases based on precedent.

statute A law enacted by a legislature.

statute of limitations A law proscribing prosecutions for specific crimes after specified periods of time.

stay A court order suspending proceedings or the enforcement of an order.

stay of execution A court order suspending the enforcement of a judgment of a lower court.

stop-and-frisk An encounter between a police officer and a suspect during which the latter is temporarily detained and subjected to a "pat-down" search for weapons.

strict liability A category of offenses that do not require the proof of criminal intent to obtain a conviction.

subornation of perjury The crime of procuring someone to lie under oath.

subpoena A judicial order to appear at a certain place and time to give testimony.

substantive due process Doctrine that due process clauses of the Fifth and Fourteenth Amendments to the United States Constitution require legislation to be fair and reasonable in content as well as application.

substantive law That part of the law that creates rights and proscribes wrongs.

suicide The intentional taking of a person's own life.

summary justice Trial held by court of limited jurisdiction without benefit of a jury.

suppression doctrine *See* exclusionary rule.

supra "Above."

surety bond A sum of money or property that is posted or guaranteed by a party to ensure the future court appearance of another person.

sustain To uphold.

tangible property Property that has physical form and substance and value in itself.

Terry-stop *See* stop-and-frisk.

testimony Evidence given by a witness who has been sworn to tell the truth.

time, place, and manner doctrine First Amendment doctrine holding that government may impose reasonable limitations on the time, place, and manner of expressive activities.

tort A wrong or injury other than a breach of contract for which the remedy is a civil suit for damages.

transactional immunity A grant of immunity applying to offenses that a witness's testimony relates to.

transcript A written record of a trial or hearing.

transferred intent Doctrine holding that if A intends to injure B but instead injures C, then A's intent to injure B supplies the requisite intent to injure C.

treason The crime of attempting by overt acts to overthrow the government, or of betraying the government to a foreign power.

trespass An unlawful interference with one's person or property.

trial A judicial proceeding held for the purpose of making factual and legal determinations.

trial *de novo* "A new trial." Refers to trial court review of convictions for minor offenses by courts of limited jurisdiction by conducting a new trial instead of merely reviewing the record of the initial trial.

tribunal A court of law.

true bill An indictment handed down by a grand jury.

trustee A person entrusted to handle the affairs of another.

"trusty" A prisoner entrusted with authority to supervise other prisoners in exchange for certain privileges and status.

UCMJ The Uniform Code of Military Justice, adopted by the U.S. Congress.
UCR The Uniform Crime Reports, compiled by the Federal Bureau of Investigation.
ultra vires Beyond the scope of a prescribed authority.
use immunity A grant of immunity that forbids prosecutors from using immunized testimony as evidence in criminal prosecutions.
uttering a forged instrument The crime of passing a false or worthless instrument, such as a check, with the intent to defraud or injure the recipient.

vacate To annul, set aside, or rescind.
vagrancy The offense of going about without any visible means of support.
vandalism The willful destruction of the property of another person.
vehicular homicide Homicide resulting from the unlawful and negligent operation of a motor vehicle.
venire The group of citizens from whom a jury is chosen in a given case.
venue The location of a trial or hearing.
verdict The formal decision rendered by a jury in a civil or criminal trial.
vice Crimes of immoral conduct, such as prostitution, gambling, and the use of narcotics.
victim A person who is the object of a crime or tort.
victim impact statement Statement read into the record during the sentencing phase of a criminal trial to inform the court about the impact of the crime on the victim or victim's family.
victimless crimes Crimes in which no particular person appears or claims to be injured, such as prostitution or gambling.
void-for-vagueness doctrine Doctrine of constitutional law holding unconstitutional (as a violation of due process) legislation that fails to clearly inform the person what is required or proscribed.
voir dire "To speak the truth." The process by which prospective jurors are questioned by counsel and/or the court before being selected to serve on a jury.

waiver The intentional and voluntary relinquishment of a right, or conduct from which such relinquishment may be inferred.
Wharton's Rule Named after Francis Wharton, a well-known commentator on criminal law, this rule holds that two people cannot conspire to commit a crime such as adultery, incest, or bigamy inasmuch as these offenses involve only two participants.
writ An order issued by a court of law requiring the performance of some specific art.
writ of *certiorari* *See* certiorari.
writ of error A writ issued by an appellate court for the purpose of correcting an error revealed in the record of a lower court proceeding.
writ of *habeas corpus* *See* habeas corpus.
writ of prohibition An appellate court order that prevents a lower court from exercising its jurisdiction in a particular case.
writs of assistance Ancient writs issuing from the Court of Exchequer ordering sheriffs to assist in collecting debts owed the Crown. Prior to the American Revolution, the writs of assistance gave agents of the Crown in the American colonies the unlimited right to search for smuggled goods. In modern practice, judicial orders to put someone in possession of property.

TABLE OF CASES

The principle cases are in *italic* type. Cases cited or discussed are in roman type. References are to pages.

INDEX

Photo Credits
Chapter 1 Courtesy of the FBI; Chapter 2 Susie Fitzhugh/Stock Boston; Chapter 3 © Spencer Grant/Stock Boston; Chapter 4 © Richard Hutchings/Photo Researchers, Inc; Chapter 5 © John Maher/Stock Boston; Chapter 6 David Karp/AP Photo; Chapter 7 Photo Researchers, Inc.; Chapter 8 Barbara Alper/Stock Boston; Chapter 9 © Richard Hutchings/Photo Edit; Chapter 10 © Barbara Alper/Stock Boston; Chapter 11 © Bettye Lane/Photo Researchers, Inc.; Chapter 12 © Paul Mozell/Stock Boston; Chapter 13 UPI/Bettmann